Catholic Dogmatic Theology ⭻ A Synthesis

BOOK 2

THOMISTIC RESSOURCEMENT SERIES

Volume 18

SERIES EDITORS

Matthew Levering, Mundelein Seminary

Thomas Joseph White, OP, Pontifical University
of St. Thomas Aquinas

EDITORIAL BOARD

Serge-Thomas Bonino, OP, Pontifical University
of St. Thomas Aquinas

Gilles Emery, OP, University of Fribourg

Reinhard Hütter, The Catholic University of America

Bruce Marshall, Southern Methodist University

Emmanuel Perrier, OP, Dominican Studium, Toulouse

Richard Schenk, OP, University of Freiburg (Germany)

Kevin White, The Catholic University of America

Catholic Dogmatic Theology ⁌ A Synthesis

BOOK 2, ON THE INCARNATION
AND REDEMPTION

JEAN-HERVÉ NICOLAS, OP

FOREWORD BY JOSEPH RATZINGER

FOREWORD TO THE ENGLISH EDITION
BY ARCHBISHOP ALLEN VIGNERON

TRANSLATED BY MATTHEW K. MINERD

The Catholic University of America Press
Washington, D.C.

Originally published as *Synthèse dogmatique:
De la Trinité à la Trinité,* © Paris: Beauchesne, 1985.
Toute demande concernant les droits de traduction,
de reproduction, d'adaptation, en quelque langue que se soit,
devra obligatoirement être adressé a Beauchesne Editeur,
7 Cité du Cardinal Lemoine 75005 Paris —
France, Editeur l'édition originale.

English Translation Copyright © 2023
The Catholic University of America Press
All rights reserved

Cataloging-in-Publication Data is available
from the Library of Congress
ISBN: 978-0-8132-3600-1
eISBN: 978-0-8132-3601-8

Contents

Foreword to the English Edition by Archbishop Allen Vigneron	vii
Translator's Preface	ix
Foreword to the Original Edition by Cardinal Joseph Ratzinger	xiii
List of Abbreviations	xv

PART 1. THE CHURCH'S FAITH IN THE INCARNATION

1.	The Scriptural Sources of Christological Dogma	3
2.	The Formation of the Christological Dogmata	21

PART 2. WHAT CHRIST IS IN HIMSELF

3.	The Hypostatic Union	47
4.	The Humanity of Jesus	135
5.	Jesus's Human Activity	216

PART 3. CHRIST'S FIRST COMING

6.	The Incarnation in the Divine Plan	263
7.	Christ's Place in Human History	295

8. The Salvation of Men by the Blood of Christ · · · · · 340
9. The High Priest of the New Covenant · · · · · 380
10. The Mediator · · · · · 411

PART 4. CHRIST'S RETURN IN GLORY

11. Christ's Return · · · · · 427
12. From Final Eschatology to Intermediary Eschatology · · · · · 466
13. The Last Things, Considered from the Perspective of One's Individual Destiny · · · · · 482

Conclusion to the Second Part · · · · · 521

Works Cited · · · · · 523
Index · · · · · 537

Foreword to the English Edition

Archbishop Allen Vigneron

———:———

In guiding the work of the Second Vatican Council, St. John XXIII and St. Paul VI made it clear that this epochal event was not for the sake of the Church herself. As their successor Pope Francis might put it: the Council was not "self-referential." The aim of the Council was the renewal of the Church as the sacrament of Jesus Christ, the Light of the Nations—*Lumen gentium,* so that she would be the ever more effective instrument for sharing the Good News. The aim of the Council was to launch the Church once more out into the deep of evangelizing the world (cf. Lk 5:4).

The Council Fathers identified the renewal of theology as a necessary dimension of this more general project of renewal-for-mission. As part of that mandate they explicitly mentioned the role that the theological achievement of St. Thomas Aquinas ought to play in achieving this aim: "In order that they may illumine the mysteries of salvation as completely as possible, sshould learn to penetrate them more deeply with the help of speculation, under the guidance of St. Thomas, and to perceive their interconnections" (*Optatam totius*, 16).

As a bishop, charged, as I am, to do my part to fulfill the Great Commission "to make disciples of all nations" (Mt 28:19), I welcome the publication of the English translation of Fr. Nicolas's *Synthèse dogmatique,* since it makes readily available to students an effective instrument for Aquinas to guide them into a deeper understanding of the saving mysteries of the gospel. And as Cardinal Ratzinger affirms in his foreword to this work, Fr. Nicolas goes about his task of exploring the mind of Aquinas with the conviction that "revealed truths are not only truths. They are principles of life, conversion, and therefore also of preaching." Thus, the deeper penetration of gospel truth that students will achieve by joining with St. Thomas to think about them with the help of Fr. Nicolas will be a blessed resource for the Church on her mission to give an account for the hope that she offers the world in the name of Christ (cf. 1 Pt 3:15).

I first became acquainted with Fr. Nicolas's *Synthèse dogmatique* when I was engaged in teaching theology to seminarians. Since then I had looked for the day when this work would be available to English-speaking students in their own language. Through the considerable efforts of the translator, Dr. Matthew Minerd, with help of those he so generously acknowledges, I have the satisfaction of seeing my long-felt need for this resource met for the good of students and professors alike. To Dr. Minerd and his colleagues I offer my sincere thanks.

A key moment in my own theological studies was when a wise professor observed in passing, "To explain a profound mystery simply you must understand it profoundly." I have made this piece of advice an axiom for my study and for my teaching. I am confident that the appearance of Fr. Nicolas's *Synthèse dogmatique* in English will aid in that profound understanding which yields in students of theology the great good fruit of their being able to offer that clear and compelling explanation of the revealed mysteries which goes by the deceptive name of "simple."

Translator's Preface

This work represents the second portion of Fr. Nicolas's *Synthèse dogmatique*, a formidable pair of tomes which, in English, will be presented as a series of separate thematic volumes. As Fr. Nicolas explains in the first volume of this English-language series of texts, *Synthèse dogmatique* is based upon a sequence of course lectures given over a number of decades. Because of these origins, his written French style can be a bit choppy at times, using formulations that are either fragmentary or idiosyncratic. The voice of the original classroom lecture texts is often obvious in the original French. Furthermore, as is particularly evident in the final volume of this series, Fr. Nicolas's own personal style is *quite* wordy, often falling into sentences that are seventy to a hundred words in length. In most cases, care has been taken to retain Fr. Nicolas's voice. However, upon consultation with Fr. Thomas-Joseph White, OP—to whom my work on this project owes a great debt—I decided it best to err on the side of readability, for these texts are destined for use in the pedagogical formation of theologians. When stylistic modification was deemed necessary, this generally required me to present a slightly more paratactic style than the more serpentine forms used by Fr. Nicolas. However, where there is a chance that I have added a nuance, I utilize square brackets (either for my added text, especially when Fr. Nicolas' meaning is not fully clear and I am aware of my own interpretive role, or to provide the original language equivalent). Moreover, Fr. Nicolas frequently utilizes a non-standard style of quoting authors, setting off in block quotes even single lines of quotation. I have worked to stylistically integrate these quotations into a standard form conformed to the style sheet of The Catholic University of America Press. On occasion, he expresses side comments / technical qualifications in small text as well. For the sake of flow, I have moved most of these to footnotes.

In Fr. Nicolas's original text, the footnotes were written in shorthand, referencing a single bibliography at the end of the lengthy volume. I have moved all bibliographical references to the footnotes for ease of reference. On occasion, I have needed to note what appear to be mistakes by Fr. Nicolas's in these notes. In general, scriptural references have been taken from the Revised Standard Version of the Bible. Where contextual rhetorical concerns did not seem to allow this, I translated the text from the French provided by Fr. Nicolas. All such citations from the Revised Standard Version are marked in the scriptural citation. For example, if a direct citation has been taken from Romans 6:1, it is cited (in footnotes) as "Rom 6:1 (RSV)."

All direct citations from Denzinger are taken from the English translation provided in the 43rd edition published by Ignatius Press. Where available, citations from contemporary non-French works have been taken from authorized translations with the relevant citation details being provided in the appropriate footnotes. All French authors have been translated anew. Because Fr. Nicolas has made slight interpretive nuances to his citations from St. Thomas, I have chosen to translate from his own translation of the Angelic Doctor but have done so with an eye to the original and always with a literal approach to Fr. Nicolas's own rendering. The same holds for his occasional citations from Patristic and Scholastic sources.

Thanks are owed to Dr. Reinhard Hütter and, especially, Fr. Thomas-Joseph White, OP, for their support in undertaking this project, as well as to Matthew Levering, who offered friendly encouragement through the long hours of working on this volume in conjunction with future portions of Fr. Nicolas's text. Likewise, gratitude is owed to the Thomistic Institute (and a kind donor) for providing funds for the overall project of translating Fr. Nicolas's *Synthèse dogmatique*. Finally, thanks are owed to all those persons involved in the editorial process without whom this volume would have been significantly more deficient, especially John Martino for his able and kind shepherding of the volume through the process of publication.

This translation is dedicated to the eternal repose of the soul of my paternal grandfather, Byron K. Minerd. Eternal memory and blessed repose!

Foreword to the Original Edition

Cardinal Joseph Ratzinger

———·———

We live in an age of excessive specialization. This assertion holds true in the domain of theology, where the number of publications has grown beyond what sight can embrace, thus making it increasingly difficult for one to have an overview of the whole of theology. In this state of affairs, we find ourselves faced with the fact that contemporary overview presentations of dogmatic theology most often are the collective work of many authors. Certainly, in such works, particular points are given thorough treatments. However, the various parts are connected to one another only in an extrinsic manner. Now, given that (according to Hegel's expression) "the Truth is the Whole," theology's current state raises problems that are not merely didactic and pedagogical. Beyond such concerns, this state of affairs also compromises the very task of theology in what is essential to it. In this regard, recall that Irenaeus of Lyon founded Catholic theology in the proper sense of the word by holding that it is based on "the primordial system" (Adv. Haer. IV, 33, 8), on the basis of what is foundational for the unity of ecclesial life. This enabled him to perceive the unity of the Old and New Covenant, of the Creator and the Savior, of philosophy and faith, and what alone can constitute the specific character of theology.

In this regard, the publication of this text in dogmatic theology by Jean-Hervé Nicolas, which matured over the course of many years of teaching, for many reasons represents a theological event of great importance. The Thomist option, which he takes as his point of departure, is not based on Aquinas's authority as such but, rather, on his theological thought, which the author receives by critically rethinking it. What is characteristic of a theology thus situated is that it is, above all, a synthesis between historical knowledge and philosophical reflection. However, it also represents the conjunction of the Church's teaching with critical reflection, as well as that of theory with practice. "Revealed truths," writes Fr. Nicolas, "are not only truths. They are principles of life, conversion, and therefore also of preaching." What strikes me in Fr. Nicolas's book is, first of all, its sure erudition in exegesis and in the history of dogmas. However, I am also struck to no less an extent by the vigor of his philosophical outlook, something that is not encountered very often today in pedagogical volumes on dogmatic theology. This philosophical outlook gives this book its depth, internal unity, and at the same time, a persuasiveness that could never arise from a more or less positivist organization of the various topics discussed therein. The reader who will allow himself to be guided by Fr. Nicolas will perceive that the ecclesiality of theology, if it is authentic, in no way impedes the power and openness of one's thought. On the contrary, it places thought in profound agreement with the great thinkers of all ages. Without such agreement, one falls into individual isolation and, in the end, into skepticism, which represents an impoverishment of the truth. Fr. Nicolas's book can assist us in drawing closer to this "unity in theology." Without such unity, the latter, inasmuch as it is theology, disintegrates. This is why I hope that this text will be broadly received by many open-minded readers.

Rome, Feast of the Exaltation of the Cross [1984/5]

List of Abbreviations

D.-Sch.	Denzinger, *Enchiridion Symbolorum*
De pot.	Thomas Aquinas, *Quaestiones disputate De potentia*
De ver.	Thomas Aquinas, *Quaestiones disputate De veritate*
FC	*La foi catholique: textes doctrinaux du magistre de l'église*, ed. and trans. G. Dumiege
In Sent.	Thomas Aquinas, *Scriptum super libros Sententiarum*
PG	Patrologia Graeca
PL	Patrologia Latina
SC	Sources chrétiennes
SCG	Thomas Aquinas, *Summa contra gentiles*
ST	Thomas Aquinas, *Summa theologiae*

PART 1

THE CHURCH'S FAITH IN THE INCARNATION

1

The Scriptural Sources of Christological Dogma

At the Council of Chalcedon in 451, after protracted struggles, patient investigations, and a slow elaboration of an adequate vocabulary for expressing in human terms a mystery that transcends human reason, the Church expressed her faith in the Incarnation.[1] The essential passage from the Council's proclamations is:

Following therefore the holy Fathers, we unanimously teach to confess one and the same Son, our Lord Jesus Christ, the same perfect in divinity and perfect in humanity, the same truly God and truly man composed of rational soul and body, the same one in being with the Father as to the divinity and one in being with us as to the humanity, like unto us in all things but sin [cf. Heb 4:15]. The same was begotten from the Father before the ages as to the divinity and in the latter days for us and our salvation was born as to his humanity from Mary the Virgin Mother of God. We confess that one and the same Lord Jesus Christ, the only begotten Son must be acknowledged in two natures, without confusion or change, without division or separation. The distinction between the natures was never abolished by their union but rather the character proper to each of the two natures was preserved as they came together in one Person and one hypostasis. He is not split or divided into two Persons, but he is one and the same only begotten Son, God the Word, the Lord Jesus Christ, as formerly

---

1. See D.-*Sch.*, 300–302; FC 313.

the prophets and later Jesus Christ himself have taught us about him and as has been handed down to us by the creed of the Fathers.²

This formula has its own history, which we will briefly summarize from the perspective of dogmatic development. For a precise exposition of the various events involved in this overall history, we refer the reader to books of biblical theology, patrology, and Church history.³

I. THE OLD TESTAMENT FOUNDATIONS OF NEW TESTAMENT CHRISTOLOGY

The Church's primitive teaching (the "apostolic kerygma") focused on presenting the facts of Jesus's life and death as being the fulfillment of the prophecies of the Old Testament concerning the Messiah.

{241} Dodd⁴ has shown, with great precision, that from early on in Christian history, the Old Testament was reread in light of the event of Jesus Christ—not in a written form but, rather, orally, by means of a methodology shared by the preachers of the Gospel. Thus, a "Bible of the Primitive Church" was gradually established, including all the *Testimonia* to which they had recourse, with Isaiah standing at the center.

This enables us to ask, more generally, what justified this use of all the books of the Old Testament. The results of such investigations can be found in Fügilster's work.⁵ It involves drawing out the funda-

---

2. [Tr. note: Text taken from the 43rd edition of Denzinger in dual Greek/Latin and English. Fr. Nicolas cites a French translation from Pierre-Thomas Camelot, *Ephèse et Chalcédoine*, Histoire des Conciles Oecuméniques 2, ed. Gervais Dumeige (Paris: Orante, 1962), 226–28. These paragraphs come from the Chalcedonian Creed, as found in Denzinger, nos. 301–2.]

3. N.B. The development of Christological dogma did not come to a halt at Chalcedon, and we will have the opportunity to study its later phases. However, the Chalcedonian formula fixes the Church's faith concerning what is called "the Hypostatic Union," that is, her faith concerning the ontological constitution of Jesus Christ, the God-Man.

4. See Charles Harold Dodd, *Conformément aux Écritures*, trans. R. Guého and J. Trublet (Paris: Seuil, 1968).

5. See Notker Füglister, "Les bases vétérotestamentaires de la christologie du Nouveau Testament," in *Les préparations de l'événement Jésus-Christ* (Paris: Cerf, 1973), 161–325.

mental scriptural categories in the Old Testament taken up in the New Testament in its proclamation of Jesus as the Christ, examining in their historical context the biblical passages corresponding to these categories and, in the end, following the development taking place outside the canonical books themselves, leading to the Judaism contemporaneous to the genesis of the New Testament.

The first of these categories is that of *the royal mediator of salvation*. It finds its point of departure in the great promise made to David.[6] The Yahwist redactor of the Pentateuch sought to theologically legitimate the Davidic kingship by connecting it to the patriarchal history, arranging it into four important historical stages, four promises (i.e., the proto-evangelium, the promise to Abraham, the blessing of Jacob, and the oracle of Balaam), leading by way of a progressive line of descent from the posterity of the woman, Eve, through the posterity of Abraham, to the posterity of David. Next, there are the royal Psalms which, on the basis of the promise made to David and taking into account the royal ideology of the whole ancient Near-East, all the while retaining its reference to historical figures, speak much more about the divine prototype of the kingship than about its historical manifestation. With Isaiah and Micah, the theology of salvation reached, from the beginning of classical prophecy, its Old Testament apogee (Is 7:10–17, 9:1–6, 11:1–9; Mi 5:1–5); then too, there are the Davidic oracles (Jer 23:5, 30:9, 33:14–26; Ez 17:22–24, 34:23ff.; 37:22, 24ff., etc.).

The second scriptural category of interest is that of *the priestly mediator of salvation*. At the beginning of the Old Testament, there are the blessings given to Levi,[7] which constitute our most important source for the priesthood prior to the Exile. Moreover, there is Psalm 110:4. Next, there are the texts of the exilic or post-exilic era. We find the theology of the temple in Ezekiel, Haggai, and Zechariah. Likewise, there is the figure of the High Priest Zechariah and the theology of the "priestly code." Paralleling the Yahwist narrative to a

---

6. See 2 Sm 7.
7. See Dt 33:8–11.

great degree, its historical arc is deliberately oriented toward the institution of the salvific function of the High Priest in the midst of the three covenants (with Noah, with Abraham, and with the family of Phinehas, the grandson of Aaron),[8] all arranged like concentric circles. This second category also includes the testimony of the Chronicler, whose writings are strongly marked with concerns related to Israel's worship, and the testimony of Sirach, which transfers to the Aaronic priestly covenant what Scripture had said about the Davidic royal covenant. This theology will develop within Levitical environs and thus will take on a Levitical character, in expectation and hope for an eschatological priestly Messiah, to whom the royal Messiah will be subordinated.

The third scriptural category is that of *the prophetic mediator of salvation*. In the people of the Old Testament, next to the political and cultic mediating functions, there is a charismatic mediating function that, far from being added after the fact to the institutional structures, is specific, primitive, and constitutive for Israel.

Therefore, the law of prophecy[9] provides us with a description of the authentic prophet, thus constituting the foundation and point of departure for understanding the prophetic, mediating function [in ancient Israel]. It presents Moses as the prototype of the prophet. The prophets whom God will arouse in each generation will be akin to Moses and are charged with a quasi-institutional function. Thus, we see a line leading from Joshua to Samuel passing through the Judges, from Samuel to Jeremiah passing through Elijah, and finally from Jeremiah to Jesus passing through Isaiah's [suffering] servant of God.

The Exile at least provisionally marked the end of the kingship and priesthood, and in the "servant" we are faced with the result of this situation, which led to the intensification of theological reflection on the prophetic function, a reflection reaching its Old Testament apogee in the "songs of the servant of Yahweh," leading for the

8. See Nm 6:25.
9. See Dt 18:9–22.

The Scriptural Sources of Christological Dogma

first time to the expectation of a salvific mediator having a clearly Mosaic and prophetic character. The servant is the typological fulfillment of the prophetic role [*est le type du prophète*]. His person and mission constitute the terminus and veritable goal of the Mosaic-prophetic tradition, all the while integrating within it the characteristic traits of the royal-priestly tradition. As Füglister remarks, the servant is the mediator *par excellence* in whom

> without a doubt, the Old Testament theology of the mediator attains its culminating point ... the hoped-for, absolute and ideal, mediator ... whose soteriological function, including both Israel and the nations, will need to unfold in two phases, one before and the other after his death for the multitudes, which brings to completion His sufferings, which bring about salvation, all the while bursting the limitations of a purely intra-terrestrial mediation.[10]

At the end of the Old Testament, when prophecy comes to disappear from Israel, the final canonical writings and texts of Qumran testify to the expectation, not only of an eschatological renewal of prophecy in general,[11] but likewise of a prophet [in general] or of the prophet of the last days, often identified with Elijah.

Besides these three great biblical categories, the Old Testament presents others that help us conceive and express the functions of a "heavenly mediator" (i.e., a supra-terrestrial and transcendent mediator) of "salvation." There is the "Angel of Yahweh," the hypostasized Divine Wisdom that, in the wisdom literature, receives the qualities and functions of the human mediators of salvation. Not only are royal prerogatives and messianic charisms attributed to it, but it is, like the "Word [*Parole*] of God that mediates creation," established from eternity, from the beginning, before the origin of the world. It reunites in itself all the conceivable mediating functions of salvation.

The expectation of salvation arises anew in the Maccabean age and is expressed in the apocalyptic writings. It has an essentially

---

10. Füglister, "Les bases vétérotestamentaires de la christologie du Nouveau Testament," 249.

11. See Jl 2:28.

theocratic orientation, but a mediating figure of salvation is formed within it and from it, namely the figure of Daniel's Son of Man.[12] This Son of Man (who is also encountered in the apocalyptic texts written after the Old Testament) will be responsible for at least one part of the functions previously attributed to the royal Messiah and to the servant of God. The Son of Man differs, however, from the Messiah-King in that the former is a celestial, transcendent, and pre-existent being, whose activity is supra-terrestrial and universal.

Thus, we can divide the saving activities attributed to the Old Testament mediators into three great groups. First, there is the king, who ultimately is the liberator, redeemer, and savior of his own people (both in war and in judgment). Next there is the priest, with his activities of pronouncing blessings and making expiation for Israel by offering sacrifices. Finally, there is the prophet, who is the specific mediator of revelation and intercession. These are the functions that the New Testament takes up and attributes to Christ, bearing witness to the extent to which soteriology, the primitive form of New Testament Christology, has its roots in the Old Testament. However, as they are presented in the Old Testament, these mediating functions present an irreducible pluralism. The New Testament will come to triumph over this pluralism by declaring how Jesus is the central reference point of all these types of mediation. All the types of mediators (which seemed to exclude one another) are reunited in the existence of the unique Jesus of Nazareth (taking place in two phases, or three, if His preexistence is taken into account). As "Son of David" or "Christ," "High Priest," "servant of God" (i.e., second Moses), and "Son of Man" (or Word and Wisdom of God), Jesus is the mediator of the ideal and complete salvation, at once royal, priestly, prophetic, and heavenly. He is the perfect mediator. At the same time, He realizes and reunites the various eschatological aspects that are separated in the Old Testament. In Him, salvation is situated as much within history as it is above it and at its end. He is

---

12. See Dn 7:13.

The Scriptural Sources of Christological Dogma

as much immanent as He is transcendent. Already realized, He is still to come.

In the person of Jesus Christ, there is an extraordinary convergence of the multiple, contrasting, and divergent traits of the Messiah announced in the Old Testament. Fr. Lagrange observed this convergence already some time ago:

> The Old Testament had designated, in many ways, him who would need to be the agent of the salvation that was to come. First of all, it was to be God Himself. A host of passages announced that God would come in person to save His people. Therefore, the salvation of Israel would be a remarkable theophany, an extraordinary manifestation of God's goodness toward His people, of His justice toward his enemies, and of His consuming and purifying holiness. On the other hand, a king was awaited, a son of David, who would ascend to the throne of his fathers and would make his nation enjoy an unheard-of felicity. Isaiah made allusion to his miraculous birth and gave him divine names ... The same collection of Isaiah contained the picture of a servant of Yahweh who would convert the peoples to Israel's faith and whose death would serve as an expiation for a great number. Daniel predicted that God would intervene to destroy the persecutors and presented a supernatural being descending from heaven to establish the rule of the saints ... The idea that one person could fulfill all these conditions seemed (and indeed, was) a difficult idea to grasp; or better yet, it would have been an unheard-of miracle, one whose mysterious nature had not yet been revealed ...[13]

Further on in the same text, he remarks:

> The fact of Jesus is the personal coming of God in a unique manifestation of goodness and is the fulfillment of the promises made to David. He is Daniel's supernatural being, though truly the Son of man. He must reign as descendant of David and as Son of Man, though, only after preaching, suffering, and being killed as Yahweh's servant. He has come in order that God's reign over earth might be recognized, so that God may be better served and more fully loved. However, it is through Him that God's reign over the elect is established, since it is by His death and grace that the elect are admitted into proximity with God. In this way, all the prophecies of

---

13. Marie-Joseph Lagrange, *Le messianisme chez les Juifs* (Paris: Gabalda, 1909), 258–59.

the Old Testament are realized and harmonized, and He who is the terminus of the promises is also He who inaugurates the future life.[14]

II. THE APOSTOLIC KERYGMA AND THE FAITH OF THE PRIMITIVE CHRISTIAN COMMUNITY

A. The Christology of St. Paul

We can gather together St. Paul's Christology (in what concerns "the being of Christ") essentially around three themes that converge by presenting Him to us as the Eternal Son of God, God Himself, having become (and, indeed, being) man without ceasing to be what He is from all eternity.

1. Christ's divine filiation

{242} The divine filiation belongs to Jesus Christ in fullness and is communicated by Him to believers through participation in His suffering and death. This is the principal theme of the letters to the Galatians and to the Romans: "We can say that the letter to the Romans is entirely dominated by the notion of filiation, which is proper to Jesus, but has been rendered participable for us through His passion and resurrection. (This is particularly present in the central section of the letter, dedicated to man's situation before and after Christ.)"[15]

See Romans 8:12–17, 29, and above all, see Romans 1:1–4, which is not directly concerned with the two natures but, rather, with the two situations of the same Jesus Christ, abased according to the flesh but exalted according to the Spirit through the resurrection, He who is said to be "The Son of God."[16] Equally, see Galatians 3:26–27 and 4:4–7.

Christ's divinity is expressly professed by St. Paul (Col 2:9, Eph

---

14. Ibid., 265.
15. Louis Bouyer, *Le Fils éternel* (Paris: Cerf, 1974), 271.
16. See *Traduction Oecuménique de la Bible* in loco, note f.; Alois Grillmeier, *La Christ dans la tradition chrétienne. De l'âge apostolique à Chalcédoine (451)* (Paris: Cerf, 1973), 35.

1:3–10).¹⁷ Likewise, see Romans 9:5 (though the exegesis of this text is controversial)¹⁸ and Titus 2:13. The *Traduction Oecuménique de la Bible* comments on this text, stating: "This is a clear affirmation of Christ's divinity."¹⁹

This theme is developed by the famous comparison of the *two Adams*, that is, the theme of the Christian's configuration to Christ through grace and the sacraments, in contrast to his or her configuration to the Old Adam received at birth. "As was the man of dust, so are those who are of the dust; and as is the man of heaven, so are those who are of heaven. Just as we have borne the image of the man of dust, we shall also bear the image of the man of heaven,"²⁰ and earlier: "For as in Adam all die, so also in Christ shall all be made alive."²¹

2. Christ's preexistence

{243} If it is true that Jesus, who was born as a man in time, is simultaneously the Eternal Son of God, we must say that He existed prior to being a man. This is the paradox of Christ's preexistence, which follows directly from the first theme, though it is expressly affirmed by Paul.

The most striking text is Philippians 2:6–11.²² Grillmeier's judgment concerning this matter can be retained:

The most natural interpretation of the passage yields the following meaning: He who was found in a divine mode of being did not wish to cling to his position in selfish exploitation. Instead, He gave himself up to the condition of kenosis (cf. 2 Cor. 8:9, δι ὑμᾶς ἐπτώχευσεν πλούσιος ὤν). But this kenosis is defined in the same sentence by a participle, λαβών! This means

---

17. On this text, see Oscar Cullmann, "Les premières confessions de foi chrétiennes," in *La foi et le culte de l'Église primitive* (Neuchâtel: Delachaux et Niestlé, 1963), 271.
18. See ibid. Also, *Traduction Oecuménique de la Bible* in loco, note m.
19. In loco.
20. 1 Cor 15:48–49 (RSV).
21. 1 Cor 15:22 (RSV).
22. See André Feuillet, "L'hymne christologique de l'épître aux Éphésiens," *Revue biblique* 72 (1965): 481–506; taken up in Feuillet, *Christologie paulinienne et tradition biblique* (Paris: Desclée de Brouwer, 1973), 83–161.

that by becoming man, the preexistent Christ, who exists in a divine mode of being, chooses a mode of existence which is a concealment of His proper being. Historical existence as man can never express what the preexistent Christ is in Himself. Because this kenosis is a "taking," or better an "adding,"[23] the first kind of being is not done away with. He who is equal with God adds something to His divinity, the form of a servant. This being which He assumes serves more to conceal than to reveal Him.[24]

This preexistence is equally affirmed in the texts that present Christ's coming as a sending, a mission.[25] The Christological hymn in Colossians 1:15–20 is focused on Jesus Christ *qua* the man Jesus. However, the assertion that He is [temporally] anterior to every creature (translated in the *Traduction Oecuménique de la Bible* as "He Himself is before all," along with the gloss, "the expression at once signifies anteriority and supremacy"), as well as the role that He is recognized as playing in creation itself ("in Him all was created ... all is created by Him and for Him") absolutely cannot belong to a man whom Paul expressly says was born in time, precisely inasmuch as He is a man. This one who is a man existed before all things, at the beginning: "He existed before being a man." What is said about Wisdom can be applied here.[26] Later on, theology will speak of "the communication of idioms" and will say, "That belongs to Him who is a man, though not on account of His humanity."

Exegetes are well justified in denouncing this interpretation as anachronistic. However, we do not mean that Paul teaches "the communication of idioms," expressly distinguishing what belongs to Jesus Christ on account of His humanity and what belongs to Him on account of His divinity. Rather, he distinguishes them *in actu exercito*, speaking about Christ as about a man, having attributes and a role belonging to Him already before creation (that is, before He is

---

23. See Grillmeier, *La Christ dans la tradition chrétienne*, 40.
24. [Tr. note: Taken from Aloys Grillmeier, *Christ in Christian Tradition: From the Apostolic Age to Chalcedon* (451), trans. J. S. Bowden (New York: Sheed and Ward, 1965), 21.]
25. See Gal 4:4 and Rom 1:3.
26. See Prv 8:22–30 and Wis 7:26.

The Scriptural Sources of Christological Dogma

a man). Therefore, he speaks of attributes and of a role that He did not receive with His humanity, attributes and a role that He does not have on account of His humanity. That is, Paul speaks of attributes and a role that Christ have from the fact that He existed before "coming into the world," on account of what He always is, God; this is what will lead reflection in faith gradually to distinguish within this man, Jesus Christ, that by which He is man (i.e., His humanity, which will be called "His human nature") and He who has this nature, He who is a man by means of that nature, though without being enclosed within the latter, namely, He who existed in the Divine Nature as Son from all eternity, what will come to be called His "person." While this distinction cannot be found in the texts themselves, it alone can render account of what is said therein.

3. *Christ as "Lord"*

{244} After the resurrection, the Christian community gave Christ the title "Lord."[27] It was, perhaps, suggested by a "cryptic" locution of Jesus of during His life, which "in the light of the resurrection would bring a growing awareness of the unexpected implications of His messiahship."[28] I am speaking of Luke 20:41–44, a citation of Psalm 110 placed anew by Luke on Peter's lips.[29]

In any case, Paul constantly attributes this title to Jesus Christ, and for a Jewish believer, the title "Lord" is equivalent to "Yahweh."[30] By proclaiming that Jesus is the "Lord" and "Savior" of the community, Paul thereby expressly attributes divinity to Him.

B. The Christology of St. John

St. John's Christological doctrine can be schematically gathered together along three axes.

---

27. Acts 2:36.
28. Bouyer, *Le Fils éternel*, 212.
29. See Acts 2:34.
30. See Cullmann, "Les premières confessions de foi chrétiennes," 169–205, 267.

1. *The Incarnation of the Logos in Jesus Christ and His Preexistence*

{245} Preexistence is expressly taught and emphasized in the prologue to the fourth Gospel. This text clearly is concerned with the Logos before the Incarnation, even prior to creation: He is "in God" (or, "turned toward God"). Of Him, it is said, "And the Word was made flesh" ("the Word began to exist in a human condition").[31] The words, "we beheld,"[32] make clear reference to the disciples' own testimony; what they saw was a man, Jesus of Nazareth, but through His deeds, words, and above all, His resurrection, they "beheld His glory, glory as of the only Son from the Father, full of grace and truth." The entire Gospel of John presents itself as being a development of this testimony: "... (these signs) are not written in this book; but these are written that you may believe that Jesus is the Christ, the Son of God, and that believing you may have life in his name."[33] The text of 1 John 1:1 makes a similar appeal to the experience of those who witnessed Christ.

Christ's preexistence is clearly affirmed many times in John's Gospel.[34] In particular, note the astonishing affirmation: "Before Abraham was, I am."[35] The *Traduction Oecuménique de la Bible* comments on this passage by noting that it is "an explicit affirmation of the preexistence of the Eternal Son in relation to that man who was Abraham." However, we must add: in relation to this other man as well, Jesus, who as a man (consider, for example, His human birth) obviously comes after Abraham.

2. *The Man Jesus is the eternal Son, present and acting in this world*

{246} The Jesus presented to us by John is manifestly endowed with a forceful human personality. However, at the same time, He

---

31. *Traduction Oecuménique de la Bible* in loco, note r.
32. Jn 1:14 (RSV).
33. Jn 20:30–31 (RSV).
34. Jn 3:16–17 and 31; 8:23.
35. Jn 8:58 (RSV).

has interpersonal relations with the Father, His Father, relations that are situated on a superhuman, eternal plane:[36]

Since the mission of the Unique Son and His Incarnation are one and the same thing, it is no less true that Christ's person is divine-human and that this person increasingly stands forth in both of these aspects, to the degree that faith acquires clarity. For John, Christ always presents believers with the traces of both His celestial and earthly origins. Never does He permit us to erect a partition between the authority and power coming to Him from on High and the weakness inherent in His flesh.[37]

3. Jesus Christ communicates the divine filiation to believers

{247} This Pauline theme is also Johannine. However, with Fr. Bouyer,[38] let us merely note one difference. For Paul, Jesus is the *first-born* among brothers who have become *adoptive sons* with Him and through Him, whereas for John, the term "son" is reserved for Christ, with this exclusive qualification: "The Only-Begotten Son." The others are "children of God," though with this specification: "and so we are" (1 Jn 3:1, RSV).

C. The Confessions of the First Christians

{248} The first community's faith is of capital importance, for the contemporary Christian community's faith is authentic only to the degree that it is rooted in the first and to the degree that the latter prolongs the former by making explicit what was already [implicit] in it. This is what is meant by the Church's apostolicity.

Oscar Cullmann carefully studied the formulas of the confession expressing this primitive faith, as it is found first of all in the books of the New Testament, though also in the post-apostolic writings.[39] These are his principal conclusions: "A first conclusion, which is important for knowing the dogmatic core of all the Christian confes-

---

36. See Jn 10:15, 3:55, 8:49–50; and in the discourse after the Last Supper.
37. François-Marie Braun, *Jean le théologien* (Paris: Gabalda, 1959–72), 71.
38. Bouyer, *Le Fils éternel*, 270.
39. See Oscar Cullmann, *Christologie du Nouveau Testament* (Neuchâtel: Delachaux et Niestlé, 1966).

sions, emerges as necessary: the point of departure of Christian faith is faith in Christ."[40]

But in what does "faith in Christ" consist? Cullmann writes: "Hence, we can conclude that Jesus Christ's divine sonship and elevation to the dignity of *kyrios* following on His death and resurrection are the two essential elements of the majority of second century confessions."[41] The original element would be his elevation: "The divine filiation is not what serves in explaining the elevation of the resurrected *kyrios*. Rather, the Christian of the first century speaks about His divine origin and later on about His return, basing his reflection upon the dignity of Christ, the resurrected *kyrios*."[42] From which he draws this third conclusion:

> Therefore, the current reign of Christ, inaugurated by His resurrection and His ascension to God's right [hand] is what stands at the center of primitive Christianity's faith. The historical and dogmatic core of the Christian confession that we are now seeking is found in the affirmation that Christ now reigns over the entire universe, that all power in heaven and on earth has been given to Him. The simplest expression of it is "Kyrios Christos."[43]

For Cullmann, this in no way means that Christ's Lordship began only at His resurrection:

> On the other hand, when the first Christians confess that "Christ is the Lord," this confession contains a precise declaration concerning the era during which it pleased God to reveal the time of salvation, a time that includes not only the present but also the past and the future. If Christ is the Lord today, this is because yesterday He was incarnate and crucified and because tomorrow He will return to judge the living and the dead. Therefore, the confession "Christ is Lord" implies a reference to Christ's earthly work and His return.[44]

---

40. Ibid., 77. [Tr. note: I have not found close parallel forms of this text in the current English translation of this text by Cullmann. Because of this discrepancy, I have translated directly from Fr. Nicolas's French text for this text and the next four.]
41. Ibid., 82.
42. [Tr. note: No citation details in Fr. Nicolas's text.]
43. Ibid., 83.
44. Ibid., 86–87.

The Scriptural Sources of Christological Dogma

The resurrection and ascension did not make Him the "Son of God." Rather, they manifested to the world that He is the Son of God, and this filiation is what was confessed by the first Christians.[45]

III. WHAT JESUS SAID ABOUT HIMSELF

"In the beginning, there was preaching about Christ." This is the famous Bultmannian formula, which seems quite contestable, for the birth of preaching about Christ still itself calls for an explanation:

> As was retorted by thinkers like Cullmann, Jeremias, and Taylor (to cite only these few names): if Jesus did not, in fact, present Himself as such (as "being aware of possessing a sovereign authority with regard to the Divine Kingdom"), as not a few Bultmannians admit today, if He stood out as a [unique] personality at this creative point, can we plausibly say that the community—or, rather, some anonymous genius in it—must have fashioned, with a magnificent simplicity, the synthesis and transfiguration of the prophetic and apocalyptic themes that the first three evangelists already unanimously attribute to Jesus? We must confess that the implausibility of the supposition is so great that it calls for a decisive argument on its behalf if it is to be convincing.[46]

A. The Title "Son of Man" and Its Reference to the Suffering Servant of Isaiah

{249} The title "Son of man" is found only in the Gospels (except in Acts 14:56, though the reference to Jesus's own words is obvious in that text), and when it is encountered, it is always placed on Jesus's lips (except in Jn 12:34, though the crowd is here merely repeating Jesus's words). It is found more than seventy times in the Gospels. If, in some cases, it is not immediately clear that Jesus is speaking about Himself when He uses this expression, in other cases, He most certainly is doing so. In the majority of cases, this is obvious. The first community certainly did not itself give this title

---

45. Along the same lines, see Joseph Schmitt, "Le Christ Jésus dans la foi et la vie de la naissante Église," *Lumière et Vie* 15 (1954): 23–42.

46. Bouyer, *Le Fils éternel*, 201.

to Jesus and did not understand it well. Thus, if it is repeated by the Gospels, we are faced with a case of Christ's authentic words.

In the Old Testament, it is one of the Messiah's titles, one that is related to his exaltation. What is entirely original (and, of itself, strange) is that in the Gospels, it is placed in close relation with the figure of Isaiah's "suffering servant." As Feuillet observes:

> The difference (between Daniel's Son of Man and that of the Gospels) consists essentially in a fact that is quite important. Whereas in Daniel the Son of Man is immutably established in celestial glory, in the Gospels, He reaches His glory only through the path of martyrdom and His expiatory death as the Servant of Yahweh.[47]

There is something incredible and absolutely new in this synthesis of the transcendent Son of Man and the Suffering Servant. Neither the Old Testament nor [inter-testamental] Judaism foresaw it.[48]

Along the same lines, Bouyer states:

> We would need to attribute this recourse (to the image of Isaiah 53) to someone other than Jesus, even though nothing, or near to nothing, in Palestinian Judaism itself drew attention to this text, above all not drawing attention to its possible interpretation along these lines. Moreover, we would need to attribute to this other person the extraordinary stroke of genius of combining this abased figure with the figure of supernatural exaltation *par excellence* (a stroke of genius so extraordinary, in fact, that the Ancient Church did not seem to have herself dared to wrap her head around it), but such an assertion would ultimately create a gratuitous and nearly-insurmountable difficulty. In order for such a paradox to have been retained at the very heart of the synoptic Gospels, it must spring from the Master Himself.[49]

Moreover, it is noteworthy that the disciples, who at this time do not seem to have wholly understood this teaching of Jesus, will lat-

---

47. [Tr. note: Fr. Nicolas cites the bibliographical entry for André Feuillet, "Les 'Ego eimi' du IVe évangile," *Revue des Sciences Religieuses* 54 (1966): 5–22 and 213–40. Neither his pagination nor the content match this article. The reference appears to be to André Feuillet, "Les trois grandes prophéties de la Passion et de la Résurrection," *Revue thomiste* 68 (1968): 69.]

48. Ibid.

49. Bouyer, *Le Fils éternel*, 206. Along the same lines, see Charles Harold Dodd, *Le fondateur du christianisme*, trans. Paul-André Lesort (Paris: Seuil, 1972), ch. 6, "The Messiah." Also see Dodd, *Conformément aux Écritures*, 110–11.

er on strive to interpret the cross and the resurrection in light of this text, as is clear in the first discourse of Acts.

Therefore, Jesus was aware of His Messiahship. However, according to the Gospels, it seems that He declined to accept "Messiah" as a title. In particular, at His trial, in response to the High Priest (according to the version reported by Matthew, which seems to provide the most exact rendering of what Jesus said), He still refuses a categorical declaration: "You say it"—that is, "It is you who say it." This is explained by the ambiguity of this title during Jesus's lifetime: Jesus's way of conceiving His role as Messiah was so opposed to what His contemporaries awaited that prior to His cross, death, and resurrection, He could not make this meaning clear and could not accept the title: "He refuses to allow Himself to be confined within an ambiguous situation regarding His Messiahship, and He gives the true meaning of His response by announcing the coming of the 'Son of man,' a celestial *persona*, as well as the privilege of the son of David who must sit at the right hand of God."[50]

B. Jesus's Filial Awareness

{250} If the title "Son of God" existed already in the Old Testament (as applied to Israel, the king, and so forth) Jesus, according to the Synoptic Gospels as well as the fourth Gospel, applied it to Himself with a peerless sense of intimacy.[51] It even seems that He sometimes simply designated Himself as "the Son" (see Mt 11:27, 13:32, and Lk 10:21–22). In the last text just cited (the great blessing pronounced by Jesus before His disciples),

> it seems undeniable that Jesus's unique filiation expresses itself as being verified in the knowledge—with all the biblical richness of that term—that He has of the Father, flowing from the knowledge the Father has of Him, that is to say, this intimacy and original conformity—"original" precisely because of His origination—that is exclusively His own.[52]

---

50. *Traduction Oecuménique de la Bible*, in Mt 26:64, note d.
51. See Joachim Jeremias, *Théologie du Nouveau Testament*, vol. 1, trans. Josse Alzin and Arthur Liefooghe (Paris: Cerf, 1973).
52. Bouyer, *Le Fils éternel*, 214.

As regards the authenticity of this prayer as being truly pronounced by Jesus Himself [we can say, with Bouyer]:

> This prayer for knowledge appears so typically Palestinian Jewish in character, and so close to the themes underlying the Sermon on the Mount (though, above all, being so powerfully original), that it is difficult to imagine that it could have been either created or substantially modified by the Church.[53]

C. Jesus's Teaching concerning Himself Is the Source of the Church's Christology

{251} If all of this is true, we must recognize that during His earthly life Jesus was fully aware of being the "Messiah" and the Son of God. Certainly, His words' profound meaning for the most part eluded the disciples when they heard Him first speak them. However, in light of the resurrection and under the action of the Spirit of Pentecost, they came to understand them. These words were the foundation for their faith and for the preaching by which they communicated this faith to the primitive Christian community.

---

53. Ibid., 215.

2

The Formation of the Christological Dogmata

I. THE AWAKENING OF CHRISTOLOGICAL REFLECTION

{252} The Church's Christological reflection began as early as the start of the second century as believers felt the need to justify the Christian faith to Jews and pagans ([e.g.,] St. Justin Martyr), as well as the need to oppose the true faith to heretical aberrations, which likewise arose at a very early stage ([e.g., as combatted in the writings of] Sts. Ignatius of Antioch and Irenaeus).

This reflection essentially includes the affirmation of faith in the unique Christ, placing the accent on both His humanity and His divinity. However, an explicit doctrine of "two natures" obviously has not yet been discovered at this point (except, perhaps, in sketched outline in Tertullian). The procedure used in this era is expressed in antithetical affirmations, which are the proclamation of the apostolic faith.

Nevertheless, "theologians" of this era were first confronted with the Christological problem from the perspective of Trinitarian theology (i.e., that of the relationship between the Logos and the Father): what is meant when we say, not that this man is God, but that the Logos is God? Then, they were confronted by what seemed to be a kind of divine mutability implied by the Incarnation. Indeed, on this point, they faced the formidable attacks of Celsus:

> So, the second century is already confronted with problems as difficult as any generation of Christian theologians had to solve. The doctrine of the "one person in two natures," much abused because of its technical terms, was the only way out of the dilemma raised by Celsus. The question was whether God had really entered history while still remaining God, the same problem with which contemporary theology is still engaged, though in a different way, in its debate with R. Bultmann. The substance of Christianity was at stake.[1]

With Tertullian, we witness the formation of a Latin Christological vocabulary, which will be found again in the *Tome* of St. Leo and will ultimately pass, with improvements into the formula promulgated by Chalcedon.

Indeed, this is not only a question of vocabulary. Here, we find the express denial of what will later be called monophysitism, that is, a denial of the idea that Christ's divinity and humanity were mixed together:

> Indeed, if the Word became flesh by a transfiguration and permutation of His substance, there will thus be a substance of Christ made out of two substances, the flesh and the Spirit, a kind of mixture, as "yellow amber" is made from mixing gold and silver. Hence, this new mixture will be neither gold—which is the Spirit—nor silver—which is the flesh—since each is modified by the other and a third thing is brought about. Thus, Jesus will not be God: He ceased, in fact, to be the Word, He who has become flesh. However, no more will He be a man: He who was the Word is not now, properly speaking, flesh. He is neither one nor the other. Far from being one or the other, He is a third thing.[2]

This theological demonstration of the impossibility of monophysitism remains a classic argument against it. Note that it is immediately connected to the primitive assertion of faith: if the Incarnation

---

1. Grillmeier, *La Christ dans la tradition chrétienne*, 150. [Tr. note: Taken from Grillmeier, *Christ in Christian Tradition*, 124.]
2. Tertullian, *Adversus Praxeam*, *Corpus scriptorum ecclesiasticorum latinorum* 2 [sic], ch. 27.

involved the mixing (*mixtura*) of divinity (*Spiritus*) with humanity (*caro*), Jesus would be neither God nor man. In such a case, He would be a "tertium quid," a third thing, as remote from Being-God as from being-man.[3]

Tertullian succeeded at formulating a remarkably precise theological vocabulary on this point, expressing the mystery in terms that will be taken up by later Latin theology. Thus, approximately two centuries later, in St. Leo's *Tome to Flavian*, we will find the following affirmation:

> We see (in Christ) a double substance, not mixed, but distinct in one, unique person, Jesus, God and man, and what is proper to each substance is preserved in such a way that the Spirit, on the one hand, performed in Him His own, proper works—miracles, works, and signs—and the flesh, on the other hand, suffered its own, proper weaknesses—hunger when Jesus is grappling with the devil, thirst when he encounters the Samaritan, tears at Lazarus's tomb, anguish to the point of death, and finally, death itself.[4]

If Tertullian's influence is only slightly apparent in the third century, it will come to be quite pronounced from the fourth century onward. Moreover, in his own work elucidating and expressing Christ's unity in two natures, St. Augustine will systematically utilize his terminology, which is already empirical enough in itself.[5]

II. THE DEVELOPMENT OF CHRISTOLOGY UP TO THE NESTORIAN CRISIS

{253} By means of an admittedly schematic division, the development of Christology up to the time of the Nestorian Crisis can be

---

3. On the meaning of the words "nature" and "substance" in Tertullian, see Raniero Cantalamessa, *La Cristologia di Tertulliano* (Fribourg: Éditions Universitaires, 1962), 94–110; on his anthropology, see ibid., 108n1.

4. Tertullian, *Adversus Praxean*, ch. 27; see Cantalamessa, *La Cristologia di Tertulliano*, 131–35.

5. See Jacques Liébaert, *L'incarnation*, vol. 1, *Des origines à Chalcédoine* (Paris: Cerf, 1968), 109–10, 124–26, 170–73.

reduced to two lines, or tendencies, which we can call the "LOGOS-SARX" line of thought and the "LOGOS-ANTHROPOS" line. These two lines crisscross each other, and these two tendencies reacted to one another up to the Council of Chalcedon (451), which attempted to synthesize them, indeed partially succeeding, though without definitively settling the conflict.

A. The LOGOS-SARX Christological Line

For theologians in the third and fourth centuries, the characteristic case of the union of two "substances" or "things" in a single being was the union of soul and body constituting man. Thus, many during this period *tended* to use this sort of union to conceptualize that of the Logos with the flesh in Christ's unified constitution.

1. *The appearance of the LOGOS-SARX schema*

{254} Origen can be called the theologian of Christ's soul. (He thought of it along the lines of his position concerning other men's souls, namely, as preexisting entities.) According to him, the union of the Logos with the flesh was brought about by the mediation of this soul. It is not clear how it would itself have been united to the Logos. Origen certainly held that such a union is real and ontological. However, he also believed that it is simultaneously a union by knowledge and love. In any case, according to him, the Incarnation consisted in the fact that, by love, the Logos united *His* soul to flesh within the Virgin.

Now, the LOGOS-SARX schema was constituted in Origen's theological line of thought, a fact that is quite paradoxical in comparison with Origen's own bent, given how this schema neglects, and often eliminates, the role of Christ's soul (for the Logos would, from this perspective, be immediately united to the flesh). It seems that Paul of Samosata's heresy (which was condemned at the Council of Antioch in 268) provoked the position of Malchion as a kind of reaction. In this case, Malchion would be a precursor to Apollinarius, who held that an acknowledgment that Christ had a human soul would make it impossible for us to acknowledge that He has a strict unity, thereby making it impossible for us to admit the mystery of the Incarnation and to provide an intelligible explanation for it.[6] Indeed, this is what would lead Origen's disciples to deviate from their master in regard to his affirmation of a created soul in Christ.

2. *The three forms of* LOGOS-SARX *Christology*

{255} LOGOS-SARX Christology is dominated by a concern to safeguard Christ's unity. This is where we find its positive aspect and its principal contribution to progress in the formulation of Christological dogmatic statements. As the LOGOS most certainly is the principle of this unity ("Jesus Christ *is* the LOGOS"), this position tends to interpret the LOGOS as being the sole principle of His life and action, disregarding the role (and sometimes even the existence) of a created, human principle of life and action (i.e., a soul) in Christ. This is the weakness of this Christology and was the reason for the trouble it aroused in the great Christological debates of the fifth century.

However, we must carefully distinguish within this theological tendency the Christologies that pushed this deficiency to the point of expressly and systematically denying that Christ had a human soul, from those that, without denying that Christ had a soul, do not know how to make room for it in their conception of Him. The first ended up in heresy, whereas the others, generally faithful to the apostolic kerygma, can be completed by later conceptual precisions and dogmatic formulations without being precluded by them.

St. Athanasius is the most eminent representative of this kind of Christology, one that is imperfect but correct. An impassioned defender of the divinity of the LOGOS, he is also a lucid and decided witness to the Incarnation. For him, Jesus Christ is the Word become man through the assumption of the flesh. The LOGOS is who exists in the flesh, all the while remaining immutable in His divinity.

---

6. See Grillmeier, *La Christ dans la tradition chrétienne*, 208.

The Lord is the LOGOS who bears the flesh, not a man bearing God. If St. Athanasius does not preclude the idea that this flesh would be animated by a created soul, he barely cares about this latter point, making no room for a "human psychology" in Jesus. This led to his troubles in responding to the Arians, who relied on Christ's "psychological weaknesses" (e.g., sadness, agony, ignorance, and so forth) in order to deny the divinity of the LOGOS. Athanasius is content to place all these experiences in the "flesh," and is also fine with minimizing their reality.

The special future significance of the Christological formula of St. Athanasius and of the Logos-sarx framework in general lies in its clear presentation of the "unity of subject" in Christ. The *Logos* is the all-dominating and sole principle of all existence and therefore of all statements about Christ. This is the superiority of the Alexandrine formula over the Antiochene, which is weakest here ... A true conception of the personality of Christ is certainly revealed here. It is an old Christian legacy, which we were able to establish as early as Ignatius of Antioch and his source, Jn 1:14.[7]

Let us add, however, that important and problematic equivocations were rendered possible on account of the confusion between the role of the LOGOS in unifying the Whole that is Christ and the soul's role in enlivening the flesh, enabling the latter to act, and itself acting in a spiritual fashion.

{256} By contrast, Apollinarius and Arius, each in his own way (though doubtlessly in dependence on the same LOGOS-SARX theological current), elaborated a Christology expressly founded on the denial of any kind of human soul in Christ. According to them, the LOGOS took the place of the soul (or, of *Nous*) in Christ's humanity, thus being immediately united to His "flesh." From here onward, however, these two are opposed to each other—indeed, Apollinarius was an ally of Athanasius against Arius—for, according to Arius, the LOGOS is not God, and all the psychological weaknesses of the man Jesus were weaknesses of the LOGOS himself, thus being a

---

7. Ibid., 255–56. [Tr. note: Taken from Grillmeier, *Christ in Christian Tradition*, 218–19.]

sign of his inferiority in relation to the Father (i.e., a sign of his non-divinity), whereas Apollinarius denied all such weakness. According to him, Christ is not truly a man but rather a "celestial man." Thus, we are in the presence of two opposed ways of "reducing" (and ultimately, of "eliminating") the mystery of the Incarnation. One path disregards the Word who is incarnate. The other disregards the very fact that He is incarnate.

On the contrary [, when it comes to Athanasius, we can say, with Grillmeier]:

> [He] never made an explicit denial of the soul of Christ and wrote no sentence suggesting the sense which Apollinarius has given to it. Precisely at this point it becomes abundantly clear that though some aspects of his Logos-sarx Christology are akin to that of Apollinarius, his thought and his picture of Christ is essentially different. His Logos-sarx framework is certainly open for an explicit doctrine of the soul of Christ. That of Apollinarius is closed.[8]

{257} Schematically, this can be summarized as follows (see figure 1, below):

Figure 1

The "Logos," the sole principle of existence and of life in Christ
- the human soul of Jesus is not denied, but is diminished: . . . . ATHANASIUS
- the human soul of Jesus is formally denied.
  - The "Logos" who takes the place of the soul is God: APOLLINAIRIUS
  - The "Logos" who takes the place of the soul is a creature: . . . . ARIUS

B. The LOGOS-ANTHROPOS Christological Line

As the LOGOS-SARX Christological tendency is founded on that part of the kerygma which affirms Christ's unity (and the fact that Christ, the man-Jesus, is the LOGOS in the flesh), the LOGOS-ANTHROPOS tendency is founded on another aspect of the mystery,

---

8. Ibid., 253. [Tr. note: Taken from Grillmeier, *Christ in Christian Tradition*, 216–17.]

which from the beginning was inextricably linked to it for faith: Jesus Christ is a true man, fully a man. When, from the very start of one's reflection, this aspect is isolated and dissociated, we find ourselves faced with the deviation of Adoptionism, whose first-known (and still-poorly-understood) manifestation was the heresy of Paul of Samosata, which was condemned at the Council of Antioch in 268.[9]

{258} Within the history of dogmatic development, LOGOS-ANTHROPOS Christology is present as a reaction against Arian Christology in the Christology of Eustathius of Antioch (d. before 337). Unfortunately, this reaction in fact led to a divisive (or dualistic) Christology, as is evidenced in the following text: "But the 'I am not yet ascended unto my Father' was not spoken by the Logos, nor by the God who came down from heaven and lives in the bosom of the Father, nor by the Wisdom which embraces all that is created, but it was uttered by a *man* formed of different members, who was raised from the dead and had not yet ascended to the Father."[10] For Eustathius, Jesus Christ is no longer *Theos sarkophoros*, the flesh-bearing God (as He was for St. Ignatius of Antioch) but, rather, *Anthropos theophoros*, a God-bearing man.

We must note a first, very important stage in the development of this Christological tendency, namely, Pope Damasus's simultaneous condemnation of Apollinarism and Adoptionism in his letters to the eastern bishops and at the Roman Council of 382.[11] In these condemnations, the reaffirmation of the kerygma has two characteristics. On the one hand, it is affirmed that Jesus Christ is the Eternal Son of God who, through the Incarnation, became a true man in the womb of the Virgin, endowed with a human body and a human soul, though without sin. However, on the other hand, this affirmation does not explain how this humanity and divinity are united in Him, nor how such impeccability is assured. Indeed, it does not even

---

9. See Henri de Riedmatten, *Les actes du procès de Paul de Samosate, Étude sur la christologie des IIIe and IVe siècles* (Fribourg: Éditions Saint Paul, 1952).

10. Cited by Grillmeier, *La Christ dans la tradition chrétienne*, 288. [Tr. note: Taken from Grillmeier, *Christ in Christian Tradition*, 248.]

11. See D.-*Sch.*, nos. 146–49 and 158–59.

seem that Damasus perceived the problem, so that the further investigations that ultimately resulted in these deviations could not be stopped by such condemnations.

We cannot here provide a history of these investigations along the LOGOS-ANTHROPOS line.[12] They bore their most elaborated fruit, on the eve of the Nestorian crisis, in the Christology of the most eminent representative of the Antiochian school, Theodore of Mopsuestia, who was Nestorius's teacher.

Theodore was a resolute adversary of Apollinarism and of Arian Christology, and he attacked the very foundation of them both (and this attack marked a great step of progress). This foundation was the conviction that the Logos is the sole principle of life and action in Jesus-Christ, his flesh only being an inert instrument by itself. For Theodore, on the contrary, Christ's human nature recovers its true internal, physico-human life, as well as its capacity to act. This enables two things to be explained. On the one hand, the "psychological weaknesses" of Christ can be sufficiently accounted for, without having them affect the Logos in His divinity. On the other hand, this outlook enables the redemptive sacrifice to be seen as an act proceeding from Christ's human decision, and this involves a penetrating theological insight into the mystery of the Incarnation. (Thus, this Christology emphasizes, well in advance, the authentic Catholic position which will be formulated in the course of the controversies of the seventh century.)

The weakness of this position begins when it comes to determining how it is that Christ is one. Theodore uses a number of formulas that seem to state that the Logos assumed a man distinct from Himself, and the metaphors that he employs are oriented toward this interpretation. (Thus, in connection with the Logos, the humanity would be like the crimson robe with which the king is clothed, which is not part of him but is honored along with him, though not in itself.) Likewise, Theodore presents the "communication of idi-

---

12. See Grillmeier, *La Christ dans la tradition chrétienne*, 279–416.

oms" as a "way of speaking" rather than as expressing the complex reality of Christ: "When they (the Divine Scriptures) speak of that which belongs to each of them (i.e., the natures) *as though we were speaking of one*, we understand what a marvelous conjunction takes place (between them)."[13]

What he lacks—and what is still lacking for theology in general at this time—is a clear distinction between "person" (or "hypostasis") and nature. This distinction had already been elaborated for the Trinitarian mystery (i.e., the distinction of the hypostases from the *ousia*). However, at this time, it had not yet come to be openly used for the Christological mystery. For Theodore, the *prosôpon* is the principle of union in Christ. However, this term does not yet have a clearly ontological meaning. Rather, it is concerned with how a concretely-realized nature is present and manifests itself, which leads to the conclusion that every concretely-realized nature (and, therefore, each of Christ's two natures) has its own *prosôpon*, even though there is only one *prosôpon* in Christ on account of the union: "For when we distinguish the natures, we say that the nature of God the Word is complete, and that (his) *prosopon* is complete (for it is not correct to speak of a *hypostasis* without its *prosopon*); and (we say) also that the nature of the man is complete, and likewise (his) *prosopon*). But when we look to the conjunction, then we say one *prosopon*."[14]

In what does this single *prosôpon* consist? It seems that Theodore's thought finds itself embarrassed on this point. He insists on the unique character of this union, in terms that tend to express an ontological union (even employing the comparison of the union between body and soul),[15] but he also speaks about it like a communication of the Logos's honor and dignity to the *prosôpon* of Christ's human nature.

---

13. Theodore of Mopsuestia, *Homélies catéchétiques*, ed. Raymond Tonneau and Robert Devresse, *Studi e Testi* 145 (Vatican City: Biblioteca Apostolica Vaticana, 1949), 201.

14. Cited by Grillmeier, *La Christ dans la tradition chrétienne*, 403. [Tr. note: Taken from Grillmeier, *Christ in Christian Tradition*, 351.]

15. See ibid., 407.

The Formation of the Christological Dogma

In conclusion, we must not say that Theodore would have denied Christ's unity, nor even that he misunderstood it. We can only say that he did not know how to intelligibly render an account of it because he did not have an appropriate conceptual apparatus at hand for the task. His Christology remains open in relation to later developments, and we can indeed say that it marks a forward step, though a timid one,[16] toward the formula of Chalcedon. Like Athanasius's Christology, though in an opposite direction, it is an imperfect, though not closed-off, Christology.

III. THE NESTORIAN CRISIS: EPHESUS AND CHALCEDON

A. Historical Remark

For a good overview of this history, consult Camelot's work, and for a more thorough study of it, refer to works of Church history and the history of dogmatic development.

B. Comparison of the Christologies of Nestorius and Cyril of Alexandria

{259} We can compare the Christologies of Nestorius and Cyril of Alexandria by considering two important texts bearing witness to a direct confrontation between these two Christologies, namely, the second letter of St. Cyril to Nestorius and Nestorius's response to it.[17] At the end of his life, in exile, Nestorius defended and developed his thought in the "Book of Heraclides."[18] For his own part, Cyril, in the course of his discussions with John of Antioch, substantially corrected his third letter to Nestorius, which notified him of his condemnation and was accompanied by the famous "twelve anath-

---

16. See ibid., 413.
17. See D.-Sch., no. 250; Camelot, *Ephèse et Chalcédoine*, 2:191–98; Gervais Dumeige, *Textes Doctrinaux du Magistere de L'Eglise sur La Foi Catholique* [Paris: Édition de l'Orante, 1969], 294.
18. See Luigi Scipioni, *Ricerche sulla cristologia del "Libro di Eraclide" di Nestorio. La formulazione teologica e il suo contest filosofico* (Fribourg: Éditions Universitaires, 1956).

emas."[19] This letter included assertions and formulas—"according to physical union," "Son by nature"—which were strongly contested at the time and which are indeed very contestable in themselves. The "symbol of union" which brought about reconciliation between the two great bishops [i.e., John and Cyril][20] expresses a Christology that is much "purer" and freed of the heavy burden that weighs upon it because of Cyril's adoption of the Apollinarist formula, "the one, single nature of the Incarnate Word"—a formula that he believed was taken from St. Athanasius!

Nestorius is obviously situated in the line of LOGOS-ANTHROPOS theology, with its characteristic strengths and weaknesses. However, in his case, this theology is closed to any future dogmatic specifications, due to his definite rejection of the "communication of idioms." It does not seem that we can interpret Nestorious's *prosôpon the union* in an ontological sense. Therefore, we can say that, despite its merits, this Christology represents a "deviation" that will need to be rectified by the Chalcedonian formula.

For its part, Cyril's Christology is situated in the LOGOS-SARX line, and his unfortunate borrowing of the formula "one, single nature" from the Apollinarists is the evident sign of this fact. Nevertheless, an obvious difference exists between Cyril and Apollinaris, namely, that Cyril recognizes that Christ has a complete humanity, with a body and soul, as well as all the *anthropina*. Therefore, his reluctance to speak of "two natures" arises from an insufficient elaboration of the concept of "nature," not from a rejection of what is meant by this [Chalcedonian] formula (i.e., the entire reality of the divinity and the entire reality of humanity are both found in Christ).[21] Cyril's considerable contribution to the correct formulation of Christological doctrine is found in his definite affirmation of Christ's unified subject, understood in light of the kerygma:

---

19. [Tr. note: Fr. Nicolas cites "Camelot, 198–207." This would refer to bibliographical entry T. Camelot, "Le dogme de la Trinité. Origine et formation des formules dogmatiques," *Lumière et Vie* 30 (1956): 9–48. As this does not make sense, he is perhaps referring to Camelot, *Éphèse et Chalcédoine*.]

20. See ibid., 209–16.

21. See Grillmeier, *La Christ dans la tradition chrétienne*, 464–65.

The Formation of the Christological Dogma

The one positive element which Cyril took over from the Athanasian and Apollinarian Logos-sarx Christology is therefore not to be underestimated. From it he formed the new Alexandrine Christology, which was the deepest expression of Christ that Greek theology was able to offer. A feature of it is the recognition of the unity of subject in Christ, the Logos. Whereas among the Antiochenes "Christ" seems to emerge alongside the Logos as a new subject of Christological expressions, in Alexandrine theology all expressions are directly orientated on the Logos.[22]

C. The "Dogma" of Ephesus

{260} Cyril's second letter to Nestorius was read at the Council of Ephesus after the arrival of the [papal] legates and was expressly approved, against Nestorius, as representing the authentic interpretation of the Nicaean Creed. Thus, it was held to express the Church's faith as it was proclaimed at Ephesus.

Obviously, the whole of Cyrillian Christology was not thereby "canonized." Nonetheless, it seems that "canonization" was indeed bestowed on this fundamental affirmation of the unity of the subject, Christ, the Incarnate Logos, to whom both what is divine and what is human really belong (and therefore to whom they are therefore justly attributed): "Furthermore, [we say] that the natures brought together in the real union [are] different and from these two only one Christ and Son results, not as though the difference of the natures was suppressed by the union, but, rather, because the divinity and the humanity have formed for us only one Lord and Christ and Son by their ineffable and mysterious coming together in unity."[23]

D. From Ephesus to Chalcedon

{261} In the Church's history, the period following Ephesus was one involving a faithful search for a reconciliation between the two Christological tendencies that were violently opposed to each other. It was also a period involving the exacerbation of the LOGOS-SARX tendency in Cyril's impassioned and blind partisans, who were at-

---

22. Ibid., 466. [Tr. note: Taken from *Christ in Christian Tradition*, 404.]
23. Camelot, *Ephèse et Chalcédoine*, 2:192. [Tr. note: Taken from Denzinger, no. 250. As noted above, this is likely from *Ephèse et Chalcédoine*.]

tached to his extreme formulas, which he himself renounced. Here, we are referring to the monophysitism of Eutyches, which was condemned by the Synod of Constantinople in 448, under the authority of the patriarch Flavian. This involved notable progress in the direction of the investigation into Christ's principle of unity (i.e., the hypostasis) and also was a clear affirmation of His two natures. Nonetheless, this latter affirmation was expressed by means of an unfortunate formula, *ex duabus naturis*, "from two natures," which Eutyches would seize on to express his doctrine: "two natures before the union" (= the union is brought about from two natures), "but only one after" (= the union fused the two into one).

However, Flavian's formula did indeed specify [these matters clearly]: "We acknowledge that Christ is from two natures after the Incarnation, in one hypostasis and one person confessing one Christ, one Son, one Lord."[24] Following this condemnation, there was the "Robber Council of Ephesus,"[25] but also the famous letter of Pope St. Leo to Flavian. Even though this letter was not able to be read at the pseudo-Council of Ephesus, it was read at Chalcedon. It represents the Latin tradition's most important contribution to the Chalcedonian definition. In the direction of this immediate preparation, we must also note the efforts of Flavian's predecessor, Proclus, the patriarch of Constantinople and his *Tomus ad Armenios*.[26] Let us note the very significant modification that he brings to Cyril's unfortunate formula: "I acknowledge one single hypostasis of God the Word made flesh," in place of, "one hypostasis of the Logos made flesh."

We can now say that the concept of hypostasis is finally prepared to enter into the Chalcedonian definition, this concept designating the unique subject in Christ, the Logos, in contrast to His two natures (i.e., the Divine Nature which this hypostasis possesses from all eternity and the human nature that He assumed in time).

---

24. Grillmeier, *La Christ dans la tradition chrétienne*, 526. [Tr. note: Taken from Grillmeier, *Christ in Christian Tradition*, 457.]
25. See Camelot, *Ephèse et Chalcédoine*, 2:95–114.
26. See Grillmeier, *La Christ dans la tradition chrétienne*, 521–25.

IV. THE FORMULA OF CHALCEDON

The "Dogma of Chalcedon": The Permanent Value of Chalcedon's Dogmatic Formulation

{262} Today,[27] a number of thinkers tend to "historicize" the formula of Chalcedon, holding that it is only a contingent expression of the faith, in accordance with the cultural situation of its era. This outlook is accompanied by a tendency to think that the same faith could be, indeed ought to be, expressed (and, first of all, thought about) in a different way today, one that would be in accordance with our current cultural situation.

This issue presents us with the entire problem of theological hermeneutics. Historically, it is very difficult to sustain the claim that the Fathers of Chalcedon intended to express the faith [solely] according to their particular conceptions. Many and sundry influences all played their role in the definition—Latin and Greek influences, as well as many different philosophical inspirations. Certainly, we cannot contest that they were guided by their concern with maintaining the faith integrally and by the sense that they had of this faith, making use of formulations that were often defective (and therefore were not merely guided along by their particular philosophical conceptions).

At the level of their preoccupations, the notions of nature and of person that they utilized to this end were not philosophical notions but, rather, were very general notions indicating what is one in Christ (the subject, designated by the name "Jesus" and the terms "the Son of God" and "the Lord") and what is twofold in Him, namely perfect in humanity (He is fully man) and perfect in divinity (He remained fully God). Even today, alongside the desire to relativize the notion of human nature, such a notion is still implicitly

---

27. See the text in D.-Sch., nos. 300–302, and the French translation in Camelot, *Ephèse et Chalcédoine*, 2:224–28; Dumeige, *Textes sur la Foi catholique*, 313. Likewise, see the brief but very good analysis in Grillmeier, *La Christ dans la tradition chrétienne*, 551–59; also, see Camelot, *Ephèse et Chalcédoine*, 2:139–50.

appealed to when one speaks of "man" and of "human rights." As a point of fact, nobody can really do without such a notion.

Catholic theology followed this middle way, which rightly illuminated the full magnitude of the mystery of the Incarnation. On the one hand, it admitted that in Jesus Christ, God and man were *one* in being and substance. On the other hand, it proclaimed His divinity and His humanity without reserve. The Council of Chalcedon provides the solution by showing the directions we must go in seeking both the unity and distinction of natures in Christ. Therefore, to the great horror of a theology inspired by Alexandrine tendencies, a distinction is made between *physis* and *hypostasis*, and the definition finds its expression thus: in Christ, there is one hypostasis, one person, one *prosôpon*, but two natures. The Council wisely added to this terminology, still in no way analyzed and fixed, some more concrete and more descriptive interpretations of its thought. It ceaselessly recalled that Christ, God and Man, is strictly "one and the same being" according to His person and subject. However, according to His nature, He is God and man without confusion. To say, "without confusion," means that there is no kind of synthesis of the two natures. To say, "without separation," means there are not two persons.[28]

C. What Is Incomplete and Open to Later Developments in the Formula of Chalcedon

{263} The formula of Chalcedon is faulted with being "static." It is indeed true that it simply tells us what Christ is, and speaks neither of His saving action, nor, in general, of His activities. It seems to consider and express Him as an abstract object, not as the historical person who is concretely engaged in salvation history (and who indeed remains engaged in it).[29]

Indeed, the discussions will continue through the course of

---

28. Alois Grillmeier, "L'image du Christ dans la théologie d'aujourd'hui," in *Questions théologiques aujourd'hui* (Paris: Desclée de Brouwer, 1963), 2:106. Also, Paul Galtier, "S. Cyrille d'Alexandrie et S. Léon le Grand à Chalcédoine," in *Das Konzil von Chalkedon*, ed. Alois Grillmeier and Heinrich Bacht (Würzburg: Echter-Verlag, 1951), 1:345–87.

29. See Walter Kasper, *Jésus le Christ* (Paris: Cerf, 1976), 356–57.

many centuries, and the Magisterium will be led (especially by the great, subsequent ecumenical councils, up to the Second Council of Nicaea in 787) to develop (and simultaneously confirm) Chalcedon's formula. Above all, it will extend this formula to the level of activities, as we will see when we study Christ's activities.

What would be false would be a rejection of the formula of Chalcedon on account of its incompleteness. The static is not opposed to the dynamic. Much to the contrary, they are both tightly interconnected. If many problems are still posed today, ones that were not thought of during the era of the Councils and the time when "classical theology" was formed (e.g., Christ's engagement in the great movements of liberation in fighting against injustices inasmuch as He is the redeemer and Liberator of man), such problems could neither be resolved nor even correctly posed if the formula of Chalcedon were repudiated [or] if it were merely neglected, for in saying "Christ" (and in making this or that assertion about Him), we would not be speaking about the Christ whom the apostles announced and in whom the Church believes. Rather, we would merely talk about an unreal being, constructed arbitrarily from manipulated data drawn from the tradition, failing to speak about the Christ of the tradition.

Normally, when we come to know a person, we pass from the "dynamic" to the "static." Indeed, a person is made known by his behavior, "in action," in his "dynamism." However, this raises the problem of who this person is, above all when we are speaking about a person to whom we are invited to give ourselves, a person we are invited to "believe"—a person, moreover, who seems quite mysterious on account of His conduct and what is said about Him. From the beginning of the Christian faith, Jesus Christ's "dynamism" referred believers back to His being: "Who do you say that I am?" And it is only natural that investigations and discussions first concentrated upon what He is, investigations and discussions that led to the formula of Chalcedon.

However, on the basis of what He is, we are led to a fuller understanding of what He has done, of that for which He has come. This forces us to pay heed to His "dynamism," which can bring new problems to light even today. These new problems do not suppress the ancient ones, nor do they render obsolete the solutions that the Church has given to them. Chalcedon's formula remains open to these developments, but if one turns away from this formula, such developments cannot fail to be deviations.

V. CHRISTOLOGICAL PLURALISM AND ORTHODOXY

{264} The mystery of Christ, in its original formulation ("this man, Jesus of Nazareth was—and is—God") includes an antinomic affirmation of *unity* (He of whom I speak, whom I call "Jesus," to whom I attribute precisely this twofold character as man and God, is one) and *duality* (He *is* man and He *is* God). I can indeed attribute different qualities to the same person (e.g., goodness and knowledge), but in the present case, we are speaking of two attributes that both intend to express *what* the designated being is, what makes him be what he is, and what distinguishes him from others. Here, when the intellect begins to reflect on its faith, it runs into what seems to be an impossibility, namely, that one and the same [thing] seems to be two different things at the same time.

A. The Double (and Complementary) Tendency in Christology

{265} We can consider the mystery of the God-Man from two perspectives. On the one hand, there is the Word who descends into humanity, taking it on in order to appear among men and to act as a man. On the other hand, we can consider it from the opposite perspective, thinking of this singular man who is elevated to the divinity in such a way that He is God and the Word.

Broadly speaking, we can say that the first tendency is that of the fourth Gospel: *the Logos became flesh*. On the other hand, the second tendency would be that of the Synoptic Gospels: "This (i.e., this man) is my beloved Son, with whom I am well pleased."[30] In other words, both tendencies can lead to a correct conception and expression of the mystery. It is the mystery of the meeting of humanity and God, a meeting that is so perfect that He in whom the meeting takes place simultaneously is God and man. It can be understood as the Divinity's descent into humanity or as the Divinity drawing humanity to Himself.

The first tendency is that of the school of Alexandria from its beginnings with Clement. It risks minimizing the assumed humanity, placing its accent on Christ's divinity. Alexandrian Christology can be characterized as a Christology of the *Word-flesh* (LOGOS-SARX). Apollinarism is the aberrant form of this tendency, which must be balanced by the affirmation that the flesh united to the Word is an animated flesh, endowed with an intellectual soul, so that we may clearly see and say that the Word assumed a complete human nature and became fully human. This is what the formula of Chalcedon will do: "Consubstantial to us according to humanity."

The second tendency is that of the school of Antioch (despite exceptions like that of John Chrysostom): "Whatever the defects of its own doctrine as sometimes expounded, it deserves credit for bringing back the historical Jesus."[31] It is ordinarily characterized as being a Christology of the *Word-man* (LOGOS-ANTHROPOS). It risked considering Jesus as a mere man united to God—a fatal error that Nestorius did not know how to avoid, indeed an error that was nearly held by his celebrated teacher, Theodore of Mopsuestia. However, it is avoidable, for the realism of the Incarnation forces us to confess that the Word became a true man without ceasing to be what He was from all eternity, God: "One and the same Lord Jesus Christ, the only begotten Son must be acknowledged in two natures, with-

---

30. Mt. 3:17 (RSV).
31. John Norman Davidson Kelly, *Initiation à la doctrine des Pères de l'Église*, trans. Celsas Tumner (Paris: Cerf, 1968), 312. [Tr. note: John Norman Davidson Kelly, *Early Christian Doctrines* (New York: Harper, 1978), 302.]

out confusion or change, without division or separation (*asunchutôs, atreptôs, adiairetôs, achôristôs*)."[32]

{266} This is where the problem of the famous formula, "assumptus homo," emerges. This formula (or other similar ones, like "suscepit hominem," etc.) was widespread in the ancient Fathers and even in St. Augustine. Then it came to be considered suspect, falling into obsolescence. In the Middle Ages, St. Thomas judged it to be erroneous and in need of a "reverential interpretation" when it happens to be encountered in the Fathers.[33] In reality, the Fathers who employ it simultaneously accompany it with the categorical affirmation that there is only one person in Christ and that the Word is who this man is.[34] [Pope] St. Damasus continues to use it at the very moment when he energetically condemns the doctrine of two sons. Its usefulness is found in the fact that it emphasizes the fact that Jesus is a concrete man, a human individual. The term "humanity," which is abstract in form, tends to obscure this fact. However, it poses the danger (which the error holding that there are two sons gradually made clear) of making the assumed man seem distinct from the Word who assumes him, thus necessarily leading the assumed man, precisely as a man, to be a person, thereby leading to a form of dualism. For this reason, this formula was progressively abandoned.[35]

B. The Double Series of Deviations in Christology

{267} "Reason" instinctively recoils before the antinomy between the two affirmations that make up the apostolic kerygma: the simultaneous affirmation of Christ's unity and of the duality of divinity and humanity in Him. Therefore, it tends to minimize (or even suppress) one of these two affirmations, in this way ending in a false clarity, obtained to the detriment of true faith in the revealed

---

32. Chalcedonian definition. [Tr. note: Taken from Denzinger as above.]
33. See *ST* III, q. 4, a. 3, ad 1.
34. See Tarcisius van Bavel, *Recherches sur la christologie de Saint Augustin: l'humain et le divin dans le Christ d'après Saint Augustin* (Fribourg: Éditions universitaires, 1954).
35. On this question, see Herman Diepen, "L'*assumptus homo* patristique," *Revue thomiste* 63 (1963): 225–45, 363–88; 64 (1964): 32–52, 364–86.

The Formation of the Christological Dogma 41

mystery. Therefore, we find ourselves faced with the following two options.

On the one hand, we can choose to sacrifice duality to unity. In other words, we can practically recognize only one of the two natures by abolishing or minimizing the other. In ancient times, Jesus's human nature was the one that was sacrificed, reducing His humanity to nothing. In this way, the reality of the Incarnation comes to be suppressed, the Word not having really become a man. In certain contemporary Christological tendencies, the divinity of Jesus is what is minimized (i.e., practically suppressed), being reduced to the fact that God manifests Himself in Jesus Christ in an exceptional manner or, drawing an example from Boff, to the fact that "Jesus was a human being who could relate to God and be in God to the point of being his Son (i.e., the personal identity of Jesus with the eternal Son)."[36] These disparate, and sometimes opposed, errors can be grouped under the terminological heading of "monism," sharing in common the fact that the duality of natures (which is an essential datum of the mystery of Christ) is practically disregarded.

On the other hand, we can choose to sacrifice unity to duality. In other words, we can minimize the unity of the subject who is simultaneously said to be God and man, thus leading one to think of Christ as two distinct beings, united to each other by an operational bond, with ontological alterity remaining. (Thus, two friends are one, indeed perhaps very intimately one, while nonetheless, remaining ontologically different from each other.) This gives rise to a second series of Christological errors, which can be grouped under the terminological heading of "dualism," meaning "duality of beings": one being who is God, another being who is man, with these two beings considered one only because of their intimate [operational] union.

---

36. Leonardo Boff, *Jésus-Christ libérateur* (Paris: Cerf, 1974), 197; on this work, see Vincent Leroy, "Leonardo Boff, Jésus-Christ libérateur," *Revue thomiste* 79 (1979): 500–503. [Tr. note: Taken from Leonardo Boff, *Jesus Christ Liberator: A Critical Christology for Our Time*, trans. Patrick Hughes (Maryknoll, N.Y.: Orbis, 1984), 197.]

1. Errors of the Monist Sort

{268} From the Church's beginnings, she found herself confronted with docetism. It seems that the author of the fourth Gospel (and above all the author of the first letter of St. John[37]) were aware of this error. In any case, it was vigorously combated by St. Ignatius of Antioch.[38] In the fourth century (though, with a prehistory since the third), such monism was found in Apollinarism. As discussed above, Apollinarius, the bishop of Laodicea, taught that the Word, the Logos, took the place of the soul in Christ, at least that of the rational soul (the *nous*), so that only the "flesh" would have been assumed. We have seen that Arius taught the same thing, though doing so in order to attribute precisely to the Logos all the limitations and inferiorities that the Gospel forces us to recognize in Jesus in relation to the Godhead. It was not easy to uncover the Apollinarist error, for those who professed it did not hesitate to affirm the integrity of Christ's humanity, understanding this as meaning that when the Word was united to the flesh He constituted an integral human composite with it.

Nonetheless, it was expressly condemned by Pope Damasus (first "tacito nomine" by his letter to bishop of Antioch, Paulinus, but then by name in 378 in his letter to the Eastern bishops).[39] Then, in the letter addressed to the same Pope Damasus by the Fathers of the Council of Constantinople I (381), we encounter an anti-Apollinarist profession of faith,[40] and in the first canon [declared by this Council], Apollinarism is mentioned in the series of condemned heresies.[41] Finally, at the Roman Council of 382, Apollinarism is expressly condemned: "We condemn those who say that the Word of God dwelling in human flesh took the place of the rational and spiritual soul,

---

37. See 1 Jn 4:2–3.
38. See Ignatius, *Letter to the Smyrnaeans*, 1:1–2, and ch. 2.
39. See D.-*Sch.*, nos. 148–49.
40. See Giuseppe Alberigo, *Conciliorum oecumenicorum decreta* (Fribourg: Herder, 1962), 24, lines 38–46.
41. See D.-*Sch.*, no. 151.

since the Son and the Word of God did not replace the rational and spiritual soul in His body but rather assumed our soul (i.e., a rational and spiritual one) without sin and saved it."[42]

From this moment, Apollinarism passed into secrecy. The texts of Apollinarius and of his disciples were circulated under venerable names, in particular, under the name of Athanasius. Thus, they were welcomed without suspicion, being used and cited by Catholic authors, in particular by St. Cyril of Alexandria. This played no small role in aggravating the Nestorian dispute.

It is in the course of this dispute that monophysitism, properly so-called, appears, on the basis of the unfortunate formulas of Cyril of Alexandria (*Mia physis tou Theou Logou sesarkômene*, "the one nature of the incarnate Word," and also, *enosis kata physin*, "union according to nature"). Cyril ultimately renounced these formulas, which he only used for expressing the unity of Christ's being. However, some of his disciples were obstinate in asserting them, especially Dioscorus, his successor at Alexandria, and Eutyches, the archimandrite of Constantinople. Originally, this error was expressed in the formula: "two natures before the union but not after." This could be expressed in another way as stating, "The union makes one single nature out of the two natures." They never were able to explain how they conceived of this fusion of humanity and divinity.

Condemned at Chalcedon in 451, monophysitism did not cease to fight against the Council, at least against its terminology concerning two natures. It reappeared in the seventh century in the form of monothelitism (an extension of monophysitism onto the level of activity [*opération*]), which was condemned at the Third Council of Constantinople in 681, as will be recalled in its proper place below.

2. *Errors of the Dualist Sort*

{269} In all the texts wherein Apollinarism is condemned, the so-called error of two sons, which divides Christ, is simultaneously

---

42. D.-*Sch.*, no. 159. [Tr. note: Translation taken from the 43rd edition of Denzinger by Ignatius Press.]

rejected. Originally, at the end of the second century, we find the theory of a certain Theodotus of Byzantium, who taught that Christ was only a man, specially united to God and elevated to the divinity after His resurrection. He was condemned by Pope Victor in around 190.

For Theodotus, his disciples, and the movement that took its birth from him, it was a question of rendering the faith rational [*rationalisation de la foi*].[43] The most important (though poorly understood) representative of this tendency, Paul of Samosata, seems to have taught that Christ was an ordinary man, with the Word existing in Him according to the manner of grace's indwelling.[44] He was condemned at the Council of Antioch in 268.[45]

The errors relating to this tendency can be grouped under the term "adoptionism," for if there are two sons united in Jesus (the Son of God and the son of man), Jesus Himself is only the son of man. If He can be called the son of God, this is only by adoption.

Historically (in the conflicts of the fifth century and then in the image of it which these conflicts left behind), Nestorianism is presented as the most typical form of this deviation. However, we have seen that Nestorius himself always repudiated the theory of "two sons" and faithfully sought to assure the ontological unity of Christ. We have also seen that, in fact, he did not succeed in doing so, such that his Christology was deviant and cannot be held to be compatible with the apostolic kerygma.

The dogmatic formula [*forme*] of Chalcedon is an admirable synthesis of all the data of the apostolic kerygma concerning Christ's being, that which He is. It expresses the truth of the Catholic faith, which is elevated far above these two deviations and rectifies them.

---

43. See Kelly, *Initiation à la doctrine des Pères de l'Église*, 126–27.
44. See ibid., 149.
45. See de Riedmatten, *Les actes du procès de Paul de Samosate*.

PART 2

WHAT CHRIST IS IN HIMSELF

3

The Hypostatic Union

{270} With Karl Rahner[1] and Aloys Grillmeier,[2] we must distinguish two things as regards Christ: *the united unity* (i.e., the union of the two natures in Christ's unity of being) and the *uniting unity* (i.e., the unifying principle of these two natures). This distinction is found equivalently in St. Thomas.[3]

This distinction is connected to the metaphysics of the one [as a transcendental property of being]. Because unity is a property of being, the one, absolutely speaking, precedes the multiple. Therefore, this unity of Christ to which the union of the two natures leads must be conceived as being anterior to the union. However, in a certain sense (the most immediately evident one), it is posterior to it, as it results from this union. Obviously, the "one[ness]" of Christ on the one hand results from the union of the two natures and, on the other, causes it in different ways and from different perspectives. The difficulty, which Rahner emphasizes, is that "classical theology" proposes the same thing (namely, the hypostasis of the Word) as the result of the union (Christ's unity, in fact, is that of the hypostasis of the Word, "a composite person," as we will see) and as the unifying principle

---

1. See Karl Rahner, "Problèmes actuels de christologie," *Ecrits théologiques*, vol. 1 (Paris: Desclée de Brouwer, 1959), 155ff.
2. See Grillmeier, "L'image du Christ dans la théologie d'aujourd'hui," 107–8.
3. See *ST* III, q. 2, a. 9, co.

(the eternal hypostasis of the Word, by being united to this assumed, individual human nature, unites Himself to the human nature, in order to constitute Christ with it). In short, it seems that the theological "explanation" of the Incarnation leads one to make the same thing play the role of the uniting unity and that of the united unity.

Given that we can consider this difficulty as residing at the heart of the theological problem of the Hypostatic Union, it will be the reference point for the order in which we undertake our investigations, which will unfold in two stages: *the united unity* and *the uniting unity*. We will conclude with a final consideration: *theological language in Christology*.

I. THE UNITED UNITY

The united unity is Christ, the Incarnate Word. The same One, the Lord Jesus Christ, is simultaneously God and Man.

A. The Word-God

{271} He is God, having the Divine Nature. How does the Word have the Divine Nature?

He has It *by identity*. In God, a real distinction does not exist between the Person who is God and the nature on account of which He is God.

He has It *as holding It from the Father*, and as, along with the Father, *communicating* It *to the Holy Spirit*. He is *unus de Trinitate*, One of the Three who are the unique God. [He is] really distinct from the other two, but the divinity by which He is God (i.e., the Divine Nature) is identically the same as the divinity of the Father and that of the Holy Spirit.

Just as He is a distinct Person, in whom the nature common to the Three subsists (by identity), so too He is a distinct Actor [*Agissant*] by the divine action, which is (indivisibly) common to the Three. This holds for immanent actions (i.e., thought and love) as well as for actions *ad extra* (i.e., creation or any other created work).

He has the divine nature *as constitutive ab aeterno*. Proceeding from the Father *ab aeterno*, the Word is constituted in His personality by the relation of filiation inasmuch as it is subsistent, that is, inasmuch as it is identical with the Divine Nature communicated to Him without being divided.[4] Therefore, His personality is perfect and infinite merely on account of the Divine Nature in which it subsists (or, which subsists in it).

The expression "God the Word" is ambiguous, and this ambiguity has caused numerous troubles and confusions in the history of dogma. If the accent is placed on "the Word," we have, "the Word who is God." Thus, the Person is placed in relief, and we then add, "The Word who is God, is also Man." However, if the accent is placed on "God," we have "God, who is the Word" (though God is also the Father and the Holy Spirit). Thus, the nature is placed in relief, and we find ourselves faced with no small difficulty in trying to say that the Word was born of the Virgin, suffered, etc., for this seems to refer to the Divinity itself. This ambiguity played a considerable role in the mutual misunderstandings between Cyril and Nestorius.

When we say that "God the Word was made man" and that "Jesus is God the Word," we must take the expression in the first sense, meaning that the Word (i.e., God from all eternity by the one and indivisible Divine Nature communicated to Him by the Father) became a man in time, assuming an individual human nature formed in Mary's womb. God the Word is the one who has received, done, and suffered all that He has received, done, and suffered in this human nature (namely, the *humana*). However, the divinity is not the one that has received, done, and suffered them.

B. The Word-Man

What we must explain is this temporal being-man of the Word which is added to His eternal Being-God. Such an explanation is theological in nature. In other words, the explanation does not claim

---

4. See §121 of the first volume of this work.

to dispel the mystery. Rather, it presupposes acceptance of the mystery by faith but partially discovers its intelligibility by showing that it is not contradictory (which would render it inadmissible for the intellect).

1. Basic explanation

It is natural for theologians to differ from each other in this search for intelligibility. Nonetheless, a basic explanation does exist, one which faith itself requires and which the Magisterium determined to be appropriate, after lengthy investigations and disputes. This basic explanation is imposed upon all theologians.[5]

a) This union is not brought about "in natura"

{272} *Nature* is taken here in the sense of *essence* (that which makes a being be what it is). Indeed, more precisely, it is taken here in the sense of meaning *a realized essence*, that is, the essence inasmuch as it is constitutive of this concrete being, belonging properly to it. In short, we are using the term as meaning the *individualized essence*, which is also called a *substance*.[6]

To say that the union of humanity and divinity in Christ is brought about *in natura* would be to say that Christ has an essence composed of humanity and divinity. Now, [there are two issues with such an assertion]. First, *it is impossible*. On the one hand, the divinity, which is Pure Act, cannot enter into composition with any creature. On the other, such a composition would lead to a total absorption of Christ's humanity, for a created essence is distinguished from the Divine Essence only on account of the former's ontological limits. Thus, if it could be ontologically united with the divinity, abolishing this created essence's limits, such a union would make it lose not only its individuality, but even every kind of specificity. In short, Christ's humanity would be dissolved in hus divinity. Second, *such*

---

5. All the elements of this "basic explication" can be found in *ST* III, q. 2, aa. 1–6, and in *SCG*, bk. 4, ch. 41.

6. See §§278–81 below. [Tr. note: The original reads "§39–42."]

The Hypostatic Union 51

an assertion in no way responds to the question posed by faith, as Christ, thus constituted, would be neither God nor man.[7]

b) Comparison with the union of soul and body

{273} This comparison is very frequent in St. Augustine,[8] and it is found in Theodore of Mopsuestia. It passed into the authoritatively recognized [*très officiel*] *Quicumque* symbol (attributed for a long time to St. Athanasius, though today it is held to be of Western origin, arising from the region of Arles, dating from approximately 430 to 450 A.D.). This creed gradually acquired so great an authority (both in the Western and Eastern Church) that in the Middle Ages it was placed on the same footing as the Apostles' Creed and the Nicene Creed and was officially integrated into the liturgy itself.[9] In it we read: "For just as one man is a rational soul and flesh, so is the one Christ God and man."[10]

At first sight, this comparison has a rather monophysitical flavor to it, which renders it suspect. Nonetheless, it is remarkable that, far from rejecting this formulation, St. Thomas accepts it by reverentially interpreting it, though explaining it in such a way that the monophysitical interpretation is ruled out.[11]

Indeed, this formula is very suggestive: in the human person, two universes flow together—that of bodies (*Nature*), in which it participates on account of matter, and that of spirits, in which it participates on account of the spiritual soul. In this, we have the classical theme about man being situated on the *horizon* (or, on the "border") between the spiritual and the bodily.[12] Therefore, if I consider the soul and the body as the two constitutive parts of human nature, it is false and unacceptable to say that humanity and divinity compose Christ

---

7. See §252, n. 2 above. [Tr. note: The original reads "§13, n. 2."]
8. See Liébaert, *L'incarnation*, 1:1 and 1:172. Grillmeier, *La Christ dans la tradition chrétienne*, 374–77.
9. See D.-*Sch.*, no. 41. [Tr. note: See no. 76 in the 43rd edition.]
10. Dumeige, *Textes Doctrinaux*, 10.
11. See *ST* III, q. 2, a. 1, ad 2; *SCG*, bk. 4, ch. 41; Cajetan, *In ST* III, q. 2, a. 2, no. 4.
12. See Aquinas, *In* III *Sent.*, prol.; *SCG*, bk. 2, ch. 68: "This opens to us ..."

in the way that the body and soul compose man. However, if I consider the human person who results from this composition, I see that he "subsists" in two distinct universes, all the while remaining one and the same [person]. On the basis of this insight, I can elevate myself (by analogy) to a consideration about how Christ's person, remaining one and the same (i.e., remaining what He is from all eternity, the Person of the Word) subsists, because of the Incarnation, both in God and in the created universe (which includes the two universes noted above, without mixing them together).

c) This union is brought about "in persona"

{274} The person is the concrete subject in whom an intellectual nature is realized. Every real being is a concrete subject, a *hypostasis*. What gives the person his dignity ("that which is most noble in all of nature") is the fact that the concrete being, the hypostasis in which an intellectual nature is realized, is endowed with thought, love, and freedom. Now, it has this endowment because of its nature: "On account of this singular nobility, the concrete individuals in whom the rational nature is realized have received a name that distinguishes them from all other substances, and this name is 'person.'"[13]

The ontological union of two or several realities necessarily comes about in a subject, in whom the realities under consideration are united. Indeed, to say that a reality is external to a subject is to say, equally, that it is external to those things that are part of the subject, which are something of it—external and therefore not united. Given that here we are obviously concerned with a subject who is a person, to say that the union of humanity and divinity in this subject is ontological is to say that it is brought about *in persona*.

However, ordinarily (on the level of our experience) every union *in persona* begins with a union *in natura*. This can be the union of two co-substantial principles (e.g., the soul and the body) in order to constitute the unique substance in whom human nature is realized.

---

13. *ST* I, q. 29, a. 1.

Or, it can be the union of the various parts of the body in order to constitute one single body, the unique body that constitutes the person along with his or her soul. Finally, it can be the union of an accidental reality with a whole, in which case the accidental reality does not constitute the substance but, rather, completes it by informing it, so that the substance is "modified" (all the while remaining essentially the same).

In the case of Christ, we must exclude every form of union of humanity and divinity *in natura* and must hold, in faith, that there is an ontological union. Therefore, we are led to affirm a union *in persona tantum*, "only in person." The Divine Nature and human nature are united in Christ's one Person such that they are not mixed together with each other in any way—neither as two co-substantial principles, nor as the members of one and the same body, nor as an accident with the substance that it modifies.

d) Appropriation of the assumed human nature by the Word

{275} This one Person of Christ has the Divine Nature. He is God. He is one of the Divine Persons, the Word. By faith, we know how He is God. He is God is by proceeding eternally from the Father in the mystery of the one and undivided divinity.

How is He a man (and how does He become one)? According to what we have said, in order to form an idea of this for ourselves, we must reflect on the relations that exist, first at the phenomenological level, between the person (the "self") and nature. As regards his nature (as a whole or in its parts), the person first manifests a relation of possession: *my* head, *my* foot, *my* will, *my* freedom, etc. Indeed, we also say, "*my* humanity" (i.e., the individual humanity on account of which I am a man). However, the person also manifests a relation that, beyond that of "having," is expressed in terms of *being*: *I am* a man, *I am* free, *I am* bodily, etc. (In scholastic terms, this is expressed as *natura de persona praedicatur in quid*, "nature is attributed to the person as an essential attribute").[14]

14. *ST* III, q. 2, a. 6, s.c.

This can be expressed by the notion of appropriation: "To say that the Word was made flesh means to say nothing other than this: He participated like us in flesh and in blood;[15] He made His own our body and was placed in the world as a man born of a woman."[16] Or again: "He who is thus made flesh or man is not a theophoric man. On the contrary, it is God Himself who has abased Himself in a voluntary annihilation, by making His own the flesh taken from a woman. Not a flesh without a soul or without a spirit, but a flesh animated by a spiritual soul."[17] The Word has appropriated an individuated, complete human nature. That is, He *has* this nature, and He *is* a man by this nature. In the strong sense that we give to this word when we apply it to our own body, to our soul and to all their parts, it is *His*:

> This appropriation is a having that results in being. Inasmuch as it is a having, it avoids all possible forms of monophysitism. Inasmuch as it is a substantial being, it entirely saves the central affirmation of faith in the Incarnation, which is a true becoming of the Immutable. Thus, we can see this theory proceed from age to age. St. John Damascene will give it a formulation that will play an important role: "He is God, He who has the divine nature; He is man, He who has the human nature."[18]

We can elevate ourselves to this vertiginous conception by means of a double, complementary analogy. However, we will need to abandon it along the way. First, there is an analogy taken from the case of *substantial parts*. Just as a man, a human person, is composed of substantial parts, thus Christ, the Person of Christ, the Incarnate Word, is composed of the substance of the Divinity and that of humanity. And the analogy's attempt to express this can be pushed further. In the case of a miracle that would give a man back a lost limb or in the case of the resurrection (wherein the human person sub-

---

15. See Heb 2:14.
16. Cyril of Alexandria, in Camelot, 193. [Tr. note: As in the previous chapter, this is perhaps *Ephèse et Chalcédoine*.]
17. Cyril of Alexandria, in Herman Diepen, *Théologie de l'Émmanuel* (Paris: Desclée de Brouwer, 1960), 8–9.
18. Diepen, *Théologie de l'Émmanuel*, 10.

sisting solely in his soul receives the addition of his body), the person preexists such events. He is not constituted by this new addition but, rather, appropriates this new limb or this body to himself. He makes it part of himself.[19]

However, we must set aside this analogy immediately, for as we have seen, in the examples given, the union first happens *in natura*, whereas for Christ human nature belongs properly to the Person of the Word, without becoming part of His Divine Nature. Therefore, another comparison can help us: the case of accidents. An accident comes unto a person already entirely constituted and becomes his, as the humanity of Jesus comes unto the Person of the Word already entirely constituted and becomes His. But here again, we must abandon the analogy, for an accident belongs to the person only by the intermediary of the substance that it informs. By contrast, the assumed humanity does not inform the divinity—first of all because the divinity is Pure Act (and therefore cannot receive any informing) and secondly because the assumed humanity is a substance that can in no way play the role of an accident.

e) Substantial union

{276} The union of divinity and humanity in Christ can in no way be called substantial, meaning that they would constitute a single substance. However, no more can it be called accidental, meaning that the united substances would each preserve its own, proper subsistence, thereby being a *distinct* being. Indeed, two things would hold in the latter case. First, Christ's humanity would be part of what the Word *has*, not what He *is* (i.e., there would not be a "predication '*in quid*'"). That is, we could not say that the Word *is* man. (Thus, given that every man is *something coming from God*, he is part of what

---

19. According to St. Thomas, the "separated soul" is not, properly speaking, a person (see *In* III *Sent.*, d. 5, q. 3, a. 2, ad 2; *ST* I, q. 29, a. 1, ad 5, and q. 75, a. 4, co. and ad 2). However, we also cannot say that man's personality is purely and simply dissolved [upon death], because the soul of this man, his awareness, and his freedom subsist with the soul. His is a truncated personality; however, precisely through the resurrection, it "reassumes" its body, which completes it.

God *has, aliquid Dei*, but I cannot—and must not—say that God is man by the mere fact of creation.) Second, to preserve the union *in persona*, we would need to say that the assumed humanity is an accident, which is absurd. In fact, given that humanity is a substantial nature, it can be realized only as a substance, never as an accident. Therefore, if this substance belongs to the Word and *is His* (as we hold by faith), this cannot be like an accident belonging to the subject that it enriches but instead like how a substantial nature belongs to the supposit (i.e., to the person) that it constitutes.

Thus, in the unique case of Christ, a middle notion must be admitted between *a substantial union* (as the parts of an individuated substance are united to each other), and *an accidental union* (as an accident is united to its substance, or as two distinct subsistents are united to each other by contact or by relation). This middle notion is *union according to subsistence*. In such a union, two distinct substances (i.e., the divinity and the humanity) are united as belonging to the same supposit, to the same Person, who subsists in both of them.[20]

Therefore, we must wholly rule out, as something contrary to the faith, the idea that there would be *two ontological subjects* in Christ (i.e., God the Word *and* a man who is distinct from Him). It would be useless to say that the second subject, the man, is not a person, for the whole, real man, the whole subject in whom humanity is realized, is a person. The mystery of the Incarnation dwells in reality, not in words.

Classically, the way of expressing this was to say, "Christ is *aliud et aliud* (one ["reality"] and another), not *alius and alius* (one [person] and another)."

2. *An attempt at a theological elaboration*

a) The disappropriation of the assumed nature

The assumed nature belongs properly to the Word. This implies that it does not belong to itself. That is, it does not constitute a new

---

20. See *ST* III, q. 2, a. 6.

person to whom it would belong as being its own, and which would be a man by means of that nature (as is the case for other men). This is a [kind of] "disappropriation." The *De fide* exclusion of a created ontological subject that would be this man, Jesus Christ, imposes upon us this notion of "disappropriation."

The subsistence of Jesus' humanity

{277} "To subsist" means "to have existence" or "to be real." Therefore, by definition, every real being "subsists." Because Jesus' humanity (obviously) is real, it subsists.

However, there are two ways of subsisting, just as there are two ways of existing. Something can "exist on its own account," as "that which exists," or something can exist as a part of a being, existing in it. Thus, we must distinguish *subsistere in se* (i.e., to be the being, *ens*, that subsists, that has existence and exercises it on its own account) from *subsistere in alio* (i.e., to contribute in some way or another in constituting the *being* that exists). In the latter case the reality envisioned is not a "quod est," a "being," but, instead, *id quo aliquid est* [that by which something is].

This is the case for an accidental form: "for an accident, to be is to inhere in a subject that is." Properly speaking, the accident is not what exists. What exists is the substance modified by it. The accident participates in the substance's existence. It makes it be the case that the substance exists in a given manner.

This is equally true for a substantial part: the bodily limb, the body itself, the soul, etc. What exists is the living being, the whole. The parts exist only in and by the whole. They do not have their own proper subsistence [precisely as parts].[21]

We saw above that the unique case of [Christ's] assumed human-

---

21. In the case of the human soul, we must say the same thing, but must specify that the subsistence of the whole, of the human person, is the subsistence of the soul communicated to the body and to all its parts. Thus, the dissolution of the composite (by death) does not entail its "de-subsistence" (i.e., its disappearance). Rather, it continues to subsist by itself. What is called (perhaps improperly) the immortality of the soul consists in this: the soul *survives* the death that dissolves the composite.

ity had to be conceived of using analogies drawn from the case of accidents and that of substantial parts. The analogy bears on this precise point, as also does the difference between the cases. Like accidents, the assumed humanity does not subsist in itself (*in se*) but, rather, makes the Word, who is eternally subsistent, be "such" (i.e., makes Him be a man). However, the assumed humanity is not an accident. It is a substance. As an incomplete substance, it is a part of the person in whom it subsists, but it itself is a complete substance.

In order for this to make sense, we must admit that even a complete substance (e.g., individuated humanity) can be non-subsistent. In other words, we must admit that individuation, by which a substance is complete, does not yet confer subsistence *in se*. Without this [distinction between individuation and subsistence], it would be incomprehensible that Jesus' humanity, which certainly is individuated and real, does not subsist in itself and does not constitute a person existing on its own account, therefore distinct from the Word.

Individuation and subsistence

{278} The "subsistent" (or "supposit," etc.) is the *substance* and, indeed, the complete substance. Every other reality is either an accident or a part of a substance.

Substance must be distinguished into *primary substance* (which is the ontological subject, the subject of *esse* and of all the accidents, the *principium quod operatur*, the principle that acts) and *secondary substance* (i.e., the universal nature that is realized in the concrete subject that is constituted by this nature).[22]

In the case of bodily beings (and, therefore, also of man), secondary substance ultimately determined in the line of essence, or ontological perfection, is still universal. It is the specific nature that can be realized only in material individuals, distinct from each other by characteristics of material origin. These characteristics do not add any ontological perfection to the essence. Nonetheless, they are

---

22. See Jean-Hervé Nicolas, "Essence et substance," *Revue thomiste* 47 (1947): 517–23.

the condition for the essence's realization; they are the individuating characteristics.

At first sight, it is possible to think that, thus completed by the individuating characteristics, the secondary substance would *ipso facto* become a primary substance, that is, a subsistent. However, above all else, what must prevent us from thinking this is the mystery of the Incarnation. Jesus' humanity is a complete, individuated substance, and it does not subsist by itself. Therefore, in order to be a primary substance (i.e., a subsistent, a "being that is and that acts"), it is not sufficient that something is a complete, individuated substance. Christ's humanity is *real*, and it belongs to the Word as His own in a real manner. Therefore, it does not belong in a real manner to a created person, constituted by it. Thus we must admit that, for each individuated nature, the constituting of a created person to which such a nature would belong is something in addition to individuation.[23]

The principle of subsistence

Therefore, we must seek out this reality which makes it be the case that this individuated nature subsists. That is, we must seek out the "principle of subsistence."[24]

---

23. Scotus, however, thought it possible to do without this addition. He resolved the problem by saying that every individuated nature is by itself a person, except in the case of the Hypostatic Union where the assumed human nature is found deprived of its natural ontological independence by the very fact that it is assumed by the subsistence of the Word (Scotus, a. 7 [*sic*]). However, is such a solution satisfactory? If every individuated nature is subsistent by itself, how could the assumption exercised on Christ's individuated human nature deprive it of this subsistence without destroying it? The subsistence of the Word is substituted for the natural subsistence of the assumed nature, though obviously it is not substituted for this nature, which itself remains while belonging to the Word. How is this conceivable, if this nature, solely because it is individuated, is subsistent?

24. The reader can refer to manuals of scholastic theology, where one can find expositions of various theories concerning the "principle of subsistence." Also see Herman Diepen, "La critique du baslisme selon Saint Thomas," *Revue thomiste* 50 (1950): 84–118; Mateo Febrer, *El concepto de persona y la unión hipostática. Revisión tomista del problema* (Valencia: Editorial F.E.D.A, 1951). [Tr. note: Fr. Nicolas also cites "Michel, c. 409–29," where he is likely referring to A[lbert] Michel, "Hypostatique (Union)," in *Dictionnaire de théologie catholique*, vol. 7, ed. Alfred Vacant (Paris: Letouzey and Ané, 1922), 437–78 and 485–86.]

It is not an individuating determination

{279} Because subsistence obviously belongs solely to the singular being that exists, it has been thought that it must be an ultimate individuating character.[25] For Christ, this individuating character would be replaced by the Hypostatic Union, which thereby would be constitutive of the assumed nature *qua* individuated. However, we have seen that the [Hypostatic] Union cannot be brought about *in natura* in any way. That is, the assumed nature can in no way be modified by the union. The assumption makes this nature belong to the Word. It does not make it be another nature (even individual).[26]

No more is it the case that it is "esse"

{280} This is the famed position of Capreolus[27] (at least as he has been interpreted). What is lacking for substance, even determined to the point of individuation, for subsisting, is quite simply *esse*. To subsist is to exist, and no finite being (even an ultimately determined being) has an essence identical with its *esse*. *Esse* simultaneously makes it exist and subsist.

In modern times, this position was taken up and vigorously defended by Louis Billot,[28] and it is still held by many of his disciples. In Christology, it leads to an explanation stating that the appropriation of the nature assumed by the Word occurs by the communication of the *eternal, Divine Being* to this nature. Indeed, if to subsist is to exist, to subsist in the Word means "to exist by the eternal existence of the Word."

---

25. See Febrer, *El concepto de persona y la unión hipostática. Revisión tomista del problema*.

26. [Tr. note: Fr. Nicolas cites "J.-H. Nicolas, 23," which correlates to Nicolas, "Enfer," in *Dictionnaire de spiritualité ascétique et mystique, doctrine et histoire*, ed. Marcel Viller, SJ (Paris: Beauchesne, 1937ff.), 4:729–45. This does not make sense, but it is not clear what entry he is referring to.]

27. [Tr. note: Fr. Nicolas only cites "Capreolus." He is likely referring to Johannes Capreolus, *Defensiones Theologiae Divi Thomae Aquinatis*, ed. Thomas Pegues and Ceslaus Paban, vol. 6 (Turin: Sumptibus Alfred Cattier, 1906), d. 5, q. 3.]

28. See Louis Billot, *De Ecclesiae Sacramentis: Commentarius in tertiam partem S. Thomae* (Rome: Apud Aedes Universitatis Gregorianae, 1924).

The Hypostatic Union

Later on, we will speak about this conception of the Hypostatic Union, which many Thomists share, though they do not, however, accept the equivalence between *to subsist* and *to exist*. In a word, let us say that even if this idea concerning the communication of the Divine *Being* to the assumed humanity could be accepted, an insurmountable difficulty would remain. Strictly speaking, [the Divine] *Being* is common to the three Persons. If the union consisted in the fact that it is communicated to the assumed nature, what would it mean to say that the Word alone has become incarnate? The three Persons together would have become a man by the communication of the Divine Being that is common to them. To this objection, the Billotists respond that what is communicated is the *Divine Being* inasmuch as it is the *being of the Word*. However, the Trinitarian processions do not introduce the least distinction, even a modal one, within the Divine Being. What the Father communicates to the Son (and the Father and the Son to the Spirit) is the unique, indivisible, undivided Divine Nature, and we can introduce no shade of distinction between the divinity by which the Father is God, and that by which the Son is God. Therefore, we can introduce no shade of distinction between the *Divine Being* inasmuch as it is the *being* of the Father, and the Divine Being inasmuch as it is the *being* of the Son.[29]

To return to the particular problem of subsistence (a problem that is metaphysical in nature, though theological inasmuch as it is part of the theological problem of the Hypostatic Union), can the equivalence between *to subsist* and *to exist* be retained? It is certain that the "subsistent" (or, "supposit" or "hypostasis," etc.) is characterized by the fact that it exists. It is that which is and which acts. However, precisely speaking, the subsistence that we are seeking is that which makes it to be the subject of existence [*l'être*], that which makes it to be an ontological subject. To merely say that it is a subject of *existence* [*l'être*] because it has *existence* [*l'être*] is to explain *prius per posterius*. Indeed, it could not receive *existence* [*l'être*] if it was

---

29. See §140 in the previous volume.

not the subject of *existence* [*l'être*]. Therefore, we must know what makes it into a *subject of existence* [*l'être*].

It is the completion of substance in the line of existence

{281} A word from St. Thomas can guide us in this investigation. With regard to the knowledge [*science*] that God has of things, St. Thomas explains in the following way the fact that the simple representation (or, idea) does not suffice for constituting such knowledge, no matter how precise it may be (up to the final determination, the individualization of the essence), for in such knowledge, in addition to the "mere representation," the will to realize what is thus represented is also needed:

> If one calls speculative science "simple knowledge," it is not in order to exclude from it the relation of knowledge to the known, for this is an inseparable characteristic of every science. Rather, one uses this term in order to exclude from it every addition from what is not of the domain of knowledge, like the existence of the things known, which the *science of vision* adds (to pure knowledge), or the relation of the will to things produced (by the science of vision), which characterizes the *science of approbation*.[30]

What is meant by the assertion, "existence is outside of the domain of knowledge"? The domain of knowledge is that of representation (i.e., the intra-mental universe), while the representation is, by its nature, wholly tendential (*intentio*) toward the thing represented, which is part of the extra-mental universe. In a realistic noetic, like that of St. Thomas, the representation coincides ([or] can coincide) wholly with the thing represented, except in the fact that the thing really exists, whereas the representation exists only ideally or intentionally.

Now, in relation to the "subject who is" (i.e., to the given being, *ens*), "existence" is act in relation to potency. Potency remains distinct from act, even when it is actualized. That is, the subject, the "primary substance," the being, remains distinct from existence, all the while being *real*, belonging to the extra-mental universe. Indeed! Subsistence is this character of reality by which primary substance

---

30. *De ver.*, q. 3, a. 3.

is distinguished from the secondary substance which is realized in it (no matter how determined that secondary substance may be). The "principle of subsistence" that we seek is what confers substance with the character of reality by which it is the subject of existence, that which is, the primary substance.

Another text of St. Thomas orients us in the same direction: "A singular is not made up of accumulated universal forms, however numerous they may be, for this assemblage of forms can be conceived of as being realized in many [subjects]." And a little later on: "Every form, of itself, is universal."[31] A primary substance realizes an ordered ensemble of forms, each of which determines the preceding: supreme genus, intermediary genus, specific nature. The individuating characteristics complete the determination of the essence so as to make it to be "the essence of a singular," of the "being."[32] Indeed! Even at this extreme point of determination, the essence is a form, that by which the subsistent is what it is. The subsistent itself is the subject in which this form is realized. The "principle of subsistence" is that by which the form becomes a subject.

In what way should we conceive of this principle of subsistence? Obviously not as a new form! By definition, it is "not representable," "not conceptualizable," precisely because it makes the essence, the form, pass from the order of representation to the real order. Scholastic thought designates it as a *mode*, by which it means a manner of existing, concerning the thing, not in itself, but in its relation to existence in a given existential situation. Here, it is the fundamental relation of the thing to existence, its reality.

For a deeper study of this solution, one should read and meditate on the text where Cajetan, who elaborated it, exposits it with depth, though not without obscurity. This is how he formulates the solution:

Just as substance, taken in the sense of "essence," is a thing made to exist in a determined manner, which we describe as "being through itself" (by

31. Ibid., q. 2, a. 5.
32. Ibid., q. 2, a. 7.

exclusion of, "being in something other than itself as are accidents," which can exist only in a subject), so too substance, taken this time in the sense of "primary substance" is a thing made to exist in a determined manner which we describe as "a being through itself apart," in such a way that it is precluded that it be in another as making up a part of it.[33]

(That is, it is precluded that it would be different from the subject that is.)[34]

In virtue of this "principle of subsistence," a primary substance is a real being, which can be broken down into two characteristics. The first is *a positive characteristic*: it is an ontological subject, which is and which acts. (By contrast, when an accident passes into reality, it is not constituted a subject but, rather, participates in the reality of a subject other than itself. That is, it subsists *in alio*.) The second is *a negative characteristic*: it is ontologically distinct from every other ontological subject. Technically: "it excludes every communication in existence with another being." Indeed, it could not, without contradiction, subsist in itself (be "that which is") and subsist in another (be a part of a "subject").[35]

Subsistence and personality

{282} As we have seen, every individual in whom human nature is realized is a human person merely because he is subsistent. The term "personality" can mean one of two things. On the one hand, it can refer to the "principle of subsistence," which makes this human

---

33. Cajetan, *In ST* III, q. 4, a. 2, no. 8.

34. In reality, Cajetan is betrayed here by an excessive intellectualism, which prevents him from following his intuition to its natural conclusion. For he seems to consider first substance itself, which can exist only as a subject, still in the mind. However, it is the real, concrete subject outside the mind. And this is why it cannot in any manner exist in another.

35. N.B. When we say that a "form" (whether substantial or accidental) "passes to reality," we obviously do not mean that it "would pass" from the intra-mental (intentional) world to the extra-mental (real) world. It exists only in the extra-mental world and therefore, properly speaking, does not "enter" into it. However, this raises the question: "How is this reality, which, as a form, coincides exactly with its representation in the intra-mental world (supposing that it can be and that it is, in fact, perfectly known), more than its representation, and what makes it be the case that it is 'real'?" Subsistence is this "more."

nature, in this individual, be real and subsistent. On the other hand, "personality" can refer to the particular dignity of a subject who is endowed with thought, love, and freedom on account of the intellectual nature that is realized in this subject. The second sense is obviously the one that we more habitually use. The first sense has the benefit of reminding us that the dignity of the person, as well as all the rights and duties that are attached to him, all arise from the intellectual nature, though they belong to a subject in whom this nature is realized and are real only as a consequence of this realization.

The depersonalization of the assumed human nature

{283} If (Christ's) human nature had not been assumed by the Divine Person, it would have its own, proper personality. And if one says improperly that the Divine Person destroyed the person (of the man), this is said in order to signify that the Divine Person, in being united to the human nature, prevented it from having its own personality.[36]

From what we have said, it follows that, in order for the human nature to be able to exist in a subject other than itself (i.e., in the Word), it was prevented from constituting a person. This differs from every other case of a newly formed human nature, which does constitute a person at the instant that it is realized. In this sense, Christ's assumed nature has been "depersonalized."

"Personality" (in the first sense of the word) is not any part of the nature, even the individuated nature. Rather, because personality's only role is to realize this nature, the aforementioned depersonalization does not involve any mutation or diminution of the assumed nature. Just as we are men by human nature, the Word is a man by it. He is consubstantial with us.

On the other hand, this depersonalization is relative. It is understood in relation to the created person who normally would have been constituted by the realized nature. In place of this person, there is substituted the eternal Person of the Word, *in whom the assumed nature finds itself personalized*. Indeed, just as this nature is the nature

---

36. *ST* III, q. 4, a. 2, ad 3.

of the Word, so too (and correlatively), the Word is the Person of this nature. Therefore, the assumed nature does not undergo *a privation of personality*. Rather, it undergoes *an elevation* to a higher, infinite personality.[37]

How can this depersonalization be brought about?

{284} Obviously, the same action that posits the nature in being (i.e., efficient causality) gives it subsistence. What is produced is the subsistent nature in this singular subject. (This is why we must reject Cajetan's bizarre idea holding that God, by His absolute power, could produce a non-subsistent substance.[38] To put such an idea another way: He could realize a non-real thing!)

Jesus' humanity was "realized" by the same action that made it subsistent in the Word, and *ipso facto* this same action prevented this nature from subsisting in itself. We will discuss this so-called assumptive action later on.

b) The Word's appropriation of the nature thus disappropriated

{285} The problem can be summarized as follows. Given that Jesus' humanity obviously is real and subsists in the Word, not in itself, we must ask ourselves what is meant by speaking of "subsisting in the Word."[39]

Explanation by actuation

In modern theology, this explanation originates in Billot and La Taille, who nonetheless make use of ancient scholastic notions. In various, original forms, this explanation currently retains great favor in the thought of many renowned contemporary theologians.

---

37. See *ST* III, q. 2, a. 2, ad 2.
38. See Cajetan, *In ST* III, q. 4, a. 2, no. 18.
39. The person is who subsists, who is the subsistent. However, he subsists according to a given nature. In ordinary cases, *the person is the subsistent nature*, and it is the same thing to say that the nature subsists in the person and that the person subsists in the nature. Now, in the case of the Incarnation where, precisely speaking, the Person is not identical to the nature, we must say *both that the Person of the Word subsists in the human nature* (i.e., subsists as a man) *and that the human nature subsists in the Word* (i.e., it subsists as the humanity of the Word).

Actuation of the assumed humanity by the being of the Word   {286} This is the first position. We have already spoken about it in relation to subsistence in general.[40] Therefore, we already considered the difficulty drawn from Trinitarian theology: the Divine Being is not proper to the Word. Moreover, we criticized the way in which these theologians think they are able to resolve this difficulty.

The specifically Christological problem remains [to be discussed]. Moreover, this problem is connected to the vaster issue concerning the relation between the Creator and the creature. Is it conceivable to say that, in relation to the creature, God may stand as act to a potency that He actuates?

La Taille attempted to resolve this problem in a well-known article, one that is still much cited and used today: "Actuation créé par l'Acte incrée."[41] His entire effort consists in distinguishing *actuation* from *information*. God cannot be an informing form. That is, He cannot enter into composition with a material cause so as to constitute a single composite with it, for He is Pure Act and does not enter into composition with the creature. Nonetheless, He can *actuate* it. That is, He can make it pass from potency to act, Himself being the actuating act. To explain this, La Taille distinguishes between *act* and *actuation*. He conceives of the latter as being an "adaptation and enabling of potency to act":[42]

In this case (= in the case wherein Uncreated Act is united as such to a created potency) there will be actuation, and there will not be information in the sense that has just been defined. It is impossible that Uncreated Act would depend in any way on any creature whatsoever. It will give of itself and receive nothing. Therefore, there will not be material causality on the side of the creature, nor consequently formal causality, properly speaking, on the side of the Act. Moreover, if there is not formal causality, no more will there be a formal effect. What will there be? There will be a communication of act to potency, a reception from Act into the potency, and a perfectioning of potency by Act, an amelioration, a change. This change is not nothing; it is something. It is certainly not the Uncreated Being, which is

---

40. See §280 in the earlier volume.
41. Maurice de la Taille, "Actuation créée par l'Act incréé," *Recherches des sciences religieuses* 18 (1928): 253–68.
42. Ibid., 260.

immutable. It is something of the created order in potency [*de créé dans la puissance*]: an infused adaptation of potency to act. However, at the same time, it is an actuation of potency by the Uncreated Act. If one asks what particular relation it supports, as such, in regard to the Act, we must respond that since it is a conjunction of potency to Act, it is the essentially inherent relation to the union, with regard to the terminus of the union.⁴³

Applied to the problem of the Hypostatic Union, this leads to the conclusion:

... if the Word forms a substantial composite with Christ's human nature, this means that it shares with it the substantial act of existence. Therefore, his human nature must receive a communication from the act of divine existence inasmuch as it is personal to the Word (i.e., coming from [*hérité du*] the Father). Here again, we have an actuation by Uncreated Act. Like before, it is a created actuation. However, this time it is a created actuation of a substantial order, not of the accidental order, since it leads human nature to existence—not to an existence of the accidental order but one of the substantial order. This substantial actuation is precisely the grace of union, a created [*sic*] grace like sanctifying grace but not, like it, purely habitual, that is, a simple accidental disposition. Rather, it is an adaptation and a truly substantial enabling [of human nature in relation] to the Word. It is not, however, a substance nor a part of a substance—no more than the substantial existence of creatures would be part of their substance, even though it actuates them substantially.⁴⁴

We are thus led to distinguish between the act in virtue of which Christ's humanity exists, (i.e., the Divine Being) and the actuation of this humanity which is something created, which makes it be the case that it exists.

Here, the contradiction implied by this explanation comes to light. On the one hand, this "created existence" [*exister créé*] appears to be some kind of intermediary between potency and act, that is, a reality that is neither potency nor act. Moreover, it is a created reality, though one that is not produced by efficient causality, that is to say, is not created. *Conversely*, the causality of the act (actuation in

---

43. See ibid., 254. See also Maurice Corvez, "Le problème de dieu," *Revue Thomiste* 67 (1967): 65–104.

44. See de la Taille, "Actuation créée par l'Act incréé," 260–61.

the active sense) is neither *efficient causality* (for efficient causality produces an effect distinct from it, which in this case would be the proper being in virtue of which the assumed humanity exists, and one absolutely intends to preclude such a being), nor *formal causality* (for the form exercises its causality by being united to a potency, which is expressly precluded and would be a form of pantheism). Now, an intermediary between efficient causality and formal causality is equally inconceivable. Either the cause is itself communicated, becoming the form of the effect (thus being formal causality), or it communicates a form distinct from itself (thus being efficient causality). It is contradictory to simultaneously say that it communicates itself and that the potency receives from this communication something other than it.[45]

{287} [Allow a technical aside.] When Fr. La Taille speaks about a substantial enabling of the assumed humanity to the Word, he refers (whether or not consciously so, it matters not) to a famous scholastic theory, namely, that of the *substantial mode*. The assumptive action would produce a "substantial modification" in Christ's humanity on account of which it would be the humanity of the Word (a theory held by Vasquez, Suárez, and the Salamanca Carmelites). It is a theory very close to that which was critiqued earlier with regard to the notion of subsistence. The following objection can be registered against it: the *raison d'être* of this "substantial mode" would be to prevent the assumed humanity from having a proper subsistence without, for that, making it subsist (as it is the Word who communicates His own, proper subsistence to it). However, if the assumed humanity does not have its own, proper subsistence, this is precisely because it has been assumed, because it has received a communication from the Word's subsistence, and not vice-versa. The communication of subsistence is logically anterior to the absence of proper subsistence, for the latter, considered apart, pertains to humanity in its ideal state, not its real state. Therefore, it does not pertain to the very humanity

---

45. On formal causality according to St. Thomas, see Cornelio Fabro, *Participation et causalité selon Saint Thomas d'Aquin* (Paris: Vrin, 1961), 381–412.

of Christ, which is perfectly real (though it is real only as assumed). If one says (with Suárez, and, as it seems, La Taille) that it is a question of "disposing" humanity to being assumed (i.e., to receiving the subsistence of the Word), one must respond that humanity is purely passive in relation to this communication of subsistence and that it is passive in relation to the Divine Omnipotence. Therefore, it does not need to be "disposed." God can do this (and we know this because He has done it), and He does it in the same way as He creates, that is, without any succession, without any kind of preparation [in a receptive subject].

Actuation of the assumed humanity by the subsistence of the Word   {288} The criticism registered earlier finds a confirmation in Grillmeier's interpretation of La Taille's thought: "He presupposes that there is a created existence of Christ's humanity. The divine act of being common to the three Persons posits, by efficient causality, the act of existence for this humanity by ordering it to the hypostasis of the Word."[46] We will see that this formula, which exactly expresses the solution toward which we will orient our own thought, certainly does not correspond to La Taille's thought, which rejects any act of existence for the humanity that would be distinct from the divine existence, as well as any efficient causality for the communication of the Word's subsistence.

Grillmeier expressly rejects the idea of a communication of the Divine *Esse* to Jesus' humanity: "Doubtlessly we must dispense with an explanation of Christ's metaphysical unity (i.e., the unity of one *res subsistens*) by way of a single act of existence." However, he retains the idea of a quasi-formal causality: "And nonetheless, we must seek after the solution in the order of quasi-formal causality—as far as the mystery of the Incarnation allows for it." But, refusing to identify existence and subsistence, he attributes this causality to the subsistence of the Word: "And if a quasi-formal causality can be found, this can only be between the 'subsistence' of the Second Person of the Holy Trinity and His humanity."[47]

---

46. Grillmeier, "L'image du Christ dans la théologie d'aujourd'hui," 108.
47. Ibid., 109. Along the same lines, see Joseph Ternus, "Das Seelen-und Bewußt-

The Hypostatic Union 71

This explanation runs into two objections, which are insurmountable in my opinion. The first is drawn from Trinitarian theology. The fundamental principle of this theology is: "All the attributes that one affirms of God are one, identical reality in Him, except where a relative opposition intervenes."[48] From this, it necessarily follows that "all the works of God outside of God are indivisibly produced by the three Persons."[49] The subsistence of the Word is distinguished in the Trinity only by His relative opposition to that of the Father and to that of the Holy Spirit. If we could conceive of a formal causality by God in relation to His creature (and all the objections registered above remain against this "actuation by Uncreated Act"), this could only come about as an action of the whole Trinity. Or, to put it another way: the form of the Godhead is common, by identity, to the three Persons; therefore, it cannot be communicated as something proper to one of them.[50]

The second objection is directly related to the present matter. We have seen that the "principle of subsistence" could not be a form that would complete substance in the line of essence, thus failing to pass out of the order of representation. Therefore, it cannot be the result of an "actuation," and therefore cannot be the effect of a kind of formal causality. This holds even if the qualifier "quasi-" is added, unless the "quasi-" were to devour the "formal." However, in that case, no part of the explanation would remain.

In any event, therefore, *at least in the ontological order*, the explanation of the Hypostatic Union as being an actuation of Jesus' humanity by the Word must be abandoned. But some theologians[51]

---

seinsleben Jesu," in *Das Konzil von Chalkedon*, vol. 3, ed. Alois Grillmeier and Heinrich Bacht (Würzburg: Echter-Verlag, 1962), 229–35; Karl Rahner, "Dieu Trinité fondement transcendant de l'histoire du salut," *Mysterium Salutis: Dogmatique de l'histoire du salut*, vol. 6 (Paris: Cerf, 1971), 49–50.

48. See §52 in the previous volume.
49. See §181 in the previous volume.
50. See Jean-Hervé Nicolas, *Les profondeurs de la grâce* (Paris: Beauchesne, 1969), 117–19.
51. See Karl Rahner, "Dieu dans le Nouveau Testament," *Ecrits théologiques* I (Paris: Desclée de Brouwer, 1959), 13–111; Karl Rahner, "Le concept du mystère dans la théologie catholique," *Ecrits théologiques*, vol. 8 (Paris: Desclée de Brouwer, 1967), 51–103;

bring this problem back by situating this quasi-formal causality in the order of knowledge or, rather, of "consciousness."

Explanation by means of consciousness-union

Here again, La Taille is the origin for the explanation under consideration, for in his famous article, he studied, as being related to "created actuation by Uncreated Act," the three forms of God's union with creatures (already formulated by classical theology): the Beatific Vision, the union of grace, and the Hypostatic Union. Along these same lines, the goal is to explain the Hypostatic Union as a singular summit of the union of grace. Indeed, in every age, theologians speak of the "grace of union." However, the Beatific Vision and the union of grace belong (it seems) to the intentional order of knowledge and love; the Hypostatic Union belongs to the ontological order. Indeed, this is true! The effort that we are studying now consists in making the two orders coincide, at least at their summit.

The great precursor here is Anton Günther (1783–1871) who, identifying consciousness and personality, made the Hypostatic Union consist in the fact that Jesus' human mind was profoundly aware of being subordinated and belonging to the Person of the Word, thus being aware that He was not an independent person. Drawing on phenomenological analyses and much more attentive to the difficulties involved in this conception, many modern theologians seek the path forward in a similar direction.

Exposition {289} On this point, Rahner writes:

We start from the axiom of a Thomist theory of knowledge, according to which being and presence to oneself are mutually causative elements of the one reality, and hence any being is present to itself in the measure in which it has or is being ... (The Hypostatic Union) is the highest think-

---

Karl Rahner, "Essai d'une esquisse de Dogmatique," *Ecrits théologiques*, vol. 4 (Paris: Desclée de Brouwer, 1966), 9–50; Léopold Malevez, "Le Christ et la foi," *Nouvelle revue théologique* 88 (1966): 1009–43; Michael Schmaus, "Sendung," in vol. 9 of *Lexikon für Theologie und Kirche* (2nd ed.), ed. Josef Höfer and Rahner (Freiburg im Breisgau: Herder, 1957–).

able, *ontologically* the highest form of being which exists at all outside of God ... But it is also (whether formally or consecutively need not be investigated here) a determination of the human reality by the person of the Word .... According to the axiom of Thomist metaphysics of knowledge just laid down, this supreme ontological determination of the creaturely reality of Christ, which is God Himself in His hypostatic quasi-formal causality, must necessarily be conscious of itself. For that which is ontologically higher can according to this axiom not be on a lower level of consciousness than that which is ontologically lesser.[52]

Rahner draws a conclusion from this correlation between being and consciousness, which is increasingly strict as the being in question is more elevated. He concludes that, for Christ, the direct vision of God is not a consequence of the Hypostatic Union. Rather, it is what constitutes it:

The result of this approach is that this divine immediacy, being a basic condition of the spirit of Jesus, is to be considered in the light of the substantial root of this creaturely spiritualness. For it is nothing else but the simple presence, to itself, the necessary cognizance of itself, which this substantial unity with the person of the Word possesses. But this means that this immediate vision of God, which is really there, is absolutely nothing else but the primal, unobjectified consciousness of being Son of God, which is *simply there as soon as*[53] the Hypostatic Union takes place. Since this Son-of-God-consciousness is nothing but the inner ontological luminosity of this Sonship, the subjectivity of this objective Sonship, which is necessarily given with the objective reality as its inner element ...[54]

And again:

The "visio immediata" is (if we may be allowed to make our point in this way for the sake of clarity) the consequence and not the presupposition of the conscious being-with-the-Logos of Christ's soul.

---

52. Karl Rahner, "Considérations dogmatiques sur la psychologie du Christ," in *Exégèse et dogmatique* (Paris: Desclée de Brouwer, 1967), 199–200. [Tr. note: Taken from Karl Rahner, "Knowledge and Consciousness in Christ," in *Dogmatic vs. Biblical Theology*, ed. Herbert Vorgrimler (Baltimore: Helicon, 1964), 253–54.]
53. [Tr. note: In the French, Fr. Nicholas notes here that he added this emphasis.]
54. Ibid., 202. [Tr. note: Taken from Rahner, "Knowledge and Consciousness in Christ," 256.]

And:

> But our Lord's self-consciousness, which we have here inferred metaphysically from the *unio hypostatica*, is—in its source and primarily at least—a given quantity which must be thought of as being situated in that substantial depth of Christ's knowledge, pointing ontically beyond itself to that with which it is united, the Logos.[55]

Here, we see the line of this investigation being sketched out. It represents a strenuous effort to make the ontological and the consciousness-relative [*conscientiel*] join back together in identity. The awareness that Christ has of being united to the Word would be this very union, which is ontological and substantial. Conceived in this manner, the Hypostatic Union is situated in the prolongation of man's aspiration toward God. It is an aspiration that finds a first realization in the union of grace and an already more fulfilling realization in immediate vision of God. At its summit, the latter is the Hypostatic Union itself. This leads Rahner to the following, astonishing idea:

> To be a man is, rather, to be completely open to self-transcendence, to tend toward this ultimate fulfillment, which remains gratuitous, to this realization of the loftiest possibility of human existence which is accomplished when, in it, the Logos himself comes to exist in the world.[56]

Thus, according to him, human nature is in obediential potency to the Hypostatic Union, or rather, it is essentially this obediential potency (the latter being understood as a positive aspiration, not as meaning a mere possibility).[57]

---

55. Karl Rahner, "Problèmes actuels de christologie," 142 and 144. [Tr. note: English taken from Karl Rahner, "Current Problems in Christology," in *Theological Investigations*, vol. 1, trans. Cornelius Ernst (New York: Seabury, 1974), 170 and 171.]

56. Rahner, "Le concept du mystère dans la théologie catholique," 160; along the same lines, see Bernhard Welte, "Homousios hemin. Gedanken zum Verständnis und zur theologischen Problematik der Kategorien von Calkedon," in *Das Konzil von Chalkedon*, vol. 3, ed. Alois Grillmeier and Heinrich Bacht (Würzburg, 1962), 69–73; Schmaus, "Sendung." [Tr. note: This was translated from the French, as no exact parallel is found in the official English translation. Fr. Nicolas's citation itself is odd, given that page 160 exceeds the boundaries of this essay in the French edition of Rahner's work. However, the text is a close parallel to Karl Rahner, "The Concept of Mystery in Catholic Theology," in *Theological Investigations*, vol. 4, trans. Kevin Smyth (New York: Crossroad, 1982), 68–69 (especially 69).]

57. See Rahner, "Essai d'une esquisse de Dogmatique," 86–89.

This idea is developed by means of the notion of "ontological abandonment":

> If this is human nature, we begin to understand more clearly—always of course within the framework of the basic mystery which is God and we—what it means to say: God takes on a human nature as His own. The undefinable nature, whose limits—"definition"—are the unlimited reference to the infinite fullness of the mystery, has, when assumed by God as *His* reality, simply arrived at the point to which it always strives by virtue of its essence. It is its *meaning*, and not an incidental activity which could perhaps be left aside, to be that which is delivered up and abandoned, to be that which fulfills itself and finds itself by perpetually disappearing into the incomprehensible. This is done in the strictest sense and reaches an unsurpassable pitch of achievement, when the nature which surrenders itself to the mystery of the fullness belongs so little to itself that it becomes the nature of God himself. The incarnation of God is therefore the unique, *supreme*, case of the total actualization of human reality, which consists of the fact that man *is* insofar as he gives up himself.[58]

Here again, ontological abandonment (which corresponds to what we have called the "disappropriation of the assumed nature") is placed in the line of voluntary abandonment, which is a religious act and, consequently, (let us already note the fact) an act of the person, not of the nature (as goes the scholastic adage, "actions pertain to subjects").[59]

Critique {290} The idea of a correlation between being and consciousness is extremely rich for Christology and is founded on a profound and important metaphysical insight: being is intelligible to the degree that it is, and it is intelligent to the degree that it is intelligible in act. Intelligence is not a perfection super-added to being. It appears as soon as one reaches a certain level of actuality (i.e., immateriality) and does not then cease to become more perfect to the degree that

---

58. Karl Rahner, "Réflexions théologiques sur l'Incarnation," *Ecrits théologiques*, vol. 3 (Paris: Desclée de Brouwer, 1963), 86 and 86n1. [Tr. note: Taken from Karl Rahner, "On the Theology of the Incarnation," in *Theological Investigations*, vol. 4, trans. Kevin Smyth (New York: Crossroad, 1982), 109–10.]

59. On this notion of ontological abandonment, see Schmaus's entry "Sendung," noted above. Also, see Malevez, "Le Christ et la foi," 1029–32.

one rises upward in being. At the summit, Absolute Being is identified purely and simply with the Absolute Intelligible, with Absolute Thought. Indeed, we can deduce from this the idea that this man who is the Incarnate Word must have full awareness of what He is. For Him, this is an existential requirement, not some form of subsequent personal growth [*un mieux-être*].

But can this be used to explain the very union in virtue of which this man is the Word? Being is what is first and fundamental in the correlation between being and consciousness, for consciousness is (and can only be) an activity, which must be conceived as consequent to being. I can think about consciousness in terms of being. I cannot think of being in terms of consciousness. I can say that every being (as soon as a certain degree of being is reached) is self-conscious. I cannot say that being is self-consciousness, for the "self" in this formula leads me back to being itself as the object of consciousness (and therefore as logically anterior to it).

If we apply this observation to the formula, "The immediate vision is the Hypostatic Union itself," we must recognize that it is impossible to make the union consist in the consciousness that Christ had of the union, for ontological union logically precedes consciousness of the union. Moreover, Rahner recognizes this fact when he admits that "[one] must appeal to ontic formulations in order to characterize the uniqueness and specific otherness of this relation to God in distinction from any religious experience of our own or of the prophets."[60] However useful and necessary the consideration of consciousness-relative union may be, if this is how things stand, such a consideration necessarily comes after the ontological explanation of the union and therefore cannot itself provide such an explanation.[61]

We must add that if Jesus Christ is at the summit of the perfection of being, this is because He is the Word. He is not there by His

---

60. Rahner, "Problèmes actuels de christologie," 145. [Tr. note: Taken from Rahner, "Current Problems in Christology," 173.]

61. See Malevez, "Le Christ et la foi," 1032.

human nature, which obviously remains (in Him, as in us) a limited essence that is inferior not only to that of God (who is pure *Esse*) but also to the essence of pure spirits. Therefore, the correlation between being and consciousness at this level of ontological perfection could not reach the supreme point of realization where it would become identity. This is realized only in God, and pure spirits are closer to it than human nature is. Therefore, it is a paralogism to conclude that in Him (in His created mind) there is an identification between consciousness and being, based on the fact that Christ is "the most elevated being," for He is the most elevated being precisely as the Word and through His Divine Being. Taken by itself, His human nature is not the most elevated being, and the consciousness of a being united to the Word is an act of human nature.

What should we think about the notion of "ontological abandonment"? A penetrating remark by Malevez can orient us toward a necessary clarification:

> At the point where we find ourselves, we have not yet established anything but the existence in Jesus of an abandonment that is given to Him, that He receives passively, so to speak, as well as the existence of the awareness of this abandonment that is undergone. Human nature is posited as relinquished, without the intervention of Christ's human freedom, and it is thus known as relinquished independent of every freely-willed ratification. In a word, so far, we understand that Christ knew Himself to be abandoned, but we do not see that He abandons Himself.[62]

Indeed, in this passage there is a grave equivocation from the notion of religious abandonment to that of ontological abandonment. The first is expressed in terms of interpersonal relation—an I-Thou relation, a Word addressed to someone. Therefore, it presupposes that, in him who abandons himself, there would be a personality distinct from the person to whom he abandons himself. Because of this supposition, it seems, on further reflection, that this outlook is altogether improper for rendering an account of the Hypostatic Union,

---

62. Ibid., 1033.

which precisely excludes a personality that would be proper to the united nature.[63]

A criticism of the same order must be addressed to the idea that each of us would aspire to the Hypostatic Union as to the ultimate realization of our own human being. It is true to say that the Hypostatic Union is such a summit for human nature in general, meaning that each man is valorized and exalted by the fact that there is a man who is the Incarnate Word. However, nobody could aspire to the Hypostatic Union without simultaneously aspiring to his own self-abolition, which would be completely contrary to an exaltation and a summit. This would involve a kind of rapprochement with the mystics of the monist sort, making the summit of the mystical ascent (a summit that is perhaps never attained but always aimed at) consist in losing oneself in the divine unity.[64] Strictly speaking, it is unintelligible to say that a desire would have the ontological abolition of the desiring person as its object.

If we examine the notion of "obediential potency" used by Rahner, we can formulate this objection rigorously. For him, obediential potency is something positive, a "tendency to become self-suspended upon the absolute God (in the ontological, not just the moral sense)."[65] He makes it be one of "the most fundamental constituents of the human essence"; "indeed, it is identical to man's essence."[66] It would seem more correct to say that obediential po-

---

63. See Schmaus, "Sendung," 179–80.

64. See Vladimir Lossky, *Théologie mystique de l'Église d'Orient* (Paris: Aubier, 1944), ch. 5.

65. Rahner, "Problèmes actuels de christologie," 143n. [Tr. note: Taken from Rahner, "Current Problems of Christology," 171n3.]

66. Rahner, "Réflexions théologiques sur l'Incarnation," 87. [Tr. note: Fr. Nicolas's statement that, for Rahner, it is "one of" the most fundamental constituents must be read in the sense of the original that he cites here. Rahner, "On the Theology of the Incarnation," in *Theological Investigations*, vol. 4, trans. Kevin Smyth (New York: Crossroad, 1982), 110: "For what does the *potentia oboedientialis* mean for the hypostatic union? What does it mean when we say that human nature has the possibility of being assumed by the person of the Word of God? Correctly understood, it means that this *potential* is not one potentiality along with other possibilities in the constituent elements of human nature: it is objectively identical with the essence of man." In the original French,

tency is the essence itself, considered as able, without contradiction, to be actuated in this manner (by the almighty power of God), not considered as positively ordered to the act in relation to which it is thus said to be in potency. In the two cases, it is indispensable to distinguish the essence considered in itself from the essence considered as realized. To say that man's essence has an obediential potency to the Hypostatic Union is to say, *in Rahner's sense*, that it is wholly itself ordered to the Hypostatic Union, as to its supreme realization. *In the other sense*, however, this would mean that it can be realized as belonging to the Word without implying a contradiction. However, if I consider *it* as already being realized in a human person, an obvious contradiction is involved in the fact that it is simultaneously realized as belonging to the Word, and it is unintelligible to say that the person in whom it is realized would tend toward the Hypostatic Union, which would be its destruction. If one retorts, "The essence, not the person, is what tends thus," we must say in response that this realized essence, precisely as realized, is identical with the person.

Conclusion {291} It is on account of his consciousness-relative union that we can say that the "ontological abandonment" which is the "disappropriation of the assumed nature" is refracted and expressed in Jesus' human consciousness in a "moral and voluntary abandonment." On account of this latter abandonment, Jesus is the perfect exemplar of the forsaken [*abandonné*] man. We can also say that human nature finds its supreme realization in Him, on account of which He is the born head of humanity, Him who has realized in an absolute manner the union with God toward which every man tends solely on account of his nature and even more so on account of his supernatural vocation. However, even though consciousness-relative union is a natural result of ontological union, helping us to understand the implications of the latter more fully, it neither can be sub-

---

Fr. Nicolas incorrectly cites "Essai d'une esquisse de Dogmatique." This has been corrected here.]

stituted for ontological union as an explanation of the Hypostatic Union, nor can it even contribute to explaining that union.

Explanation by the "assumptus homo" theory

{292} The term "assumptus homo" is used for a theological conception of the mystery of the Incarnation holding that the humanity assumed by the Word would constitute an individual human, distinct from the Word, though ontologically united to Him so intimately that this individual human would make up only one person with Him, all the while remaining a distinct subject of being and activity.

This theory was set forth boldly and vehemently by a modern theologian, Déodat de Basly,[67] and was taken up by his disciple Léon Seiller in a form that is perhaps more rigorous.[68] It was exposited and critiqued by Herman Diepen and more recently by Aloys Grillmeier.[69] Fr. Galtier has presented a brief, more favorable exposition of it (though his exposition remains quite reticent).[70] Its earlier form can be found in the first of the medieval opinions reported by Peter Lombard[71] and critiqued by St. Thomas.[72]

Exposition of this theory {293} A perfect summary of this thesis can be found in Déodat himself.[73] From this summary, we can draw the following exposition.

---

67. A Franciscan who died in 1937.

68. [Tr. note: The note reads "Seiller-Diepen, 1: Fr. Diepen shows that it is undeservedly that this Christology is claimed to be that of Scotus." However, it is not clear to what bibliographical entry he is referring here. See L. Seiller, "La psychologie humaine du Christ et l'unicité de personne," *Franziskanische Studien* 31 (1949): 40–76 and 246–74.]

69. See Grillmeier, "L'image du Christ dans la théologie d'aujourd'hui," 111–26.

70. Paul Galtier, "La conscience humaine du Christ. A propos de quelques publications récentes," *Gregorianum* 32 (1951): 525–68.

71. Peter Lombard, *Sentences*, bk. 3, d. 6, nos. 2 and 3.

72. See *ST* III, q. 2, a. 6; Hyacinthe-François Dondaine, "Notes doctrinales thomistes," in *Saint Thomas d'Aquin. Somme théologique, La Trinité* (Paris: Cerf, [1946]), 1:214–58 and 2:383–453.

73. Déodat de Basly, *Scotus-Docens, ou Duns Scot enseignant la philosophie, la théologie, la mystique, Supplément de La France franciscaine* (Paris: La France Franciscaine, 1934), 254–57.

The Hypostatic Union 81

The Christological fact. In virtue of the *deifying susception* [*susception déitante*], an individual human is found united, ontologically *subjoined*, to the Word of God, without ceasing to be an "autonomous" subject (independent in the sense that He depends on God neither more nor less than any other individual human being).

This union constitutes a *Relational Static Theandric Whole* and in no way constitutes a *Third Thing* [*Res tertia*]. (That is, the two beings, the Man and the Word, are united without composing a third being.)

In this Whole, there is only one *person*, the *Word*, for although man is *an intelligent individual*, he does not have the character of being a person on account of the fact that he is united to an already-existing person. However, this in no way reverberates on his behavior, for by contrast, the man is the autonomous actor in this Whole, not the Word (because the Word does not act without the Father and the Holy Spirit). This is what Fr. Déodat calls *the reversal of autonomies*.

The verbal expression of the Christological fact. From the perspective of logic, the Whole thus constituted is a *complex subject*, that is, a group of two subjects taken together. One of the two is the principal subject, and that is what I state first. If I say "Word-Man," I turn my attention to the Word and directly make an attribution to Him. If I say, "Man-Word," the contrary is the case. When the predicate is drawn from the first of these terms (the suppositum [*mot support*]), the copula "is" signifies *identity*: "The Word-Man is the Son of God"; "The Man-Word was born of the Virgin Mary."

When, on the contrary, the predicate is drawn from the second (the attribute [*mot apport*]), the copula signifies *connection*, not identity: "The Man-Word is the Son of God = Man is united (subjoined) to the Word who is the Son of God"; "The Word-Man was born of the Virgin Mary = the Word is united (subjoined) to the Man who was born of the Virgin Mary." In the first case, we have predication *in recto*. In the second case, we have predication *in obliquo*.

The essential difference between this procedure, which Déodat calls "predicative reciprocation," and the classical procedure, "the communication of idioms", which we will discuss below, is that the latter involves an attribution to a single subject of predicates, belonging to it on account of either nature, whereas the former procedure involves attributing to one subject that which belongs to another subject (one that is intimately united to the other but distinct from it). Logic does not authorize such an attribution. If the attribution is valid for both subjects, it can only be made in the plural, by means of a conjunctive proposition that is resolved into two propositions: Peter and Paul *died* in Rome. When the subject of the attribution is an group of subjects taken together, there is only one attribution, precisely because there is only one logical subject: "The crowd backed away." In no case is it legitimate to attribute to a subject a predicate that does not hold true for it but, instead, does for another subject.

An observation. For Fr. Déodat, "Jesus Christ" is the proper name of the *Assumptus homo*. It is said of the Word only *in obliquo*.

Arguments in favor of this theory {294} The theory is founded on the following three principles.

- *First principle:* A realized singular human nature always and necessarily constitutes a human individual, the subject of being and activity.
- *Second principle:* The Word could not be this principle of human being and activity, for this would amount to identifying the Absolute with the non-absolute, the Creator with the creature.
- *Third Principle:* The Word cannot be this principle of activity for the additional reason that He is not an autonomous actor, that is, capable of an action distinct from that of the Father and of the Holy Spirit.

In virtue of these principles, every Christological doctrine that does not admit the *Homo assumptus* (namely, that of St. Thomas) will be accused of Apollinarism.[74] To avoid the accusation of Nestorianism, *psychological personality*, which is full and entire in the *Homo*

---

74. See Déodat de Basly, *Inopérantes offensives contre l'Assumptus Homo*, Supplément à La France franciscaine (Paris, 1935), 126.

assumptus, is distinguished from *metaphysical personality*, which is of a static and extrinsic order. What results is a unique form of solitude in the order of being, the fact that a human individual exists who does not possess his own personhood but who also is not assumed by a Divine Person.

Thus, Christ has a full psychological personality. However, He is not a *person* because the Person of the Word has assumed Him. The assumption of the self modifies psychological personality in no way: if Lucifer were assumed by the Word, he would remain fully himself, and there would be perfect continuity of consciousness before and after the assumption.[75]

Criticism of the homo assumptus *theory*   {295} *Criticism from the point of view of logic.* The copula "is" always signifies the identity of the *thing* to which the subject is related with the *thing* to which the predicate is related. To contest this is to violate the principle of noncontradiction, which governs all of logic.

A complex subject in logic is a *single subject* in which two or many extrinsic intelligible determinations are gathered together. What unites them into a unique logical subject is the unity of the *ontological subject* in which they are realized (e.g., *a musician-man*). On the contrary, the subject *Man-Word* (or *Word-Man*) is a grouping of two subjects which are both conceptually and really distinct. Consequently, such a subject constitutes a *double logical subject* that can in no way be the subject of a unique attribution—above all of an attribution that would be verified only for one of the subjects that are united in it.

True predication *in obliquo* would consist in attributing to a subject a predicate that belongs to it only on account of an intelligible determination that indeed belongs to it in reality, but not by rights (i.e., by the requirements of [the subject's] concept). For example: *The philosopher is a good pianist.* Where the unity of a real subject does not exist, no predication *in obliquo* is valid.

---

75. See Seiller, "La psychologie humaine du Christ et l'unicité de personne," 262–63.

Criticism from the point of view of metaphysics. Every individual in whom human nature is realized is a person. The distinction between (human) *subject* and *person* comes down to the distinction between *hypostasis* and *person*, a distinction which some thinkers in the Middle Ages wished to draw. It should be rejected for the same reasons [as those registered against such medieval explanations].[76]

Criticism from the point of view of theology. The theologian must render account of the various data of faith in a satisfying manner. The theology of the *Assumptus homo* is unable to do so on multiple heads. Indeed, it runs into problems concerning the following points of doctrine.

As regards the unity of the person and the duality of natures: the human nature of Christ is conceived in such a manner that one cannot, without incoherence, deny that it is a human person distinct from the Word.

As regards the divinity of Christ and the divine maternity: in accord with what we have said, to say that Christ is God *in obliquo* is, in fact, to say *that He is not God* but, rather, is only united to God. Likewise, to say that Mary is the mother of God in the sense that she is the mother of a man ineffably united to God is to say, in fact, *that she is not the mother of God*. The Word is not *born* of her. Rather, He is united to him who is born of her.

As regards the unique filiation: to say that the Word communicates His natural filiation to the *Homo assumptus* is to fall into self-contradiction, for a communicated filiation is not natural.

To say that Christ is a natural son of God *in obliquo* is to leave open the question of knowing what He is *in recto*. If He is a "subject" which is distinct from the Word, there is no valid reason to affirm, as the Church teaches, that He is not an adoptive son. Consequently, He would be capable of another filiation than that of the Word, one that can obviously only be adoptive. In response to this, it has been said that adoption necessarily presupposes a preexisting subject, and

---

76. See *ST* III, q. 2, a. 3.

Christ could not have been adopted because He was assumed from His conception. However, this kind of response resorts to a gratuitous and inexact affirmation: every non-natural filiation is adoptive, even if it is bestowed from the first instant, as was the case for the Virgin. The *Homo assumptus* is not, *in recto*, a son by nature. He is a son by grace. Therefore, He is an adoptive son.

Refutation of the arguments in favor of this thesis {296} The argument of tradition. In defense of this position, a multitude of texts are pulled together, ones saying "susceptus homo," "susceptus hominem," etc. To use these texts as teaching that there is a distinction between the *man-Christ* and the *Word* is to force their sense, imposing on them a determinate meaning that they do not have in the writings of their authors. They only mean that Christ is truly a man, all the while being God, and that the Word assumed humanity into the unity of His Person.

What justifies this overarching interpretation is that these texts most energetically and simultaneously affirm Christ's unity (especially the unity of filiation), His divinity, and also that the *Word*, in Christ, was born, suffered, and died. The reference made to the Patristic tradition by the theologians of the *Assumptus homo* is invalidated by the fact that they find themselves obligated to interpret these texts by means of their distinction between *predication in recto* and *predication in obliquo*, for at the very least, we can say that this distinction is utterly foreign to the authors of the texts thus interpreted.[77]

{297} *The truth of Christ's humanity*. Classical (and Catholic) theology does not diminish the truth of Christ's humanity in any way. The latter is concrete and living, subsistent, personalized, acting, and the master of its acts. However, the person who is and acts through this nature is not distinct from the Word. *He is* the Word.

Inasmuch as He is a man, the Word behaves (both externally and interiorly) as a man. He *loves* the Triune God with a created love.

---

77. See Diepen, "L'assumptus homo patristique."

He prays to the Triune God. He humbles Himself before the Triune God, submits His will to the Trinity's, etc. In order to recognize this, we do not in any way need to make the Man-Christ into a subject who is distinct from the Word. It suffices that one recognize this sort of mysterious composition of the Person of the Word subsisting in two natures, that is, the very mystery of the Incarnation. We will examine this point later.

The Word is not an autonomous actor in relation to the Father and the Holy Spirit {298} *Indivisibilia sunt opera Trinitatis ad extra.* This principle holds for all the activities that the Persons produce by the Divine Nature that is common to them. It does not hold for Christ's human actions, as the human nature, which is their source, belongs to the Word only as to Him who subsists in it. *The Word who is man acts in man* by means of the human nature that He has made His own by becoming incarnate. This human action is proper to Him because this human nature is His own, to the exclusion of the Father and the Spirit.

Conclusion {299} As Fr. Grillmeier states: "By the Church's taking of a position with regard to a disciple of Fr. Déodat, namely Fr. Leon Seiller, this extreme Christology of the 'homo assumptus' has been excluded as a possible path for the Church's theology."[78] With the same author, we will note the same is not true for theologians who, following Fr. Galtier, seek to distinguish in Christ a "psychological self" which would be distinct from the Word, though wholly referred to Him.[79] This is not a theology of the *assumptus homo*, for these authors strongly affirm the unity of subsistence. This unity of subsistence is precisely what one must ultimately attempt to explain.

Explanation by the real relation of union

This is the explanation that St. Thomas proposes, which we must explain and justify. We will also need to try to integrate into his ex-

---

78. Grillmeier, "L'image du Christ dans la théologie d'aujourd'hui," 115.
79. See §358 below.

planation certain insights encountered in the preceding solutions. They needed to be critiqued, but they cannot be totally rejected.

The hypostatic union is a real, predicamental relation   {300} Jesus' human nature belongs to the Word in an utterly real manner, and He is a man by means of it in an utterly real manner. But, furthermore, this belonging does not modify the nature in itself, for by this nature He is a man among men, "consubstantial to us."[80] Now, in the entire field of created reality and being, only relation can be real without modifying the subject referred (by the relation). This is why the Hypostatic Union really affecting Jesus' human nature can be nothing other than a real relation.

On the other hand, relation can be real without its co-relation (i.e., the opposed relation) being real. In other words, there are non-mutual relations (in which case only one of the correlative relations is real). Now, we will see that it is impossible for the relation of the Word to the assumed nature to be real, for this would imply a change in God.[81]

This notion of real relation furnishes an account for the mystery. Indeed, we have seen that this mystery could be expressed only in terms of *belonging*. The assumed nature belongs to the Word as His own. Only the notion of relation can express this belonging. However, one will object that in the case of an ordinary man, "personalization" is not brought about by a relation, and it is not clear how a mere relation can explain the subsistence and realization of Jesus' human nature.

We must respond as follows. In the ordinary case, there is an *identity* between the person and the realized nature, meaning that the relation of belonging that we would establish between the person and the nature would be a rationate relation [*relatio rationis*]. In the Hypostatic Union, the Person is and remains distinct from the nature that subsists in Him and by Him. For this reason, the belonging can

---

80. Formula of Chalcedon; see D.-*Sch.*, no. 301.
81. See §308 below.

be only a real relation. However, we should not say that this relation makes the human nature subsist, rendering it real (no more than the "principle of subsistence" in a mere creature renders the latter real). The nature is rendered real by a divine action, namely, the assumptive action.[82] However, the relation is that on account of which this nature is real. In other words, it exists only as belonging to the Word. The reality of this nature consists in the fact that it is "of the Word."

Many Thomist theologians have held that this relation is a "transcendental relation." (A transcendental relation adds nothing to the referred being. It is the referred being itself, considered as itself being wholly referred to another.) This notion of transcendental relation, which was held by "classical" Thomism, has been vigorously attacked as being intrinsically contradictory and wholly foreign to St. Thomas.[83] Whatever may be the outcome of this discussion [concerning the legitimacy of the notion of transcendental relation], it is quite difficult to say that the Hypostatic Union adds nothing to the assumed humanity and that it is nothing. Jesus' humanity has something that the ordinary man's humanity does not have, namely the fact that it is referred to the Word as to its own person. This relation can be conceived of only as being predicamental (unless this transcendental relation is said to be part of the individuating principles of Jesus' humanity, but we have critiqued this explanation).[84]

Hypostatic union and creation

{301} Creation is the fundamental divine action *ad extra*, not in the sense that every divine action *ad extra* would be a "creation," but in the sense that all the other divine actions *ad extra* presuppose creation. In other words, the effect of all other such actions is first, in its

---

82. See §318 below.
83. See Anton Krempel, *La doctrine de la relation chez Saint Thomas, exposé historique et systématique* (Paris: Vrin, 1952). [Tr. note: For a brief discussion of this philosophical topic in English, see "Translator's Appendix (Minerd)" in Reginald Garrigou-Lagrange, *Philosophizing in Faith: Essays on the Beginning and End of Wisdom*, ed. and trans. Matthew K. Minerd (Providence, RI: Cluny Media, 2019), 116–19.]
84. See §278 above.

The Hypostatic Union

very specificity, a "creature." We can draw significant illumination by comparing the Hypostatic Union to creation.[85]

We will not speak here about the Incarnation as a (transcendent) terminus of creation, as giving it its ultimate meaning.[86] However, we will compare the effect of the creative act for an ordinary creature with the effect of the assumptive action for Christ's humanity.

Both confer subsistence upon the effect. The creative act makes the creature subsist in itself. The assumptive action makes the assumed nature subsist in the Word. In both cases, this dependence upon God for subsistence is expressed by the notion of relation. Passive creation (*creatum esse*, to be created) is reduced to a relation of total dependence upon God.[87] Just as "passive creation" is the relation by which the created being is referred to God as to the principle of its being, so too the Hypostatic Union is the relation by which Jesus' humanity is referred to the Word as to the principle of its subsistence. In the case of creation, the relation, inasmuch as existence [*être*] presupposes the substance (because existence is an ontological accident, and every accident presupposes its subject), even though according to its formal notion it is presupposed by this substance, as it is a relation to the very principle of this substance's existence.[88] In the same manner, in the case of the Hypostatic Union, the relation of union presupposes Jesus' human nature as its subject but is simultaneously presupposed by it, for this humanity is real and subsistent only as the humanity of the Word (i.e., as referred to Him).

We must also note a difference. The assumptive action does not give *existence* to Jesus' humanity (at least if one accepts our critique of the theory of actuation). It only gives subsistence to it. Therefore, it presupposes another divine action by which Jesus' humanity receives existence.[89] Thus, a double relation of dependence with regard to God must be recognized in this humanity. One such dependence will

---

85. See Rahner, "Problèmes actuels de christologie," 134–38.
86. See section 3, ch. 1 below.
87. See *ST* I, q. 45, a. 2.
88. See ibid., a. 3, ad 3.
89. See §317 below.

be related to God the Creator (the three Persons who are the unique Creator). The other will be related to the Word in whom, alone, it subsists as His own.[90]

The subject of the relation of union   {302} In general, the subject of a relation is the being that is referred to another. However, here a grave difficulty arises. Jesus' human nature is what is referred. It is not a being, for it is not a "subsistent."

St. Thomas says (or seems to say) that this subject is [Jesus'] human nature.[91] However, he makes an important distinction between "human nature inasmuch as it is at the terminus of its assumption to the divine hypostasis" and "human nature considered in itself, that is, abstractly."[92] Let us note that, in the second case, it is still a question of Jesus' human nature, not of human nature *in universali*. Therefore, it is a question of distinguishing the same human nature considered sequentially *as concrete* (i.e., as subsisting in the Word, making the Word to be this Man who is Jesus) and *as abstract* (i.e., as what is realized and concretized by the subsistence of the Word).

This places us on the way toward the solution. The subject of the relation of union is Jesus' human nature considered as belonging to the Word, this nature being rendered concrete by belonging to the Word. In ordinary cases, the concretized nature and the person in whom it is concretized are identical. The mystery of the Incarnation consists in the fact that the human nature on account of which the Word is a man is really distinct from the Person who subsists in it and in whom the nature subsists. Therefore, one can consider this nature apart from the Word and in relation to Him.

The terminus of the relation of union   {303} Normally, St. Thomas presents the Divine Nature as being the terminus of the relation of union. In

---

90. As regards the general problem concerning the essential role of the notion of relation in theology for *real knowledge* of God's effects precisely as His effect, as well as for real knowledge of God Himself, see §§305–8 below.

91. See *ST* III, q. 2, aa. 7 and 8.

92. Ibid., a. 8.

fact, it is a question of the union of two natures in the sole Person of the Word. However, he sometimes speaks about the relation of the human nature to the hypostasis of the Word.[93]

This is not a useless subtlety. Two problems must be distinguished (in a way that will perhaps need to be discussed). On the one hand, there is the problem of the union of the two natures with one another. On the other hand, there is that of the union of the human nature with the Divine Hypostasis.[94]

The solution is analogous to that given for the subject of the relation. The Divine Nature subsists in three Persons. The Hypostatic Union is certainly the union of two, though concrete and subsistent, natures. They are united precisely on account of their subsistence in the unique Person of the Word. Therefore, the terminus of the relation of union is the Divine Nature subsisting in the Word. Or, if one so prefers, the terminus of this relation is the Divine Nature as constituting the Person of the Word. Or, again, the terminus of this relation is the relation that is constitutive of the Person of the Word inasmuch as this relation is subsistent.[95]

Therefore, the idea of a double relation of the human nature (i.e., with respect to the Divine Nature and the Person of the Word) must be rejected as a superfluous and ultimately unintelligible complication. The Hypostatic Union is a single relation of the human nature that the Word has made His own to the Divine Nature inasmuch as it is His own from all eternity.

The foundation of the relation of union   {304} A relation is real when it has an ontological foundation in its subject. Thus, it exists in the extramental world, not on account of the act of the mind referring one terminus to another. The mind can only perceive such a real relation. It cannot make it. Such is indeed the case for the Hypostatic Union. It is not the believer's mind that places the humanity of Jesus

---

93. See ibid., a. 7.
94. See Rahner, "Problèmes actuels de christologie," 158.
95. See §121 in the previous volume of this work.

in a privileged relation with the Godhead (for example, on account of the fact that Jesus would be the man in whom we discover the greatest proximity to God, or Him through whom the Word of God is strikingly proclaimed to us, etc.). Rather, this relation exists independent of any and all intellectual activity (even, as we have seen, independent of Jesus' own consciousness). In virtue of this relation, Jesus *is* Man and God. Therefore, we must find a real foundation in Jesus' human nature for the relation of union.

For those who admit the theory of actuation by Uncreated Act, the solution is simple: "This foundation is nothing other than this nature inasmuch as it is transcendentally actuated, in its created being, by the subsistence of the Word."[96] [Or, as Rahner puts it:] "The Hypostatic Union is an ontological appropriation of a human nature by the person of the Word. But it is also ... a determination of the human reality by the person of the Word."[97] If the refutation that we have provided against this theory is exact, this is only a false form of clarity.

As we have seen, a number of scholastics have described a "substantial mode" which would affect human nature, preventing it from being enclosed in its own, proper personality, reserving it for the Word as being able to belong only to Him.[98] This was one possible solution for our problem. This *modus substantialis* would be the foundation from which the relation of union would flow forth. However, we have not retained this explanation. The assumed nature is in no way modified by its assumption to the subsistence of the Word.

Therefore, we must say that the foundation we are seeking is the same, singular substance of Jesus' humanity itself. Taking up our comparison with creation once again, let us say that as the relation in which the "being created" consists is founded immediately on the substance of the creature as receiving its *esse* from God, so too the relation in which the Hypostatic Union consists is founded immediately on the substance of the assumed humanity inasmuch as it is

---

96. Grillmeier, "L'image du Christ dans la théologie d'aujourd'hui," 127.
97. Rahner, "Considérations dogmatiques sur la psychologie du Christ," 199–200. [Tr. note: Taken from Rahner, "Knowledge and Consciousness in Christ," 253.]
98. See §287 above.

The Hypostatic Union 93

appropriated to the Word by the assumptive action, not inasmuch as it is actuated by its *esse* (for, from this latter perspective, it founds the relation of "being created," like all other created realities).

Here we reach the limit of our explanation, and we must recognize this fact. We have no conceptual means for determining and specifying the assumptive action's effect in the assumed humanity (i.e., its "appropriation" to the Word). A number of Thomists here speak about a transcendental relation to the Person of the Word, which would found the predicamental relation of union. (For the topic of creation, the same thinkers speak of a fundamental relation of the creature to the Creator, which would found the predicamental relation of "creation.") This can be said, but it is hardly illuminating. It is certain that Jesus' humanity is referred to God by a double relation: one to the Triune God inasmuch as He is the Creator, the other to the Word, as to Him whose nature it is. This is quite real but, in the end, exceeds explanatory possibilities.

C. On the Use of the Notion of Relation in Theology and Its Realistic Scope

When we come to define the various kinds of creaturely dependence upon God (and, conversely, God's "mastery" or "Lordship" over His creatures), we find only concepts that are relations. That is, we find that we must make use of that which has the least degree of reality in the entire order of reality: "Relation has the weakest being."[99] Does this not involve a reduction of this dependence to nothing or nearly nothing?

1. *The problem*
a) The principal cases where theology must have recourse to relation

Creation

{305} "If creation introduces something into the creature it is only something relative."[100] We cannot hold that creation involves

---

99. *De pot.*, q. 8, a. 1, ad 4.
100. See *ST* I, q. 45, a. 3.

a "matter," a "patient" on which the creative action would be exercised, receiving the creative action. For this reason, the "being created" (i.e., what makes the contingent being be a creature) is surprisingly reduced to a simple relation to God the Cause. Likewise, the creative action is reduced to a (rationate) relation (*relatio rationis*) from God to His effects.

The Incarnation

"The union about which we are speaking is a unique relation between the Divine Nature and the human nature on account of which they come together in one person, that is, [the person] of the Son of God."[101] We explained this earlier.

Eucharistic presence

"When we say that Christ is under the Sacrament, it is a question of a singular relation that He has to this sacrament."[102]

The presence [of the Trinity] through grace

"What is included in the notion of mission is a relation of the Divine Person to the terminus to whom He is sent, so that He begins to be there in some manner."[103]

b) Difficulties

First, *in the creature*. It seems that this removes all reality from the creature's dependence upon God. First, and fundamentally, it seems to remove all reality from what I express in saying that it is a creature, namely, its *creatum esse*. Next, it seems to remove the entire reality of the Incarnation. If the Hypostatic Union is reduced to a mere relation, in what does the singularity of Jesus' humanity consist in comparison with every other man's humanity? How can a relation, which presupposes the referred subject, really prevent this human-

---

101. *ST* III, q. 2, a. 7.
102. *ST* III, q. 76, a. 6. See the third volume of this work.
103. *ST* I, q. 43, a. 1. See §204 of the first volume of this work.

ity from constituting a "subject" (i.e., a person)? And likewise, for the Eucharist, how can the identification of the offerings with Christ be explained by a simple relation of these offerings to Jesus Christ?

Second, *in God*. If being the Creator, being man (in what concerns the God-Man), being present in the Eucharist, and indwelling in the spirit of the believer, are all only relations of the immutable God to His distant creature, with God remaining, as it were, enclosed in His inaccessible transcendence, does all of this still mean something real for Him? Moreover, this seems pertinent as we must say that these are rationate relations (*relationes rationis*) in Him, so that we may preserve His immutability. In these conditions, all the trouble taken in explaining how He creates, how He becomes man, etc., are defeated: He did not really create, He did not really assume a human nature, etc.

2. *The realistic scope of these explanations by means of relation*
a) The absolute is implied in the concept of the relative

{306} Relation concerns a subject, which is an absolute (i.e., a being subsisting in itself). This subject is what is referred, and it is therefore necessarily implied in the concept of relation. Thus, it is clear how a relative concept can be a valid (noetic) instrument for knowing the absolute. The concept of "son" at least implies a living thing, as well as the generative action by which it has come forth from another living thing of the same species.[104]

b) Application to the creature's relation to God

{307} Every real relation has a foundation that, in the subject that is referred, is the determination on account of which the subject is referred. Thus, the relation of filiation is founded on the generative action inasmuch as it is received in the living thing that has come forth

---

104. N.B. Let us recall that, in the Trinity, the relations do not refer to a subject that is distinct from themselves. However, this does not mean that they are *lacking a subject*. They are their own, proper subject for themselves. (See §92 in the previous volume.) Thus, even at this summit, and for what concerns the concepts by means of which the believer's mind can "attain" the Divine Reality, the relative concept implies an absolute concept.

from another. In the case in which the relation arises from the divine action by which the creature depends entirely upon the Creator, the very substance of the creature immediately founds the relation. That is, the subject is referred according to all that it is, according to its substantial being. Thus, the relative concept, which directly represents the relation itself, indirectly attains the being considered in its complete reality.

Thus, to say that the Hypostatic Union is a relation is to say that we know it by means of a relative concept. However, this concept implies and connotes the complete reality of the assumed humanity, making it known inasmuch as everything is referred to the Word as to the person who has it, properly, as His own and is a man by it.

Similarly, creation is a relative concept that directly expresses the created being's relationship of total dependence upon God. However, it connotes the whole reality of this being, known precisely as referred to God.

c) Application to God's relation to creatures

{308} God's relation to creatures can only be a rationate relation (*relatio rationis*) for God is utterly immutable, and while relation itself is not produced by an agent ("relation," the ancients said, "is not the terminus of a movement," a passage from potency to act: *ad relationem non datur motus*), it does come about in the referred subject because of a change that is produced in it, making it acquire the foundation from which the relation flows forth as soon as the terminus is posited. (Thus, to have begotten is, in a man, a determination from which flows forth the relation of paternity in relation to a son who has come forth from him.) We can conceive of no change [in God] that would make Him become the Creator, nor of any such change that would make it be true that the Word has become a man.

Nonetheless, are we not faced with the scriptural formula: "The Word was made flesh"? This shows that, in order for us to conceive the reality of the created being and of the assumed being (of Jesus' humanity), we find ourselves forced to double the utterly real relation of the creature to the Creator and of the assumed humanity to the Word by means of a correlation constructed by our reason and whose subject is the Absolute, God [as regards creation], [and] the Word [as regards the assumptive action in the Hypostatic Union]. This is the only noetic means that we have for knowing and saying that God is really the Creator and that the Word is really a man. It is real because God is the real terminus of the relation of creation and the Word is the real terminus of the relation of union. However, ordinarily, the terminus of a real relation is also (and simultaneously) the subject of a correlation. On account of His transcendence, God cannot be the subject of a real relation to the creature. Nonetheless, as it is impossible for us to think about the transcendence of God, who is infinite (for, we can only affirm this transcendence), we need to construct this relation, which in fact, is a rationate being [*ens rationis*]. Nonetheless, by means of this relation, we can indirectly and negatively attain God as Him to whom the creature is really referred in order to exist, in order to subsist:

> Given that God is referred to the creature by the same reason by which the creature is referred to Him, and given that the relation of dependence exists in the creature in a real manner, God is the Lord in a real manner and not only according to the conception of reason. Indeed, if He is called the Lord, He is so called as the creature is submitted to Him (that is, in a real manner).[105]

The sole relation that in reality unites God and the creature is the relation of the creature to Him, and the reality of the divine attribute of Lordship is sufficiently assured by the fact that He is at the terminus of this relation. God's relation to the creature constructed by us from the start is not real. Nonetheless, it is used to attain and speak about this reality. And similarly, I can conceive and speak about the Incarnation's reality only by the proposition, "The Word has become flesh," which translates only this: "Flesh has been assumed by the Word, and therefore the Word is really a man, some-

---

105. *ST* I, q. 13, a. 7, ad 5.

thing that He was not." However, I must simultaneously affirm that He has undergone no real change and no becoming.

3. What is the source of the fact that concepts pertaining to God are relative concepts?

{309} This [relativity] comes from the fact that we cannot know God directly by means of concepts that represent Him. Because God is infinite—according to intelligibility as much as according to being—no concept can contain Him. On the other hand, all our concepts come from experience, and God is not in the field of our experience, which cannot shed its sensible dimension (even when such experience is spiritual): "All knowledge has its origin in sensation." Therefore, we can know God only as the transcendent terminus of the relation of creatures to their Cause. The concepts that we use for knowing Him are drawn from our experience and first of all represent created perfections. They can be of use for knowing God only in virtue of the act of the analogical judgment that, applying them to this transcendent terminus of the relation, makes these concepts transcend themselves so as to aim at Him who is beyond all the objects of our understanding. This means that only relative concepts can serve as the concepts by which we attain God. This rule is valid for revelation itself (and therefore for theology), for in order to reveal Himself to Man, God made use of human concepts, elaborated by man on the basis of his experience.[106]

I. THE UNITING UNITY

Up to this point, we have fixed our attention on the problem of the "united unity," that is, the union of humanity and divinity in Jesus Christ. The Person of the Word is the principle of this union. Indeed, it consists in the fact that this man, Jesus (constituted by this singular human nature), and the Word (constituted by the Divine

---

106. Vatican II, *Dei Verbum*, no. 12; Jean-Hervé Nicolas, *Dieu connu comme inconnu* (Paris: Desclée de Brouwer, 1966), 238–50.

Nature that He holds from the Father) are one and the same person. We will now consider the same problem from the perspective of the "uniting unity," that is, from the perspective of the Word inasmuch as He subsists in Christ's human nature and in this way unites humanity and divinity in Himself.[107]

A. The Word, the Uniting Unity

1. *The Word, the principle of the Hypostatic Union*

Karl Rahner raises this problem, which can be summarized as follows: we can explain the union of the two natures in Christ by means of the unity of the Word's Person (union in *persona*). However, the union of the human nature to the Person of the Word must still be explained. Where is the uniting unity in this union? It cannot be the Person of the Word, as He is a part of the united unity in the union thus considered.[108]

a) The communication of the Word's subsistence to the human nature

{310} We saw above[109] that the Divine Person communicates His subsistence to the human nature. That is, because of the assumption [of Christ's human nature, in the Hypostatic Union] (which is a real action), this human nature exists only as the nature of this Divine Person.

This is conceivable only on account of the Divine Person's infinity.[110] Indeed, given that what is proper to a person is the substantial unity by which he is distinct from every other substance than the substance that constitutes him, we could ask ourselves how an already-constituted person could receive a substantial nature into himself and make it subsist as something belonging to himself. However, the Divine Person is infinite, constituted by the Divine Nature, which is infinite. No created nature is foreign to the Divine Na-

---

107. See *ST* III, q. 3; Vincent Leroy, "L'union selon l'hypostase d'après Saint Thomas d'Aquin," *Revue thomiste* 74 (1974): 205–43.
108. See Rahner, Problèmes actuels de christologie," 158n1.
109. See §300 above. [Tr. note: The original reads "§61."]
110. See *ST* III, q. 3, a. 1, ad 2.

ture, for in fact, every created essence is a finite participation of the unique and infinite Divine Perfection.

We are not here concerned with "demonstrating" even the mere "possibility" of this "integration" of the assumed human nature into the eternal subsistence of the Word. Rather, we are only concerned with showing that it is not impossible, not contradictory: "It is not contradictory to the very idea of a person that it would be communicated in such a manner that it would subsist in many natures."[111] However, this is conceivable only on account of the ontological infinity of the Divine Person: "However, *on account of His Infinity*, it is proper to the Divine Person that the two natures could come together in Him, not accidentally but according to subsistence."[112] Indeed, the Divine Person is constituted by the Divine Nature. (Strictly speaking, we must say that He is constituted by the subsistent relation that is identical with the Divine Nature[113] and that the Divine Nature is infinite. That is, It "includes" in Its supereminent simplicity all the perfections realized in a manifold and finite manner in creatures.)[114] Thus, a finite nature is not foreign to the Divine Nature and for this reason is not, of itself, external to the Divine Person in such a way that the latter would not be able to extend Himself to it and assume it into His subsistence without losing His own incommunicability: "And this is why when the Person of the Word assumes the human nature, He does not extend Himself outside the Divine Nature but, much to the contrary, He elevates to Himself that which is below (this Nature)."[115] Such an extension would be impossible for a created person, not because he is a person (that is, it would not be in contradiction with the idea of being a person), but rather because He is *finite*.

We have seen how we can come to some understanding about this joining of human nature to the Person of the Word by making

---

111. Ibid.
112. ibid. [Tr. note: reading *en elles* as *en elle*, based on the Latin original *in ea*.]
113. See *ST* I, q. 29, a. 4. Also, see §121 of the previous volume.
114. [Tr. note: The closing parenthesis does not exist in the original.]
115. *De unione verbi*, a. 1, ad 14.

use of its analogies with accidents, on the one hand, and substantial parts, on the other.[116] What is unique and elevated above everything that we can conceive is the idea of a union *in persona tantum* (i.e., a joining to the person without a prior joining to the nature so as to constitute one, single nature.)

In virtue of this "joining" of an individuated human nature to His Person (and on account of this communication of subsistence), the Word is Himself the man whom this nature thus subsisting constitutes (yet all the while remaining distinct and infinitely other from this human nature). The Word is *He who has a human nature* and who for this very reason is a man by it, as the person whom this nature would have formed would have been if the assumptive action had not occurred.

Therefore, there is a "united unity" between these two termini (namely, the Word and the human nature). However, must we find a distinct uniting unity? Here, the united unity is the Incarnate Word, who is purely and simply identical with the eternal Person of the Word. Indeed, here there is more than *a union* of two distinct termini. There is an *identity* of the Eternal Word with the man who subsists in this human nature.

b) The Word as terminus of the Hypostatic Union

How can a Divine Person, in His distinction, make human nature subsist?

{311} The problem can be formulated as follows: is not such an action making a created nature subsist [in the Word] an action *ad extra*? Therefore, is it not an action that is common to the three Persons? In this case, it would not make sense to say that, among the Divine Persons, only the Word is Man: "One of the Trinity suffered," as the Scythian monks said.

St. Thomas's response is as follows. Inasmuch as the assumption [of the human nature in the Hypostatic Union] is an action, it is produced by the three Persons together. However, the terminus

---

116. See §275 above.

of this action (i.e., the communication of subsistence) can be proper to a Person: "The Three Persons together made it be the case that this individuated human nature is united solely to the Person of the Son."[117]

To understand this response, recall that although the three Persons act undividedly as regards efficient causality exercised in creating or within the created universe, each Person in His distinction can be the terminus of a relation from the creature to Him. We saw this in our discussion about interpersonal relations of knowledge and love.[118] This is equally verified for this ontological relation of the assumed nature to the Word in which the Hypostatic Union consists, for in this relation, the Word is the terminus toward which the creature is directed outside of itself, the Word Himself being immobile, immutable, and distinct.

By contrast, for those who hold that the Hypostatic Union is a communication of the *Divine Being* to the human nature, it seems impossible to explain how the three Persons are not incarnated together, given that the Divine Being is absolutely one and common to the three Persons.[119]

Could a different person than the Word have become incarnate?

{312} This is a question that the medieval theologians themselves raised, and it has been taken up by some modern thinkers as well. Rahner at one time suggested that it must be answered affirmatively,[120] but he then, later on, vigorously combated this hypothesis.[121] Michael Schmaus declares the matter to be inconceivable from the perspective of the relationship between the *ad extra* divine missions and the intra-Trinitarian relations.[122]

---

117. *ST* III, q. 3, a. 4.
118. See §198 in the first volume of this work.
119. See §280 above.
120. See Rahner, "Le concept du mystère dans la théologie catholique," 159.
121. Rahner, "Dieu Trinité fondement transcendant de l'histoire du salut," 94–95.
122. Schmaus, "Sendung," 185–87.

The Hypostatic Union

St. Thomas resolves the question affirmatively,[123] though adding, "It was supremely fitting that the Person of the Son would be the Person who becomes incarnate."[124] What does St. Thomas mean by "fittingness"? According to Marie-Dominique Chenu[125] and Ghislain Lafont,[126] ["arguments of fittingness"] are investigations into the intrinsic intelligibility of an event that depends on the divine freedom, though a freedom ruled by a sovereign wisdom. Max Seckler adds an important bit of precision:

> However, the term "fittingness" does not indicate a deficient mode of knowledge. Instead, it indicates the "a priori" that is logically necessary for a free historical event. Essential structures do not obligate one to the act, but when there is an act, it is revealed as being in conformity with such structures.[127]

If this is how things stand, Schmaus's position rejoins that of St. Thomas, despite the apparent opposition between the two. However, in my opinion, it is not true to say that the question was posed only from the vantage point of the *potentia absoluta* of scholasticism in its period of decline. St. Thomas intended to emphasize that the Son did not make the assumed nature subsist on account of what is proper to Him as a person, by which He is distinguished from the two other Persons but, rather, by what He has in common with the two others (i.e., subsisting in the Divine Nature). However, if I consider the Incarnation in relation to salvation history (i.e., as the mission of the Divine Person to humanity), then the Son alone can be sent in this manner because the mission to be accomplished corresponds to what is proper to Him personally and would not correspond to what is personally proper to the two others.[128]

---

123. See *ST* III, q. 3, a. 5.
124. Ibid., a. 8.
125. See Marie-Dominique Chenu, *Introduction à l'étude de Saint Thomas d'Aquin* (Paris: Vrin, 1954), 262–63.
126. See Ghislain Lafont, *Structures et méthode dans la Somme théologique de Saint Thomas d'Aquin* (Paris: Desclée de Brouwer, 1961), 306–7.
127. See Max Seckler, *Le salut et l'histoire* (Paris: Cerf, 1967), 41.
128. See §145 in the previous volume.

c) The composition of the Person of the Incarnate Word

In what sense can one say that the Person of the Word is composite?

{313} This expression appears for the first time in the fourth anathema of the Second Council of Constantinople:

> If anyone ... does not confess that the union of God the Word with the flesh animated by a rational soul and intellectual soul took place by way of synthesis, that is, according to the hypostasis, as the holy Fathers have taught, and consequently denies that he has only one hypostasis who is our Lord Jesus Christ, one of the Holy Trinity, let him be anathema.
>
> ... The Holy Church of God, rejecting these two impious heresies, confesses the union of God the Word with the flesh as being by synthesis, that is, according to the hypostasis. For in the mystery of Christ, union by synthesis not only preserves from confusion what has come together but also tolerates no division.[129]

The canonization of the word "synthesis" for indicating the personal, Hypostatic Union is remarkable in this anathematization; with allusion to the *unus de Trinitate* that was the initial problem of the case of the Three Chapters, one can say that it constitutes the truly original element of the definition. The expression *enosis kata synthesin* indicates the *composition* of the hypostasis thus formed by the union of the Word with the flesh because "not only does it safeguard the non-confusion of the elements from which the union is brought about, but it also excludes every kind of division." It was good that the Council, which wished, in accepting the word "synthesis," to make a concession to the monophysites, explained in a precise manner the meaning of this word, which was dear to the Severians. It is to be noted, moreover, that the formula of Chalcedon is taken up and approved again by the Council; the union by synthesis is the equivalent of the Hypostatic Union: the Church professes the union of the Word God with the flesh *kata synthesin, oper esti kath upostasin*.[130]

---

129. D.-*Sch.*, nos. 424–25. [Tr. note: Taken from the 43rd edition of Denzinger.]
130. See Michel, "Hypostatique (Union)," cols. 485–86.

The idea was taken up again and developed by the great doctor of the Greek Church, St. Maximus the Confessor.[131]

St. Thomas takes up Peter Lombard's expression. Lombard expresses it as though it is traditional[132] and connects it expressly to John of Damascus, where he explains it thus: "Thus, although there is a single subsistent there, nonetheless there are two distinct reasons for subsisting."[133]

At first sight, this is shocking. Is not the Divine Person infinitely simple? Moreover, the nature [of a given person] is part of [that] person—the person is the whole. As there are two natures that remain distinct, we must also say that this Whole who is the Person of the Incarnate Word is composed of the Divine Nature which is subsistent (in the Word) and the human nature which is subsistent (in the same Word). But how can we conceive of the idea that the divine, infinite nature would be a "part"?

Therefore, we must say that the Divine Person is infinite and that nothing is really added to Him. Also, this "composition" comes from our manner of conceiving. Here again, the case of creation serves as a reference point. All creatures, taken together, add nothing to God. Nonetheless, they are real and distinct from God. For this reason, I cannot conceive of their reality without thinking that they are part of the totality of being and, therefore, that the Divine Being is another part of this totality. However, I must simultaneously affirm that the Divine Being is the Whole and that the being of creatures adds nothing to Him.

Can one speak of a human personality of Christ?

{314} The Person of Christ subsists in his human nature. Is a person who subsists in the human nature something different from a human person?[134]

---

131. See Juan-Miguel Garrigues, "La personne composée du Christ d'après S. Maxime le Confesseur," *Revue Thomiste* 74 (1974): 199–200.
132. See Lombard, *Sentences*, bk. 3, d. 6, no. 4.
133. *In III Sent.*, d. 6, q. 2, a. 3; see *ST* III, q. 2, a. 4.
134. See J.-H. Nicolas, *Les profondeurs de la grâce*, 234–38.

The expression is found in Peter Lombard (*Sentences*, bk. 3, d. 14, no. 10): "*Hominis persona.*" St. Thomas comments (*In I Sent.*, q. 1, a. 1): "persona divina fit persona huius naturae humanae [a Divine Person becomes the person of this human nature]." In the *Summa theologiae*, St. Thomas says that, by the Incarnation, the Word became "hypostasis naturae humanae [the hypostasis of a human nature]" (*ST* III, q. 16, a. 1, ad 1) and that in the expression "Deus factus est homo," this "homo" designates (*supponit*) "not the bare person of the Son of God but, rather, Him inasmuch as He subsists in a human nature" (a. 6, ad 3). Now, for him, "hypostasis of a human nature" is exactly the same thing as "human person": "Beyond [the notion of] hypostasis, person only adds a determinate nature" (q. 2, a. 3). His commentator Cajetan understood him in this way: "Therefore, from the union of this soul and this body, what must be constituted is either a new person or the previously-existing [*antiquam*] person. And the latter is what we find in Christ" (*In ST* III, q. 2, a. 5, no. 11). Before him, St. Albert said: "Indeed, He is not this human person except through the personality of the Son of God, not by any created person" (*De incarnatione*, tr. 3, q. 3, a. 5 [Cologne ed., vol. 26, p. 203]) Was this not prefigured in St. Irenaeus's expression, which returns in the leitmotiv found in *Summa contra gentiles* III (12.3, 16.7, 18.6, 19.1): "Filius Dei factus est filius hominis," the Son of God has become the son of man? (Also, see Nazarius: "Verbum incarnatum duplicis habens hypostasis rationem, divinae sc. et humanae" [The Incarnate Word, having the *ratio* of a twofold hypostasis, namely divine and human]).[135]

This expression is shocking at first sight, as we have seen that the mystery of the Incarnation precludes that the assumed humanity would have its own, proper personality: "One person in two natures." However, while we needed to speak about the "depersonalization" of the assumed humanity, this was in order to show that the Word appropriated this nature, which thus was disappropriated (i.e., not belonging to a person formed with it and in it), and made it

---

135. Cited by Yves-Marie Congar, "La Personne-Eglise," *Revue thomiste* 71 (1971): 622–23.

His own. A person who has a human nature which subsists in Him or a person in whom this nature has subsistence is a human person.

What we absolutely must avoid is the idea that this would be a human person distinct from the Word. It is the Word who has become a human person without ceasing to be a Divine Person. It seems that this would be a valid and necessary expression of the mystery of the Incarnation.

Moreover, this expression enables us to refute the fundamental objection that we already encountered: how would Jesus be a true man, fully a man, if He were devoid of what makes up the most precious value of a man (i.e., personality)? If one responds that He has the Divine Personality, what is meant by such a response? Does the *Man-Jesus* have the Divine Personality? This can only be understood in the way discussed above: a personality that a man has is a human personality. Therefore, we must say that, *in becoming incarnate, the Divine Person became a human person*, without ceasing, for all that, to be a Divine Person, the Second Person of the Trinity.

Another consideration can be added to this. From what has been said, it seems that a nature cannot exist without subsisting, without being subsistent. Now, for a human nature, being subsistent and being personalized are the same thing, as the person is the subject subsisting according to and in the human nature.

By contrast, see the explanations by Fr. Galtier in opposition to this.[136] He so strongly insists on the absence of any sort of human personality in Christ and on the separation between the Divine Person and the assumed nature that only two outcomes seem possible on his account. Either this nature must be considered to be unreal (which is utterly opposed to what Galtier holds), or it must be made into a distinct ontological subject, to which one would refuse personality only *pro forma* [*auquel on ne refuserait d'être une personne que pour la forme*] (which is certainly contrary to Galtier's intention). In order to assure the real consistency of the human nature, we ab-

---

136. See Paul Galtier, *L'unité du Christ. Être. Personne. Conscience* (Paris, 1939), 126.

solutely must acknowledge that it is personalized. In order to preclude that, thus personalized, it would constitute a distinct ontological subject, we must admit that it is personalized by the Word. That is, we must admit that the Word is the human person of whom it is the nature. Indeed, in the end, this is the way that St. Thomas envisions these matters: "The human nature does not constitute the Divine Person properly speaking. Rather, it constitutes it inasmuch as the Divine Person is denominated by this nature."[137] How is the Divine Person denominated by the human nature if not [by the expression] "human person"?

This fundamental datum remains (a datum which, for Galtier, is the foundation and justification for the radical distinction that he draws between the Divine Person and the assumed nature): whereas the subsistent nature and person are identical in the case of an ordinary man, in the case of Christ, we obviously must rule out such an identification between the Person of the Word (whom we say is the "human person" corresponding to Jesus' human nature) and this nature, even if this nature is considered as subsistent. This grave difficulty can and must be resolved as follows. Jesus' subsisting human nature does not constitute a subject and a person distinct from the Word. It exists only as His own. He makes it subsist by making it His own. Also, all the while being distinct from this nature (as the Creator is distinct from His creature), He subsists in it: He who is the human person of whom this nature is "constitutive"—with an immense difference (and here we are faced with the mystery), however, namely, the fact that this nature does not constitute Him as a Person (*He preexists it*) but only makes it be the case that He who is a Person from all eternity by the Divine Nature that He holds from the Father becomes a human person in time. These considerations are important for making it clearer that Christ was fully a man, a man among men.

It is also important for resolving difficult theological problems concerning Jesus' human condition, which are first raised by an at-

---

137. *ST* III, q. 3, a. 1, ad 3.

tentive reading of scriptural texts and then by reflection in faith. In particular, it helps in the resolution of the key problem concerning Jesus' submission to the Father, for the three Persons are equal in majesty, power, and authority. Therefore, we must say that Christ was submitted to Himself! In what sense can we say this? It is not a question of saying, "Human nature was submitted"; rather, it is a question of saying, "Christ, according to His human nature, was submitted." And "Christ" is the *Incarnate Word*.[138] Therefore, we must admit that the Incarnation introduces a new aspect and a new qualification into the Word Himself (even if this is only according to our manner of conceiving things):[139] [He] who is indeed a "human person."

The kenosis of the Word

{315} This brings us to the difficult theological question of the kenosis of the Word. It is well known that this theme finds its origins in the Christological hymn of Philippians 2:5–12 (RSV), especially in the words, "but emptied Himself (*heauton ekenosen*), taking the form of a servant, being born in the likeness of men."[140]

Some hold that this "emptying" is a reference to the Incarnation itself. Others (like Lamarche) believe that it is first of all a question of the crucifixion. However, these latter do not in any way contest that the Incarnation is at least in the background. Today, some use this text as an occasion for justifying the theme of the "death of God": God was made man, He is no longer God, there is only a man! This does not deserve our attention.

---

138. See *ST* III, q. 20, a. 2.

139. See §316 below.

140. For the exegetical study of this text, see Paul Henry, "Kénose," in *Dictionnaire de la Bible*, vol. 5, ed. Louis Pirot and Robert André (Paris: Letouzey et Ané, 1950), 7–161; Paul Lamarche, "Le prologue de S. Jean," *Recherches des sciences religieuses* 52 (1964): 497–537; Lamarche, "L'hymne de l'épitre aux Éphésiens et la kénose du Christ," in *L'homme devant Dieu, Mélanges offerts au P. H. de Lubac* (Paris: Aubier, 1963), 147–58; Feuillet, "L'hymne christologique" (taken up in *Christologie paulinienne et tradition biblique* [Paris: Desclée de Brouwer, 1973]). [Tr. note: The second entry by Lamarche is not cited in the original, though it seems that Fr. Nicolas may have meant to include this from his bibliography. Also, for this entry, Fr. Nicolas does not cite the volume number for the chapter by Lamarche.]

It seems that the idea of the Word becoming a human person by the Incarnation (and then, inasmuch as He is a human person, shorn of the honor owed to a human person, humiliated, and finally deprived even of His human life) is apt for rendering an account of this strange and difficult notion. Indeed, if we were to remain content with saying that a human nature is what was emptied in this way, we find ourselves deprived of every means for interpreting the kenosis as an emptying of the Word Himself (and above all as being related in some way to the Incarnation). It is clear that to be a man is not an emptying for human nature (making abstraction from the Word). However, when we consider that the Word of God would be made man, that He would be this man, and first this little child in the womb of Mary, a fact which scandalized Nestorius, we cannot fail to think that this was a tremendous abasement for him.

However, this holds from the perspective of our manner of conceiving (and of attaining to some degree) the Divine Reality. In Himself, the Word could not be really affected by this abasement. And this introduces us to the ever-difficult problem of the immutability of the Word in the Incarnation.

2. *The immutability of the Word and Christ's coming into being*

{316} The mystery of the Incarnation places us once again before the problem of the relations between God and creatures (though it does so in a particularly "uncomfortable" manner). The creature begins to exist, it changes, it ceases to exist; in the case of man (which is of utmost interest for us here), this creature is "historical." God does not change in any way. He is the Eternal One. However, given that He certainly is in relation with the creature, whom He rouses and leads to Himself, how is this divine immutability compatible with the modifications of God's relation to creatures according to the phases of their existence?

In the case of the Incarnation, the problem is pressing, for through the Incarnation, God has entered into history and has made Himself "historical." In maintaining His immutability, do we not, in a way, shatter the reality of the Incarnation? However, were we to sacrifice His immutability, would we not suppress the Incarnation in another way, for if the Word is not immutable, He is not God![141]

a) The classical position
"Every change is situated on the creaturely level."[142]

---

141. A question arises concerning the "mutability" that the mystery of the Incarnation would seem to require us to introduce into God Himself. (In fact, it is a question intimately linked to that concerning the "suffering of God" that is posed by the mystery of the redemption—"unus de Trinitate passus est"—a question that supposedly is not sufficiently resolved by the classical formula of the Councils and of the Fathers, "The Son of God suffered in the flesh.") Indeed, this problem gives rise to profound discussions in theology. The principal studies which one should consult concerning it are as follows.

Arguing that God (the Christian God) truly is mutable: Hans Urs von Balthasar, *Le mystère pascal*, in *Mysterium Salutis*, 12:13–275; Hans Küng, *Incarnation de Dieu. Introduction à la pensée théologique de Hegel comme prolégomènes à une christologie future*, trans. E. Galichet and C. Haas-Smets (Paris: Desclée de Brouwer, 1973) ; Heribert Muhlen, *Die Veränderlichkeit Gottes al Horizont einer zukünftigen Christologie. Auf dem Wege zu einer Kreuzestheologie in Auseinandersetzung mit der altkirchlichen Theologie* (Münster, 1969); Italian translation, *La mutabilità di Dio come orizzonte di una cristologia futura. Verso una teologia delle croce in discussion con la cristologia delle Chiesa antica*, trans. Rosino Gibellini (Brescia: Queriniana, 1974) ; Jürgen Moltmann, *Le Dieu crucifié. La croix du Christ, fondement et critique de la théologie chrétienne*, trans. Bernard Fraigneau-Julien (Paris: Cerf-Mame, 1974) ; Jean Galot, *Il mistero della sofferenza di Dio* (Assisi: Cittadella Editrice, 1975) ; *Dieu, souffre-t-il?* (Paris: Lethielleux, 1976) ; Piet Schoonenberg, *Il est le Dieu des hommes*, trans. M. Claes (Paris: Cerf, 1973).

Arguing on behalf of the inviolable immutability of God (the Word was made flesh while remaining perfectly immutable in Himself, the Father and the Spirit remaining immutable like Him): Carlo Cantone, "Dio in divenire, una nuova gnosi," *Salesianum* 37 (1975): 69–91; Michel Gervais, "Incarnation et immutabilité divine," *Revue des Sciences Religieuses* 50, no. 3 (1976): 215–43; Luigi Iammarone, "Il 'divenire di Dio' et Giovanni Duns Scoto," *Miscellanea Francescana* 77 (1977): 45–94; Jean-Louis Leuba, "Temps et Trinité. Esquisse d'herméneutique doctrinale," in *Temporalité et Aliénation. Actes du Colloque organisé par le Centre international d'Etudes humanists et par l'institute d'Etudes philosophiques de Rome (Rome, 3–8 jan. 1975)* (Paris: Aubier Montaigne, 1975), 365–75; Andrea Milano, "Il 'divinire di Dio' in Hegel, Kierkegaard e san Tommaso d'Aquino," in *Studi Tomistici* 3 (Rome: Città Nuova Editrice, 1974), 284–94; Jean-Hervé Nicolas, "L'Act pure de saint Thomas et le Dieu vivant de l'Evangile," *Angelicum* 51 (1974): 511–32; "Aimante et bienheureusement Trinité," *Révue thomiste* 78 (1978): 271–91, taken up again in *Contemplation et vie contemplative en christianisme* (Fribourg / Paris: Éditions Universitaires / Beachesne, 1980), 138–87. Likewise consult: Evert H. Cousins, "La temporalité de Dieu dans la théologie du devenir," in *Temporalité et Aliénation* (Paris: Aubier Montagne, 1975), 139–59.

142. *ST* III, q. 16, a. 6, ad 2.

b) Objections

In at least two places in Karl Rahner's works,[143] we can find a quite brilliant and profound questioning of this classical solution. In its essentials, his criticism consists in the following argument. To explain the Incarnate Word's entrance into history and His becoming historical (i.e., His *acta et passa*) by saying that it is only in His humanity that He is "historical" (i.e., that He began, that He matured, that He went through a series of events, etc.) is to walk right past the mystery that tells us that "the Word Himself became flesh," that He suffered, died, and resurrected, in short, that He underwent a historical process of becoming: "What does this (the communication of idioms) mean if the actual human reality predicated of the Logos as Person does not change the Logos, and so does not make Him something which He would not be without this humanity?"[144]

In the second text cited, we find an attempt at a personal solution, which unfortunately is not sufficiently developed. It consists in this: "God can become something, He who is unchangeable in Himself can *Himself* become subject to change *in something else*." And this is explained by means of a development of a remarkably scholastic workmanship (though of the loftiest and most profound scholasticism), in which it is said that, in His infinite transcendence, the Absolute has the power of becoming finite: "The Absolute, or more correctly, He who is the absolute, has, in the pure freedom of His infinite and abiding unrelatedness, the possibility of Himself becoming that other thing, the finite; God, in and by the fact that He empties *Himself* gives away *Himself, poses* the other as His own reality."[145]

---

143. See Rahner, "Problèmes actuels de christologie,» 150–55; Rahner, "Essai d'une esquisse de Dogmatique," 90–101; Jean Galot, *Vers une nouvelle christologie* (Gembloux: Duculot, 1971), pt. 2.

144. [Tr. note: Taken from Rahner, "Current Problems of Christology," 179.]

145. Rahner, "Réflexions théologiques sur l'Incarnation," 93. [Tr. note: Fr. Nicolas incorrectly cites "Essai d'une esquisse de Dogmatique." Text here taken from Rahner, "On the Theology of the Incarnation," in *Theological Investigations*, vol. 4, trans. Kevin Smyth (New York: Crossroad, 1982), 113–14.]

c) Returning to the classical solution

Rahner's critique fully holds against a conception of the Hypostatic Union like what we find in Galtier, where the union of human nature to the Word leaves the latter in His distance, so that He is not the one who really suffers and dies, even though suffering and death must be attributed to Him. However, can Rahner's own solution be accepted? In order to affirm, within the transcendent Divine Reality, the conjunction of two attributes that are (and remain) distinct on our conceptual level (e.g., thought and love, which are one in God; the relative and the absolute, which are one in the *Res divina*),[146] one of the two must not be the contradiction of the other. Otherwise, we will fall into contradiction in our affirmation, and strictly speaking, contradiction is unthinkable and unreal. Now, while "Absolute" and "Relative" are not contradictories,[147] "immutable" and "mutable" quite surely are. To hold that God, on account of His omnipotence, has the ability to "become finite," to "go out of Himself," to "become historical Himself," ultimately means that we hold that God has the power to cease to be God!

However, the classical solution must be deepened in light of the protest that is raised against it. To this end, note well that the "terminus" is part of the relation and, in a real relation, everything is real. Therefore, the "terminus" is real. In the creature's relation to God in general [i.e., in creation], and especially in the relation of Christ's humanity to the Word, the terminus (i.e., God [in the case of creation] and the Word [in the case of the Hypostatic Union]) is real [precisely] as the *terminus of the relation*—He is really the terminus of the relation.

Thus, we will not say (like Galtier) that only the assumed nature is submitted to becoming. Inasmuch as the Word is the terminus of the relation of union, He is really engaged in this becoming. He is the one who was born of the Virgin, who lived, suffered, died, and

146. See §103 in the previous volume.
147. See §101 in the previous volume.

was resurrected. This is what the formula, "The Word has become a human person," intends to express.

However, He remains immutable in Himself. It is true that, despite all the explanations provided, this remains profoundly mysterious for us. It is the very mystery of the Incarnation. I cannot think about it without the assistance of the [conceptual] categories pertaining to the domain of relation, and I can justify (as was attempted above) the value of these categories for real knowledge of the Word inasmuch as He is incarnate. At the same time, I must continue to affirm that the categories of the Absolute, which exclude all real becoming, apply to Him.

Therefore, the Word *in Himself* does not experience becoming. However, *insofar as He is a human person* (and He is such on account of the assumed nature's real relation to Him), He is engaged in human becoming—even if His own relation to this nature is a rationate relation (*relatio rationis*).

B. The Assumptive Action

1. The action which produces Jesus' humanity

{317} Obviously, Jesus' humanity is a created reality. It is produced by God, the First Cause. He does so by the motion exercised, as the First Cause, on Mary's generative faculty, a motion that has a miraculous character because, thus moved, a woman all by herself produces a fertilized egg, the point of departure for a new organism. Additionally, there was the creation of the spiritual soul (as happens for every new human being). On account of this divine action, Jesus' humanity, like every created reality, is referred to God by the relation of total dependence in being that is creation.

2. The assumptive action, properly speaking

{318} If this human nature thus produced is not "enclosed on itself" in order that it may constitute a distinct human person, this is because another divine action is simultaneously exercised on it, "appropriating" it to the Word by making it be the nature of the Word. This action is the assumptive action.

As we have seen, the Word is the terminus of this action. This means that by this action, the Word was made (and has become) a human person—by a change to this human nature, not by a change to which He would be subject. The entire Trinity is the principle of this action because it is an action of efficient causality. In reality, this nature subsists in the Word. It exists only as the nature of the Word. As St. Thomas expresses this: "The three Persons together made it be the case that the human nature is united solely to the Person of the Son of God."[148] The "change" in the human nature did not consist in it being intrinsically modified. Rather (as we have tried to show), it consisted in it being ordered to the Word as His own. This action remains very mysterious, and we cannot produce a precise idea of it for ourselves because we lack any corresponding concepts that could be drawn from our experience.

C. The Unity of Christ's Being

1. Christ is one "being" (Unum Ens)

{319} The "being" [in question] is the "ontological subject," the "suposit," *quod est*. To say that Christ is ontologically "one," a unique being, follows immediately from the fundamental affirmation that He is a single person, a single ontological subject, at once God and Man.

What is mysterious is that this unique "being" has two essences or natures. That is, He is a unique Someone (*unus Quis*) to whom two natures (*duo Quid*) must be attributed. I must say that He is both this (God) and that (Man). Classically, this is expressed as follows: He is not *alius et alius*, but *aliud et aliud*. Given that the two natures are real, certain people thought that we could say that *Christ is two*. However, this attribution is obviously false (and even contradictory), for it first posits the subject as being one (Christ) but then has a predicate which removes this unity. Yes, each of the two natures is real, but the same *res* is constituted by each of them. The same one who is God by the Divine Nature is man by the human nature.[149]

---

148. *ST* III, q. 3, a. 4.
149. See *ST* III, q. 17, a. 1.

2. Christ has only one existence (Unicum Esse)

a) The principle

{320} A given being [*l'étant*] is called a being on account of existence [*être*]. Existence is the act having as its receptive subject the "being" that is actualized by existence. It is clear that if we have one "unique being," we can have one "unique existence."[150]

b) The Cajetanian interpretation

{321} Cajetan gave a famous interpretation for this principle (or rather for the application made of it by St. Thomas to the case of Christ). His interpretation became the classic position of the Thomist school.[151] In every [finite] being essence and existence [*l'essence et l'existence, ou "être"*] are distinct. We said that there are two "essences" in Christ. According to this interpretation, there would be only one existence, given that there is only one person. This means that Jesus' human essence (or, human nature) is "actualized," made to exist, by the eternal existence of the Word communicated to it.

We have already encountered this idea with regard to the Hypostatic Union.[152] The difference between Cajetan's position and that of Billot consists in the fact that Cajetan does not identify "subsistence" and "existence." Likewise, he did not make the Hypostatic Union consist in the communication of the Word's *esse* to the human nature. However, for him this communication is a consequence of the union.

c) A brief critique of this interpretation

{322} This interpretation was attacked by Herman Diepen,[153] who was followed by many Thomists (including Jacques Marit-

---

150. See ibid., a. 2.
151. See Cajetan, *In ST III*, q. 17, a. 2.
152. See §286.
153. See Diepen, "La critique du baslisme selon Saint Thomas"; "L'unique Seigneur Jésus-Christ," *Revue thomiste* 53 (1953): 28–80.

ain).¹⁵⁴ Following these critiques, it was reexamined to its foundation and defended by Albert Patfoort.¹⁵⁵ It was reexamined with regard to this work, and newly criticized, by J.-H. Nicolas.¹⁵⁶ The criticism is wholly concerned with the impossibility of conceiving this actuation of a created nature by Uncreated Act (a criticism registered above as well).¹⁵⁷

It is also subject to criticism precisely as an interpretation of St. Thomas. In all of the five well-known texts dedicated to the unity of existence in Christ, St. Thomas never speaks about the *existence* by which Jesus' human nature exists. He speaks about the existence of Christ, who is the Word Incarnate, not about the existence of the assumed nature. What he says is that the Word existed from all eternity and did not begin to exist as a person by beginning to be a man: "The Son does not have existence purely and simply from the human nature, for He exists from all eternity. Rather, from the human nature He only has the fact that He is man."¹⁵⁸

d) The assumed nature's substantial existence and the Word's personal existence

{323} Normally, a nature, a secondary substance, becomes subsistent, a primary substance or supposit (or person), at the moment when it is realized. The existence that it thus receives, which is the ultimate terminus of the productive action, is both the existence of the supposit as *what is* (*ut quod*) and the existence of the nature as *that by which it is* (*ut quo*).

The distinction between existence inasmuch as it is of the nature and inasmuch as it is of the supposit (*esse prout est naturae* and *esse*

---

154. See Jacques Maritain, "Sur la notion de subsistance," *Revue thomiste* 54 (1954): 242–56.
155. See Albert Patfoort, *L'unité d'être dans le Christ d'après Saint Thomas. A la croisée de l'ontologie et de la christologie* (Paris: Desclée de Brouwer, 1964).
156. See Jean-Hervé Nicolas, "L'unité d'être dans le Christ selon S. Thomas d'Aquin," *Revue thomiste* 65 (1965): 229–60. One can add, against the Cajetanian interpretation: Leroy, "L'union selon l'hypostase"; and in defense of it: Corvez, "Le problème de dieu."
157. See §286 above.
158. *ST* III, q. 3, a. 1, ad 3.

prout est hypostasis)¹⁵⁹ is a rationate distinction (*distinctio rationis*) of minimal importance. Also, it does not appear in metaphysical texts concerned with the real distinction between essence and existence.

However, note well that in Christ human nature is realized without constituting a supposit. Rather, it is adjoined as a second nature, a second substance, to the preexisting supposit, the Word. Here, in this fact, we find ourselves faced with the mystery of the Incarnation. To say that it is realized is to say that it receives existence, the act without which it would remain in the state of pure potentiality, which comes down to saying that it would not be realized. To say that it is assumed by the Word is to say that it is assumed existing, with its existence.

However, to say that the Word is preexistent is to say that this existence cannot be attributed to Him and that the Word does not acquire existence by acquiring the human nature. This man existed before being man: "Before Abraham was, I am."

Moreover, the rule of the communication of idioms¹⁶⁰ does not enable us to attribute this existence to Him. Indeed, an attribute that belongs to the Word essentially on account of His Divine Nature cannot be said of Him by participation, even if the human nature *of itself* would justify this attribution for the person to whom it belongs. This is because "essentially" and "by participation" are opposed qualifications for one and the same form. Thus, in speaking about Christ we cannot say that He is *a man of the Lord* [*homme du Seigneur*], for on account of his Divine Nature *this man* is *the Lord*. Likewise, we cannot call him *an adoptive son* (even though His soul is filled with the grace of filial adoption) because He is *Son according to nature* on account of His Divine Nature.

The same is true here. We cannot say that the Incarnate Word, *this Man*, exists *even as a man* (i.e., from the being that belongs to His human nature). In this, we discover again St. Thomas's insistence upon Christ's *sole existence*. Scotus, on the contrary, will say that the

---

159. See *In I Sent.*, d. 37, q. 3, a. 1; *ST* III, q. 2, a. 6, ad 3.
160. See §328 below.

Word exists a second time as man.[161] But then, what is the *principium quod* of this existence which has the nature only as its *principium quo*? Who exists by this existence?

According to someone like Matthew of Aquasparta, before Scotus, and then according to Scotus and his school, the assumed nature exercises this existence in an exceptional manner. It would exist by it as a distinct *quod* because it cannot affect the Word Himself.[162] Many modern theologians incline toward a similar formula, which has the great danger of leading to a duality of supposits. It is clear that a Thomist cannot accept such a solution.

Therefore, we must say that the only, unique *quod* of this *quo* (the assumed nature being the Word) is He who is the *what is* corresponding to this *existence*—though inasmuch as through the Incarnation He has become the supposit of this existing nature. That is, this is so first of all without Him being really affected by this existence. Furthermore, it is so without this existence being able to be attributed to Him in any way (unlike cases of accidental *esse*, which also do not really affect Him yet nonetheless can be attributed to Him because they can concern the Word only inasmuch as He subsists in human nature, in contrast to the substantial existence which can be attributed to Him only inasmuch as He subsists purely and simply and therefore inasmuch as He subsists in the Divine Nature). Thus, through created grace, Christ's soul receives a participation in the Divine Life, and the Word Incarnate is the one who lives by this participated Divine Life. However, one can in no way say that He is an adoptive son, for He is already a son by nature. Just as on account of His soul filled with grace He cannot be said to have a second filiation and be a son a second time, so too on account of His existing human nature, He cannot be said to have a second existence (even a secondary one) and to exist a second time.

---

161. See Edgar Hocedez, *Quaestio de unico esse in Christo a doctoribus saeculi XIII disputata, Textus et documenta, Series theologica* 14 (Rome: Pontificia Universitas Gregoriana, 1933), 120.

162. See ibid., 56–57.

The notion of integration can validly render an account of this mysterious relationship between the substantial existence that makes the assumed human nature exist in time (and therefore in reality) and the personal, infinite, and eternal existence of the Word. The latter does not become existent. Rather, He integrates the temporal existence of His humanity into His eternal existence, just as He integrates humanity itself into this Whole that He constitutes from all eternity by appropriating it to Himself. Thus [by way of a kind of analogy], at the resurrection, the body will begin again to exist without having a new existence. The person existing solely through His soul will integrate to His personal existence the existence that the body will receive so that it may exist, not apart, but as the body of this person who existed before it resurrected. Of course, this is a very defective analogy, for the personal being of the resurrected person will be expanded by this extension to the body. However, the comparison bears precisely on the fact that the person will not receive a new existence from the resurrection, even while it comes to exist anew corporeally.

Therefore, it seems that in order to fully assure personal unity in the two natures without violating the fundamental metaphysical principle of the foundational ordination of *ens* to *esse* (*ens dicitur ab esse*) that requires us to recognize the rigorous correspondence between unity of *ens* and unity of *esse* (which Scotus did not recognize), we do not at all need to have recourse to the metaphysically impossible scenario holding that the assumed nature would have a real existence without having its own proper *existence*, by virtue of the Word's *existence* alone. It is of capital importance that we free an essential thesis of Christology (one which is worth the struggle) from another, unsustainable thesis which can only compromise it (see figures 2–4, facing).

The first conception of Christ's existence is the Cajetanian position. The second is that which we have chosen and which we think is St. Thomas's. The third is, in its first part, Scotus's conception and that of the theologians who follow him, at least on this point. In its

The Hypostatic Union

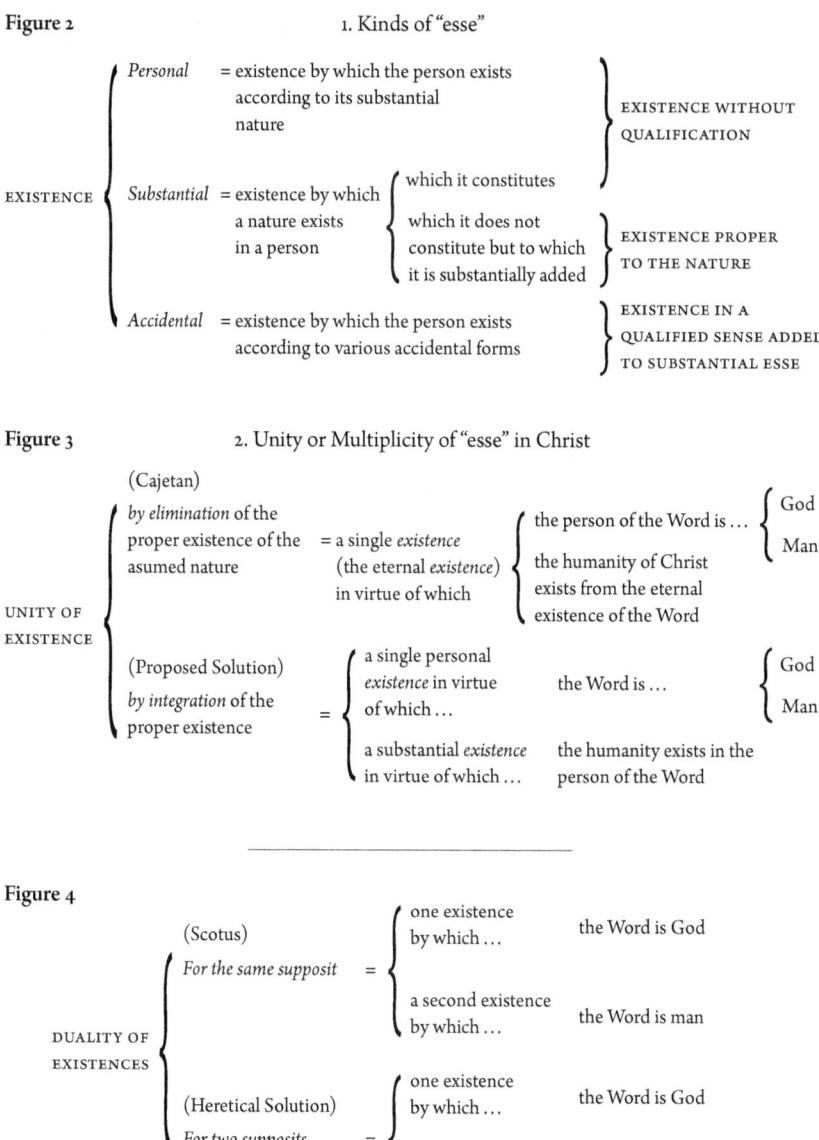

Figure 2. 1. Kinds of "esse"

EXISTENCE
- *Personal* = existence by which the person exists according to its substantial nature } EXISTENCE WITHOUT QUALIFICATION
- *Substantial* = existence by which a nature exists in a person { which it constitutes; which it does not constitute but to which it is substantially added } EXISTENCE PROPER TO THE NATURE
- *Accidental* = existence by which the person exists according to various accidental forms } EXISTENCE IN A QUALIFIED SENSE ADDED TO SUBSTANTIAL ESSE

Figure 3. 2. Unity or Multiplicity of "esse" in Christ

UNITY OF EXISTENCE
- (Cajetan) *by elimination* of the proper existence of the asumed nature = a single *existence* (the eternal *existence*) in virtue of which { the person of the Word is … {God, Man}; the humanity of Christ exists from the eternal existence of the Word
- (Proposed Solution) *by integration* of the proper existence = { a single personal *existence* in virtue of which … the Word is … {God, Man}; a substantial *existence* in virtue of which … the humanity exists in the person of the Word

Figure 4.

DUALITY OF EXISTENCES
- (Scotus) *For the same supposit* = { one existence by which … the Word is God; a second existence by which … the Word is man
- (Heretical Solution) *For two supposits* = { one existence by which … the Word is God; a second existence by which … the assumed nature exists as though it were a distinct supposit

second part, we have the assertion that there are two supposits in Christ, which is incompatible with the Church's faith.[163]

D. Christ's Preexistence

1. Jesus Christ existed before being a man

{324} From all that we have said, it is clear that the mystery of the Incarnation involves the "preexistence" of Christ as one of its essential elements: this person, Jesus Christ, who is a man (a "human person"), is the eternal Person of the Word. Therefore, He preexists the being-man of Jesus Christ. "He existed before being man." Correctly understood, this "before" (the "pre" included in "preexistence") must not be understood as indicating temporal anteriority as, precisely speaking, it designates anteriority with regard to time itself, in relation to the whole of temporal succession. Eternity is not "before" time, for it coexists with the totality of time, transcending and enveloping it. However, for this reason, it coexists with the part of time anterior to that in which Christ lived His human life, which enables us to say—indeed, requires us to say—that the Person of Christ, this person who exists as a man from the moment of the Incarnation, existed as a Person before this moment: "Before Abraham was, I am."[164] This "preexistence" is interpreted today by some authors either in a maximalizing or a minimizing sense.

2. Christ's preexistence understood in a maximalizing sense

a) Presentation of the theory

{325} Fr. Benoît[165] developed a new and original theory of Christ's preexistence. His theory intends to do justice to the scriptural texts that are related to it. He believes that these texts are interpreted inexactly and deficiently when they are read as only expressing the fact that the Word preexists in the Trinity:

---

163. See §269 above.
164. Jn 8:58. See André Feuillet, *Le prologue du IVe évangile* (Paris: Desclée de Brouwer, 1968), 32 and 115; *Le sacerdoce du Christ et de ses ministers* (Paris: Editions de Paris, 1972).
165. See Pierre Benoît, "Préexistence et incarnation," *Revue biblique* (Paris) 77 (1970): 5–29.

The Hypostatic Union 123

Let us gather the *fruits of this brief investigation*. All the texts that we have recalled envision the Incarnation as the passage from one state of life to another, a change of condition for the same subject, Jesus Christ. Whether they directly express this passage by using the terms "mission," "descent," "coming," and "manifestation," or whether they suggest a state prior to this passage, they always give the impression that Jesus, the concrete and historical person who had been known while living on the earth, did not wait for this moment to really exist, although He would have existed in a different situation from that of His earthly one. Before taking on our human nature, with its concrete conditions as a poor, humble life, subject to the Law, freighted with sin, etc., He was already engaged in salvation history and associated with mankind's destiny. He was present from the time of the Old Testament, acting in the formation of the chosen people and preparing His own coming among men. And it was not the Second Person of the Trinity, in His eternal and transcendent existence, who thus appeared as being involved in our history. It was indeed Jesus Christ, already at work in the divine plan of salvation before assuming our human existence in the womb of the Virgin Mary.

This New Testament way of thinking and speaking poses a problem and invites us to revise our own thought and speech. Take care to understand this correctly. It is not a question of placing in doubt the two natures of Jesus Christ (i.e., His divine and human natures). Nor is it a question of placing in doubt their union in one person who is the Word. Even if it is not expressed in the New Testament in this manner, this dogmatic formulation is perfectly valid and overlays with its philosophical concepts a sure datum of Revelation. Thus, it is something held *De fide*. Rather, the precise question is this: is the union of the divinity and humanity, which is brought about at the moment of the annunciation, an absolute beginning before which the Word only subsisted at the heart of the Trinity? Or, was it not preceded by a mysterious but real situation wherein the future God-Man already preexisted, although in a different manner than our own manner of existing? And if this is how matters stand, how can we conceive this superior mode of existence, which is neither that of the Pure Divine Transcendent Being, nor that of the man Jesus after His earthly birth?[166]

But how is this mysterious preexistence of the "future God-man" to be conceived, thus situated between Jesus' earthly existence and the Word's eternal existence? Deliberately ruling out any docetist

---

166. Ibid., 19–20.

or Origenist interpretation, the author proposes a philosophical explanation that essentially consists in distinguishing a "time of God" placed between human time and eternity. He presents this "time of God" as "an adjacent [*mitoyen*] domain, where divine eternity and human duration intersect in realities that have their own times [*ont leur temps à elles*]."[167] It is the time proper to salvation, the time of salvation history (distinct from our history), and this is the time of Jesus Christ's preexistence:

> This Jesus, already God and man prior to the annunciation, whom we have glimpsed in Paul, and in John, is a creature, the first-born of every creature, and for that reason does not belong to the pure eternity of God. He must already come from some sort of duration, some sort of time. And nonetheless, He is not, of Himself, enclosed in our ephemeral, perishable human time. He exceeds it and transcends it. He precedes it and follows it. He is already prior to the ages, our human ages, and He contributes to the creation of them; and He remains prior to the ages, ruling as *Kyrios* and penetrating with His glory the renewed cosmos of the eschatological era. His work of incarnation and redemption precisely consists in descending into human time so as to elevate the latter to God's time. By the very real fact of His conception in the womb of Mary, He enters into our human time, into our ephemeral world. He takes on its conditions and its servitudes. He assumes a *body of flesh*.[168] Then, having accomplished His work by the cross and the resurrection, He returns to the plane and duration of the celestial realities from which He had descended, renewed in Himself by this human race of whom He has taken charge, whom the Father created in Him and whom He has introduced, in His glorified person, into the restored and definitive kingdom of God.[169]

This theory is inspired (doubtlessly in an unconscious manner) by the quite widespread conviction holding that only the *physical* is what is *real*. Indeed, Christ's preexistence in all of salvation history, as well as His preexistence before the Incarnation, is a certain, traditional theme. This presence is already realized for creation, the latter being the first act and point of departure for salvation history.

---

167. Ibid., 26.
168. Col 1:22.
169. Benoît, "Préexistence et incarnation," 27.

If no other way is seen for assuring this presence and action which is the physical presence and action of the Man-Jesus, one is led to seek (against all likelihood) some kind of presence of this man, Jesus Christ prior to the Incarnation.

However, there is another way that influence can be exercised over history, indeed one that is decisive, namely influence through final causality. The whole of salvation history is oriented to Christ (by the efficient-causal action of the whole Trinity together, and therefore, by the action of the Word with the Father and the Spirit—the action of the Word who from the Incarnation onward, will be the man Jesus Christ). Thus, creation itself and evolution, as well as the permission of sin, in whatever way one explains the latter, are all oriented to Christ. Hence, we can say that Jesus Christ is the principle of salvation history. First, He is this principle as the Word, because He conceived, willed, and realized this history from its start, along with the Father and the Spirit. Then, He is the principle as the Incarnate Word insofar as salvation history was thought, willed, and realized from the beginning (including, therefore, the Incarnation) in function of Him, the God-Man. This can and must be said, without, for all that, claiming that He existed as a man before the Word was incarnate (i.e., at a time prior to the historical moment of the Incarnation). An expression in the text cited above reveals that this latter assertion would be contradictory. Indeed, in speaking of this preexisting Jesus Christ, Fr. Benoît says that "He assumes a fleshly body" at the moment of the Incarnation. Does he mean that He preexisted without a fleshly body? This would not be Jesus Christ! And when did He assume the soul, if He does not do this at the same moment as when He assumed this fleshly body?

b) Critical examination of the "philosophico-theological" explanation

Real time is not an external framework in which the existence of a bodily being would unfold and could just as well, remaining the same, pass from one temporal framework to another. The very existence of a bodily being is temporal. Properly speaking, there is not an encounter between time and eternity whose conjunction would produce an intermediary time. There is the coexistence of God (whose "duration" is without succession) and the material universe (whose duration is successive, having time as its measure, one that is successive like it and with it). It is not that we only lack the words and concepts needed for thinking about this "intermediary time." Rather, the very notion is unthinkable and contradictory. It comes down to considering the idea of a thing to be realized (here, the idea of Christ in God) as though it were real.

On the other hand, how can one admit without inconsistency that Jesus Christ was really born at a moment of time and that He lived his human history, if He already existed as a man? Despite the author's express intention and his very clear declarations, if we allow ourselves to follow the natural bent of this explanation, we would find ourselves to be irresistibly led to a form of docetism, asserting that the events of Jesus' earthly life, His earthly existence itself, would not be real.

c) Critical examination of the scriptural foundations

As one critic remarks,[170] this concern to retain an extreme and intransigent literalism leads to an impasse, for one is thus required to say that the biblical texts attributing preexistence to Jesus do not apply to the historical Jesus (at all) but, rather, to the preexisting Jesus of salvation history. Now, the historical Jesus is the one who speaks in these texts (or to whom these texts are attributed), so that if they do not apply to Him, they lose all of their reality.

On the other hand, the rejection of the classical interpretation of these texts (which holds that they are concerned with the Person of Jesus, who is a man but who is also God, who is the Second Person of the Trinity and for this reason exists from all eternity) rests on a misunderstanding. We are told that, according to their immediate and general context, they can only be related to Jesus entirely, the

---

170. See Bernard Rey, "Théologie trinitaire et révélation biblique," *Revue des sciences philosophiques et théologiques* 54 (1970): 648–49.

God-Man. But why must this be the case? Because the full meaning of the term "person" has not been grasped, as well as the fact that it expresses the Whole, constituted from its ontological parts, encompassing them in its unity. The human nature's union with the Divine Person does not leave the former exterior to the latter. On the contrary, as we have seen, by this union the Divine Person draws the assumed nature to His unity, making it His own, which means that He made it part of Himself.[171] Thus, everything that Jesus Christ says about Himself, He says it (like every man) about His Person. However, His Person is the Word, a Divine and eternal Person, who existed before being a "human person." Concerning this person, Jesus could speak, in full truth, about things that belonged to Him in His eternal existence, not in His human existence.

To say that Jesus Christ is "preexistent" is to say that His Person, whom He expresses by saying "I" and whom we express by saying "Him" or "He," existed before being a man. And this renders account of the fundamental biblical theme that *He was sent into the world*, that He has *come into the world*, etc., doing so in the most literal way while nonetheless preserving the mystery involved here.

3. *Christ's preexistence understood in a minimalist sense*

{326} Claiming to fully and entirely restore the human dimensions of Christ, a contemporary trend in Christology tends to minimize His preexistence, sometimes to the point of practically abolishing it, reducing it to the fact that "Jesus is God's presence in history. He is God, God the Son. Consequently, this identity and difference belong to God's very being, which implies that Jesus always was one with God." If, as Pierre Benoît holds, the texts concerning [Jesus'] preexistence are concerned with the Incarnate Word precisely as incarnate, according to these theologians He does not speak of any other existence than His earthly one, for "God's very divinity can

---

171. See §311 above. [Tr. note: The original reads "§73." This would correlate to §312, which seems to be wrong.]

no longer be thought of without Jesus, the Son."¹⁷² The same author adds, "The language of preexistence and the Incarnation should be interpreted within this same context. It intends to signify Jesus' unity with God and to say that this unity is everlasting [est de toujours]. It is a question of a symbolic representation enabling us to affirm the inseparability of Jesus and God." The following text of Schoonenberg provides a good contextualization concerning the scope of such language:

> Jesus Christ is one, unique person, and He is a human person. What then remains, in addition, for a Divine Person? Nothing *to the degree* that this Divine Person would stand in the way of the human person. Nothing *to the degree* that it would introduce a doubling of subjects or an I-Thou relation within the unique Christ. Does this mean that a preexisting Divine Person of the Word—and, at the same time, a preexisting Trinity in God—would be for this very reason purely and simply denied? No, it is denied only to the degree that it is an obstacle to the being of Jesus Christ inasmuch as He is a human person. The preexistence of the Word as a Person and that of the Trinity cannot be denied for the same reason that it cannot be affirmed. In saying this, I understand "preexistence" as meaning: existence in God Himself "before" His creation and His economy of salvation, understanding that the term "before" cannot be interpreted temporally. "Before" is a temporal image signifying "transcendent to" (which is a spatial image) or "independent of." Now, we know nothing about God such as He is independent of His creation or of the work of salvation (that is, inasmuch as He transcends them). He has not communicated Himself to us in this manner. Positively, this means that we cannot speak in a reasonable [sensée] manner and do not have the right to affirm or deny anything about the Word who is alongside God (or, rather, concerning the Trinity of God), unless we do so in relation to creation and the Incarnation (and to the gift of the Holy Spirit).¹⁷³

These affirmations, Rey adds, in no way mean that the language of preexistence must be abandoned. Such language is a symbolic

---

172. Rey, "Théologie trinitaire et révélation biblique," 651. See also his *Le cheminement des premières communautés chrétiennes à la découverte de Dieu* (Paris: Cerf, 1972). Also, read the latter alongside the critique by Vincent Leroy, "Bulletins," *Revue thomiste* 73 (1973): 494–96.

173. Cited by Rey, "Théologie trinitaire et révélation biblique," 652.

manner of expression needed for affirming Jesus's union with God. However, it will be necessary to avoid every representation of Jesus' preexistence that would lead one to conceive of the existence of a preexisting Son alongside His temporal manifestation, Jesus of Nazareth:

> The Eternal Son cannot be separated from the Man-Jesus, writes Pannenberg. We must always bear in mind that this is only a question of two aspects of the same Jesus Christ. And nonetheless, the eternity of Jesus' filiation ... can no more be thought of in the individuality of this man living at a determinate time and in a determinate place.[174]
>
> And we thus come to the limits of thought and conceptual expression. At the same time, we must hold that Jesus is the "Eternal" Son of God and that the Son is none other than this Jesus, without being able to express this datum of faith in a coherent conceptualization. Faith is here led to dialectical and even paradoxical formulations. It must accept them as necessary and due to the spatio-temporal conditions of our imaginative representations, which force us to speak about a descent (i.e., the incarnation) and an ascent (i.e., the ascension). Critical attention will ceaselessly need to accompany the procedure in order to prevent one from transforming what is only the imaginary consequence of a conclusion into a starting point for a Christological or Trinitarian reflection.[175]

How could one subscribe to these views which, though out of a concern to avoid saying anything about God that would not be scriptural, ultimately render Scripture's words incomprehensible? What we are taught in Scripture and what the Church has received and guarded jealously as the divine teaching is that Jesus is the manifestation of God because He really is God. This is meaningless if one does not admit the preexistence of Him who is a man from the time of Jesus' birth, this man whom we call Christ and who from all eternity was and is God, the Son of the Father.

Moreover, we can add that these affirmations asserting that God would have manifested Himself to men in Jesus and that He would be God's presence to the world are perfectly arbitrary assertions out-

---

174. Cited in ibid.
175. Ibid.

side of Christian faith. Can an enterprise like Pannenberg's,[176] this "Christology from below" seeking to verify Jesus' divinity on the basis of His historical reality, succeed? If Jesus' divinity is acknowledged, this can only be through faith, as a mystery that defies every possibility of verification, historical or otherwise: "It is not flesh and blood that have revealed it to you." Merely considering Jesus' historical reality, however illustrious one may hold it to be, one could not demonstrate [by reason alone] for anyone (or for oneself) that Jesus is the man in whom man can and must encounter God. It is clear that a host of men reject such an assertion, and one can say only that this would be contrary to reason, absurd.

III. CHRISTOLOGICAL TERMINOLOGY

"We fall into heresy through thoughtless words."[177]

A. Communication of Idioms (of Attributes)

{327} This is the fundamental rule of Christological language. I can designate Christ by using the concrete term corresponding to each of the two natures: God, Man.

I designate one and the same subject by using the words, "The Incarnate Word." Therefore, in order to designate Him in one way or another, I can attribute to Him the properties that belong to Him on account of either of His two natures. Therefore, I can designate Him as the subject of one nature (e.g., Man) and attribute to Him properties that belong to Him on account of the other nature (e.g., "born of the Father before all the ages"). Thus, I can say, "This Man (Jesus) is eternal, almighty, etc. God (the Word) is man, born of the Virgin

---

176. See Wolfhart Pannenberg, *Esquisse d'une christologie*, trans. Arthur Liefooghe (Paris: Cerf, 1971); cf. Albert Patfoort, "Bulletin de théologie dogmatique. Christologie," *Revue des sciences philosophiques et théologiques* 51 (1967): 312–17, and "Compte-rendu du livre de Pannenberg W., Autour d'une problématique théologique," *Angelicum* 51 (1974): 312–19; and I[gnace] Berten, "Bulletin de Christologie protestante," *Revue des sciences philosophiques et théologiques* 54 (1970): 157–65.

177. *ST* III, q. 16, a. 8 (citation of the Ordinary Gloss under the name of St. Jerome).

Mary, etc. *Unus de Trinitate passus est,* 'one of the Trinity suffered.'"

This is first of all a linguistic rule. However, it also is a logical rule, founded on being. The logical subject is one because the ontological subject is one. Language, whether divinely inspired or guaranteed by the Spirit's assistance, here plays the role of introducing one to the mystery. Therefore, it cannot be said that this is mere wordplay.

B. Concrete Applications of the Rule of the Communication of Idioms

1. Designation of a subject in whom the union of natures occurs

{328} The unique subject in whom the union of the two natures comes about can be designated:

- either by means of a term that expresses Him in His complexity: *Christ, Jesus, Incarnate Word, Son of Man*
- or by means of a term that indicates Him as the concrete subject of one of the two natures:
- *Man* (the context indicates that it is this singular man whom I designate)
- *God* (likewise, the context indicates that it is a question of the Second Person of the Trinity)
- *Son of God* (likewise, the context indicates that it is a question of [He who is the] Son by nature)

2. Attribution of properties of one of the two natures to this unique subject

In whatever way I designate this unique subject, I can attribute to Him the properties that belong to Him on account of either nature: *this man is God; God is this man; this man was before Abraham; God suffered.*

3. Exceptions

a) First exception

If an attribute that would belong to the unique subject in virtue of the human nature itself excludes an attribute that would belong to Him in virtue of the Divine Nature, the attribution is illegitimate and erroneous.

"Christ is the legate [*légat*] of the Lord." This attribution is false, not because Christ is not sent by the Lord, the Father, but rather, because He also is the Lord, the Son, and because the attribute "Lord" and the attribute "legate of the Lord" are incompatible with each other.

"Christ is the adoptive son of God." This attribution is inadmissible, not because Christ does not have filial grace in Himself—for men receive it from His fullness—but, rather, because according to His Divine Nature, He is the Son by nature, and being a son by nature and being an adoptive son are opposed to each other. By becoming incarnate, the Word did not cease to be what He was from all eternity and therefore did not lose any of His divine attributes. However, we need to be more precise here. None of the attributes belonging to Christ on account of His human nature essentially (*per se*, that is, those that necessarily belong to every man on account of the fact that he is a man) can be included in this exception [*aucun ... peut être dans ce cas*]. Without this, the Incarnation would be impossible. It can only be a question of existential attributes, that is, of attributes that belong to the subject on account of the fact that He is a given man, not on account of the fact that He is a man.

Indeed, by assuming a true humanity, the Word made all the properties of human nature His own. Therefore, they are not incompatible with the Divine Nature.

b) Second exception

If an attribute belongs to Christ only on account of one of the two natures, and it could possibly seem that it is attributed to Him also on account of the other, a specification must be stated in one's expression. For example, if one says, "Christ is created," one must add, "According to the assumed nature." Likewise, if one says, "Christ is everywhere," one must add, "According to the Divine Nature."

c) The meaning of the addition: "inasmuch as He is man,"
"inasmuch as He is God"

It is the (Incarnate) Word who is God and Man. Likewise, when I say, "Inasmuch as He is a man" or "Inasmuch as He is God," I do not mean "The human nature" or "The Divine Nature." Rather, I mean, "The Word considered as Man," or "Considered as God." In accord with the explanation proposed earlier, "Inasmuch as He is man," means, "The Word inasmuch as He is a human person."

When the subject is so specified, it is clear that I can attribute to Him only a property that belongs to Him in virtue of the nature which is thus placed in relief. Thus, I can say, "Christ, inasmuch as He is a man, suffered," but not, "Christ, inasmuch as He is a man, created the heavens and the earth with the Father and the Holy Spirit." (However, this does not hold for the assertion, "Christ is created," for the Word can in no way be called "created." But indeed, we can say that that on account of which the Word is called, and is, a human person—namely, the assumed human nature—is created.)

4

Jesus's Humanity

{329} These were tendencies on the fringe, yet Gnosticism at any rate came within an ace of swamping the central tradition. The fact that it did not do so was in large measure due (apart from an astonishing feat of pastoral care on the part of the ecclesiastical authorities) to the unwavering insistence in the rule of faith, as expressed in the liturgy, catechetical teaching and preaching, that the Son of God had really become man. This fundamental datum ensured that the Christological scheme of the primitive Church reproduced the pattern laid down in the New Testament—one Christ, at once human and divine, flesh and spirit.[1]

We must now speak about this humanity by which the Word really is a man. While humanity is one and common to all men with regard to the essence of humanity itself, it is realized in each [human person] under a proper existential mode, including, with its individuating characteristics, an ensemble of qualities, all of which are included in the common nature's virtualities. However, they are realized more or less in each person, sometimes not at all in particular individuals, without this meaning that one person is more human than another. Rather, this different kind of realization only means that one person is more or less perfect in his humanity, and also per-

---

1. Kelly, *Initiation à la doctrine des Pères de l'Église*, 151. [Tr. note: Taken from Kelly, *Early Christian Doctrines*, 142–43.]

fect in a different way. Such differences also include individual deficiencies, "shortcomings" in possible human perfection, without this meaning that such deficiencies would be so great that they would abolish the human essence.

In Christ, the common human nature is realized under an exceptional existential mode, namely, as belonging to a Divine Hypostasis. This implies, first of all, within the insuperable limits of this nature, the loftiest possible realization of human nature's virtualities. Certainly, this is not [precisely speaking] *in virtue of the Hypostatic Union*, for the Divine Person assumes the nature and does not modify it. Rather, this height of human perfection in Christ exists *on account of the Hypostatic Union*. That is, by considering things from the perspective of the Divine Wisdom, we can say that if the Word becomes a man, He cannot fail to be a man in whom human nature is fully realized with the perfections that are necessary so that He would not be less a man. Nonetheless, we still need to determine which "perfections" a man must have so that he would not fall short in relation to human nature, as well as those whose absence does not imply, of themselves, such imperfection, for it is impossible that all the virtualities of human nature be realized in one and the same individual.

However, there are not only "natural" virtualities. There are "supernatural" ones as well. That is, there are virtualities that cannot be realized by solely natural agents (e.g., parents for the individual's constitution; personal efforts, with assistance from other people, institutions, and circumstances such as culture, virtues, etc.), but that God can realize. On the one hand, He can realize such virtualities because He is Almighty. On the other, such realization is possible because human nature is susceptible to being actualized in this manner beyond its natural virtualities, to being elevated and enlarged up to the point of being able to attain the very object of the divine activities, God in His mystery, through its own proper activities (i.e., of thought and love). Such virtualities are real, for in its ontological structure (i.e., in its "nature"), the created spirit has a radical capacity for these activities. However, they are "supernatural" virtualities because the created spirit is radically incapable of realizing them itself, by its own, proper efforts, however much assistance it may receive from other creatures (whereas it can develop its natural virtualities through its own efforts).

In what pertains to man's "natural virtualities," contingency (and, therefore, in the end, the divine freedom) plays its own role with regard to the ensemble of second causes that were executed for bringing about the formation of Jesus's humanity: Jesus was an individuated man, situated geographically, historically, and culturally. This existential and contingent aspect of Jesus's human personality cannot be abolished on the pretext that the Incarnation is a fact concerning human nature in its universality. Even though Jesus's teaching sets forth absolute truths for us, indeed the very truth of God, it is profoundly marked by the Jewish culture of His era. His human behavior is simply that of the Son of God in the flesh and that of a man of His era and of His milieu. If the Incarnation had taken place at another time, in another human milieu, this behavior would have been different and, yet, the same. Thus, "following Christ" does not involve a material imitation of what Christ did. Rather, it requires each person to transpose what is universal in Christ's behavior, not its contingent modalities, into his or her own milieu and era. In a course on Christology, we have little to say about these contingent aspects of Jesus's humanity, except to note them and to specify that they are part of the concrete Incarnation such as God conceived, willed, and realized it.

On the other hand, there is a degree of perfection in the development of these natural virtualities that is required by the Hypostatic Union itself, so that such perfection would be found in the Incarnate Word in whatever contingent conditions in which the Incarnation might be realized. However, given that the Hypostatic Union (which, obviously, is supernatural) is the principle of this perfection, even the natural perfection, of Jesus's humanity, this natural perfection of His humanity is inseparable from the perfection of [His] supernatural virtualities.

Jesus Christ is the Son of the eternal God who has become a true man without ceasing to be God. Two inviolable principles will direct our investigation into what Jesus's humanity must have on account of the Hypostatic Union: first, the inalienable requirements of the infinite dignity of the Person of the Word; second, the similarly inalienable requirements of the truth of His being-man.

In classical theology, the term *co-assumpta* is used for the positive and negative attributes thus acknowledged in the assumed humanity on account of the union. Positive attributes are grouped under three headings: attributes of holiness; attributes of knowledge; attributes of power. The attributes of power pertain to Christ's powers over the forces of nature. However, given that these powers can only be limited on account of the requirements of the truth of [His] human nature, they are studied, instead, in relation to the "negative attributes."

Indeed, human nature necessarily brings with itself the limitations and conditions of humility. First of all, it brings with itself subjection to God and all that this implies. Likewise, it includes a kind of subjection to the forces of nature and to the determinism found in nature. Nonetheless, these "conditions of humility" clearly are realized in very different degrees for different individuals. Did not the dignity of the Divine Person of the Incarnate Word require them to be reduced for Him solely to that which is inevitable for every man because he is a man? And even the Divine Omnipotence can withdraw the requirements of nature, for according to tradition, at man's origins, God exempted him from many natural servitudes. Would not such an exemption have been sovereignly fitting for the God-Man, not only on account of His infinite personal dignity but also on account of His perfect innocence?

Still, in contrast to this, Scripture presents Jesus Christ as being submitted to the worst sufferings and humiliations, as well as to the worst of deaths. We are presented with the Person of the Word "suffering," after the fundamental abasement of the Incarnation itself, the ultimate abasements at the very heart of the human condition. We will see that the reason for this is found in the requirements for accomplishing His redemptive mission. However, we cannot fail to pose the question: What abasements are compatible with the dignity of the Person, and which ones, by contrast, could not be "co-assumed" by the Word? Therefore, this chapter will successively treat the attributes of holiness, the attributes of knowledge, and the abasements of the Incarnate Word during His earthly life.

I. THE ATTRIBUTES OF HOLINESS

A. The Hypostatic Union and Grace

1. Christ's holiness and grace

{330} Holiness is one of God's attributes. It is His infinite perfection, considered as the terminus of the rational creature's religious relation to Him whom the creature recognizes as the Creator, master, and sovereignly perfect one, Him in relation to whom the creature variously expresses his reverence (i.e., adoration), recognition (i.e., thanksgiving), confidence (i.e., prayer), and as necessary, repentance (i.e., penitence).

Historians of religion describe this terminus of the religious relation as arousing sentiments of reverential fear and of distance: "the sacred." The latter often appears in the Bible, with the theme of Yahweh's glory and majesty: "[They] said to Moses, 'You speak to us, and we will hear; but let not God speak to us, lest we die.'"[2] However, another sentiment is provoked by being aware of God's perfection, namely, the recognition of His justice and rectitude, and even more so, of His goodness and mercy.

This brings to light the two principal components of the religious sentiment, and they refer to God's holiness under two conceptually distinct but inseparable aspects. On the one hand, there is the perfection of His Being, from which His omnipotence and sovereign authority follow. On the other hand, there is the perfection of His goodness, from which His infinite love for creatures and the

---

2. Ex 20:19 (RSV) (and the two chapters 19 and 20).

perfect rectitude of His action in the world flow. Thus we can distinguish between holiness of being, which corresponds to "the sacred," and holiness of activity. The two are proper to God in the sense that He alone is holy "by essence," the Holy One, the *Thrice-Holy One*.

Can God's holiness, with its two aspects, be communicated to creatures? This doubtlessly must be possible, for all throughout the Bible, as well as in the Church's traditional language, the qualification "holy" is attributed to creatures. But how? It is sometimes attributed to inanimate beings—a place, a building, etc. Clearly, given that such a created being is incapable of free activity (i.e., an activity whose rectitude would depend on the creature itself), such cases do not involve a participation in rectitude of activity. Therefore, it is a question of a participation in ontological holiness. But still, how? In itself, such holiness is wholly proper to God, because it flows from the infinite perfection of the Divine Being. Hence, an inanimate creature can be holy only as a sign, as a manifestation, as something holding the place of the Divine Majesty for man, evoking it and rendering it present. Therefore, such "holy" creatures are ones chosen by God to manifest Himself and His presence in a permanent or transitory way.

This manifesting function can also be imposed upon men: prophets, priests, kings, etc. From this perspective, the holiness thus conferred on them does not depend upon their activity and, consequently, does not depend upon their moral goodness (nor, moreover, upon their natural perfection). They are not holy in themselves. They refer to the Thrice-Holy God.

But men can also participate in the "holiness of activity [*opération*]," and indeed, Christ's entire redemptive work is ordered toward this participation. This is possible because, as we have seen, God's own, proper goodness, which "rules" (according to our manner of conceiving) His activity, assures its absolute rectitude, and this goodness (understood as a love that gives and is self-diffusive) can be communicated to rational creatures as the object of their loftiest activities and as the "ultimate end" of all their earthly activities.

Thus, we also have the divine participation in this order of the good and activity. In short, this participation is divinization.[3]

Clearly, such a communication in God's life and goodness can be brought about only by grace. Grace is a gift that elevates the created person above the level upon which it would remain by its nature alone. It elevates the created person to the level of divine activities. Therefore, holiness is a gift of grace. Is this likewise true for Christ inasmuch as He is a man? Given that He has a created nature, it seems that this would be the case. However, how can we conceive that the Word would have God's holiness as a kind of grace? Is not His person holy by itself?

2. *The subject of Christ's grace*

{331} Above all, we must bear in mind that grace is the freely-given [*gratificateur*] love of God. In loving His spiritual creature with a paternal love, God makes the creature His son. The Father's eternal love for the Word is eminently natural. It is of God's nature to blossom forth in three Persons who are distinct and bound together, not only by ontological relations but likewise by the intentional relations of knowledge and love, for the intentional and the ontological are identical in God.[4]

Now, we have seen how and in what sense the Word "became" a human person *in tempore*. It is a becoming that involves no alteration for Him. Nevertheless, there is a new fact, namely, that a man who previously did not exist now is the Word. Along the same lines, we must say that the Father's eternal love for the Word "became" love for this human person whom the Word "became." Therefore, it "became" a freely-given [*gratificateur*] love, a love of grace, without ceasing to be a natural love (if we consider the Word in Himself).

We find ourselves led anew to discover in the mystery of the Incarnation the sublime meeting of the natural and the supernatural, of the creature and the Creator. Already, God's creative love seemed

---

3. See §§232–33 in the previous volume.
4. See §§136 in the previous volume.

to be a prolongation of the intra-Trinitarian love. Here, in Christ—if we consider creation as wholly ordered (at least *de facto*) to the Incarnation—the intra-Trinitarian love becomes love for Him who is the principle of all creatures, *primogenitus omnis creaturae*. Therefore, the subject of Christ's grace (i.e., of all the gifts of grace that make up Christ's holiness) is this Man, Jesus (i.e., the Incarnate Word *qua* incarnate), not the *humanity* considered separately, for "grace" designates interpersonal relations.

3. *The grace of union*

{332} Nobody can doubt that the Hypostatic Union is the supreme gift of God to His creation, the loftiest grace, the source of all other graces. But again, to whom is this gift given? To the universe taken as a whole, having the Incarnation as its supreme coronation? Doubtlessly. However, the universe is not what is hypostatically united to the Word of God. No more can we say that the gift was given to mankind taken as a whole. It is given to this singular human nature, Jesus's humanity.

Will we say that Jesus is the subject of the grace of union? However, what does this grace entail if not the fact that the assumed nature is ontologically united in the Word to the Divine Nature itself? Now, how could we say that it is a grace for the Word to have the Divine Nature?

Obviously, the fact that the Word is God is not a grace. Nor can we say that the fact that He is a man is a grace. However, for this man, the fact of being the Word is indeed a grace. By "this man," I mean, "the human nature personalized by the Word." And in this sense, the fact that human nature, which is common to all men, would be personalized by the Word in one of its realizations, is a grace for all men.

This grace is uncreated. It is not a *participation* in the Divine Nature. Instead, it is God Himself giving Himself to His creature. It is first and foremost a gift bestowed to this man, Jesus, who receives something that is not a mere created gift [like the supernatural grace of sanctification shared by all men] but, rather receives the gift of being the Word, of being God. By the mediation of this gift, God gives Himself to men and to all creation: "One (of the two graces that are found in Christ) is the grace of union, which consists in this gift which has been freely given to human nature: to be united to the Son of God Himself, according to the unity of the Person."[5]

4. Created grace in Christ's soul

{333} Created grace is the ensemble of gifts bestowed upon a spiritual person, making him or her participate in the divine nature and life. Above all, it is sanctifying grace, which transforms the soul itself, making it into an immanent principle of the Divine Life (just as the soul by its nature is a principle of human life), radically "divinizing" it. Next, created grace is made up of the "virtues" (principally the theological virtues) which irradiate from sanctifying grace, elevating the spiritual faculties to the level of the divine object, enabling them to perform acts of knowledge and love of God in His mystery, acts of the Divine Life. By means of these acts, the divinized human person vitally communes with the Divine Persons. Finally, created grace is made up of the "actual graces" by which God Himself, as the fountainhead of the Divine Life communicated in the soul (*intimior intimo meo*), animates this new life from within, a life which is at once the Divine Life and that of this living being, the divinized, created person. The Gift of the Spirit is constituted by this entire ensemble of gifts.[6]

Must we hold that such gifts exist in Christ?[7] Given that the grace of union is infinite, certain theologians think that it excludes these created gifts. How and in what way would the Person who is God by nature need to be divinized? Moreover, Scripture and tradition present Jesus to us as a man on whom the Spirit of God rests and who is moved by Him. (Cassian is an example of an ancient author who denied, or at least overlooked, the necessity and existence

---

5. *ST* III, q. 7, a. 11.
6. See J.-H. Nicolas, *Les profondeurs de la grâce*, 87–229.
7. See ibid., 240–48.

of created grace in Christ.[8] Among modern thinkers, this denial is expressly developed by Felix Malmberg.)[9] In reality, far from excluding created grace, the grace of union calls for it and requires it.[10]

In the order of being. While Jesus's human nature is "divine" in the sense that it belongs to the Word of God as His own, it remains, in itself, merely humanity. Human nature can itself be divinized, in itself, through grace. However, being made to belong to the Word does not "divinize" human nature in itself. It only grants this nature a title to receive this Gift from God.

In the order of activity [*opération*]: "Action is proportioned to being." This man, Jesus, is the Word of God. He is God. It belongs to Him to act divinely, through this human nature that He has assumed and by which He is a man without ceasing to be the Word. However, in order to be the immanent principle of a Divine Life, human nature must be amplified and elevated by grace. Therefore, if the assumed nature were not enriched by grace, we would be faced with this paradox: the Word who has become man would remain alienated, precisely as a man, from His own Divine Life.

In the order of the mission. By the mediation of the God-Man, the supreme and infinite gift that God gives of Himself to His creation must spill over onto all men and onto the universe. However, the "grace of union" is obviously incommunicable. Therefore, it must be the case that He makes the source of living water flow forth from within the God-Man's very humanity. Then, this water must be poured out upon the whole world: "If anyone thirsts, let him come to me and drink. He who believes in me, as the scripture has said, 'Out of his heart shall flow rivers of living water.' Now this he said about the Spirit, which those who believed in him were to receive."[11]

---

8. See Grillmeier, *La Christ dans la tradition chrétienne*, 458.
9. See Felix Malmberg, *Über den Gottmenschen* (Freiburg; Herder, 1960), 71–88.
10. See *ST* III, q. 7, a. 1.
11. Jn 7:37–39 (RSV).

5. Christ's holiness

{334} Jesus's humanity is holy on account of the Hypostatic Union. It is holy because it belongs to the Word as His own. In classical theology, this is called "Christ's substantial holiness." On account of this holiness, Christ's humanity is worthy of adoration in itself, in each of its parts, and in the very images that represent it.[12] This can be connected to the Eucharistic realism of certain Fathers (e.g., Gregory of Nyssa, John Chrysostom, and Cyril of Alexandria), who held that physical contact with Christ's flesh is sanctifying for the recipient of the Eucharist.[13] Furthermore, Christ's humanity is holy through the created grace that divinizes it in itself.

Although certain authors speak about two forms of holiness, this is not the best way to express these matters, given the fact that there is only one Person in Christ—for while a "thing" can be holy (in the sense of being "sacred"), the person [himself or herself] is what is holy in the case of a personal being. Therefore, it is better to say that Jesus Christ's holiness is principally constituted by the Hypostatic Union. It is the very holiness of God. However, it includes and incorporates the holiness that confers the gifts of created grace to Christ's soul, a holiness that is only the continuation of God's holiness within the assumed nature, just as the Word's human activity is the continuation of the Hypostatic Union.

B. The Fullness of Grace in Christ's Soul

Here, we are concerned with the fullness of Christ's created grace. Relying on the dictum from John 1:14, "Full of grace and of truth," classical theology spoke of the fullness of grace in Christ's soul. (In fact, in this text *charis* directly designates "the divine goodness that rests on humanity in order to fill it with its benefits."[14]

---

12. *ST* III, q. 25, a. 1.
13. See Jules Gross, *La divinisation du chrétien d'après les Pères grecs, contribution historique à la doctrine de la grâce* (Paris: Gabalda, 1938), 232–33, 258–59, 287–88.
14. See Feuillet, *Le prologue du IVe évangile*, 115.

However, as "God's love makes goodness gush forth in the things that it touches,"[15] this term can be extended without misinterpretation to designate the created grace that God's love for the Son, having become man, makes arise in the assumed humanity in order to enrich, exalt, and "divinize" it.)

1. *Grace without measure*

{335} The true scriptural foundation of this notion must be sought out in the repeated affirmation that Jesus is the "Beloved Son" who has life in Him. Especially: "He who receives his testimony sets His seal to this, that God is true. For He whom God has sent utters the words of God, for it is not by measure that He gives the Spirit; the Father loves the Son, and has given all things into his hand."[16]

a) The totality of the gifts of grace

Grace, in part (indeed, the principal part) is common to all those who receive it: it makes them participate in the Divine Life. It "divinizes" them. However, for the needs of earthly life this grace has multiple virtualities whose actualization is not necessary for each person but instead is necessary in particular people for the sake of the whole—necessary for the Church, not for the individual person of the believer. For example, there is the pastoral charism, the sacerdotal power, charisms in general, and so forth. Moreover, we can say that even from the perspective of divinization, certain traits of grace common to all are accentuated in certain people, while others are accentuated in others: *mercy* in someone like St. Vincent de Paul, *poverty* in St. Francis of Assisi, *missionary zeal* in St. Francis Xavier, *the desire to sacrifice his life as a witness* in St. Ignatius of Antioch, and so forth.

Given that Christ is the highest point of the actualization of grace, we must say that all the virtualities of grace were actualized

---

15. See *ST* I, q. 20, a. 2. [Tr. note: Closing quote missing in original.]
16. Jn 3:33 (RSV).

in Him.[17] Nonetheless, there are two important values of grace that traditional theology excludes from the soul of Christ, even during His earthly life: faith and hope. What should we say about them and how should we understand what is said?

Did Christ have faith while on Earth?

{336} We will see later on[18] that a very ancient theological tradition, with deep scriptural roots, holds that while Christ lived on earth He had immediate vision of the Divine Essence. We will take a position on this subject, ourselves remaining in line with this tradition. If we take this point as being granted for now, at least provisionally, the exclusion of faith in Christ seems to go without saying. Theological faith—about which we are speaking here—is incompatible with vision because its object is the Divine Truth precisely as not seen [through direct vision]. We obviously mean that it is not seen by the intellect, given that the Divine Truth is wholly spiritual and unperceivable by the senses. "Vision" here means the intellectual intuition of a truth that is imposed upon the mind in a dazzling and immediate manner, without investigation and without reasoning, solely by the very light of that truth itself. We have seen that the perfect revelation of God is found in such vision. It is a revelation in which, without any intermediary, the Truth which is God Himself elevates the created mind to His vertiginous loftiness, showing Himself by uniting himself to the created mind, and making Himself be seen or, rather, making the creature see Him.[19] Below this level, when it is a question of a truth at once so lofty and so simple, we have only imperfect revelation. Such revelation is brought about through words that make it known while simultaneously hiding it. Only one kind of knowledge can correspond to this imperfect revelation, however lofty or profound it may become: faith, which consists in holding as true what is spoken, while remaining mysterious,

---

17. See *ST* III, q. 7, aa. 2–8.
18. See §§350–51 below.
19. See §170 bis in the previous volume.

obscure, and unverifiable.[20] He who comes to see no longer needs to believe. He who does not yet see can know the mystery of God—the mystery of His intimate life, the Trinitarian life, the mystery of His designs and that of His self-communication to men, the mystery of the Son in the Incarnation, that of the Spirit in and through the Church, the mystery of His paternity through the grace of divine filiation—only by relying upon His word, by faith.

If, during the time of His earthly life, Christ saw God by His human mind, we must say that He did not have faith. However, this does not diminish His grace in any way, for the [Beatific] Vision is the terminus and summit toward which faith leads. Faith fades away before vision, for the same truth that faith knows imperfectly and obscurely shines forth in full light in vision. Conversely, if, as a number of theologians think, Christ did not have the vision of God in his soul, we would need to acknowledge that He had the loftiest, purest, and richest faith. However, it would remain faith, with the limitations inseparably inherent to faith by its very nature—unless one were to say that He did not know the whole mystery of God, which is absurd, given that His mission consisted in revealing this mystery to men.

However, certain theologians among those who admit that Christ had the vision of the Divine Essence during His earthly existence, speak (indeed, profoundly) of what they call "Christ's faith."[21] Could this opposition between faith and vision perhaps be less rigorous than we hold that it is?

In reality, when using the expression "Christ's faith," these theologians are not thinking about the very knowledge of faith. Rather, they are thinking of this other element of faith, which in certain regards is as important (or even more important), namely the believer's confidence in Him who speaks, his personal engagement in relation with Him. From this perspective, Christ's faith is total and super-exemplary.

---

20. See §167 in the previous volume.
21. See Hans Urs von Balthasar, *La foi du Christ* (Paris: Cerf, 1968); Malevez, "Le Christ et la foi."

Nonetheless, it seems that this does not avoid falling into an equivocation. It is true that what gives worth to grace and to the sanctifying power of faith is the total confidence with which one abandons one's autonomy, even one's intellectual autonomy, to the Father and simultaneously to the Word "who illuminates every man." However, knowledge of the revealed truth is what, in itself, constitutes faith. The voluntary movement of welcoming the Divine Truth, without which faith would be impossible, is part of faith in him who has faith (unless there is only a wholly dead residue in the mind of the person who received this truth and then wholly turned himself away from it without however repudiating it, without ceasing to hold that these things that no longer interest Him are true). However, it obviously endures, indeed more strongly, and is more totally rousing when faith fades away before vision. If Christ had the vision of the Divine Essence[22] from the beginning of His existence as man, without a doubt He had a very lofty degree of filial confidence in relation to the "Father of lights." With a great desire, one that was completely filled yet never extinguished, he welcomed this truth that was given to His human mind. However, the knowledge that He had of the Divine Truth was conditioned neither by this confidence nor by this desire. Instead, they sprang from it.

When it is thus disconnected from the knowledge of faith, is this confidence which certain people call "Christ's faith" something different from hope? Here, however, traditional theology holds that Christ likewise did not have the theological virtue of hope.

Did Christ have hope while on Earth?

{337} Let us immediately say that the traditional reasons for excluding hope from Christ's fullness of grace are much less certain.

---

22. [Tr. note: Throughout his texts, Fr. Nicolas often uses "vision" where in English "Beatific Vision" would normally be used. Because of a qualifying point made below in §405, concerning Christ's experience of the vision of the Divine Essence during His pre-resurrection existence in contrast to after His crucifixion, I have chosen to render the pre-resurrection of "vision" (when by itself) as "vision of the Divine Essence" in most cases when "vision" alone would be clunky.]

Indeed, there are even scriptural texts that could well incline one to think the contrary. As we will see, Jesus's cry on the cross, "Why have you abandoned me?," certainly is not a cry of despair but, rather, is related to hope, pushed to the very heights of its power for relying on the divine promises, even down into the greatest depths of dereliction. And, indeed, there is an echo of this "hope against every hope"[23] in the famous verse of the Letter to the Hebrews: "In the days of his flesh, Jesus offered up prayers and supplications, with loud cries and tears, to Him who was able to save him from death, and he was heard for his godly fear."[24]

Moreover, it is undeniable that Christ awaited many benefits from his Father, the first of which was His resurrection and exaltation. There also was the reconciliation of the world with God, the fruit of redemption that He would bring about upon the cross, though it remains a pure grace for its beneficiaries: "For the wages of sin is death, but the free gift of God is eternal life in Christ Jesus our Lord."[25] He desired them and awaited them in complete confidence, founded on the promise that had been made to Him through the whole history of Israel, all the prophecies, and His own, incomparable spiritual experience. And nonetheless this did not depend on Him as a man, and on the cross, He experienced, up to the point of the most terrible agony, the feeling of being abandoned—all without yielding His certitude in the divine aid, a certitude that, in the peace of the resurrection, He recalled to His disciples on the way to Emmaus, reproaching them for losing hope: "Was it not necessary that the Christ should suffer these things and enter into his glory?"[26] For His own part, He never lost it. What would that be if not hope?

Nonetheless, St. Thomas, who obviously recognizes the reality of Christ's hope thus delimited, refuses to hold that it would be the

---

23. Rom 4:18.
24. Heb 5:7 (RSV).
25. Rom 6:23 (RSV).
26. Lk 24:26 (RSV).

same as the theological virtue of hope.[27] He explains this by noting that the first object of theological hope is union with God in vision. Everything else (including earthly joys) that is also the object of theological hope nonetheless exists only in function of the principal object which precisely makes hope a theological virtue, namely, inasmuch as they derive from union with God or contribute in one's progress toward it. As soon as this principal object is lacking—as holds for Christ, because on this earth He was, as a man, fully united to the Father and the Spirit through the vision of the Divine Essence, as well as through the love that irresistibly flows forth from such vision—the other goods, all while being the object of hope, would not suffice for specifying the theological virtue of hope or for creating it in Christ in His earthly existence while He was still moving toward His "bodily glorification."

It is understandable [*permis*] that one may not be convinced by this argumentation. First, how can one not wonder what this hope for the resurrection, "bodily glorification," and the reconciliation of the world with God is if not the theological virtue of hope? In addition, the distinction that St. Thomas draws between the essential glory that union brings with it and the accidental glory that is the glorification of one's body seems too cut-and-dry of a distinction. Beatitude and glory are a single whole and, even if the vital and irradiant nucleus of this whole incontestably is the [Beatific] Vision, with the love that is inseparable from it, bodily glory (not only the glorification of the body but also that of the entire human being, considered in his bodily dimension) is not only accidental and, as it were, super-added to it. The spiritual union with God that Christ experiences in His humanity is not increased in itself by the resurrection. However, it draws toward it the whole part of His humanity that, through a mysterious effect of the economy of salvation, did not yet share in it, now engulfing it in that resurrection. At the moment when the entire glory and joy of the resurrection flooded over

---

27. See *ST* III, q. 7, a. 4.

the lower parts of Jesus Christ's spirit, sensibility, and flesh, the resurrection itself is what mysteriously expanded, at last unfurling itself in all of its dimensions. Therefore, we must not hold that the principal and determining object of theological hope is truly external to the immediate object of His earthly hope.

With regard to the achievement of the redemption, while it is in a sense relegated to the end of the world, in another sense (one that is more restrictive here), it is already given, because all the graces given to men up to the end of time are, and will be, caused (by way of merit and satisfaction, as well as by way of efficient causality as well) by the power of the cross of Christ. As we will see below, they were entirely given to Christ with His bodily resurrection and glorification. Therefore, we can validly extend to Christ's state of glory what we said concerning what He had on earth prior to His passion and resurrection. Without a doubt, He currently no longer hopes. He now has what had been promised to Him.

Similarly, the elect in heaven no longer hope, even in their bodily resurrection. This does not mean that they do not care about the resurrection. Rather, it is already given to them with Christ's resurrection, in which they already participate in the vision of God. However, we will discuss all of this when we come to discuss eschatology.

b) Infinite grace

{338} "Without measure"—does this mean "infinite"? In what sense can Christ's created grace be called infinite?[28] It can be infinite in the sense that, in the real economy of salvation, it is the greatest grace, containing all those that are given (or ever will be given) to created persons.

Why? The reason that St. Thomas gives, one of great depth, is that Jesus's created grace is directly and immediately connected to the grace of union, which is the absolute summit of grace. This continuity between intentional union (through knowledge and love) and

---

28. See *ST* III, q. 7, aa. 11–12.

ontological union (through the communication of the Word's subsistence to the assumed human nature) is a central and essential aspect of the mystery of the Incarnation. If we critiqued it earlier,[29] our concern was registered only to the degree that one would like to reduce ontological union to intentional union, misunderstanding what is unique and proper to it. It remains true that the Hypostatic Union is the summit of humanity's union with God and that every union effected by grace is measured in relation to it. In Christ's soul, the two forms of union are connected, within the unity of His Person, in such a way that intentional union receives a relative infinity, *in ordine gratiae* (i.e., within the limits of the order of grace, which belongs to the created, and therefore finite, sphere for it includes personal creatures, though inasmuch as they are elevated to union with God even through their activities) from the fact that Christ, being the Word, is united through His human activities to the Godhead in a way worthy of the Word (i.e., at a degree of intimacy transcending that to which any created person whatsoever is led by God's Spirit). This gives it a kind of absolute [character] within the order of salvation such as it has been conceived and realized by God.

In these conditions, it is futile to ask whether Christ could have received a more abundant grace. It would have been a "more" that is only quantitative, without importance, a "more" that would not really have drawn this human person, who was the Divine Person Himself, closer to God.[30]

2. Grace given in full from the beginning

a) St. Thomas's position

{339} According to St. Thomas,[31] Christ's grace, which was infinite in the sense that was just specified, was at the apex of its perfection from the beginning of His earthly existence, meaning that

---

29. See §290 above.
30. For the history of the problem, see Jan Rohof, *La sainteté substantielle du Christ dans la théologie scolastique* (Fribourg: Éditions Saint Paul, 1952).
31. See *ST* III, q. 7, a. 12.

it did not need to grow (in distinction from grace in the cases of all the saints, including the Virgin Mary). The principal reason that he gives for this is that the vision of the Divine Essence is the ultimate fruition of grace, given that it is the highest point of union to God. Given that Christ had this vision from the beginning of His earthly existence, the grace that was given to Him was at the ultimate terminus of its development. In his response to an objection,[32] he suggests another reason, one that is perhaps more profound. Here, he says that the divinizing grace in Christ's soul was wholly ordered to the grace of union and in some way proportioned to it, according to a measure that was certainly fixed by the Divine Wisdom, though in such a manner that this grace was fitting for the Son of God made flesh. Given that the grace of union was obviously given from the first instant and does not have degrees—it is purely and simply infinite—the sanctifying grace that derives from it, aroused in Jesus's soul by the same love by which the Father loves the Son, could only be perfect from the first instant, without needing to increase so that it might arrive at its perfection.

b) Objections

This thesis seems too systematic to many, and serious objections have been raised against it. They are too important and too justified for us to pass on without examining them.

Christ is truly and fully a man. The Hypostatic Union does not modify human nature in Him. Now, by his very nature (and therefore essentially), man is a developmental being, at least during the earthly phase of his destiny. On account of this developmental character, redemption is accomplished progressively in mankind and in each person. Do we not run contrary to the realism of the Incarnation if we refuse to hold that Christ would have experienced such progress in His grace?

Later on, we will discuss the problem concerning the attribution

---

32. See ibid., ad 2; equally, a. 13.

of the vision of the Divine Essence to Christ during this life. Once again, we are for now provisionally holding that this is a granted fact of Christology. Jacques Maritain tried to reconcile the idea that Christ's grace is progressive with the affirmation of this vision during His earthly life.[33] It does not seem that Maritain truly succeeded in this, for the vision of God is the terminus of one's progress in grace, as it is by revealing Himself that God gives Himself.[34] It seems contradictory to say that, *with regard to the perfection of grace*, one and the same person would simultaneously have arrived at the terminus [of grace] and still be in a state of progress [toward its perfect fullness]. While St. Thomas teaches that Christ on earth was simultaneously *viator* (i.e., in a state of progress) and *comprehensor* (i.e., at the terminus), he nonetheless takes great care to specify that this is true from two different perspectives (i.e., in relation to two formally different termini). On the one hand, there is beatitude inasmuch as it concerns only the soul (i.e., inasmuch as it is spiritual, essential beatitude). On the other hand, there is beatitude inasmuch as it is communicated to bodily existence (i.e., the goods that bring beatitude to its integral perfection [*les biens qui intègrent la béatitude*]).[35]

Here, we are formally concerned with the fullness of Christ's grace. Does this perfection of grace exclude every kind of progress during His earthly life, or on the contrary, can we admit that it is realized only at the resurrection? In this case, it would certainly be necessary to preclude immediate vision of the Divine Essence during Christ's earthly life, with all the difficulties that such a rejection raises from the perspective of his knowledge [*science*] and consciousness.[36]

c) Attempt at a solution

Everything comes down to this fact, which is the very mystery of the Incarnation: in Jesus, the Person is preexistent, perfect, and in-

---

33. See Jacques Maritain, *De la grâce et de l'humanité de Jésus* (Paris: Desclée de Brouwer, 1967), 47–92.
34. See J.-H. Nicolas, *Dieu connu comme inconnu*, 358–75.
35. See §337 above.
36. See §§361–63 below.

finite. Christ's human nature does not make this Divine Person be a person but, rather, only makes Him be human. This means that the development of human perfection in Jesus implies no progress in personal perfection *qua* personal, whereas in our case, personality develops gradually with our nature.

Formally speaking, grace is a personal perfection. It is defined by interpersonal relations between the creature and God. Certainly, these are relations founded on modifications of human nature itself (*habitus* [pl.]). However, they concern the person as such. In my opinion, this is the profound and necessary reason why we cannot admit that there is progress in Christ's virtue.[37]

This explains, at once, why this fullness of grace given from the beginning of His life is not opposed to the realism of the Incarnation. The assumed nature is certainly developmental. However, this does not entail that His grace develops and undergoes progress, for this does not entail that his personality, even human [in the sense discussed earlier], is developmental, as is the case for us.

Fr. Galot contests such reasoning, given that we are here considering a concrete modality of the Incarnation that cannot be deduced *a priori*.[38] Nonetheless, it is a question of the very law of the Incarnation, namely, the independence of the Person of the Word in relation to the [assumed human] nature.

However, does this exclude every kind of progress in the life of grace? While Christ's person is not developmental, He lives in accord with His grace only through the acts which have His nature as their source and focal point. If His human nature is developmental—and it is—some sort of development must be found, if not in grace itself, at least in the activities of the life of grace that are produced by this nature and by the faculties super-elevated by grace.

Indeed, there is a text in scripture to which Jacques Maritain lays claim, one that, in fact, seems to prove him right: "Jesus progressed

---

37. See *ST* III, q. 2, a. 12.
38. See Jean Galot, *La conscience de Jésus* (Paris: Lethielleux, 1971), 140–43.

in wisdom and in stature, and in grace before God and man."³⁹ The *Traduction Oecuménique de la Bible* translates "in favor" instead of "in grace." This does not change the meaning of the text, for grace is simultaneously God's favor as well as that which places the favored man near to God. This text makes a precise, and even literal, allusion to another text from the Old Testament: "Now the boy Samuel continued to grow both in stature and in favor [*grâce*] with the LORD and with men."⁴⁰ Does this comparison invite us to acknowledge some kind of progress in Christ in what concerns grace itself?

St. Thomas proposed an interpretation of Luke's text that can put us on the way to a resolution:

Someone progresses in wisdom and grace in two ways. On the one hand, the very *habitus* of wisdom and of grace grow. Now, Christ did not progress in this sense. On the other hand, one performs works that are wiser and more remarkable, and in this sense He progressed in wisdom and grace, as well as in age. Indeed, to the degree that He advanced in age, He performed more perfect works, so that He manifested that He was a true man both in the things of God and in the things of man.⁴¹

However, let us first note that he is not speaking about a progress that would be merely apparent in nature. The "ut se verum hominem demonstraret" must not be understood as though it was only a question of Christ "appearing" to be a true man, for St. Thomas's Christology does not contain the least trace of docetism. This is why I translated the *ut* as "so that He manifested that He was a true man." As regards the "sapientiora et virtuosiora opera," there is no reason that we should limit ourselves to thinking only about external and visible works. The "works" of the supernatural *habitus* are first of all internal acts of knowledge and love.

Therefore, the solution could run as follows. In order to perform an act of charity or of (supernatural) wisdom, it is not enough for one to have the corresponding *habitus*, even at its loftiest degree. Be-

---

39. Lk 2:52.
40. 1 Sm 2:26 (RSV).
41. *ST* III, q. 7, a. 12, ad 3.

yond this, the faculty that must vitally elicit this act (i.e., the intellect, the will, or both together) must be able to act, indeed with its maximal natural vitality. Now, in a human being, this happens only after a lengthy process of development, which moreover, is not directly concerned with the spiritual faculty itself but, rather, with the sense faculties, the senses, and also their bodily organs, all of which must necessarily be used by the spiritual faculty in man so that it may exercise its own, proper act. A newborn can receive a very lofty grace at baptism. He or she should grow and develop so as to reach the point when his or her spiritual faculties will be able to elicit supernatural activities at the level of the *habitus* that is in him or her. Until this point is reached, he or she will grow in the life of grace without, necessarily, his or her grace itself growing. Of course, in a mere man, this grace could grow (and, indeed, normally should grow) thereafter and even should grow in the child under the action of the Eucharist. However, when it comes to the case of Christ, we can admit that His grace could not grow, given that it was at its summit from the first instant of the Incarnation, simultaneously admitting, however, that He grew in the life of grace until He arrived at the fullness of His "human stature," both psychologically and physically.

In his *Catena aurea*[42] entry for this verse in Luke's Gospel, St. Thomas brings together two Patristic texts that indicate this idea. He cites Gregory Nazianzus as writing, "He is said to have progressed according to humanity, not that the latter itself grew, being perfect from the beginning"—obviously, it is a question of humanity considered in the values coming to it through grace, for the assumed humanity obviously developed from infancy onward—"but because it manifested its perfection only gradually." Likewise, he cites Theophylact:

> The natural law does not permit a man to make use of wisdom that is superior to that which corresponds to one's bodily age. Therefore, the Word was a perfect man, being the Power and Wisdom of the Father. However, because something needed to be accorded to our nature's behaviors so that His contemporaries would not think that He was a fantastical be-

---

42. Catena Aurea, *In Lk* 2:52, Marietti, no. 14.

ing, as a man He manifested Himself gradually to the degree that He advanced in age and was judged increasingly wise by those who saw Him and heard Him.

Moreover, we will see that, in contrast to St. Thomas, contemporary theology justly admits that during the first years of his life, Jesus, like every infant, was "unconscious" and not yet prepared to make use of His superior human faculties. Therefore, we must acknowledge that there is a difference between, on the one hand, the possession of grace and of all the supernatural *habitus*, and, on the other hand, the use of these *habitus*. Along the same line of reflection, we can think that when Jesus began to use His *habitus* of wisdom and of charity, the acts that He produced did not correspond to the perfection that grace and the virtues had in Him, all the while being the most elevated and purest acts that He could elicit at this moment of His human development.

In this way, we can reconcile the very profound and necessary idea of the fulness of grace in Christ's soul from the first instant of the Incarnation with not only the text cited from Luke, but also with the requirements of the "truth" of the Incarnation. It seems that this is the way that one can do justice to what is essential in Maritain's insights.

C. Capital Grace

{340} While grace is first of all God's paternal- and friendship-love for man, we must say that all men are loved in Christ. He is the New Adam in whom the whole of humanity is included (as we will discuss later).[43] Moreover, He is the New Adam who bears this humanity in His spirit and in His heart.

Earlier, we said that the Father's eternal love for the Son in the Trinity becomes, through the Incarnation, the Father's love (and the whole Trinity's love) for the Son become man, the Man-Jesus.[44] This love is what is prolonged into a personal love for each believ-

---

43. See §435 below.
44. See §331 above.

er to the degree that he adheres to Christ through faith (and love).

Just as God's love for the Man-Jesus brings to birth grace (and all the gifts that it includes) in His soul, so too does this love include the promise and offer of grace to all men, realizing this gift in each believer. Thus, capital grace is not another, additional grace in Jesus. The grace that He receives "as the Unique Son full of grace and of truth"[45] is a capital grace, a grace given, in Him first, to mankind. Indeed, every grace given to men through the course of salvation history is derived from the grace initially given to Jesus. This should not be understood materially, as though it involved a kind of bodily transfusion. Rather, it should be understood spiritually, for grace is born in the soul under the irradiation of God's love. Indeed, it is in Christ that each man is loved, in continuity with the love through which the "beloved Son" is loved.

In the third part of this *Dogmatic Theology*,[46] we will see that the Church's grace derives from this fullness of grace which is in Christ.

II. THE MAN-JESUS'S KNOWLEDGE DURING HIS EARTHLY LIFE

{341} The Incarnate Word has the Divine Nature and therefore has an infinitely perfect knowledge of God, which He has in common with the Father and the Spirit. This is one reason why it is very difficult to interpret what the Fathers say about "Christ's knowledge [*science*]." In virtue of the rule of the "communication of idioms," the divine knowledge [*science*] and all its perfections can be attributed to the Man-Jesus. However, the problem that we are addressing here is that of the knowledge that He had "inasmuch as He is a man." Therefore, we are concerned with addressing His human knowledge. If certain perfections of the Divine Nature can be communicated to the assumed human nature, this happens in a participated manner and not such as they are in God.

---

45. Jn 1:14.
46. That is, in the next volume to be published in English.

However, matters are not completely the same in the case of the perfections of Christ's knowledge as they are in that of His gifts of holiness. The latter make their recipient a participant in the very nature of God. That is, they are supernatural and *grace-given*. Therefore, they come immediately from God and are first bestowed upon the Divine Person, the Word who subsists in the assumed nature. They derive immediately from the Father's intra-Trinitarian love for the Son and from the Son's intra-Trinitarian love for the Father. Consequently, from the beginning, they are at the summit of perfection and are "developmental" neither through their cause (which is the eternal love), nor through Him who receives them, the Word.

Intellectuality, as well as the knowledge by which it is actualized, is a perfection of human nature. Certainly, like all natural perfections, it comes from God, though not through grace. This means that inasmuch as understanding and knowledge are human, they come to the person of the Incarnate Word from the assumed nature, which itself is developmental.

Nonetheless, there is a knowledge that comes from God and itself is a gift of grace: supernatural knowledge, begotten in the human intellect through revelation. Here again, however, matters are not completely the same for the cases of holiness and knowledge. Here below, revelation uses natural means of knowing and, therefore, makes use of the activity of nature. While faith is itself a grace, the knowledge of faith is acquired—not in the sense that it would be the fruit of human discovery but, rather, in the sense that it must be received by an act of the intellect, can progress, and arouses an entire intellectual labor. In Christ's case, the developmental character of human nature must therefore play its role and have its effects in this matter.

There is another difference between the cases of knowledge and holiness. The perfection of holiness includes a kind of totality (at least a relative one), for it is defined in relation to the good, which includes total perfection (at least tendentially). Thus, he who turns away from God on any single point loses all holiness. By contrast, the perfection of knowledge, which is defined in relation to the truth, does not include this totality, for a particular truth remains a truth and brings a perfection to the intellect that knows it, even if many errors concerning other points coexist with it. For all the more reason, we in no way need to know all truths, nor even need to aim at knowing them. (Moreover, the intellect is not a faculty of tending toward an object but rather is a faculty whose activity consists in being assimilated to the object.) Here again, by the intermediacy of the assumed nature, the person of the Incarnate Word can be thus partially perfected by the truth.

Nonetheless, at the summit of revelation and of supernatural knowledge, the gift of knowledge and the gift of grace coincide in *immediate Vision of the Divine Essence*. There, the Divine Essence immediately informs the created intellect. It is a pure grace, indeed, the complete perfection of the intellect. It is not obtained at the terminus of some progressive investigation but, instead, is purely given all at once. Therefore, we can say that it is given to the person. However, if it was given to the Person of the Word in His human nature from the first instant of the Incarnation, would not such a gift remove all possibility of development? And, therefore, all of its reality as well? This issue can make the problem of the fullness of grace present itself once again.

Therefore, we will successively study the following topics. First, we will consider the man Jesus's natural knowledge on earth. Then, we will consider His supernatural knowledge, as well as how we must think about the conjunction and synergy between His natural and supernatural forms of knowledge. Finally, we will consider a problem that is posed today with insistence and which merits being treated apart, namely, Jesus's human [self-]consciousness on earth.

A. Jesus's Natural Knowledge during His Earthly Life

{342} Physical sufferings, along with the emotions that they cause, naturally affect the person himself, at least when one has a unitary anthropology, like the one that certainly underlies the thought of the biblical authors and that likewise was quite deliberately elaborated by St. Thomas. However, it is understood that they can be "assumed" (*co-assumed*) by the Word because they reach the person in the inferior part of himself (i.e., the sensible part), not the superior part (i.e., the spiritual part), which characterizes the person as such. The human person—and this is a fundamental principle in morality—must "integrate" the movements of sensibility, subordinating them, by his reason and freedom, to the foundational movement of his will, which is a spiritual faculty (although the human good toward which it tends includes a sensible dimension). The Stoic seeks to deny and reject the movements of his sensibility from his personal depths. The Christian neither denies nor rejects them. He takes them up into an existential project which is elaborated by his reason (itself illuminated by faith) and embraced by his will. By taking up suffering and by really experiencing it, not only in His sensibility but also in His will ("a tendency toward the good on the part of the whole person"), Christ opened up a way in which suffering and weakness may be personalized and ennobled, thus ruling out the idea that they would undermine one's personal dignity.

Is the same true for knowledge? Man's cognitional imperfections and limitations are all too manifest. Because they are connatural to him, they do not undermine the dignity of the human person. However, they certainly denote his radical imperfection *inasmuch as he is a person*, that is, inasmuch as he is a spirit. This fact led to a twofold temptation, which we can find in the Patristic tradition, as well as in [the history of later] theology. On the one hand, there is the temptation to deny that Christ has this kind of purely human knowledge while on earth. On the other hand, there is a temptation to exempt Him from its imperfections and limitations.

1. The existence of natural human knowledge in the Man-Jesus
a) The realism of the Incarnation requires us to acknowledge that Jesus had such knowledge

{343} We cannot reasonably deny that Christ, who had a true human nature, also had (indeed, as a necessary consequence [of the

Incarnation]) human knowledge. "Every being is made for its activity," and knowledge is the highest activity in which a human being is brought to his completion and comes to full fruition (when this activity arrives at its perfection). To say that the Word is a man and that He does not act in a human manner would be to render the Incarnation meaningless.

Indeed, we must also add that it was through human acts that Christ redeemed men (for, inasmuch as He is God, He could neither offer Himself in sacrifice, nor merit, nor pray, nor make satisfaction). Knowledge is not only the highest and most characteristic of human actions, it is the principle from which all of a man's human acts proceed. Finally, as we have seen, Christ is the revealer of the Father, He by whom God is given to man by revealing Himself. We will see that Christ could reveal to us what He knew through His divine knowledge only by making use of human knowledge of these same truths.

The difficulty lies in taking this fundamental affirmation all the way to its conclusion. Indeed, human knowledge has characteristics that result strictly from man's ontological structure and, therefore, are necessarily found in every man. Let us briefly recall a relevant fact: the human intellect is a "blank slate on which nothing is written." Human knowledge begins with sensible perception, from which "phantasms" are formed in the sense faculties (and also in the cogitative power's sketches of judgment). This is the basis for the intellect's development, attaining its object (i.e., being) by abstracting it from the phantasms, gradually proceeding forward by means of conceptual composition and division and through reasoning, to increasingly more precise and vaster knowledge of the being presented to its experience (that is, the quiddity, or essence, of material things).

However, it does all of this in such a way that it can never, under pain of being cut off from its object, cease to remain in contact with the being of material things through the intermediary of perception and imagination: "The intellect cannot know without concurrently turning to the phantasms."[47] Certainly, the human intellect can also

---

47. *ST* I, q. 84, a. 7.

know immaterial beings (and above all, God), but it does so by way of analogy and by remaining in permanent contact with the being of material things. The abstraction by means of which it in some manner "constructs" its object is, according to St. Thomas, the activity of a second intellectual faculty [*sic*], the agent intellect. Without the agent intellect, the intellect properly speaking (i.e., the passive intellect) would remain empty and in a state of pure potency to knowledge.

In a number of his works, St. Thomas masterfully identified and explained this characteristic mode of human knowledge.[48] It seems to go without saying that everything that he says about the nature of the human intellect and about its manner of knowing must be fully applied to Christ, whose complete humanity St. Thomas so strongly emphasized on the basis of the Incarnation.

And nonetheless, he hesitates and obviously recoils before the consequences of such an application. In the *Scriptum*,[49] he refuses to admit that Christ had "experiential knowledge [*science*]" (that is, according to his terminology, knowledge acquired from sense experience and through abstraction). However, in the *Summa theologiae*, he retracts this assertion, constrained by the requirements of the Incarnation's realism. Christ was fully a man and had an agent intellect. We cannot hold that this human faculty would have been inoperative in Him, like a useless ornament.[50] Nonetheless, the very order of questions in the *Summa theologiae* dedicated to Christ's knowledge[51] already shows that experiential (or, acquired) knowledge [*science*] holds the last and least important place among the various types of science or types of knowledge which St. Thomas acknowledged that Christ had. On the other hand, he pushes the perfection of this acquired knowledge to the extreme, stating that Jesus knew everything through this form of knowledge. If it progressed, this was only until he reached the age of manhood and, even then,

---

48. See *ST* I, qq. 79, 84, 85ff. Also see parallel texts.
49. *In* III *Sent.*, d. 14, especially aa. 2 and 3.
50. See *ST* III, q. 9, a. 4.
51. See *ST* III, qq. 9–12.

such progress occurred without Him having been taught, by either human masters or angels.

What is the source of these kinds of reticence and this manifest distortion in relation to St. Thomas's own analysis of human knowledge? An in-depth textual study, first considering the text of the *Scriptum* and then that of the *Summa theologiae*, makes it quite clear why he came to these conclusions. According to St. Thomas (and according to the truth of the matter) intellectuality is the first property of a spiritual being and, likewise, spirituality is the foundation of personal dignity. Therefore, in light of this fact, he is opposed to the idea that Christ's intellect could have existed in an initial state of pure potentiality, passing slowly and with difficulty from potency to act, like an ordinary man's intellect, for if this were the case, the very person of the Incarnate Word would have been in potency (i.e., would have been imperfect), not only by the imperfection inherent to every created nature—something that is the immediate consequence of the Incarnation—but imperfect with regard to the perfection possible to a human being. In particular, St. Thomas does not admit, even in the *Summa theologiae*, that Christ could have been taught by a mere creature, whether man or angel, for even as man, He is the Word, "the true light who, coming into the world, illuminates every man."[52]

b) Therefore Jesus, in His humanity, was subject to limitations in His knowledge

However, how would the Incarnate Word have had a true human intellect, one having the same nature as ours, without this intellect functioning in accord with the human intellect's natural mode of activity? This mode necessarily implies:

- First, *progressivity*: for while the passage of the human intellect from potency to act is, in itself, a spiritual process that, of itself, could be instantaneous, it in fact depends on sense experience

---

52. Jn 1:9.

and the activity of the internal senses, which are obviously submitted to temporal succession.

- Second, *an indefinite progressivity*: for man can never exhaust the whole field open to his knowledge by making use of the ways of abstraction, composition and division, and reasoning.

- Third, *a progressivity that not only concerns the individual but mankind taken all together*. Man is a "political animal," that is, a social animal, and this social and communal dimension affects him also in his spiritual activities, in his knowledge. The progress of human knowledge takes place collectively, from generation to generation. Even if an individual is endowed with the loftiest of genius, his knowledge is necessarily dependent on his era's state of culture and on his environment. If he can precede his contemporaries and open up new ways for them (and even then, only in a determinate domain of knowledge), he cannot be detached from them and know things that will be able to be known only many generations after him. (That is, he cannot know them in such a way that his knowledge [*science*] would be, strictly speaking, incommunicable to his contemporaries.) This is obvious in the order of the sciences (in the modern sense of the word): how can one know the astral universe or the composition of the living cell before the existence of the instruments (e.g., the telescope, the microscope, etc.) needed so that one might have the experience that is the necessary basis for such kinds of knowledge? However, this is true also in the philosophical domain, more clearly so in the philosophy of nature, for it is more immediately dependent on the sciences. (For example, it is undeniable that the discoveries of psychology and of the other human sciences enable heretofore impossible developments in [philosophical] anthropology.) However, this is true also, though to a lesser degree, for metaphysics. Even though its object, being, may be seized on the basis of the simplest experiences, better knowledge of particular beings enables a new deepening (or at least new extensions) of this fundamental metaphysical knowledge, the intuition of being. For example, one can think of the enrichment brought to metaphysics ([i.e., the metaphysics] of being) by what is sometimes improperly called "the discovery of the subject." Even though they were aberrant in themselves, the developments of idealism have enabled us to see more fully the intellect's domination over the material universe and to place this in much greater relief, even if the [human] intellect depends on the material universe in some way, etc.

- Fourth, *consequently, a progressivity that necessarily implies that every human individual, even the greatest of all possible geniuses, depends on other men*: A child learns to read. He does not reinvent the alphabet. In every science that he will cultivate (and perhaps illuminate), he learns what was discovered before him, indeed from living masters. Having reached the apex of knowledge in a given science, he continues to learn from others, at least through reading, dialogue, etc.

- Fifth, *such progressivity does not take place without forms of ignorance*: Through experience, reasoning, teaching, or simple intellectual exchanges, we discover things that we did not know and that we were unaware of. Therefore, we cannot retain this idea proposed once upon a time by various theologians, holding that Christ was omniscient, at least as concerns His human knowledge. Now, this ineluctably poses the grave problem concerning the forms of ignorance Christ would have experienced.

2. *The forms of ignorance experienced by the Man-Jesus*

a) The testimony of the Gospels

{344} The "theological thesis" of Christ's omniscience is an example of a topic occasioning the most lamentable sorts of conflicts between exegetes and theologians. As we have seen, it is the fruit of a theological deduction *taking its basis from Scripture* (in the sense that the principle of this deduction is the Hypostatic Union, which the theologian knows from Scripture and holds as being true on account of Scripture's authority), though *not on the basis of the image of Jesus Christ given by Scripture.* In the Gospels, Jesus does not seem to know all things in advance. He poses questions, and most importantly, in all the expressions of his knowledge, He appears to be very dependent on his cultural milieu, speaking the same "language" as the doctors and popular preachers of His time (even if He opens up unsuspected horizons to His listeners by means of this language). Nothing in His words or behavior leads us to suspect that He would possess scientific or philosophical knowledge foreign to this very particularized culture. If Jesus seems omniscient in the Gospel, this is solely in the domain of religious knowledge, in the domain of revealing the mysteries of God, and even in this domain His knowledge seems to be limited, as we see in His famed remark concerning the Judgment Day.[53]

The theologian can say that Scripture does not absolutely impose the image of a Christ who is unaware of many things and instructed by men. However, the exegete can rightly respond to him that nothing in the Gospels verifies the theologian's thesis of a Christ who is omniscient during His earthly life. It is clear that if, as we have seen, the very reasoning the theologian uses for arriving at his thesis must be contested and rejected, this thesis can no longer be supported.

b) The theological thesis of omniscience and the tradition

{345} St. Thomas's position,[54] like that of all his contemporaries, is wholly dependent on St. Augustine's influence. The latter connected ignorance to sin in a strict manner. For this reason, he refused to acknowledge that Christ experienced ignorance:

He came in the likeness of the "flesh of sin" in order to remove the body from sin, the very infirm body, in which, with its infantile members inapt for every use (for knowledge), the rational soul was gravely jeopardized

---

53. See Mt 24:36 and Mk 13:32.
54. See Jules Lebreton, *Les origines du dogme de la Trinité* (Paris: Beauchesne, 1919), 1:513–44, note C.

by a wretched ignorance. I cannot believe that such ignorance was found in any way in this child, in whom the Word was made flesh so as to dwell among us. I cannot imagine that the Christ child experienced this infirmity of the spirit itself which we see in infants.[55]

Likewise, in a famous passage in which he describes the human misery following on sin, he places ignorance in the first place, as the very source of such misery:

What else does this horrible depth of ignorance, whence comes every error, which receives all the sons of Adam into its dark bosom, denote if not that man cannot be freed by Him (by Christ) without labor, grief, and fear?[56]

It is also in Augustine that we find, for the first time, an express formulation of the affirmation that Christ had the Beatific [sic] Vision[57] throughout His life here below.[58] He systematically interprets Christ's ignorance as being the result of a choice not to reveal his knowledge.[59] St. Thomas will adopt this interpretation.[60]

Note that the same conception was formed, though later, in Greek Patristic authors. In the course of the controversy with the Agnoetae (in the sixth century) every sort of deficiency in Christ's knowledge came to be rejected, and the texts of the ancient Fathers were reinterpreted as meaning only an apparent ignorance: Christ took our physical infirmities on Himself but did not take on the ignorance which we experience. Such a doctrine was very firmly proposed by Maximus the Confessor in the seventh century and was approved in a lively manner by St. Gregory the Great in his letter to Eulogius[61] as corresponding exactly to the Latin tradition.

---

55. St. Augustine, *De peccatorum meritis et remissione*, PL 44, bk. 2, ch. 29, col. 180.

56. Augustine, *La Cité de Dieu*, Oeuvres de Saint Augustin (Paris: Desclée de Brouwer, 1959–60), bk. 17, ch. 22.

57. [Tr. note: See note 22, regarding the choice to distinguish between Fr. Nicolas's general language of "Vision" and "Beatific Vision."]

58. See Paul Galtier, "L'enseignement des Pères sur la vision béatifique dans le Christ," *Recherches des sciences religieuses* 15 (1925): 54–68.

59. See Augustine, *De diversis quaestionibus LXXXIII liber unus*, Oeuvres de St. Augustine 10, q. 60 and q. 65; 1, bk. 1, ch. 23.

60. See *ST* III, q. 10, a. 2, ad 1.

61. See PL 77, 1096–99.

In reality, this doctrine was not that of the ancient Fathers. Even before the Arian and Apollinarist controversies, St. Irenaeus interpreted the key text concerning the ignorance of the Day of Judgment[62] as being destined to give us an example of humility: "Therefore, if the Son did not blush in referring to the Father for knowledge of this day, and if He spoke the truth, we should no more blush at reserving the loftiest questions to God."[63] Indeed, he appeals to Christ's word: "The Father is greater than I."

In the fourth century, we encounter, on the one hand, Apollinarism, which disregards Christ's humanity, and, on the other hand, Arianism, which makes the Logos as such to be a creature. Arius abused the meaning of the words, "The Father is greater than I." In response to him, it was said that Christ did not know as man but that He knew as God. This ignorance as man was also an argument against the Apollinarists.

St. Athanasius, who was above all preoccupied with assuring the equality of the Son and the Father, fluctuates on this point, and he came to speak about an apparent ignorance. However, he was the person who uttered the principle pertaining to this subject: "Christ willed to take our infirmities on Himself so as to heal all of them."[64]

As regards Cyril, [following Bouyer, we can say,] "With greater hardiness than any other Father, he went so far as to admit a true ignorance in Christ and to make it into a touchstone concerning the reality of His incarnation in our flesh."[65] By following his inspiration in this matter, the author of *De Sectis* (which was once attributed to Leontius of Byzantium, though it was in fact written by an unknown author at the end of the [sixth] century) goes so far as to say about it: "Most of the Fathers admitted that Christ did not know certain things. Since He is altogether consubstantial with us and since we

---

62. See Mt 24:36; Mk 13:32.
63. Irenaeus of Lyon, *Adversus Haereses, libri quinquie, Libri I–II*, ed. U. Mannucci, in *Bibliotheca sanctorum Patrum et scriptorium ecclesiasticorum* (Rome: [Ex Officina Typographica Forzani et Socii, 1907]), bk. 2, 28:6–8.
64. See PG 9, 621–24.
65. Bouyer, *Le Fils éternel*, 406.

ourselves do not know certain things, it is clear that Christ Himself also had forms of ignorance. And Scripture says about this: 'He progressed in age and in wisdom.' This means that He learned what He did not know."[66]

Therefore, the idea that Christ was unaware of nothing during His earthly existence was not an idea held at first by believers. Rather, such a claim gradually emerged in Christian thought. On the one hand, Scripture certainly reports forms of ignorance attributed to Christ, and these texts were first taken in their obvious sense. Then, the difficulty of admitting true ignorance in Him who is the Word, the Wisdom of God, was encountered. This difficulty was aggravated by heretical interpretations of these texts, some drawing from them an argument for denying the equality of the Son and the Father. Thus, the general orientation turned toward an interpretation holding that it would be a question of only an apparent ignorance or toward a "mystical" interpretation (which is found already in Origen) holding that this pertains to Christ's body, the Church, and not to Christ Himself. With St. Augustine, the principle of the theory of omniscience was formulated: ignorance is not an infirmity like other infirmities; it is connected to sin and cannot be assumed, no more than the *fomes peccandi*[67] could be. Systematically developed, this principle leads to the medieval thesis holding that, during His earthly existence, Christ had knowledge of everything that a man can know, whether naturally or supernaturally.

c) The forms of ignorance experienced by Christ and the dignity of the Incarnate Word

{346} We can be certain that knowledge is part of the perfection proper to human nature. Therefore, a person who is deficient in the order of knowledge is deprived of an element of his personal perfection. To put it another way, the normal development of human

---

66. Cited by Bouyer in ibid.
67. [Tr. note: "The tinder for sin" (or, disordered concupiscence); this will be discussed at the end of this chapter.]

personality includes, as an essential element, progress in the order of knowledge.

However, this does not mean that every kind of ignorance is a diminution of personal dignity, nor, conversely, that personal dignity grows with every acquisition of knowledge [*savoir*]. While knowledge [*science*] is a human perfection, omniscience is not, as we have seen. The human person's real progress in the perfection of knowing necessarily includes choices and, therefore, forms of ignorance— both those which are imposed by the state of culture at a given moment, but also ones that are deliberate. Moreover, for the case of an ordinary man, we must add those forms of ignorance that are imposed by his human limitations.

If the Word became a human person, this means that He accepted the limits proper to the human person. Here again, we find an example of His "kenosis." What we can say is that these forms of ignorance do not come from His individual limitations. No man was superior to Him in the ability to learn.[68]

d) The forms of ignorance experienced by Christ and the requirements of his redemptive mission

{347} It is commonly said that, during His earthly life, Christ held under His gaze all the men of all times, in their individual situations. We can find this claim being made by Pius XII[69] and by Pius XI as well: "Now if, because of our sins which also were as yet in the future, but were foreseen, the soul of Christ became sorrowful unto death, it cannot be doubted that then, too, already He derived somewhat of solace from our reparation."[70] Note, however, that Pius XII speaks expressly about the science of vision, not about knowledge [*science*] of the human mode, and that Pius XI does not specify the knowledge [*science*] in question. Likewise, St. Thomas claims that the science of

---

68. See Karl Rahner, *Exégèse et dogmatique* (Paris: Desclée de Brouwer, 1967), 195.
69. See Pius XII, *Mystici corporis*, AAS 1943, 230. [Tr. note: see par. 75 of the encyclical.]
70. Pius XI, *Miserentissimus redemptor*, par. 13. [Tr. note: Taken from official Vatican translation.]

vision extends to all the events of salvation history.[71] With regard to knowledge [*science*] of the human mode, he only says that "through His acquired knowledge [*science*] He knew everything that can be known by the action of the agent intellect."[72]

The reason why St. Thomas claims that Jesus's knowledge [*science*] of vision extends to all the events of salvation history is drawn both from Christ's personal dignity and from His role as the universal judge. However, this role belongs to Him on account of His resurrection, and His redemptive mission itself in no way requires Him to have known men's sins in detail. He had perfect religious knowledge of man's sin and of the situation of man's sinfulness [*pécheur de l'homme*] before God. This was sufficient.

e) The forms of ignorance experienced by Christ and His perfect innocence

{348} St. Augustine's reason remains: ignorance would be part of the state of sin. However, if we see that, on the contrary, this is inherent to the human condition, we will thus know that this assertion is not universally true. The ignorance that is part of the state of sin is ignorance of God and of the image of God in man. Obviously, such ignorance must be excluded from Christ.

Likewise, we cannot find "error" in Christ. It is one thing not to know, whereas it is a completely different thing to know falsely, to misunderstand. Error is an evil. Of course, it is not always a moral evil. However, because it is an evil of the intellect, it is an evil affecting the person as such. It cannot be found in the Incarnate Word. (However, it is not precluded that He would have participated in the common and naturally inevitable errors of the men of His cultural milieu.)

---

71. See *ST* III, q. 10, a. 2.
72. See *ST* III, q. 12, a. 1.

B. Jesus's Supernatural, Human Knowledge While on Earth

{349} Earlier, we established that Jesus had in His human mind, through grace, knowledge of the mysteries that are accessible to man only by revelation.[73] However, knowledge through grace (or, supernatural knowledge) is bestowed upon men, in general, in two stages. The two successive phases of revelation correspond to these two stages. *Faith* corresponds to *imperfect revelation*, through human words, images, concepts, and propositions. It is an adherence to the revealed Divine Truth, which remains obscure for the believer's intellect. However, man holds it as being true on account of the authority of God who reveals. On the other hand, vision in the full light of God corresponds to *definitive revelation*, which occurs through the immediate union of the Divine Truth, which is the very essence of God, with the intellect of the beatified person. It is the culmination and endpoint of revelation, in which God gives Himself, in His personal reality, to the spiritual creature.

We are not questioning whether Jesus had the vision of the Divine Essence in His human soul after His resurrection and even from the moment of His death. However, do we need to think that, like other men, He first benefited from imperfect revelation and that He needed to "believe" without "seeing" during His earthly life? Does the realism of the Incarnation, which led us to extend the Incarnate Word's participation in the limitations of the human intellect very far when we studied His "natural knowledge" now lead us to equally acknowledge that He underwent limitations and imperfections in His supernatural knowledge, as takes place in other men?

The obstacle to affirming this is that, before being a human activity into which the human intellect necessarily introduces the limitations and imperfections proper to its nature, supernatural knowledge is a gift of God, a grace. And we were led to exclude the idea

---

73. See §333 above.

that the grace given to Christ would have been progressive.⁷⁴ Therefore, must we say that Jesus, already on earth, had immediate vision of the Divine Essence?

1. Did Christ have immediate vision of the Divine Essence while on Earth?

In a well-known decree (June 5, 1918), the Holy Office responded to a question: "One cannot teach with security (*tuto*) that Christ on earth did not have the knowledge of the blessed."⁷⁵ This response expressed the common teaching of theologians from the time of the Middle Ages onward. It is a teaching that is still held by many theologians of great renown, though it is no longer one that we could claim is universally admitted by theologians (nor, above all, by exegetes).

a) Scriptural and traditional arguments

{350} The two texts that are cited as teaching this are John 1:18 and Luke 10:22, as well as Matthew 11:27. Exegetes such as Lagrange, Boismard, and recently André Feuillet hold that the first text ("No one has ever seen God; the only Son, who is in the bosom of the Father, He has made Him known" [RSV]) seems to provide "strong support" (Lagrange) for the "theological thesis."⁷⁶

As for the second text, it shows in an arresting manner that the revealing power originates in a direct knowledge, a vision, and not in a revelation that would have been made to Him.⁷⁷ However, Scripture here also orients us in the same direction by its silences. Indeed, it is remarkable that there never is a question concerning Christ's faith. He is never presented to us as an example for this. He is the "pioneer and perfecter of our faith."⁷⁸ He is not Himself a believer:

---

74. See §339 above.
75. D.-*Sch.*, 3645–47. [Tr. note: Fr. Nicolas has altered the text to allow it to be readable outside of the terse question and answer format of dubia.]
76. See Feuillet, *Le prologue du IVᵉ évangile*, 126–36.
77. See Jean Mouroux, *Le mystère du temps* (Paris: Aubier, 1962), 112–13.
78. Heb 12:2 (RSV). [Tr. note: Fr. Nicolas apparently has wrongly cited Heb 2:10.]

In any case, it remains incontestable that the Johannine Christ is presented as being a direct witness of the divine world. He says that He has "seen" and "heard" nearby to the Father. And this knowledge [*science*] of Christ is the suspension point for the faith of all other men, including the eyewitnesses of His existence, who never "saw" nor ever "heard" in that manner. This is the reason why Christ is the only revealer whom humanity has ever known.[79]

As regards the Tradition, before St. Augustine we do not find a clear expression of this "theological thesis" that Christ had immediate vision of the Divine Essence here below. However, we likewise do not find the idea that He would have had faith. Moreover, we have seen the increasingly-marked opposition of the Fathers to the idea that the Incarnate Word would have been truly ignorant of something. It seems that for them there would have been a compenetration (which they neither explain nor thematize, but which they instead "felt," so to speak) between Jesus's human knowledge and His properly divine knowledge. In this general sense, we can see a kind of preparation for the theory that St. Augustine was the first to express. [As Trembelas writes:]

The Lord acquired this incomparable perfection (as supreme teacher and prophet) on account of the Hypostatic Union of His human nature with the Divine Nature of the Word, thanks to which He draws forth from His intimate depths, *saying what He has heard and bearing witness to what He has seen*, not only in His condition of eternal and beginningless preexistence with the Father and the Holy Spirit, but also during His earthly life when He preserved an uninterrupted communion with the Father, *as a Son of man being in heaven* and *judging as He had heard from the Father*.[80]

b) Theological arguments

{351} Can we establish with certitude, through theological reasoning, that Christ had the immediate vision of the Divine Essence while on earth? Obviously, on the basis of such reasoning, our cer-

---

79. Feuillet, *Le prologue du IVe évangile*, 132.
80. Pangiotis N. Trembelas, *Dogmatique de l'Église orthodoxe catholique* (Paris: Desclée de Brouwer, 1957), 3:171–72.

titude would not be that of faith but would, instead, be that which is proper to theological reasoning, a certitude completely depending upon the value of the reasoning offered on its behalf and upon its binding force.

The first argument. As we saw above, this first argument is drawn from the personal dignity of the Incarnate Word. A quite remarkable modern expression of it is found in Jean Mouroux.[81] Against this, an objection has been raised: "It is not in the nature of grace to imply the actual possession of glory. Rather, it leads to this possession in the hereafter."[82]

This objection places in question the fullness of grace given to Christ from the first instant of the Incarnation. Above, we saw the reason why we must acknowledge that Christ's grace was fully perfect from the start. This entails the thesis affirming the vision [of the Divine Essence during Christ's earthly life]. Indeed, this immediate vision is not a super-added gift. It is the supreme fructification of grace. Whoever has grace without vision is in progress toward the latter. Such a person is purely and simply in the state of being on the way, a *viator*.

In Jesus, human nature is progressive, just as it is for every man. We have seen that this necessarily implies that He had an acquired, progressive, and limited knowledge, which is the perfection proportioned to His intellect. However, in any man whatsoever, the Beatific Vision is not the terminus of such progression. It is in no way an "acquired" form of knowledge but, instead, is "given." There is merit in relation to this gift on the part of man. However, merit belongs to the order of progress in grace and not to the order of intellectual perfection. Because the former kind of progress must be excluded from Christ, the progressivity we must accord to Him in the intellectual order in no way enables us to situate the immediate vision of the Divine Essence at the terminus of His intellect's development. At whatever moment of such development that it would be given

---

81. Mouroux, *Le mystère du temps*, 111 and 111n21.
82. Galot, *La conscience de Jésus*, 143.

to Him, this vision would already be completely and totally "given."

In short, because grace is given to Jesus's soul at its ultimate degree of fructification from the first instant of the Incarnation (on account of the personality of the Word from whom it results), this grace includes the immediate vision of the Divine Essence. This is theologically certain. However, the theologian has the burden of interpreting this gift in function of all the data that comes to him concerning Jesus's human psychology—scriptural data and data coming from theological reflection concerning the requirements of human nature, of man's earthly condition, and of the redemptive mission.

The second argument. This argument is drawn from the redemptive mission:

What is in potency is led to act by that which is in act. [For example,] something through which other things are heated must itself be hot. Now, man is in potency to the knowledge [*science*] had by the blessed, which consists in the vision of God, and he is ordered to it as to his end. Indeed, the rational creature is capable of this blessed knowledge inasmuch as he is made in God's image. Now, men are led to this end, beatitude, by Christ's humanity ... Therefore, it was necessary that the blessed knowledge consisting in the vision of God be found in Christ in the supreme degree, for the cause must always be richer than what it causes.[83]

An objection can be registered against the seemingly too metaphysical character of this argument (i.e., "the passage from potency to act can happen only under the action of a being already in act"). More directly, the following objection has in fact been registered:

Is the Christ who communicates salvation and who gives the Beatific Vision Christ in His earthly condition? Is it not, rather, the glorious Christ, the resurrected Christ? Nobody can doubt that this glorious Christ possesses the Beatific Vision. However, evidence would need to be furnished as regards the life of Christ here below.[84]

To this, we must respond that Christ obtained the vision of the Divine Essence for men through the acts of His earthly life: first by re-

---

83. *ST* III, q. 9, a. 2.
84. Galot, *La conscience de Jésus*, 143.

vealing the mystery of God, then through His passion and sacrificial death, and finally through His resurrection.

If we place the argument within the purely theological perspectives of Christ's mediation, thus setting aside its overly metaphysical formulation, it presents a compelling case. He is the *mediator*, He who unites men to God, and the Beatific Vision is the summit and consummation of this union. We cannot admit that He, as a man, would have needed to be united to God. In such a case, He would have needed mediation, whereas He is, in fact, the first and unique mediator. We will see that it is difficult to see how the Word, inasmuch as He is Incarnate, can be the mediator between man and God, that is, the Trinity of whom He is a member). It would not make sense to say that He would, moreover, be a beneficiary of this mediation inasmuch as He is a man.

The third argument. This argument is a modern one drawn from the requirements of Christ's [self-]consciousness. Christ proclaimed that he is the "Son of God," and our faith rests upon this primordial affirmation. Therefore, He needed to be aware that He was the Son of God. However, how could He be aware of this without the vision of the Divine Essence, given that the Person of the Word can only be "experienced" by immediate vision?[85]

Conclusion. These arguments are convincing. We still must ask how this immediate vision was compatible with knowledge that was human in its mode.

2. *How should we understand that Christ was* simul viator et comprehensor *while on Earth?*

{352} To say that Christ had vision of the Divine Essence from the first instant of His human life means that He already was a *comprehensor* during His earthly life. That is, He was someone who had arrived at the ultimate terminus of His human destiny. However, the very idea of the Incarnation as a [divine] mission includes the

---

85. See §§361–63 below.

The Humanity of Jesus

idea that Jesus led a true earthly life, that He "lived among men" and walked among them.[86] Moreover, it is clear that the image of Christ presented to us by the Gospels is that of a man fully participating in the life of men, that is, as a *viator*. Moreover, the redemptive acts would be incomprehensible without this being the case, for suffering and death do not partake in the state of the *comprehensor* as such, any more than does sacrifice.

Redoubtable problems are posed by the simultaneous conjunction of two "states" in the same person, with each state appearing to exclude the other. First, there are problems from the perspective of "beatitude," which intrinsically includes the state of *comprehensor* and seems incompatible with suffering and death. We will examine this problem later on when we speak about Christ's vulnerability. Moreover, problems are posed from the perspective of the Man-Jesus's situation in relation to the ultimate end. How should we understand that He has attained this end (something entailed by the state of *comprehensor*) and simultaneously was on the way toward it (which is entailed by the state of *viator*)? Above,[87] we encountered the solution proposed by St. Thomas, a solution that I accepted. However, our present difficulty remains. How can we reconcile, simultaneously within the same person, the knowledge that is the immediate vision of the Divine Essence (a knowledge that is complete, clear, certain, and free from all error) with the partial and obscure knowledge of a *viator*, a knowledge which includes ignorance and, if not personal errors, at least some kind of participation in the collective errors of His era and cultural milieu?

St. Thomas strove to resolve this difficulty in two stages. (Moreover, he does not seem to have dwelled on it at length.) First, he thinks that the immediate, transcendent, and ecstatic vision "erupted" into a multitude of *species* (i.e., intelligible representations) in Christ's intellect. This is akin to his explanation of the knowledge had by the angels in heaven. Thanks to such *species*, they can direct-

---

86. See §227 above.
87. See §339 above.

ly know created natures in a representation that would be proportioned to them.[88] Next, he holds that Christ knew everything that can be naturally known by the human intellect (i.e., in an abstractive and discursive manner) and that this kind of knowledge [*science*] was abolished neither by His vision of the Divine Essence, nor by His infused knowledge [*science*], for one and the same thing can be known in different ways, by different "noetic means" (*media*).

However, we must admit that St. Thomas is a bit awkward when He explains the usefulness of this third form of knowledge [*science*], which only seems to bring the complete fulfillment of His human faculties, though not a necessary increase in knowledge:

> Human perfection required that knowledge be realized even in a form which includes a relation to phantasms (drawn from things). This does not mean that the first form of fullness discussed above (i.e., infused knowledge [*science, scientia*]) does not by itself suffice for the human mind. However, it was necessary that this mind also receive this particular perfection which the human intellect receives from its interaction with the phantasms.[89]

a) The vision of the Divine Essence was not a knowledge [immediately] directing His daily behavior

{353} Using the insights of Karl Rahner[90] and Jacques Maritain (which are quite different, though they converge upon this point),[91] we must orient ourselves toward the idea that immediate vision of the Divine Essence is an absolutely transcendent knowledge that wrenches to itself the person who looks upon it, rendering him incapable of considering creatures in themselves and for themselves. Certainly, he knows them, but does so *in Verbo*, without being able to pull his attention away from the Word in whom he knows the Trinity, as well as all things as in their cause. Therefore, he is incapable of being interested in them for their own sake and, thus, is also incapable

---

88. See *ST* I, q. 58, aa. 6–7; III, q. 9, a. 4.
89. *ST* III, q. 9, a. 4, ad 2.
90. Rahner, "Considérations dogmatiques sur la psychologie du Christ," 199–204.
91. Maritain, *De la grâce et de l'humanité de Jésus*, 49–64.

of acting upon them (and, moreover, with them). St. Thomas likewise orients us in this direction when he justifies the fact that the angels in heaven require an infusion of *species* (or, intelligible representations) from God. By means of such *species*, the angel is, so to speak, freed from this paralyzing ecstasy, thereby being placed in relation to them and thus able to know them in themselves, in a manner conformed to his own nature. We could say that the immediate vision of the Divine Essence is a knowledge proportioned to God alone[92] and that He alone can act on creatures in the universe (by creating it, governing it, divinizing the personal creature, etc.) under the guidance of this knowledge (which, obviously, is neither transcendent nor ecstatic for Him). The creature to whom it is granted by grace cannot act in this way, and this is why the knowledge that is connatural to that creature not only is not something superfluous for him but is, indeed, utterly necessary.

However, we discover that it is impossible to follow St. Thomas here when he believes that we must hold that, during His earthly life, Christ had this kind of knowledge, like that had by the angels, through infused intelligible representations. We cannot follow him here because this kind of knowledge does not belong to a human intellect, at least when it is united with the body. The reason that St. Thomas proposes—namely, that because Christ's intellect is in potency to all intelligibles, it must be fully actuated from the first moment [of the Incarnation]—is quite difficult to admit. First of all, Christ had a human intellect, and it is connatural for the human intellect to pass, slowly and laboriously, from potency to act.[93] Moreover, the constitution of the human intellect is such that it can know only by abstraction and returning to the phantasms. Therefore, it cannot know by means of the intelligible representations which would come from on high without phantasms and without a connection to reality by the intermediary of perception.

Therefore, we must say that natural human knowledge, acquired

---

92. See *ST* III, q. 9, a. 4.
93. See §343 above.

on the basis of perception and internal images, was not incompatible with the knowledge [*science*] of vision, for it responded to a cognitional need and covered a field of knowledge that escaped His vision of the Divine Essence, on account of the latter's transcendence and perfection, not on account of its imperfection.

On the other hand, it could seem impossible that a man, living among men and acting in communion with them by means of his natural human knowledge, could simultaneously see the Divine Essence. Indeed, without any doubt, this remains a profound mystery. By noting that there is no "opposition" between the vision of the Divine Essence and knowledge through "infused intelligible representations" (and therefore that their conjunction in the Man-Jesus is not impossible), St. Thomas gives us the key to this difficulty, for this observation applies just as much to natural human knowledge [*science*], the only one that we hold that Jesus had at the same time as the vision of the Divine Essence. By saying that they are not *opposed* to each other, we therefore also mean that *it is not impossible* for the two of them to be realized together in one and the same subject. Here again, we cannot directly prove that it is possible. Therefore, one first must be convinced by all the reasons that we gave on behalf of the claim that Jesus, on earth, had the vision of the Divine Essence and, therefore, that it is possible for this transcendent knowledge to coexist with natural human knowledge, along with natural behavior in relation to things, men, and events. But the person who does not accept these arguments is charged with resolving the immense problems posed by the idea that Jesus progressed toward God in the obscurity of faith while Himself being God and, as man, the revealer.

b) The problem of immediate vision alongside ignorance

{354} By fully pressing onward to the ultimate consequences of this transcendence of the Man-Jesus's immediate knowledge by the vision of the Divine Essence over all His human conduct (which includes His speech, as well as the formation of images, "affects," and concepts at the foundation of this speech), we can understand and acknowledge that the real forms of ignorance that we believe we must admit, as regards His natural knowledge, are compatible with the omniscience which is an obvious property of His vision of the Divine Essence. Without some kind of artifice, how can the same man not know what He knows and know what He does not know? Every example that could be drawn from the life of an ordinary man is obviously inadequate and paltry, for the ordinary man only has one way of knowing everything he knows: the human way, through abstraction and reasoning. If we acknowledge that Christ's natural, "experiential" knowledge could not express His immediate vision of the Divine Essence during His earthly life (a vision which, according to an expression drawn from Maritain, remains in "the heaven of his soul" without "passing" into His earthly conduct), we can admit that such conduct remains really marked by the limitations and imperfections inherent to the natural knowledge that rules it and that it expresses. Therefore, it likewise remains marked by [forms of] ignorance, as well as by inquiries and hesitations.

To express this non-communication between the two forms of knowledge, Jacques Maritain spoke of a "partition." This image seems unsatisfactory to me, for it evokes the idea of an express intervention by God, preventing a communication that would have been "natural." Admittedly, St. Thomas orients us in this same direction by his own language, which refers to the "Divine Will, which retained beatitude within the soul, thus preventing it from flowing over onto the body" and sense powers. This was how he explained the fact that the "beatitude" of the "superior part of the soul" (which is equivalent to the expression "heaven of the soul" used by Maritain) did not prevent suffering and agony from being felt (indeed, in his body and the sensibility, though, moreover, even in the inferior part of his spiritual soul).[94] However, note that Christ would in no way have been a *viator* if this "overflow" onto the superior powers had existed in Him. Indeed, He would not have partaken in human life, and the Incarna-

---

94. See *ST* III, q. 14, a. 1, ad 2.

tion would have been meaningless.[95] The same must be said concerning the communication between the knowledge of vision and His natural knowledge. The latter would have been rendered impossible by such a communication, for it would have become radically useless and meaningless.

If we presuppose the Incarnation such as it was realized—that is, as a real partaking in the earthly life of men by the Word become man (in order to, at a later stage, make them partake in His life as the Son in heaven)—it "naturally" follows that there was a non-communication between Christ's knowledge of vision and His natural knowledge, without requiring us, however, to appeal to a new and particular intervention by the Divine Power. This is part of the mystery of the conjunction of the state of *comprehensor* and of *viator* in the Man-Jesus. It is not a new mystery.

c) The synergy of two forms of knowledge
Communication between the two forms of knowledge [sciences]

{355} However, this non-communication could not be total. This is so for two reasons. *The first reason* comes from the very meaning of the Incarnation. As we have seen, Christ is the revealer in an utterly fundamental way [*essentiellement*]. Immediate vision, which quasi-necessarily was befitting to His dignity as Son of God, was "given" to Him inasmuch as He is a man. If He became a man, this was "for us men and for our salvation."[96] Thus, if immediate vision of the Divine Essence is found in Christ from the first moment [of the Incarnation] precisely because of who He is, it also (and simultaneously) has a meaning for man. This meaning is expressed by the evangelist John thus: "No one has ever seen God; the only Son, who is in the bosom of the Father, he has made him known."[97] He is the revealer because the transcendent and inexpressible Divine Truth, which He attains in its transcendence by immediate vision of the Divine Es-

---

95. See §355 below.
96. This will be developed and explained below in §§425–30.
97. Jn 1:18 (RSV); see also Mt 11:25–27 and Lk 10:22.

sence, is refracted in His intellect and sensibility, as well as in a human language (made up of concepts, images, and words). By means of this language, He communicates this truth to men.

Let us add the following *confirmatur.* Only the testimony of Scripture can tell us with certainty that Christ had this vision on earth. Now, it is quite clear that the apostles knew what they knew about the Incarnate Word through His earthly conduct, which, of course, was interpreted under the light of the Holy Spirit acting in them through the charism of inspiration. In order for Him to be able to reveal, even in a veiled manner, that Jesus had the vision of God, some aspect of this vision, therefore, needed to pass into His conduct.

The second reason why this non-communication could not be total is drawn from [philosophical and theological] anthropology. We can neither understand nor admit the notion that two forms of knowledge would exist in one and the same intellect, in one and the same mind, without there being any communication between them. The non-communication spoken of above is concerned with the objects of these two forms of knowledge. In short, Christ's knowledge of an object had by means of one of these forms of knowledge, according to its proper mode, did not enable Him to know this object by means of the other form of knowledge (according to the latter's own proper mode). However, knowledge is an act of the intellect. The same faculty, the same mind, elicited two kinds of acts of knowledge, and this established a subjective kind of communication between them, not an objective one.

Subjective communication

{356} St. Thomas profoundly analyzed this type of communication within one and the same faculty (or between many faculties) in one and the same person (i.e., in one and the same "subject"), above all in the domain of affectivity.[98] As regards intellectual activity, we can find at least the beginning of such an analysis in the notion that

---

98. See *ST* I-II, q. 77, a. 1; *De ver.*, q. 22, a. 9, ad 6; cf. also *ST* I-II, q. 9, a. 2, and q. 10, a. 3.

wisdom directs inferior intellectual acts from on high.[99] In what concerns our present problem, along these same lines, we also find the interpretation that he provides, as regards Christ, concerning the coexistence of the vision of the Divine Essence alongside knowledge through infused *species* in the minds of the blessed. This latter knowledge, which would be a kind of "remote disposition" to the vision of the Divine Essence, becomes an effect of the vision when the latter is given and flows from it: "And similarly, infused knowledge remains in Christ at the same time as beatific knowledge [*science*], not as a way leading to beatitude but, rather, as being in some way strengthened (*confirmata*) by beatitude."[100]

Confirmata indicates an influence, though subjective, related to the strength of the mind's adherence to the truth, its strength of judgment. And this can lead us to a conception that St. Thomas took from Dionysius the Areopagite, though interpreting the idea in his own original way: the illumination of a superior angel can communicate [knowledge] to an inferior angel not (only) by augmenting the knowledge that the latter has, but [also] by making it know better what it knows by means of its own representations, "by strengthening its intellective energy."[101]

Indeed, intellective energy, *virtus intelligendi*, is expressed by the metaphor of light, for to know is not to act upon the known thing so as to modify it. Rather, it is to be the other according to form (not through a material identification but operatively and through a kind of spiritual transparency). What is lacking in the light is also lacking for the power of the [intellect's] adherence. (In the case of faith, this is completed by the will to believe, though the overall gift of faith is called the *lumen gratiae* or *lumen gratuitum* because this gift enables man to know truths that he did not know without it, even though he knows them obscurely.)[102] When we speak about a superior [act of]

---

99. *Sententia super Metaphysicam*, prologue; *ST* I-II, q. 57, a. 2, co. and ad 2.
100. *ST* III, q. 9, a. 3, ad 2.
101. *ST* I, q. 106, a. 1.
102. See *ST* I, q. 106, a. 13.

knowledge strengthening [*confortant*] an inferior one, we are speaking about illumination. This is true whether this superior knowledge arises from another intellect (as in the case of one angel illuminating another or in the case of God illuminating the created mind by means of the *lumen gratiae*) or from the same intellect (as in the case of the knowledge of vision "strengthening" [*affermissant*] Christ's natural knowledge while He existed on earth). Through such an illumination, the inferior knowledge is not enriched as regards the object known but, rather, as regards the strength of [the knower's] adherence and as regards the continuity between the inferior truths known by the inferior knowledge [*science*] and the transcendent truth (in which the inferior truths only distantly participate, for the truth is one). As already noted, we believe that we must rule out the idea that such inferior knowledge [*science*], thus illuminated, existed in Christ as knowledge through "infused representations," akin to that which is had by the angels. Nonetheless, we still can retain St. Thomas's insights concerning the derivation of inferior knowledge from Christ's knowledge of vision, applying these insights to Jesus's "natural" (i.e., abstractive and discursive) knowledge as a man. In short, we can say that His human knowledge was not derived from His vision of the Divine Essence but, instead, was illuminated from within His intellect by this vision, thus being placed in continuity with it. Such continuity was subjective and dynamic in character, not objective.

In this way, we can incorporate the insights of Karl Rahner and Jacques Maritain into a mutually-complementary synthesis. For Rahner, Jesus's immediate vision is "the primal, unobjectified consciousness of being Son of God, which is simply there as soon as the Hypostatic Union takes place." In order to "describe it in an approximate manner without distorting it," he compares it to "the subjective basic condition of the human spirit in general," in virtue of which

<blockquote>this act of attending not to himself but to external objects is still inspired by this knowledge of himself, inarticulate, non-reflective, perhaps never reflected upon at all. It is a simple "self-possession" which is not reflected</blockquote>

in clear consciousness and not translated into terms of objects, but which even when looking away from itself is still present to itself, precisely in the manner of this seemingly colourless basic condition of a spiritual being and of the horizon within which all traffic with everyday objects and concepts takes place.

Thus, in Jesus, the immediate vision

is therefore not to be regarded as being the vision of an object. Thus, the ontic and ontological thoroughness and completeness of this immediacy is in no way affected. This immediacy is precisely what we mean when speaking of the *visio immediata*, except that any idea of an object presented to it must be avoided, such as we are accustomed to think of in our usual model for representing a vision.[103]

We cannot purely and simply say that Jesus's vision of the Divine Essence was not an objective face-to-face [vision], for that is quite precisely what vision of the Divine Essence is. However, we can (and must) say this in relation to Christ's natural knowledge (i.e., the knowledge acquired by way of abstraction and reasoning), which obviously does not attain the Divine Essence directly and immediately but, rather, unfurls itself against a background of light whose hidden source was the vision. Jacques Maritain situates this vision in what he calls the "supra-consciousness," the background spiritual domain from which all of the mind's intuitions proceed. This vision can only be concretized and objectified by means of Christ's constructed and conscious knowledge. In the two cases, the continuity between vision and natural knowledge is assured by a subjective communication, not an objective one.

In virtue of this illumination, Christ knew the mysteries of grace by means of His knowledge of the human type. On this point, one could compare the illumination we have spoken about to the illumination involved in prophecy. The latter involves forms of knowledge

---

103. [Tr. note: These quotes are not cited here Fr. Nicolas's original. They are taken from Rahner, "Knowledge and Consciousness in Christ," 256–58. The second, brief quotation is taken from Fr. Nicolas's text, as a correlative is not readily discernable in the official English translation of Rahner's text.]

that are naturally acquired by the prophet, but by illuminating them with a supernatural light, God uses them so as to enable the prophet to know the mysteries of grace.[104]

This explains what is meant when we say that Jesus did not have faith. By His natural knowledge, He did not immediately attain the mystery of God but, rather, did so by a kind of detour through creatures. Nonetheless, the light by which He attained the mystery of God through this detour was neither the "light of faith," nor the light of prophecy. Instead, it was the overflowing light of His vision of the Divine Essence (a vision that was His own, thus setting Him apart from mere prophets),[105] illuminating His natural representations and placing them in continuity with it.

This leaves room for Him to have acquired knowledge of the revealed doctrine by the natural means of teaching and reading, or even by representations aroused in his mind by God. Jesus read the Bible and truly (humanly) learned from it what He himself taught in it (through His divinity). Indeed, before reading the Bible, he heard it read and interpreted, perhaps first by his mother. According to a suggestive expression of Jean Mouroux, we might say that "He learned God."

This also leaves room for a superior equivalent to the "infused contemplation" experienced by mystics here below, through an intimate experience of the Divine Reality and of the Divine Persons by the created mind [*esprit*], though under the inspiration of the Holy Spirit. It is an experience that, for the mere man, is realized in faith (and, therefore, in obscurity). As regards Christ, although it belonged to the sphere of His "natural" knowledge (in the sense of "natural" meaning the human intellect's connatural mode of know-

---

104. See *ST* II-II, q. 173, a. 2. We must, however, note that St. Thomas admits that prophetic knowledge can also include *species* miraculously formed by God in the prophet's mind, imagination, or senses. In any case, he thinks that the essential characteristic of prophetic knowledge is the judgment by which, under the light of prophecy, the prophet reaches the mysteries of grace that God wishes to make known to him, doing so through the things thus represented (whether miraculously or naturally).

105. See ibid., a. 1.

ing), it was experienced in this light proceeding from His vision of the Divine Essence.

This continuity, in the depths of Jesus's created mind, between the natural, humanly acquired and humanly exercised knowledge, on the one hand, and the knowledge of vision, on the other, has been extended to all believers by the act of revelation and is prolonged in them by the "light of faith." This is how Jesus is the revealer, the teacher of all humanity regarding the things of salvation. His "natural" knowledge of the mysteries of grace is prophetic for others, not for Himself.[106]

C. Jesus's Human Self-Consciousness

{357} The term "[self-]consciousness" is used to express the idea of the experiential knowledge one has of oneself. Modern philosophy, in its most certain acquisitions, has emphasized that [self-]consciousness is one of the characteristics of persons, indeed the most fundamental one. We cannot hold that personality is identical with [self-]consciousness. (Indeed, such an assertion is hardly intelligible.) However, we can be certain that what primordially distinguishes persons from mere supposits is [self-]consciousness, the power of knowing oneself (even if this power is still virtual during a period of one's existence, as happens for every human being, or even throughout the entire earthly existence of those who suffer from profound mental debility).

Moreover, the ancients were not unaware of this. Indeed, they were the ones who had perceived and emphasized the close and indissoluble bond between "personality" and "spirituality." Likewise, they were the ones who characterized the spiritual faculty as having the capacity of the *perfecta reditio ad seipsam*, the power to take hold of itself and to take hold of the knowing subject as an object of its activity. If this is how matters stand and if Jesus Christ was a Divine Person subsisting in an individuated human nature—a "human person," according to the terminology that I proposed above—we must acknowledge that He had a human [self-]consciousness. That is, His

---

106. See *ST* III, q. 7, a. 8.

human intellect was capable of a *perfecta reditio ad seipsam*, and, indeed, achieved it, knowing itself, knowing the spiritual soul that acted by it, knowing the person who was the man constituted by this soul united to the body that it informed.

However, in what concerns Christ, there is a specific problem that has been posed in recent days. It is an extremely difficult question: how could He be humanly aware of His divine self? This refers to a human act, that is, an act elicited by the human nature and its faculties. However, it is an act that is intentionally divine (i.e., an act whose object is the very person of the Word).

Traditionally,[107] "reflex consciousness" is distinguished from "direct consciousness." The latter is the self-perception that accompanies every psychic phenomenon. (It is more often called "spontaneous consciousness.")[108] The former is express knowledge of the "subject" in his opposition to the "object." It is obtained through a "reflection" by the knowing subject on his acts and states [of mind] so that he may extract the self-knowledge that is implied in it and place it in the foreground.[109] Let us add that self-consciousness, whether spontaneous or reflective, entails and integrates into itself love of self, which itself can also be spontaneous or reflective.[110]

1. The human consciousness of the divine self in Jesus

a) The theory of a "psychological self"

{358} In[111] short, this theory involves the idea of attributing to Christ not only a human consciousness (something that is absolute-

---

107. See C[arlo] Molari, "Aspetti metafisici et funzionali della conscienza umana di Cristo," *Divinitas* 4 (1960): 265.
108. See André Lalande, *Vocabulaire technique et critique de la philosophie*, 7th ed. (Paris: P.U.F., 1956), 173–75.
109. See *De ver.*, q. 10, a. 8; *ST* I, q. 87, a. 1.
110. See Jean-Hervé Nicolas, "Amour de soi, amour de Dieu, amour des autres," *Revue thomiste* 56 (1956): 5–42. On this question of human self-consciousness in Christ, I defer to Galot, *La conscience de Jésus*. This work presents a precise and detailed analysis of the indispensable biblical data, a critical exposition of the principal positions, and the personal taking of a position. Among the studies that he cites, see especially Hermann Diepen, "La psychologie humaine du Christ," *Revue Thomiste* 50 (1950): 515–62, and Galtier, *L'Unité du Christ*.
111. See Galot, *La conscience de Jésus*; Galtier, *L'unité du Christ*; Galtier, "La conscience

ly required) but a human "self" [*moi*], constituted by the human nature without itself being a person. This "self" would belong to the Person of the Word (similar to how we can speak of a plurality of "selves" regarding the same person: *I* compel *myself* to do this or that, etc.). The object of Jesus's human consciousness would have been this human "self," the center of His human psychological life. Moreover, Jesus would have known (through His vision of the Divine Essence, according to Galtier) that this human "self," whom He thus would have been aware of, was related, in reality, to the Word. That is, He would have known that it was the "self" of the eternal Son of God. This would mean that His [self-]consciousness was filial.

Galot quite rightly criticizes this theory by insisting on the fact that what consciousness attains is the person. The "self" can be distinguished from the "I" only because the "self" is the "I" inasmuch as it is engaged in a state of particular [self-]consciousness. The "self" partially reflects the "I," but still, it is itself that it reflects. The person is not only a "metaphysical" reality. He is the concrete human being. The person is he who lives, feels, knows, etc. In short, he is the "psychological self."

b) Theories situating Jesus's human [self-]consciousness at the very point where the Hypostatic Union is established

{359} This is how Galot translates Karl Rahner's and Jean Mouroux's theories (to which we could add those of Jacques Maritain). As we have seen, Rahner held that Jesus's vision of the Divine Essence assured this non-objectified experience of the self, which accompanies all of our acts and all of our acts of knowledge. By means of this experience, in everything that Jesus did or felt, He had the habitual sense of being the Son of God. However, this feeling could be objectified only by being thematized in particular acts of knowledge, acquired through experience and reflection on experience. For Mari-

---

humaine du Christ: A propos de quelques publications récentes," *Gregorianum* 32 (1951): 525–68; Galtier, "La conscience humaine du Christ," *Gregorianum* 35 (1954): 335–46; Diepen, "La psychologie humaine du Christ."

tain, the vision of the Divine Essence is indeed an objective knowledge that Jesus had of the Word and of being the Word. Moreover, through an interior illumination of His "natural" knowledge (into which Maritain introduces, following St. Thomas, knowledge [*science*] of the angelic type, through infused "representations") this knowledge makes it be the case that "knowledge of His own divinity emerged in Jesus from His intellect's first act." According to Jean Mouroux, Christ's self-consciousness as the Son of God is situated at the summit of His soul. There, this soul escapes from the existential condition of other men: "It emerges all at once beyond the merely human condition, beyond the shadows of the unconsciousness, into the light of God."[112]

Galot objects to these explanations, saying that consciousness must be attributed to the Person of the Word engaged in human existence, not to Jesus's soul, which, at its summit, would participate in some way in the divine condition. Moreover, his criticism of the positions of Rahner and Mouroux is very rapid and somewhat superficial. Above all, he admits neither that the immediate vision of the Divine Essence could resolve the problem of Jesus's human self-consciousness, nor even the fact of this vision.

c) Galot's own position

{360} The structure of Christ's act of consciousness does not require any other extraordinary element than the Hypostatic Union itself. In virtue of the hypostatic unity [*sic*], the person of the Son assumes a human nature and performs human activities. Among these activities, there is self-awareness, which moreover is inherent or underlies all of His activity of knowing and willing.

He appeals to the elevation of human nature and not to the Beatific [*sic*] Vision, which he says is wholly different from [self-]consciousness and therefore would not resolve the problem. This elevation of human nature is "implied in the Hypostatic Union ... and [it] results from the fact that His human activity is performed by the di-

---

112. See Mouroux, *Le mystère du temps*, 111.

vine person. This means that Jesus became aware of His divine self as spontaneously and easily as any man becomes aware of himself."[113] If we wonder how His Divine Person can be reached by a simple human act, we should note that [self-]consciousness in general only attains the self as engaged in determinate psychic states, colored by them and characterized by them: "Therefore, it is not a question of grasping a self in a pure state, such as He reveals Himself to Himself in the divine nature."[114] Nonetheless, the divine self is indeed what is thus characterized and attained by [self-]consciousness.

It seems that the essential point of this solution is that, on account of the Hypostatic Union, His human nature itself received an ontological increase in the dynamic order:

> We touch here upon the mystery of the hypostatic unity [sic]. The Incarnation is nothing other than the crossing, by the person of the Word, of the distance that separates God from man. Therefore, the disproportion has been bridged. It seems that one should say that the Incarnation entailed, for the assumed human nature, a supernatural ontological elevation that extends its activity to the divine "self" of the Word. This elevation enables the human activity of [self-]consciousness to be set in motion by a divine "I" and to perceive reflexively the divine "self".[115]

Critique. This position rests on an outlook (which we will see is wholly untenable) holding that the Person of the Word would exercise an action on the [assumed] human nature. The ontological superelevation imagined here would consist in the adaptation of [the assumed] human nature to such a motion. This motion, as well as this disposition, must be rejected.

Despite Galot's warning against the monophysite temptation of imagining a penetration of human nature by the Divine Nature, it is impossible to not detect this grave theological fault in the notion of an ontological elevation of [the assumed] human nature solely on account of the Hypostatic Union. In reality, the problem remains com-

---

113. Galot, *La conscience de Jésus*, 179.
114. Ibid., 121.
115. Ibid., 177.

pletely open. Galot believes that he resolves the problem posed by the disproportion between Jesus's human consciousness and its object, the Word, by appealing to the Word as the principle of this act of consciousness: "If we keep in mind that the Word is involved from the start of the act of consciousness, we will be less astonished to find Him at the end." In reality, as we saw above,[116] if the human nature's belonging to the Word renders its reception of the gifts of grace and divinization morally necessary (so that the Word in His humanity, inasmuch as he is man, would not be a stranger to the mystery of the Divine Life), it does not replace this grace and does not render this nature capable of knowing, by itself, God in His mystery and of loving Him in His Persons, without a super-elevation of His soul and faculties.

However, could we correct Galot's position and simply appeal to this grace? Galot himself goes down this path by studying the possibility of a "mystical intuition" in Christ's soul, enabling Him to attain the mystery of His person. This solution is seductive, and one undoubtedly must have recourse to it if one has decided to set aside any appeal to immediate vision of the Divine Essence. However, this is a deceptive solution, for the consciousness that the mystic has of God (and of himself in his relationship with God) is obscure and intermittent. Can it fulfill the conditions required by Christ's "self-consciousness," such as it is expressed with power, clarity, and unshakeable firmness in the words by which He reveals His divinity? It cannot, unless we were speaking of Jesus's "superior mystical experience," which we accepted above. However, this presupposes the immediate vision of the Divine Essence and does not replace it!

d) Avenues for arriving at a solution

Immediate vision and self-consciousness

{361} If man's [self-]knowledge is obscure and non-objective in nature,[117] this is because the direct object of human intellectu-

---

116. See §333 above.
117. That is, without noetic content, only the existence of the "self" being grasped in an experience that is profound and sometimes very lively, though obscure.

al knowledge is the being of things given to experience, not the "self." Spontaneous [self-]consciousness only accompanies the act of knowledge of an object. To know himself reflectively, a man must detach himself from the object that he knows so that he may fix his attention on the knowing subject. However, the latter does not become the object of a new act of knowledge. Rather, it is a question of a pure experience that the knowing subject has of himself on the occasion of knowledge of an object. According to the results of St. Thomas's very detailed analysis,[118] it is an experience of the subject's *an sit*, its existence, not its *quid sit*, what it is.

This is not the case for the self-knowledge experienced by a purely spiritual being such as an angel. The angels do not know themselves by means of reflex knowledge (i.e., on the occasion of knowledge of another object). Instead, the angel is his own primordial object of knowledge. He knows himself through a pure self-transparency, through a knowledge that is in no way abstractive, but on the contrary, is perfectly concrete. That is, it is a knowledge in which the *quid est* is attained with the *an est*, the essential with the existential.

For all the more reason is this true in the case of God, who is the sole object of His own knowledge. The act of immediate vision of the Divine Essence elicited by the Man-Jesus (i.e., by His human soul, by His human intellect) attains the Trinity, the Word *as an object*. However, for what pertains to the Word, it attains the Word as the same subject who sees, for this man who sees is the Word. How could this not be an act of knowledge in which the subject knows Himself as the subject, while nonetheless being a wholly-objective [*objectuelle*] and wholly-luminous act of knowledge?

For all that, this does not entirely resolve the problem that is posed by the disproportion between Jesus's human act of [self-]consciousness and its object, the divine self. Certainly, grace and the light of glory enable Jesus's created mind to cross the distance that separates it from His uncreated self. However, as we have seen,

---

118. See *De ver.*, q. 10, a. 8.

in Christ during his time living on earth, the knowledge of vision did not belong to His human mode of knowledge. Now, the [self-]consciousness that we seek to explain is the self-consciousness that Christ had as a man living among men, speaking to them about Himself and about His Father.

"Acquired" or "elaborated" self-consciousness could not, by itself, reach Christ's "self"

{362} In speaking about Jesus's "acquired" or "elaborated" consciousness (still here considered during His earthly life), I am referring to the self-consciousness that He formed in Himself, as happens in other men, on the basis of experience. As was said above, such knowledge is either spontaneous or reflex.

Against Galtier (and with Galot), we have rejected the idea that this knowledge could have as its object a purely psychological "self" which would be the "human nature." Against Galot, we have rejected the idea that Christ could be aware of his unique "self," the divine "self," by means of a "natural" act. We have judged that knowledge through faith would be insufficient for assuring this self-awareness, even were it to include in itself the loftiest mystical knowledge that one may have in faith. (Here, let us note another reason for this, namely, the fact that mystical knowledge is "negative" in its very structure. By contrast, self-knowledge is affirmative, even when is obscure.)

It follows that, without immediate knowledge [of the Divine Essence], self-consciousness would be impossible for Christ while He lived on earth. Despite the criticism that Galot registers against me,[119] I take up here what I wrote in 1953:[120] "We must say that if it did not have the Beatific [sic] Vision, Christ's soul would have been aware of a mystery. His consciousness would not be enclosed in a human 'self,' which, in fact, does not exist and, in any case, would be powerless to attain His 'self,' which is divine." This point constitutes one of the theological arguments in favor of Christ being accorded

---

119. See Galot, *La conscience de Jésus*, 135.
120. Jean-Hervé Nicolas, "Chronique de théologie dogmatique," *Revue thomiste* 53 (1953): 423–24.

the immediate vision of the Divine Essence in His humanity from the time of His earthly life.

The Man-Jesus's integral self-consciousness

{363} From what we have said, it follows that the problem of the self-consciousness that Jesus humanly had can be sufficiently resolved neither by His vision of the Divine Essence alone, nor by His elaborated [self-]consciousness. His vision of the Divine Essence is useless on the level of His earthly life, not only for Him to be able to express to other men what He is but even for Him to be able to express it to Himself. Likewise, by itself, His elaborated consciousness is powerless to attain Jesus's "self." Thus, neither of these suffice for us to be able to respond to the question, "How did He know that he was the Son of God?" Instead, what we could call "the Man-Jesus's integral self-consciousness" is constituted by the conjunction and lived synthesis of both forms of knowledge.

Above, we tried to explain, in a general way, this "conjunction" of vision-knowledge and knowledge in a human mode. As regards His [self-]consciousness, the light coming from the vision of the Divine Essence is projected onto His elaborated [self-]consciousness (to the degree that it was formulated). Thus, from the awakening of His elaborated [self-]consciousness, Jesus knew Himself, on account of the vision, to be the Son of God. The vision of the Divine Essence was able to exist for a time (e.g., during the time of His infancy) without His elaborated self-consciousness. At this time, He lacked what I have called His "integral human self-consciousness." However, His elaborated [self-]consciousness never lacked this illumination by the vision of the Divine Essence, without which, as we saw above, such elaborated knowledge would be impossible.

Thus, I reject the criticism that Galot registers against me: "Moreover, even the first act of consciousness that this theory proposes remains difficult to understand."[121] A "first act of [self-]consciousness,"

---

121. Galot, *La conscience de Jésus*, 136.

The Humanity of Jesus

which would then be completed by the vision of the Divine Essence, does not exist. Rather, there is a first act of consciousness bathed in the light of His vision of the Divine Essence, receiving from this light the fact that it is an achieved act of [self-]consciousness.

2. *The progress of Jesus's human self-consciousness*

This manner of conceiving and explaining Jesus's human self-consciousness enables us to fully accept and integrate the insights of modern Christology concerning progressivity in Christ's [self-]consciousness into a frankly Chalcedonian Christology, without falling into incoherence.[122] Indeed, if Christ's self-consciousness has "humanly elaborated consciousness" (which by its nature is progressive) as one of its components, His integral consciousness will also be progressive along with it.

a) The years of Jesus's unconsciousness

{364} With Galot, Jacques Maritain, and many others,[123] we must not hesitate to speak of the awakening of self-consciousness in Jesus. Such an awakening implies that the Word made flesh experienced the night of childhood during His first years. This is part of the kenotic truth of the Incarnation. This mysterious night was not illuminated by the transcendent light of the vision illuminating the "heaven" of His soul. (Note the difference here, however, from Galot, who does not admit this vision of the Divine Essence.) However, His awakening of [self-]consciousness does not include any progress in grace itself, which is at its summit of realization (as is this vision) from the start. Instead, this awakening only involves disposing the psychological instruments necessary for the exercise of this grace.[124]

His awakening of [self-]consciousness was itself progressive, as it is for every man. However, we must hold that, from its first dawn-

---

122. Galot, *Vers une nouvelle christologie*, 107ff.
123. See Galot, *La conscience de Jésus*, 103ff., and Maritain, *De la grâce et de l'humanité de Jésus*, 119ff.
124. See §339 above.

ing, it was a self-consciousness of being the Word and at the same time of being a man. This is necessary, as Maritain writes, "because it is entirely unthinkable that the fact of *being God* would have one day erupted in the consciousness of an adolescent who up to this moment would have been aware of himself without being aware of such a fact, while, on the other hand, he would have already formed for himself the idea of God."[125] However, even more, it is necessary simply because this adolescent absolutely would not have been self-conscious if He was not aware that He was the Word. This does not prevent us from speaking of a child's self-consciousness, for we can say that the elaborated [self-]consciousness which was an integral part of this self-consciousness for a time had this character.

b) The progressive awareness of His mission

Exegetes invite theologians[126] to go so far as to admit the fact of progress in Jesus's awareness about how He must accomplish His mission, that is, by sacrificing His life. Can the theologian follow this invitation? Jacques Maritain was vigorously opposed to this idea.[127] Indeed, it seems difficult to believe that Jesus did not know from the start that He must give His life in sacrifice for men's sins. (Moreover, the exegesis that François-Marie Braun proposes concerning Jesus's words to His mother at the Wedding Feast of Cana leans in this direction. According to Him, the passion and death would have been present to Jesus's consciousness from the start as "The Hour for which He had come."[128])

However, progress in this self-awareness, which the Synoptic Gospels seem to note, could be admitted as an explanation of a muffled certitude which would be present from the start, without being incompatible with Him having a real hope of leading the Jewish peo-

---

125. Maritain, *De la grâce et de l'humanité de Jésus*, 123–24.
126. See André Robert and André Feuillet, *Introduction à la Bible* (Paris: Desclée de Brouwer, 1959), especially 68:59–61.
127. See Maritain, *De la grâce et de l'humanité de Jésus*, 113–15.
128. See François-Marie Braun, *La Mère des fidèles* (Casterman, 1954), 50ff; *Jean le théologien* (Paris: Gabalda, 1959–72), 3:137ff.

ple to Him. If we must acknowledge that Christ had a truly human [self-]consciousness, we must acknowledge that, like every human [self-]consciousness, this involved obscurity and the imperfect coherence between various sentiments that, at a given point of implicitness, do not existentially exclude each other, even though one of them cannot be explicitated completely, without, by that very fact, excluding the other.[129]

c) Existence of a psychological subconscious?

{365} As modern psychology has discovered, every man has a part of himself that is subconscious, a whole world of impressions and images that exercise more or less of an influence on his thought and deliberate behavior. Such impressions and images themselves are not only not actually perceived, but also cannot yet be perceived, for they are, as it were, buried in the psyche.

There is no reason to deny that Christ had an "subconscious," if by that term we mean that which, in an organic form of life, escapes the normal possibilities of perception. This is part of the human condition. Moreover, if we use the term "subconscious" to designate that which, without being actually perceived, is susceptible to being perceived (e.g., the phenomenon of "involuntary memory" brought to light by Proust), there is no reason why this would be unworthy of the Incarnate Word, for it is natural for man not to be actually aware of everything that takes place within himself and of everything that He knows. This is obvious in the subconscious state of sleep, which undeniably is part of the image of Jesus presented in the Gospels.

However, we must resolutely exclude pathological subconscious, provoked by psychological traumas and itself provoking "disordered" conduct. This kind of subconscious, which can be very purifying [*purificateur*] [when uncovered], in itself is an offense to

---

129. On this question concerning Jesus's progress in self-consciousness, one can consult Hans Urs von Balthasar, "La foi du Christ," in *La foi du Christ* (Paris: Aubier, 1968), 23–79. Also, see Maurice Nédoncelle, "Le moi du Christ et le moi des hommes à lumière de la réciprocité des consciences," in *Problèmes actuels de christologie* (Paris: Desclée de Brouwer, 1960), 201–26.

the person's dignity, diminishing what makes up his essential dignity, self-mastery. Yet is it not part of the human condition for every man to have a psychological subconscious that is not perfectly reducible to the full light of consciousness? In this case, the incomplete self-mastery resulting from such subconscious would not be an offense to the human person's dignity. Instead, it would be one of the limitations that his person has on account of the fact that he is human, inasmuch as he is a person.

In this case, the assumption of this subconscious would also be part of the kenosis of the Word. However, this is a question that is too vast and complex for us to be able to consider it more deeply so as to arrive at a firm conclusion concerning this matter.

III. THE ABASEMENTS OF THE INCARNATE WORD DURING HIS EARTHLY LIFE

{366} As we discussed earlier,[130] the Incarnation itself involves a kenosis of the Word. It is a kenosis which begins in His being-man and is naturally prolonged in His participation in the conditions of being human, with its limitations and the weaknesses included in it, placing the human person in relation to God first of all and then in relation to the forces of the universe, as well as in relation to those of created wills.

Can we hold that such dependence existed in the person of Jesus, who is the Word? In becoming incarnate, can the Word really make Himself dependent upon creatures? If we were to deny this, many of the traits of Jesus's personality emphasized in Scripture (e.g., hunger, the need to sleep, suffering violence, etc.) would need to be done away with (which is obviously unacceptable). However, beyond this, such a denial would once again risk making His humanity seem ghostly or mythical. Nonetheless, it is a certain fact that Scripture also tells us about extraordinarily powerful traits attributed

---

130. See §315 above.

The Humanity of Jesus 205

to Jesus's personality. How can these be reconciled with the traits of weakness, and how can both of them be reconciled with the realism of the mystery of the Incarnation?

A. The Bodily Vulnerability by Which Jesus Was Submitted to Suffering and Death

{367} It is a primordial datum of the dogmas of the Incarnation and the Redemption that Jesus would have really experienced suffering and death. This is a feature that is indubitably part of the image of Jesus that the Gospels present to us. It is not only a question of the forms of violence exercised against Jesus but also of the sufferings that are part of the human condition: hunger, thirst, fatigue, and so forth.

1. The Word assumed the sorrowful and humiliated human condition

St. Thomas provides three reasons to explain this vulnerability. The first is drawn from the requirements of the redemptive mission, which required the Savior to be vulnerable so that He could really (and voluntarily) take the punishment of man's sin upon Himself. The second is drawn from the proper requirements of the Incarnation. The experience of suffering (at least as something really threatening) is such a part of the human condition (at least as we know about it through our experience) that the Incarnate Word's humanity would not have seemed true if He had presented Himself in way that would have implied immunity from such forms of suffering. Finally, the third and consequent reason is that the Incarnate Word also wished to give us the example of "patience" in relation to this hard and painful aspect of our human condition.[131]

More than the others, the second reason opens the way for us to understand the matter: given the world as it is, the Incarnation would not be true if Christ had not partaken in the condition of other men. It would not be "true" [*vrai*] (or rather, "plausible" [*vrai-*

---

131. See *ST* III, q. 14, a. 1.

semblable]). Using a more modern turn of phrase, we can say that it would not have a meaning for us and, consequently, would not be believable. Nonetheless, we find ourselves faced with a particular difficulty if we acknowledge, as we must, a close relationship between sin and the sufferings that afflict humanity. Should not Jesus's perfect innocence (i.e., His total non-participation in human sin) preclude the existence of this kind of "vulnerability"?

We must respond that this connection, existing in other men, between suffering and sin (a connection that is, moreover, difficult to specify) is not found in Jesus in the same way. His sufferings and death are related to sin, though not to His own sin. They are related to the sin of the men whom He has come to save. He bore this upon Himself, in their situation as sinners, partaking in their sinful condition (born of sin), but not in their sin. This will be studied in its rightful place, namely, in relation to the mystery of the redemption.

2. The Person of the Word was really affected but in no way degraded by the humbled condition that He assumed

{368} It is natural for a human person to be dependent on the external and internal forces that are exercised upon him. In becoming man, the Word accepted this as an element of the human personality that He took on. This is an aspect of His kenosis. To the question that was posed—namely, "How is this vulnerability compatible with the Incarnate Word's dignity?"—St. Thomas proposes this response:[132] by voluntarily accepting them, both by His human will and by His Divine Will, Jesus "personalized" them, integrating them into His personal existence. He changed this necessity into freedom.

This precludes, first of all, the form that this vulnerability takes on in other men—more or less in all—when it is aggravated by an insufficient and disturbed development of personality, arising from natural difficulties or from a wicked use of freedom. By assuming human nature and becoming man, the Word did not cease to be what

---

132. See *ST* III, q. 14, a. 2.

He was. He could not be diminished in His personality by the assumed nature. Now, a human nature is diminished as a person by physical deficiencies and, above all, by psychic deficiencies that affect the individuated nature in which his personality is realized, whatever benefits he may draw from God's grace. (Such benefits are substitutes that compensate—and indeed, go beyond mere compensation—for the wounds of personality, without mending it for as long as one lives here below.)

Therefore, we must think that the individuated nature in which and by which the Word was a man (i.e., a "human person") was perfectly healthy and integrated in all ways. By contrast, we are not required to follow St. Thomas when he writes: "His spirit had power over His flesh so as to prevent it from suffering any injury whatsoever. The soul of Christ had this power from the fact that it was joined to God in the unity of the person."[133] In reality, Jesus is presented to the world as being submitted to limitations that are part of the human condition. St. Thomas is here thinking of Jesus's words, "No one takes [my life] from me, but I lay it down of my own accord."[134] However, the meaning of these words are sufficiently safeguarded (indeed, in accord with the complete truth concerning Jesus human condition), if one acknowledges that He consented to His death and passion in complete freedom.

The true and immense power that the Incarnate Word had in relation to His bodily vulnerability, which He shared in common with other men, is this prodigious self-mastery that He had in the midst of the worst sufferings and humiliations which are described for us in the Gospels. In this, we find the profound meaning of the classic expression: "He took on suffering and death." We must not think of a particular, human volitional act by which He would have allowed His flesh to suffer. This "permission" was included in the "willing of the Incarnation"—a divine volitional act, obviously, though one fully and completely accepted by the human will. By fully agreeing to

---

133. *ST* III, q. 47, a. 1.
134. Jn 10:18 (RSV).

suffer and die, He made His sufferings and death His own, freely integrating them into His project of human existence. In this way, He completely dominated them, without, for all that, modifying their painful reality. He did not suffer less, but He did not allow Himself to be overwhelmed by suffering.

As regards the extraordinary powers that Jesus exercised during His earthly life ([i.e.], miracles), they were the demonstration of His "divine condition," by which He was more than a man, and He performed them for the accomplishment of His mission. Inasmuch as He was a man, He exercised them as an instrumental cause. We will discuss matter this later.

B. Jesus's Psychological Vulnerability during His Earthly Life

1. *The reality of the passions in Jesus Christ*

{369} Inasmuch as it is the form of the body, the soul partakes in its vulnerability. And it is obvious that every bodily "lesion" reverberates upon the sensibility. In other words, "pain" is a psychological phenomenon. But, moreover, the portrait of Jesus traced out in the Gospels includes sufferings that are properly and formally psychological (e.g., sadness, anguish, and also, moreover, expressions of joy, anger, etc.).

Given that Jesus is fully a man, He had a sensibility—and a very rich, very refined one, for this is part of human perfection as such. We can say that this sensibility would have made Him experience suffering (and also physical pain) to an exceptional degree for two reasons. On the one hand, this was so on account of His very perfection (as human experience shows). On the other hand, this was so on account of His "willingness to suffer" spoken of above. To say that He permitted His "flesh" to suffer means that He permitted these psychological sufferings which are related to the "flesh" in the sense that all the "passions" of the sensibility have a physiological component. Also, this holds in the more immediate biblical sense of "flesh," which is taken in the sense of "the man Jesus in His earthly reality."

However, be on guard concerning the ambiguity of the term "passion." In a perfectly "right" human person (i.e., a person who is interiorly ordered and wholly ordered to God), the passions are not less lively and less intense but, rather, are intrinsically submitted to and consonant with reason (the latter itself being intrinsically submitted to and consonant with the Holy Spirit).[135] This is the case for Christ in His humanity, and we must say with St. Thomas that He had the same passions as us.[136] However, our own experience teaches us that the passions such as they are stirred up in us are, on account of sin, the cause of interior disorder and draw us away from God. Therefore, we must also add that Christ had the same passions as us, though in a different manner. These passions made Him psychologically vulnerable. That is, His soul (His psyche) was "passible," submitted to all the impressions of the sensibility. Was it also spiritually vulnerable? This is what we must examine.

2. *The reality of temptations*

{370} The Gospel narrative concerning the temptations of Christ poses exegetical problems which we cannot take up here. However, they also invite the theologian to ask himself how we are to understand what this incitement to evil, undergone in the desert, can mean for the Incarnate Word. Must we say, as is ordinarily said, that He was tempted "only by an external suggestion"?[137] However, a famous text of Scripture invites us to perhaps ask ourselves if He was not, in fact, really tempted. That is, it invites us to ask whether temptation itself had not been taken on by Him in some way: "For we have not a high priest who is unable to sympathize with our weaknesses, but one who in every respect has been tempted as we are, yet without sin."[138] This final trait marks the limit that our investigation cannot cross.

---

135. See *ST* I-II, q. 24, a. 3; q. 59, a. 2; q. 68, a. 1.
136. See *ST* III, q. 15, a. 4.
137. See *ST* III, q. 41, a. 1, ad 1. [Tr. note: This appears to be the reference. Fr. Nicolas cites "Som. Théol. 3, 41, 1um".]
138. Heb 4:15 (RSV).

In general, "temptation" consists in presenting the tempted person with an object that is "good" *for him* in some respect. In other words, such an object corresponds to this or that aspiration of his and therefore is susceptible to awakening his desire and, subsequently, to provoking his will, then his pursuit, leading to his taking possession of this "good" and to his enjoyment thereof. However, it is an object that, considered in relation to his true good, is an evil *for him* because he could not desire it, will it, possess it, and take joy in it, without renouncing his true good, without turning away from God. To experience this object as good and as desirable within himself (i.e., in his sensibility or in his spontaneous will) is in no way evil because this is conformed to the spontaneous movement of nature toward its good. Evil begins to creep in when there arises a desire soliciting the deliberate will to choose against the total good of the person, against that good which must rule his action. Therefore, we must establish a distinction which is rather subtle but well-founded, namely, between *to experience a good as desirable* and *to desire this good*.

The first kind of experience can be admitted in Jesus, and this gives more force and truth to the fine arguments given by St. Thomas to explain why Christ underwent temptation. (He draws these reasons from tradition, as well as from the aforementioned text from the Letter to the Hebrews.) Thus understood, temptation introduces the moral struggle into Jesus's psychology. However, this struggle does not take the form of a combat between good and evil in the depths of Jesus's soul. The good was totally triumphant in Him from the first moment. Rather, this struggle takes on a form expressing the fact that the accomplishment of God's will is, during His earthly existence, often painful and even shattering. The scene of Gethsemane stands as a striking testimony to this.

3. Jesus's psychological vulnerability and the beatitude of the vision of the divine essence

{371} This necessary realism which we must apply to all of Scripture's descriptions showing us Jesus in pain, anguish, and psychological distress returns us once again to a problem that we have already encountered. As we said, during His earthly life, He would have found Himself simultaneously in the state of *viator* and that of *comprehensor*.[139] How can the worst of moral sufferings be reconciled with the beatitude and peace that accompany the vision of God?

Will we join Karl Rahner in contesting the idea that the vision of the Divine Essence would by itself be beatifying? Given that it is the spiritual being's definitive grasp of the Absolute Good, which is also the good toward which he tends by all his aspiration, it cannot fail to bring with itself happiness, at least to the degree that it fills his entire being. Nonetheless, to the degree that this good could not be possessed in some part of the person who sees God, we can hold that this portion of shadow and of not-yet-satiated desire would be rendered much more dolorous by the coexistence of the fullness of light and joy that is the vision of the Divine Essence found in the same mind [*esprit*].

Let us only mention a further qualification so that we may immediately avoid the odd idea of certain sixteenth-century theologians (e.g., Melchior Cano, Juan Maldonado, et al.) which would hold that Christ's vision of the Divine Essence would have been interrupted during the passion. This idea, which nobody holds today, leads to a host of problems. If the vision of the Divine Essence must be suspended in order for the pains and anguishes of the passion to be real, this would come down to saying that Christ would have only seemed to partake in the human condition during the rest of His life. Moreover, the vision of the Divine Essence is inalienable [*inamissible*] by its very nature.[140]

We must return to St. Thomas's explanation: "By a dispensation

---

139. A "viator" is a man on the march toward eternal life (and therefore during earthly existence for an ordinary man). A "comprehensor" is he who is already at the ultimate terminus, in the next life. To say that Christ living on earth had the immediate vision is to say that He was simultaneously "viator" and "comprehensor" (*ST* III, q. 15, a. 10). We already encountered this problem in §339. It arises here again.

140. [Tr. note: This last, briskly stated point, seems to be an allusion a teaching such as is found in *ST* I-II, q. 5, a. 4.]

of Christ's divine power, beatitude was retained within the soul, so that, not overflowing onto the body, it took away neither passivity nor mortality."[141] Nonetheless, we must understand this more broadly of the whole of the human being inasmuch as He is a *viator*, not as a new and quasi-miraculous disposition from God, but rather, as a result of the Incarnation itself, which was willed as such (i.e., as a partaking in the earthly life of men by the Incarnate Word). This explanation does not introduce artifice into Christ's psychology (no more than does the explanation that we provided concerning the coexistence of a really limited human knowledge [*science*] alongside His knowledge [*savoir*] of vision). It is true that the beatitude attached to the vision itself can concern only the superior part of His soul, given that this vision is wholly spiritual. It spreads out over the whole person by "reverberating" upon the other "parts" of the soul, and it is not inconceivable (although it remains very mysterious) that this reverberation would have been prevented. This was so in virtue of the willing of the Father (and of Christ Himself) that the Incarnate Word would partake in the human condition, in the situation of *viatores*.

Classical theology explains the texts of Scripture showing that Christ merited glory by His obedience up to death by presenting the glory of the resurrection as the reverberation of God's glory within all of Christ's being, a glory which He had already participated in at the summit of His soul. We will study this in the third section of this volume, but it does not seem that this interpretation does violence to the texts, above all to the Johannine texts where the passion itself is presented as manifesting Christ's glory.

In order to penetrate in some paltry way into the mystery of this coexistence of beatitude and temporal anguish, with its interior and exterior sufferings, in Christ's soul on earth, we can appeal to the testimony of the mystics. To a much lesser degree, though really so, these mystics know this interior division: an unspeakable joy in the

---

141. *ST* III, q. 14, a. 1, ad 2; q. 15, a. 5, [ad] 3.

C. The Spiritual Vulnerability of Jesus and Its Insurpassible Limits

1. Jesus's sufferings in His human spirit

{372} Within a human person, we can legitimately distinguish various levels of "passion," of suffering (or of joy). However, decoupling them would involve a kind of artifice, and even more so if one were to separate them. We denounced this kind of artifice in the account that attributes Christ's sufferings to His body, in opposition to His soul. Every suffering is psychological, and the most formally "psychological" sufferings have a bodily element. It would be a similar artifice if one were solely to place these sufferings in the sensibility, in opposition to the spirit. The Gospels present Jesus as "rejoicing in His spirit," and also suffering in His spirit. The paroxysm of this suffering, which was formally spiritual—all the while including sensible elements—is expressed by His cry on the cross: "My God, my God, why hast thou forsaken me?"[142]

The descriptions furnished by mystics teach us that the same sufferings, which are properly spiritual, are also compatible with peace and profound serenity. Above, we discussed the interior division within Jesus, between the "heaven of His soul," where He was established in His beatitude, and His temporalized being, immersed in time and history. By analogy to the case of the mystics, though at an incomparably more-elevated degree, this division within Christ does not separate His human spirit from His sensibility but, instead, traverses His very spirit.

2. Jesus's absolute inability to sin during His earthly life

{373} "One who in every respect has been tempted as we are, yet without sin."[143] The entire scriptural doctrine of the redemption is

---

142. Mt 27:46 (RSV); Mk 15:34.
143. Heb 4:15 (RSV).

founded on the fact that Christ saved sinners, with Himself remaining sinless. Theologically, we must connect Christ's absolute inability to sin [*impeccabilité*] to the very dogma of the Hypostatic Union. Sin is a relation (more specifically, a rupture of relation) between the created person and the Divine Persons. While the act of sin has as its principle one (or several) faculties and, ultimately, one's nature (for Christ this would obviously be His human nature), sin itself affects this act inasmuch as it is free, that is, inasmuch as the person engages himself through it and does so against God.[144] Hence, if we were to attribute sin to the Incarnate Word, we would divide Him in His very personality and, in the end, deny the Hypostatic Union.

[However, St. Thomas enunciates a universal principle in this matter which raises a question:] "If we consider its nature, the angel can sin just as easily as any rational creature whatsoever; and if any creature is able not to sin, it holds this as a gift of grace."[145] In virtue of this universal principle, should we not say that Jesus, *considered in His human nature*, is radically capable of sinning? Is this not part of the "human condition" that He assumed, as we saw above, so as to assure the full "truth" of the Incarnation?

However, what can the formula "considered in his human nature" mean for Christ? We have seen that Jesus's human nature exists and is real only as belonging to the Word, as the nature by which the Word is a man. Now, as we have also seen, this is already a grace, the highest of all graces, the "grace of union." If one contrasts nature to grace (i.e., what a created person has by nature to what he has by grace), as St. Thomas does in the text cited above, it is contradictory to speak of the Word considered solely in His human nature, as this human nature cannot be considered apart from the grace that makes it be the nature of the Word. This grace is what renders the man Jesus incapable of sin [*impeccable*]. This is not the case for the saints, including the Virgin Mary. In her case, we can consider what she has by grace ([e.g.,] her perfect innocence and absolute preser-

---

144. See §§487–88 below.
145. *ST* I, q. 63, a. 1.

vation from sin) and what she has by nature ([e.g.,] a radical capability to sin).

3. *The exclusion of every kind of "tinder for sin"*

{374} The "tinder for sin,"[146] concupiscence, presupposes the capacity to sin. It is a capacity for sin that is not yet actualized in a determinate sin, though it is marked by a positive propensity toward it. (In contrast, the capacity to sin, of itself, is only a non-impossibility of sinning.) However, do we not encounter here again the problem of the truth of the Incarnation? Is Jesus a man like us if He did not know the great test, the moral struggle against sin that haunts us?

We must once again reflect on the meaning of such a struggle. It draws its human value from the complete or partial victory to which it leads, not from the situation of conflict and incertitude in which it partakes. The person who has triumphed over sin in himself, not the sinner, is the person who is most truly human. This is what Christ's situation was from the very first moment of the Incarnation. Christ did not need to battle against sin in Himself because, from the first moment of His human existence, He was perfectly innocent, just, and holy with the very holiness of God, which the Word bears with Him and in Him, which He could neither lose nor diminish by becoming a man. But from this first moment, He is holy *in a human manner*, that is, inasmuch as He is a man, sin thus being excluded from His human spirit. It is more than vanquished, for it has not been able to creep into Him. Therefore, He never needed to rid Himself of it. Jesus triumphs over sin in the world on the basis of this absolute domination over sin in Himself. That is, He triumphs over it in humanity in general and in each person who accepts the grace that comes from Him.

---

146. [Tr. note: I am taking the French "foyer de péché" as translating the traditional Latin *fomes peccati*, which I here translate following the official English of the Universal Catechism of the Catholic Church as "tinder for sin" (no. 1264).]

5

Jesus's Human Activity

"Every being is made for its own proper activity." Activity is a being's ultimate actuality, *actus secundus*, its blossoming forth. Jesus manifested Himself and made Himself known as God through His activities: "He went about doing good."[1] The Church proclaimed that He was God, and theology has attempted to explain what this means. However, turning from the human-Divine Being of Christ, we necessarily return anew to His activities. They appear to be (and are) human, as Christ Himself appeared to be (and was) a man. However, must they not also be divine, just as this man, Jesus, was also God? And in what sense can we understand this to be the case? To put the matter directly: this question represents the prolongation of the question of the Hypostatic Union onto the dynamic level. Up to this point, it was treated on the static level. But, just as (and because) Christ is one BEING (*ens*) in two distinct and united natures, so too He is one AGENT by two distinct and united activities.

---

1. Acts 10:38 (RSV).

I. CHRIST'S TWO ACTIVITIES AND THEIR UNION IN THE HYPOSTASIS OF THE WORD

A. The Data of the Problem

1. The data of faith

{375} There is the general datum of the Incarnation's realism, which requires us to *truly* recognize that the Word, having become man by the Incarnation, really behaved and really acted as a man. Every minimization of His action's human character (and *a fortiori* every suppression of it) would represent a more or less open return to the aberrant tendency that we designated under the general term of "monism."[2] On the contrary, this same realism requires us to recognize that it is the Word who is this man, Jesus. Therefore, it requires us to recognize that it is God the Word who acts in this way as a man, and that He does not cease to act as God when he becomes man. Therefore, we must also avoid *separating* the human and divine activities in Christ. Such a separation would be a more or less open return to the dualist aberration.

Historically, the end of the sixth century (after the Second Council of Constantinople) and the whole of the seventh century were occupied with the argument concerning *monoergism* and *monothelitism*, professed more or less openly and more or less expressly by the intractable monophysites. Here, on this point, I refer the reader to texts of ecclesiastical history for further details.[3] *Monoergism* consists in conceiving Jesus's humanity as being totally passive under the action of the Word, meaning that Christ would not have had a properly human activity. *Monothelitism* pushed this conception to the extreme, denying the very existence of a human will in Christ. This represents a resurgence of Apollinarism.

The Church's doctrine on this precise point of Christology was

---

2. See §268 above.
3. See Christoph Schönborn, *Sophrone de Jérusalem* (Paris: Beauchesne, 1972); *L'icône du Christ, Fondements théologiques*, Paradosis XXIV (Fribourg: Éditions Universitaires, 1976).

defined at the Second Council of Constantinople (681). The decisions of the Roman Council of Lateran (649) are very important as well. At this Council, the Church of Rome definitively fixed its position, which was defended thereafter by the pope's legates to the Third Council of Constantinople.

The certain data of faith can be summarized as follows, and this data must be safeguarded and used by every theology that wishes to be acceptable:

1. Christ had (and has) a human will and a human willing which are at the root of all His human actions. This will has all the characteristics of a human will: above all, freedom (with regard to all the objects of any free activity of willing), as well as the functioning of this freedom and its dependence on reason in particular.

2. Given that He was the Word, Christ also had the Divine Will as His own. As a single agent, He acted in a simultaneously divine and human manner.

3. The Word is the only Divine Person who has the assumed human will as His own. On the other hand, "His" Divine Will is the single will common to the three Persons.

4. Without ceasing to be entirely free, His human will was strictly incapable of sinning. That is, at least in the sense that every human will *should* submit itself to the Divine Will, He could not fail to submit His human will to His Divine Will.

5. His human willing, as well as all the human actions that depend upon it, were meritorious before God.

2. *Human person, human activity, human nature*

To understand how the theological problem is situated, we must focus our attention on certain notional and terminological clarifications.

a) The unification of various human actions and passions by the will

{376} Human activity is multiform, as is human passivity. What gives it ontological unity is the person. One and the same person has undergone, undergoes, and will undergo all the various impressions to which his various faculties are subjected. He has produced, produces, and will produce all the various actions which have his various faculties as their immediate principle.

How does this ontological unity become an operative unity? In other words, how does the person's ontological and static unity unify all his actions and passions dynamically? *By the will.* The will is the *appetitus totius personae* (the inclination of the entire person toward the good). By means of the will, the person as such (in his unity and his complexity) is ordered to his good (in its unity and complexity), allows himself to be "permeated" by it, and chooses and commands all the actions by means of which he gradually tends toward his effective realization. It is in his will that he experiences joy and suffering, arising from the good or evil that affects him in whatsoever of his parts.

It is absurd to operatively dissociate the person from his will, imagining that the person as such could act in some other way than by his will or could be affected without his will being reached. In every human activity, the person is the principle *quod agit* (who acts), and the will is the principle *quo agit* (by which the person acts)—just as the person is what exists, and nature is *that by which it exists as such* (as a human person, angelic person, or Divine Person).

Nature is the ultimate *principium quo*. Indeed, the will is the faculty in which and by which the inclination of the nature toward its good is realized. We have said that it is the *appetitus totius personae*. However, we could equally say that it is the *appetitus totius naturae*, for the good of the person is the good in which his nature is brought to completion in its perfection.

b) *The will and the sense appetite*

{377} The sense appetite is also an inclination of the person toward his good, not toward his total good but, rather, toward the sensible good, which is part of his total good. Obviously, it has a kind of independence in relation to the will. Indeed, it possesses its own spontaneity, for the sensible good can attract the human person by its own attraction, absolutely, and not only inasmuch as it is integrated into his total good.

This leads to a kind of "division" within the person (i.e., the struggle of the flesh against the spirit). However, it is a provisional division, which makes itself felt during the phase of deliberation. The person must decide, or, rather, he integrates the sensible good into the total good, rejecting the particular object that cannot be integrated in this way, accepting and ordering that which is susceptible to such integration. Or, on the other hand, he organizes his total good in function of this particular object which he decides to make his own.

Once again, the will, the *appetitus totius personae*, is the principle of this unification. It is by the will that the sensible object is accepted or rejected. Even in the extreme case of the person who purely and simply follows his (sense) instinct without an act of will ratifying it explicitly, this non-intervention involves an acceptance sufficing to render the instinct and the act (of which it is the principle) voluntary (except in cases when the will really is paralyzed and prevented from intervening).

Thus, the duality of appetites in the human person is not translated by a true duality of activities: the human act, even when its immediate principle is the sense appetite, is a human act (i.e., an activity of the human person precisely as human) only inasmuch as it depends upon the will.

c) Nature, the ultimate *principium quo* of activity

{378} Generally speaking, a being's nature is the radical principle of its activity. A given being acts in a given manner because it has a given nature. Being what it is by this nature, it has a given end (corresponding to this nature), and it acts in such a manner (according to this nature, on account of this end). The faculties are not little, more or less independent, beings grafted onto the fundamental being, which would be the nature. They are a determination of this nature, actualizing the latter in the line of its activity, rendering it capable of effectively producing a given activity, to which it is ordered by itself. Properly speaking, the faculty is not the principle of activity. Instead, the principle is the nature, determined and completed by its faculty. (We cannot here examine why such a finalization is necessary.)[4]

The other faculties enable the nature to produce one of the activities for which it is made. As we have seen, the unifying principle of all these activities (and passions) is the will's activity: love first, then, in consequence, the effective willing [*le vouloir réalisateur*] that places all the faculties into action. Therefore, even though the will's activities are partial as well (in the sense that it is a determinate and particular activity), it nonetheless has a general character. As we have said, the acts elicited by the other faculties are human acts, acts of the human person, precisely through the will's activity. Thus, the will is the general principle of the person's activity and therefore of the nature's activity because the person acts (as a *principium quod*) only through the nature (the *principium quo*).

Therefore, the will, the unique *principium quo* of all human acts inasmuch as they are human, the unifying principle that makes all these acts, however various that they may be—constitute *a single human activity* and is the faculty in which nature is actualized and expressed as a total principle of the person's activity. Therefore, we have, on the one hand, the person and, on the other, the nature determined by the will. *The person* is the unifying *principium quod* of all the actions and passions produced or undergone by the human individual. *The nature determined by the will* is the unifying *principium quo* of all the actions and passions produced or undergone by the person, inasmuch as the latter is constituted in his being by his nature.

3. Will and [self-]consciousness

{379} Some say that [self-]consciousness is the unifying principle of all the acts, states, and passions produced or undergone by

4. See *ST* I, q. 54, aa. 1–3.

the person. This is true in the sense that by [self-]consciousness the person knows himself as the unifying *principium quod* [of his actions and state], thus relating these acts and these states to himself. Therefore, it also is the unifying principle as *quod*. This does not mean that [self-]consciousness would be identical to the person. Rather, it is this spiritual act by means of which the person is rendered more or less transparent to himself.

The will is a unifying principle in a different manner, namely, as a *principium quo*. Roughly speaking, we can say that, from the perspective of the unification of the human being's acts and passions, [self-]consciousness is situated on the side of the person (*principium quod*), whereas the will is situated on the side of the nature (*principium quo*).

4. *The problem of Jesus's human activity*

{380} In Jesus, there is one Person and two natures. Moreover, there is the preexistence of the Person in relation to the human nature. Therefore, there is a disjunction between the *principium quod* of activity, which is unique, and the *principium quo*, which is twofold. Therefore, there also is the possibility of the Person acting on one of the two natures (i.e., on the human nature) by means of the other.

The duality of *principia quo* requires a duality of activities, for the natures are not founded on a third superior nature (and therefore no more can we say that the wills are founded on a third superior nature). Here we must note a difference, which we will encounter later, between the duality of appetites in the ordinary human person and the duality of wills in Christ. The two appetites belong to a single nature. Therefore, the sense appetite is not autonomous but instead is by nature incorporated into the will, at least in that the sense appetite's inclination to its own good is incorporated by the will and experienced by it. Indeed, this is so even when this incorporation happens through a voluntary acceptance of the sensible spontaneity and not through the abatement of the latter. Thus, as we have seen, it is a single human activity. By contrast, given that Christ's two wills belong to two distinct and unmingled [*inconfusibles*] natures, they are principles of two activities that are distinct and unmingled.

However, the person is engaged in one's activity—in love and willing, as well as in the act by which this willing is accomplished. Now, Christ's person is one. How is His person not "torn asunder" by this double engagement? In order to avoid such a scission, He must in some sense unify them. Thus, we must seek out the way that the *principium quod* brings the duality of *principia quo* back to unity. Thus, we now, on the dynamic level, find ourselves faced with the problem of Christ's unity, which we heretofore have considered on the static level of His ontological structure.

Therefore, we can summarize the problem facing us as follows. Christ is *one who wills by two wills, one who acts by two activities*. How is His unity safeguarded in this duality of activities? Or, indeed, how does Christ remain "one inasmuch as He is an agent," despite the duality of His activities?

B. Various Solutions

1. Theandric activity

{381} The expression comes from [Pseudo-]Dionysius. In the strong sense of the term, it would mean that Christ's two activities (i.e., the human and divine activities) would have their foundation in one of the activities [i.e., His divine activity]. It seems that this conception was proposed in the seventh century and was accepted by Sergius, the patriarch of Constantinople. It is at least what is expressed in the seventh of the anathemas composing the formula of union elaborated in 631 for reconciling the Egyptian monophysites with the Church. It condemned anyone who denied "that there was only one, single Christ and Son, bringing about divine actions and human actions by a single theandric activity, as St. Dionysius says."[5]

It may seem that this position has been definitively abandoned.

---

5. See Johannes Dominicus Mansi, *Sacrorum Conciliorum nova et amplissima Collectio* (Florence, 1758ff.; Venice, 1799ff.; Paris / Arnhem / Leibzig, 1901–27), 9:564–68.

However, it is necessary to reconcile with it the conception expressly held by Parente and by Galot.[6] According to them, the Word would have His own, proper action (distinct from that which He exercises *ad extra* along with the Father and the Holy Spirit). Therefore, He would have an action that would not proceed formally from the Divine Nature but instead from the Person of the Word in His distinction, being exercised over the assumed will. Thus, Christ's human activity would be "theandric" as proceeding from two subordinate principles, the human will and the Word.

This position, which has been vigorously critiqued by Diepen, Galtier, and myself, is not admissible. From the perspective of Trinitarian theology, no divine action *ad extra* can be proper to one of the Persons. Every divine action must have the Divine Will, which is identical with the Divine Nature and common to the three Persons, as its efficient principle. From the perspective of Christology, the Word, inasmuch as He is a human person, can will and act only by His human will, and *therefore cannot act upon it*. Once again, inasmuch as He is a Divine Person, He can act only by the Divine Will and undividedly with the Father and the Spirit.

Under this motion of the Godhead, Christ's human will necessarily remains a human will, without mixing with the Divine Will. If it can be called "theandric," this is only in the sense that the Divine Person of the Word is its *principium quod* so that, on the one hand, it is divine, as being an activity of the Word, all the while being a human activity and, on the other hand, in the Word, it is united to the properly divine activity, and "communicates" with it, according to the famous expression of St. Leo: "Each *form* (or, *nature*) does that

---

6. Pietro Parente, "Unità ontological e psicologica de l'Uomo-Dio," *Euntes docete* 5 (1952): 337–41; Galot, *La conscience de Jésus*, 126–27; Diepen, "La psychologie humaine du Christ"; Galtier, "La conscience humaine du Christ"; J.-H. Nicolas, "Chronique de théologie dogmatique," 424–25. [Tr. note: Fr. Nicolas cites a third bibliographical entry for Parente, which does not exist in his bibliography in the original. Perhaps he meant to cite the second entry, Pietro Parente, *L'Io di Cristo* (Brescia, 1955). He also cites the article by Diepen as being pages 415–31. The article (in full) is actually found on pages 515–63. As this seems to be the only entry matching the citation, I have corrected the pagination.]

which is proper to it, in communion with the other."[7] We will need to determine precisely what this "communion" involves.

2. *The autonomy of Christ's human will*

{382} This position was taken early in the twentieth century by Tixeront and presented by him as expressing the Church's own doctrine against monothelitism.[8] He expressed it in an outstanding manner, and his formulation finds itself taken up today by those who hold this position: "The divine and human activities of the Word must be considered as forming two parallel series, each having the personality of the Word as the condition for their existence, though proceeding from each of the two natures as from their true efficient principle."[9] The single person of Jesus is the single subject of attribution for all these activities and passions, and this alone unifies the two series. Nonetheless, they remain as external to one another as an ordinary man's acts remain external to the divine acts that are exercised upon him. There is no special subordination of Jesus's human will to His Divine Will on account of the Hypostatic Union.

This theory was developed in such a manner that it aroused a desire to discover a "psychological self" in Jesus's humanity. Such a "self" would play the role of being the *principium quod* in relation to His human acts, a role ordinarily played by the person.[10] This "psychological self" would not be a person. It would belong to the Word so that the ultimate *principium quod* of these acts is indeed the Word. However, once again, there would be no "communication" between His human and divine acts. The same Person acted simultaneously by human acts and divine acts.[11]

---

7. D.-*Sch.*, no. 294. Cf. *ST* III, q. 19, a. 1, ad 1. [Tr. note: Selection from Leo translated from original so as to maintain the parenthetical remark by Fr. Nicolas. The 43rd edition of Denzinger, with English translation, translates *forma* as "nature."]

8. Joseph Tixeront, *Histoire des dogmes* (Paris: Gabalda, 1911), 3:160–92; cf. Diepen, "La psychologie humaine du Christ," 554–62; Diepen, *Théologie de l'Émmanuel*, 275–93.

9. Tixeront, *Histoire des dogmes*, 3:173.

10. See §358 above.

11. See Galtier, *L'unité du Christ*. See also his "La conscience humaine du Christ. A propos de quelques publiations récentes," *Gregorianum* 32 (1951): 525–68; "La conscience

{383} *Critique.* The principal (and, in my opinion, insurmountable) objection raised by this explanation is the disconnection that it establishes between the static (or, ontological) and dynamic (or, operational) orders. The Person, who is unique, would remain rigorously restricted within ontology, without Himself being engaged in [Christ's] activity. For this "engagement," a "psychological self" is substituted, seemingly playing the role of a "vicar" or a "procurator," charged with acting the place of the Person and in His name.

However, in that case, there are only two possible options. Either this "psychological self" is the Person Himself, considered as engaged in and by human activities. In this case, the problem arises anew, for we must admit that the same, unique Person is at the same time engaged in His divine activities, and these two engagements must be unified on the *level of activity*. Or, on the other hand, this "psychological self" is a distinct actor. In this case, it is not clear how this distinct operational subject could fail to be a distinct ontological subject, for the "agent" cannot not be a "being." Then, if it is a "being" having an intellectual and volitional nature, how is it not a person? The attribution of all human actions and passions to the Word seems to be a pure logical or juridical artifice, as though one said: "I consider everything that you will do as things done by me; I consider everything that will be done to you as things done to me." Now, the Hypostatic Union is situated in the order of reality, not in that of juridical fiction.

We saw above that this attribution must be explained by the very grace of the Hypostatic Union.[12] However, this would not be intelligible if we must acknowledge that Jesus's human will is autonomous in relation to His Divine Will. If the Person of the Word is, in truth, the only subject of attribution of the human acts of Jesus, we can indeed see why it would be sovereignly unsuitable for sin to be intro-

---

humaine du Christ," *Gregorianum* 35 (1954): 335–46; Diepen, "La psychologie humaine du Christ"; "L'unique Seigneur Jésus-Christ"; *Théologie de l'Émmanuel* (Paris: Desclée de Brouwer, 1960); Nicolas, "Chronique de théologie dogmatique," 415–31.

12. See §373 above.

duced among these acts. However, it is not at all obvious how or why this would be [completely] impossible:

> Therefore, far from a person determining the mode of action and behavior of His nature, it is exactly upon it that his own depends. Consequently, the "depersonalization" of a nature cannot entail for it any modification of its mode of acting, of its behavior. Such is what we find in Christ's case: with the exception of sin, despite the depersonalization of His human nature, it remains similar to ours in all things. In relation to everything that is not sin, it has a comportment like our own, that is, acting as a non-"depersonalized" nature would act, though elevated like it to participation in the divine nature by grace and enriched like it by all the gifts and aids that the divine munificence and holiness can lavish on a created being united to one of the Three Persons.[13]

Very well. But how are we to explain this exception that is made for sin: "with the exception of sin"? If the man Jesus has the same comportment as an ordinary man, enriched by all possible graces, He is intrinsically capable of sin. Therefore, it is conceivable that He, the Word Incarnate, could sin. This cannot be admitted, for sin would shatter His personality, as we have seen.[14]

3. St. Thomas's solution

{384} St. Thomas affirms[15] first of all "Christ's unity of activity."[16] He forcefully affirms the reality and integrity of Jesus's human activity, which is mixed with the divine activity in no way.[17] According to him, Christ's unity inasmuch as He is an agent (*unitas in operando*) is assured on three heads:

1. By the fact that His human will was wholly moved and ruled by His Divine Will, or by the fact that His human nature was moved by His Divine Will as an instrument.[18]

---

13. Galtier, "La conscience humaine du Christ," 234.
14. See §373 above.
15. Carefully read *ST* III, qq. 18 and 19.
16. See *ST* III, q. 19, prol.
17. See ibid., a. 1.
18. *ST* III, q. 18, a. 1, co. and ad 4; q. 19, a. 1.

2. Again, by the fact that Christ entirely followed His Divine Will by His human will, as a friend follows a friend's will.[19]

3. Or, finally, as an animated and conscious instrument follows the impulse of the principal cause using it.[20]

This complete subordination is not the same as an ordinary saint's subordination [to God]. It is proper to Christ and is formally connected to the Hypostatic Union:

> Hence, Christ's human will had a mode of acting determined by the fact that it belonged to a divine hypostasis. This mode consisted in the fact that it always moved itself at the least sign (*ad nutum*) of the Divine Will.[21]

Therefore, St. Thomas's solution can be summarized in the following manner. Christ was a single agent (the same one, *being* man and God, *acting* humanly and divinely) by two wills and two activities, which are *ordered in relation to each other* so that His human will was totally subordinated to His Divine Will, moved and ruled by it, exactly willing what the Divine Will willed. (By His two wills, Christ willed the same thing.) Nonetheless, His human will was not deprived of its own, proper free movement. Indeed, it was subordinated in this way spontaneously and freely. This subordination had its proximate principle in created grace (i.e., habitual grace and actual grace) and its radical principle in the grace of union.

Flowing from the same principle (i.e., the unique Person of the Incarnate Word), the two activities converged, not only toward one and the same end but also upon the same object and together produced one and the same result.[22] Note, however, that our verbs here are in the past tense because, in this section, we are considering Jesus Christ from the perspective of His earthly life. Currently, in His eschatological status, He does not stop BEING the Incarnate Word, ONE in two natures. Consequently, He still has two wills and two ac-

---

19. See *ST* III, q. 18, a. 5, co. and ad 2.
20. See *ST* III, q. 18, a. 1, ad 2.
21. *ST* III, q. 18, a. 1, ad 4.
22. See *ST* III, q. 19, a. 1, ad 5.

tivities. (Thus, He "makes intercession on behalf of His own"[23] by means of His human intellect and will.) However, now that His human mode of acting is totally at the terminus of its course (*comprehensor*), it obviously is different than the mode according to which He acted during His earthly life, and He accomplished the work of our salvation on earth according to this latter mode of activity.

C. The Complete Subordination of Christ's Human Will to His Divine Will

1. *The only solution*

{385} As regards the criticism of the theory of the parallelism of two series of activities, it is clear that the Person of the Word, the one Person of Jesus, is engaged in His human activities [*opérations*] and that He is responsible in them, not only juridically and morally but first of all really, given that He is the person who wills and acts by the human will. Therefore, we absolutely must acknowledge that He has a real power over this human will.

On the other hand, as we also have seen, person and nature cannot be separated in order to attribute any power to Him without qualification, an action that would not simultaneously belong to the nature. Just as the person exists by his nature, he cannot act except by his nature, that is, by his will. Therefore, he cannot act *upon* his nature and *upon* his will. If, in an ordinary man, the person is engaged in and by his willing, this is because this willing is his own. He is the one "who wills and acts," the will being the *quo*. Therefore, how should we understand the idea that the Incarnate Word had the power of acting *over* his human will?

We must recall that before being a human person in time (on account of the assumed human nature), the Word is from all eternity a Person constituted by the Divine Nature. His primary power of willing and of acting is the Divine Will. If He assumes a human will and makes it His own, so that He is the one who wills and acts by this

---

23. Heb 7:25.

will, He can do so only as a Divine Person (i.e., as a Person having a Divine Will and divinely willing even what He humanly wills). Here in the dynamic order, we must apply the principle: "without ceasing to be what He was" (that is, someone willing by the Divine Will), "He became what He was not" (one who wills by a human will).

This implies a complete subordination of the human will to the Divine Will. Indeed, the Divine Person must be able to act upon His human will and hold it in His hand so as to be engaged by it. However—and let us repeat the fact—the person acts only by his will. The solution is that the Person of the Word acts upon the assumed will *by means of His Divine Will*, and this action is omnipotent. In saying this, we completely eliminate the inadmissible idea that the Person of the Word would act directly upon the human nature without the intermediary of the Divine Will. However, an objection arises: what is "Jesus's Divine Will"? There is only one Divine Will, one Divine Willing, common to the three Persons. Are we not thus thrown back into the parallelism theory, holding that Jesus's human will was certainly submitted to God's will, as a just man's will can and must be, but no more than this and in no different manner?

To resolve this difficulty, we must return anew to the very mystery of Christ's ontological constitution, for the mystery of His twofold and unified activity is nothing other than its prolongation on the level of dynamism. The assumptive action is common to the three Persons as regards efficient causality [*l'efficience*]. The three Divine Persons together are the principle of this action. It is proper to the Word in the sense that the Word alone is the terminus of this action resulting in the assumed nature being made His own, thus making it a human person: "Thus, that which is an action in the assumption [of the human nature to the Word] is common to the three Persons. However, as regards its terminus, this assumption is related to a single Person and not to the others. Indeed, the three Persons made it be the case that the human nature is united solely to the Person of the Word."[24]

---

24. *ST* III, q. 3, a. 4. See §311 above.

In the same way, we must say that the Divine Willing by which Jesus's human will is moved is the willing of the Father, the Son, and the Spirit together. However, the human willing that is at the terminus of this moving action is the willing of the Word alone. Therefore, I can say that the Word moves HIS human will by HIS Divine Will, exactly in the same sense as I can say that the Word (alone) IS a man by the assumed nature. In this way, we thus provide a response to Galot's objection: "Is this not to misunderstand the fact that the human acts emanate from the Person of the Word and not from the two other Persons?" The Incarnate Word acts on His human will by the Divine Willing, which emanates from the three Persons together. The will moves and all the acts proceeding from it emanate from the Word alone, *inasmuch as He is a human person*.

What can it mean to say that the Divine Will moves the human will if not that God wills for this human will that which He Himself wills? To say that Jesus moves His human will by His divine will is to say that under the divine motion, Jesus's human will wills what the Divine Will wills, and this Will is also Jesus's will. In other words, Jesus willed by His human will the same thing that He willed by His Divine Will in relation to the same object.

"In relation to the same object": clearly, the Divine Will infinitely exceeds the human will. Therefore, we cannot say that Jesus willed by His human will everything that He willed by His Divine Will. There are objects of the Divine Will that cannot be objects of the human will (such as the creation or conservation of creatures in existence). However, Jesus could will nothing by His human will which He had not first willed (according to a priority of nature) by His Divine Will.

2. *The motion of the Divine Will over the human will*

How should we conceive of this motion exercised by the Divine Will upon the human will? Obviously, we must refer to the general problem concerning how God acts upon the human will. There are two kinds of motions that can be exercised upon the will: *efficient-*

causal motion, which is exercised upon the will so as to make it will effectively; and *objective motion*, which leads it to will by presenting it with a determinate object.²⁵

a) Efficient motion: operative grace

{386} God alone can act upon the will by efficient causality, for He alone is interior to it. (Here, I refer the reader to the general problem concerning physical premotion.) In the supernatural order, the ordinary way that God acts on the human will is a simple motion (or, cooperating grace). The will normally is determined by means of deliberation, weighing the pros and cons of various objects of the will that are proposed to it. The divine motion brings about all these acts of reason and of will, up to the final one which is choice. We are not concerned here with the question of how freedom is respected. That to which God moves is a free act.

By means of deliberation, the will moves itself on the basis of a prior act of willing: "Given that I will this end, what means should I will?" Therefore, we must initially admit a first act of non-deliberated willing, namely, the willing of the end. For this first act of willing, the divine motion does not pass through the process of deliberation. Reason is moved to judge concerning a good, and the will is simultaneously moved to will it.²⁶ This first act can be perfectly free, but it can in no way be a sin. The judgment of goodness that rules this act of willing can only be perfectly right because it comes immediately from God.²⁷ It is an act of human willing for which the human will has secondary-causal responsibility [*responsabilité seconde*], God having the first responsibility for it.

This sovereign intervention by the Divine Will takes place many times in the course of a human life, and it can take place very often in the order of grace. Indeed, in this order, the human person is often called upon to make decisions that exceed him, for he is situated in

---

25. See *ST* I-II, q. 9, a. 1.
26. See ibid., a. 4.
27. See *ST* I, q. 63, a. 5.

the midst of the order of objects pertaining to the Divine Life. This is *operative grace*. Here, we find the same process described earlier: God makes one judge concerning the good, not according to one's prior conceptions (i.e., not through deliberation) but according to His divine conception (by inspiration). Simultaneously, He makes the person will in accord with this "inspired" judgment. This is encountered in two domains. First, it is encountered in conversion. (The sinner obviously cannot judge that it is good for him to prefer God's will in preference to his own, basing such a choice on his prior conceptions, which are characterized by the preference of self over God.) Then, it is encountered in the Holy Spirit's interventions through the Gifts of the Holy Spirit. Such interventions are increasingly frequent to the degree that the process of divinization grows, and consequently to the degree that the objects that are presented to the will are more and more purely divine.

In this way, Jesus's human will was moved by His Divine Will *in all of His willings*. We must imagine this as being an intimate and infallible collaboration [*connivance*], not a form of a continuous constraint. Every decision formed in the divine "counsel" concerning an object of Jesus's human acting was immediately formed in Jesus's human counsel, on account of the conjunction of the two minds (i.e., the divine and the human mind) in the unity of the Person and on account of the perfect *consonance* between the two wills that results from this. By His human will, Jesus could not will anything else, for this alone seemed good for Him to will *hic et nunc*. (This is the meaning of St. Thomas's example of friends joined in mutual agreement: this is the opposite of constraint.)

Nothing prevents us from saying that, like our own, Jesus's human spirit was dwelt in by and moved by the Holy Spirit. However, for Him, His own Person is the one who "sent" the Spirit. Thus, we must simultaneously say that He Himself moved His human will by His Divine Will.[28]

28. See J.-H. Nicolas, *Les profondeurs de la grâce*, 184–227 and 246–47.

b) Objective motion: Jesus's obedience

{387} It is natural for the will to be moved by its object, that is, to be attracted by the good that is presented to it. The good is presented to the will by the intermediary of the intellect, which knows this good and appreciates its (always relative and contingent) goodness. Many and sundry causes can act upon the will by this means. First, and obviously, the sense appetite and all its stimulations can act upon it. However, there also are the persons who act upon it, either by presenting the good and by emphasizing its desirability (by seduction), or by way of counsel, or by prayer, or authoritatively by prescribing what ought to be willed. God thus acts in a thousand ways on man in order to draw him to the good, either by making use of creatures, by interior graces of light, by graces of attraction, etc. He also acts authoritatively by giving commandments and prohibitions (and counsels as well, but this question goes beyond our current discussion).

Thus, every man is guided in his choices by God's will, conceived as the source of these commandments and prohibitions. He can disobey. However, in that case he does not choose the true good and, thus, sins. God's objective motion is not constraining. It is situated in the order of the presentation of the good and the order of incitement to choose it. In the case of Jesus, Scripture is quite clear that His Father's commands extended to all of His life's acts. He had a mission to fulfill, one that was specified for Him in the least of its details: "Must not the Scripture be fulfilled?"

In His case, there was complete concurrence between God's efficacious motion and His objective motion. The former, in the form of a judgment concerning the goodness conforming, in His human mind, to that of the Divine Mind, led Him to will what the Father (and He Himself with the Spirit) willed in each circumstance. The objective motion presented him with the command that made Him humanly know this Divine Willing to be fulfilled.

There are theologians who hold that such obedience would not have been compatible with freedom, on account of His inability to sin. Such thinkers would say that insofar as Jesus could not sin, He could not disobey, thus meaning that if God's command extended to all His acts His willing would not have been free. Let us note that if this were true, we would need to reduce Jesus's human freedom to His minor acts, for we can be certain that the essential acts of His human existence were commanded of Him, something that we know on the basis of what He Himself expressly said. In reality, the fact that the order has been given does not, by itself, diminish freedom in any way. It is addressed to freedom. As regards His inability to sin, it does not mean that Christ was deprived of the freedom to sin but, instead, that He could not *will to sin*.

3. *The great objection: did Jesus have self-mastery?*

a) The objection

{388} According to the outlook that has been presented, Jesus's human will seems completely "servile." On the one hand, what it must will was prescribed for it in the smallest of details. On the other hand, it was moved in such a manner that it had no possibility of deliberating. Thus, it was deprived of all ability to make a decision.

Now, this seems contrary to the dignity of the human person. One can acknowledge that psychological freedom is preserved. However, this annihilates freedom in the conventional sense of the word, understood as the power to dispose of oneself and to choose the direction in which one will be engaged by one's action. Thus, He would be like a slave who could at no moment decide for himself what he will do. For many, this situation seems to be wholly incompatible with Jesus's human dignity. Once more we encounter the same difficulty as discussed before: on the pretext of safeguarding His divine dignity, do we not diminish His human dignity to the point of reducing the Incarnation to nothing? "We know what a man's will is."[29]

---

29. Hyacinthe-François Dondaine, "Bulletin de théologie dogmatique," *Revue des sciences philosophiques et théologiques* 35 (1951): 609–13.

b) First response

{389} We must first analyze this inquiry concerning independence in the name of human dignity.

First, *from the perspective of obedience*, the obligation to obey human authorities is founded on human nature's social dimension. Man is not purely and simply a part of a social whole but simultaneously is a person (i.e., a whole, having a value on his own account and capable of directing himself). Therefore, in order for this obligation to obey to remain fully compatible with human dignity, it is associated with two things. On the one hand, it is associated with the real ability of making his own the decision that has been made. This normally includes participation in the decision and, in any case, free assent to it. On the other hand, it is associated with room being left for individual initiative, as far as the requirements of the common good allow for it in a given situation.

If personality is considered in its horizontal dimensions (i.e., in relation with other human persons and with earthly realities), to the degree that the part taken in the elaboration of the decision is greater, so too is the individual initiative greater, as well as the affirmation of man as a person; indeed, all the greater in that case is his personal dignity. However, this no longer plays a role when it is a question of the person taken in his vertical dimension (i.e., considered in his relation to God), for *inasmuch as the created person is a person*, he is totally dependent on God. First of all, he is ontologically dependent. Then, in consequence, he must also be operatively dependent, seeking in all things to do God's Will.

If God's express commandment does not extend to all of each person's acts of will, this is not the case so that one's power of decision may be preserved before God Himself. This is so because the majority of men play only a limited role in salvation history. However, for each person, the voice of conscience, which must be heeded, is the voice of God.

The more a man is engaged in salvation history, the more he has (by the divine choice) an important role to play in it. Therefore, God's will is also expressed for him in more precise commandments. Thus, we have the examples of the patriarchs, prophets, apostles, and so forth. Beyond every measure, the Man-Jesus, the living and active center of the whole of salvation history, had to fulfill a mission that could leave no room for an initiative arising from his human "counsel." Everything was ruled by God. Human dignity is in no way diminished by the obligation to obey God.

{390} Second, *from the perspective of the motion of grace*, given that grace in general, and operative grace in particular, are required on account of the limitations and insufficiencies of nature in the supernatural order, it could seem that the more a man progresses in the line of divinization, the less he needs grace. This is the Pelagian illusion. In reality, the gap between the divinized creature and the divine object cannot be spanned, meaning that God must continuously give Himself to the creature gratuitously (by grace), indeed all the more intensely and completely as their union becomes more intimate and more profound.

Thus, the more the process of divinization grows, the more the creature is concerned with the divine object in its purity. (Indeed, below the Beatific Vision the mediation of created objects is always involved. However, these become increasingly transparent.) Therefore, he must all the more be borne aloft by grace. Thus, he who has penetrated into the domain of the mystical life begins to be under the rule of the Gifts of the Holy Spirit, indeed increasingly so to the degree that he progresses.

We absolutely must not compare this submission to the Holy Spirit's direction (which is realized by ever more frequent and continuous operative graces) to pressures that are exercised on the will in the temporal domain. Every pressure exercised on the will by other created wills (in the form of threats, promises, or urgings) undermines the native independence of the will. They are sometimes good and necessary, but this is precisely to the degree that one's personality is insufficiently developed, poorly disengaged from the pressure of the sensibility or from external pressures. The greater a man's personality, the more he himself chooses his ways in full independence. (Obviously this does not mean that he does not take account of others' advice, demands, and wishes. However, even granting this, he judges by himself what is fitting to will and do and is led in accord with his judgment.) On the other hand, the motion of the Holy Spirit goes in the direction of personality's development:

> The Divine Good to which the Holy Spirit moves man is his true good. It is that to which his fundamental willing, both as natural and as supernaturalized by charity, is inclined with all its weight, so that the judgment concerning goodness that grace makes him perform without deliberation is the judgment to which deliberation would have tended, though obscurely and less efficaciously. There is a perfect correspondence between what man wills most profoundly and what the Holy Spirit makes him will.[30]

According to St. Thomas, this is why "the Holy Spirit suppresses servitude when, through love, He inclines the will toward the true good *to which it is ordered by nature*."[31] Thus, "totally possessed by the Holy Spirit, Christ's soul was also totally directed by operative grace, which assured the perfect harmony of His human will with His Divine Will, the Divine leading the human, which was, in its depths, in agreement with it former, indeed, freely so."[32]

c) A second (and radical) response

{391} What are we referring to when we speak about Jesus's human dignity? "Dignity" formally and directly concerns the person. Therefore, we must say the same concerning independence. It is not the will that is independent. Rather, it is he who wills [*le "voulant"*] who is independent. In the case of an ordinary person, this distinction is unimportant, for the ordinary person is dependent or independent solely in and by his human will. And if his human will is dependent on another will, this means that the person is dependent on another person. By that very fact, there is a limitation of his dig-

---

30. J.-H. Nicolas, *Les profondeurs de la grâce*, 217.
31. *SCG*, bk. 4, ch. 22.
32. J.-H. Nicolas, *Les profondeurs de la grâce*, 217.

nity, in the way we specified above. However, in Christ's case, the human person is also and simultaneously the Divine Person. The will to which the human will is submitted is not another person's will. However total this dependence may be, it does not affect the person and in no way diminishes His dignity, which is infinite.

To this, Fr. Galtier objects:

> Assuredly too, it is quite certain that this Man, the Incarnate Word, would remain autonomous and free, even though He would not be so by his human will. However, without real autonomy and real freedom (in this will), we cannot speak of Him having autonomy and consequently cannot speak of Him having a properly human form of obedience.[33]

The response is that autonomy can belong only to a person, and in order for it to be human it suffices that this person truly be a human person, which is the case for the Incarnate Word.

This "composite" Person always acted in accord with his own decision. Such a decision taken simultaneously in the divine counsel and in human counsel, with the latter totally dependent upon the former. By submitting His human will to the Divine Will, He submitted His own will to it.

The two responses mutually complement each other, for it is indeed true that the Incarnate Word performed an act of complete obedience to God through this submission of His human will. However, He was God Himself and, with the Father and the Spirit, was simultaneously He who ordered and He who obeyed. This creates a paradoxical situation which we will examine later on.[34] In any case, it is certain that such obedience could not undermine His personal dignity. It is also certain that His human life was completely dependent upon the divine initiative through this complete submission of His human "counsel" to the divine counsel. However, we have seen that when the divine initiative is communicated to the created spirit through operative grace, it does not impinge upon human initiative. On the contrary, it makes it blossom forth.

---

33. Galtier, "La conscience humaine du Christ," 241.
34. See §§510–12 below.

{392} Therefore, within the framework of our solution, we must affirmatively respond to the question that we posed: "Did the Man-Jesus have self-mastery?" He had self-mastery, first of all because the "Man-Jesus" is the Word, as well as because in every way He, the Word, was the One who sovereignly directed and moved His human will by His Divine Will. However, we also must say that this total subordination was the very opposite of servitude for this human will—and therefore also for the Word considered as a human person, and thus submitted to the Father (and to Himself as well as to the Holy Spirit). It was the perfect freedom of the children of God. This freedom does not consist in independence from God (a wicked and impossible independence). Instead, it consists in complete independence from all creatures, an independence which, precisely speaking, has as its foundation complete dependence upon God, a dependence fully accepted through love. The more a man is possessed by God, the more he possesses himself and possesses the universe.[35]

4. Christ's human will and His human activity

a) The problem

{393} By his will, a man directs his other actions, both internal and external. Thus, the complete sway that the Word had, by His Divine Will, over His human will extended to all and each of the actions that are themselves under the sway of His human will.

However, are all the actions having man as their subject under the sway of his will? Obviously not. First of all, there is all the physiological activity that escapes his will completely—at least the direct movement, for one can act voluntarily on it by external stimulation. There also is his sensibility. The ancients already saw quite well and recognized that the sense appetite was a principle of spontaneous action, one that is not automatically submitted to the will. However, they thought that every movement of the sensibility not

---

35. See St. John of the Cross, *Oeuvres complètes*, trans. P. Cyprien de la Nativité de la Vierge, OCD, ed. P. Lucien-Marie de Saint-Joseph, OCD (Paris: Desclée de Brouwer, 1959), 1304–5.

controlled by reason (i.e., irrational) and, therefore, independent of the will (which is connected to reason) was a disorder. Such a disorder would be culpable every time the will had the real possibility of intervening but would be non-culpable when this intervention was rendered impossible in an existential situation which was itself non-culpable (sleep, for example, or mental distress). The discoveries of modern psychology force us to correct this way of seeing things. Doubtlessly, there are great psychological disorders arising from the unconscious. However, it does not seem that we can say that the very existence of the unconscious (and the subconscious even more so) is a disorder. Nor, consequently, does is seem that we can say that the fact that our acts partially evade our reason and our will is a disorder. Finally, do we not need to recognize, *in the will itself*, non-deliberate movements, prior to every deliberation, which are the will's spontaneous reaction in the presence of what is presented as being good or bad for the person (e.g., the horror of suffering and of death or the movement of joy in the presence of him whom one loves and the manifestations of his love)?

What about Christ as regards these matters? If we were to remove this sensible and spiritual spontaneity, would we not dehumanize Him? If we were to grant Him volitional power over His physiological reflexes, would we not mythologize His humanity? However, on the other hand, if His human will did not have power over all His actions, how can the Incarnate Word be the agent of these actions? Indeed, He directs His human life by acting on His human willing by means of His Divine Willing.

b) St. Thomas's position

{394} St. Thomas's position is ambiguous. He is obviously caught between two exigencies that he does not seem to have reconciled. On the one hand, the preponderant importance that he gives to reason in the conduct of human life makes him reject the idea that there would have been an irrational aspect in Christ's activity. This goes so far that he tends to grant that His human will even had power over His physiological reactions—either by simply accepting that they be produced[36] or even by having the power of preventing them (though He did not wish to make use of this power).[37] However, on the other hand, paying heed to everything that Scripture says to us about Christ, St. Thomas reflected at length on the drama of Gethsemane, and on Jesus's words, "Not as I will, but as you will," and he admitted that the spontaneous movements of the sensibility and even of the will, independent by nature from reason and from the deliberate will, occurred. They were subordinate to the human will's decision, and therefore to the Divine Will's decision, because they were voluntarily accepted and in no way hinder his deliberate will.[38]

c) Critical reflections

{395} Christ's acceptance (through His Divine Willing and human willing together) of the natural determinism of physiological reflexes and psychological spontaneity is nothing other than His acceptance of the human condition. This is one aspect of the kenosis of the Word. It seems impossible to say that this acceptance rendered these actions "voluntary" for His human willing (and, therefore, also for His Divine Willing considered *as specifically the will of the Word*—that is, as we have seen, in its relation to His human willing).

We must certainly say that Christ experienced these physiological reactions as "acts of man," not as "human acts,"[39] as is the case for us as well. Can the same be said for spontaneous movements of the sensibility and of the will? On the one hand, we must say that the person is truly engaged only by his definitive act of will in relation to the good: choice. On the other hand, the person is indeed the one who reacts spontaneously in the presence of good or evil. His choice can be a triumph over this first impression, but it neither abolishes nor abnegates it.

---

36. See *ST* III, q. 19, a. 1.
37. See *ST* III, q. 47, a. 1.
38. See *ST* III, q. 18, aa. 5–6.
39. [Tr. note: See *ST* I-II, q. 1, a. 1.]

Similarly, the Word truly was the one who experienced a violent movement of recoil in the face of suffering and death, and He did not experience this only in His sensibility.[40] Indeed, this movement of recoil was incorporated into His free acceptance. He accepted death as being something horrible for Him, experienced as being horrible, and the same Divine Willing that made Him will this humanly, also made Him recoil before it.

Therefore, from the start (that is, at the first presentation of the passion), there is a duality of willings. At first, by His human willing, Christ refuses what God wills (something which He Himself wills by His Divine Will). It is in a second stroke [*dans un deuxième temps*] that the unification is made, through the integration, in choice, of this overcome (but always present) recoil. As regards the question of an "irrational" part (therefore of a non-voluntary part) arising from the subconscious into Christ's activity, we discussed this matter earlier.[41]

II. JESUS'S HUMANITY AS THE INSTRUMENT OF HIS DIVINITY

{396} This complete dependence of Jesus's humanity upon His divinity is classically expressed by the notion of "instrumental causality." The expression itself goes back to St. Athanasius and was made classical by St. John Damascene.[42] It was utilized and analyzed by St. Thomas.[43] Can it be retained, and if so, in what sense? Is it capable of illuminating the problem for us?

A. Statement of the Problem

However closely a human will may be dependent upon the Divine Will, even when the latter acts continuously through operative grace, the activity of the creature is never attributable to God

---

40. Although, St. Thomas seems to say that the agony happened only on the level of the sensibility. See *ST* III, q. 18, a. 6, ad 3.
41. See §365 above.
42. St. John Damascene, *De fide orthodoxa*, PG 94, 1060.
43. See *ST* III, q. 18, a. 3, ad 2; q. 19, a. 1, co. and ad 2.

as though He were the agent. However holy and however inspired Mary's acts may have been, they were in no way acts of the Holy Spirit. Why? Because a created person is a *second cause* in relation to his own, proper acts. He must be moved by God to do them, but he is the one who does them, the one who is engaged in them. He realizes himself and actualizes himself in them.

This is not the case for Christ. His acts are the acts of the Word. We have seen that they can be the acts of the Word only on account of the action that the Word, through His Divine Will, exercises on His human will. In order for this action to make it be the case that these acts, which are produced by the moved human will, would be acts of the Word who moves this will, the latter must be an instrumental cause, not a second cause.

But is this intelligible? Instrumental causality pertains to a work to be done. The instrument is used by the principal cause to produce an effect exceeding the instrument's own, proper virtualities. It cannot perform this act by itself. However, it can concur in the production of such an effect through [the application of] the principal cause's power. Thus, we can conceive of the idea that Jesus would have produced and produces supernatural effects by His humanity as by an instrument in the production of miracles (e.g., when He commanded, by human voice and will, the winds and the sea), even the great miracle of His own resurrection, and in the works of grace. But how can we think of this in regard to His immanent activities, His own acts of willing and contemplating? Indeed, in those cases, the activity itself is the effect produced. The human faculty is the proper and perfectly proportioned cause of this effect, as it is second act in relation to the faculty which is in first act.

B. Instrumental Causality in General

{397} Generally speaking, an instrumental cause is a cause that actually participates in the causality of a superior cause (i.e., in the very action by which it produces its effect), which draws the instrument into its movement. The instrument is thus taken up and elevated formally as a cause. Now, given that it is a question of actual elevation, we must also add, "inasmuch as it is a cause causing in act." Thus we have the following principle, which is absolute in this matter: the instrument must have its own proper action and must make its own contribution in the action that it performs in common (though in a subordinate manner) with the principal cause.

This presents various difficulties, which we will consider later on when we speak about the causality of the Church through the sacraments. However, in the case before us now, in order to understand in what sense one can speak of instrumental causality for Jesus's human will, it is important to carefully distinguish the various ways in which this principle plays out. St. Thomas makes use of it in these various ways.[44] This leads to two successive distinctions.

1. First distinction: inert instruments and active instruments

{398} It is a recognized fact that in the very activity in which the instrument is engaged by the principal cause, the instrument itself is always active. However, there are instruments that have no other activity than that which is conferred upon them by the principal cause (e.g., a hammer or a brush). Other instruments, by contrast, have their own, proper activity, and this activity is what the principal cause uses (e.g., radium). In the second case, the instrument is indeed elevated to produce an effect that surpasses it (e.g., the treatment of a tumor). However, its action obeys the laws that are proper to it, coming from its nature. The principal cause must respect the proper nature of this action in order to make it serve its ends. Therefore, we have two distinct actions (i.e., that of the instrumental cause and that of the principal cause) that converge in a single action (i.e., the action that produces the destruction of the cancerous tissue). What is this action? It is the action of the instrumental cause (radioactivity), though oriented and channeled by agent's will and own activity.

---

44. See *ST* III, q. 18, a. 1 and 2; q. 19, a. 1, co. and ad 2.

2. Second distinction: how the motion of the principal cause is exercised

{399} We must distinguish an *non-ensouled instrument* (on which one can exercise only motion by efficient causality) from a *ensouled instrument* (which, as such, can be moved only by an action exercised upon its psyche, by way of final causality). Thus, as a *ensouled instrument*, an animal, precisely as an animal, can be moved only by an action that is exercised on its sense appetite, by the intermediary of the imagination which presents an object to it, arousing appropriate reflexes so that it may react to this object in accord with man's will. *Ensouled* instruments must themselves be distinguished into the purely animal psyche and the spiritual psyche (i.e., man). A man can be acted on [precisely as human] only by being made to will what someone else wishes to make him do. However, does this not make us pass beyond instrumental causality, which is situated in the order of efficient causality?

In the case of an animal's *ensouled activity*, given that this psyche is determined, one can exercise an efficacious pressure upon it. Therefore, one can make it act instrumentally in accord with the will of the person who trains it. In the case of man, this is no longer the case. A wholly efficacious pressure cannot be exercised upon a man's will, and the stronger and more disengaged this will is from the sensible [order], the less the notion of instrumental causality will play a role. Therefore, we do not have in our experience a case wherein the human will plays an instrumental role. The Aristotelian example of the slave is only a distant approximation and a simple illustration.

However, God can act on the human will efficaciously, all the while respecting its proper mode of willing (i.e., according to a personal judgment and freely). As we have seen, this is the way the Word moves His human will by His Divine Will.

C. Application to the Relations of Jesus's Human Will to His Divine Will

{400} Our first distinction enables us to see that the instrumental role attributed to Jesus's humanity in no way undermines the reality and specificity of His human activity. The second distinction shows that instrumentality does not, of itself, take anything away from Christ's human mode of acting. The instrumental action of a person can be conscious and free in the case where the principal cause is the Divine Will.

If we now return to the first distinction, we can understand how even an immanent action can be produced by instrumental causality. Indeed, in the case of what we have called an "active instrument" (i.e., that which has a proper action), such an instrument exercises this action under the motion of the principal cause and through the latter's power, as well as in service of the end pursued by it. This does not mean that this motion modifies the action of the instrumental cause. (Under the action of the principal agent, radium does not radiate differently than when it acts by itself.) However, the principal agent orders this action to a determinate effect to be produced (e.g., the destruction of a tumor). And in order to attain this effect, it directs the radium's action to precise places in the patient's body, regulating the time and intensity of each application. In this manner, one can say that radium is only the instrumental cause of the tumor's destruction. Similarly, under the motion of the Divine Will, Jesus's human will and intellect produce their proper activity, a fully human activity, which is the simultaneous effect of the two wills: "Thus, the activity that is elicited in Christ by the human nature inasmuch as the latter is the instrument of the divinity, is not a different activity from that of the divinity. The salvation by which Christ's humanity saves is not different from that performed by His divinity."[45]

---

45. *ST* III, q. 19, a. 1, ad 2.

D. What Does Jesus's Human Activity Receive from the Divine Motion?

{401} This "divine character" of Jesus's human activities must be distinguished from that which created grace confers, enabling them to have the divine mystery itself as their object and to be supernatural and meritorious. This latter characteristic comes to them from human faculties that have been super-elevated by grace, and it is also found in the activities of the righteous, who are created persons. What we are concerned with is Christ's activity's unique character as having an infinite value, being activities in which the Word Himself is engaged (and, hence, also their singular character as being morally indefectible). Just as Jesus's humanity is deprived of a proper personality (i.e., is "depersonalized") because it has been assumed to participate in the Word's subsistence[46] without, however, being diminished (neither in itself, given that personality is not an element of the nature's perfection [*qua* nature],[47] nor as regards His dignity[48]), so too is His human activity in no way diminished by the fact that it is only instrumentally produced by human faculties (neither in itself, given that it remains the second act of the will and of the human intellect, nor as regards its dignity, given that it receives an incomparable and infinite dignity from the fact that it is the Word's activity).

E. The Instrumental Causality of Christ's Humanity in Works and Miracles

{402} This is a controversial question, above all in what concerns the production of the works of grace. We will study it *ex professo* in relation to the sacraments, for it arises there in its full amplitude. One great difficulty is involved in imagining how such an action can be exercised. Must there not be some contact with the subject on which one acts? For the works of grace, St. Thomas makes

---

46. See §§283–84 above.
47. See *ST* III, q. 4, a. 2, ad 2.
48. See *ST* III, q. 2, a. 2, ad 2.

use of the sacraments for the establishing of this contact. However, does this not still leave a necessary point unaddressed, namely the contact between Christ's humanity and His mysteries, as well as the sacraments themselves? And beyond this, there are graces that are conferred without the intervention of the sacraments (at least their effective intervention).

In passing, St. Thomas proposes an explanation regarding miracles which we will discuss so that we may investigate whether it might not be extended to the works of grace. He states that, in miraculous activities, the instrumental causality of creatures consists in the fact that "by them, in some manner, the divine willing (*imperium*) is presented to nature."[49] And, in another place, he specifies that "God can make use either of man's interior movement, or of his word."[50]

I can only indicate the solution here. It will consist in saying that Jesus acted and acts on the world (and, indeed, on persons in their justification) by His human *imperium*, instrumentally traversed by the energy of the divine *imperium*. In any case, this joins back with the traditional idea that this power of doing miracles and of justifying was a permanent gift possessed by Jesus, one connected to the Hypostatic Union.

III. THE MERITORIOUS VALUE OF CHRIST'S HUMAN ACTS ON EARTH

{403} A very general notion of meritorious action can be expressed as "acting in such a way that one obtains from God (for oneself or for others) a grace in such a way that one's action would be the reason why God granted this grace." If we accept this notion of merit, we must hold that the idea that Christ merited while on earth is a fundamental truth of Christology. Scripture expressly presents us with the glory of His resurrection as being the recompense for His

---

49. *De pot.*, q. 6, a. 4.
50. *ST* II-II, q. 178, a. 1, ad 1.

obedience. Likewise, the justification offered to men and accorded to all those who believe is also the fruit of His obedience and sacrifice. Nonetheless, it is not easy to see how the Word, even the Incarnate Word, could merit: one merits before God, but can God merit?

A. Statement of the Problem

1. Reminders concerning the notions relating to merit

{404} In general, every action is done in order to procure a good, whether for the agent himself, for another agent, or for both: "Every agent acts in view of the good as an end." However, man's final end (i.e., communion with the Divine Persons) cannot be produced by a human action. God gives Himself. He is not "taken by force." Nonetheless, man draws closer to his final end and at last arrives at it through his own actions. Without this being true, his freedom would be meaningless. This antinomy is resolved by the notion of merit. Man acts in such a way that God, in recompense, gives him His eternal life: "Two conditions are required for meriting: a situation wherein one can merit (*status merendi*) and the power of meriting."[51]

The status merendi. In order to be able to merit, one must act in view of a good that one does not yet possess. He who attains the final end acts (and, indeed, still acts in virtue of the final end). However, he acts "on account of the goodness that he has, not in view of acquiring it." In other words, such a person does not merit.

The term *status comprehensoris* is used for the situation of the person who has the final end in his grasp, and the term *status viatoris* is used for the situation of the person who is on the path toward it. Only the latter can merit, without this meaning that the other ceases to act supernaturally. On the contrary [the latter is more in act supernaturally than the person living in *status viatoris*].

This is the reason why we cannot accept the idea of progress in eternal life. This idea, taken up today by certain theologians, is based upon a fact that is recognized by all, namely that the Beatific Vision

---

51. *De ver.*, q. 29, a. 6.

(in which eternal life consists) is limited for each [created] person (indeed, existing in various degrees for each person who partakes in it). No created intellect can embrace the infinite Divine Being and know it inasmuch as He is knowable.[52] However, for each person, the union with God at which he has in fact arrived by grace is the ultimate end. He acts on the basis of this end and not as though it were an end toward which he tends. For this reason (among others) his supernatural activities (of which the highest, source, and rule of all the others is precisely the Beatific Vision to the degree that it is granted to him) cannot merit a superior degree of vision. It is undeniable that God could, if He willed, grant a superior degree to a person. However, in the general context of salvation history, such a gift would seem to be without a reason: what God wills to give to this person, He gives him in full at the instant of the person's glorification.

The *facultas merendi*. The first condition for an activity to be meritorious is *freedom*. Indeed, it is through freedom that an agent is engaged in his activity and that, from this fact, an interpersonal relation, founded on this action, can be established between him and another agent (him for whom there is question of meriting). By a non-free action, the agent is only placed in relation with the reality on which he acts, and this relation is determined by the efficacy of his action.

Every free action places the created person in a particular relation with God, for, created by God, even in his freedom, he is responsible before God for the use of his freedom. Does this mean that the created person merits eternal life by any right use of his freedom whatsoever? No. Right use of freedom is measured by the ultimate end, such that what the free person can merit is the bestowal of this end upon him, giving him possession of the end toward which he tends and according to which he acts.

Now, eternal life can be the end toward which the created person tends only if God calls him to it and orders him to it by His grace.

---

52. See *ST* I, q. 12, a. 7.

The virtue of charity (poured into our hearts by the Holy Spirit) is what orders to eternal life the free actions that he performs. Therefore, to merit eternal life, meritorious activity not only must be free but also must proceed from grace and charity.

2. The difficulty of finding in Jesus on Earth the conditions needed for meritorious action

{405} First, *from the perspective of the status merendi.* We have seen that while He was on earth, Christ had the immediate vision of the Divine Essence, which is the essence of participated eternal life. It is true that He was still able to experience suffering and humiliation during His temporal life. For this reason, one cannot simply call such vision "beatific." However, it is a happiness inherent to life with God, which is not separable from Him, and He had this, a radiant nucleus of eternal happiness, while on this earth. Thus, how can we understand that He would have been able to merit eternal life, which He had in its essence from the start of his life?

Moreover—and this objection is more radical—we have seen that grace itself was connatural to Him because He was the Son of God.[53] Given that eternal life has grace as its principle (indeed, being grace itself), it belonged to Him by right and could in no manner be merited by Him—neither in what is essential to it, nor in its complements and prolongations. Therefore, the Son of God cannot merit. *Confirmatur:* merit can be understood only as a personal relation between the person who merits and God. Therefore, in Christ, it would arise from his Person, who is divine, not from his human nature, which alone is created.

Second, *from the perspective of the facultas merenda.* We have seen that Jesus's human activity was free. On the other hand, it quite obviously proceeded from grace and charity. Yes, but precisely speaking, His charity was not free—not that He would be lacking in something but, on the contrary, on account of its fullness. He who sees

---

53. See §331 above.

God is not free to not love Him. This is not because He would be constrained but, rather, is because the absolute good, which the *viator* seeks without finding it in its purity among earthly objects—and this is the reason why He is free, remaining always unsatisfied by what is offered to his love—is present to Him in its brilliance. Freedom is the search for God. He who sees God has found what he sought: love gushes forth from his depths, from the depths of his will, drawing him along irresistibly. This love is more than free, being the very principle of freedom (and, at the same time, its summit). However, he is not formally free.

Hence, how could a non-free charity be the principle that renders an activity meritorious, even if this activity is free in relation to its object? He who possesses the ultimate end remains free in relation to everything that is not that end, but not in relation to the end itself.

B. Examination of the Objection Drawn from the *Facultas Merendi*

1. St. Thomas's response

{406} Christ did not merit by His charity inasmuch as it was the charity of Him who had arrived at the ultimate terminus (*caritas comprehensoris*). Rather, He merited it inasmuch as it was the charity of Him who is still in progress toward the end (*caritas viatoris*). For He was simultaneously at the terminus (*comprehensor*) and en route (*viator*). And this is why obviously, no longer being a *viator*, He is no longer in the situation of being able to merit (*status merendi*).[54]

2. *Christ's charity in* quantum erat viator

Obviously, there are not two charities in Christ. Generally speaking, charity has two kinds of acts. On the one hand, there are *its proper acts* (i.e., love of God and neighbor), by which it is a distinct virtue (indeed, the highest of all virtues). On the other hand, there is *the orientation that it impresses on the acts* of other faculties, making

---

54. *ST* III, q. 19, a. 3, ad 1.

it into a universal virtue (with regard to the extent of its influence). As we have seen, the proper acts of Jesus's charity were beyond freedom. However, it also was the directive principle of acts that He accomplished on earth as *viator*, and these acts were free.

3. *"Participated charity"*

To understand how these free acts could be meritorious on account of a charity that itself was not free, we must appeal to a key concept of Christian morality, namely, the fact that charity is the form of the virtues.[55] Every virtuous act in the "righteous person" receives from charity its ordination to eternal life (as well as its ordination to conformity with Christ, etc.). Charity, properly speaking, remains external to this act, which is specified by its own object. Nonetheless, the impulse and orientation toward the supernatural end are intrinsic to the act. Inasmuch as it is free, it is ordered to eternal life, and it has this orientation from charity, not from the particular virtue from which it proceeds.

With Cajetan, we can say that the act thus oriented by charity is an act of charity by participation.[56] Thus, we have a free act, ordered to the ultimate end not yet possessed (to the degree that Jesus is still a *viator*) and informed by charity. Thus, all the conditions of merit are fulfilled, at least from the perspective of the *potestas merendi*. Is the same true as regards the *status merendi*?

C. *Examination of the objection drawn from the* status merendi

{407} To the degree that Jesus was a *viator* while He was on earth, He also existed in the state of meriting (*status merendi*). On the other hand, inasmuch as He was Savior, He was engaged in salvation history, which developed progressively—not only in relation to the Church (the "time of the Church," which extends up to the world's end) but also in relation to Jesus's personal destiny, for He

---

55. See *ST* II-II, q. 23, a. 8.
56. See Cajetan, *In ST* II-II, q. 23, a. 8.

accomplishes salvation through His temporal acts, from His conception to His resurrection. Therefore, during His earthly life, the salvation of humanity was set before Him as the end toward which He tended.

D. What Christ Merited

During His earthly life, and especially through His sacrifice, Christ merited both "bodily glorification" and the salvation of humanity.

1. Bodily glorification

{408} Scripture clearly indicates that after His death Christ was glorified by His resurrection and as a recompense for His sacrifice. Is it a question of [meriting] the Godhead itself, as certain heretics believed? We cannot accept this interpretation precisely on account of all the reasons we have for affirming that Jesus's divinity was taught by Scripture and believed in from the start by the Church as being constitutive of His being and as belonging to Him from the beginning [of the Incarnation].

Hence, expressions saying that Jesus received the "name that is above every name," the title "Lord," and so forth at His resurrection must be understood in the way they were understood from the beginning as being a question of the external and public manifestation of His glory, which was hidden up to that point. But what is meant by the expression *glorificatio corporalis*, which St. Thomas employs? It is clear that "glory" belongs only to a person. Therefore, "bodily" can here only mean the complete human person, inasmuch as he is bodily. Therefore, the *glorificatio corporalis* is the glory affecting the person even into his bodiliness.

This "glory" can only be understood in opposition to and in contrast with the deprivations and humiliations that reached His person, having their principle in bodiliness: sufferings and death. It is clear that the entire person is who was affected, reaching even in His soul. Likewise, it is in His soul as well, indeed principally so, that He is glorified through this liberation from His deprivations and through the splendor of His resurrected body.

The difficulty is found in seeing how this glory is a distinct object of merit, in relation to interior, spiritual glory. Indeed, Jesus had the latter from the start, and it seems that "bodily" glory would naturally flow from it. On the other hand, for the blessed in heaven, there is also a dissociation between spiritual glory (which they already have) and the "bodily" glorification that they will have only at the resurrection. However, can we say that the saints in heaven merit their resurrection?

We must give two successive responses. *First*, "bodily glory" is a distinct object of merit in the sense that it is a distinct element of the complete glory which has been promised to the human person and which the latter can merit. Certainly, it flows from spiritual glory. However, it remains distinct from it, and if this derivation is not, in fact, immediate and if a person is found in the situation of being already in possession of spiritual glory without yet having bodily glory, the latter becomes, by the same fact, the object of merit separately. *Second*, the saints in heaven are in no way in the state of *viator*. Therefore, they are no longer in a state subject to the possibility of meriting, and this is why the bodily glorification that they will receive at the resurrection is *already merited* for them. Christ on earth was in the state of way and therefore His bodily glorification could be the fruit of His merits.

2. *Why Christ had to merit His bodily glorification*

Scripture most certainly teaches that Christ, in fact, merited His bodily glorification. We can find the following two reasons for this fact.

a) *It is more dignified to merit that which can be merited*

{409} This is the reason given by St. Thomas.[57] It must be glossed as follows. Inasmuch as bodily glory naturally flows from

---

57. *ST* III, q. 19, a. 3.

spiritual glory, it would have normally accompanied Christ's spiritual glory from the start. This spiritual glory was given without prior merits because the Incarnate Son of God could not be deprived of it, even temporarily, during the time needed for meriting it, and bodily glorification would have normally been given with it as well. However, given that bodily glory was deferred for soteriological reasons, it became worthier and more honorable to merit it rather than to merely receive in due course.

However, we can ask whether the Incarnation would be conceivable without a temporal interval existing between spiritual glory and bodily glory. It seems that the bodily glorification could only be eschatological, and the Incarnation implies that the Incarnate Word led a human, "historical" life during the normal time of an earthly human existence.

If, hypothetically speaking, Christ came to a sinless world, His earthly existence would not have entailed suffering and death, though it would have entailed submission to the natural conditions of human life. In this case, would not the principle proposed by St. Thomas hold? Would we not need to say that He would have merited His bodily glorification?

b) Merit for others presupposes merit for oneself

{410} Merit for others can be conceived only as an extension of merit for oneself. If the latter did not exist at all, there would not have been in Christ a point of departure from which the meritorious scope of His free actions, performed in charity, could be extended to others. "Although He was a Son, He learned obedience through what He suffered; and being made perfect He became the source of eternal salvation to all who obey Him."[58]

3. *How Christ was able to merit salvation for men*

The whole of soteriology is founded on the meritorious worth of Christ's mysteries in relation to the salvation and justification of

---

58. Heb 5:8–9 (RSV).

men. However, do not salvation and justification depend on one's personal return to God?

a) The inclusion of all men in Christ

{411} St. Thomas speaks about the mystical inclusion of the Church's members in Christ.[59] However, is it not true that Christ merited for men who are not yet part of the Mystical Body? And is the act of returning to God by which a man becomes a member of Christ accomplished without grace? If it is an effect of grace, is it not true that this grace was merited by Christ?

Mystical inclusion presupposes ontological inclusion. We will see[60] that the latter must be operative and cannot be static (for Jesus, being a true man, could only be a human individual, distinct from all others, and hence "external" to them). Man is foundationally ordered to God, to union with God, and individual men and women commune in this dynamic order. In Jesus, the God-Man, this dynamic tendency common to all humanity finds its absolute realization so that the communion that all men have with each other *through their very nature* is already a communion in Christ. This communion, only sketched at the beginning of every human life, needs to be actualized in each person by his free action (in faith and through the sacraments).

This sketched-out, initial communion sufficed for Christ's personal actions (the interior acts of charity and of penitence, as well as external ones of expiatory sufferings and death) to be actions of all men together, so long as they exist in Christ. This is how His acts were meritorious for them. However, this is possible only because they were meritorious in themselves, in other words, because they were meritorious for Jesus Himself first of all. And this merit has value only for the person who actualizes his initial communion with Christ through his own personal action.

---

59. See *ST* III, q. 19, a. 4.
60. See §§ 434–35 in section III below.

b) Christ's merit in relation to the grace given to each human person

{412} This grace by which a man believes in Christ and becomes one of His members is obviously the fruit of Christ's merits. In reality, it is nothing other than the grace of the remission of sins actualized for this member of mankind. But why is it not given to all? We must firmly hold that it is really offered to all and that he to whom it is not given has rejected it (granting that this acceptance or rejection takes place in the depths of consciousness and that, for a great number of men, external signs do not exist for enabling them to judge whether grace has been accepted or refused). Grace is what makes one say, "Yes." Man's will alone is what says, "No." This is the mystery of grace.

c) Christ's merit and Christian merit

{413} Just as every human individual appearing in the world becomes a new living being who lives a human life, though also a new sinner, so too anyone "reborn of water and the Spirit" becomes a new righteous man, with grace as his own, that is, having personal relations with God. This means that he himself, through his own acts, which are free and performed in grace, really merits eternal life and makes satisfaction for his sins.

However, neither this grace, nor the merits that follow it, add to the grace and merits of Christ. It is Christ in him (and by him) who loves God and pleases Him by His actions. Here we have, without a doubt, the solution to the antinomy that sets faith in opposition to works. Works done outside of faith are useless before God. However, works done in faith please God and are meritorious, for they are a mere prolongation of Christ's works. By faith and the sacraments, this continuity between the Christian's works and those of Christ is established.

PART 3

CHRIST'S FIRST COMING

Christ is the Savior. He came to bring salvation to men, and from the beginning He was believed in and preached about in terms of this salvific mission. Having studied "what Christ is in Himself," we now approach the question concerning the reason for His coming and what He did during His earthly existence, as well as how He did it. That is, we will now undertake a study of *the salvation brought about by Jesus Christ*.

INTRODUCTION: THE NOTION OF SALVATION

{414} *Christian salvation*, the salvation that is announced by the Gospel, is *liberation from sin* (i.e., liberation from the wrath of God provoked by sin) and *the definitive happiness of man in God's company, eternal life*. In a word, *salvation is the definitive reconciliation of man with God*.[1]

---

1. A full bibliography concerning the notion of salvation would be immense. For a first introduction, one will fruitfully consult *Mysterium Salutis*, vol. 1 (Paris: Cerf, 1969), "Introduction générale," by Johannes Feiner and Magnus Löhrer, and "Théologique fondamentale de l'histoire du salut," by A. Darlapp. To this, one could add: Bernard Catão, *Salut et Rédemption chez S. Thomas d'Aquin* (Paris: Aubier, 1965); Stanislaus Lyonnet, *Les étapes de l'histoire du salut selon l'épître aux Romains* (Pairs: Cerf, 1969); the collective work, *Foi et Salut selon S. Paul*, Analecta biblica 42 (Rome, 1970); Jean-Pierre Jossua,

Even though salvation may also be presented in the Old Testament as being a liberation from temporal servitudes (first of all from the servitude of the people in Egypt, a liberation which is the very image of salvation), the notion of salvation is *an eschatological notion*, for it consists essentially in that which is the fruit of this liberation: being with God, in peace and happiness and being protected by Him against all evils.

The question concerning the relationship between this eschatological salvation and temporal liberations within history, considered in themselves, need not be treated here.[2] There is no doubt that the Gospel has a liberating value in relation to all of man's alienations in his earthly life (and requires us to work on behalf of such liberation). However, this liberating value can only be understood in light of its essential and characteristic nature: God's salvation is first of all, and principally, liberation from sin.

This salvation was brought to the world and accomplished by Jesus Christ, the God-Man. We spoke above, in general terms, about the Word's mission.[3] Here, we are concerned with studying the Incarnation of the Word as bringing to man eschatological salvation, eternal life with God by means of the remission of sins. In short, we are concerned with reflecting on this article of the Nicene Creed: "We believe ... in one Lord Jesus Christ ... *who for us, men, and for our salvation*, descended from heaven ..."

Le salut incarnation ou mystère pascal, chez les Pères de l'Eglise de S. Irénée à S. Léon le Grand (Paris: Cerf, 1968), and *Saviour God: Companion Studies in Concept of Salvation Presented to E. O. James* (Manchester: Manchester University Press, 1963); André Feuillet, "Le temps de l'Eglise d'après le IVᵉ Evangile et l'Apocaplypse," *Maison-Dieu* 65 (1961): 60–79.

2. This question will be treated in the fourth section of this volume.
3. See §§226–30 in the first volume.

6

The Incarnation in the Divine Plan

Today, the question of "meaning" is understood in the following way: "What meaning does the Incarnation have for me (or, for contemporary man)?" However, first and foremost, the Incarnation is an act of God. Thus, the very first question that must be asked is, "For what end did God decide to become Incarnate?" This does not exclude the preceding question. On the contrary, it furnishes the principle for its solution, for the Incarnation could have no other meaning for man than that which God willed to give it. As we will see, this meaning is likewise the meaning that it has for man.

I. THE INCARNATION'S MEANING IN RELATION TO GOD

A. The Ultimate Reason for the Incarnation

{415} The ultimate reason for the Incarnation is God's love—love, whose property is to give. One always gives oneself through love, by the means of a good that is one's own and that one communicates to another, and the two are united in the common possession of this good. This is the great metaphysical principle that commands the entire order of action: *bonum diffusivum sui*, the good is self-diffusive. If every agent, as such, simultaneously brings its effect back to itself, this is precisely because the good that it communicates to its effect is its own proper good and because the agent communicates this good to its effect so that it may exist in communion with it.

Every action by God *ad extra* is a communication of the divine good because no good exists at the principle of the divine action other than the divine good. And it is a pure communication to the other (i.e., to the creature), for God has nothing to acquire through His own action because He is infinitely good from the start. It is a pure gift and can only be explained by love. However, while every action *ad extra* is a pure communication of the divine good, we can distinguish, following Cajetan, three successive strata of communication, constituting three orders.

Through creation, God communicates Himself to His creature in the form of an ontological participation. The creature's being [*l'être*] is not God's being (which would be pantheism). Instead, it is a participation in it, in the form of a distant and partial imitation. By its very being, the creature resembles God, and the ensemble of all creatures reflects the Divine Perfections. This being constitutes the first goodness of things that strive, by that very fact, to increasingly resemble God and to be united to Him from afar, by means of their own proper goodness, which is a goodness that is created but is, nonetheless, a participation in God's goodness.[1]

Through grace, intellectual creatures are elevated, as we recalled earlier, to participate in the very activities of God. God communicates Himself to them, not by the mediation of a created goodness, but such as He is in Himself, as an object of knowledge and love. Obviously, this is still a participation because the created person remains a distinct person and a limited being which obviously has activities which themselves are also limited and created. Nonetheless, through these activities he takes part in the divine good itself, not in a distant imitation thereof. Indeed, he "possesses" the Divine Persons by being possessed by them.[2]

---

1. See *SCG*, bk. 3, ch. 2–25.
2. See §§207 and 208 in the first volume.

Finally, through the Incarnation, God communicates Himself to the creature in a substantial manner. This does not mean that the created being would become the Uncreated Being or would enter into composition with Him. Rather, it means that the Word has become a man by assuming a created human nature and that, consequently, *this man is the Word*. In the person of the Word made flesh the ontological conjunction between the created and the Uncreated is achieved. This is an infinite communication: this man, Jesus, is good with the very goodness of God.

This means that the Incarnation is the supreme realization of the good's self-diffusive character. It is fitting that that which is sovereignly good would sovereignly communicate itself. And the act of self-communicating is the very act of love. We can express this in a different way: it is fitting that He who is infinite love would give Himself infinitely, and this is what is realized through the Incarnation.[3]

B. The Freedom of the Incarnation

{416} Through the course of the ages, and again today, great minds are inclined to think that even though the Incarnation is not necessary in itself, it would be indispensable as the fulfillment of creation, giving creation and man their meaning, without which they would be incomprehensible. Ramon Llull (1235–1316),[4] Nicolas Malebranche (1638–1715),[5] and Maurice Blondel (1861–1949) are all examples of people who have spoken along these lines.[6]

According to such a conception, the three orders we have spoken about would constitute a single order that God would will or

---

3. See *ST* III, q. 1, a. 1. Also, see Cajetan's commentary on this article.
4. See B. Nicolau Tor, "El primado absolute de Cristo en el pensamiento Luliano," *Estúdios Lulianos* 2 (1958): 297–313.
5. See Martial Guéroult, *Malebrance: Le cinq abîmes de la providence* (Paris: Aubier, 1959), 2:114–36.
6. To express this, Blondel invented the term "Pan-Christism" [*panchristisme*]. [Tr. note: Fr. Nicolas also cites "Blondel, 3, I, 44." There is no third entry for Blondel in the bibliography. The first entry is Maurice Blondel, *La pensée*, vols. 1–2 (Paris: Aubier, 1934). The second entry is Maurice Blondel and Pierre Teilhard de Chardin, *Correspondance*, commented upon by H. de Lubac (Paris: Beauchesne, 1965).]

not will. (Therefore, it would be offered to the free divine decision). However, these three orders, thus constituting a single order, could not be dissociated. Any one of them could not be willed without the others being willed as well by the same act of freedom. Did St. Thomas not provide an explanation for these thinkers when he said that it is fitting that the sovereign Good would communicate Himself sovereignly?

1. Every communication of the divine goodness is free

{417} It is extremely difficult even to pose the problem, for the divine freedom never was situated at a moment antecedent to [the Divine] choice, placed before many hypotheses. (Indeed, we cannot even conceive it thus.) And, there are not a multitude of divine acts of willing. By a single willing, which is His eternal willing, God willed Himself first (this willing is the infinite friendship in which the Trinitarian life consists) and then the whole of creation, His entire work, *ad extra*. However, in relation to this willing, this work is a contingent object which is willed only by a free decision, and such a free decision could be not willed.

To say that it is fitting that the sovereign goodness would sovereignly communicate Himself, that the infinite love would infinitely give of himself, does not suppress the radical contingency of this object in relation to the divine willing. This contingency is essential to it. It comes from the fact that God has His infinite goodness in Himself, meaning that no other good whatsoever can be added to Him. Moreover, He is the absolute giver of every good other than His own and therefore can receive nothing from it which He would not already have. Thus, none of these goods that differ from His own correspond to a deficiency that would be found in Him, thus making it necessary for Him to will it. Therefore, by its very nature, every communication of the divine goodness *ad extra* depends on a free decision. Every act of God's love for His creatures is a love that is given in perfect freedom.

Will we then say that the three orders together constitute a single object of willing? This would mean that one of these orders could not be willed without the others being willed. Now, while it is indeed true that the hypostatic order cannot be willed without the order of grace being willed and likewise that the order of grace cannot be willed without man being willed ([and] called to become a child of God) and that man cannot be willed without the whole material universe being willed, the opposite is not true. Of themselves, man and the material universe could be willed without the grace of the children of God being willed, as well as the grace of the Hypostatic Union. Why? Because the inferior order is not of itself and by an intrinsic requirement ordered to the good whose communication constitutes the superior order. Therefore, by itself, it constitutes an object of distinct willing. Thus, the superior order depends on a free decision in relation to the inferior order. We must be more exact in our wording, however, for there are not several successive decisions in the Divine Reality. We must say that, in relation to the single free willing by which the universe in fact was willed, the three orders constitute three contingent objects that are willed together and ordered in relation to one another, though in such a manner that this very ordering is contingent, freely decided, and willed by God from all eternity.

Consequently, the decision on behalf of the Incarnation is not, of itself, included in the decision to create. Therefore, we cannot *deduce* it from the decision to create, which is first known by us (on the basis of the fact of creation), as is done by the Christian thinkers mentioned above (and by their numerous imitators) through this sort of reasoning: if God decides to create, He must necessarily decide that the Incarnation will take place, for without it His work would remain unfinished and unworthy of Him.

Of course, God's decision to bring about the Word's Incarnation modifies the decision to create and the decision to call man (and the angels) to His communion. That is, the real universe that God conceived and willed is a universe wholly ordered to Christ, one that could not, itself, not be ordered to Him. But we know this because the Incarnation has been revealed. We could not know it in any other manner. Moreover, the revelation of the Incarnation does not bring man the response to a question that he posed. Rather, it brings something unheard of and utterly unexpected, and nonetheless it is immediately present to his awareness as that which entirely fulfills his expectations.

2. *The sublime good of the Incarnation adds nothing to God's goodness and grandeur*

{418} We will see what a sublime valorization the Incarnation gives to the entire created universe and to man first of all. Given that the entire universe has no other meaning than to glorify God, God receives through the Incarnation the greatest glory that the creature could render to Him. And yet, this glory adds nothing to what He possesses in Himself. It does not lead to any increase for Him in any way, for the Infinite Good cannot acquire any kind of increase whatsoever. Every creaturely homage, even when it comes forth from the Incarnate Word's human heart and spirit, adds nothing to the eternal manifestation and proclamation of His glory, the Word in the intimate depths of the Trinity.[7]

Thus, the principle *bonum diffusivum sui* can be verified in God alone in its absolute purity. This purity is so disconcerting that the principle seems to disappear. We must pass through the negative way [of analogy], as we do for every transposition of a created good to God. However, the "negative way" would lead to nothing if the "way of eminence" were not joined to it.[8] This "absolute purity" consists in the purity of the act of giving. To give is to communicate one's own good to another without drawing from it any benefit for oneself, doing so through the giver's pure love for the one to whom he gives, exclusively for the sake of his own good. This can never be absolutely realized in creatures, for even utter disinterest does not prevent the giver from himself receiving some kind of increase

---

7. See Bouyer, *Le Fils éternel*, 473–75.
8. See *ST* I, q. 12, a. 12.

through his own generosity. God is the one who is infinitely good in Himself, infinitely happy in the absolute fullness of the Trinitarian life. The three Persons are perfectly self-sufficient, meaning that they cannot receive any growth in goodness, beatitude, or life from creatures, indeed from any creature whatsoever—including even Christ's humanity—nor from the universe of creatures. Certainly, the goodness of creatures is willed by God and loved by Him. Nonetheless, it is willed by a totally disinterested (and therefore perfectly free) love. For God's infinite love, any finite good is a contingent object that is not necessary in any manner, neither through itself (for it is good and loveable only because it is loved), nor by any need whatsoever on the part of God.

Thus, at its infinite summit, the good's proper character as having an intimate tendency to communicate and radiate itself includes the absolute freedom of the gift. Every such gift is freely communicated, so that every gift given by God is given through love and through a free decision in His depths, without any external pressure. The whole of creation is subject to the possibility of not existing (and thus, of not being good, of not being loved). And were God to have not created, He would nonetheless be Infinite Love. This means that the Incarnation can glorify God only by being a gift given to men by pure love, by a totally free and gratuitous decision.

3. *The Incarnation really glorifies God*

{419} So understood, it glorifies Him. Indeed, on the one hand, it manifests God's infinite goodness and His transcendent perfection, making it burst forth "externally." By "externally" I mean "in the created universe," wherein the Incarnate Word (who, certainly, is God, the Word, but whose humanity, by which the Word is a man, is created) is the crowning, the sublime summit, to which (as we will see) all the rest is ordered, giving the universe and man their meaning and true dimensions. However, this manifestation is not for God, who is infinitely aware of His grandeur and does not need to see it outside of Himself as in a mirror. Likewise, we must add that this manifestation causes the rational creature to glorify God, by thanksgiving and praise, which find their perfect expression in Christ's soul and heart, and in the Church, in every man who wills it in union with Christ. This so-called external glory rendered to God does not add to His intrinsic glory: "glorify thou me in thy own presence with the glory which I had with thee before the world was made."[9]

However, it nonetheless is real, for Christ is real, as is His body, composed of all men who are bound to Him as His members. Their praise and thanksgiving are real, and the Trinity to whom they are addressed is thus really praised and blessed. It is not true that this external glorification would be useless for God in the sense that He would despise it or simply be indifferent to it. It is useless to Him in the sense that God does not need it. Nonetheless, He really gave what He gave through pure love and in pure gratuity, and what He gave is precisely the ability to praise Him, to really glorify Him.

II. THE MEANING OF THE INCARNATION IN RELATION TO MAN

{420} If the Incarnation, considered from God's perspective, is a pure gift, we must also say that it is a gift for man, for it can be a gift for the universe, its enrichment and its consummation, only if it is a gift for man, who provides the very possibility of consciousness for the universe itself [*est la conscience de l'univers*]. Therefore, we must ask: What does the Incarnation bring to man?

A. It Seems That It Brings Nothing to Him

The Incarnation makes it be the case that an individual human is the Word of God. However, what interest do other men have in such a "promotion"? If a human group can feel affected and exalted by the exaltation of one of its own ([e.g.,] a hero), this is because such an exaltation does not make that person pass beyond the hu-

---

9. Jn 17:5 (RSV).

man sphere. Thus, each human person can project his own desire onto him, making him into a "model." However, how can we make a God-Man into a hero? On the one hand, one might reduce the word "God" to "a superior man." In that case, we are faced with something quite different. (Thus, we can see here precisely why Jesus did not wish to take on the appearance of a hero.) On the other hand, the formula could be taken in complete seriousness. In that case, it would seem that such a man, who would truly be God, would be utterly foreign to humanity, having passed into another sphere. But then, what can be brought to other men by the fact that one of them would have been elevated so high that He ceased to be a man like the others. Is He not now far beyond their possible concerns?

For the same reason, He cannot (so it seems) constitute a "model" for them. That is, it seems that He cannot constitute an example whose behavior they could imitate. Such a reaction is rather common, saying something like, "Christ was God. He knew neither sin nor weakness. We cannot compare His situation to our own." In short, one could easily say: "What is the point of such a God-Man's activity?"

An answer does exist: "to free us from sin." However, this again is problematic. Man's alienation consists neither solely nor principally in an external form of servitude, from which one could be delivered by an intervention which itself would be external. Man's servitude is interior, and man must himself be freed. Therefore, his "liberator" must be a man who is alienated like others, one who frees himself, leading the others. A God-Man by definition is non-alienated [*désaliéné*] from the beginning, and has neither the need nor the possibility of being freed (unless it is, instead, said to be an alienation that is more profound still, one that nothing can remedy).

B. Christ, the Perfect Realization of Humanity

{421} There is a profound affinity between the human person and the Person of the Word, for the human person is characterized by his aptitude for wisdom, finding his perfection in wisdom.[10] This affinity is what makes it possible for the Word to become a human person, a man through the Incarnation. To say that "Christ is like unto us according to humanity" is to say, "He is a man like us (on account of this human nature that is like unto ours)," and not only, "He has a human nature like ours." He is fully man, indeed a perfect man.

The perfection that the Divine Personality brings to the assumed humanity is not foreign to humanity. It infinitely realizes that to which humanity (in each person) tends with all its spiritual weight: union with God. Theologians like Karl Rahner, Welte, and others interpret this as meaning that each man would have an "obediential potency" to the Hypostatic Union, a potency that would be expressed in a positive inclination and desire. This runs into an insurmountable objection: the Hypostatic Union excludes every human personality that is distinct from that of the Word, whereas the person is the one who existentially experiences [human] nature's aspirations. How can we conceive of the idea that a person really aspires to a perfection which includes his own abolition? As soon as human nature is realized and concretized in a human person, it ceases to be open to the Hypostatic Union.[11]

Nonetheless, it does not cease to tend toward union with God, the highest possible union *for a created person* (that is, as we have seen,[12] the intentional union of knowledge and of love). Now, while the Hypostatic Union is of another, superior order, as an absolute form of man's union with God (to the point of identity with the [Divine] Person) it lies in the line of this intentional union. Put another way, we could say that the aspiration to the Hypostatic Union is inconceivable for a given human person because this would be an aspiration for one's own abolition. However, for the humanity that is realized in this person, the Hypostatic Union is situated, at infinity, in the line of his aspiration toward God, as though being realized in

---

10. See *ST* III, q. 3, a. 8.
11. See §290 above.
12. See §§267–68 above.

a solely human person would be a limitation imposed upon its aspiration toward God, while simultaneously being, in fact, a realization of this aspiration that, without it, would remain abstract alongside the nature itself.

Thus, when the Word is made flesh and becomes a human person (without ceasing to be a Divine Person), the universal and irrepressible aspiration of humanity is realized in Him. It is an aspiration that is so profound and so complete that it is found in each person before every deliberate choice. It is the foundational movement of the human being, what Blondel called the "willing will." Thus, through the Incarnation, humanity is not wrenched from the sphere of what is human. On the contrary, it is exalted to the summit of what is human—all men participate in this exaltation.

C. Christ, the Model for Every Man

{422} If Jesus Christ is an exceptional man, this is because, as a man, He is perfectly and universally a man. (The hero attains a very lofty but particular human perfection through the extreme development of one part of human perfection, often to the detriment of other parts.) Certainly, He is also God, but His divinity modifies His humanity in nothing. It makes it perfect according to the creative intention and, for this reason, exemplary for all men in their own effort to be fashioned in God's image.

Paradoxically, His perfect and total innocence draws Him closer to every man. Sin does not really draw men closer to one another. On the contrary, it separates them, closing each person in his self-love and in his egoism. By contrast, to the degree that someone is united to Him, such a person is also united to all men in what is most profound in them, that which is most essential and authentic in them: their aspiration toward God.

When Jesus seems inimitable in His behavior, this is not because this behavior is particular, corresponding to an ideal foreign to others. Rather, it is perfectly consonant with the ideal that each person carries buried in himself, the ideal that he projects onto his particular objectives. If He is inimitable, this is because through one's own sin, one is profoundly alienated and can say, "I do not understand my own actions. For I do not do what I want, but I do the very thing I hate."[13]

D. Liberation from Sin

{423} Precisely speaking, Christ presents man with the possibility of being freed from sin, and this gives meaning to the Incarnation for man. Christ restores man to himself by restoring him to God and by exalting him. To respond to the objection presented above, we say, still in the same line of reflection, that far from being external to the alienated man, Jesus Christ is wholly interior to him. Man's alienation, at least during his earthly life, is not complete and absolute (in contrast to the angel who, as a purely spiritual being, is irreversibly engaged through his first act of freedom and therefore cannot be saved if he has gone astray through this act). However profoundly man may be committed to his self-love, he can be saved because he retains in the depths of his spiritual being the freedom to extract and free himself by turning toward God, for it is indeed entirely true to say that this liberation can be brought about only through an act of freedom, given the role of the will in this process.

Now, Jesus Christ represents and realizes the man who is free in relation to the servitude about which we are speaking. However, as will become clearer below, He does not do so as someone who externally looks upon the condition of alienated men but, rather, Himself partakes in the consequences of their alienation and is the first fruits of their liberation.[14]

13. Rom 7:15 (RSV).
14. Indeed, Christ obviously represents all of this for man only according to His mystery as the God-Man (and, therefore, only from the perspective of faith). It is not at all reasonable to seek out the meaning that the Incarnation could have for contemporary man if by "contemporary man" one means "him who refuses to believe." The Incarnation has a meaning immanent to itself, the meaning that God gave it, and it is not man's role to give it a meaning. However, as the Incarnation is a gift of God to man, this meaning is a meaning for man, one that he must discover—or rather, that must be revealed to him. It can be presented before [the listener has] faith because of the aforementioned

III. THE MEANING OF THE INCARNATION IN RELATION TO CHRIST HIMSELF

Therefore, Christ is the supreme gift given to man by God. However, He also is a Person: the eternal Person of the Word, though having become a human person through the Incarnation. Therefore, we must ask ourselves, "What is Incarnation's meaning for the Incarnate Word Himself?"

A. The First-Born of Every Creature and Head of Creation

{424} It is a traditionally incontestable view, one rooted in Scripture, to say that Christ is the summit and crowning of the creative work, that everything that exists, especially man, exists for Him and for His glory.[15] Note that the Fathers of the Church, from St. Irenaeus onward, expressly interpreted [Genesis's words about man being] "made in the image of God" as meaning that Christ is the man who exists perfectly as the image of God and that other men are the same only thanks to Him, by being conformed to Him.[16]

Therefore, He is the one who gives creation its meaning. This is not opposed to what was said above about the freedom of the Incarnation, for the universe that God freely decided to create includes the three aforementioned orders,[17] ordered in relation to each other, so that the order of natures is intrinsically ordered to the order of grace, and both together are ordered to the hypostatic order. When we speak about the freedom of the Incarnation, we do not at all intend to speculate about another hypothetical creation (i.e., a creation, on this hypothesis, existing without the Incarnation or with-

---

correspondence between the mystery and man's profound aspirations. However, it can be perceived only in faith.

15. See Thomas R. Potvin, *The Theology of the Primacy of Christ According to St. Thomas and Its Scriptural Foundations* (Fribourg: Éditions Saint Paul, 1973). This contains a bibliography up to the date of its publication in 1973.

16. See *Dictionnaire de spiritualité ascétique et mystique*, 6:812–22 and 7:1401–25.

17. See §414 above.

out the supernatural elevation of the order of grace). Rather, we are asking whether this connection and ordination are in fact necessary or contingent in this real universe that God conceived, willed, and realized. To admit that it is contingent is to admit that it could have not been willed, though [this recognition] also [entails an admission] that God, in fact, willed it, indeed, freely. In willing it, He who is the immutable One conferred upon it a *de facto* necessity. This could have been different, but this cannot [now] be different, for God conceived and willed it in this manner.

Therefore, one can say with Mouroux: "The meaning of cosmic time is properly religious, Christological, and theological,"[18] and "Temporal creation is the first act of salvation history." However, how can this be reconciled with the other aspect of the mystery of the Incarnation we spoke about above, namely the fact that Christ came so as to free man from his sins? This is a fundamental theme: The Incarnation is the essential and decisive phase of salvation history. However, does this not mean that Christ exists *for man* instead of man being *for Christ*? Moreover, does this not irredeemably compromise Christ's primacy?

B. The Incarnation and Sin

1. The thought of the Fathers

{425} The medieval problem concerning the "motive of the Incarnation" was not posed by the Fathers, who did not dream of considering the hypothetical situation of a universe without sin. Instead, we find in them the data whose conflicting nature will give birth to the problem. These are the two fundamental data which are difficult to reconcile. First, the Christ about whom they speak is always the real Christ, the Savior, who suffered for men's sin, who rose from the dead, and who divinizes man by snatching him away from his sin. They never separate the Incarnation from the cross and the resurrection. Second, this redeemer Christ was willed by God from the

---

18. Mouroux, *Le mystère du temps*, 57 and 91–92.

beginning. He gives the work of creation its meaning and is its fulfillment.

This emerges quite clearly in the series of texts cited by Myrrha Lot-Borodine in her *La deification de l'homme*.[19] "Like his predecessors, St. Gregory Nazianzen founds the realism of the Incarnation on its redemptive finality ... He has taken on the whole of man, except for sin, so that he may save every man from his sin."[20] And Gregory himself:

If, on the contrary (the Word was made man) so as to abolish the condemnation of sin by sanctifying the similar by what is similar to it, just as it was necessary for Him to take on flesh because of the condemnation of the flesh and a soul because of the condemnation of the soul, so too it was necessary for Him to have a spirit because of the condemnation of the spirit which in Adam had not only sinned but had presented the first symptoms of evil, as doctors say about sicknesses ... What was in need of salvation is that which was assumed; therefore the spirit was assumed."[21]

How can we fail to pose the question: "And what if man had not sinned?" This question springs up several times in the work of Maximus the Confessor.[22] Here, we first of all encounter the idea that the Incarnation, considered as the descent of the Word into suffering and death, gives the world its meaning, being the reason why the world was created.[23] Then, we also encounter the problem of man's original fault. It consists in the fact that man chose to turn himself toward nature instead of giving himself over to the contemplation of God. However, this is what makes the history of the world possible. It is also presented as the choice of the sensible instead of the spirit. Sin has exiled us in the currently existing world. Nonetheless, the state of innocence is not a mythical state. Standing between Origen's

19. See Myrrha Lot-Borodine, *La deification de l'homme* (Paris: Cerf, 1970), 52–57, and Jossua, *Le salut*.
20. Vincent Leroy, "Bulletin de patristique," *Revue thomiste* (1979): 642.
21. Gregory of Nazianzen, *Orationes*, PG 35–36, 59. Also, see Jean Kirchmeyer, "Grecque (Église)," in *Dictionnaire de spiritualité ascétique*, 6:822.
22. See Hans Urs von Balthasar, *Liturgie cosmique. Maxime le Confesseur* (Paris: Aubier, 1957), 2.
23. See ibid., 204–7.

position (holding that souls fell into bodies following upon sin, as a consequence thereof) and that of Gregory of Nyssa (who held that God, in His foreknowledge of the sin of nature, immediately created the consequences of the transgression, namely sensibility and, above all, sexuality), Maximus chooses a radical solution, namely, the idea that creation and the Fall coincided: "For Maximus, the bronze doors of the divine home are slammed remorselessly shut at the very start of our existence."[24] Thus, according to Maximus, man must not look behind him (toward the lost fatherland) but, rather, must look forward so as to find his point of departure at the terminus [of this forward-pointing orientation]: "Seeking his end, man encounters his principle, who stands where the end is ... For as I have said, he must not seek the principle behind him, but rather, must envision the goal that is set before him in order to know the forsaken principle in the end, this end which man could not foresee at the start."[25]

This is a highly metaphysical intuition, though one with redoubtable implications: if sin appears at the instant that existence appears, will not God, who is the author and source of existence, be the cause of sin? Note that, when St. Thomas found himself faced with the problem of sin's origin in the angelic world, this will be the reason why he refuses to situate sin at the first instant of the angel's existence.[26]

Will it be said that Maximus holds that sin is necessary? He denies this expressly. However, we must recognize that this denial is not (or does not seem) completely coherent with the whole [of his thought]: for it seems that if man had not sinned, God's plan could not be realized. One is thus paradoxically led to the position that is directly opposite of the one that will be held by the later theologians who will envision the problem concerning the motive of the Incarnation. Indeed, for them, man frustrated the divine plan by sinning.

---

24. Ibid., 135. [Tr. note: Taken from Hans Urs von Balthasar, *Cosmic Liturgy: The Universe According to Maximus the Confessor*, trans. Brian E. Daley (San Francisco: Ignatius Press, 2003), 187.]

25. Maximus the Confessor, *Questions to Thallassius* 59, PG 90, 631D.

26. See *ST* I, q. 63, a. 5.

The Incarnation in the Divine Plan

We must recognize that this outlook is at once more rational and more religious.

2. The theological problem concerning the motive of the Incarnation

{426} Thus does the celebrated *quaestio* arise: "If man had not sinned, would Christ have come?" The question was introduced into the history of theology by Rupert of Deutz (1075–1130), who seems to have resolved it affirmatively,[27] and it became a classic question in scholasticism. However, thus posed, it seems to be in the typical form of a false dilemma. How can the theologian reason outside the real order of salvation in which He is engaged, not only for his personal destiny, but even in his thought?

However, as often happens, a poorly posed question touches on a problem that is real and cannot be evaded. We must consider the real Incarnation, the historical Christ, and we can ask ourselves about the relationship that this Incarnation has with man's sin. Did Christ come in order to redeem man, thus meaning that man's sin would be the reason for His coming? Or did He come to assume headship over the universe? In this case, as regards the mission of the Word, the redemption is thus conceived as being an annexed task that He accomplished because He was here, not the task that was His reason for being here. In the first case, it is not clear how the Incarnation is for His glory and His exaltation. In the second case, it is not clear how the Incarnation itself belongs to salvation history.

3. Various positions

a) The coming of Christ as something independent from sin

{427} This is the position best known as formulated by Duns Scotus, adopted by the whole Scotist school, as well as by many other theologians and Christian philosophers ([e.g.,] those who were noted above with regard to the freedom of the Incarnation). Before

---

27. See Leo Scheffczyk, "Die heilsökonomische Trinitätslehre des Rupert von Deutz und ihre dogmatische Bedeutung," in *Kirche und Überlieferung. Festschrift für J. R. Geiselmann* (Freiburg: Herder, 1960), 90–118.

Scotus, it was already the position of St. Albert the Great, though in a much less affirmative manner.[28] Prior to him, Robert Grosseteste, Odo Rigaldus, and the *Summa* attributed to Alexander of Hales can all be cited.[29]

According to Scotus,[30] Christ had been willed first and above all, independent of the very existence of all other things (and, therefore, for all the more reason independent of an event that would happen in the universe, such as sin). The decision to realize the Incarnation is so perfectly independent from every other decision that "Christ would still have been predestined even if there had not been any other creatures than Him." Thus, Christ is willed primarily for Himself, to the point that we can ask ourselves about the use of all the rest, as God finds in Christ all the glory that the creative action pursues and since Christ, it seems, did not need a universe to crown. He has full worth by Himself.

According to Scotus, the "motive of the Incarnation" (i.e., the reason why God freely chose to have the Word become Incarnate) is not the perfection of the universe—as it was for the theologians and philosophers cited above. Instead, he held that it was because God willed to have, outside of Himself, someone who responds to His love, and in order for this someone to perfectly respond to His love, He could only be a Divine Person, the Word. However, to be "outside of himself," this Divine Person needed to make a creature be his own and needed to become (according to a terminology that is not that of Scotus) a human person.

---

28. Albert the Great, *Opera Omnia*, ed. Emil Borgnet (Paris: Vives, 1890–99), 28:360–62.

29. See Thomas-André Audet, "Approches historiques de la Somme théologique," *Etudes d'histoire littéraires et doctrines* 17 (Montréal, 1962), 7–32.

30. For Scotus's thesis, interpreted by modern Scotists, see Jean-François Bonnefoy, *La primauté du Christ selon l'Ecriture et la Tradition* (Rome: Herder, 1959); for the history of this position, see Jean-François Bonnefoy, "La question hypothétique, 'Utrum si Adam non pecasset' au XIIIe siècle," *Revista Española de Teologia* 14 (1954): 327–68; E. M. Caggiano, "De mente Joannis Duns Scoti circa rationem Incarnationis," *Antonianum* 32 (1957): 311–34.

b) The position of the "Thomists"

{428} St. Thomas opined—though with the nuances that we will come to discuss—on behalf of a negative response to the question. After this, his school took a position that was opposed to the view articulated by Scotus, though not taking into account the nuances of St. Thomas's response (and, above all his "existential" manner of posing the problem). They categorically declared: "Christ would not have come [if man had not sinned]."

Following in this line, there are several ways to envision Christ's "predestination" (i.e., the decision on behalf of the Incarnation) in relation to sin. On the one hand, with Cajetan,[31] one may hold that the decision to create is *of itself* (i.e., in the order of divine decrees, such as our mind establishes them, though not without a foundation) prior to the decision on behalf of the Incarnation, which was made only *praeviso peccato*. On the other hand, with the Salamanca Carmelites,[32] one may agree to say that the Incarnation was decided upon first and above all, though specifying that it was decided upon in the way it was realized (i.e., as redemptive), thus meaning that God permitted sin so that this decision could be realized. However, this poses problems in relation to God's permission of sin.

c) St. Thomas's position

{429} Although St. Thomas, both in the *Summa theologiae* and in the *Scriptum*,[33] accepts the question as it was posed in the schools, it is remarkable that in the *Summa* he no longer resolves it from the hypothetical perspective but instead takes up an existential one: "It is better to say that the work of the Incarnation was ordered by God as a remedy against sin, meaning that if there had not been sin, the Incarnation would not have taken place." Therefore, it is a question directly of saying why He did what He did (i.e., why, in fact,

---

31. See Cajetan, *In* ST III, q. 1, a. 3.
32. See Salmanticenses, *Cursus Theologicus*, In III, tract. 21, disp. 2, dub. 1.
33. See *ST* III, q. 1, a. 3; *In* III *Sent.*, dist. 1, q. 1, a. 3.

the Word was Incarnated), not what God would have done if there had not been sin. His mentioning of the hypothesis that there would not have been sin to redeem comes to reinforce this position. The motive is redemption (positive affirmation): if there had not been a need for redemption, this motive, the only one that we know, would not have existed (negative affirmation of the same position). However, this is immediately adjusted: other motives are possible, and therefore, we cannot conclude with certitude that the Incarnation would not have happened without this motive.

This position is rigorously connected to the recognition that the Incarnation is a free act on the part of God. However great this good who is Christ may be, [the Incarnation] is not imposed necessarily upon God. It is contingent in relation to the divine willing. We cannot deduce it in any way. Therefore, it is purely and simply impossible to respond to the question in the hypothetical form in which it is posed.

4. The redemptive Incarnation and the primacy of Christ

{430} If the Incarnation was undertaken on account of man, in order to save him, how can we still maintain that Christ was willed for Himself and the world for Him? How can we maintain His primacy over all creation? Below,[34] we will see why the role of being the redeemer fell to the God-Man. However, if this role fell to Him, He Himself is much more than this, and it is not a question of enclosing Him in His redemptive function (as so-called functional theology logically tends to do). As soon as the Incarnation has been undertaken, the hypostatic order can only be that to which everything else is ordered, for which all is done, and to which all belongs, so that it may all be related to the Father by it. He is the one in whom the consciousness that man has of himself and of the world takes on its full dimensions.

However, it is urged and objected that if Christ came in order to save man and at the same time in order to unify the universe and rule it, the Incarnation has two distinct ends that are irreducible to

---

34. See §491 below.

one another. Hence, we would need to say that the end of the Incarnation is man's salvation, not Christ Himself. Thus, Christ would be placed at the head of the universe only as an afterthought.

The response to this objection is found in the distinction that must be made between the "motive" and the "end" of the Incarnation. The end of the Incarnation can only be Christ's glory, a created end because every other created good is subordinated to it, as well as the glory that this loftiest communication and manifestation of His Infinite goodness obtains for God. However, we have seen that even this lofty good that is the communication of God's goodness through the Incarnation is a contingent object in relation to the divine will, one that depends upon a free decision. Because this end is not imposed upon the Divine Will as necessary, there must be a reason for willing it rather than not willing it. This reason is the "motive" for it.

Obviously, a perfectly sufficient motive would indeed be the inherent value [*la valeur propre*] of this end, and this is why the theologians who say that Christ was not willed for any other reason than Himself do not say something irrational or impossible. Other motives would still be conceivable. What St. Thomas says to us is that the redemption is the only motive that God has revealed to us, meaning that it is also the only one that we can affirm with certitude. However, this "motive," this "reason why God decided," is not the "end" of this decision, which is and can only be Christ Himself, that is, this sovereign communication of the divine good that was made to Christ in His humanity, and through it to mankind and to the whole universe.

It is still more difficult (and profoundly mysterious) to determine the place of sin in the ideal series of divine willings. Obviously, sin is not the object of a divine willing. However, in whatever way one explains it, one must admit that it is an object of the divine knowledge. God chose for the Word to become Incarnate in view of man's sin. From this perspective, the decision to create the world and man, as well as the decision to call man to communion with Him, has a kind of priority over the decision on behalf of the Incarnation (for man's sin could not have been foreseen prior to the decision to create).[35] Is this compatible with Christ's primacy, which requires the world and man to exist for Christ and therefore requires them to have been willed only in function of Him? No, if one admits that man's sin (mysteriously total and collective) had really interrupted the execution of the divine plan. The Incarnation then appears as a recovery of an interrupted work, ordered this time to Christ. From the ruins of his first work, God has fashioned one that is greater and more beautiful. Once again, it is a question of an order among the various objects of the unique divine willing to create the world such as it is, not a plurality of divine decisions.

While giving greater respect to the freedom of the Incarnation—and consequently its characteristic as a great act of mercy for man—this conception simultaneously provides a better account of salvation history. Salvation history is not the simple and quasi-automatic realization of ideal necessities. It is made up of unpredictable divine interventions and of no-less-unpredictable decisions on the part of human freedom.

C. Teilhard de Chardin's Notion of the Cosmic Christ

{431} According to Teilhard de Chardin's conception, in order for this primacy of Christ to be real, it must consist in the organic union of Christ with the world.[36] Blondel reproached Teilhard for insisting that such union would be physical.[37] In truth, this "organicism" is a myth, not an intelligible theory. (Such physical penetration of Christ, in His physical reality, into the heart of things, is not thinkable.) It forces into a purely imaginative schema this certain truth: the ordering of all things to Christ. How can we conceive of this truth in intelligible terms?

---

35. [Tr. note: There is no closing parenthesis in the original.]
36. See Pierre Teilhard de Chardin, *Oeuvres*, 13 vols. (Paris: Seuil, 1955–76), 9:39–44: "Note sur le Christ universel."
37. See Blondel and de Chardin, *Correspondance*, 23, especially 23n12.

D. The Ordering of All Things to Christ

{432} We must reject the dilemma stating that Christ's primacy over the universe either is something purely juridical and does not penetrate into the heart of reality or, otherwise, is "organic" and physical. Between the two horns of this dilemma there is room for the realism of final causality, which is founded on the reality of the good and that of activity. To the degree that every being is, it is good. Its goodness is as real as its being.

This goodness comes from the being [*être*] that it already possesses, which is its good and richness. It also comes from all the increases it undergoes in this being up to its ultimate perfection. It tends toward this ultimate perfection (i.e., the consummation of its initial perfection) with all its "weight" (*amor meus pondus meum*), drawing close to it so that it may at last attain it by its activities. (This is true for the being that is spiritual, or at least partially spiritual [i.e., man], for the purely material being never attains its ultimate fulfillment. This fulfillment is ever placed before it, and it dies or disappears without ever attaining it.)

Christ is the immanent end of the universe, and all beings tend toward Him in this realistic manner. Man not only tends toward Him. He is finally united to Him (or at least can be united to Him) by his spiritual activities. Thus, while remaining ontologically distinct from all the beings of the universe, Christ exercises His primacy in a real way, drawing all things to Himself because all things were created for Him.

IV. THE RECAPITULATION OF ALL THINGS IN CHRIST

{433} Therefore, the Incarnate Word was sent for man's redemption. He accomplished this mission by giving His life as a sacrifice and by receiving it anew through the resurrection. But, by the Incarnation itself, man's salvation has already begun. In the Man-Jesus, the image of God, which was eroded by sin, is already restored, for this man is the Word, the eternal and perfect image of the Father. He restored it by realizing, in Himself first of all and perfectly, the divine intention to make man in His image. He restored it inchoately and virtually in all of humanity because mankind was in some way contained in Him. In the Incarnation, the recapitulation of all things in Christ already begins. The Incarnation is already redemptive.

However, how can we understand the idea that all men are included in Christ? The immediate response that comes to mind is the inclusion of all men in Christ's capital grace, and this solution is correct. However, would His capital grace itself be conceivable if Christ did not contain all men in Himself already on the level of nature, so that the grace given to Him *tanquam unigenitus a Patre*, as the Father's only-begotten Son, involves all of them in Him?

A. The Inclusion of All Men in Christ according to Nature

{434} Prior to any reflection and explanation, we are here in the presence of an intuition of faith, one that appears in the most ancient tradition of the Church. [As Charles Journet remarked,] "The inexhaustible riches of this theme represent a permanent acquisition for Christian teaching."[38] This theme was taken up at Vatican II.[39] What we must seek out is an explanation that intelligibly accounts for this basic intuition.

1. Discussion of the explanation by ontological inclusion

The idea of the inclusion of humanity in Christ at first developed under a Neo-Platonic inspiration.[40] Without always expressly saying it, the unity of human nature is mentioned in order to say that in being made man the Word assumed the whole of humanity, which

---

38. Charles Journet, *L'Église du Verbe incarné* (Paris: Desclée de Brouwer, 1951), 2:337. See Emil Mersch's classic book, *Le corps mystique du Christ. Études de théologie historique*, vols. 1–2 (Paris: Desclée de Brouwer, 1951).
39. See Vatican Council II, *Gaudium et Spes* (December 7, 1965), no. 22.
40. See Henri Rondet, *Gratia Christi* (Paris: Beauchesne, 1948), 91–97.

also exists in all other men. Mersch[41] provides a chronological exposition of this point of Patristic thought. Several Fathers, especially St. Cyril of Alexandria, also make recourse to the Eucharist to explain how Jesus's individual humanity penetrates the humanity of all men. J.-P. Jossua calls for a great deal of nuance in the "incarnationist" theory (i.e., the theory holding that the Incarnation itself was redemptive, a theory which can be found in the Greek Fathers). He holds that, according to the Fathers, mankind is included in Christ above all at the resurrection. And yet, this anthropology remains a Platonic one, holding that even though the humanity assumed by the Word was not a universal humanity it is identical with our common nature so that the Word is united in Christ to all men.[42]

This idea was taken up by Leopoldo Malevez.[43] It represents a kind of reinterpretation of the same theory in line with an Aristotelian anthropology. According to Malevez (at least at one time in his career, for he would later provide another explanation, as we will discuss below) a form would bring with itself all the riches of the nature, which the matter would limit to a single individual. All the possibilities of human nature not actualized in this individual (on account of the limitation imposed upon the form by matter) would virtually exist in each individual so that each human person would include all the others in himself as unrealized possibilities. Thus, the inclusion of all men in Christ would be explained by the general condition of human nature, which is found in every other man as well, and not by His singular condition.

This last observation suffices to make clear the unsatisfactory nature of his explanation. What we are seeking to explain—namely, the inclusion of all men in one man—is a characteristic of Christ, not something that He would share in common with other men. He alone is "the New Adam." On the other hand, it is easy to see

---

41. See Mersch's text cited above.
42. Jossua, *Le salut*, 13–44.
43. Leopoldo Malevez, "L'Église dans le Christ. Étude de théologie historique et théologique," *Recherche de Science Religieuse* 25 (1935): 257–91 and 418–40; Yves-Marie Congar, *Sainte Eglise*, Unam Sanctam 41 (Paris: Cerf, 1963), 483.

that this interpretation of the hylomorphic theory does not hold. The form itself is what is individuated, even if this individuation is brought about by matter. It is a limited realization of the ontological perfection of human nature so that the "possibilities" of this nature in this individual person do not have any reality. They are "logical possibilities." Moreover, note that in such a conception, human personality finds itself quite devalued. Indeed, while the person must be conceived as including all other personalities in himself, he himself remains very undetermined. A person is fully himself only by not being what others are.

Let us also note the position expressed by Glorieux, who would like it to be the case that in Christ, on account of the Hypostatic Union, the individual nature (i.e., the assumed nature) would be identical with the universal nature [of humanity].[44] However, this would tend to strip the Incarnation of its reality, for the universal nature,[45] precisely as universal, is not real, and it can be realized only in a particular individual nature. It is contradictory to say that it would be realized in an individual while also retaining its universality. Finally, there is the Teilhardian conception of an organic unity; however, we already critiqued this above.

2. *Recourse to dynamic inclusion*

{435} Having explored these various possibilities, we must say that mankind's inclusion in Jesus Christ cannot be entitative. The reality of the Incarnation, as well as the reality of each human person in his permanent distinction, mean that, in His ontological constitution, Christ must be a human individual who is distinct from all others. They are not part of Him; nor are He and they part of a vaster whole in which both would lose their distinction and autonomy.

However, we cannot content ourselves with an inclusion that would be merely intentional and moral. This would lead us to weak-

---

44. Palémon Glorieux, "Le mérite du Christ selon Saint Thomas," *Revue des Sciences Religieuses* 20 (1930): 622–49.

45. [Tr. note: Reading "la nature universelle" for "la nature individuelle."]

en the aforementioned intuition of faith. There is a third option between entitative (static) inclusion and intentional (moral) inclusion: dynamic inclusion.[46] In each human individual, human nature is the principle of a fundamental ordination to this concrete good, God. On account of [man's] divinization [through grace], it is an ordination that finds its terminus in personal communion with God. Radically by his nature and formally by his vocation to divine filiation, man is *capax Dei*.

In the man Jesus Christ, humanity realizes this fundamental aspiration as in an absolute summit. Also, the natural and existential tendency (*voluntas ut natura*) which, prior to every proper activity and choice, orders to God the man called by God and redeemed, likewise orders him to Christ as to the perfect model through whom man's return to God necessarily passes. Now, the entire dynamism that a being exerts in fulfilling itself is pre-contained in its tendency toward its end. Thus, given that man can find his fulfillment only in Christ by rejoining Him through man's own proper activities of understanding and love, therefore prior to any activity on his part, he is already in Christ on account of his dynamic ordering to Christ.

However, as soon as the person is capable of an act of self-disposition (i.e., an act of freedom), he can refuse such fulfillment, separating himself from Christ. Indeed, although man is "naturally" ordered to God, he can "freely" turn himself away from Him, thus bringing about, in the depths of his spiritual being, a kind of divorce between his will's fundamental movement (i.e., his willing will) and the free movement by which he chooses to seek the realization of his fundamental desire in a good that is not his true good (i.e., his willed will). Just as he separates himself from God, this man separates himself from Christ (at least, such as Christ is really present to his awareness). Nonetheless, as long as man has the power of returning to God (i.e., as long as he lives upon earth), he remains virtually included in Christ. It is only through his last act of choice (by which

---

46. See J.-H. Nicolas, *Les profondeurs de la grâce*, 248–52.

he commits himself in an irreversible manner) that he definitively cuts himself off from Christ (if this choice is a rejection).[47] This explanation can be connected to St. Thomas's use of the notion of image in his explanation of man's return to God.[48] One must not forget that, for St. Thomas, man is dynamically the image of God.

B. The Inclusion of All Men in Christ's Grace

1. How all men are loved in Christ

{436} Above all, grace is the eternal love by which God loves the person who exists in grace, for God's love is what renders the beloved being worthy of love. The eternal love by which the Father loves the Son is not a grace. It is the infinite friendship between the Persons at the heart of the Divine Nature.[49] However, as soon as the Word "becomes" a human person through the Incarnation, this love—identically the same love—becomes a grace. This grace is the *grace of union*.[50] It is a love that is at once *natural* (inasmuch as its object is He who is the Son by nature) and *grace-given* (inasmuch as its object is a man in whom the human nature is exalted by this very love to the point of substantial union with the divinity).

In the Incarnate Word, this love encounters all of humanity, which is included in Him in the way that we explained above. He encounters all of humanity in it in the way that this humanity is contained in Him, that is, by the mediation of human nature and its fundamental inclination toward God. Given that this nature is personalized in each man, each man's person is reached by God's love in Christ.

However, we have seen that [human] nature's inclination toward God must be personalized in each person, through each person's own freedom. If the act of freedom ratifies and personalizes this tendency, the human person thus finds himself loved for himself, in his

---

47. For a solution very close to this one, see Malevez, "Le Christ et la foi."
48. See Lafont, *Structures et méthode*, 265–90.
49. See §§148–49 in the first volume.
50. See §332 above.

personal distinction, and as a result, is justified and divinized. This justifying and divinizing love by which he is loved is an extension of the love by which the Father loves the Incarnate Son. If, on the contrary, he rejects this love, the aforementioned divorce is brought about; though on the level of the love of God, this divorce could be expressed by the words used by St. Paul in designating the situation of the Jewish people in relation to God: "As regards the gospel they are enemies of God, for your sake; but as regards election they are beloved for the sake of their forefathers."[51]

This enables us to resolve a very grave difficulty which arises concerning grace. We often have had the occasion to recall this fundamental principle which rules all the problems concerning God's relation to creatures: There is no change in God. Therefore, I am only able to distinguish one of God's acts by considering Him in relation to a change brought about in the creature by this act. Hence, what can be meant by saying, "God calls men to Himself," inasmuch as man has not responded to the call and, therefore, inasmuch as the change brought about by grace is not produced in him? In short, what is the real content of the notion of "vocation"?

> Every divine willing *ad extra* is defined by the terminus that it posits. Therefore, if the divine decree that presided over creation was a decree concerning men's vocation [*destination*] to the Kingdom, this vocation must be translated by some kind of effect in our inmost depths. Some kind of disposition in us, an ordination to the goods that were promised to us, corresponds to the decree immanent in the divine willing. It is an ordination that, moreover, must be conceived in terms of desire ... Given that the Kingdom is not yet given to us but, instead, has been proposed as an end, the interior disposition connaturalizing us to it therefore took on the form of being a tendency and attraction.[52]

Some have tried to resolve the difficulty by imagining that in each man, in the economy of salvation, nature is already "modified" by a supernatural "existential." For such thinkers, this "existential"

---

51. Rom 11:28 (RSV).
52. Leopoldo Malevez, "La gratuité du surnaturel," *Nouvelle revue théologique* 15 (1953): 561–86 and 673–68.

is not yet grace to the degree that there has not yet been a free response. However, on account of it, our nature no longer belongs to the order of "mere nature."[53]

The better solution is to say that the post-lapsarian act of calling mankind [*l'acte de vocation du genre humain*] is included in the willing of the Incarnation, that is, in the love with which the Father loves the Incarnate Word. There is a change in the creature—not yet in individuals but, instead, in mankind, which is really affected by the Incarnation. Before the Fall, it was included in the divinizing act that filled the first human couple with grace.

2. *How all men are loved by Christ*

{437} Inasmuch as Christ is also a man, He is a person endowed with knowledge, love, and freedom—human knowledge, human love, and human freedom. It is impossible that this inclusion of all men in Him, prior to every act [by a given human person], according to nature and according to grace, would not be translated upon the level of consciousness. That is, in His human consciousness, Christ bore all men within him, knew them, and loved them.

In Jesus's human heart, this love is the reverberation of God's love and its first realization. Thus, it is not enough to say that all men are included in Christ in the sense that He bears them in His thought and love. However, when a "real" inclusion has been assured, this second, intentional, and conscious inclusion not only does not become useless, but rather, emerges as something completely necessary. One cannot imagine that it would be lacking.

3. *How every grace comes from the fullness of Christ*

{438} God's freely-given love for His creatures is the source of all the gifts of grace by which they are justified and divinized. Given that God's love for men is the extension of the Father's love for the Incarnate Word to each person (to the degree that the latter is freely

---

53. This is the position of Karl Rahner that Malevez relates in the work cited above.

open to this love), we must also say that all the gifts of grace given to men are the outpouring within them of the gifts—and, first of all, the primordial gift of the Spirit—given to Christ in His human soul. In short, in the actual economy of salvation, every grace is "Christic."[54]

CONCLUSION

Thus, it is profoundly true that Christ is the only one who is just before God, the only one worthy of love. However, this exclusivity does not exclude other men from true and interior justification, for such an exclusion would be the failure of the redemptive mission and, therefore, of the Incarnation. In Christ, all men who accept Him (in faith) are loved, justified, and saved.

However, in order for each person to be able to personally adhere to Christ and thus accept God's justifying love, the obstacle of sin which paralyzes man's natural movement toward God (and therefore the movement of faith) must be abolished. For this, it was necessary that the Incarnate Word accomplish His redemptive mission. That is, bearing sinful mankind in Himself, He offers it with Himself, in sacrifice, and through His resurrection, He receives new life (in Himself first but for all men). This is something we still must study, in due course. However, to accomplish this mission, it was not enough that the Word become a man through the ineffable gift of the Incarnation. It was necessary that He espouse the destiny of sinful man, Himself remaining without sin. It was necessary that He place Himself within human history.

{439} Here is where one would normally place a question that occupied many of the Fathers of the Church,[55] one that St. Thomas treats quite briefly, namely the question concerning the moment of Christ's coming.[56] "Why did He come at this moment of history?," the

---

54. See J.-H. Nicolas, *Les profondeurs de la grâce*, 281–304.
55. See Oscar Cullmann, *Christ et le temps* (Neuchâtel: Delachaux et Niestlé, 1966); Jean Daniélou, *Théologie du Judéo-christianisme* (Paris: Desclée, 1958); and Auguste Luneau, *L'histoire du salut chez les Pères de l'Eglise* (Paris: Beauchesne, 1964).
56. See *ST* III, q. 1, aa. 5–6. [Tr. note: The original incorrectly reads "*ST* I."]

ancients asked themselves. "Why so late?" And, indeed, they did not know how late it was. However, one could also ask oneself: "Why so early?" For can one think that the Christian era is "the last age of the world"? This question can be treated from a historical point of view, which would present the history of this theme in Christian thought. However, from the point of view of dogmatic theology, it does not seem possible to present anything more than mere conjecture.

7

Christ's Place in Human History

Christ redeemed, sanctified, and glorified the human family by becoming a member of it. In order to become the head of humanity, He first needed to be part of it. The whole theological meaning of the Virgin Mary lies in this fact: through her, the Word, in becoming man, truly and really became a member of humanity. First of all, through her, He knew the generation which is natural to human beings (which is also part of the assumed humanity). Moreover, through her as well, He who came from on high placed Himself within human history by thus coming forth from historical humanity.[1]

---

1. Bibliographical note. For an introduction to Marian theology, see Louis Bouyer, *Le trône de la sagesse* (Paris: Cerf, 1957); René Laurentin, *Court traité sur la Vierge Marie* (Paris: Lethielleux, 1967); and Marie-Joseph Nicolas, *Theotokos, le mystère de Marie* (Paris: Desclée de Brouwer, 1965). For biblical sources, see the collective work *Maria in Sacra Scriptura: Acta congressus mariologici in Republica Dominicana anno 1965 celebrati* (Rome: Pontificia Academia Mariana Internationalis, 1965); Michel Cambe, "La 'charis' chez S. Luc," *Revue biblique* 70 (1963): 193–207; Jean Daniélou, *Les évangiles de l'enfance* (Paris: Seuil, 1967); André Feuillet, *Jésus et sa Mère d'après les récits lucaniens et d'après S. Jean* (Paris: Gabalda, 1974); René Laurentin, *Structure et théologie de Luc I–II* (Paris: Gabalda, 1959); René Laurentin, *Les évangiles de l'enfance du Christ. Vérité de Noël au-delà des mythes* (Paris: Desclée de Brouwer, 1982); Xavier Léon-Dufour, *Les évangiles et l'histoire de Jésus* (Paris: Seuil, 1963), 343–53; Stanislas Lyonnet, *Le récit de l'Annonciation et la maternité divine* (Rome: Institute biblique pontifical, 1956). On the development of Marian dogma, see Jean Galot, "L'immaculée conception de Notre-Dame," in *Maria* (Paris: Beauchesne, 1964), 7:10–116; "Le mystère de l'assomption," in ibid., 155–237; Charles Journet, *Esquisse du développement du dogme marial* (Paris: Alsatia, 1954). On Marian

I. THE DIVINE MATERNITY

{440} At least from the time of the fourth century, the Church has used the title "Theotokos" as a designation for Mary. It was solemnly proclaimed at the Council of Ephesus in 431. This definition is first of all Christological. From the start, the Church was aware that Mary is the mother of Jesus. The affirmation that, for this reason, she is the mother of the Word is a form of the affirmation that Jesus is the Word. It is a way of proclaiming Christ's unity.

The story of the annunciation is much richer than the simple assertion that Jesus was born of Mary. Already, it indicates that this Jesus whom she will conceive is the Messiah and that He is God ("He ... will be called the Son of the Most High"). Likewise, it indicates that she conceived virginally, as well as the fact that she believed and is commended for her faith (not in the narrative of the annunciation but in that of the visitation). The whole narrative tends to show that her consent was sought and obtained.

The task of understanding this title, as well as that of drawing out its implications, falls to the theologian. One controversial question lies in knowing whether this title of hers alone expresses the essence of the mystery of Mary, meaning that everything that can be known and said about her is connected to it or whether it must be supplemented by other considerations that would also be in Scripture. This is the ordering principle of Mariology. We will not treat this question for its own sake but only as the occasion necessitates.[2]

---

dogma at Vatican II, see *Lumen Gentium* (November 21, 1964), ch. 8; also, *La Vierge Marie dans la Constitution sur l'Église, Etudes Mariales* (Paris: Lethielleux, 1965) and *Maria in Sacra Scriptura*. On the ecumenical aspect of the Marian question, see *Etudes Mariales*, nineteenth, twentieth, and twenty-first volsumes; also, Max Thurian, *Marie Mère du Seigneur, figure de l'Église* (Taize: Presses de Taize, 1963).

2. See Laurentin, *Court traité sur la Vierge Marie*, 190n15 and n16. M.-J. Nicolas, *Theotokos*, 104–7.

A. The Formal Constitutive of the Divine Maternity

1. The concurrence Mary brought to the Incarnation

a) The formation of Christ's humanity

{441} *Verbum caro factum est* must be understood without there being any change in the Word. What is new is the formation of this humanity and its assumption—this humanity by which the Word is Man.[3] We cannot distinguish any order of priority between these two actions (the formation of Christ's humanity and its assumption). The formed nature is what was assumed. However, it was formed only as the Word's humanity. It can be conceived of as concrete and existing only if it is also conceived of as being assumed.

b) The role of Mary in the formation of Christ's humanity

The role of parents in ordinary cases of generation

{442} In every case of generation we find: the action of parents (as second causes) for the formation of the body; the divine moving action in relation to this action (as First Cause); and the divine (creative) action producing and infusing the soul. What the parents form is a human body, that is, a body that can be animated only by a spiritual soul, by this individual spiritual soul. What God creates is the soul corresponding to this body, the soul that informs and forms this body, called for by the parents' generative action.

This is the reason why the parents are truly the begetters of this human person. This human person is what is at the terminus of their action. Through them, this human person receives a communication in human nature and human life. The creation of the soul by God emerges as the natural and necessary completion of their generative action. The father and mother together are the cause of this generative action. Each exercise a causality that is partial, complementing the other's causality.

---

3. See §275 above.

Application to Christ's generation

{443} In the case of Mary's generative action, we find the miracle of the virginal conception. (Below, we will attempt to specify the nature of Mary's virginity.) In a word, by a miracle, God enabled the generative action of the woman, which by its nature is partial and incapable of producing a new living being as its effect, to produce the initial cell of the new organism by itself alone. This miracle was brought about by a particular action by God upon the generative activity of the Virgin.

Mary's generative action, thus miraculously rendered fruitful without the normal complement of a man's generative action, normally moved by God as a second cause and normally completed by the creation of the soul that it calls for, produced this new human being, Jesus. This is the simultaneously occurring assumptive action which makes the humanity thus formed in and by Mary to be the Word's humanity and made this human being be the very Word become man.

In any case, this new human being was a person, and on account of her generative action, Mary was the mother of this person. Mary is the mother of this *new man who is born in the world*;[4] she is the mother of the Word, as this man is the Word. This fact cannot be changed by the fact that, through the assumptive action, this new human person would be the preexisting Person of the Word. We do not need to imagine that this would have required some kind of super-elevation of her generative action. Just as the Word assumed an individuated human nature that was wholly like ours, so too and for the same reason, this humanity was formed through a generative action that was natural (apart from the miracle of the virginal conception). This generation, even if virginal, would have produced a mere man if the assumptive action had not intervened.

---

4. See Jn 16:21.

The role of Mary in the Incarnation itself

{444} Certain theologians have imagined that Mary would have played a causal role in this assumptive action. Most of them make this claim in terms of instrumental causality. Some go so far as to speak of principal (secondary) causality. This is completely impossible. Instrumental causality must contribute in producing the principal cause's effect. It is nothing without this contribution. Now, the effect here is the Incarnate Word precisely as incarnate. That is, it is the fact that this new humanity belongs to the Word.

Now, we can say the following: on the one hand, this humanity never was anything but the Word's humanity. We cannot conceive of any "space" between the formation of this humanity, on which the Virgin's instrumental causality would have been able to exercise itself, and this humanity's appropriation by the Word. The case of the "assumption" is the same as that of creation insofar as neither of these cases allow for any created causality, even instrumental causality.

On the other hand, we cannot conceive of any preparation or disposing of humanity for the Hypostatic Union. The latter is brought about immediately through God's intervention, making this singular humanity be the humanity of the Word at the instant when this humanity is formed. Human nature only brings to this its aptitude for being assumed, its "obediential potency" (i.e., human nature's general characteristic of being assumable).

Moreover, such causality is completely useless in relation to the divine maternity. Even if, *per impossibile*, Mary had concurred instrumentally (or as a second cause), she would not have been the mother of God on account of this. She is the mother of God fundamentally because, by her natural generative activity (miraculously led to the terminus of its activity without a masculine complement), she begot this new human being who is the Word made man on account of the assumptive action. She is the mother of the Word as she would have been the mother of the created person who normally would have been constituted if the assumption of the humanity to the Word had not taken place.

2. The relation of the divine maternity

a) The divine maternity is a unique relation of Mary to the Word

{445} Generally speaking, maternity (as well as paternity) is a relation. It is a relation founded on the communication of existence, that is, on the fact that the human nature by which the child is constituted as a man has been communicated to him by his parents through generation. In other words, it is founded on the fact that he communes with them in an individuated human nature with the same biological heredity and not only in human existence in general.

This relation, founded on the very constitutive nature [of the person] (and therefore in what is ontologically most profound for the person), unites the person of the parents to that of the child. It is, as it were, the ontological nucleus around which all the various interpersonal relations that will come to exist between parents and children will be formed. Thus, the divine maternity consists fundamentally in this singular ontological relation of Mary's person to the Person of the Word (in His distinction, for only the Word became incarnate). The whole ensemble of relations of grace (which are interpersonal relations)—first of all between Mary and the Word, but also between her and the two other Persons—unfold from there.

b) The assumed maternity

{446} Can one speak, as several theologians have, of an "assumed" maternity? The expression presents a grave danger of equivocation. One risks passing from "assumed maternity" to "assumed mother." Quite obviously, Mary is a mere creature, a purely human person who in no way was [hypostatically] assumed. Indeed, one must forcefully hold that this is the case. (Moreover, we have already seen that the concept of an "assumed person" is contradictory in itself.) However, this expression can be understood in an acceptable sense. Indeed, a relation is specified by its terminus. Thus, by assuming the humanity formed by Mary, the Word simultaneously assumed the generative action itself and the relation founded on this, so that we can say that He elevated to Himself Mary *in the exercise of her maternity.*

Thus we have the profound insight expressed by Cajetan: "(Mary) who alone touched, by her own proper activity, the limits of the Godhead when she conceived, bore, and gave birth to God."[5] This connects back to what St. Thomas himself wrote:

> Christ's humanity (because it is united to God), created beatitude (because it is the fruition of God), and the Blessed Virgin (because she is the Mother of God) has a dignity that is in some manner infinite, coming to them from the infinite good who is God. This means that nothing can be made that would be better than these three things, for there is nothing better than God.[6]

Thus, on the one hand, Mary's generative action was "natural" (apart from the *miracle* of the virginal conception). On the other hand, the divine maternity that it founds is supernatural to the highest degree, just as the assumed humanity is natural and nonetheless exists at the highest supernatural degree because it is the humanity of the Word:

> There is a twofold miracle In Christ's conception: one is that a woman gives birth to God; the other that a virgin gives birth to a son. For what pertains to the first, the Blessed Virgin solely brought her obediential potency to the conception ... However, for the second, the blessed Virgin had a passive, natural potency, that is, a potency susceptible to being brought to act by a natural agent ...[7]

c) The divine maternity and the hypostatic order

{447} Above, we spoke about three degrees of communication in the divine goodness, constituting three orders: the order of na-

---

5. Cajetan, *In ST* II-II, q. 103, a. 4.
6. See *ST* I, q. 25, a. 5, ad 4.
7. *In III Sent.*, d. 3, q. 2, a. 2, ad 1. Note that when St. Thomas speaks of passive potency to designate the natural power that the woman has to beget, he does so on account of the conceptions of his era which granted to the feminine principle only a passive role in procreation.

ture, that of grace, and that of the Hypostatic Union (i.e., the order of the Incarnation).[8] We must first note that this threefold communication is brought about by means of relations. Through creation, every creature is fundamentally ordered to God as to its efficient and exemplar principle and as to its end. Through grace, the spiritual creature is ordered to God in His mystery as to the object of his activities and as to his end. By the Hypostatic Union, the assumed humanity is ordered to the Word as to the Person of whom it is the humanity and who, through this humanity, is man.

Next, we must note that these three orders are themselves ordered in relation to each other so that they constitute, in the end, a single order, whose ultimate principle is the Hypostatic Union. We have seen how the whole universe is ordered to man, the image of God and called to communion with Him, as well as how man is ordered to Christ as to the supreme realization of his natural and supernatural vocation, union with God.[9] Nonetheless, these orders, thus unified, remain distinct. It is indirectly, by being itself and being ordered to its proper end that nature is moreover ordered to grace; and it is indirectly, by being ordered to Christ and to communion with God in Christ that man is ordered to the Hypostatic Union.

Let us consider now the divine maternity. It is directly ordered to the Incarnate Word. It exists only by and for the Incarnation of the Word. This is why many theologians say, and with good reason, that she belongs to the hypostatic order. Still, we must understand these theologians aright and not make them say that Mary herself is hypostatically united to the divinity. If she belongs to the hypostatic order, she does so through her activity, not through her being (unless indirectly, in the sense that she exists as the mother of God only in the hypostatic order). This will have important consequences for situating her in the order of grace.

---

8. See §415 above.
9. See §421 above.

B. The Grace of the Mother of God

{448} We have spoken about what formally constitutes [Mary's] maternity. It is the generative action terminated, because of the assumptive action, at the Person of the Word. However, in ordinary maternity, we only have the generative action. If maternity is a relation of person to person, it is obviously composed of an ensemble of interpersonal relations of knowledge, love, and exchanges of all kinds. This is "natural." However, in Mary's case, it is a question of a Son who is God. These interpersonal relations, which are included in every case of maternity, are, like maternity itself, at once "natural" and "of grace."

1. The very grace of the divine maternity

a) By itself, the divine maternity is a unique grace

{449} If the divine maternity is supernatural (i.e., the generation of the Word) for the same reason that it is natural (i.e., the generation of a new human being), we must say that it is a grace. It is true that it is always ordered to the Incarnation, as is the assumed humanity itself. However, humanity as such is not a subject of grace. When we sought the subject of the singular grace that is the Hypostatic Union, we were led to say that it was the Word Himself, inasmuch as He is this man and inasmuch as He became a human person. Given that the mother of God is a person, she is a subject of grace. She is the one who is graced with this singular gift of being the mother of the Word.

Here, we encounter a principle that commands the entire economy of salvation, one that finds a privileged application in Mariology. On the one hand, all creatures are at the service of God, and in particular, every created participation in salvation history is first of all a service wholly ordered to God (and to Christ). However, on the other hand, everything that God does *ad extra* is for the exaltation of the creature. Therefore, when He makes use of a free creature for the work of salvation, which is the gift that He makes of Himself to spiritual creatures, the creature that He uses is the privileged beneficiary of the good that he himself is called upon to spread forth in cooperation with God. Thus, the Word willed to have a mother in order that He may become incarnate (and, therefore, willed this for the sake of all men). However, to have been chosen to fill this role is, for Mary, a singular honor and a unique grace.[10]

b) The divine maternity implies the graces of holiness

{450} Maternity in general normally engages the entire woman in relation to her child—in knowledge, love, and self-gift. This holds true all the more for the divine maternity. In this case, the Son is a preexisting and perfect Person, who can be loved totally from the start and for whom Mary's personal feelings will not be changed. Moreover, it is a virginal maternity, which gives her maternal love the singular characteristic of being a mother's first and exclusive love.

However, because this love has the Word as its object, it cannot be a merely natural love. It is the love by which the divinized creature loves her God. Like the fundamental relation of maternity, Mary's maternal love and all the interpersonal relations between her and her Son are at once natural and supernatural. As supernatural, they can proceed only from grace. As natural, they are called for by maternity itself: maternal feelings proceed naturally from the ontological relation of maternity.

That is, the grace of the divine maternity implied the gifts of holiness. Without these gifts, Mary would have been a mother who was unaware of her own maternity, which thereby would have been something foreign to her. If God calls a woman to become His mother, He cannot fail to grace her with the gifts of grace without which she could be His mother only in a bodily manner. In other words, without such gifts, she would be a mother in a nonpersonal

---

10. Mary was not "chosen" from among existing women, for she was willed and created only so as to be the mother of God, so that her call to existence is unable to be dissociated from her election. She is, nonetheless, by this election, distinguished from all other women.

and nonhuman manner. According to the expression of St. Augustine, "She conceived the Word of God in her mind [*esprit*] before she conceived Him in her womb."

Objection: Mary could have received and loved her child as an ordinary child, having for him the human, though natural, feelings that every mother feels for her child.

Certainly. However, here we encounter anew the requirements of the mystery of the Incarnation. Jesus was not an ordinary child. His destiny called for Him to be a great religious leader, to be proclaimed the "Son of God." Indeed, from the first moment of His life, He was "the Son of God." If the divine maternity is, as we have said, an immense grace, it necessarily entails that the maternal sentiments resulting from it in some manner (yet to be determined) focus upon the Divine Person of this infant. Without this, it would be an unconscious maternity, if not as maternity as such, then at least as the divine maternity.

This complex fact of the divine maternity itself, and of all the gifts of grace that it calls for so that Mary may fully be the mother of God in a personal manner, has been called "the integral concept of the divine maternity."[11] For example, a being is essentially a man as soon as he is constituted through the composition of matter and a spiritual soul, although he will integrally be a man only when he acquires the organic, psychological, spiritual, and moral development required by human personality, which is constituted solely by the composition of the soul and the body. In like fashion, Mary is constituted as the mother of God essentially by the ontological relation founded on her generative action. However, she is integrally the mother of God only through the ensemble of gifts of grace that enable her to elevate her heart and mind [*esprit*] to the level of her singular maternity.

---

11. M.-J. Nicolas, *Theotokos*, 104–6.

c) The divine maternity is a loftier grace than the gifts of holiness

{451} The relations between the grace of divine maternity with the graces of holiness can be compared to the relation which exists between the grace of union in Christ and the created grace that places His soul at the level of His Divine Personality. The grace of union is the loftiest grace, uncreated grace. Obviously, we will not say that the grace of the divine maternity is uncreated. However, it is through it that Mary is connected, in the way that we have explained, to the hypostatic order, whereas by the graces of holiness, she belongs to the order of grace, which is inferior.

However, an objection will be registered here: if the grace of union is superior to all the created graces by which Jesus's soul was enriched, this is because the grace of union is the Divine Nature itself, hypostatically united to His human nature. It is a personal grace: Jesus is infinitely holy, given that, through the Hypostatic Union, He is the Word Himself, the holy One of God, the holy God. In contrast, Mary is only a created person, and as a person, she is rendered holy only by the gifts of holiness. Jesus Himself proclaimed the superiority of the gifts of holiness: "Blessed rather are those who hear the word of God and keep it."[12]

One must absolutely concede that the bare divine maternity, without the graces of holiness, would leave Mary in a religious situation very inferior to that of the saints. She would "materially" participate in Christ's holiness (somewhat like a sacred object in a temple), but her person as such would not be holy. However, if we admit that the gifts of holiness are conferred upon her on account of her divine maternity and that the latter calls for them, thus in this way being part of her divine maternity, then we can see that the comparison is not concerned *with the divine maternity in contrast to the graces of holiness*, but instead is concerned *with the interior reality of the integral divine maternity, thereby considering the elements that compose it*. Here, the divine maternity emerges as the source and principle of all her

---

12. Lk 11:28 (RSV).

holiness, placing the latter in an order set apart (i.e., the hypostatic order) in relation to that of other saints.

If grace is first of all God's eternal love for created persons, and in the second place the gifts that enrich the person and render her worthy of this love, divinizing her on account of God's eternal love, we must say that God loved Mary (in a way that was inseparable from the Father's love for the Incarnate Word included in this love) precisely as the mother of God and made her the mother of the Word, not only *corpore* but *mente*, filling her with the graces without which she could not be a worthy mother of God. This situates Mary's predestination in relation to Christ's. In predestining the Incarnate Word as such (i.e., inasmuch as He is a human person) to the Hypostatic Union,[13] God simultaneously predestines Mary to be the mother of the Incarnate Word.

All the other effects of grace, whether in Jesus's soul or in Mary, are the second (although inseparable) effects of this first predestination. The predestination of the other saints is also included in Christ's predestination[14] in the sense that their holiness exists for the glory of Christ and is an effusion of Christ's grace. However, inasmuch as it is the predestination particular to them, it is related, as to its ultimate and principal terminus, to their particular holiness. In short, Mary was *first* predestined *to be the mother of God*, and then, on account of this, she was predestined to the loftiest individual holiness. Other saints are predestined simply to their particular holiness.

Nonetheless, other saints can also have a role, sometimes a very important one, to fulfill in salvation history: St. Peter, St. Paul, the great doctors, etc. The difference in Mary's case is that, *from the perspective of their salvation*, the fulfillment of this role is ordered to their salvation and their sanctification, whereas, for Mary, conversely, her salvation and her sanctification are ordered to making her, in the full and integral sense of the term, the mother of God. And this is because the divine maternity is an integral part of the Incarnation

---

13. See *ST* III, q. 24, aa. 1 and 2.
14. Ibid., aa. 3 and 4.

(such as it has in fact been conceived and decided upon by God). It is related not only to the application of salvation to men but to the very existence of salvation, to God's gift of the Savior to men.

2. *The graces of holiness in Mary on the Earth*

a) Mary's faith

{452} Although certain theologians, even in our days, have believed it possible to attribute to Mary an immediate vision of the Godhead (most holding that this was transient, though some holding that it was habitual), we must unhesitatingly and in conformity with tradition, as well as in conformity with what the Gospel tells us about her, say that she purely and simply had faith.

What was the object of this faith? Before the annunciation, it was the faith of Israel, though in all its purity and depth. At the moment of the annunciation, was it revealed to her that her son would be the Word Himself? It indeed seems that the evangelist's intention would be to tell us this.[15] On the other hand, there are other passages in the Gospel that seem to indicate an ignorance precisely about her Son's Divine Nature.[16]

There is at least one theological argument in favor of saying that her Son's divinity would have been revealed to her. Although it is doubtlessly not decisive, it is strong and is drawn from what we said earlier concerning the requirements of an integral divine maternity. In order for her to be able to fully be the mother (indeed, the willing mother) of this Son, would she not need to know that He is the Son of God? Note, however, if she received Him as the Messiah and the Savior at this first instant, that would be enough.

In order to avoid unduly overstating the data of Scripture, the theologian can have recourse here to the notion of "implicit faith." Mary's faith could only explicitly be related to the Messiahship of the

---

15. See Laurentin, *Structure et théologie de Luc*, 165–68; with reservations, René Laurentin, "Bulletin sur la Vierge Marie," *Revue des sciences philosophiques et théologiques* 55 (1970): 269–328.

16. See Feuillet, *Jésus et sa Mère*, 120–21.

Son who was announced to her. However, in the light of Old Testament themes like that of the "Son of Man," understood in the wholly new light shed upon these themes by the annunciation, this Messiahship could have been enriched for her by the idea of this son's "preexistence," which implicitly contained the divinity of his Person, His eternal filiation, and so forth. In any case, we must hold this was *a faith that had as little conceptual content as possible*. It would be principally consist in a very lofty mystical (obscure) contemplation with the minimum of noetic content required for such contemplation. Indeed, this would explain the difficulties and hardships of this faith she would have experienced, as well as its growth throughout the course of Jesus's life as He manifested who He was. It was not easy for her to believe that this child, who was so similar to others (despite his extraordinary "wisdom"), was the Son of God! Certainly, this faith grew, not only subjectively, but objectively. That is, Mary did not cease to grow in knowledge of her Son while she lived on earth.

b) Mary's charity

{453} By charity, the righteous person enters into personal relations with God, which includes distinct relations with each Divine Person. Mary's love for the Word was a maternal love. With regard to the Father, she partook in her Son's filial love, more than any other saint, for she was enveloped, as we have said, in the Father's love for the Incarnate Son. On the other hand, we risk equivocation if we say that she was the spouse of the Holy Spirit. Let us only say that for her, as for every saint, He was the agent of her predestination, He who led it along its way, though first of all to the prodigious terminus that is the divine maternity. In a manner proper to her, He was the one who simultaneously brought about in her the miracle of the virginal conception as well as the mystery of the assumption of this humanity conceived by her to the Person of the Word, thus assuming, as we have seen, her maternity. This is what the angel's mysterious expression means: "The Holy Spirit will come upon you" (Lk 1:35, RSV). This does not mean that the Holy Spirit would have acted alone, without the Father and without the Son. Rather, it is a question of a proper work of love, which therefore is justly appropriated to Him.[17]

Finally, if Jesus is essentially the Savior and if she received Him as such, she therefore embraced all men in her charity in a maternal form, which we will specify later.

c) Charisms

{454} Many Mariologists are pleased to attribute all possible charisms to her (and sometimes even impossible ones). We must not forget that charisms are graces given to a person in view of a mission to be fulfilled in the order of salvation. Jesus had all the charisms because He is the source of every grace, He upon whom the Spirit rested and by whom the Spirit is sent forth into the world. However, what charisms are required by Mary's mission?

Doubtlessly, the charism of revelation was required in a wholly exceptional manner, which she received at the annunciation and also at the cross. As for the other charisms, Scripture invites us to respect her modesty. She gave Christ to the world and she let Him act for the sake of its salvation, without herself acting (except, as we will see, in a wholly spiritual manner, which did not require charisms).

II. THE HOLINESS OF THE MOTHER OF GOD

{455} To say that the divine maternity is the reason for the graces of holiness that Mary received does not mean in any way that these graces could be deduced *a priori* as being required, taken together and each in particular, for the divine maternity. The existence of these graces and their proper form are revealed to us by Scripture and tradition. The role of the theologian is not to deduce them but to explain them by the divine maternity. This is why we must speak of "reasons of suitability" and not of "proofs." (Here, one must un-

---

17. See §192 in the previous volume of this work.

derstand the term "suitability" in a strong sense: if she received such a grace, this is because it was suitable to the mother of God in order for her to be a worthy mother of God.)

A. The Virginity of the Mother of God

1. The Church's faith in Mary's perpetual virginity

{456} It[18] is undoubtedly the case that the virginal conception is taught at least by the first and the third Gospels. The authors of these texts certainly intended to speak (and indeed expressly did speak) of virginity in the obvious sense of the word. That is, they spoke of a conception brought about in and through Mary *sine virile semine*, without any previous sexual union. Those who seek today to interpret this virginity in another sense (e.g., as expressing only that Jesus comes from on high, that He is a gift of God to humanity, etc.) do not do justice to the evangelists' express intentions.

From the beginning of the Church's history, this was accepted and taught. The idea of perpetual virginity (i.e., after Jesus's birth) imposed itself very quickly upon the Church's consciousness, despite the great exception of Tertullian. So too, a little later on (though already universally, at the Council of Ephesus) the idea of virginity in birth (*in partu*) imposed itself as well. We can consider the Church's faith as being fixed on this point by the third canon of the Council of Lateran (649), which "only wished to express in a more explicit manner a doctrine reported by the Greeks at the fifth Ecumenical Council (II Constantinople) when they declared Mary 'ever-virgin.'"[19] This is the canon in question:

If anyone does not, following the holy Fathers, confess properly and truly that holy Mary, ever virgin and immaculate, is Mother of God, since in

---

18. Bibliographical note. See José Antonio de Aldama, "La maternité virginale de Notre-Dame," in *Maria*, 7:119–52; *Etudes Mariales* 21 (1971); Laurentin, "Bulletin sur la Vierge Marie," 291–304; Jean-Hervé Nicolas, *La virginité de Marie. Étude théologique* (Fribourg, 1962), and "Vierge jusque dans l'enfantement," *Ephemerides Mariologicae* 21 (1971): 377–82; and M.-J. Nicolas, *Theotokos*, 88–94.

19. Georges Jouassard, "Marie à travers la patristique: Maternité divine, virginité, sainteté," in *Maria*, vol. 1 (Paris: Beauchesne, 1949), 139n18.

this latter age she conceived really and truly, without human seed from the Holy Spirit, God the Word Himself, who before the ages was born of God the Father, and gave birth to Him without corruption, her virginity remaining equally inviolate after His birth, let him be condemned.[20]

2. The virginal conception of Jesus

a) The virginal conception is first of all a privilege of Christ

{457} The virginal conception is presented in Scripture and was understood by the Church as being a privilege of Christ. St. Thomas[21] proposes four reasons for this, three of which are deeply rooted in the tradition. The third of his reasons, which is very contestable in itself and in relation to St. Thomas's own doctrine concerning the transmission of original sin, strongly reflects Augustinian influence, on a point where St. Augustine was rightly not followed by the Church. We can add two more reasons to the ones offered by St. Thomas, one that is taken from the exposition found in the Dutch Catechism and perhaps another reason still, drawn from the human and Christian meaning of virginity.

First reason (from St. Thomas)

Christ comes to reveal His Father: He is the Son. This fact can be interpreted as follows. Although a father and mother are equal, constituting a single principle of generation, and although the relation of filiation therefore finds its terminus in the two together, we can say that on the phenomenological plane, the maternal relation comes to our awareness as a relation of service and the paternal relation as a relation of authority. In fact, the divine maternity, *as maternity*, was at the service of the redemption and therefore of the redeemer. Human paternity would have also been a relation of service (and, indeed, Joseph's adoptive paternity was such), but this would not have been *as paternity*.

---

20. D.-*Sch.*, no. 503.
21. See *ST* III, q. 28, a. 1.

Second reason (from St. Thomas)

The Word Himself was conceived and born a second time. There is great suitability in the idea that this second conception (to the degree that it is possible in the case of a true human birth) would resemble the first, the new being thus conceived proceeding from the depths of the mother's being, without coming in any way from something external. ("The depths of Mary's being" must be understand as meaning the Holy Spirit, *intimior intimo meo*.)

The term "corruption" in St. Thomas's text raises concerns for some. It must certainly be understood in a physical sense. However, even when it is thus understood, it has a disagreeable resonance, giving the impression that sexual union represents an infringement upon the woman's integrity and upon her purity. We will see that this is not how virginity needs to be understood.

Third reason (from St. Thomas)

At first, it is surprising to see original sin connected to sexual union as such, along with a joining of the *theological* notion of "concupiscence" with that of "pleasure and sensible joy" (i.e., the *psychological* notion of "concupiscence")! This is all the more surprising because when St. Thomas himself expressly speaks about original sin, he explains its transmission in an utterly different manner. Likewise, when he speaks about concupiscence, he does not identify it with sensible pleasure, which he declares to be natural and good in itself. It is equally surprising to see this declaration that, if Christ had been conceived in an ordinary way, He would have contracted original sin. We have seen that Christ's inability to sin is an inalienable prerogative of His Person and therefore could be found in the assumed humanity in whatever manner it might have been formed. It seems that in drawing up his article, St. Thomas simply reported contemporary explanations without critiquing them.

Fourth reason (from St. Thomas)

In whatever way the thirteenth verse of John's prologue is read (and it indeed seems that a reading in the singular must be abandoned, "To him whom neither ... nor the will of man begot"[22]), it indicates a wholly spiritual birth, a birth whose sole principle is God, a birth from on high.[23] It is wholly certain that Christ's birth would be the image and exemplar of the Christian's rebirth. From this perspective, Jesus's virginal birth finds its meaning in symbolizing the Christian's rebirth.

Fifth reason (drawn from the "Dutch Catechism")

The virginal conception and birth emphasize and manifest Christ's character as coming from on high (preexistence) and as being a descent by God into humanity, not a summit to which humanity would have arrived by its own effort.[24] This does not imply that we need to retain the ancients' conceptions in matters of embryology, holding that the woman would have a purely passive role in generation. Indeed, it is clear that, in a virginal conception, the woman is first of all purely passive ([i.e., through her] obediential potency [to such a miraculous intervention by God]), given that her own proper genital activity is able to bring about conception only under an absolutely new divine action which depends only on the divine initiative:

> Mary is a virgin in order to signify that God is the one who begot Christ and that the Savior is not a superman, the fruit of human effort toward deliverance. Neither blood (i.e., human heredity) nor the will of the flesh (i.e., the effort of the sinful creature) are at the origin of our eternal salvation. God alone is there, in His eternal design, having predestined the Vir-

---

22. See Feuillet, *Le prologue du IVe évangile*, 76–80.
23. See Jn 3:7.
24. See the Dutch Catechism, 106–9. Let us only note that if the annunciation to Mary concerning the coming of Jesus into her, and by her to the world, resembles many other annunciations in the Bible concerning the birth of a man sent by God, it has this unique characteristic: it is the only one which announces a virginal conception and birth, whereas all the other cases involve ordinary births.

gin Mary in order to beget in her and give birth by her his Unique Son, the Savior of the world. All is from Him and through Him in this first act of the Incarnation.[25]

Sixth reason (drawn from the meaning of virginity)

We will see how and in what sense (voluntary) virginity is a "spiritualization of the flesh," an anticipation (in earthly life) of the eschatological situation of man wherein the flesh will only exist in service of the spirit. In this sense, and in this sense alone, such virginity is the exact opposite of "concupiscence," which is the "carnalization" of the spirit. The Incarnation, which ultimately aims at bringing about man's perfect spiritualization (something which is eschatological), is itself (and, indeed, first of all) a work of the Spirit alone. The virginal conception fully brings this to light.

b) The personal value of Mary's Virginity

{458} What has been said for maternity holds for virginity. If the Word needs His conception to be virginal in order for Him to be humanly born, then the woman called to become His mother, to conceive and give birth to Him and to always live in maternal relations with Him, must be a virgin in a personal manner (i.e., deliberately and voluntarily). We have seen that no other meaning can be given to the expression that Luke places on the lips of Mary at the annunciation: "How shall this be, since I have no husband?"[26]

The material and the formal in virginity

Virginity is a bodily state, that of a person who has not experienced sexual union (or its intimations). This is its material element. However, it is also a spiritual state, that of a person who, in full consciousness and will, has wholly renounced sexual union.[27]

---

25. Thurian, *Marie Mère du Seigneur, figure de l'Église*, 47.
26. Lk 1:34 (RSV).
27. See J.-H. Nicolas, *La virginité de Marie*, 22–32.

The material element

St. Thomas, as well as the ancients in general, have been strongly critiqued because they defined female virginity by the abstention from sexual sensations and by bodily integrity. It is true that, beyond all the sensations connected to the exercise of sexuality, we must see human love in it. This human love has sexual union only as a component, and precisely speaking, it is what bestows the fully human value upon the sexual union in which such love is expressed. Let us only say that it is easy to reintroduce into their analyses of virginity (or of chastity in general) the element which, by rights, is principal and which, in fact, unfortunately passes into the background in a host of cases: namely, one's abstention from human love. But we would commit a different error if we neglected sexual union itself, as well as sexual impressions, as things being pertinent in this matter. It is not by the abstention from any human love whatsoever that virginity can be defined. Rather, it is defined in terms of abstention from this precise form of human love which finds its natural expression and fulfillment in sexual union, and therefore, it is also defined in terms of a total abstention from sexual union itself.

As regards bodily integrity, it is a concern in virginity only as a natural sign. Such a sign can be lacking without virginity being affected in reality. Or, conversely, such a sign can be found even where virginity properly speaking does not exist.

The formal element

It is clear that the mere bodily state of virginity is not, of itself, a personal value. In order for it to have such a personal value, it must be expressly willed. Thus, it is the "external act," with the intention [*propos*] of virginity being the internal act. (Here, we use the term "act" to refer to a state constituted by the absence of an act—that is, the absence of an external act, not an absence of an internal act of will.) A human act is composed of the external act and the internal act.

If we restore the interpersonal relations of love to their rightful place in the exercise of sexuality, though without losing sight of the very sexual union in which these relations are expressed and consummated, we can say:

> The intention of virginity consists essentially in the deliberate and definitive renunciation of the (full, that is, also bodily) gift of one's person to another created person as well as the reception of that gift from the other. Because this gift is accompanied by forceful emotions and strong, sensual impressions, the intention of virginity is also the renunciation of these emotions and impressions, even when experienced outside of this gift. And we must concede to the ancients that, on the psychological level, the mutual gift of persons in sexual union is first present to awareness as being enveloped in these sensible attractions, so that, concretely, these joys of sensibility are what is renounced when one decides to remain a virgin, even though there is much more contained in this renunciation.[28]

Integral virginity

In order for it to be integral, virginity must include this twofold material and formal composition. Setting aside every moral description of things, virginity does not exist if the material element is lacking, even if the bodily state of virginity was lost through violence and against one's will. Of course, in this case, the moral value of virginity remains whole and intact. However, virginity itself has been snatched from such a person, and the damage suffered consists precisely in this fact.

Nonetheless, the case of violence suffered is ambiguous, and given that the intention of virginity was not in itself attained, we could say that virginity remains as a personal value. (However, the bodily element must not be considered as being without importance for the human person and his or her manifestations.) In any case, when the bodily state of virginity voluntarily ceases (even when this happens in a legitimate manner), the intention of virginity can no longer be taken up. Its object (namely, the bodily state of virginity) is lacking.

Conversely, the bodily state of virginity without the intention of

---

28. Ibid., 31.

virginity is not integral virginity. This is obvious if the bodily state of virginity is preserved only through constraint (for example, through sociological constraint). This represents the opposite situation to that wherein virginity is lost through violence. However, this also applies to the wholly normal and right case of him or her who contemplates human love and sexual union for the future, all the while deliberately preserving his or her virginity for the present time.

Therefore, along with the bodily state of virginity, integral virginity includes the deliberate intention of remaining in this state. If this intention is virtuous (i.e., if it is formed on account of God, for God), it is the virtue of virginity in the strict sense. As regards bodily integrity for the woman, it pertains to virginity only to the degree that it is a sign and symbol of it, as we said above.

Mary "ever-virgin"

{459} From what we have said, it follows that, in order for the divine design concerning the virginal conception of the Incarnate Word to be fully realized, it was necessary that the woman who should conceive Him should thus be integrally virgin, *mente et corpore*. Thus, we here find ourselves faced with the "intention of virginity" which is suggested by Luke 1:34. The same is perhaps also suggested by Luke 1:27, if we must translate *pros pathenon emnestaumenen* as "a married virgin," as several exegetes propose.[29] We would thus have a kind of enigma, which Mary's response to the angel would then come to illuminate. However, note that, according to Matthew 1:17, Joseph had not yet taken Mary into his house.

Can we speak of a "vow of virginity" [which Mary would have taken]?[30] Obviously, we must exclude all juridical form from this notion of a vow. If it is merely identical with an "intention of virginity" formed in devotion to God, we would thus have the *desiderium virginem permanendi* spoken of by St. Thomas, and it seems that we must admit this. It is clear that this "intention of virginity" of itself excludes all forms of sexual relation after Jesus's birth. This gives

29. See Laurentin, *Structure et théologie de Luc*, 175–89.
30. See Augustine, *De virginitate*, PL 40, 397–428; *ST* III, q. 28, a. 4.

us the virginity after childbirth (*virginitas post partum*) perceived by Christian consciousness, supported on a very firm and very ancient historical tradition.[31] Very early on, this consciousness was expressed by the title, "The Virgin Mary."

Virginity in birth

{460} Here we find ourselves in the presence of something that the Church firmly believed from very early on in her life: in giving birth to Jesus, Mary knew neither the sufferings of childbirth nor the tearing of the *claustrum virginitatis*. There have been strenuous discussions about this topic in recent years.[32] For what pertains to the sufferings of childbirth, let us only note that the modern experiences of delivery without pain have brought to light how the liberation of the woman from suffering in delivery personalizes the maternal action of bringing a child into the world. This brings to light the great suitability of this tradition in relation to Mary's personal participation in the divine maternity. The only thing that one could ask oneself about is the relationship between this and virginity.[33]

As regards the maintenance of bodily integrity, we must primarily see it as having a symbolic value, founded on the body's role as the expression of the person. Along these lines, the hymen—which from a purely biological point of view is of no importance—could be seen as being the natural sign and symbol of virginity. By miraculously preventing the tearing of the hymen, God would have willed to preserve, in being born from her, not only virginity itself but even that which belongs to it merely as a sign.[34]

c) Mystery and miracle in the virginal maternity

{461} What is most important in the virginal maternity is the mystery of virginity, that is, its meaning—both for Jesus and for

---

31. See Laurentin, *Court traité sur la Vierge Marie*, 175–77.
32. See ibid., 177–80; Laurentin, "Bulletin sur la Vierge Marie," 357–58.
33. For the tradition on this point, see Georges-Matthieu de Durand, *Saint Cyrille d'Alexandrie. Deux dialogues christologiques*, SC 97 (Paris: Cerf, 1964), 204n1.
34. See J.-H. Nicolas, "Vierge jusque dans l'enfantement," 377–82.

Mary. Nonetheless, in the final analysis, there is the physical fact of Mary's preserved virginity, for virginity includes a bodily element that could not be eliminated without introducing idealism into anthropology. From this perspective, it is a question of a "miracle," or of many miracles—the miracle of parthenogenesis, the miracle of the virginal birth. A painstaking study of these miracles has been undertaken in light of modern science.[35] It does not seem that theology has much to gain from such investigations. Again, what is important is the firm recognition that this miracle is the ontological basis without which the mystery would no longer be anything but a religiously motivated mental construction.

3. The virginity and holiness of the mother of God

{462} What is the meaning of virginity as a personal value for Mary? How does virginity a value for one's holiness?

a) The Christian meaning of virginity

Virginity is the renunciation of an authentically human good

In valorizing virginity, one must not disparage and scorn the values that it comes to renounce: the mutual love of man and woman, parental love, and the joys of the flesh.

The mutual love of man and woman

[The mutual love of man and woman was] instituted by God Himself as the normal path for the development of human persons on earth. Sanctified by the sacrament, St. Paul proposes it as an example of the union of Christ and the Church. While human love can have a solely secular value (one that can be found just as much without any reference to God and to Christ), it also has a value for the holiness of the believer who lives this love in accordance with his or her faith.

---

[35]. See Cletus Wessels, *The Mother of God. Her Physical Maternity: Reappraisal* (River Forest, Ill., 1964).

Parental love

For human beings, parental love is much more than the realization of the biological instinct for reproduction. It is a participation in God's creative love. For believers, it is a participation in salvation history. Both universal human experience and Scripture assure us that children are, for man and woman, one of the loftiest and most intense satisfactions of human existence.

The joys of the flesh

Integrally making up part of human love and corresponding to the sensible and bodily dimension of human existence, the joys of the flesh also are part of the normal development of the human person, to the degree that they are integrated into an authentic and legitimate human love. If someone is a believer and lives one's love in faith, these joys also have a value for one's holiness. They are also sanctified by the sacraments and by faith.

Virginity is holy only on account of the good for the sake of which these human values are renounced

Therefore, virginity is neither holy nor sanctifying of itself. To determine whether it is, one must understand why a person intends to be a virgin. It could spring from egoism or pride. Clearly, in this case, far from being holy and sanctifying, virginity would be a diminution and an obstacle [to holiness]. It could spring from a desire to free oneself for purely temporal tasks. In this case, if these tasks are worthy of pursuit, virginity is a moral choice, one that can, in faith, be sanctifying. However, of itself, such virginity does not have a particular value for one's holiness. In order to have a value for one's holiness, one must renounce the goods of conjugal union for the sake of a superior good, for God. In that case, we must ask how and why can the intention to seek after God and to love Him incite one to renounce human goods that God Himself has proposed to man?

Love of God and the renunciation of conjugal union

Scripture expressly teaches that virginity chosen in view of being exclusively dedicated to love of God (and of neighbor) has a value for one's holiness that is superior to the values for one's holiness connected to conjugal union.[36]

The ancients most especially saw how the sensible emotions of sexual activity constitute an obstacle to union with God. On the one hand, they easily draw man far from God by the violence of the desires that they arouse. On the other hand, even when they are legitimate, they arouse an absorption of reason in sensibility, which seemed to them, in itself, to be a diminution of man. Some Fathers of the Church (for example, St. Gregory of Nyssa) expressed the strange idea that, in the state of original justice, the propagation of the human species would have occurred by other means. (This idea has been taken up in our days by Mitterer, who thinks that parthenogenesis would have been the ordinary law!)[37] Someone like St. Bonaventure thought that these sensible emotions, this effervescence of the flesh, would have been absent from sexual union. St. Thomas strongly took a position against these conceptions which misunderstand the reality of what it means to be human.[38]

One cannot deny that carnal concupiscence is, in fact, one of the great causes leading men to become distant from God. Nor can one deny that such concupiscence is quite difficult to master, so that it constitutes a *de facto* obstacle to seeking God. However, the value of virginity must be judged in relation to conjugal chastity, not in relation to debauchery. Is human love (in this case, conjugal love and parental love) an obstacle to love for God? Here again, we must respond, *in principle*, "no." Love for God can integrate and assume all legitimate human loves, which themselves can indeed be ordered to

---

36. See Lucien Legrand, *La virginité dans la Bible* (Paris: Cerf, 1964).

37. Albert Mitterer, *Dogma und Biologie der heiligen Familie nach dem Weltbild des Hl. Thomas von Aquin und dem der Gegenwart* (Vienna: Herder, 1952).

38. See *ST* I, q. 98, aa. 1 and 2.

the former. However, *de facto,* human love has a demanding character rendering this perfect subordination to the divine love difficult. Given the exclusivity and absolute character belonging to the mutual love of man and woman, one thus risks substituting the beloved person for God, if not completely (which would be a perversion), at least partially. Hence, the impulse of pure charity is constrained and impeded.[39] This enables us to understand how a Christian would form the idea of reserving for God his entire capacity to love and would thus choose virginity to this end.

This again presupposes man's existential situation, wounded as he is by original sin. One could perhaps prolong this reflection and bestow a singular value upon virginity not only on account of the disorder that risks slipping into the purest of human love, but as a consecration to the love of God alone. Here, we find ourselves faced with the great traditional theme of spiritual marriage (a theme that requires delicate handling but one that, nonetheless, cannot be repudiated) wherein God holds the role of the spouse for the consecrated person. He is the One who is exclusively loved and for whom one renounces all things.[40] In making this choice, one is not concerned with removing a possible evil from one's life. (Or, in any case, one is not only concerned with this and, indeed, is not principally concerned with this.) Rather, one is concerned with preferring a greater good to a lesser one, one that is still authentic and itself belonging to the way of holiness.

Finally, Christianity doubtlessly also here includes the themes of conformity to Christ and imitation of Mary. This is the highest motive from the perspective of Christian faith. It is the motive to which all the others are ordered. However, this motive of course pertains only to those who come after [Christ and Mary]. It is not what explains Mary's virginity.[41] If virginity has a value for one's holiness,

---

39. See Jacques Maritain, *Carnet de notes* (Paris: Desclée de Brouwer, 1965), ch. 7.
40. See Pierre Adnès, "Mariage spirituel," in *Dictionnaire de spiritualité ascétique et mystique,* 10:388–408.
41. See J.-H. Nicolas, *La virginité de Marie,* 32–50.

it also includes the inclination to communicate the good of grace. However, it likewise includes the renunciation of human fecundity. This gives rise to another precious aspect of the Christian theme of virginity, namely, spiritual fecundity. By giving Mary's virginity its full fecundity without suppressing it, her virginal maternity fulfills this aspiration to fecundity.

b) Virginity is part of the perfection of the divine maternity

{465} Every maternity includes the mother's consecration to the child who is born from her (a partial and relative consecration, but a real one). In its full "integrity," the divine maternity includes a total consecration by the mother to the Word, achieving in the spiritual and personal order the quasi-physical consecration that results from generation. As we have seen, virginity is the effect and sign of such a consecration.

B. The Fullness of Grace in Mary

We have already spoken about "Mary's graces of holiness on earth" and showed how they are connected with the divine maternity.[42] Here, it is a question of holiness considered as excluding all sin. The Church only gradually became aware that Mary's singular holiness ruled out all participation in human sin.[43] In short, as we have seen, the development of this awareness passed from the fact of Jesus's virginal conception to an awareness of how perfect virginity had a personal value for Mary's holiness. From here we pass on to the idea of her holiness of life.[44] St. Ambrose presents her as the example of consecrated virgins, and with St. Augustine, we arrive at the idea that she was exempted from every sin: "With the exception of the Virgin Mary, concerning whom, out of honor for the Lord, I wish to raise no question concerning the possibility of sins..."[45]

---

42. See §§452–54 above.
43. See Jouassard, "Marie à travers la patristique," 1:69–158; Jean Galot, "L'immaculée conception de Notre-Dame," in *Maria*, 7:10–116.
44. See Jouassard, "Marie à travers la patristique," 81.
45. St. Augustine, *De Natura et Gratia*, Oeuvres de Saint Augustin 21:321 and 609–10.

Following along this line of thought, through many adventures and resistances, though under the pressure of the People of God's piety much more than through theologians' speculation, the Church arrived at the affirmation of Mary's Immaculate Conception, which was solemnly proclaimed as a dogma of the Church in 1854 by Pope Pius IX. Mary's perfect holiness was connected to the *kekharitomenè* of the angelic salutation. The Immaculate Conception represents the point of departure for this holiness if we consider things from the perspective of her real development in grace. However, from the perspective of the Church's awareness concerning her fullness of grace, it represents a point of arrival.[46]

1. *The privilege of the Immaculate Conception*
a) Belief and the theological obstacles that it encountered

{464} Clearly, the question of knowing whether Mary was or was not conceived in sin is connected with explicit awareness concerning the doctrine of original sin and its transmission to all men. It is well known that this doctrine was clearly formulated by St. Augustine on the occasion of Pelagian denials. Through the course of these discussions, the problem of Mary's conception was raised as an objection to the doctrine of original sin. Julian of Eclanum cited the case of the Virgin Mary as an objection to this doctrine. (Indeed, this presupposes that, from this era, the Christian people generally rejected the idea that any sin could be attributed to Mary.) He objected to St. Augustine, "If one thinks Mary was submitted to original sin, one thereby delivers her over to the devil."

St. Augustine then responded with the famous phrase which through the course of the centuries would block progress toward [an acknowledgment of] the Immaculate Conception in the domain of theological research (though not in that of piety): "If we do not in-

---

46. See Laurentin, *Court traité sur la Vierge Marie*, 25 and 212; Lyonnet, *Le récit de l'Annonciation et la maternité divine*, 91; Jean-Hervé Nicolas, "L'innocence originelle de la Nouvelle Eve," in *Etudes Mariales* (Paris: Lethielleux, 1958), 15–35; Thurian, *Marie Mère du Seigneur, figure de l'Église*, 29–37.

scribe Mary in the lists of the devil on account of the condition of her birth, this is because this very condition of her birth had been undone by the grace of renewal."[47] Despite certain authors' desire to present this phrase as a first affirmation of her privilege, it in fact certainly submits Mary to the common condition of humanity as regards its participation in Adam's sin. In fact, this is how he was understood by the great theologians of the Middle Ages ([e.g.,] St. Albert, St. Bonaventure, and St. Thomas). During this time, popular piety developed in the direction of recognizing such privileges, feasts of the conception of Mary were instituted, and in 1439, the schismatic council of Basel defined it as a dogma. There were then several declarations of the sovereign pontiffs, the most renowned of which is that of Alexander VII in 1661.[48] The Council of Trent allowed the question to remain open.[49]

b) The theological difficulties that this privilege raises

{465} Opposition from theologians was not caused by *a priori* systematic considerations. Rather, their concerns were based on their consideration of wholly essential and certainly-revealed salvific truths. Theological reflection was able to overcome this obstacle only when the means for bringing this privilege into accordance with these truths was discovered. All the theologians who claimed (or who still claim) to simply bypass these truths followed (or still follow) a false route.

The universality of original sin

In whatever way one explains the transmission of original sin, a fundamental revealed truth remains certain: by themselves and without grace, all men are sinners and stand in need of grace in order to be saved. Here, we find ourselves faced with the entire dia-

---

47. St. Augustine, *Opus imperfectum contra Julianum*, PL 45, 1418. Moreover, he elsewhere says explicitly that "Mary's flesh issued from a sinful source." See Augustine, *De genesi ad litteram*, Oeuvres de Saint Augustin 49: 201.
48. See D.-*Sch.*, nos. 2015–17.
49. See ibid., no. 1516.

lectic of faith and works, as well as the dialectic of law and grace. The law is good. It becomes an instrument of death for man because he is evil. Works are not evil in themselves. They are prescribed by God, and man will be judged by his works. However, the works of man without grace are valueless before God because without grace man is a sinner.

If we say that a single human person escapes this sinful condition by his own birth, do we not thus relativize this condition? Does this not represent an admission that it is not impossible for man to be saved by his own powers? It will be said, "Christ escaped this condition." However, this is precisely a point where the parallelism between Jesus and Mary cannot be sustained. Although sin finds its source in nature, it [likewise] affects the person [who has this nature]. Therefore, He escaped all of sin's effects because the Person of the Word absolutely does not allow for sin. She, however, is a human person. Thus formed by nature at the moment of her conception, participating in human nature in accord with her personhood, she cannot fail to participate in its sin (or so it seems).

The universality of the redemption

Christ is the mediator, the source of all grace, and He exercises His mediation through His expiatory death and His resurrection. The theologians who, even today, hold that Mary was not formally redeemed, say that this does not prevent it from being the case that she would have received Christ's grace. However, the grace spoken of in Scripture is the remission of sins. Christ's merit in obtaining this grace is the fruit of His expiatory death, which once again demonstrates that this grace has the essential characteristic of being a [form of] pardon. Likewise, if one simply says that Mary was not redeemed because she did not need to be redeemed, one thereby removes her from Christ's grace.

A difficulty immediately follows from this: such a claim involves removing her from the human community, which is a community of the redeemed. This would lead to a Mariological conception which would place Mary between mankind in need of redemption and Christ the redeemer, thus *externally coming along* so as to cooperate in the redemption of men. As we will see, this position is inadmissible.

c) The way toward a resolution and the dogmatic definition

{466} There can be no doubt that St. Thomas (along with the theologians of his era) formally precluded the privilege for the reasons noted above.[50] Scotus is the one who cleared the way by being the first to elaborate the liberating notion of "preventive redemption," for there can be no doubt that Scotus held that Mary was preserved from human sin (which she normally would have contracted at her conception) solely by a grace coming from Christ (in anticipation of His merits), a formally redemptive grace.[51]

The words referring to the idea of preventive redemption, *sublimiore modo redempta*, redeemed in a more sublime manner, are found in the Bull, though not in the text of the definition. Nonetheless, they give the sense of the words *intuitu meritorum*, in view of [Christ's] merits, which are part of the definition itself.

One may ask, "Must we hold on [divine] faith that Mary was really redeemed?" It seems that the correct response is, "Yes." However, this affirmation would not principally be based upon the text of the definition, which could be (and, indeed by some is) interpreted in a different manner. Instead, such an affirmation would be based on a reason that goes much deeper: on account of the universality of redemption, which certainly is something held on [divine] faith.

d) The first redeemed person

{467} Thus, Mary was not merely free from sin from the first moment of her existence (as was Eve). Her preservation from sin was brought about through a special grace, through a "privilege." However, the very nature of this privilege precludes one from considering

---

50. See *ST* III, q. 27, a. 2.
51. See M.-J. Nicolas, *Theotokos*, 118–20; Carolus Balić, *La pensée de Scot sur l'Immaculée Conception* (Rome: Academia Mariana Internationalis, 1954).

Mary as first existing without this privilege (as it were, mixed in with the crowd) only thereafter receiving this privilege (thus, passing out of the crowd). Indeed, at the very moment when this person was constituted, she was privileged. How can this be expressed if not in a hypothetical form: "Mary would have contracted original sin if she had not been preserved by the grace of the mediator."[52]

In this case (as in many others), the hypothetical mood of this question does not intend to make us consider a non-existing state of affairs (and therefore, as non-existing, a state of affairs without any theological interest and beyond our grasp). Rather, it here intends to highlight an aspect of that which exists by bringing to light its true relationship with its cause. Thus, to say that the universe could have not existed is simply one way of expressing the fact that, in its given reality, it is contingent.

The notion of preventive redemption

{468} The person and his nature together make up a single principle of being and of activity, though each from a different perspective. The person is *quae est et quae operatur,* that which is and that which acts. The nature is *quo est et quo operatur,* that by which it is and by which it acts. This [distinction] is again found in sin, which first of all is "an evil of free activity" and secondly is "an evil of (personal) being." The person is *quae se avertit a Deo,* he who turns himself away from God, and *quae est peccatrix,* he who is a sinner. The nature is *qua persona se avertit a Deo,* that by which the person turns away from God, and *qua est peccatrix,* that by which he is a sinner.

However, there is a considerable difference between so-called personal sins (i.e., those committed by the person) and original sin. For the first kind of sins, the nature by which and in which the person sins is the individual nature as such. (It is through his freedom, inasmuch as it is his own, that the person sins.) In contrast, the source of the state of original sin is not an act of the person's

---

52. See Carolus Balić, *Joannes Duns Scotus Doctor immaculatae conceptionis* (Rome: Academia Mariana Internationalis, 1954), 16.

freedom. Rather, it is his participation, by means of his individuated nature, in the common nature of humanity. Given that the person is constituted in his singularity by the individuated nature as such, we can say that, in the first case, the person is the one who stains the nature (*macula peccati*), whereas, in contrast, in the second case, the nature is what stains the person.

Now, generation is the means by which the person participates in the common human nature. Therefore, through generation he participates simultaneously in humanity and in the sin that is common to humanity. (Here, we set aside the particular problem of the transmission of original sin. However one explains it, it remains the case that it is by becoming a man that the person becomes sinful, and he becomes a man through generation.)

What is meant then by the expression, "*Mary would have* contracted original sin"? It means that the cause through which she exists—and she exists as a human person, thus obviously a real cause, given that she really exists—by its own weight and inclination, simultaneously would have made her sinful by one and the same action. The grace of the Immaculate Conception prevented this cause from producing this effect. More exactly, it prevented Mary from receiving (from that cause's effect) a participation in human sin at the same time that she received a participation in human existence [from that same cause].

Therefore, we are here concerned with a real grace, that is, with a real action by God on the person of Mary, thus preserving her from a real evil. It was not real in itself, for it was precisely what was prevented. Nonetheless, it was real in its cause. Thus, if a combatant is hit on the head by a bullet, and the latter is deflected by the curve of his helmet, he can say, "Without my helmet, I would have been killed," and he says something real, even though the predicate "killed" is unreal.

Can we say that this grace of the Immaculate Conception is a "remission of sins"? Obviously, this can be true only in a particular sense. There is not a remission of real sins. However, the grace of the Immaculate Conception does most perfectly for Mary what the grace of the remission of sins does [for all others]. It "purified" her, rendering her pure by God's mercy, a person who naturally (i.e., according to the natural activity of the causes of her existence) would have been a sinner.

To understand this, we must recall that the remission of sins is much more than a mere pardoning of sins. (Indeed, this notion is inapplicable in the case of Mary.) It is the abolition of the state of sin. It makes it be the case that the beneficiary no longer is a sinner but, instead, is a just person.[53] If there was no sin to abolish in Mary's case, meaning that there was not a passage from injustice to justice, it remains true that the justice accorded to her by grace is a triumph over sin. It represents the extreme case for the realization of justification. We can in no way say that Mary was sinful.[54] However, a truth can be extracted by the following sort of affirmation (one that is scandalous for a Catholic): Mary was the privileged object of God's mercy toward sinful man; the Gospel expression, "I have not come for the just, but for sinners," is absolutely realized in her.

Finally, this preventive redemption is in no way an exception to the necessity of Christ's death on the cross for man's salvation (a necessity in the order established by God). It is by the merits of this death (*intuitu meritorum Chrisi Jesu salvatoris humani generis,* in view of the merits of Jesus Christ, the Savior of the human race) that this singular grace was accorded to her. That is, it was accorded *first to Christ,* just as all the graces bestowed upon men in general are bestowed through Christ's merits (before the Incarnation just as much as after it, and outside of explicit membership in the Church just as much as through the Church's sacraments). In other words, it was accorded to Christ Himself "on account of His obedience." Obviously, this anticipation does not render Christ's death useless for those who benefited from it in advance, for they have benefited from it, which is eternally present in the divine plan of man's salvation.

---

53. See *ST* I-II, q. 113, aa. 1 and 2.
54. See Thurian, *Marie Mère du Seigneur, figure de l'Église,* 29–37.

The term and notion of debitum peccati

{469} Cajetan introduced into our problem a notion that has been violently critiqued, namely, the notion of a *debitum peccati*, a debt of sin.[55] He explained this privilege as follows. Like every child of Adam, Mary has a *debitum peccati*. Therefore, this *debitum* was remitted for her by grace at the very moment of her conception. He pushed to the extreme the idea, one that was traditional [*classique*], that sin is a debt owed to God. Thus, Scotus said that, at his conception, man is a *debitor justitiae originalis*. That is, if man could not present himself to God with original justice, he was therefore in the situation of an insolvent debtor. (Note that the image itself has a basis in the Gospel.) For Cajetan (and here he doubtlessly exceeds the image's limits), sin itself is what is owed to man: he must be a sinner.

First of all, the legalism of this conception is troubling, at least in how it is expressed. Moreover, it is difficult to see what reality the image can apply to when treated in this manner: who is "obligated" by this debt? Would it be man? However, it does not make sense to say that one is obliged to be a sinner. (The idea of a moral debt here finds itself to be bizarrely inversed. The sinner has a debt toward God *because he is a sinner*. However, he obviously does not make satisfaction for his debt by being a sinner.) Would it be God? It is likewise meaningless to say that God is obliged to allow man to become a sinner, for man is a sinner by standing in opposition to God and not in dependence upon Him. The application of this conception to the Holy Virgin is no easier. How can one say that the immaculate Mary had an obligation to be sinful or that God would have the obligation to leave her be touched by sin?

In reality, it seems that Cajetan was betrayed by his fondness for condensed formulas. He substituted a substantive, *debitum*, for a conditional verbal form that is related, by its very structure, to that which does not exist and never did (whereas the substantive, by its

---

[55] See Cajetan, *De immaculata conceptione Beatae Mariae Virginis, Opuscula Omnia*, vol. 2, opusc. 1 (Venice, 1594).

very form, indicates that which is). One is thus led to find something real in Mary corresponding to the *debitum peccati*. Moreover, the term *debitum* is a juridical term which calls to mind juridical relations (in this case, something wholly out of context), whereas the verb *debere* extends broadly outside the juridical domain.

However, Cajetan employs a much more accurate expression when he speaks about the *necessitas contrahendi peccatum*.[56] Here, we again find our explanation: the *necessitas contrahendi* is situated in the relation of the person of Mary to the real causes of her being (i.e., her parents), who simultaneously would have been the real causes of her sinful situation if the grace of the Immaculate Conception had not intervened. Therefore, we are concerned here with a reality, not an abstraction ("Christ did not die for an abstraction," as Fr. Bonnefoy has said). Yet this reality is very poorly expressed by the term and image of *debitum peccati*, which introduces into Mary that very thing which it is her privilege to have been preserved from, any kind of participation in human sin.

e) The meaning of this privilege

The Immaculate Conception and the divine maternity

{470} Karl Rahner and Max Thurian[57] both insist on an idea which we already encountered in relation to the divine maternity, namely, that Mary was predestined by the same act as Jesus Himself. Her holiness is that of the mother of God, and it absolutely excludes all sin. Here again, it is necessary to say that Mary's Immaculate Conception is first of all a privilege of Christ. This is the line of thought along which the piety of the People of God principally developed.

The triumph of the redemption

If the grace of the Immaculate Conception is a redemptive grace, it is certainly the highest achievement of the redemption. It was fit-

---

56. See Cajetan, *In ST* I-II, q. 81, a. 3, no. 1.
57. Karl Rahner, "L'immaculée conception," *Ecrits théologiques* (Paris: Desclée de Brouwer, 1966), 4:145–59. Also, see the work of Thurian cited above.

ting that the measureless efficacy of the redemption would manifest itself through this triumph over sin (and the assumption, in the same line, is the triumph of redemptive grace over death). Scotus strongly emphasized this point. We must add that this makes the Immaculate Conception the paradigm of every justification. Thus, Mary emerges as the figure of the Church.

Mary, the perfect example of "justification by faith"

Justification is real, and it makes one good. It divinizes the person who is the object of it. However, this feeling of being justified excludes all pride, for it is a righteousness "not by works but by faith." The Immaculate Conception is the absolute image of grace conferred without any merit, before any work. For this reason, Mary is the perfect image of the justified person, who draws from her own holiness the reason for her humility.

2. *Preservation from all sin*

{471} [The preservation of Mary from every sin is] a privilege recognized for the Virgin very early, universally from the time of the Council of Ephesus[58] and ever since. It was defined anew at the Council of Trent.[59] St. Thomas gives three reasons for it, all of which are traditional.[60]

a) The grace of the Immaculate Conception and the grace of preservation from all sin

"If one considers (any free creature) in what it holds from its nature, it can sin, and every creature whom we can say cannot sin holds this from a gift of grace, not from her natural condition."[61] On the other hand, the grace which actually "divinizes" the believer is not of itself a guarantee against future sins. This is clear in Scripture, which

---

58. See Jouassard, "Marie à travers la patristique," 69–158.
59. See *D.-Sch.*, no. 1573.
60. See *ST* III, q. 27, a. 4.
61. See *ST* I, q. 63, a. 1.

places the believer on guard against the danger of being unfaithful. This is clear at the outset of salvation history, for at its very beginning, man had grace and nonetheless sinned. In these conditions, how should we understand the idea that Mary's initial grace included immunity from later sins? As we have seen, it was a triumph by Christ over sin (which was not the first grace given to humanity). It was the effect and expression of God's intention for the person of Mary, an intention to preserve her from sin.

Could Mary's own will frustrate this divine intention? In itself, yes, because it is capable of sin and because sin consists precisely in the free creature withdrawing from God's love. However (and here we find ourselves faced with the mystery of grace), if created freedom can really withdraw from grace, the latter can prevent created freedom from doing such. In fact, original sin includes in itself, virtually, all the other sins that man commits. Each sin is committed in imitation of the first man and those following on him. Mary's initial grace was a total victory over sin in her, a victory that abolished the very root of sin.

b) How we should conceive the grace of preservation from sin

We have seen that Christ's exemption from every sin was a property and effect of the *grace of union*. Christ, the Incarnate Word, could not sin. He was absolutely incapable of sin. This is not the case for Mary. While the divine maternity is the reason for this preservation from sin, it is not its cause. It was sovereignly suitable that the mother of God would be exempt from all sin. However, it was not absolutely impossible for her to sin. She remained capable of sin, both by her nature and personally.

The grace that preserved her from sinning is sanctifying grace, which, as we have seen, precludes every tendency in her toward sin (i.e., concupiscence) and also perfectly connaturalized her to the divine good. However, given that every free creature *in via* (i.e., not yet definitively united to the divine good, which happens only through the Beatific Vision and beatific love), remains radically capable of sin (on account of the disproportion between her person, which is finite, and the infinite good to which the person is ordered), we must also think of the continuous action of the Holy Spirit through operative graces [working in Mary for this kind of preservation for her entire existence as a *viator*]. The Holy Spirit who made her into His temple from the first moment of her existence did not cease to lead her [throughout her whole life].

c) Exemption from concupiscence

{472} It is universally admitted that, through the grace of the Immaculate Conception, Mary was exempted from the misery that is man's tendency to sin—*concupiscentia* or the *fomes peccati*. However, this was not expressly introduced into the definition, and it seems that this was intentional.[62] Indeed, the meaning of this notion should first be specified.

In a broad sense, *concupiscentia* could designate the sense appetite's spontaneity, as well as that of the will itself, faced with an object being presented to it as something good. In this sense, *concupiscentia* is not the *fomes peccati*, given that such a spontaneous reaction is "natural." However, we must admit two qualifications. On the one hand, this spontaneity is, for man, a cause of sin (obviously, a non-necessitating cause). Indeed, by following it when the object is not conformed to the true good and to the Divine Will, the free will is borne toward an apparent good (*conversio*), *being thus turned away* from the true good (*aversio*). On the other hand, the state of original justice obviously did not include in itself the abolition of this spontaneity, which is a form of richness. Instead, it provided for the perfect submission of the instinct (even the "spiritual" instinct) to man's deliberate will so that the latter could not be surprised [in its activity]. This submission was brought about through grace.

In the strict theological sense, *concupiscentia* refers to this spontaneity inasmuch as it is independent of reason, as an irrational force,

---

62. See J. Alfaro, "La formula definitoria de la immaculada concepción," *Virgo immaculata*, vol. 2 (Rome, 1956), 201–75.

one that is contrary to the movement of the free will toward the true human good. Considered in this way, however one explains it, it is a consequence of original sin. This consequence is not suppressed by baptism, which effaces original sin and all of its personal consequences. Why? Because baptism finds the *fomes peccati* established in the person purified by it. It is intimately united to original sin but, nonetheless, is distinct from it. Indeed, of itself, it is neither a sin, nor a punishment, but a congenital deficiency.

Translating man's ontological complexity as a being made of flesh and spirit onto the dynamic plane [of human activity], this state of soul takes the form of a conflict of tendencies [in the human person]. It likewise translates onto the dynamic plane [of human activity] this paradoxical situation of a finite creature ordered to an infinite good and ruled by it in its goodness. If it is a punishment, this is in reference to the sin committed at the beginning of human history through the common nature that is realized in this person, a nature which is stripped of its primitive harmony only as a punishment for this sin. Baptismal grace totally suppresses sin and, consequently, all penal obligation without, for all that, suppressing this deficiency in nature. When separated from sin, it is no longer either culpable or penal for the person but, instead, is only the occasion of the struggle and of victory. However, this does not prevent it from being the case that, by its nature, it inclines one to sin.

If the grace of the Immaculate Conception involves the total exclusion of concupiscence, this is because it has abolished its cause: in the human person called by God and fallen, what is first is his participation in human sin. The *fomes peccati* follow from there. In Mary, this participation in sin never existed. The grace that preserved her from it radically suppressed concupiscence. The redemption of which Mary was the object was perfect from its first instance.

3. *Mary's participation in humanity's earthly punishments*

{473} Mary certainly participated in the human condition. However, is not the latter, at least in part, a consequence of sin? Hence, how can we reconcile all of this, by which we can call this condition "sinful" (in the sense that it affects man on account of the fact that he is a sinner), with the dogma of the Immaculate Conception?[63]

a) The Immaculate Conception is not the restoration of the state of original justice in Mary

The state of original justice is now but a past stage of salvation history. If Mary belongs to the order of redemption, she does not belong to the order of humanity's first innocence.

b) Mary Suffered the Painful Condition of Humanity

On this point, we see her difference from Christ. The Word "assumed" the punishments connected to the human condition following on sin. Given that He was the Word, He was able to remove these punishments from it. He willed to endure them so that He may redeem sin by suffering and, in the end, deliver man from it through His resurrection. Mary, however, comes forth from humanity, and she receives, along with the human nature from which her human person is formed, the human condition. By grace, she is exempt from all participation in sin. However, the "common punishments" are not sinful. They remain extrinsic to sin (as a punishment remains extrinsic to fault). Mary did not "assume" them, as Christ did. She was naturally submitted to them. Obviously, accepting them fully by love and uniting them to Christ's sufferings, she made them into an instrument of redemption (not of purification for herself, as she is entirely pure from the beginning by grace).

c) Did Mary know death?

For the Christian, to the degree that he is a Christian, death is not a punishment but instead is the ultimate conformity (according to the Christian's earthly being) to Christ. This is why it seems that we must say that Mary knew death.[64]

---

63. See J.-H. Nicolas, "L'innocence originelle de la Nouvelle Eve," 15–35.
64. See Laurentin, *Structure et théologie de Luc*, 182–84; M.-J. Nicolas, *Theotokos*, 173–84.

4. *The growth of grace in Mary*

{474} Mary grew in grace from the first moment of her existence up to her passage into glory. In this, she differs from Christ. For as we have seen, Christ was not submitted to development in His very person, and before being an enrichment of nature (and from this perspective we can indeed speak of a form of progress in the manifestation and the exercise of Christ's grace) grace is an interpersonal relation between the human person and the Divine Persons.

Three stages can be distinguished in this growth: preparation for the divine maternity; participation in Christ's redemptive mission; and the end of her earthly life in the Church, beginning after Christ's resurrection.[65] Laurentin distinguishes five stages. Between our first and second stages, he introduces the divine maternity, which, in fact, certainly introduced an immense novelty into the development of the immaculate one's grace. In the same way, he numbers as the separate, final stage the consummation of Mary's grace at the assumption.[66] In any case, the assumption must be considered in light of this growth. It is the ultimate victory of redemptive grace, its victory over death.[67]

---

65. See *ST* III, q. 27, a. 5, ad 2.
66. See Laurentin, *Court traité sur la Vierge Marie*.
67. On the Assumption, see Galot, "Le mystère de l'assomption," in *Maria*, 7:155–237.

8

The Salvation of Men by the Blood of Christ

{475} The Incarnation itself is already redemptive in the sense that in Christ man is already restored, having again become (indeed, with an incomparably superior perfection) an image of God, divinized. Nonetheless, the salvation of all men required something else. For the sake of this salvation, the Incarnate Word poured out His blood in expiation. He had to obtain from God the grace of the remission of sins for sinful men. This is the mystery of the *redemption* which, although intimately connected to that of the *Incarnation*, remains distinct from it and poses specific problems for the theologian.

From all the texts of Scripture (with the prophecy of the fifty-third chapter of the Book of Isaiah related to the sufferings of the servant of God for his people always in the background), the idea emerges that Jesus poured out His blood in order to obtain the grace of the remission of sins and of new life for those who come to believe in Him, a new life which is the same as the life He Himself received at the resurrection and which He communicates to believers. Or, again, we may say: He poured out His blood in ransom for men's sins and has thus redeemed them.[1]

---

1. See Braun, *Jean le théologien*, 3:139–93. Lucien Cerfaux, *Le Christ dans la théologie de saint Paul* (Paris: Cerf, 1954), 95–125; Cullmann, *Christologie du Nouveau Testament*,

The Salvation of Men by the Blood of Christ 341

This doctrine was preached from the start without dispute. The doctrine of salvation was itself precisely what served to place other dogmatic truths in relief: the *reality of the humanity* of Christ, for if He is not truly a man, He did not truly suffer and we are not saved; His *divinity*, for if He is not God, He was not able to divinize us. The Pelagian heresy is what placed this dogma into question and was the occasion for the formulas into which the Church expressed it. Among these formulas, that which Trent proclaimed condensed it thus: "Christ ... merited for us justification by His most holy Passion on the wood of the Cross and made satisfaction for us to God the Father."[2]

I. INADMISSIBLE THEOLOGICAL EXPLANATIONS

A. Explanation by the Rights of the Devil

{476} This strange explication, holding that the price of our redemption,[3] namely, the human life of Jesus, was given, and His blood was poured out, in ransom to the devil who held sinful man in servitude, needing to receive a "just"[4] recompense, arose from a

---

48–73 and 206–12; André Feuillet, "Le logion sur la rançon," *Revue des sciences philosophiques et théologiques* 51 (1967): 365–402, and "Les trois grandes prophéties de la Passion et de la Résurrection," *Revue thomiste* 67 (1967): 533–60; 68 (1968): 41–75; *Jésus le Sauveur, Lumière et Vie* 15 (1954); Pierre Grelot, "La théologie de la mort dans l'Écriture Sainte," *Vie Spirituelle Supplément* 77 (May 1966): 143–93; Jacques Guillet, "Le titre biblique de Dieu vivant," in *L'homme devant Dieu*, 1:11–23; Joachim Gnilka, "Rédemption," *Encyclopédie de la Foi* (Paris: Cerf, 1967), 4:11–13; Stanislas Lyonnet, *De peccato et redemptione*, vol. 1: *De notione peccati* (Roma: Pontificio Instituto Biblico, 1957); Lyonnet, *De peccato et redemptione*, vol. 2: *De* vocabulario redemptionis (Rome: Pontificio Instituto Biblico, 1960), and *Les étapes de l'histoire du salut selon l'épître aux Romains* (Paris: Cerf, 1969); and Léopold Sabourin, *Rédemption sacrificielle. Une enquête exégétique* (Paris: Desclée de Brouwer, 1961).

2. Council of Trent, *Decree on Justification*, ch. 7 (Denzinger, no. 1529). Also, see the formula of the council of Querzy (Denzinger, no. 624).

3. For the history of the theology of redemption, see Jean Rivière, *Le dogme de la redemption. Étude historique* (Paris: Lecoffre, 1905); Rivière, *Le dogme de la rédemption. Étude historique* (Louvain: Bureaux de la Revue, 1931); Rivière, "Rédemption," in *Dictionnaire de théologie catholique*, 13:1912–2004; Henry Ernest William Turner, *The Patristic Doctrine of Redemption* (London: [Mowbray, 1952]).

4. See Rivière, *Le dogme de la rédemption*, 373–486. Paul Synave, "La passion du

univocal use of the notions (and images) of *servitude* (as applied to sin) and of *redemption* (as applied to the act by which Christ freed man). Thus, certain thinkers sought after the person *to whom* this ransom had been paid and came to think of him who in Scripture personifies sin inasmuch as man is a "slave of sin." This idea goes back rather far in the history of the theology of redemption. It was already suggested by St. Irenaeus, was clearly proposed by Origen, and was made use of by certain Fathers such as Gregory of Nyssa. However, in all eras, it has encountered opponents and does not deserve to be called traditional. In any case, even in the ancient authors who use it, it is balanced by the "mystical" or "physical" conception of the redemption which we recalled earlier.[5] For the ancient Fathers, it was never a complete explanation of the redemption, nor doubtlessly the principal one.

B. Explanations by the Imprescriptible Rights of God

{477} This is the Anselmian explication. First of all, we must say that, despite its grave imperfections, it played an essential role in the formation of the theology of redemption. St. Anselm definitively excluded the theory of the "rights of the devil" from the field of theology. In a very lively and very profound way, he saw that sin of *itself* requires an infinite reparation because it is an infinite offense and that, therefore, the drama of the redemption did not play out between Christ and the devil but, instead, between Christ and His Father. He introduced into theology the key notion of satisfaction, which alone enables us to "explain" the mystery (within faith). However, he introduced excessive legalism into his own explanation, thus distorting it. In this way, far from being a wasted attempt at theological reflection, his failure indicated the way to be followed in order to arrive at an explanation that is satisfying for reason and for faith.[6]

Christ et les droits du démon," in *Saint Thomas d'Aquin. Somme théologique, La Vie de Jésus* (Paris: Cerf, n.d.), 3:270–78.

5. See §433 above.

6. See St. Anselm, *Pourquoi Dieu s'est fait homme*, ed. and trans. René Roques, SC 91 (Paris: Cerf, 1963); René Roques, "Introduction," in *Anselme de Cantorbery, Pourquoi*

1. The Anselmian criticism of the theory of the rights of the devil

{478} St. Anselm poses the theological problem of the redemption in striking terms, excluding overly simplistic explanations (which we see again today). Indeed, it is not enough that we would admire the abnegation of Jesus in His passion and His love for men (so that we may attempt to imitate it). We must first explain why and in what way men needed Him to die for them.[7]

He refutes the explanation by the rights of the devil by decisively showing that it is incoherent to speak of a devil having a real right over men, as well as to speak of a kind of duty on the part of God's justice in relation to the devil. God is the master of the devil as of man, and if man by sin lives under the yoke of the devil, this is on account of a mysterious disposition that God can recall at His pleasure, not in virtue of an acquired right.[8]

2. Sin considered as a theft committed against God: a theft against his "honor"

{479} Man as a person (i.e., by his free will) totally depends upon God. He owes God the submission of his whole person. First of all, this is an interior submission (i.e., rectitude of will). Moreover, it is an external submission (i.e., the fulfillment of prescribed works, but if, against his will, he is prevented from performing them, God is not *inhonoratus*, just as, conversely, He would not be "honored" by works done without this right will). In its essence, sin consists in refusing this submission. Anselm conceives of this as a "theft" (as a result of a univocal perception of the [term] *debitum*). However, note that the very person of man is what is first of all "stolen" from God. Moreover (as another manner of conceiving of the "damage" done to God), sin is a "disorder" and therefore a subtraction of good

---

Dieu s'est fait homme, SC 91 (Paris: Cerf, 1963), 9–190; Rivière, *Le dogme de la redemption* (Paris: 1905), 291–323.

7. See Anselm, *Pourquoi Dieu s'est fait homme*, bk. 1, ch. 6.
8. See ibid., ch. 7.

from the universe, which belongs to God. If it is a theft, sin calls for and demands the "restitution" of what has been stolen. And beyond this, it also calls for compensation for the damage thus caused. And, obviously, this compensation must, on the one hand, correspond to the damage and, on the other hand, must entail a "gratuitous" deliverance (i.e., a deliverance that was not otherwise owed).[9]

3. *God Himself cannot pardon sin without this restitution*

{480} The fundamental idea—and one that is fundamentally just—is that God cannot tolerate disorder, which infringes on His proper good and is the principal injustice. To tolerate it would mean that He would be rendered unjust toward Himself. Consequently, according to Anselm (and here his position ceases to be true) it would mean that God *must* either punish the sin (in a manner proportioned to its gravity, that is, by an eternal punishment) or, if He wishes to pardon it, must require for pardon an adequate reparation (namely, *satisfaction*).[10]

4. *Only Christ can give this satisfaction by giving his life*

{481} Man can give nothing that He does not already have, for he wholly belongs to God. And, even if he could give God something "of himself" which would not otherwise be owed to God, this would be a paltry compensation. Here, we are in the presence of the profound idea (one that is just in itself, though receiving a defective presentation in Anselm) that sin is an infinite offense, calling for an infinite satisfaction. The reasoning runs as follows. It is not just for man to disobey God, even in a small thing, for anything in the world, for the world itself and for a thousand worlds. Therefore, by sinning, man steals from God something that is more important than the entire created order. Therefore, this damage cannot be balanced out by anything created. This means that God alone can make satisfaction, for who can have as his own a good that is superior to every created

---

9. See ibid., ch. 11.
10. See ibid., ch. 13 and 19.

good, if not God Himself? However, man is the one who must make satisfaction, as man is the one who sinned. There is only one solution: the God-Man.

As on the other hand, systematizing one of St. Augustine's insights, Anselm thinks that God Himself needs man to be saved in order that he may take the place of the fallen angels, the Incarnation thus emerges as being necessary as it is the only means that God has for realizing His design: "Thus, since this superior city must be completed by men, and since this could not be the case without the aforementioned satisfaction being assured, a satisfaction which God can make but which man alone must make: the God-Man must be the one who makes it."[11]

5. Critical examination of the Anselmian explanation

{482} The primordial intuition that we noted remains the principle of every explanation of the redemption: sin *of itself* requires an infinite reparation. However, the following three sub-points must be recognized and accepted.

a) This in no way diminishes the divine freedom for pardoning

God is not enveloped in the order that He assures. On the contrary, this order depends on His free will, and He can therefore freely pardon. He is not accountable to anyone.[12] It is true that He cannot tolerate disorder. However, His pardon is not a mere *condonatio*, an "amnesty." God's love is truly effective. The love of God who pardons rectifies the sinner's will[13] and, consequently, reestablishes the order violated by sin.

b) This does not justify a juridical conception of sin

Anselm saw very well that, through sin, what man takes away from God is not a *thing-good*. What He takes away is himself, a *person-*

---

11. See ibid., bk. 2, ch. 6.
12. See *ST* III, q. 46, q. 2, a. 3.
13. See *ST* I-II, q. 113, q. 1.

good. However, he did not know how to draw the consequence of this. It is not a question of a theft but of a rupture in interpersonal relations. And, once again, it is indeed true that, as long as this rupture remains, pardon does not exist, because, by its very nature, pardon reestablishes the connection between God, who is offended, and man the sinner. However, indeed, once this bond comes to be established, the pardoned man finds himself anew in love, with the evil of sin also being abolished.

c) This does not justify a juridical conception of satisfaction

In the same way, this "restitution" required by sin must not be conceived of as a thing-good. (God has every good in Himself.) Instead, it must be conceived of as the restoration of the broken connection on the part of man. Therefore, if this connection was first restored by the divine pardon, satisfaction would become useless. Moreover, note that Anselm does not indicate how the death of Christ was able to be a "restitution" for God.

C. Explanation by Penal Substitution

{483} According to Scripture, Christ suffered and died "in place of sinners." Given that death is the "chastisement for sin," it was natural enough to express this by saying that Christ was chastised in our place. Moreover, it is what is suggested by Isaiah 53:5 (RSV): "Upon Him was the chastisement that made us whole, and with His stripes we are healed." Suggestions of this kind can be found in the most ancient tradition,[14] though not in a systematic form. Indeed, the theme "Jesus paid the debt for all," uses the notion of "substitution" more than that of punishment.

This notion of the "punishment" of Christ has little echo in the Middle Ages. (It is not St. Anselm's way of speaking, as we have seen.) However, we do find it exposited in a curious text of Dante which Rivière cites. In this text, St. Anselm's "satisfaction" becomes synon-

---

14. See Rivière, "Rédemption," col. 1941.

ymous with "chastisement" to the point that, if the death of Christ had not taken the form of a penal sanction conferred by a legitimate judge, it would not have caused our redemption.[15]

This is the notion that Luther, and then Melanchthon, will place at the center of their theology of redemption: God has placed all our sins upon Christ. Thus, we read in Luther:

> Be you Peter the renegade or Paul the persecutor.... Consequently, you must pay and satisfy for all men, and I see only sins in them. Therefore, it is necessary that He die upon the cross. Thus, it rushes upon Him and puts Him to death. Through this, the world is freed and purified of its sins.[16]

And Melanchthon:

> We must set forth God's admirable plan, according to which, given that He is just and experiences a horrible anger in response to sin and also willed that this utterly just anger be appeased, He poured out His anger on the Son of God because He pled for us.[17]

Calvin equally shares in this overall approach (although an extensive theology of mercy can be found in him as well), holding that, overwhelmed by the thought of God's judgment, we find our rest only by considering Jesus Christ condemned in our place:

> We could not escape God's horrible judgment. In order to remove it from us, Jesus Christ suffered being condemned before a mortal man and appearing evil and profane ... When He was led to the tribunal like a criminal (both in order for some formality of justice to be held against Him, arguing the case from testimony, and in order for Him to be condemned by the very mouth of the judge), we see Him here condemned in the place of sinners so that He may suffer in their name.[18]

This theme of penal substitution developed with insistence in the Churches [sic] arising from the reformation in the seventeenth

---

15. See Dante Alighieri, *La Monarchie*, in *Oeuvres complètes*, ed. La Pléiade (Paris, 1965), 698–700.
16. Martin Luther, *Commentary on Galatians Martin Luthers Werke* (Weimar, 1883ff), 40:432–40.
17. Cited by Rivière, "Rédemption," col. 1552.
18. Jean Calvin, *Institution chrétienne* (Genève: Labor et Fideles, 1967), 262–63. [Tr. note: No date provided by Fr. Nicolas.]

and eighteenth centuries. Then, it was violently critiqued and rejected.[19] During the same era, it certainly at least leeched into the teaching of the Catholic pulpit,[20] if not into Catholic theology. However, it is not tenable.

On the one hand, "punishment" gives "satisfaction" to the "offense" (whether in a particular person, society, or even God) only if it reaches the offender. Representing the "anger of God" as a violent sentiment (doubtlessly triggered by sin but having lost its reference to the sinner to the point of needing, in order that it be appeased, a certain quantity of chastisement undergone by anyone) is not only an impiety but moreover is an absurdity. On the other hand, what characterizes "punishment" is the fact of being "suffered," of being contrary to the will of the sinner. Now, a fundamental biblical notion in this matter is the idea that Christ freely suffered and that He voluntarily gave Himself over to death, as we will see. Hence, it cannot be a question of a chastisement, properly speaking, but of a free action undertaken by Christ. To say that Christ took upon Himself the chastisement that was owed to us is a shortcut. He took upon Himself sufferings and death, which are the punishment of sin. However, as soon as He took them upon Himself freely, they were not a punishment for Him. Another explanation will need to be sought out.

D. Minimizing Explanations

{484} Conversely, minimizing explanations also exist, ones which entirely remove objective efficacy from Christ's death, making it into only a testimony of love, an encouragement to undertake the redemptive process for oneself. Already in the Middle Ages, Abelard, in reaction against the notion of being liberated from the yoke of the devil, reduced Christ's passion to being only an example.

Within Reformed theology (indeed, already in the sixteenth cen-

---

19. See Rivière, *Le dogme de la rédemption. Étude historique* (Louvain, 1931), 355–428.
20. Jacques-Bégnigne Bossuet, *Oeuvres oratoires de Bossuet*, ed. J. Lebarq (Paris: Desclée, 1914–26), 3:361–86. [Tr. note: I have added the final publication information, which Fr. Nicolas does not provide explicitly, though he cites Lebarq's edition.]

tury), Socinus held a position against the punishment-satisfaction doctrine of the Reformers, though also against any kind of satisfaction theory of redemption. [According to him,] each person can and must expiate his sin by penitence. Christ's death contributes to it only through the love and confidence that it inspires in us or by the advantage we draw from the assurance of having an efficacious intercessor in heaven.[21]

Hesitations exist today on the subject of the true nature of sin, based on a tendency to once again put into question the notion of "an offense to God" underlying the theology of sin and the theology of redemption. These hesitations incline many contemporary theologians, even Catholic ones, toward solutions of this kind. In such solutions, the objective value of the passion and the death of Christ (namely, their value antecedent to every act of awareness and acceptance by man) is, if not denied, at least unexplained and, consequently, neglected.

As an extreme case in Catholic theology, the curious theory sketched out by Schoonenberg can be mentioned. According to him, Christ's passion and death, far from being an undertaking that would liberate man, would be sin itself, the rejection of grace (and therefore of God) by man.[22] What saves us is the resurrection, through which the Father, by raising Jesus, frees man from his sins, by first freeing them from the enormous sin of having put Christ to death (a sin in which all the others are summed up).

This theory is strictly inadmissible in Catholic theology, for without any doubt, through the attestation of Scripture and the teaching of the Church from her beginning, we are told that it was *through his death and resurrection* for men that Christ "redeemed" them, freed them from sin, and justified them (at least if through faith they accept this death and resurrection). Moreover, this theory is unsustainable solely from the perspective of reason. On the one hand, only a very

21. See Rivière, "Rédemption," col. 1954.
22. Piet Schoonenberg, *L'homme et le péché*, trans. Michel Martron (Tours: Mame, 1967).

restricted number of people really took part in the decision to kill Jesus, and it is not clear how the whole of humanity could be guilty of this "sin." On the other hand, if the condemnation of Christ was, in fact, the rejection of the author of grace ("He came to his own home, and his own people received him not," Jn 1:11, RSV), those who decided to kill him were not aware of this and certainly could be perfectly innocent. Moreover, let us note that such a theory, which rests on no exegetical or historical foundation, is a purely arbitrary speculation, which cannot be taken into consideration in sound theology.

E. Conclusion

{485} Therefore, two things must be explained. On the one hand, one must explain [the fact] that Christ's passion, death, and resurrection were the cause of salvation—that by them, solely by them and because of them, God accorded to men the grace of the remission of sins and, with the obstacle of sin thus being removed, has rendered unto them the grace of divinization. On the other hand, one must explain that this redemptive mission of the Son was itself a pure grace, a gift from God ("God so loved the world that he gave his only Son," Jn 3:16, RSV), not an incomprehensible requirement of the divine justice. The notion of "vicarious satisfaction" is the key to this explanation—the only one.

II. THEOLOGICAL EXPLANATION OF THE REDEMPTION BY THE NOTION OF "VICARIOUS SATISFACTION"

A. The Introduction of This Notion into the Theology of Redemption

{486} St. Anselm's great merit is to have introduced into theology this notion of "satisfaction," even if his use of it was uneven.[23] The two inseparable notions offense-satisfaction that he extracted in their mutual relation remain the notions that must be used in or-

---

23. In addition to the studies already noted, see J. Rivière, "Sur les premières applications du terme 'satisfactio,'" *Bulletin de littérature ecclésiastique* 25 (1924): 285–97 and 353–69.

The Salvation of Men by the Blood of Christ 351

der to understand the redemption. St. Anselm introduced the notion of satisfaction without explaining it, as something self-evident, although he was the first to use it for explaining the redemption. In fact, the notion is found in the Fathers and theologians before him, as well as in liturgical texts.

In the former (already in Tertullian[24]) *satisfactio* is employed for designating the sinner's penitential acts. In ancient liturgical texts, it is employed in prayers made to the saints: he who prays relies upon the "satisfaction" of the saints. It is in the texts of the Mozarabic liturgy that we see the term *satisfactio* attributed for the first time to the Eucharistic sacrifice, *pro satisfactione saeculi elinquientis*, then to the sacrifice of the cross. There, it is said that Christ was our "vicar."[25]

After St. Anselm, the notion became standard in the theology of the redemption.[26] St. Thomas pushed the analysis of this notion of satisfaction much further. He saw this notion as expressing an act of reparation for sin through the fulfillment of a painful, penal work, though one that has the character of being voluntarily taken up, indeed by love, instead of being suffered, as it were, as a chastisement.[27] I will attempt to show that the notion of vicarious satisfaction, when sufficiently elaborated, is indeed the notion that explains redemption.[28]

B. Analysis of the Notion of Satisfaction

1. The theological notion of sin as an offense against God

a) The components of sin

{487} In a human act, one must distinguish the *physical act* from the *moral act*.[29] The physical act is a given human action, ordered to

---

24. See Tertullian, *Traité du baptême*, SC 35 (Paris: Cerf, 1953), ch. 20, 1.
25. See Jean Rivière, "Sur les premières applications du terme 'satisfactio,'" *Bulletin de littérature ecclésiastique* 25 (1924): 362–64.
26. See Paul Galtier, "Satisfaction," in *Dictionnaire de théologie catholique*, 14:1129–1210.
27. See Catão, *Salut et redemption*, 78–94.
28. Against this, see Catão (in pages 79–80 of the work cited above), who contests that this is the "master notion" of the theology of redemption for St. Thomas; see also Christian Duquoc, *Christologie II: le Messie* (Paris: Cerf, 1972), 175–81.
29. For the biblical notion of sin, one can refer to Lyonnet, *De peccato et redemptione*, vol. 1: *De notione peccati*, and Lyonnet, "Péché," *Vocabulaire de théologie biblique*, 936–46.

realize (or attain) a determinate object of human activity. The moral act is the same action, though considered formally as an act of freedom, in which the person, as such, engages himself. That is, he chooses to do this action and to pursue a given objective through it, on account of a given final end that he has made his own. In this way, he orients his destiny, whether the choice proceeds from an engagement that is anterior though now renewed and confirmed by this choice or, whether, through this choice, he repudiates his prior engagement, engaging himself in another, opposite direction. In the latter, we find ourselves faced with a case of "conversion" in the neutral sense, that is, as much from good to evil as from evil to good.

It is clear that sin belongs to the moral order. There can even be sin without a physical act, without action ([i.e.,] sins of omission). In the moral act of sin, two aspects must be distinguished. On the one hand, there is the *conversio*, which is this very engagement in question. On the other hand, there is the *aversio* which is, in this engagement, the repudiation of the true final end (for man's final end is not optional).

The *conversio*: the person can engage himself only in relation to his own good or at least with that which he considers as being his good. If he can be (practically) deceived by placing his good in objects in which that good does not indeed exist (*bonum apparens*), the error cannot be total. Total or absolute error does not exist. In other words, absolute evil (for "evil" is the name of the "error" of free choice, error in the matter of moral action) does not exist. That is to say, first of all, the object of sinful choice is always a particular good for man, a particular realization of the aspiration of the whole man toward the good. Every man, if he is sufficiently discerning and attentive to himself, can "understand" another person's sin. That is, he can discover in himself the perspective which was able to make this object seem suitable to the sinner so that he would thus have seen his good in it.

In other words, to push the point further, the end in relation to which the sinner engages himself through this choice is not absolutely wicked. Self-love, which is the immediate principle of the *conversio*, is natural and perfectly orderable to love of God, to charity. It is the first movement of the will, the point of departure of the whole process of love, as much for right love as it is for perverse love.[30] Thus, whether we are concerned with the immediate object of choice or with the engagement of the personal destiny that is implied in this choice, the *conversio* is not evil *by itself*. And this must illuminate many modern discussions bearing on various domains of morality (e.g., abortion, contraception, extramarital sexual union, even sexual aberrations). In order to justify these behaviors morally, one must do more than identify the human values that certain behaviors arouse or preserve.

The *aversio*: what makes for the malice of the *conversio* is always the *aversio* that it entails. When I engage myself in a given moral orientation, itself implied in a given particular choice, I turn myself away, *by that very fact,* from the orientation that God imposes on me (not by an arbitrary willing but, instead, by the creative act concretized in my nature, as well as by the supernatural vocation concretized in grace). I give myself an evil orientation, and the choice in which the latter is concretized is evil, not because of the good on account of which I have made this choice but because, in choosing this good, I turn myself away from the true good. The self-love that commands this choice is a preference of self to God.

Every particular moral law finds its justification in the fact that, in relation to a given field of human activity and for a given person situated in given circumstances, it is the determination of the fundamental moral law of obedience to one's human vocation and his vocation as a child of God in Christ. There is a perfect coincidence between this twofold vocation and man's ordination to his final end.

Indeed, man's final end is the "good of God." The final end of man is his true good, that for which he was made. In it alone does his being blossom forth in achieved goodness. However, it is also the "good

---

30. See J.-H. Nicolas, "Amour de soi, amour de Dieu, amour des autres."

of God," for already the creative act and, in a much loftier manner, man's supernatural vocation both order him to God. Man himself is the good of God, His glory. And this glory is entrusted to him because, in distinction to inferior beings, the free person does not passively "undergo" his ordination to God but instead has the ability to "order himself" to God, an ability that has, as its redoubtable counterpart, the ability of being "disordered" in relation to God. How this disordering does not really prevent the creative intention from being realized, even though the disordering is quite real on the creature's side, is a different problem, which we cannot take up here.

b) The three aspects of sin

{488} Thus considered, sin can be studied at the following three levels. First, *it is a transgression*, a transgression of the moral law that it violates and simultaneously a transgression of the fundamental moral law. Note that from this perspective, it is, of itself, *a transitory act*, for its object is a temporal good, one that is often quickly forgotten, in any case, one that will not be willed forever.

Second, *it is an offense against God*. Created freedom, *as such*, is subordinated to God. Man's self-consciousness, which is at the basis of his freedom, is—if it is right and conformed to nature and grace, in which God's will is expressed—an awareness of his essential subordination inasmuch as he is a person. The free acceptance of the true final end flows from such awareness, that is, the acceptance of God as Him in whom and by whom it is realized. Here, even alongside speculative ignorance concerning God, such an act of freedom envelops a kind of existential knowledge of God, which can even be the support for grace in an "atheist of good faith."[31] Conversely, the refusal to know this subordination, the refusal to know God as the final end, as the absolute Good to whom all the others ought to

---

31. See Jacques Maritain, "La dialectique immanent du premier acte de liberté," in *Raison et raisons* (Fribourg: Egloff, 1947); J.-H. Nicolas, *Les profondeurs de la grâce*, 478–83; and "Universalité de la médiation du Christ et salut de ceux qui ne connaissent pas le Christ," in *Acta del Congressso internazionale Tommaso d'Aquino nel suo settimo centenario* (Naples, 1976), 4:269–73.

be referred, is a refusal of God, a denial of God, even in the person who speculatively professes God's existence. Sin abolishes God, not from the real universe, but from one's personal universe. Thus, we have this profound observation by St. Thomas: "As regards the evil that is sin, the good to which it is opposed is, properly speaking, the uncreated good. Indeed, it is contrary to the fulfillment of the Divine Will and to the fulfillment of the divine love, by which the divine good is loved in itself and not only in as much as it is participated in by the creature."[32]

Therefore, we could think about these matters as follows. Just as there is an intentional infinity (i.e., the infinity of the object to which the free creature called to communion of life with the Trinity is fundamentally ordered) in the opening of the free person to God by desire and love—an opening ultimately filled by the acts of Beatific Vision and love[33]—so too and in the opposite direction, there is also an intentional infinity in the self-enclosing in which sin consists, even though the self in which one encloses oneself is finite, for this enclosing includes the rejection of this infinite object to which the person is open by nature and by [the] vocation [of grace]. From this perspective, sin is an "offense" against God, for it is the refusal to recognize the dignity proper to God, the denial of His infinite goodness on account of which every true good is referred to His. This is how the characteristic evil of sin as such is a "privation of the infinite good."

One also speaks of the infringement of the universal order. One must understand quite clearly that we are not speaking here about some sort of abstract order, nor of a static order (like the order of a building, of a garden, or of a city). It is a question of the ordering of the whole universe to God, an ordination for which man, indeed each man, is responsible. This is so not only because he is part of the universal order and because, through his freedom, he must order himself, this part of the universe, to God. However, this is more pro-

---

32. *ST* I, q. 48, a. 6.
33. See §170 in the previous volume of this work.

foundly the case because it belongs to him to be the universe's conscience and, for this reason and for his part, to order the universe to God, insofar as the universe is aware of itself in him.

Third, *it is the counter-love of God*. The ordering of the universe to God, inasmuch as the human person is responsible for it, is first of all a question of "justice,"[34] the justice of the creature in relation to God, "God's rights." However, beyond justice, it is a question of love, for it rests entirely upon the creative act, inspired by love. Indeed, it is only the concrete realization, outside of God, of the infinite love by which the three Persons eternally refer to the two others.[35]

The creature's love must correspond to God's creative love and, above all, to His love of communion. Without this correspondence, this love of God becomes objectless, for it is a question of a personal love, something which calls for reciprocity. Sin, indeed every sin, at its depths is the rejection of this love. However, it is a "positive" rejection, the love of self *against* God, a counter-love.

The refusal to love God comes from the *aversio*. However, the *conversio* is such a counter-love on account of the *aversio* that it entails. St. Augustine provides an expression which provides the most penetrating insight concerning sin: "Thus, two loves have fashioned two cities; the love of self to the point of contempt for God fashions the earthly city, and the love of God to the point of contempt of self fashions the heavenly city."[36]

Fourth, *the permanence of the rupture with God*. If sin considered as a transgression is a transitory act and if the situation that it determines, even a lasting one, is transitory of itself, this is not the case if one considers it as being a rupture with God, that is, a *counter-relation*. Indeed, the relation is an interpersonal relation between the creature and God, and sin is the rejection of this relation. Such a relation is permanent, like the persons united through it. For as long as the sinful person remains before God (i.e., indefinitely), not repu-

---

34. See *ST* I-II, q. 113, a. 1.
35. See §§157–59 in the first volume of this work.
36. St. Augustine, *La Cité de Dieu* (Oeuvres de Saint Augustin, 33–37), XIV, 28.

diating his *aversio* by a contrary *conversio*, he remains, having sinned, opposed to God. His offense and his counter-love do not pass away. He is completely engaged in them.

2. *Reparation for sin*
a) God cannot accept the disorder of sin

{489} This would be for Him to deny Himself, for it would be to accept the independence that is proclaimed by the creature in his sinning. Such an acceptance would be the ratification of this denial of God in which sin ultimately consists, and, from this fact, would be to render it real. It is inconceivable that God would accept being repudiated and rejected from the personal universe of the sinner, for this acceptance would make this denial pass into the real universe, which is meaningless.

It in no way follows that God could not remit sin without having first obtained a sufficient reparation for it. Above, following St. Thomas, we critiqued the Anselmian view, which violates God's transcendence, enclosing Him in an order that is created and totally dependent upon Him, something imposed for every creature, but in any way not imposed for God Himself.[37] He who made man in his freedom can rectify his will by acting on it from within by His grace and can thus reestablish the order that man had disrupted by sinning.

At first sight, this means of reestablishing man in justice seems the one that would be most conformed to mercy. However, upon a deeper examination, this impression is dispelled.[38] In any case, God is sovereignly free. At the same time, He is love and He is mercy. If He freely chose to reestablish order by means of an adequate compensation for sin, let us always remember that His mercy is what shines forth in this fact.

---

37. See §482 above.
38. See §496 below.

b) The compensation for sin

As disorder exists in free will, this compensation is situated at the level of free will and not that of things. Therefore, it involves no legalism. It is a question of "compensating" for the rupture in interpersonal relations by means of an act having such a nature as to make the conflict caused by sin cease, an act that, unlike the divine act of mere pardon with the restoration of justice, proceeds from the sinner as a reparation for his sin. This act can be nothing other than conversion.

The sinner makes the conflict end by being converted, by returning, of himself, into [right] order. *Of itself,* this conversion is painful. It is not brought about without the will being broken. The person must be rid of himself and must do "injury" to himself. Conversion to God is essentially a *love,* for it is by his love that a person is ordered to God. However, when the point of departure is the *counter-love* that is sin, love takes on the painful and mortifying form of *penitent love*[39] with which *death to oneself* is necessarily included. Moreover, on account of the human person's profound need to express his spiritual movements in a sensible way, interior penitence tends, by its proper requirements, to be expressed in external afflictions, in penitential acts. Indeed, this is all the more the case as interior penitence is livelier.

Allow a remark here. Sin places the free creature in an objectively disastrous situation, making him lose God, who is his true good, cutting off friendship with God, whom the free creature, in his essential vocation, is called to love above all else. However, sin simultaneously prevents the sinner from being aware of this. He loves himself more than God, and therefore does not mourn the loss of the love of God. He has preferred apparent goods and does not mourn the loss of the divine good. *Paradoxically,* it is at the moment when he gives up his sin that the sinner is aware of his misery and experiences its painfulness and horror. This is an analysis that is confirmed by

---

39. See J.-H. Nicolas, *Les profondeurs de la grâce,* 469–71.

Christian experience, above all in the saints. The greater one's love is, the more intense is one's penitence, and the more ardent is one's felt need to express this penitence through voluntary afflictions—whether they be freely chosen or whether they be imposed, though freely accepted.

In a sense, it can be said that the penitent chastises himself.[40] However, there is only a material coincidence between penal afflictions and penitential afflictions. Formally, they are wholly different. The former are undergone against the will of him who suffers them, and they shatter him. The latter are in accord with his will, and they free his love.

c) Satisfaction

{490} From what we have said, we can say that the (internal and external) process of penitence follows upon conversion of heart. Now, conversion of heart is an effect of grace. Indeed, one must guard oneself against the Pelagian temptation that would wish to imagine that the created person could return to God in virtue of the very freedom by which he is turned away from God. The whole of Scripture rejects this idea. The creature is justified (rendered just, converted) by grace, not by his works.

Theological reflection can discover the reason for the necessity of divine grace in conversion. Conversion is necessarily an act of charity because it is a question of taking the path opposed to sin, which was a counter-love, in the sense of being the refusal of the love of communion that God offered man by calling him to supernatural life. In turning himself away from God, the sinner does not purely and simply fall back into the natural order, for he remains one who is called [to the life of grace]. Therefore, his *aversio* is a wound in him, the privation of his true good (not only of his supernatural good, but also of his natural good which, by the fact of this vocation, exists only as encompassed within the supernatural good). However, he falls into his natural limits, being deprived of the grace which

---

40. See the citations of St. Thomas in Catão, *Salut et redemption*, 87n1.

provides him with the only way of transcending them. Grace is necessary for him to transcend these limits anew.

A second reason arises from sin's character as an offense against God. It belongs to God to pardon. If the initiative in turning away from God comes from man, in order to efface the sin by turning back to God, the initiative can come only from God. Now, the Divine Will has the power to realize what it wills [*est réalisiteur*]. The offense being abolished by the recovered *rectitudo voluntatis*, what the divine willing of pardon realizes is precisely this *rectitudo voluntatis*. No divine pardon is conceivable without a divine action rectifying the will, an action of grace. (This is said against the very widespread conception, found even in the scholastics following upon Scotus, holding that pardon is an act of God without any other effect than exemption from punishment, which is the absence of an effect, not an effect.) For God, pardoning does not merely involve dispensing a guilty person from punishment. Instead, by His grace, which rectifies the will, it renders innocent the person who was rendered guilty by his disordering. This grace does not suppress freedom, and conversion is, quite obviously, an act of freedom. However, by His grace, God moves the will to freely convert.[41]

God could bestow this grace independent of any creaturely activity. This would be the simple *condonatio* by which God would pardon the sinner without having received the slightest compensation from him, bringing him back to Himself by His all-powerful grace. Against St. Anselm, St. Thomas firmly maintains this freedom of God in relation to the very order that, of itself, requires the fault to be repaired by the person who committed it.[42] Naturally, such a conversion would also precede the penitential activity discussed earlier. However, this very activity would purely be an effect of grace and would in no way be its cause. And the grace in question is that of the remission of sins.[43] "Satisfaction" is what designates the action

---

41. See §496 below.
42. See *ST* III, q. 46, a. 2, ad 3.
43. See J.-H. Nicolas, *Les profondeurs de la grâce*, 472–73.

of the created person returning to God after having sinned and obtaining from Him the grace of the remission of sins. It has the same structure as the creature's penitential activity. However, it precedes the gift of grace and provokes God's pardon.

d) The vicious circle of satisfaction

{491} It is here that we come back to the great Anselmian idea. Because man cannot convert without grace, and because satisfaction can proceed only from a heart that is already converted, it is impossible for him to make satisfaction for his sin. God alone could do this because conversion proceeds from a divine initiative. The only solution to the dilemma is the one which God found: it is necessary that God become man, in order to divinely perform a deed that would be human.

First, the infinity of the satisfaction required. To abolish the offense of sin, which is infinite, the satisfaction must also be infinite, always remembering that this is understood as being within the domain of interpersonal relations, as we have seen. However, in opposition to the offense whose "value" is taken from the dignity of the person offended (so that when the offended person is God, this "value" is infinite), satisfaction draws its "value" from the dignity of the person who makes satisfaction. Thus, a solely human person could in no way make satisfaction in the strict sense of the term.

Second, the necessity of grace for making satisfaction. Because, as we have seen, satisfaction follows on conversion, it is an act inspired by charity, and there is no charity without grace.

Third, only the God-Man can make satisfaction. A human person who would be only a human person either would participate in man's sin or not. In the first case, in order for him to be able to make satisfaction (and then imperfectly, because he could not offer an infinite satisfaction), he would first need to receive the grace of conversion, which itself is the grace of the remission of sins. Therefore, his satisfaction would follow upon pardon, which would be given by a simple condonatio. In the second case, he would not need to convert, nor, consequently, to perform any penitential deed for himself. In order for him to be able to perform a penitential deed that would have the value of making satisfaction for other men's sins, he would need to receive a "capital grace." The bestowal of this grace, which would be God's pure gift for this person who, of himself, does not include other human persons in himself, would already be the thus-granted grace of the remissions of sins—again by a simple *condonatio*—to sinners.

This is not the case for the Incarnate Word. On the one hand, He can offer a satisfaction of infinite value, for while He is capable of a reparative human deed, this deed is performed by the Word and therefore has an infinite value. On the other hand, if He can perform this deed for all men, it is because He contains all of them in Himself, naturally and supernaturally, not by a super-added divine gift but precisely on account of the Hypostatic Union, which constitutes Him as the Incarnate Word.

An objection may be raised: One could respond to this that the very grace of the Incarnation—made to all men, as we have seen—is already the grace of the remission of sins and therefore the latter is bestowed by a simple *condonatio*.

However, this is not exact. For, as we have seen, man is not freed by the Incarnation alone. The Incarnation renders possible the deed by which man's liberation is obtained, though it was obtained precisely through the performance of this very deed. Now, the grace by which it was possible for Christ to make satisfaction for all men belongs naturally to Christ inasmuch as He is the Word, being a grace for Him only inasmuch as He is a man. Therefore, the Person of the Word naturally possesses this grace in virtue of which He makes satisfaction for all men. Thus, this latter is not yet, of itself, the grace of the remission of sins for sinful men.

C. How Christ's Passion and Death Freed Man from Sin

1. *The satisfying value of Christ's passion and death*

a) Christ's penitent love

{492} From what we have said, we can see how this value can arise only from Jesus's interior sentiments and above all from His charity.⁴⁴ On this subject, we have spoken about *penitent love*. Can we speak of penitent love in the case of Jesus, who never knew sin? Yes, by appealing to the realism of the Incarnation. Because all of humanity is⁴⁵ included in Christ (in the way we strove to explain earlier), He represents all of them before God—not only juridically but really.

However, penitent love could not be included in Christ with the sins that accompany it, for the Hypostatic Union excludes all sin. However, it is included in it with this characteristic of having sinned. We noted above that penitence is all the livelier as charity is greater. In Christ, humanity is aware of its sin and detests it. Thus, although Christ Himself had no part in sin, Christ's charity is penetrated with penitence because of the sin of the men whom Christ bears in Himself and who, in Him—to the degree that they are in Him—are freed from their sin and reject it.

This can be seen in the words of St. Paul: "For our sake he made him to be sin who knew no sin, so that in him we might become the righteousness of God."⁴⁶ The exegesis of this text has a long history.⁴⁷ According to Latin exegesis, it is a question of "sacrifice for sin," and Sabourin defends this exegesis with good arguments.⁴⁸ Below, we will see that, far from being opposed to an interpretation of the passion as a form of satisfaction, the sacrificial interpretation, on the contrary, implies it. Thus, I do not think that I depart from the exegetical position holding that "made sin" is equivalent to "sacrificed for sin" by proposing that Jesus, without having been personally implied in sin, lived the situation of the sinner in His consciousness, doing so with an infinite intensity, as the convert is aware of his sin from the moment that he rejects it. And (analogically) as the material universe, in man's mind, is aware of itself, its dependence upon

---

44. On this subject, one will fruitfully refer to Marie-Joseph Nicolas, *Théologie de la résurrection* (Paris: Desclée, 1982), 207–50.
45. See §435 above.
46. 2 Cor 5:21 (RSV).
47. See Sabourin, *Rédemption sacrificielle*, 15–162.
48. See ibid., 153–60.

God, and its ordination to God, so too mankind in Christ is aware both of its foundational ordination to God and of the sin by which it has turned itself away from Him.

b) Christ's sufferings and death

{493} Nonetheless, one can ask—and this is one of the aspects of the mystery of redemption—why this penitent love of Jesus should lead Him to the terrible satisfaction of the passion. Indeed, it was terrible and, so it seems, useless. In fact, given that, in any event, the quasi-infinity of His charity on the one hand and the infinite dignity of His Person on the other both gave an infinite value to whatsoever satisfactory deed that He would have chosen to do, why go to these extremes?[49]

In this, we find ourselves faced with a mystery. It is a mystery of love that St. Paul expresses when he writes: "Why, one will hardly die for a righteous man—though perhaps for a good man one will dare even to die. But God shows his love for us in that while we were yet sinners Christ died for us. Because, therefore, we are now justified by his blood, much more shall we be saved by him from the wrath of God."[50] But the question is posed once again: What need did we have for the gift of His life if He could have freed us at a lesser cost?

St. Thomas's response to this new theological aporia is one of great profundity and indeed seems to show the direction in which the solution must be sought: Christ wished to free mankind "not only by exercising His power, but also by an act of justice,"[51] and for this, He sought to give a satisfaction that was capable of recompensing for sin, not only by the exceptional conditions that His Divine Personality gave to any of His human deeds, but by the very nature of this satisfaction.

In line with this, and in conformity with the fundamental idea of satisfaction which consists in an external work whose essential role

---

49. See *ST* III, q. 46, a. 6, ad 6.
50. Rom 8:7–9 (RSV).
51. *ST* III, q. 46, a. 6, ad 6.

The Salvation of Men by the Blood of Christ 365

is to be the bodily expression of penitent love, we can say the following. Christ's charity, precisely because of its intensity (which, moreover, would have been able to dispense Him from every burdensome external work), drove Him to perform a satisfactory work that would be really proportioned to Him. Now, the external work that, of itself, is the most proper for expressing interior penitence is the gift of one's own life, for if love in general includes self-gift to the beloved being (a total and absolute gift when it is a question of the love of the free creature for God, and above all when it is a question of the love of communion, charity) "penitent love" confers upon this self-gift, as we have seen, the character of being "a death to oneself."

Nothing can better express this—the *abneget semetispum* of the Gospel—than the gift, or at least the offering, of His own life *for the beloved being*, for God. Such a gift obviously cannot take the form of a suicide—which would not be a death *for God*, for it is by living that the living person glorifies God who gave life to him. However, it can be performed, first, by consecrating his life, his activity, and his good to the service of God. Then, it can be performed by voluntarily accepting death (and, to begin with, sufferings, which are an anticipation of death) from the hand of God, for if the living person can neither put himself to death, nor put another to death, God remains the master of this life, which He gave to the creature. Beyond all the particular circumstances of each person's death, beyond all second causes, he who dies hands his life over to God. Penitent love is expressed in this self-renunciation, which finds its loftiest expression in a voluntarily accepted death.

In this way, we can explain the meaning of Christ's sufferings and death. It is not a question of separating them from the *penitent love* of which they are the expression, on which they totally depend. St. Anselm's reasoning—it would be necessary to offer to God something that would be of greater value than the whole created order, such as was Christ's life—left intact the question: in what way was Christ's death a gift offered to God, one that was agreeable to Him and accepted by Him? It is necessary to respond: what was agreeable to the

Father and superabundantly compensated for every sin in the world is Jesus's penitent love, expressed by His suffering and His death.[52]

We will see that, in what concerns the death to which Christ voluntarily delivered Himself, the notion of "sacrifice" is indispensable for understanding how it was the gift of His life to God. This inseparable ensemble (the penitent love of Jesus expressed by the passion and by His death) is what was his "satisfaction for the sin of the world," the deed by which the whole of mankind in the person of its head came back to God like a prodigal child. Here, it is a question of a human deed, a human undertaking. However, its value is infinite because the human person who performs it in the name of all is the Word, *unus de Trinitate*.[53] But how are we to understand, precisely, that this deed that Christ alone performed would have a value for all men?

2. How all men are implied in Christ's work of satisfaction

a) Response by appealing to the inclusion of all men in Christ

{494} To respond to this fundamental question, St. Thomas appeals to Christ's capital grace:

Grace was given to Christ not only as to a singular person, but as to Him who is the head of the Church, that is, in such a way that from Him, it can flow over upon His members. Thus, His works have the same relation to Himself and to the others [i.e., His members] as the works of another man, when he is in a state of grace, have in regard to himself.[54]

And he specifies: "The head and members are [united] together as one mystical person."[55]

To understand this response in full, one must refer to what was said above about capital grace[56] and recall that, in fact, this characteristic of Christ's grace as affecting all men in Him results from the

---

52. See *ST* III, q. 48, a. 2.
53. See *ST* III, q. 46, a. 12.
54. *ST* III, q. 48, a. 1.
55. ibid., a. 2, ad 1.
56. See §340 above.

Hypostatic Union. Therefore, these works can make satisfaction for the sin of all on account of the Hypostatic Union and not only on account of a divine decree to consider Christ's deeds as though they were performed by all men and for each of them. Naturally, the Hypostatic Union results from the free decision of the Father *to give His only Son*, but this decision includes all the gifts of grace given to men by Christ's mediation: "He who did not spare his own Son but gave him up for us all, will he not also give us all things with him?"[57] However, this way of resolving the problem gives rise to several further questions.

b) Questions

Men are part of the mystical body of Christ only when they have been redeemed and have accepted the redemption. Is it not a vicious circle to say that Christ's act redeems them because they are His members? The response is that, in virtue of the inclusion of all men in Christ from the time of the Incarnation, every man is a member of Christ *virtually* from his conception, being part of mankind, which is entirely included in Christ.[58]

But then, why only virtually? If the redemption was accomplished by one for all, why do they not all receive grace and immortality by being born, insofar as the redemption has been accomplished? The response, first of all, is that this is part of Christian faith. Each person must personally respond to the appeal made by God, in and by Christ, so that redemption may be accomplished in him and for him. How should we understand this point?

To do so, one must appeal to the anthropology that underlies theology. Man is *a part of a whole*, with which he is united, namely, mankind, and more particularly is united with this or that group of men. However, he is simultaneously a *whole*, a person. In virtue of the first characteristic, he is engaged in a shared, common destiny. In virtue of the second, he must, through his own freedom, freely

---

57. Rom 8:32 (RSV).
58. See *ST* III, q. 8, a. 3. Also, see §435 above.

make his destiny his own, doing so in accord with the common destiny in which his own is involved. Jacques Maritain tried to explain this by his[59] distinction between personality and individuality.[60] The distinction between *nature* and *person* can be used, if it is interpreted correctly: each man is a person in whom a universal nature is realized, human nature. Through his nature, he belongs, *inasmuch as he is a person*, to the ensemble of individuals in whom this nature is realized. Through his personality, he constitutes, *inasmuch as he is the same (individuated) nature*, an independent whole. Therefore, *on account of his nature* (human nature, but already existentialized in "mankind," constituted by descent from "Adam" and redeemed by Christ), each man is, by his conception and his birth, in solidarity with Adam in sin, and in solidarity with the new Adam in grace. *On account of his personality*, it belongs to him to accept one of these two solidarities and to refuse the other.

However, we find that there is a difference on this point. Solidarity with the old Adam is a *given* for the person, who is constituted by the nature received from the old Adam through the generative action and all the successive generations. Therefore, the person is born in solidarity with the sinful Adam, and his later personal choice (when consciousness and freedom awaken in him) can be only the taking of a personal position in relation to this primordial solidarity, whether he accepts it or rejects it. Solidarity with Christ, on the con-

---

59. [Tr. note: Maritain's distinction is, in fact, originally posed by Marie-Benoît Schwalm, OP, and it is used variously throughout the career of Fr. Reginald Garrigou-Lagrange. See Marie-Benoît Schwalm, *Leçons de philosophie sociale* (Paris: Bloud & Cie, 1911), 2:417–40; "Individualisme et solidarité," *Revue Thomiste* 6 (1898): 66–99, especially 81ff. See Reginald Garrigou-Lagrange, *Le sens commun*, 1st ed. (1908) and 4th ed. (Paris: Desclée de Brouwer, 1936), 347–49. Also, in Garrigou-Lagrange, *The Trinity and God the Creator*, trans. Frederic C. Eckhoff (St. Louis: Herder, 1952), 155–56. See also Reginald Garrigou-Lagrange, *Christ: The Savior*, trans. Bede Rose (St. Louis: Herder, 1950), 119ff.; *De beatitudine* (Turin: R. Berruti, 1951), 85–87 and 372; "The Subordination of the State to the Perfection of the Human Person According to St. Thomas," in *Philosophizing in Faith: Essays on the Beginning and End of Wisdom*, trans. Matthew K. Minerd (Providence, RI: Cluny, 2019), 183–204.]

60. See Jacques Maritain, *Du régime temporal et de la liberté* (Paris: Desclée de Brouwer, 1933), 56–75.

trary, is only offered to him, and in order for it to become effective, he must accept it and choose it. (This is the meaning of the "dynamic" characteristic that we have recognized for the inclusion of men in Christ. It concerns man inasmuch as he is the principle of his activities, so that it must be actualized by the fundamental choice that orients all of the person's activities in one direction or another.)

Therefore, in order to personally participate in the redemption accomplished by Christ for all men, each man must adhere to Christ freely (i.e., by being able to not adhere) and, by this same choice, dissociate himself from sinful Adam. This adherence itself has a twofold, antinomic character. On the one hand, it is instantaneous and definitive because it is spiritual, taking place at the depths of man's spirit. On the other hand, it is developmental and at every moment susceptible to being withdrawn because the human person has a bodily dimension that affects even his spirit.

Considered as a spiritual decision, adherence to Christ is faith, in the scriptural sense (including all the acts that constitute conversion).[61] However, on account of the bodily dimension of the human person (except for the case of involuntary impossibility) this faith must be concretized in the external reception of the sacrament [of Baptism].[62] Faith thus concretized is *of itself* definitive and total.

However, on account of man's bodily dimension, it is developmental and fragile. By saying that it is developmental, we wish to draw attention to two necessities. On the one hand, it must be externalized through all the acts of the Christian life, good works. On the other hand, it must integrate all the person's tendencies, for he bears in himself, with "concupiscence," the inclination to apparent goods which must be renounced in order for one to fully adhere to Christ. It is *death to sin*; the Christian must repudiate the works of sin and *"crucify the flesh with its lusts."* Living the life of the resurrected Christ, the Christian must live according to the Spirit and produce *the fruits of the Spirit*.

61. See J.-H. Nicolas, *Les profondeurs de la grâce*, 452–71.
62. See the first part of the next text in this series.

It is *fragile*, for in the course of this spiritual struggle against the flesh, the Christian can be conquered and can repudiate his solidarity with Christ thus being placed back into solidarity with sinful Adam (obviously, without this being a "reviviscence" of original sin). Finally, this same bodily dimension leads the Christian, even on account of his spiritual adherence, to bodily conformity with Christ the redeemer through suffering and death. As we have refused to view Christ's death as being a chastisement, so too suffering and death are not a chastisement for him who belongs to Christ. Instead, they are a participation in Christ's satisfaction, in which he is asked to participate personally and freely. In the Christian, it is Christ who continues to suffer and die.[63]

c) Objective redemption and subjective redemption

{495} In classical theological terminology, the expressions "objective redemption" and "subjective redemption" are used to distinguish redemption inasmuch as it is the work of Christ, superabundantly sufficing to free all men from redemption inasmuch as each man makes it his own in the way that we explained above. This terminology can be critiqued on two heads: on the one hand, as we have seen, Christ's work is a personal undertaking and therefore is itself *subjective*; on the other hand, through his personal adherence, the believer enters *objectively* into Christ's redeeming act.

3. *God's mercy and justice in the redemption thus understood*

{496} By His redemptive action, Christ *merits* God's pardon for men. Inasmuch as He is man, He acquires a kind of "right" to the grace of the remission of sins. Does not this assertion end up situating the redemption in the order of justice, thus, contrary to Scripture's testimony, removing it from the order of grace? In no way, for at the fountainhead of this justice achieved by Christ there is this primordial grace that is the Incarnation itself: "God so loved the world

---

63. See Jean-Hervé Nicolas, *L'amour de Dieu et la peine des hommes* (Paris: Beauchesne, 1969), 61–72.

that he gave his only Son" (Jn 3:16, RSV). God's mercy toward sinful man superabounds precisely in the fact that He enabled him to freely come back to Him, emerging from his sin through a free action.

This way of delivering man from his sins is certainly much more attentive to the human person's dignity. In fact, it allows him to participate in his restoration, instead of receiving it passively. Certainly, for each particular human person, everything begins with God's free gift, the gift of initial grace. However, that which is a pure grace for each individual man was merited by the man Jesus who bore all men in Himself. The remission of sins is the fruit, not the principle, of the satisfactory act by which sinful man is brought back to God. Thus, if God demanded satisfaction for sin, this ultimately was for man's sake, not for God's, for in both cases, His glory consists in His mercy.[64]

D. How All the Other Aspects of Christ's Passion Are Connected to the Satisfaction He Made

{497} Up to this point, we have explained the efficacy of Christ's passion and death in relation to man's liberation solely by means of the notion of satisfaction. Now, Scripture and tradition emphasize many other reasons for this efficacy. Christ's passion merited for us the grace of the remission of sins, and at least according to the Thomists, as well as St. Thomas himself, it is the *efficient cause* of it. It "redeemed" man from slavery to sin. It was a "sacrifice agreeable to God," who responded by the gift of His grace. Therefore, it is not an excessive to reduce everything to the notion of "satisfaction" as to the key notion [for understanding Christ's sacrifice upon the cross]? Bernard Catão thinks that "for St. Thomas, satisfaction is not the master notion, that which would enable us to understand that in which the redemptive value of the Cross consists. It is only a good analogy, which *among others* helps us to understand why the Savior's human act was one of humiliation, suffering, and death on the Cross."[65]

---

64. See *ST* III, q. 46, a. 3.
65. Catão, *Salut et rédemption*, 79–80 [Tr. note: emphasis in original].

As for St. Thomas's own thought, an attentive reading of question 48 of the *Tertia pars* (even in light of the presentation that Catão provides for it) leads to a completely contrary conclusion. Moreover, theological reflection finds that this conclusion is necessary. If the passion was meritorious, this can be understood only in relation to satisfaction. For the principle of merit is charity, and any other deed whatsoever performed by Christ, inspired by the same charity, would also have been as meritorious. Therefore, the notion of merit by itself does not in any way explain why it is precisely by suffering and dying for us that Christ saved us. As we have seen, this is explained only by the requirements of penitent love. Therefore, it is only explained by the satisfactory meaning of these sufferings.

The passion of itself was redemptive. However, in relation to St. Anselm, we have seen that a question arises, making us strive to understand how Jesus's human life was able to have a "price" for God and how it was "precious"[66] to Him. As we have seen, this question can be responded to only by appealing to the satisfactory value of Christ's sufferings and death, and this is what St. Thomas expressly does.[67]

Christ's death is sacrificial. This is not in doubt and is essential. However, if sacrifice in general is the primary external act of the virtue of religion, it does not, of itself and necessarily, symbolize man's death, the destruction of his sinful self in order to free the true self and to surrender it to God. This presupposes sin. The sacrifice offered by the God-Man in the name of humanity would never have taken on this bloody form if there had been no sin to remedy. And we have seen that this redemption can be explained only in terms of being a form of satisfaction.[68]

Thus, *satisfaction* is indeed the key notion enabling us to explain

---

66. See §§486–91 above.
67. See *ST* III, q. 48, a. 4.
68. See Marie-Joseph Nicolas, *Théologie de la résurrection*, 239–43; also see the express study of the notion of sacrifice in the treatise on the Eucharist in the third part of this course [in the third English volume].

what we are looking for, namely, the relation of Jesus's passion and death to God's bestowal of the grace of the remission of sins. However, it in no way excludes the other aspects of the passion. Much to the contrary, it brings them together in their integral unity.

III. NECESSITY AND FREEDOM IN CHRIST'S PASSION

Historically, Christ's passion seems like a defeat, as something imposed externally and *undergone* by Jesus, a catastrophe. On the other hand, from what we have said, it seems that it was expressly willed and that it was the work whose performance was the reason for the sending of the Word. We must reconcile these two aspects.

A. Christ Suffered and Died Because He Willed It, as He Willed It

{498} Christ's freedom in relation to His passion is marked out clearly by the evangelists. According to them, He voluntarily hands Himself over to death, fully aware that He is doing what He must do and that He is not merely undergoing the events taking place in his life. Doubtlessly, St. Thomas goes too far when he says that Christ's will would have a power over His own body such that His freedom would have been active in the fact of His suffering and death.[69] It is better to interpret this along the lines of what Rahner says concerning death as the supreme act of freedom.[70] Needless to say, if we can say that our death is an act of freedom, this is wholly verified of Christ in a singular and unique manner.

---

69. See *ST* III, q. 47, a. 1.
70. See Karl Rahner, "Pour une théologie de la mort," *Ecrits théologiques*, vol. 3 (Paris: Desclée de Brouwer, 1963). Claude Geffré, "La mort comme nécessité et comme liberté," *Vie Spirituelle* 492 (1963): 264–80.

B. Christ Gave Himself Over to His Passion through Obedience

Through obedience, but freely? Earlier, we discussed the problem that is posed by the reconciliation of Christ's complete freedom and His obedience, taking into account His radical inability to sin.[71]

C. Therefore, the Father Willed That His Son Suffer and Die

{499} St. Paul assures that the Father "did not spare His own Son but gave him up for us all."[72] His "expression brings to mind the sacrifice of Isaac."[73] It includes an implicit reference to the "suffering servant" of Isaiah: "God handed him over for our sins."[74] The Father "handed over His own Son." What does this mean? Obviously, it is not a question of an act of "betrayal." God's design, the plan of man's salvation, conceived by the three Persons together, includes the Incarnation and the Redemption. Inasmuch as He was a man, the Incarnate Word accepted this plan and submitted Himself to it, and this plan consisted in the fact that He would take on, and be put to, death.

Similarly, the Father "handed over His own Son" in another sense, for it is clear that God could have delivered Jesus from the hands of His enemies. He did not do this, for such an intervention, inspired by a particular [act of] mercy, would have been contrary to the plan of salvation, the latter inspired by [God's] utter mercy. This finds an application in the entire mystery of evil and that of the suffering of innocents.[75]

---

71. See §387 above.

72. Rom 8:32 (RSV).

73. *Traduction Oecuménique de la Bible*, in loco.

74. Is 53:6. [Tr. note: The RSV reads: "the LORD has laid on him the iniquity of us all."]

75. Jürgen Moltmann pushed to an unsustainable point the idea that the Father would have handed His Son over to death and would have "abandoned" Him, introducing into the intimate depths of the Trinitarian mystery a conflict between the Father and the Son, a claim which is unthinkable and totally foreign to Scripture. See Jürgen Moltmann, *Théologie de l'espérance* (Paris: Cerf, 1970); J.-H. Nicolas, "Aimante et bienheureuse

D. Those Who Killed Christ Did So Freely

{500} If those who killed Christ were the instruments of the execution of the divine plan, they obviously were not such consciously and deliberately. They had another end in sight. Was it necessarily evil? No, and we must take very seriously Jesus's words on the cross: "They know not what they do." In any case, their end obviously was not "to kill God," and they in no way thought that they were doing this. The accusation of deicide—an accusation that is, alas, too often made!—is not only abhorrent; it is absurd.

Conclusion

{501} Like the Incarnation, the Redemption is a work of freedom. Indeed, it is a work of divine freedom and therefore a work of Jesus's freedom inasmuch as He is God: *He came* in order to give His human life. Moreover, it is an act of Jesus's human freedom, as well as an act of men's freedom, be it blind or misdirected: He gave His life for the remission of man's sins.

IV. THE SOTERIOLOGICAL VALUE OF CHRIST'S RESURRECTION

The importance of Christ's resurrection in apostolic thought and preaching, in the awareness of the early Christian community, and also in the Patristic tradition,[76] is too great [to be ignored], and a soteriology that would minimize its role is unacceptable.[77]

Trinité," 271–73. Certain Catholic theologians follow him along these lines, even if they will not go as far as he did. Nonetheless, this interpretation, which is in no way required by the most realist theology of the redemptive sacrifice, inadmissibly violates the total union of the Father and the Son in being, thought, and love, a union which is an integral part of the Trinitarian mystery.

76. See Jossua, *Le salut*.

77. See Marie-Joseph Nicolas, *Théologie de la résurrection* (Paris: Desclée, 1982), 207–50. François-Xavier Durrwell, *L'Eucharistie, présence du Christ*, 2nd ed. (Paris: Ed. Ouvrières, [1971]).

A. Christ's Resurrection, the Response of the Father to the Oblative Love of the Son

{502} In Scripture, Christ's resurrection comes to be seen as the recompense for His obedience.[78] In general, it is presented as the conclusion of the passion. The adversaries of God's design placed Him to death, but God did not permit it to be the case that His Christ would remain in death: "This Jesus God raised up, and of that we all are witnesses."[79]

Indeed, the resurrection comes to be seen as giving the true meaning to the difficult idea that the Father handed His Son over to death and also (correlatively) that the Son handed Himself over to death through love and obedience. The Father's command would remain incomprehensible if this death must be the definitive defeat. To the Son's abandonment into the hands of the Father, there mysteriously corresponded the Father's abandonment of the Son to all the forces of evil. This would be a betrayal and inconceivable denial of the Son's trust if this abandonment must be definitive. In truth, if the Father abandoned His Son up to the point of death, this is because He is powerful enough to intervene even in death and to deliver Him from it. The resurrection superabundantly justifies the Son's abandonment to the Father, even if on the cross this abandonment was felt by Jesus, in the depths of His human being, as a trial without measure.

Moreover, St. John and St. Paul present the redemption as Christ's battle against both sin and death, with the latter simultaneously being the effect and the symbol of sin. If Christ were not to have risen from the dead, then He would have been defeated by death and, therefore, by sin. In other words, He would have died in vain. Thus, we can say that, *from the Father's perspective*, the passion calls for Christ's glorification after the humiliation. Likewise, *from the Son's perspective*, we can say that it calls for His victory over death.

---

78. See Phil 2:9.
79. Acts 2:32 (RSV). See Acts 4:10.

B. Christ's Resurrection and Man's Salvation

Christ's resurrection is not only a kind of divine compensation granted to Christ upon the accomplishment of the redemption. It is intrinsically part of the redemption itself.

1. Christ's resurrection, the manifestation of the salvation that has been accomplished

{503} If Christ's salvific work is not merely an interior work performed by Him, then salvation itself, the remission of sins, and grace cannot be purely interior realities. We will see that, *for each believer*, these realities are externalized by the sacraments. But, at their source, *for the whole Church*, it was necessary that they be externalized and manifested. Christ's resurrection is this externalization and manifestation for the whole Church (which the sacraments prolong and extend through the ages to each person). This manifestation is an intrinsic part of the work itself.

As a radiant manifestation of God's power and grace at work for man's salvation, Christ's resurrection is constitutive of the object of faith. This is the source of its capital importance in the Christian *kerygma*: "If Christ has not been raised, your faith is futile and you are still in your sins."[80] Exegetes agree in saying that the evangelical preaching comes forth from the apostles' "paschal experience."[81]

2. Christ's resurrection and our own

a) The eschatological character of Christ's resurrection

{504} Through[82] His resurrection, Christ does not return to His historical, earthly life. He is situated outside of history, at the terminus and consummation of salvation history. This point is given particular emphasis in the narratives recalling His apparitions. In them,

---

80. 1 Cor 15:17 (RSV).
81. Joseph Schmitt, *Jésus ressuscité dans la prédication apostolique, étude de théologie biblique* (Paris: Gabalda, 1949). Rudolf Schnackenburg, "La christologie du Nouveau Testament," in *Mysterium Salutis: Dogmatique de l'histoire du salut* (Paris: Cerf, 1974), 10:13–236.
82. See M.-J. Nicolas, *Théologie de la résurrection*, 129–82.

Jesus appears suddenly and disappears suddenly as well. He no longer lives with the apostles, and shows Himself to them only to assure them of His resurrection, or to confer to them the mission of evangelizing the world (and through them, to the Church). Note that St. Thomas saw this point very profoundly.[83]

In this sense, Christ's resurrection is not "historical." It is not situated in history. It is outside of history. By it, Christ entered personally (inasmuch as He is a man) into eschatological time. However, to say that it is not historical *in this precise sense* is not to say that it was not an event that really took place. That is, not having taken place in historical time, this event is not knowable by historical methods, at least directly. Yes, it can be known indirectly, for our historical time touches eschatological time in this event. What we can *know historically* is the testimony of the disciples, a testimony that precisely makes us know that eschatological time has already arrived for Jesus and that they have, in some manner, *touched* it, thus being able to announce it with assurance.[84]

b) Christ's resurrection, the principle and cause of our resurrection

{505} That Christ's resurrection is the principle and cause of our own resurrection is St. Paul's doctrine: "But in fact Christ has been raised from the dead, the first fruits of those who have fallen asleep. For as by a man came death, by a man has come also the resurrection of the dead. For as in Adam all die, so also in Christ shall all be made alive."[85] The theological explanation of this doctrine is diffi-

---

83. See *ST* III, q. 53, a. 3.
84. Concerning the apostle's testimony regarding the real event that was the resurrection of Jesus, see the following works: Pierre Benoît, *Passion et résurrection du Seigneur* (Paris: Cerf, 1966); Cerfaux, *Le Christ dans la théologie de saint Paul*; André Feuillet, "La découverte du tombeau vide en Jn 20, 3–10 et la foi au Christ ressuscité," *Espirit et Vie* 19 (1977): 257–84; Jacques Guillet, "Les récits évangéliques de la résurrection," *Les Quatre Fleuves* 15–16 (1982): 7–21; M.-J. Nicolas, *Théologie de la résurrection*, 93–128; Béda Rigaux, *Dieu l'a ressuscité* (Gembloux: Duculot, 1973); Joseph Schmitt, *Jésus ressuscité dans la predication apostolique, étude de théologie biblique* (Paris: Gabalda, 1949).
85. 1 Cor 15:20–22 (RSV).

cult. St. Thomas's interpretation is strikingly realistic in character.[86] We will return to it in the third volume in relation to the causality of the sacraments.[87]

In short, all men are involved in this resurrection in virtue of their initial inclusion in Christ: "resurrected with Christ." The final resurrection will be the personal actualization of this resurrection *in Christo*. It will be the continuation and renewal of the action by which Christ was resurrected—an action that is brought about by the whole Trinity, though one that is the action of the Father in a special way inasmuch as it reaches the Son and, for this reason, prolongs in time the Father's relation to the Son. It is an action of which Christ, through His humanity, is also the instrument. His soul takes up and revivifies His body, doing so under the almighty action of God.

c) Christ's resurrection, the principle and cause of the grace conferred to men

{506} Scripture certainly teaches that Christ's resurrection is the principle and cause of the grace conferred to men. Grace is the believer's participation in the life of the resurrected Christ.[88] The resurrection is the ultimate effect of the Redemption, just as death is the effect of sin. That is, for each person the resurrection begins with the remission of sins and the life of grace.[89]

Conclusion

{507} All this would be empty wordplay if Christ's resurrection did not really take place, if Christ does not *truly now* live with His twofold human dimension, as someone who is spiritual and embodied, though in conditions of life that, properly speaking, are unimaginable and unrepresentable for us, given that our thought is always dependent on the conditions of historical existence.

---

86. See *ST* III, q. 56. Jean-Hervé Nicolas, "Réactualisation des mystères rédempteurs dans et par les sacrements," *Revue thomiste* 58 (1958): 41–50.
87. See §§745–47 in the third volume of this series.
88. Cerfaux, *Le Christ dans la théologie de saint Paul*, 65–71.
89. *ST* III, q. 58, a. 2, ad 4.

9

The High Priest of the New Covenant

{508} The Letter to the Hebrews is centered on the idea that Christ is the High Priest of the New Covenant.[1] This does not mean that this is the only scriptural text where this property of Christ is mentioned and emphasized, for it occupies a place that is certain, although less immediately perceptible, in the fourth Gospel.[2] This topic cannot be overlooked in Christology.

However, a preliminary question must be examined. A priest is at the service of God for men. In order to introduce the question of Christ's priesthood, St. Thomas writes, "He served the Father in the exercise of His priesthood." In fact, this is obvious, for priesthood can be defined only in function of worship, that is, in function of all of the virtue of religion's external acts, principally that of sacrifice. By the virtue of religion, the rational creature renders to God the

---

1. See Albert Gélin, "Le sacerdoce du Christ d'après l'épître aux Hébreux," in *Études sur le sacrement de l'ordre* (Paris: Cerf, 1957), 43–76; "Le sacerdoce de l'ancienne alliance," in *La Tradition sacerdotale* (Paris: Mappus, 1959), 27–60; Ceslas Spicq, *L'epître aux Hébreux* (Paris: Gabalda, 1952), 1:291–324 and 2:110–312 ; Albert Vanhoye, "Le Christ grand-prêtre selon He 2, 17–18," *Nouvelle revue théologique* 91 (1969): 449–74. [Tr. Note: The second entry for Gélin has been added to this list of citations. Fr. Nicolas cited it in the bibliography without any corresponding footnote reference.]

2. See Braun, *Jean le théologien*, 2:69–102. André Feuillet, *Le sacerdoce du Christ et de ses ministers* (Paris: Editions de Paris, 1972).

homage of adoration, thanksgiving, and voluntary submission that is owed to Him as the Creator, He who is the source of all the goods of nature and of grace. In Christology, this raises the grave problem concerning the relationship between the Incarnate Word to the Father. To say that He is a priest is to hold that He is inferior to the Father and submitted to Him. How is this compatible with His infinite personal dignity, by which He is equal to the Father?

I. THE RELATION OF THE INCARNATE WORD TO THE FATHER

A. Jesus's Submission to the Father

{509} This submission is proclaimed in the clearest and most explicit way in the Gospels. It is an integral part of Jesus's character as it appeared to those who witnessed His life and in the way that they described and presented it to us. Here, it suffices to recall the numerous texts of the fourth Gospel where He Himself proclaims that He does the will of the Father in all things. However, this is equally found in the Synoptic Gospels, in particular in the garden of Gethsemane. The Letter to the Hebrews speaks expressly about His obedience to the Father: "Although he was a Son, He learned obedience through what He suffered,"[3] and according to St. Paul, it is precisely by this obedience that He made reparation for sin, the root of which is disobedience: "For as by one man's disobedience many were made sinners, so by one man's obedience many will be made righteous,"[4] and "being found in human form He humbled himself and became obedient unto death, even death on a cross."[5] All these texts find, on this precise point, their condensed form in the famous expression, "The Father is greater than I."[6] Moreover, indeed as a sign of this submission (though a sign that adds a specific note to it), the

3. Heb 5:8 (RSV).
4. Rom 5:19 (RSV).
5. Phil 2:8 (RSV).
6. Jn 14:28 (RSV).

four Gospels present Him to us (indeed, on a number of occasions) as praying to His Father.

These texts were abundantly used by the Arians for establishing the Logos's inferiority in relation to the Father, who would have been the only true God, the Logos being a creature, elevated above all others but inferior to God. However, our faith, supported by numerous texts wherein Yahweh's prerogatives are attributed to Christ, where He is even expressly called "God," where He is sent with the Spirit, at the same level as God the Father, professes that the three Persons of the Trinity together are the one God, each infinite and equal in dignity and in power—the very dignity and power of God.[7]

Thus, how are we to interpret the first texts so that we may do complete justice to what they say (thus recognizing a true inferiority and true submission of Christ in relation to God), without, however, this inferiority (as well as the submission resulting therefrom) undermining the Logos's equality with the two other Persons in the unique and indivisible Trinity?

1. Inasmuch as He is man, Christ is inferior to the Father

{510} Obviously, we must make recourse to the distinction [between Christ *inasmuch as He is man* and *inasmuch as He is God*]. It is *inasmuch as He is a man* that Christ is said to be (and was) inferior to the Father. Nonetheless, the difficulty remains, for submission and dignity directly affect the person, not the nature. (Thus, we can understand what is meant when it is said that Christ was born of the Virgin Mary, suffered, and so forth *inasmuch as He is a man* was born of the Virgin Mary. We are indeed referring to the Word, though considered as subsisting in [His assumed] human nature, as He who does and suffers what He did and suffered by means of His human nature, in it.)[8] However, if I say, "the Word, inasmuch as He is a man, submits Himself to the Father," does this not contradict [this other certitude of faith]: "The word is equal to the Father"? For, whether this be *inas-*

---

7. See the first section of the second part above.
8. [Tr. note: This closing parenthesis is missing in the original.]

much as He is a man or otherwise, it remains the case that the Word is inferior to the Father, and therefore cannot be His equal—unless we were to say or think that Christ, inasmuch as He is a man, is another person than the Logos. However, as we have seen, this solution, one that is too simple, is incompatible with faith in the Incarnation.

a) The Man-Jesus's submission to God

Our reflection must begin with this man, Jesus of Nazareth, such as the Gospels present Him to us. He proclaimed His submission to God. This submission is obviously founded on the created condition of this human nature according to which He is a man. However, we also believe that this man is the Word. Therefore, we must not hesitate to say that, in becoming man, the Word became a subject of God. He is the one who is the subject of this creaturely relation to God, even though He Himself is not a creature. Indeed, it is founded on the assumed human nature, which in Him does not make the person, Who is preexisting, exist.

This can be understood, it seems, only by the traditional notion of a "composite person", which we have transcribed as "the human personality of the Word" or "the Word by His Incarnation has become a human person." To say that Christ, *inasmuch as He is a man*, is submitted to God is not to say only that His human nature is wholly dependent on God, who created it and who governs it. (This is a truism.) It is to say that, *inasmuch as He is a human person*, He is placed in a situation of inferiority in relation to God. This is the most profound point of the kenosis.[9] However, "becoming what He was not, He did not lose what He was." *Inasmuch as He is a Divine Person*, He remains God, equal to the other two Persons.

b) The submission of the Word, inasmuch as He is a man, to Himself inasmuch as He is God

{511} God the Creator is the Father, the Son, and the Spirit together. To say that Christ, inasmuch as He is a man, is submitted to

---

9. See *ST* III, q. 20, a. 1, ad 3.

God is to admit that the Word, inasmuch as He is a human person, is submitted to Himself inasmuch as He is a Divine Person. This cannot be anything but disconcerting for reason. St. Thomas proposes illustrations from our experience,[10] but they are distant approximations. Nonetheless, it is not contradictory (and therefore, not irrational), for the idea of a "composite person" enables us to avoid pure and simple submission of oneself to oneself.

Once more, our mind is here faced with the mystery of the Incarnation. We do well to keep in mind this eminently paradoxical situation of a single Divine Person subsisting in two, distinct, substantial natures, not mixed into a third thing. Also, we do well to keep in mind the nature of the mystery present here, namely, the fact that one of these two natures is God's nature and the fact that the Person who thus subsists, no longer only in the Divine Nature, but in a created nature, is an uncreated Divine Person.

c) The special submission of the Incarnate Word to the
Person of the Father

{512} Founded on [God's activity of] creation, the submission of the Incarnate Word as such to God has the entire Trinity as its terminus. However, there is another foundation: the mission, for by the Incarnation, the Son is "sent" to the world.[11] The Father is the one who sends the Son. Therefore, the submission founded on the mission of the Son is a special relation of the Incarnate Word to the Person of the Father. For this reason, it is ordinarily expressed in relation to the Father.

These two foundations are not heterogeneous. Both are concerned with the Word only on account of the assumed nature, for if the Word proceeds eternally from the Father, in order for there to be a mission, in addition to the procession, there must be a "new manner of existing for someone,"[12] in this case belonging to the Word on ac-

---

10. See ibid., a. 2, ad 2 and ad 3.
11. See §227 in the previous volume in this series.
12. See §§204–5 in the previous volume.

count of the assumed nature. However, they are distinct. The first concerns the Word only indirectly. (The Word is not created; He is the Person in whom a created nature is realized.) The second concerns Him directly, for He is the one who is sent, although it implies the nature because it belongs to the Word inasmuch as He is Incarnate.

2. *Christ's prayer*

{513} Prayer holds too great and too significant a place in Jesus's earthly life for us to content ourselves with merely mentioning it in passing. It is a characteristic aspect of His submission to the Father and of His "inferiority," for prayer in general (even if one can address oneself to an equal) presupposes that the thing being asked for is not in the power of the person praying but, instead, in the power of the other person who, at least on this precise point, is superior to him. When it is a question of prayer addressed to God, it is an act of the virtue of religion, for "by prayer, man reveres God, in the sense that he submits himself to Him and recognizes in praying that he stands in need of God as the Author of all his goods."[13]

a) Prayer and the conformity of the created will to the Divine Will

However, prayer presents theological reflection with a peculiar difficulty. Prayer is the creature's act recognizing God's complete sovereignty over it, a recognition of His grandeur and goodness. However, at the same time, it seems contrary to a complete submission by the creature, given that prayer is a kind of pressure exercised by the creature on God so that He may do His will for it. This leads to frequent, well-known objections against the very idea of prayer. On the one hand, there are those who advocate "pure love," radicalizing the requirements of abandonment to God's will, holding that spiritual perfection is found in refusing to ask anything of Him (a prescription that is obviously opposed to the words of the Gospel). On the other hand—and, alas!, a position expressed even by theologians—there are others who, radicalizing reason's requirements in the oppo-

---

13. *ST* II-II, q. 83, a. 4.

site direction, claim that it is absurd to think that God will alter His project under pressure coming from His creature, therefore claiming that prayer, which would be such a form of pressure, is irrational.

This is not the place to enter into a discussion of these problems.[14] It was necessary to recall them in order to introduce the classical response that is made to these objections. God Himself is the one who arouses His creature's prayer, for He does not wish only to give it this or that good but, instead, wishes to give it in response to His creature's prayers and in fulfillment of them.[15] Granted this response is enigmatic enough in itself. Moreover, with regard to Christ's prayer, it gives rise to a redoubtable difficulty.

In what concerns prayer in general, the response that we are considering holds that prayer is a second cause, thus applying this general rule to it: the effect is willed by God as something produced by this cause.[16] Now, this application does not seem to take into account the unique way that prayer is a cause. Prayer does not produce the effect in question. It inclines the Divine Will to produce it. For this reason, this case returns us to God's Will as the cause of the effect. It will cause the effect, doubtlessly, by means of secondary causes, but not by means of the prayer itself, as the latter does not directly produce anything. Therefore, we find ourselves led to introduce into the Divine Will itself a distinction between what is "ordinarily" willed, as resulting from the order of causes that God wills, and what is "extraordinarily" willed, as resulting from an intervention of the Divine Will in this order of causes in favor of the person who prays. This intervention does not include a real modification in the divine willing, for God willed from all eternity both this order of causes from which a given result must happen as well as the modification of the result, obtained by the prayer that He Himself aroused. However, if we place the act of prayer back into the existential context of

---

14. See Jean-Hervé Nicolas, *Contemplation et vie contemplative en christianisme* (Fribourg / Paris: Éditions universitaires / Beauchesne, 1980), 109–16 and 263–77.
15. See *ST* II-II, q. 83, a. 2.
16. See *ST* I, q. 19, a. 5, ad 2 and a. 8.

the person who prays, without knowing the divine project in which his own prayer has its place, it is truly a question of doing something, at the level of second causes, from which the expected result arises (or can arise), if God grants the prayer.[17]

b) The unknown future presupposed by Christ's prayer during His earthly life

{514} Can we purely and simply extend this analysis to Christ's prayer? The difficulty does not arise from the perfect conformity of Jesus's human will to the Divine Will, for this conformity is a paradigm for all free and divinized creatures, toward which they must tend. Indeed, perfect prayer would be that in which such a conformity would be perfect. The difficulty is found in His perfect knowledge of the divine project, on the one hand, and [on the other hand] in the very perfection of His prayer which, founded upon the mutual love of the Father for the Son and of the Son for the Father, would seem to need to be always answered.

A lively perception of this twofold difficulty led St. Thomas to an interpretation of Christ's prayer that is not entirely satisfying. Relying on the words pronounced by Jesus when He had just resurrected Lazarus, "Father, I thank thee that thou hast heard me; I knew that thou hearest me always, but I have said this on account of the people standing by, that they may believe that thou didst send me,"[18] and following the interpretation of many of the Fathers, St. Thomas seems to hold that Christ did not really pray but, rather, in order to invite us to pray, only spoke the words of prayer which were not of real use for Himself: "Given that He Himself was God and man, He wished to present a prayer to the Father, not that He was powerless (to realize what He asked for) but, instead, did so for our instruction."[19] Likewise, he writes: "Indeed, as we have said, Christ willed

---

17. See ibid., a. 7, ad 2.
18. Jn 11:41–42 (RSV).
19. *ST* III, q. 21, a. 1. To the Patristic citations that this article contains, one can add the others found in the *Catena aurea* on Jn 10, no. 8.

to make use of prayer addressed to the Father in order to give us an example of prayer and also to show that His Father was the Author from whom He proceeds eternally according to the Divine Nature, as well as from whom He holds, according to His human nature, all His good."[20]

This minimizing of Christ's prayer is somewhat unsettling. The text of St. John used in justification for it does not say this, and in any case, it cannot be extended to the whole of Christ's prayer, which is so strongly attested to in the Gospels. There can be no doubt that He truly prayed. In what concerns the perfect knowledge that Christ had on earth regarding God's designs, we must have recourse to the distinctions to which we had recourse as regards Christ's knowledge [*la science du Christ*].[21] By His human, "earthly" knowledge, even illuminated by the transcendent focal point that was the immediate vision He had of the Divine Essence, Christ did not know all things. Certainly, He knew at every moment what the Father willed of Him. However, it would not have been compatible with the reality of His situation as a *viator*, a "wayfarer," a man living in the midst of men and with them, to have the divine design (even concerning all the events of His earthly existence, and even more so, of salvation history in its totality) placed before His eyes like a "storyline written in advance" which He would have only needed to realize in its exact lines. Nothing in the Gospels invites us to admit this. In fact, they all turn us away from such a claim. The exercise of freedom in earthly life—which is a forward march, indeed a march into the unknown of the future—does not take place without discoveries and ever-new decisions. We have seen that what must be absolutely, though uniquely, recognized in the case of Christ is the perfect and total agreement of each new decision of His human will with the divine decision. This leaves room for this unknown domain of the future necessary for freedom and also for authentic prayer.

20. *ST* III, q. 21, a. 3.
21. See §§352–54 above.

c) The fulfillment of Christ's prayer and the freedom of those for whom He prays

{515} What does it mean to say that this is necessary for prayer? The Catholic faith recognizes that the saints in heaven, and the Virgin Mary in an eminent manner, have a power of intercession to which the Church has continuous recourse in her liturgy. Moreover, she asks Christ Himself to intercede for her and for the world, making her own prayer pass through Him. Nonetheless, it is impossible to think that in the Beatific Vision the elect pray without knowing what God has decided. Doubtlessly, they do not know salvation history in its details. However, according to St. Thomas, each of the blessed knows what is personally of interest to him and therefore knows what he prays for.[22] Because there is nothing in salvation history that does not fail to interest Christ and the Virgin personally, they cannot be unaware of any of it.[23] How is this prayer possible if they know in advance what God has decided and if they do not will anything other than what God has decided?

It is here that the way that St. Thomas explains Christ's prayer offends the heart the most, though it also offends the mind [*esprit*]. Confronted with the problem of the fulfillment of this prayer, which could not fail, alongside the Gospel's narrative telling us that, while hanging upon the cross, Christ prayed for those who were the cause of His death—that is, for all men, because He was killed on account of all our sins—St. Thomas comes to say that Jesus prays only for the predestined![24] Already in the commentary on the *Sentences* of Peter Lombard, he explained the non-fulfillment of the prayers of the saints by saying that they do not ask for what they know that God does not will.[25]

This seems certain when it is a question of temporal benefits, for what God essentially wills for man is his salvation, and He can will

---

22. See *In* IV *Sent.*, d. 45, q. 3, a. 2.
23. For Christ, see *ST* III, q. 10, a. 2.
24. See *ST* III, q. 21, a. 4, ad 2.
25. See *In* IV *Sent.*, d. 14, q. 3, a. 3.

temporal goods for them only in function of salvation. However, can it be said that God does not will man's salvation? This would lead us into the vortex of debates pertaining to predestination, and we cannot take them up in full. However, some observations are necessary. In the text cited from the *Scriptum*, St. Thomas recalls the famous distinction between *God's antecedent will* and *His consequent will*, though he does so in order to say that what God wills by His *antecedent will*, He does not will purely and simply. However, if we refer to this distinction as He explains it, at length in the *Scriptum* and in a more condensed way in the *Summa theologiae*,[26] we find ourselves led to nuance this assertion heavily.

In fact, the only thing that prevents God's antecedent will from being a pure and simple willing (and therefore prevents it from passing over to being a consequent will) is the sin of the free creature. And it is necessary to add that [this really also involves] his obstinacy in sin, for as long as a man lives on earth, God is near, ready to pardon all His sins, provided that he converts. Now, it is an absolute principle in St. Thomas (indeed, one that must serve as the hermeneutic criterion for understanding and, eventually, rectifying all his formulations in this domain) that "in no way does God will the evil that is sin, which is a privation of the ordination (of the free creature) to the divine good."[27]

Thus, it is not in the Divine willing that we must seek after the reason why God does not purely and simply will a given person's salvation. Instead, we must seek after this reason in the created person's will. Thus, the most perfect conformity of created willing with the divine willing—in the saint, in the Virgin, and in Christ Himself—is not opposed in any way to prayer having as its object the salvation of all and of each person. The mystery is not found in the non-fulfillment of such prayer but, rather, in the created wills ability to be opposed, through sinning, to the omnipotent willing of God. However, the study of this mystery falls to another chapter in theology.

26. See *In I Sent.*, d. 46, q. 1, and d. 47, q. 1; *ST* I, q. 19, a. 6, ad 1.
27. *ST* I, q. 19, a. 9.

d) The desire and hope that animated Jesus's prayer during his earthly life

{516} These shadows must not obscure the remarkable analysis of Christ's prayer by St. Thomas. Taking up what he had explained concerning Christ's two wills, he shows, through a very profound interpretation of Jesus's agony in Gethsemane,[28] that the very realism of the Incarnation requires us to recognize a kind of contrariety between these two willings, for the sense appetite, and also what he calls the *voluntas ut natura* (i.e., the spontaneous movement of the will in the presence of the object), are naturally repulsed by what is opposed, at least immediately, to the "proper good" of the person and to everything that "does evil" [to him]: suffering, death, and moral and spiritual punishment. It is only at a second moment that the created will, considering that the same thing is willed by God and entering into His design (which is a design of love, in which the proper good will be found again and will blossom forth, even though it is temporarily frustrated and crushed) and deliberately conformed to the divine willing, chooses that which it feels to be an evil but which it judges to be a good, the Absolute Good, of which the proper good of the creature is only a subordinated part. Thus, the perfect conformity of Christ's human willing to the divine willing is an overcome contrariety—overcome without hesitation and without the least reticence, certainly, but not without there being, at the heart of this acceptance, the persistence of the desire to be delivered from this evil that He accepts: "Father, if it be possible, let this cup pass from me."[29]

This desire is what Christ's prayer expresses. Moreover, there is His desire for all the goods that had been prepared for Him according to the divine design, "the glory which [He] had with [the Father] before the world was made,"[30] namely, the overflow of the glory of His divinity onto His humanity. This overflow was suspended, as it were, by a mysterious disposition of Divine Providence, so that,

---

28. See *ST* III, q. 18, a. 6.
29. Mt 26:39 (RSV).
30. Jn 17:5 (RSV).

living among men a life similar to their own, suffering and dying at their hands and for them, He could redeem them. According to His Divine Will, He was the author of this disposition, together with the Father and the Holy Spirit. According to His Divine Will, He fully accepted and ratified it: "He did not count equality with God a thing to be grasped, but emptied Himself, taking the form of a servant, being born in the likeness of men."[31] At the same time, He was occupied with the desire for this glorification of His humanity to be accorded to Him, in accord with the divine design, and this was the object of His prayer: "In the days of His flesh, Jesus offered up prayers and supplications, with loud cries and tears, to Him who was able to save Him from death, and He was heard for His godly fear."[32]

St. Thomas did not wish to interpret this trusting desire as though it indicated that Christ had the theological virtue of hope, because the formal object of theological hope is perfect union with God in the [Beatific] Vision, and Christ did not have need of attaining this Good, given that He had received it from the beginning [of the Incarnation].[33] However, it is a question, here too, of a good not yet possessed, but promised, one that Christ awaited from the Father's mercy with a wholly certain trust, for if the glorification of His humanity was owed to the Word on account of His divinity, it was a free gift of love for the man whom He had really and fully become. St. Thomas says that this desire and expectation constitute a "kind of hope." If it is not theological hope, what should we call it? In any case, this is little more than a question of words.

B. "My Father and Your Father"

1. *Christ was not the subject of filial adoption*

One of the most ancient forms of dualism in Christology was *adoptionism*. According to this doctrine (or, these doctrines) the man Jesus would have been the son of God by adoption. The princi-

---

31. Phil 2:6–7 (RSV).
32. Heb 5:7 (RSV). See *ST* III, q. 21, a. 3.
33. See *ST* III, q. 7, a. 4. Also, see §337 above.

ple of this position holds that the man Jesus is a person distinct from the Word: the Word is the Son by Nature; Jesus is a son by adoption. It represents the theory of two sons, a theory that was expressly condemned by the Church.[34] However, in repudiating every form of dualism, one could be tempted to believe and say that Christ as man is an adoptive son. Did He not have the grace of filial adoption?[35]

This must be completely rejected. Filiation not only affects the person (like submission and inferiority), it is constitutive of the person—not directly when it is a question of a person who is only human, but indeed indirectly, in the sense that the person is constituted by the individual nature, received from those who have begotten it and for this reason founding a relation from the person of the child to those of his parents. And this relation is what filiation is.

However, given that Christ's person is purely and simply preexistent, it is in no way constituted by [His assumed] human nature. It is constituted by the eternal filiation: "The Word does not hold His being purely and simply from His human nature, for He exists from all eternity. From it He only holds the fact that He exists as a man."[36] Likewise, and for the same reason, it is not from the grace conferred on Him inasmuch as He is a man that He holds that He is the Son, purely and simply, but instead that He exists and acts humanly as the Son who exists from all eternity. Thus, although created grace of itself brings along filial adoption—so that, when communicated to men, it makes them be adoptive sons—it therefore could not make Christ an adoptive son because He is the Son, independent of created grace and from all eternity.

2. *The filial adoption of Christians*

If Christ's created grace does not produce filial adoption, this is because it is prevented in the way we have discussed. It remains true that of itself, given that it is a participation in the Divine Life,

---

34. See §269 above.
35. See §340 above.
36. *ST* III, q. 3, a. 1, ad 3.

it makes one a child [of God], re-begetting those who receive it, themselves not being sons by nature. Filial adoption exists through a participation in Christ's filiation, not in the grace of union through which Christ is the Son of God, but in created grace, which, *in Him*, derives from the grace of union. Christians are made "in conformity to the image of his Son."[37]

A question thus arises. The terminus of Jesus's natural filiation is obviously the Father, the First Person of the Trinity. Must we likewise say that filial adoption has the Father as its terminus? If not, it is not the same filiation. If it does, must we attribute to the Person of the Father, in His distinction, the re-begetting action in which adoption consists? However, this is a real action, and every divine action *ad extra* is indivisibly an action of the three Persons of the Trinity.

St. Thomas (in *ST* III, q. 23, a. 2) judges that filial adoption has its [relational] terminus in the whole Trinity because it is founded on an action common to the three Persons. Many theologians today still maintain this position.[38] However, a number of other theologians hold the opposite position, principally out of a desire to understand the obvious sense of numerous scriptural texts where "God" manifestly refers to the First Person of the Trinity.[39]

Once more, we find ourselves faced with a conflict between "theological reason" and an affirmation drawn from Scripture. *A priori*, the latter should prevail. However, one must not forget that theological reason is wholly dependent on faith and is also founded on Scripture. In the present case, the principle, expressly recognized since the fourth century, that God's activities *ad extra* are actions of the whole Trinity, is founded on the absolutely fundamental biblical truth of God's unity.

---

37. Rom 8:29.
38. See Stanislas Dockx, *Fils de Dieu par grâce* (Paris: Desclée de Brouwer, 1948), 22–23; Journet, *L'Église du Verbe incarné*, 258–67 and 360–62; Lafont, *Structures et méthode*, 268.
39. See Rahner, "Dieu dans le Nouveau Testament," 85; Henri Rondet, *Essai sur la théologie de la grâce* (Paris: Beauchesne, 1964), 119–23; Mattias-Joseph Scheeben, *Les mystères du christianisme* (Paris: Desclée de Brouwer, 1947), 177–82.

Instead of exacerbating the conflict, in cases like this, we must strive to find a resolution. I have proposed such a reconciliation elsewhere in greater detail.[40] In sum, I propose that, in the ensemble of relations that constitute "filial relations," we should distinguish ontological filiation (founded on the generative action) from the interpersonal relations of love, respect, submission, and so forth, that are woven around it. In the case of adoption, in men, there is a kind of separation involved: a mere juridical relation is substituted for generation, and the aforementioned interpersonal relations are woven around it. This kind of distinction can be found in the relations constituting our filial relation to God. The primary, ontological relation of regeneration, founded on God's action *ad extra*, has the three Persons together as its terminus. However, the interpersonal relations that are woven together around it have the Person of the Father in His distinction as their terminus.

Thus, we have an explanation for the fact that Scripture invites us to have filial feelings in relation to the First Person, the Father of our Lord Jesus Christ, as well as the fact that Christian experience, as it has been expressed by numerous spiritual authors, proves the reality of such sentiments in those who strive to live according to Christ's grace, the formal effect of which is, as we have seen, the uniting of the believer to the Trinity (i.e., to each of the three Persons distinctly).[41]

II. CHRIST'S PRIESTHOOD

We can now address the very question of Christ's priesthood.

1. Priest according to the order of Melchizedek

a) Christ is a priest

{517} In the Letter to the Hebrews, Christ is presented as being the High Priest of the New Covenant. If Christ is a priest in a unique way, nonetheless, there is a fundamental similarity between His priesthood

---

40. See J.-H. Nicolas, *Les profondeurs de la grâce*, 415–24.
41. See §§209–16 in the first volume of this series.

and the Levitical priesthood. In short, Christ perfectly realizes that to which the Levitical preisthood powerlessly tended,[42] and on the other hand, the latter has a prophetic meaning in relation to Christ's priesthood. However, if Christ did not belong to the tribe of Levi and is called a "priest according to the order of Melchizedek," this is to emphasize His singularity and His excellence in relation to the whole Levitical priesthood. He is not one Levitical priest among the others, even the most excellent one. He is a priest in different way. His priesthood is different.

St. Thomas founds Christ's priesthood on His role as mediator. Christ came to reconcile man with God, to make him return to grace, and to grant him the adoption of sons through the Gift of the Holy Spirit. He did this first of all in His own Person[43] and then by sacrificing His life.[44] To offer sacrifice is the priestly activity *par excellence*. Certain theologians have even wished to reduce all of Christ's activity to this and to find there its *raison d'être* so that, according to them, it could be sufficiently "defined" by it, in the sense that the Hypostatic Union would directly and formally make Him "the priest." This is, on the whole, the position of the French School. A substantial presentation of it can be found in Héris.[45]

This position cannot be retained. Indeed, the priest is defined in relation to worship, especially in relation to sacrifice, which is the primary act of worship, that to which all the others are related.[46] Now, while every human activity must be ordered to God (and, consequently, while every act of freedom by which a man is turned away from God is an "offense"), the acts of religion by which man renders God the honor that is owed to Him are a human activity. These are not even the principal acts [of his activity], for the object of these

---

42. See Spicq, *L'epître aux Hébreux*, 2:126.
43. See §433 above and §529 below.
44. See §492–93.
45. See Charles-Vincent Héris, *Le mystère du Christ* (Paris: Revue des jeunes, 1928); Héris, "Le Verbe incarné," in *Saint Thomas d'Aquin. Somme théologique* (Paris: Cerf, n.d.), 3:352–59.
46. See Congar, *Sainte Eglise*, 269–73.

acts is not God Himself but, rather, the cultic signs by which interior religion is expressed. By contrast, "theological" acts have God Himself in His mystery as their object.[47] Inasmuch as He is a priest, Christ rendered perfect worship to the Father—for Himself first of all, then for all of humanity—and on His cross He "inaugurated the worship of Christian religion."[48] Just as Christianity cannot be reduced to "Christian religious worship," Christ cannot be enclosed in the notion of "the High Priest of the New Covenant."

In particular, Christ's essential revealing function, which we have seen is an integral part of the mission of the Word,[49] cannot be confused with His priestly function. Nor can His royal and priestly functions be identified with each other, even if they are closely connected,[50] with the royal (or "pastoral") function of Christ consisting in leading to God the people whom He redeemed by His blood.[51]

b) Christ is the sole priest of the New Covenant

{518} The relation between Christ's priesthood and the ministerial priesthood on the one hand, and the universal priesthood on the other, will be studied in connection with the sacrament of orders. Briefly stated, Christ's sacrifice is the unique sacrifice which efficaciously frees man from sin, placing him back into grace with God. All the preceding sacrifices had their value only on account of Christ's sacrifice, which they prophesied. Every sacrifice other than His has now objectively become a form of sacrilege. If this sacrifice is the only one that is pleasing to God, this is because Jesus Christ, who offers it, is the only priest who is approved by God. This is the whole meaning of the Letter to the Hebrews. It likewise is the meaning of 1 Timothy 2:5–6a (RSV): "For there is one God, and there is one

---

47. See *ST* II-II, q. 81, a. 2.
48. *ST* III, q. 62, a. 5.
49. See §230 in the previous volume.
50. See Spicq, *L'epître aux Hébreux*, 2:238ff.
51. See Heb 13:20. Journet, *L'Église du Verbe incarné*, 1:168–70. J. G. Riedlinger, *J'espère en Jésus-Christ* (Paris: Desclée de Brouwer, 1964). Olivier Rousseau, "Autour de l'idée de la royauté du Christ," *Concilium* 11 (1966): 115–26. Also, §432 above.

mediator between God and men, the man Christ Jesus, who gave Himself as a ransom for all."

2. *The formal constitutive of Christ's priesthood*

{519} The same theologians to whom we alluded above (i.e., those of the French School or those under its influence) think that Christ is formally constituted a priest by the Hypostatic Union itself. The grave drawback to this outlook was noted above as well:[52] Christ's priesthood would express, by itself, the whole richness of the mystery of the Incarnation. Another drawback is that it would be scarcely understandable how men can participate in Christ's priesthood, for precisely speaking, the Hypostatic Union is that by which He is unique and distinct from all other men.

Along the same line of thought, it seems that this conception would lead, in fact, to the false conception of the priest as a "super-Christian." (This was denounced, though not without some excesses, by Jacques Maritain.)[53] Indeed, if one is a Christian through an effusion of Christ's grace, he who by the sacrament of orders would receive something belonging to the order of the grace of union (which we have seen is of another, infinitely superior order) would, by that very fact, be placed above all Christians *in the very order of grace*. And how then can we conceive of the "universal priesthood of believers," if not as a metaphor without any bearing on reality?

Nonetheless, it is certain that if Christ is the sole priest of the New[54] Covenant, this is on account of the Hypostatic Union. Therefore, we must say that Christ is constituted as a priest by created grace (deriving in Him from the Union, though distinct from it).[55] This grace, with its priestly dimension, is what He communicates to His Church, as we will see in the third part of this course.

---

52. See §517.
53. See Jacques Maritain, "A propos de l'École Française," *Revue thomiste* 71 (1971): 463–79.
54. [Tr. note: Reading "la nouvelle Alliance" for "l'ancienne Alliance"]
55. See Journet, *L'Église du Verbe incarné*, 2:247ff.

3. Priest and victim

{520} Today, some exegetes place the sacrificial character of Christ's death in doubt. Without being able to enter into this debate here, I believe that we can still maintain the traditional position, which relies upon many convergent texts drawn from the Gospels[56] and the other books of the New Testament.[57] From a theological perspective, it could be objected that, in order for it to be a sacrifice in the strict sense, Jesus's passion and death lack the character of being a cultic act. Some have wished to find this cultic character in the interior oblation made by Christ on the cross.[58] However, worship is something external, and interior oblation does not suffice for making Christ's death into a "ritual." La Taille "imagined" [sic] that Jesus would have made His death into a ritual in advance at the Last Supper.[59] This is quite artificial.

This objection rests on too narrow of a concept of the "cultic." Obviously, Christ's passion and death present no characteristics of a liturgical ceremony. But why? Because, liturgy is made up of signs which are related to a reality. In the case of the liturgy of the New Covenant, this reality surely is the passion and death of Christ, though it is also referred to by the liturgy of the Old Covenant, which was prophetic in relation to the New. In order for Christ's death and passion to be cultic, it suffices that it be sacrificial. That is, Christ on the cross would have really offered His life to the Father in full awareness and with full freedom for the remission of man's sins. It is cultic without being liturgical, though it is the principle of the whole of the liturgy.[60]

Therefore, in Christ priest and victim wholly coincide. Note that this identification is, in a sense, the law of every sacrifice. The ex-

---

56. See Braun, *Jean le théologien*, 3:139–72. André Feuillet, "Les trois grandes prophéties de la Passion et de la Résurrection," *Revue thomiste* 68 (1968): 42–46.

57. See Sabourin, *Rédemption sacrificielle*.

58. See A[lbert] Michel, "La messe chez les théologiens postérieurs au concile de Trente. Essence et efficacité," in *Dictionnaire de théologie catholique*, vol. 10, col. 1192.

59. See Maurice de La Taille, *Mysterium fidei. De augustissimo Corporis et Sanguinis Christi sacrificio atque sacramento* (Paris: Beauchesne, 1921), vol. 1, cc. 3 and 4.

60. See *ST* III, q. 62, a. 5.

ternal sacrifice has a value only as a sign of the internal sacrifice by which the created person offers himself to God, at once as belonging to Him (however, it is fitting that he accepts and ratifies this ontological dependence by an act of his freedom) and as a repudiation of the sin by which he intentionally drew back from this dependence (i.e., as having turned back to Him). Ordinarily, the coincidence does not go beyond symbolic identification, given that the victim is physically different from him who offers it, symbolically representing the latter.

All men are included in Christ's sacrifice, not as constituting another priest or other priests but, rather, as internally (and externally through the sacraments) ratifying Christ's sacrificial offering and as offering themselves with Him. Thus, we have the universal priesthood. This self-offering along with Christ is first performed symbolically and then continues through the course of the Christian life up to death.

III. MARY'S ASSOCIATION WITH CHRIST'S SACRIFICE

This participation in Christ's sacrifice, a participation which is common to all the redeemed and by which each believer receives the benefit of redemption on his own behalf, is obviously found in Mary, as much as it is found in all other believers and indeed more perfectly, for she was the most perfect believer. (We speak here of Mary on earth, during the first days of the Church.) In modern times, the question was raised asking whether or not she would have participated in the redemptive sacrifice itself in its reality and not only in its sacramental renewal.

A. The Theme of the New Eve

{521} This is a very ancient theme, going back to St. Irenaeus: Mary is associated with Christ as Eve was associated with Adam.[61] According to Braun,[62] the theme would have existed already in St. John,

---

61. On the birth and development of this theme, see *Études Mariales*, 1954–57. Also, see Laurentin, *Court traité sur la Vierge Marie*, 42–44.

62. Braun, *La Mère des fidèles*.

along with a soteriological meaning. Mary's presence at the foot of the cross in the Johannine account of the passion, which refers in detail to the prophecies of the Old Testament, would be a willed evocation of the first couple, Adam and Eve. In fact, however, this theme was exploited in a soteriological sense only much later on. The general idea maintained that Mary was Jesus's companion in the work of salvation, as Eve was Adam's companion in that of perdition.

B. Mary, Companion of Jesus from the Beginning of the Incarnation

{522} We have already seen that the Incarnation itself is already redemptive in the real history of salvation.[63] Now, what emerges from the third Gospel's account is that Mary's consent was expressly required for the Incarnation. We have interpreted this in function of the divine maternity. However, can we push this reflection further and see in this consent not only the acceptance of the Incarnate Word as her son but also the acceptance of the Savior as such, thus here seeing a first participation in His redemptive mission, comparable to her participation in the Incarnation? This is what St. Thomas seems to advance in a text which is almost a "hapax" in his work. In any case, he himself did not draw this consequence from what he says in that text. (One would search in vain in him for this idea of Mary participating in the reality of the redemptive sacrifice.) Nonetheless, the text in question opens a promising path forward in this direction.

This is the fourth reason that he proposes for explaining the meaning of the annunciation: "[It was fitting] in order to render manifest that there is a kind of spiritual marriage between the Son of God and human nature. On account of this, by means of the annunciation, the consent of the Virgin was solicited, standing in place of all of human nature."[64] This idea is sketched out in the *Scriptum*. Nonetheless, there is a difference between the two texts. In the oldest text, the "marriage" consists in the union of the Divine Nature and human nature (i.e., the assumed nature) in the Person of the

---

63. See §433 above.
64. *ST* III, q. 30, a. 1.

Word.⁶⁵ (This does not leave much meaning to the image of marriage—although, in this sense, it would be traditional—for, given that the assumed nature is deprived of its proper personality, there is hardly a place for the idea of the interpersonal relation in which marriage consists.) In the text of the *Summa theologiae*, by contrast, it seems that is a question of "human nature" in the sense of "mankind," *totius humanae naturae*. That is, it seems to be a question of the union that the Son of God contracted with the ensemble of men by the fact of the Incarnation, a union finding its scriptural expression in the theme of the Church as the spouse of Christ.⁶⁶

Hence, Mary was called to consent to the Incarnation "in the name of all men." This is related, though at the very source of grace, to the primordial principle of salvation: all is a grace, a pure gift of God. However, because God's gift is the gift of a personal God (the Holy Spirit) made to persons, it can be really bestowed only if it is freely accepted. This is found in the destiny of each person ("to all who received Him, who believed in His name, He gave power to become children of God").⁶⁷ However, at the annunciation, it was necessary that He who is the very grace of salvation, already containing all graces, would be freely accepted by the humanity whom He came to save. Mary's role in salvation history was to give, in the name of all, this necessary consent to salvation as a whole.

Such reflection leads one to the theological justification for the topic of Mary's spiritual maternity which, moreover, has a scriptural foundation (a disputed one, doubtlessly, but one that is recognized by many exegetes) in the words of Jesus on the cross to His mother and John, such as they are reported by the fourth Gospel. We will return to this when we discuss the relationship between Mary and the Church.⁶⁸

Like Scheeben, must we speak of her "spousal maternity" (*Bräut-*

---

65. See *In III Sent.*, d. 3, q. 3, a. 1.
66. See M.-J. Nicolas, *Theotokos*, 146–47.
67. Jn 1:12 (RSV).
68. See §707 in the next volume.

liche Mutterschaf)? This is also an idea taken up recently by Gonzalo Gironés.[69] There are difficulties involved with this image. It seems more adequate to say that, on account of the unique conditions of the divine maternity (the preexistence of the Son, as well as the consent asked of Mary, not only in relation to the child to come but in relation to a Divine Person who will become her child on account of her consent) it includes, beyond the total reality of maternity, the reality of spousal union, the latter being found within the divine maternity itself and not as something added to it.

C. Mary's Association with Christ in the Redemption Itself

{523} The[70] title of co-redemptrix is held in suspicion by a growing number of theologians. Indeed, it seems to say that Christ is not, Him alone, the redeemer—He would be, for His part, a *co-redeemer*. This obviously cannot be held. Thus, many, like Journet, prefer to emphasize that the Church's participation in the Redemption found its perfect and outstanding form in Mary. However, can we not recognize that Mary has a singular role in the very act of reconciliation?

Above all, we must exclude absolutely every association of Mary with Christ's priestly act. If ministerial priests in the Church are associated with it, this is in a purely sacramental manner, as sacramental representatives of Christ the High Priest and as His pure instruments. Now, we have no scriptural, traditional, or theological foundation for attributing to Mary this function, which she could

---

69. See Gonzalo Gironés, *La humanidad salvada y salvadora* (Valencia: Anales del Seminario de Valencia, 1969). [Tr. note: This was cited by Fr. Nicolas in the body of the text.]

70. See Braun, *La Mère des fidèles*; Bouyer, *Le trône de la sagesse*, 229–51; Jacques Bur, *Médiation mariale* (Paris: Desclée de Brouwer, 1955); Clément Dillenschneider, *Marie au service de notre rédemption* (Haguenau: Maison Saint-Gérard, 1947); Feuillet, *Jésus et sa Mère*, 59–69; Michel de Goedt, "Bases bibliques de la maternité spirituelle," in *Etudes Mariales* (Paris: Lethielleux, 1959), 3–53; Journet, *L'Église du Verbe incarné*, 2:382–453; Theodore Koehler, "Les principals interprétations traditionnelles de Jn 19, 25–27," in *Etudes Mariales* (Paris: Lethielleux, 1959), 119–55; René Laurentin, *Le titre de co-rédemptrice* (Paris: Lethielleux, 1951); M.-J. Nicolas, *Theotokos*, 150–69.

have fulfilled only during her earthly life and after the foundation of the Church.[71] As regards the priestly act by which Christ offered His life in sacrifice on the cross, we have seen that He is the sole priest of the New Covenant. Like all human beings, Mary was redeemed by this act, although in a singular manner. She could not be the principle of it because she spiritually exists only in dependence upon it.

To escape this impasse, an idea was proposed by M.-J. Nicolas, which seems to open an interesting path for research: Mary could have been able to contribute to the redemptive sacrifice, not as priest but as victim. This is founded, first of all, on the meaning of Christ's sufferings as the expression of His love,[72] and on this idea that St. Thomas expresses thus: "He suffered every kind of human suffering."[73] Therefore, we could say that [Mary's suffering as victim] is compassion, which is a kind of human suffering playing a considerable role in human destiny, though one and the same person cannot experience such compassion at the same time as his or her own suffering. In compassion, we can see the personal association of Mary with Christ plays out in a unique manner at the foot of the cross. She was there in order to add the weight of her compassion to the redemptive passion of her Son, constituting with Him a single victim in two persons, a victim that He offered, in a priestly manner, in sacrifice. Of course, Mary, through all her charity, was associated with this offering, though this association was a simple, personal adherence to what Christ accomplished alone as a priest; however, it was not essentially different from that to which the whole Church is invited, along with each believer in her through the centuries that would follow, namely, the personal adherence by which the universal priesthood is exercised.

This line of reflection must not be neglected, and it certainly pro-

---

71. See René Laurentin, *Marie, L'Église et le sacerdoce*, vols. 1–2 (Paris: Lethielleux, 1952–53).
72. See §493 above.
73. *ST* III, q. 46, a. 5.

vides precious illumination on these matters. There is another one, however, and it is one that will doubtlessly go further. It is based on the role that Mary played in the Incarnation, giving her consent in the name of all of mankind made present by her.[74] Now, the Incarnation is redemptive in the divine intention, meaning that to consent to the Incarnation was for man—and for Mary who represented man before God—to consent to salvation. However, as we have seen, the Incarnate Word redeemed man and saved him by giving His life for him on the cross—"for him," that is, by at once substituting Himself for him and on his behalf. Each person is called to enter personally into this redemptive action of Christ, as we have seen, for if salvation is God's gift given to all of humanity, it is also a personal gift to each person, consisting in the restoration of the personal relations of each person with the Divine Persons entailed by the remission of sins and divinization.[75] However, is it not also necessary and most important that man's participation in the redemptive work accomplished by Jesus Christ for him be accepted and ratified by him at its beginning and at the very moment when it is accomplished? Man cannot be a mere spectator of the redemption. He is implied in it. Mary's role at the foot of the cross, as a prolongation of the role that she had to play and that she did play at the annunciation, is to represent mankind before Christ so that she may consent to His sacrifice and make it her own—so that she may offer herself with Him in reparation for sin. The consent of each person through the course of his own earthly existence is thus only the personalization of that which the whole of mankind gave in Mary to the sacrifice of Christ.

It has been objected against this, however, that Christ is the one who properly plays the role of representing humanity before God. Hence, when the same role is attributed to Mary, does this not fall into the snare which is a constant risk for Mariology, namely that of not being able to attribute to the Virgin a unique value in relation to what grace confers on all those who receive it without thereby en-

74. See §522 above.
75. See §494 above.

croaching upon the incommunicable prerogatives of Christ? Doubtlessly, a lively perception of this danger is what makes not only Protestants, but also many Catholics, defiant with regard to Mariology on the levels of doctrine and the spiritual life.

However, the snare is inevitable in any case, indeed especially in the latter. For while Christ, the man whom the Word has become, represents the whole of Adamic humanity—sinful, repentant, and reconciled humanity—before the Father (and before the whole of the Trinity), Mary represents humanity before Christ. Indeed, she does so precisely at the moment when He takes this humanity into Himself in order to bring it back to the Father; she speaks in its name, consenting to this deed performed by the Savior on behalf of humanity, one which, however, must first of all be consented to, making it its own: "Jesus represented humanity inasmuch as He is its Head, inasmuch as He offered Himself for man's sins. Mary represented humanity inasmuch as she is the first member of the mystical body. In the name of all mankind, she had to adhere to the sacrifice of the Head."[76]

This is why one can say with Fr. Bouyer: "The faith that saves, in all of us, will never be anything other than a communication in what Mary's faith was on Calvary. And Calvary itself will be redemptive for our humanity because, from the time of Calvary, our humanity in Mary believed that we are reborn in Jesus's death, because we are reborn as sons of God by being reborn as sons of Mary in it."[77] This is the profound and true meaning of this classical (though often so poorly interpreted) formula that says that Mary is our mediatrix next to the mediator. We will encounter it soon enough below.[78]

D. Mary's Merit and the Redemption of Men

{524} It is clear that this act by which Mary accepted and offered her sufferings next to the cross was greatly meritorious, to the mea-

---

76. Bur, *Médiation mariale*, 497.
77. See Bouyer, *Le trône de la sagesse*, 244.
78. See §537 below.

sure of her charity. If one admits that these sufferings contributed to the very act of our redemption, one must also admit that her merit, united to that of Christ, contributed to our salvation. Great debates have arisen among mariologists regarding the nature of this merit. It is neither possible nor very useful to take them up here. Let us only say that it cannot be conceived as completing Christ's merit in any way, as though it added something to it. Here again, we must recall that Mary's holiness is first of all the fruit of Christ's merit. Therefore, it is a question of a merit that presupposes Christ's infinitely sufficient merit, far from being something added to it.

Therefore, this cannot be a merit *de condigno*, that is, a merit that by itself would suffice for obtaining for men the grace of salvation from God. It can be only a merit *de congruo*, that is, a merit that is a reason for the granting of a prayer, according to the expression of St. Thomas: "Indeed, if man constituted in grace acts in accord with God's will, it is fitting according to the proportion proper to friendship that God would act in accord with man's will by saving the other person for whom he prays."[79] As for her participation in Christ's redemptive sacrifice, it is therefore a question of the eminent realization, in Mary, of an effect of grace in general, though also a unique realization of this effect, for although this merit is only *de congruo*, it has the unique characteristic of having the salvation of mankind for its object, not the salvation of one or of some individuals.

IV. THE GLORIOUS CONSUMMATION OF CHRIST'S PRIESTHOOD

{525} Here, we ask ourselves simply what becomes of Christ's "priesthood" in glory. Traditionally, it is said that He is a "priest for eternity." What does this expression intend to express? According to St. Thomas, given that the priestly activity by its nature is an activity of *viatores*, it has no *raison d'être in patria*, at least after the redeemed

---

79. *ST* I-II, q. 114, a. 6.

people, following Christ and in virtue of His sacrifice, come to enter into the true "holy of holies," that is, into the glory of the Trinity. Christ's priesthood will henceforth endure in its effects and in Christ, inasmuch as He will Himself remain the cause of these effects.[80]

After him, an entire school of theology was formed, which again had important representatives, according to whom Christ in glory does not cease and will not cease to offer to the Father the sacrifice of Himself made once upon a time on Calvary. Here, we find ourselves faced with the theory of the heavenly sacrifice, which will be considered later in relation to the Eucharistic sacrifice. However, sacrifice is the eminent act of the virtue of religion by which man, on the way toward God (and therefore still distant from Him, and moreover, though in a different manner, distanced by sin) comes back to God so that he may arrive, in the end, at complete union. According to St. Augustine's famed words: "Therefore, sacrifice is the complete work that contributes to uniting us to God in a holy society, that is, the entire work referred to this end, the only good by which we can be truly happy."[81]

The sacrifice of Calvary is the work by which Christ reconciled humanity with God, gathering it from all the places where it was dispersed in the region of dissimilitude. Having accomplished this work, "He entered once for all into the Holy Place, taking not the blood of goats and calves but His own blood, thus securing an eternal redemption."[82] The redemption having been obtained and the work of reconciliation having been achieved, it is not clear what foundation there could be for the idea that Christ must ceaselessly offer His sacrifice, as though the Father had not fully accepted it: "For by a single offering He has perfected for all time those who are sanctified."[83]

It is sometimes asked: What name do you give to this act by

---

80. See *ST* III, q. 22, a. 5.
81. Augustine, *La Cité de Dieu*, Oeuvres de Saint Augustin 34:444.
82. Heb 9:12 (RSV).
83. Heb 10:14 (RSV). [Tr. note: Fr. Nicolas incorrectly cites 9:14.]

which the Incarnate and glorified Son does not cease to give Himself to the Father if you do not wish to call it a "sacrifice"? However, this self-gift is included in charity and is not distinct from it. In the act of loving, there is a gift of self, and if this love is total, engaging one to one's depths, without any part of the person being held back—as was the case for Jesus Christ from the first moment of His earthly existence and as is the case for each of the elect when he has arrived at full union with the Trinity—there is also a complete self-gift. The role of sacrifice is to be the means by which charity, inspiring the virtue of religion (which has sacrifice as its principal external act), strives to realize union with God, bearing in itself the very aspiration and desire for such union. Its place is located in the "in-between state" that is the state of the *viator*: this passage between the sketched and tendential union with God that charity assures by itself and the fully realized union with God in which it finds the terminus of its movement. Certainly, the virtue of religion does not cease to be active when union with God is fully realized. The elect in heaven do not cease to praise the Trinity and to bless Him. However, this does not make them closer to Him, nor do they thus return to Him. Rather, they are in Him, they belong to Him, they live in this "holy society" toward which they advanced through their external acts of the virtue of religion, as well as by the acts of all the virtues, when they were still on the road toward beatitude.

In what concerns Christ, however, although His priestly activity does not aim at bringing Him closer to the Father, from whom He has never been distant, we nonetheless must distinguish two stages in this activity, the second of which comes after His glorification. The first and essential stage was the sacrifice of Calvary, and it found its consummation in Christ's resurrection and glorification. The second is pursued throughout the entire "time of the Church" and consists in believers' participation in Christ's sacrifice and resurrection through faith and the sacraments. Here again, Christ the priest is the one who principally acts, applying His sacrifice to men, though by means of the Church, as we will see in the third volume of this work. Moreover, according to the words of the Letter to the Hebrews, "always living to intercede in favor" (for those who advance toward God through Him), He prays to the Father for the pilgrim Church. However, when the Church's earthly pilgrimage is brought to fulfillment, there will no longer be anything to ask for her. All that will now be needed is that her praise and benediction be brought forth and conveyed to the heart of the Trinity. This will no longer be a priestly activity, for she will be one with Him, the "Whole Christ." This is why St. Thomas says that if Christ's priesthood is eternal, this is because the goods that it procures are eternal. Its exercise is what exists in time.[84]

---

84. See *ST* III, q. 22, a. 5.

10

The Mediator

{526} In general, a mediator is a person whose role is to reunite separated persons (and who indeed has the power to do so). To say, with Scripture[1] and with the whole of tradition, that Christ is the universal and sole mediator between man and God is to express formulaically the fundamental truth of salvation history proclaimed by Peter at the beginning of the apostolic ministry, a truth that is a constitutive element of the kerygma: "And there is salvation in no one else, for there is no other name under heaven given among men by which we must be saved."[2] This also means that this term, "mediator," expresses and sums up what Jesus Christ is for God and man. Certainly, the ultimate explanation of the Incarnation is God's love, His propensity to give Himself, His *hesed*. However, the mediator, He in whom He can give of Himself, is precisely what God has given to man through this communication.

I. THE INCARNATE WORD'S MEDIATING ROLE

A. The "Minister of Reconciliation"

{527} At the starting point for the work of salvation, there stands man's sin, man separated from God by sin. Christ came to reconcile

---

1. See 1 Tm 2:5.
2. Acts 4:12 (RSV).

man with God, or rather: "God was reconciling the world to Himself."³ What is certain is that "through Him we (Jews and Pagans) both have access in one Spirit to the Father."⁴ The same sin that separates man from God introduces separation between men, for the essential, profound, and principal unifier for all men is their common ordination to God, an ordination that sin disturbs and paralyzes without wholly abolishing it. Also, Christ's role as mediator at the same time involves "[gathering] into one the children of God who are scattered abroad."⁵

B. The Joining of the Creature to the Creator

{528} Even independent of sin, there is a radical separation between man and God on account of God's perfect transcendence. Certainly, creation represents a kind of crossing of this distance by God Himself. Through creation, He is immanent to His creature, present at its depths. However, He remains the wholly Other. Even the spiritual creature is infinitely distant from Him, of itself incapable of entering into a communion of life with Him. From the start, God also wished to fill in this distance by the gift of grace, divinization. The personal meeting between the creature and the Creator is brought about in that grace. It is a permanent meeting, communion, eternal life.

Now, was a mediator necessary for this encounter to take place? When it is posed in this way, the question in reality is the same as that concerning the necessity of the Incarnation: given the Creator's design, which not only involves bringing spiritual creatures into existence but also involves their elevation to a participation in His life, was the Incarnation necessary? Without a doubt, we must respond negatively, for God undergoes no external necessity. What He did through the mediator could have been done without Him. What is certain, however, is that the mediator does indeed exist: Jesus Christ,

---

3. See 2 Cor 5:19 (RSV).
4. Eph 2:18 (RSV).
5. Jn 11:52 (RSV).

the Incarnate Word. Hence, His mediation cannot solely consist in reconciling sinful man with God. It is through Him and in Him that the spiritual creature's personal encounter with the Divine Persons is brought about, an encounter which quite precisely is salvation, divinization, and eternal life.

C. The Man-Jesus, Mediator on Account of the Hypostatic Union

{529} It is tempting to think that the Word is a mediator through His very divinity, inasmuch as He is God. Note, however, that in this case the Incarnation would become useless (if its ultimate *raison d'être* truly is mediation, while the Word would be a mediator without the Incarnation). In reality, the Word in the Trinity cannot be a mediator. On the one hand, He is One God with the Father and the Spirit and therefore is completely "next to God." On the other hand and for the same reason, He is transcendent in relation to man, by the very transcendence of God.

In order to be a mediator, it was necessary that He become a true man, though without ceasing to be God. There, once again, is the whole mystery of the Incarnation. A true man, who partakes in the being and conditions of men, including the wretched conditions of sin—though without partaking in sin itself, for sin separates from God and the mediator must be united to each of the two termini being united—yet without ceasing to partake in the Trinitarian life.

However, in order to understand this sufficiently, one must not stop at the distinction and union of the two natures, stating: by His human nature the Word partook in the condition of men, and by His Divine Nature in the divine condition. For it is in some way through the two parts of Himself that the "composite person" would touch the divinity and humanity together, without, however, joining them. As we have seen, Jesus's humanity is full of grace and "divinized" only on account of the Hypostatic Union, all the while remaining plunged into the wretched condition suffered by men. "Jesus's humanity," therefore, is the Word inasmuch as He is a human person.

Thus, the Man-Jesus is the one who is a mediator. As we have seen, inasmuch as He is a man, He submitted Himself to the Father and to the whole Trinity, while nonetheless being profoundly united to it by the communication of grace. Inasmuch as this man is and remains the Son of God, He is the head and king of humanity, while nonetheless being profoundly united to all men, both by the shared human nature ("consubstantial to us according to humanity") and by the shared condition coming from sin.

From the first moment of the Incarnation, the perfect (and definitive) meeting of sinful man (snatched from his sin) with God is established in Him. Indeed, He Himself is a man (not a sinner, but "one who is penitent"), containing all men in Him, and simultaneously is God, partaking in the Trinitarian life, not only through His Divine Nature but also in His humanity which is divinized to the highest degree by grace. In short, what constitutes Him as the mediator is indeed the grace of union, though inasmuch as divinizing grace results from it in His human spirit.

Here, the Virgin's essential role in salvation history is clear. It is through her that the Word was born of the race of Adam in order that He may become man, thereby taking part in humanity in its reality, in humanity separated from God. And, in this way, the latter can rejoin God in Him.

II. THE MEDIATING OFFICES OF THE INCARNATE WORD

If men come back to God *in Him*, it is again necessary that they come back to Him *through Him*, so that each man, personally, may take part in this encounter. A born mediator, He accomplished the mediating offices on earth and, indeed, does not cease to do so.

A. The Reconciliatory Office

{530} We have seen how by His death and resurrection He has reconciled the world with God. We need not revisit this here.

B. Revelatory Office

{531} We have insisted on this aspect of the Incarnation: the Second Person of the Trinity, who became incarnate, is the Word, He in whom the knowledge of God is expressed. By His hypostatic existence, He is the "Revealer." This does not mean that revelation would be necessary, as the procession of the Word is necessary. Rather, it means that if God freely wills to reveal Himself, it belongs to the Word to be the revealer.[6] He is the "true light that enlightens every man [who] was coming into the world,"[7] and "in many and various ways God spoke of old to our fathers by the prophets; but in these last days God has spoken to us by a Son ... [who] reflects the glory of God and bears the very stamp of his nature, upholding the universe by his word of power."[8]

We have seen[9] that Christ exercised His revealing function on the basis of the immediate vision which was a participation in His divine knowledge within His created mind: "No one has ever seen God; the only Son, who is in the bosom of the Father, He has made Him known."[10] The revealing mediation had Jesus's human speech as its instrument, which immediately expressed His human knowledge. However, this latter, itself in touch with the immediate vision of the Divine Essence, was the expression of the unique and infinite divine Word in concepts and in human images, in a host of particular truths. This breathtaking transmutation of the transcendent Divine Truth into particular, partial human truths was brought about in Jesus's human mind, and this is what revelation is. It is also through Jesus's mind that our faith knowledge, founded on the apostolic preaching that transmitted Jesus's teaching to the world, really rejoins the transcendent Divine Truth and therefore His Being. We humanly know God such as He is in His transcendent divinity.

---

6. See §230 in the first volume of this text.
7. Jn 1:9 (RSV). [Tr. note: Fr. Nicolas incorrectly cites Jn 1:29.]
8. Heb 1:1–3 (RSV).
9. See §355 above.
10. Jn 1:18 (RSV).

This is what Jesus Christ's revealing mediation consists in.[11]

Now, revelation culminates in the Beatific Vision, where God is unveiled in full light. Every revelation tends toward this, finding its fulfillment and terminus there. Must we say that Christ continues His mediating function at this terminus? Or, on the contrary, must we say that it is effaced at this moment? The Catholic Church teaches as a matter of faith, basing herself on St. Paul and on St. John, that the elect in the hereafter immediately see the divine face, that is, God in three Persons, the Persons in the Essence, the Essence in the Persons. However, this in no way precludes the continuation of Jesus Christ's revealing function in eternity. Indeed, we have seen that face-to-face vision is rendered possible and realized only through this supreme gift of grace that is the "light of glory." The latter is called a "light" because the Trinity is rendered "visible for man's mind" by it. However, it is not an objective light which would illuminate the object and make it visible (for the Trinity, by itself, is pure light). Rather, it is a subjective light which makes the created mind capable of seeing what it did not see, not because that thing was obscure but, on the contrary, because it was too purely luminous. The ultimate source of this light obviously is God Himself ("God makes Himself seen"). However, the immediate source is the created mind [*esprit*] of Jesus himself, enriched with a light of glory which has a singular elevation and intensity. Thus, whereas the Orthodox seem to understand Jesus's mediation in the vision of the elect as being an objective mediation (holding that the elect would see the Divine Nature in the resplendence of Jesus's face), Latins, without in the least denying this mediation, situate it in the subjective order. According to them, the elect immediately see God, but the gift of grace in virtue of which they can see God derives in them from Jesus Christ. Therefore, it is truly in Him that they see the Trinity.[12]

---

11. On the revealing mission of the Incarnate Word according to St. John, see Ignace de La Potterie, *La vérité dans Saint Jean*, vols. 1–2 (Rome: Biblical Institute Press, 1977).

12. See §174 in the previous volume.

C. Priestly Office

{532} We spoke about this above. It consists in offering men to God and in conferring to men the grace in which God is given to them as Persons. It is continuous, ascending and descending, back-and-forth, like Jacob's ladder. In reality, it is first descending, for the Trinity already gives Itself to man in Jesus Christ, sent by the Father, and offers Itself to all men. Then, the ascending movement occurs: the return of the sinful man to God in Christ. Setting out from there anew, there is a descending movement: the resurrection of Christ and, through it, the communication of the grace of the remission of sins and divinization to all believers. In response to this, a new movement ascends upward: thanksgiving, imploring the gift of other graces, and so forth. All of this back-and-forth descending and ascending is accomplished in the composite person of Jesus Christ. Men partake in it as belonging to Jesus Christ and by being included in Him.

We have seen in what sense one can say (and, in my opinion, in what sense one cannot say), that the priestly function of Christ remains in eternity. The solution is similar to what we have said for the revealing function. The grace of divinization, which blossoms forth into the "light of glory," was merited by Christ's priestly activity on earth and given to all believers by the glorious Christ. The elect now continue to derive it from Christ's grace, though not as the effect of a new priestly action which would be a continuous offering of the sacrifice accomplished once and for all. Moreover, this ceaseless thanksgiving by the elect in heaven obviously passes through Christ. With Him they constitute the "whole Christ."

III. SECONDARY MEDIATIONS

{533} Christ is the sole mediator. Does this also mean that man must be purely passive in this twofold ascending and descending movement of mediation? If it is a question of drawing close to God, will we not need to conceive of his action as though it were added to Christ's? Consequently, will it not be the case that he himself is a mediator for himself and for others, someone whose mediation would be added to Christ's? Here, we find ourselves faced with a dilemma whose solution is vital for our understanding of the salvation brought about by Christ.

A. The Notion of Subordinate Mediation

{534} On this topic, St. Thomas writes: "However, nothing prevents it from being the case that some others (i.e., those who are not Christ) would be called mediators in certain respects inasmuch as they cooperate in the union of God and of men in a dispositive and ministerial fashion."[13] And he further specifies: "The priests of the new law can be called mediators between God and men because they are ministers of the true mediator and because in His name they confer the sacraments of salvation to men."[14]

Christ's unique and universal mediation allows for secondary mediations: *not by way of substitution*, for nothing can substitute for Christ's mediation, which is universal and necessary (in the real economy of salvation); *not by way of complement*, as though Christ's unique mediation were insufficient for reconciling man with God and stood in need of completion (in reality, far from completing Christ's mediation, all the other mediations rely on it and draw their value from it); but, rather, *by way of being a service*. Christ's mediation uses secondary mediations *so that it may be exercised*. This is not because His unique mediation is incapable of producing its effect on its own but, instead, is due to His mercy, so that He may enable the redeemed to really participate in the work of salvation. By His mediation, Christ not only saves men but also enables them to act for their own salvation and to aid in the salvation of others.

---

13. *ST* III, q. 26, a. 1.
14. See ibid., ad 1.

B. VARIOUS SUBORDINATED MEDIATIONS

1. Elementary mediation

{535} "Elementary mediation" is that of each person's freedom. Christ's grace is not substituted for the freedom of the person on whom it is exercised but, instead, makes him freely turn away from sin, convert to God, and choose and then realize the works of righteousness: "For just as you once yielded your members to impurity and to greater and greater iniquity, so now yield your members to righteousness for sanctification. When you were slaves of sin, you were free in regard to righteousness."[15]

Already at the moment of conversion, at baptism, the adult is not passively justified. He cooperates in his justification by the act of conversion. This is even truer in penance, where his own acts are the matter of the sacrament. Then, under the action of grace, he performs acts that merit eternal life. The merit of the just person does not add its efficacy to the efficacy of Christ's merits because, on the contrary, Christ is the one who merits for him the grace of meriting.[16]

Moreover, one can say that the believer is *simul justus et peccator* in a true sense. He is righteous in one respect and unrighteous in another. The ungodly man is already virtually righteous inasmuch as he is already in Christ in whom reconciliation is accomplished. The righteous man on the earth is still a sinner inasmuch as he still is partially under the sway of sin. Thus, we can say that the same man, inasmuch as he is righteous and under Christ's action, brings back to God his own sinful being, turning himself away from sin.

{536} This elementary mediation, exercised by each person in relation to himself by accepting Christ's mediation through faith and allowing it to be exercised in him, can also be performed for the sake of another person's salvation—not, certainly, by meriting, properly speaking, the grace that alone can save him but, instead, by interceding for him and by substituting oneself for him in some way,

---

15. Rom 6:19–20 (RSV).
16. See §413 above.

through the unitive virtue of charity which makes such a mediator one in Christ with the person whom he loves. We have already cited this expression of St. Thomas: "If someone fulfills God's will, it is fitting, according to the laws of friendship (which is above every law) that God fulfill his desire by according him the salvation of that other person."[17]

This is how this circulation of grace is established in the Mystical Body, thus assuring the vital unity of the body and the communion of all in love, a circulation finding its fountainhead in the source of grace, Jesus Christ, the head of the Mystical Body, though then putting to work the participation of his members. And when such members are spoken of, one must think also of the men who do not yet belong to the Mystical Body but have their place marked out within it because Christ died for all and because all are called.[18]

Here again, this mediation does not add anything to Christ's mediation. On the contrary, the latter provides the former with its efficacy. It serves Him, and it is Christ's mediation that is exercised by it. Nonetheless, it is not superfluous, and what eminently holds for the case of Christ's prayer,[19] also holds, in its own measure, for the prayer of the person who prays with Him and through Him. That is, the grace bestowed upon a member is indeed the fruit of another's prayer, without, for all that, that other person's prayer being a principle differing from God's merciful will and Jesus Christ's redemptive willing. By summoning believers to pray for one another and also to pray for those who do not believe, and by bestowing upon their prayer, through a pure act of mercy, a power that it could not have by itself, God has willed to elevate His creature to the dignity of being a cause in the supernatural order as well, one that is subordinate but real, thereby causing the communication of the gift of His life, His beatitude, which He wishes to grant to all.

---

17. *ST* I-II, q. 114, a. 6. [Tr. note: Fr. Nicolas incorrectly cites a non-existent a. 16.]
18. See *ST* III, q. 8, a. 3.
19. See §513 above.

2. The Church's mediation

{537} The Church's mediation, about which we will speak at length in the third volume of this work, first of all includes all of these particular mediating activities exercised by each person for himself and for others—all of them together, though much more than their mere sum. This is so because the communion established among all the members of the Church through charity constitutes a personality which exceeds (while embracing) all the particular personalities gathered therein, and in this personality, each person, far from losing himself, is exalted.[20] Thus, the Church is the one who, by her members and by their grace-filled activity (i.e., their activity inspired by charity), assures in a communitarian fashion the mediation that we have spoken of, in the service of Christ's mediation.

This does not mean that it would not simultaneously be individual, for each person exercises it with his mind, his heart, his body as well, and with his grace. However, in each person, this mediating activity is mixed with sentiments that are not purely charitable. It is weak and troubled. All of these forms of dross fall into the Church's communion, and if each person, by his individual mediation, takes part in the Church's own mediation, this part finds itself purified, valorized, and exalted. In short, the mediation that each person must exercise for oneself and for one's neighbor takes on its value as concurring with the Church's mediation. And the latter can be considered and called a mediation next to the divine mediator—not as though Christ would not be immediately in contact with the men whom He saves (for He is the mediator by His Spirit whom He sends to them and who conforms and unites them to Him) but, rather, as meaning that Christ saves men in and by the Church, thus making them members of Christ by becoming members of the Church. The latter, as we will see in due time, is the place of grace, the place where it is given as well as the place wherein the life having it as its principle unfolds.

20. See the first section of the next volume.

However, this mediation by the Church also takes on other forms that are proper to her. In order to communicate the fruits of His redemption to men, Christ makes use of the Church in her pilgrim and earthly realization. Through her, He continues to give the world His word which illuminates and purifies, to communicate His grace in the sacraments, and to direct His people toward eternal life. Certainly and obviously, these mediating activities exercised by the Church are performed by the men who are her members. But here, although they apply, indeed must apply, their personalities' resources of nature and grace in her, it is in the name of the Church that they act, as representatives of her All of this will be examined at length in its proper place.

3. Mary's mediation

{538} Mary's[21] mediation must be understood and situated within the framework of the Church's mediation. We will see the impulse and simultaneous purification that the parallelism of Mary and the Church brings to Mariology, a parallelism which was seen very early in the Church's life and which has received renewed appreciation of late. They mutually envelop one another and are illuminated by one another. In what concerns mediation, it is in no way a question of giving the Virgin a role in what we have called properly ecclesial mediation. First of all, such mediation is exercised only in and by the pilgrim Church, and therefore is not concerned with the members of Christ who have passed into the Church *in patria*. (In the case of Christ Himself, He exercises such mediation because He is rendered present and active in the continued work of saving the world through the pilgrim and earthly Church.) However, we will also see that, even during the time when Mary still lived upon earth, she did not participate in this mediating activity. Therefore, it is a question of the mediation that Mary exercises (both throughout the last peri-

---

21. See *Études Mariales* [(Paris: Société Francaise d'Études Mariales,) 1961–63]; *La maternité spirituelle de Marie, Actes du VIIIe congrès marial national, Lisieux 5–9 July 1961* (Paris: Lethielleux, 1962); and Jean-Hervé Nicolas, "Compte-rendu du livre de Febrer M., El concepto de persona y la union hipostatica," *Revue thomiste* 55 (1955): 186–88.

od of her earthly existence, as well as in her current existence in definitive union with the Trinity) through her spiritual action, essentially through her prayer for men—both in her prayer *on their behalf* (descending mediation) and in her prayer in *substitution before God* (ascending mediation).

Mary exists at the heart of the Church.[22] If in this communion of persons that is the Church, each person acts not only for himself—in order to grow in grace and to act according to grace—but also for the others, Mary's mediation has an exceptional character from the fact that, by standing in the place of all humanity at the moment of this sacrifice, she participated in the redemptive sacrifice whence comes the whole of grace.[23] For this reason, her mediation is universal. By her intercession, she participates in Christ's communication of all grace (and not only of particular graces) to the Church. And this intercession is totalizing. That is, her thanksgiving and blessing gather together and unify all thanksgivings, all benedictions, and all the praises of all the other members of the Church, integrating them into a movement toward God which is that of the whole Church personalized in her.

{539} Will it be said that this universality and totality of Marian mediations are an object of faith? We must always be prudent when it is a question of saying that something must be believed, and the Church alone can make such a declaration in the end. Up to the present day, she has not spoken of the universal Marian mediation, and it is unlikely, indeed probably not desirable, that she one day declare it [through an act of extraordinary Magisterial action]. She has made it the object of her ordinary teaching, and this justifies the theologian in striving to establish it. What is of first importance in this effort is to assure that Mary's mediation does not infringe on Christ's unique mediation. Without the latter, the idea of her own universal mediation would not be acceptable. However, if she adds nothing to Christ's mediation, is it not vain and pointless?

22. See Journet, *L'Église du Verbe incarné*, 2:382–453.
23. See §523 above.

God needs no instrument, no intermediary, in order to pardon His creature's sins, in order to divinize it and make it enter into the Trinitarian life. No creature can cooperate with Him without that creature having been aroused by a grace which fully comes from God Himself, who calls this creature to this action, thus providing the means for this service. However, God does nothing artificial, and when He enables a creature to serve Him, He enables it to render an authentic service that becomes indispensable in the order of things freely instituted by Him. Indeed, it is a gift of grace to be thus rendered really necessary for the communication of grace to others—a gift of grace that, as a principle of created mediations, itself has its principle in Christ's mediation to which all the others, as a result, are subordinated.

Thus, Mary's mediation was not necessary for Christ so that He may save the world—no more than the mediation of the Church herself was necessary for this. However, He really made her a mediatrix so that her mediation has become indispensable for men in the economy of salvation that He willed and realized. Understood in this way, Marian mediation can be recognized together with the unrestricted profession of Christ's unique mediation.

PART 4

CHRIST'S RETURN IN GLORY

{540} The *eschata* are the "last events" of salvation history. Eschatology is the part of theology that, in the light of what is said in Scripture and the Church's tradition, strives to reflect on these events in order to understand them better, doubtlessly, but also and above all, in order to come to understand salvation history, which finds its ultimate fulfillment in them.

"Classical theology" is commonly reproached for having neglected eschatology.[1] However, Max Seckler has shown that, at least in what concerns St. Thomas's thought, this reproach is unfounded.[2] "Classical theology" is, in fact, quite occupied with the "last things," though perhaps in a non-eschatological manner. As Congar remarked, it provides a kind of physics of the last things.[3] That is, it reflects on the *eschata* more as a determination of what must happen than as something giving meaning and an orientation to the Church's life today. Vatican II placed this essential dimension of the Church in relief:

The Church, to which we are all called in Christ Jesus, and in which we acquire holiness through the grace of God, will attain its full perfection only

---

1. See Hans Urs von Balthasar, "Eschatologie," in *Questions théologiques aujourd'hui* (Paris: Desclée de Brouwer, 1963), 2:269–97; Karl Rahner, "Eschatologie," in *Lexikon für Theologie und Kirche* (2nd ed.), 3:1094–96.
2. See Seckler, *Le salut et l'histoire*, 12–13.
3. See Congar, *Sainte Eglise*, 601.

in the glory of heaven, when there will come the time of the restoration of all things (Acts 3:1). At that time the human race as well as the entire world, which is intimately related to man and attains to its end through him, will be perfectly reestablished in Christ (cf. Eph. 1:10; Col. 1:20; 2 Pet. 3:10–13).[4]

Coming forth from the eternal Father's love, founded in time by Christ the Redeemer and made one in the Holy Spirit, the Church has a saving and an eschatological purpose which can be fully attained only in the future world.[5]

"Classical theology" is also reproached for having considered the "last things" nearly exclusively from the perspective of our individual destiny. This reproach is also founded. However, as we will see, one must not fall into the reverse excess and overlook the personal aspect of eschatology. The communion of believers is only realized in persons, and its consummation will also be the fulfillment of personal destinies. Without this, eschatology would become unreal. Vatican II in no way passed over this aspect of eschatology in silence, an aspect that is also essential:

For before we reign with Christ in glory, all of us will be made manifest "before the tribunal of Christ, so that each one may receive what he has won through the body, according to his works, whether good or evil" (2 Cor. 5:10) and at the end of the world "they who have done good shall come forth unto resurrection of life; but those who have done evil unto resurrection of judgment" (Jn. 5:29; cf. Mt. 25:46).[6]

Therefore, we will successively study: eschatology from the universal point of view, intermediary eschatology, and eschatology from the personal point of view.[7]

---

4. *Lumen Gentium*, no. 48.
5. *Gaudium et Spes*, no. 40.
6. *Lumen Gentium*, no. 48.
7. See an organized bibliography in Michel Dupuy, *Bérulle et le sacerdoce* (Paris: Lethielleux, 1969). Von Balthasar, "Eschatologie"; Jean Galot, "Eschatologie," in *Dictionnaire de spiritualité ascétique et mystique*, 4:1020–59; Journet, *L'Église du Verbe incarné*, vol. 3, ch. 3; P. Molinari, "Caractère eschatologique de l'Église pérégrinante et ses rapports avec l'Église céleste," in *Augustinus Magister, Congrès international augustinien, Paris, 21–24 September 1954, Communications. Études augustiniennes* (Paris, 1954), 3:1193–1208; Donatien Mollat, "Jugement," in *Dictionnaire de la Bible*, 4:1321–94; Cándido Pozo, *Teología del más allá* (Madrid: BAC, 1968); and Rahner, "Eschatologie," 1083–98.

11

Christ's Return

I. THE ESCHATOLOGY OF THE NEW TESTAMENT

{541} What characterizes the New Testament's eschatology in relation to that of Israel before Christ is that in the New Testament, the "day of the Lord," the eschatological event, has already arrived with the Pascha of Jesus (His passion, death, and Resurrection).[1] This remains the sure insight for explaining what is essential to Christian eschatology in its New Testament sources. Jesus's words, as they are reported to us by the Gospels, which seem to announce the Parousia as being imminent (whether during His lifetime, or soon after His death), have given rise to various theories.[2] From the Catholic perspective, one cannot accept an explanation, like that of Cullmann himself,[3] which presupposes that Jesus would have been deceived and therefore would not have foreseen the "time of the Church," much less its duration. On such a hypothesis, the Church, such as it is, would not have been founded by Christ but would have somehow

---

1. See Cullmann, *Christ et le temps*, 59–61; André Robert and André Feuillet, *Introduction à la Bible* (Paris: Desclée de Brouwer, 1959), 776–84. [Tr. note: Fr. Nicolas also cites "Mollat, op. cit., p. 650 note i," which would presumably refer to Mollat, "Jugement," 4:1321–94. This does not make sense from the perspective of pagination. There are no entries in the bibliography that appear to be candidates for this pagination.]

2. See Oscar Cullmann, *Le salut dans l'histoire. L'existence chrétienne selon le Nouveau Testament* (Neuchâtel, 1966), 23–58; Mollat, "Jugement," 1353–54.

3. See Cullmann, *Le salut dans l'histoire*, 196–210.

been organized for the sake of filling the void left by His departure.

These various explanations abusively privilege certain New Testament texts to the detriment of others. Yes, the kingdom of God is presented as being imminent, but Jesus refuses to satisfy the curiosity of the apostles concerning the hour and the day of His return. The apostles organize the Church's life as though it is to last indefinitely (that is, without a definite endpoint). Jesus promises His presence to the apostles "to the close of the age."[4] He entrusts His Church to Peter, giving him true authority over her (the power to bind and unbind), here again without a temporal limitation.[5] Even if it seems that the apostles and first Christians believed that Christ's return would take place during their earthly life, this is not asserted in any way. On the contrary, we can see that they admitted, in a kind of second step, that this would only happen later on, that is, in a future that is wholly undetermined.[6]

The true reconciliation is found in the tension between the "already" and the "not yet" characterizing the Church's life.[7] Thus, the kingdom of God is already here, in our midst. (It was already here when Christ lived on earth, and this presence is continued by the Church, which is his body.) However, at the same time, it is to come. Christ's return is announced for an undetermined day, which will be the Day of Judgment and also the day of the resurrection.[8] St. John's phrase is first of all holds true for the Church: "It does not yet appear what we shall be."[9] Jesus told the apostles about the persecutions they would suffer while fulfilling their mission, while simultaneously promising them His presence, that of the Holy Spirit. St. Paul emphasizes this paradox of the Christian life in the most gripping manner. In the Letter to the Romans, he marks out the necessity of participat-

---

4. Mt 28:20 (RSV).
5. Mt 16:18–20; Jn 21:15–19.
6. See Jn 21:23, 2 Cor 5:1–10, Phil 1:19–26.
7. This famed formula is owed to Oscar Cullmann.
8. Mt 24:37–50, 25:13, 26:29; Lk 17:24; Jn 6:40, 44, 54; Rom 2:5–16, 13:12; 1 Cor 1:8; 2 Cor 2:14; 1 Thes 5:2, 4; etc.
9. 1 Jn 3:2 (RSV).

ing in Christ's death, in His crucifixion, first by baptism, then through the new life [lived by Christians],[10] and by means of this, promises participation in His resurrection: "For if we have been united with Him in a death like His, we shall certainly be united with Him in a resurrection like His,"[11] and "if children, then heirs, heirs of God and fellow heirs with Christ, provided we suffer with Him in order that we may also be glorified with Him."[12] He presents us with the entire creation waiting to partake in the freedom and glory of the children of God, and the latter themselves also are presented as awaiting their deliverance in the future: "For in this hope we were saved."[13] And note too that in his later letters, he presents this promise as being already realized in the very midst of one's trials and in conditions appearing to be forms of servitude: "and you were buried with Him in baptism, in which you were also raised with Him through faith in the working of God, who raised Him from the dead";[14] "But God, who is rich in mercy, out of the great love with which He loved us, even when we were dead through our trespasses, made us alive together with Christ (by grace you have been saved), and raised us up with Him, and made us sit with Him in the heavenly places in Christ Jesus."[15]

The meaning of this mysterious design of Providence is clearly marked out: for the believer (and therefore for the community of believers that is the Church up to the end of time) it is a question of first being crucified with Christ before participating in His glory. The mysterious words, "Was it not necessary that the Christ should suffer these things and enter into His glory,"[16] also apply to the Church. But as she is the body of Christ, she already mysteriously participates in the life that He received at the resurrection and in

---

10. Rom 6 and 8.
11. Rom 6:5 (RSV).
12. Rom 8:17 (RSV).
13. Rom 8:24 (RSV).
14. Col 2:12 (RSV). [Tr. note: Fr. Nicolas incorrectly cites Phil 2:12.]
15. Eph 4:4–6 (RSV).
16. Lk 24:26 (RSV).

the glory with which His Father glorified Him "with the glory which I had with thee before the world was made; Father, I desire that they also, whom thou hast given me, may be with me where I am, to behold my glory which thou hast given me in thy love for me before the foundation of the world."[17]

In this way, the "day of the Lord" announced by the whole Bible is indeed essentially the day of Jesus's resurrection, which inaugurates the messianic times. However, all the glory and triumph of this day in what concerns the Church remains hidden under the temporal reality of suffering, hesitations, sins, and all the transgressions of her members, in faith:

> It seemed certain that at the moment when the Kingdom of heaven would come to touch the earth, it would immediately burst the fragile envelope of time, dissipate sorrow, cast out death, renew all things, and transfigure the universe. Indeed, should it descend for anything other than this? But, behold, on the contrary, that its power is covered with signs of weakness and its grandeur with signs of humility. Behold that its eternity slips silently under the unchanged outer bark of time. Behold that its felicity is immersed in the very ocean of our trials. It was made so as to disperse suffering, temptations, and death, and behold that it chooses to live in the midst of them so as to tame them, seeking not—alas!—to eliminate them but only to illuminate them. The law of its radiation ought to be a law of glorious transfiguration and behold that it wishes to be first of all and for long centuries only a law of sorrowful sanctification. We expected it in its radiance as the heavenly kingdom, and behold: it has come to us with the traits of a pilgrim and crucified kingdom.[18]

Thus, the "day of the Lord" is broken down into two series of temporal events that are separate but so intimately connected that the second are already pre-contained in the first and will only make manifest what was hidden in them: the events of the first coming of Christ (His birth, life, passion, death, resurrection) and the final events, those of the second coming of Christ in glory, which He announced before the full Sanhedrin at the moment when He had

---

17. Jn 17:5 and 24 (RSV). [Tr. note: Fr. Nicolas incorrectly cites 17:4 instead of 17:5.]
18. Journet, *L'Église du Verbe incarné*, 3:625.

been judged: "You have said so (that I am the Messiah, the Son of God). But I tell you, hereafter you will see the Son of man seated at the right hand of Power, and coming on the clouds of heaven."[19] This is the Parousia, which must mark the end of time, the fulfillment of the redemption by the resurrection of the dead, the judgment, and the dazzling manifestation of the kingdom of God (with the exclusion of those who refused it while on earth).[20]

II. ESCHATOLOGY AND SALVATION HISTORY

The "eschata" are not only the events that will come at the end of time. They are the terminus of a development having arrived at its fulfillment. They are not only the terminus of salvation history but also are the end toward which salvation history tends, in which all the promises that have put it into motion and do not cease to bear it toward its consummation are definitively realized. That is, the salvation brought about by Jesus Christ is essentially historical. But how should we understand this?

A. The Historicity of Salvation

{542} To say that a given reality is "essentially historical" is to say, *first*, that it has an ontological structure (an "essence") that is fixed and immutable in itself, while nonetheless being submitted to development (therefore to movement), such that it remains the same ("essentially") all the while changing (existentially)—for example, a living being, whose law of development is inscribed in its essence. *Second*, that it has a "past" (that is, its present state is the end point of an earlier development); and that it has a future (that is, this present state itself is pregnant with further development and "becoming"). And *third*, that this process of becoming itself has a terminus, beyond which it is no longer a historical reality, for this terminus is the complete realization of the so-called historical being, of the be-

---

19. Mt 26:64 (RSV).
20. See Lk 12:9.

ing in development. In short, a historical being is situated between a beginning, before which it did not exist, and an end, after which it is, in fullness, that which it has become through its historical development. In other words, pure historicity is unthinkable. Such pure historicity would be a being that would be a pure becoming, without anything that becomes and without becoming anything.

B. The Historicity of Christ

{543} Christ was a historical being. First of all, there was the development of His own human being from His conception up to the end of His earthly existence. There also was the fulfillment of His redemptive work through His preaching of the kingdom and through the essential acts of His passion, sacrificial death, and resurrection. This development unfolds in time. It was historical.

At the point of departure, there is the Incarnation, the establishing of the Incarnate Word. Through it, the eternal Word entered into history according to His human nature, not according to His Divine Nature, which remains immutable and in which He remains immutable and eternal. The man Jesus who is the Word was a historical being. This stands in contrast to the views of the Lutheran theologian Jürgen Moltmann, who has been more or less followed by a number of Catholic theologians, who would like it to be the case that, through the Incarnation, the Word, as well as the Father who sent Him, would have become historical in His very divinity, thus being submitted to change and suffering.[21] However, if God can be submitted to change, He is not God, and how then can we affirm His existence? We have no direct experience of it and can affirm Him only as the first, immutable Cause of the changing universe, the necessary Being who provides the foundation for contingent being. If He is neither necessary in Himself, nor immutable, what will He

---

21. See Jürgen Moltmann, *Théologie de l'espérance* (Paris: Cerf, 1970), and *Théologie de l'espérance, II. Débats* (Paris: Cerf, 1973); Jean-Hervé Nicolas, "L'acte pur de saint Thomas d'Aquin et le Dieu vivant de l'évangile," *Angelicum* 51 (1974): 511–32, and "Aimante et bienheureuse Trinité."

be if not a being in the universe, incapable of explaining the universe, invisible and imperceptible, whose existence could be affirmed only arbitrarily and in an irrational manner? At bottom, we are here (in Moltmann) faced with the Lutheran conception of faith, an unconditioned and absolutely primary acceptance of God's Word, an acceptance of His promise, precluding every rational justification. But how could one accept the Word of God if every rational verification of the existence of the God who speaks were impossible?[22]

The development that Jesus knew during His earthly existence affected the Incarnate Word precisely as Incarnate, that is, the Word Himself, though according to His human nature. It did not modify His ontological structure, which was given from the first moment of the Incarnation, but instead deployed it in time. During His earthly life, Jesus was a "wayfarer," *en route* toward a terminus, which He himself defined as His human being's full and definitive participation in the glory that He had from all eternity according to His Divine Nature: "I glorified thee on earth, having accomplished the work which thou gavest me to do; and now, Father, glorify thou me in thy own presence with the glory which I had with thee before the world was made."[23]

The ultimate terminus of this development is the resurrection. Through it, Christ entered into eschatological time, beyond history. He is fixed in glory—a glory that is not a static perfection, arrested in inactivity. It is a glory that is a perpetually outpouring, intense life, an immobility that is not inert but, instead, is the end point of a movement whose entire energy is condensed into this point. Our thought is historical in the sense that it is conditioned by space and time. We find it impossible to represent to ourselves a life thus having arrived at the terminus of history, having passed out of history, and nonetheless continuing to unfold itself. Nonetheless, the very notion of historicity of necessity leads us to recognize and affirm this passage out of history, for history cannot be conceived of as being

---

22. See §§6 and 7 in the previous volume.
23. Jn 17:4–5 (RSV).

an indefinite movement. It tends toward an end, which gives it its meaning, which is a future for it and for the being thus engaged in history. This future would be unreal (and therefore incapable of giving history a meaning) if it could never arrive and if, at least, it were conceived of as never being able to arrive. The future that has thus arrived becomes a permanent present, this present in which life, far from coming to a halt, finds its definitive and full fruition. The Incarnate Word found this fruition in the glory of His exaltation.

C. The "Time of the Church"

{544} We have seen why Christ's redemptive work must be pursued on earth through the succession of generations.[24] Salvation continues to be realized in history, whereas the Savior, in His individual destiny, has already passed outside of history and into the eschaton. The sign and instrument—the sacrament—of salvation is the Church.[25] She is engaged in history. Salvation history continues in her and through her.

However, it is continued on the basis of Christ's saving work accomplished once and for all:

> And by that will we have been sanctified through the offering of the body of Jesus Christ once for all ... But when Christ had offered for all time a single sacrifice for sins, He sat down at the right hand of God, then to wait until His enemies should be made a stool for His feet. For by a single offering He has perfected for all time those who are sanctified.[26]

This saving work accomplished by Christ in the days of His flesh, when He was still in history, is not only something past for the Church, a past to which she would refer herself, and on whose basis she would develop herself in history. It encompasses the past, the present, and the future of the Church. In the next volume, we will see that the Church's sacramentality—especially in its primary form in the sacraments properly so-called—has the precise role of assur-

---

24. See §494.
25. See sect. 1, ch. 1 of the next volume.
26. Heb 10:10–14 (RSV).

ing this active presence of Christ the Savior and of His salvific mysteries to all generations.

This entire history from Christ's resurrection (and from the Church's birth) to His return (the Church's consummation) is the "time of the Church." Like all history, it is made up of a past, a present, and a future. However, it is completely encompassed in the permanent present of the resurrected Christ.

D. The Authentic Historicity of the Church and Providence

{545} According to Moltmann, it is essential to history that it be open to an indeterminate future, an opening founded on God's promise in Christ's resurrection, an opening that not only cannot be *known* in advance but, moreover, one that actually remains undetermined in itself. This leads him to reject the idea of Providence, which he holds to be the equivalent of *fatum*, something which would presuppose, according to him, that everything has played out in advance. In contrast, the "kingdom of God," the object of the promise, is essentially the "new creation," something absolutely new, which not only is not contained in the present but which contradicts it:

> In the eschatology of the prophets, the horizon of the promise, both in its breadth and in its depth, reaches the limits of what can be described as cosmic finitude. When, however, the moving historic horizon of the historic hopes reaches these *eschata*, then there arises the possibility of abandoning the point of perspective in history and reading the course of world history backwards from the end now contemplated, as if universal history were a *universum*, a predetermined cosmos of history. Numerical speculations from ancient cosmology are introduced in order to provide an order or the periods of world history corresponding to the spatial order. The world empires are fixed. The *eschaton* becomes a *fatum*. Then the place of election, which determines the ground of obedience and hope, is taken by providence, which determines events ... The place of the *eschaton* which is brought about by God in his freedom is taken by a historical finale that comes about in the course of time. The place of the faithfulness of God to which, in his freedom, the fulfillment of the promised future is entrusted is taken by the plan of God which is firmly established from the beginning

of time and gradually disclosed by history. In place of a historical theology we have a theology of history and in place of a historical eschatology comes an eschatological contemplation of history.[27]

In addition to Moltmann's particular conceptions, we here are faced with a fundamental critique of the very idea of Providence, which [from his perspective] would destroy history. Providence is conceived as being a pre-established plan, making history into the simple execution of it, having the mere appearance of spontaneity and freedom. (Thus, it would be a stage play, acted out in accord with a text written in advance, in which all the actions and reactions of the actors are set beforehand, having only appearances of free discovery and chance.) Against such a conception of Providence, the aforementioned criticism is perfectly justified and irrefutable. There is no true history when everything is given and done in advance. (What characterizes the scenario presented in a stage play is that it can be reenacted indefinitely, whereas, by contrast, what characterizes history is the fact that it is irreversible: we cannot repeat it.)

However, this conception of Providence is false and a caricature. Providence is an act of God and, for this reason does not itself exist in time. The divine eternity—and therefore Providence—embraces the whole of time in its eternal present and is not submitted to succession. By its very nature, history is successive. The past is fixed by free actions (and also by events) which have taken place (and for this reason cannot not have taken place, thus requiring that there be a necessity of fact). The present is the fixing of one of the possibilities that were indeterminately contained in the past, being brought about through free realization and events produced [by non-free agents]. The future remains undetermined, depending on free actions and events that exist only when they will be produced, that is, when the future will have become the present. The "divine plan" according to which history unfolds is not anterior to history but, instead, is simultaneous with it.

---

27. Moltmann, *Théologie de l'espérance*, 145 and 241–46. [Tr. note: Taken from Jürgen Moltmann, *Theology of Hope: On the Ground and the Implications of a Christian Eschatology*, trans. James W. Leitch (New York: Harper and Row, 1967), 135.]

What is "to come" for man is the fruit of the mysterious conjunction of God's freedom and man's freedom. It is future only in relation to the freedom exercised by man, who alone exists in time. In relation to God's freedom, it is a pure present. However, although it is present to God, this does not mean that it is somehow wholly independent from man's freedom (as though one were to say, "Whatever man may do, this will happen"). What is present to God is the free and spontaneous accomplishment of man's will, which is also conditioned by events which themselves depend upon second causes (i.e., other free causes and natural causes).

So conceived, far from suppressing the spontaneity and unpredictability of history and far from removing the indetermination that is essential to it, Providence arouses them and guarantees them. It is not a "scenario written in advance." The "scenario" is composed by God and by man to the degree that it is performed, and it exists only as performed and factually realized; however, in its very progress, it is always present to God.

If we apply this to eschatology, we can say the following. The *eschata* are things to come for man, undetermined, and dependent on his freedom. However, they are also present to God, determined not in advance but, rather, as they will be for man when they will have happened for him.[28] However, they are also determined by God's intellect and will. Here, we are faced with the mystery of Providence: history is simultaneously that which God makes it to be from all eternity and that which man makes it to be in time. As for sins, which are so intimately inserted into its warp and woof, man is the sole author of them. However, God foresees them, permits them,[29] and orders them, thus giving them a place in His plan.

Inasmuch as they depend on the divine freedom, the *eschata* were able to be revealed to man. Therefore, this revelation is not only the promise of as yet undetermined events—the new heavens and the new creation—but also the partial and obscure unveiling

---

28. See *ST* I, q. 14, a. 13.
29. "Permits them": in the sense that He does not prevent them from being produced.

of what must happen, thus enabling man, in faith, to order his free actions in the direction that God prescribes for them. One can and must study eschatology in theology, in the light of this revelation of the *eschata*—not in order to describe in advance what will come to pass but, rather, in order to discover the meaning of the present time of the Church, which is wholly pregnant with this future and which also must be born of the freedom of men and from the spontaneous unfolding of events.

E. The Last Events (The *eschata*)

1. The parousia

{546} The Greek word *parousia* means "presence" or "coming." In the New Testament, it designates the arrival of the Lord Jesus at the end of time.[30] This announced return of Christ is the ultimate terminus of Christian eschatology. It will mark His definitive victory over sin: "For He must reign until He has put all His enemies under His feet. The last enemy to be destroyed is death."[31] This will be the end, that is, the definitive achievement of the redemptive work and of salvation history.

Concerning this subject, can one join Moltmann in speaking of "Christ's future"?[32] From what we have said, it follows that we cannot, properly speaking, speak of "Christ's future." The glory that He received definitively at His exaltation will receive no increase, though it will be manifested in all men, those who have believed in Him and to those who have rejected Him: "You will see the Son of man seated at the right hand of Power, and coming on the clouds of heaven."[33] "Christ's return" will be an event for the Church in relation to Christ, an event that will mark the end of her earthly history.

On the other hand, this event is the furthest point in the Church's future. It is so, first of all, in the sense that it lies in the future for her.

---

30. Mt 24:3, 27, 37, 39; 1 Cor 15:23; 1 Thes 2:19, 3:13, 4:15; 2 Thes 2:1, 8; 2 Pt 1:16.
31. 1 Cor 15:25–26 (RSV).
32. See Moltmann, *Théologie de l'espérance*, ch. 3.
33. Mt 26:64 (RSV).

It is likewise so in the sense that there will no longer be a history for the Church but, instead, the definitive and permanent fruition of the life that already exists in her though as still growing and fluctuating, currently submitted to the trials and changes of history.

One can perfectly say, with the Protestant reformers, that the kingdom of God is found *tectum sub cruce et sub contrario*.[34] This connects back to the great Pauline idea that the believer here below is simultaneously "crucified with Christ" and "resurrected with Christ," which holds true first of all for the Church herself. The "delay of the Parousia" which obviously so strongly affected the first Christian communities, in every era remains a trial and temptation for the Church. It is *a trial for her faith* because all the appearances are contrary to Christ's victory, which she proclaims and announces, just as under the cross all appearances were contrary to Christ's awareness of His divine filiation and mission. She experiences *the temptation* either to establish herself in this world wherein she is bound to live out her hope or to escape from it, whereas she must precisely "always be ready to justify (her) hope"[35] before the world and to communicate her hope to it.

It is in speaking of his *parousia* that the Lord said: "But of that day and hour no one knows, not even the angels of heaven, nor the Son, but the Father only."[36] The Church received a mission, that of "[making] disciples of all nations, baptizing them in the name of the Father and of the Son and of the Holy Spirit, teaching them to observe all that I have commanded you; and lo, I am with you always, to the close of the age."[37] Therefore, Christ is invisibly present to His Church until the end of the world, which will be marked by His return in glory, His "parousia." Meanwhile, the Church must at once "be in the world" ("as thou didst send me into the world, so I have

---

34. "Hidden under the cross and under its contrary": Moltmann, *Théologie de l'espérance*, 239.
35. 1 Pt 3:15.
36. Mt 24:36 (RSV); see Mk 13:32.
37. Mt 28:19–20 (RSV).

sent them into the world")[38] and not be "of the world" ("they are not of the world, even as I am not of the world").[39]

She lives in expectation of this return, all the while continuing to fulfill her mission: "For as often as you eat this bread and drink the cup, you proclaim the Lord's death until He comes."[40] "He who testifies to these things says, 'Surely I am coming soon.' Amen. Come, Lord Jesus."[41] Along these lines, the reader should refer to the beautiful pages written by Journet concerning the Church's impatience for the return of Christ.[42]

2. The resurrection of the dead

{547} We saw above how the resurrection of the dead was included, announced, and promised in Christ's resurrection. "But in fact, Christ has been raised from the dead, the first fruits of those who have fallen asleep."[43] The resurrection of the dead is essential to the New Testament's eschatology: "The will of the Father is that I not lose anyone ... but that ... I raise him on the last day."[44] It is inseparable from Christ's resurrection: "But if there is no resurrection of the dead, then Christ has not been raised."[45]

Although in certain texts it would (or could) seem that only the just will be resurrected to life, St. John is unambiguous in the opposite direction. He speaks of a "resurrection of life" and of a "resurrection of condemnation."[46] It is vain to attempt to represent to oneself an event that will not belong to the historical universe, which structures our own thought and imagination. Instead, it will belong to a new, eschatological universe. This does not mean that it must not be real, for the eschatological times will be fully real, the consummation and fruition of the complete reality of the world.

---

38. Jn 17:18 (RSV).
39. Jn 17:16 (RSV).
40. 1 Cor 11:26 (RSV).
41. Rv 22:20 (RSV).
42. See Journet, L'Église du Verbe incarné, 3:626–33.
43. 1 Cor 15:20 (RSV). See §505 above.
44. Jn 6:39–40.
45. 1 Cor 15:13 (RSV); see verses 12–33.
46. See Jn 5:29 and Rv 20:5–6.

What one can do is propose an intelligible, theological interpretation of the "how" of this event—an interpretation that must at one and the same time safeguard its reality and present this reality as something beyond imagination and even thought. We said that its "reality" must be safeguarded. Therefore, to resurrect a being is to give it life after it would have lost it. This implies that this being who lost his life once again exists.[47] In order to exclude absurd imagery concerning the recovery of a body that has long since corrupted, dissolved, and disappeared, one must appeal to an anthropology that is at once realistic and spiritualistic. The human person is composed of the spiritual soul and of matter, of which the soul is the form. That is, the soul is what organizes the matter into a human body which it vivifies and unifies. By it, the body is constituted as a human body, indeed, as this individual human body, the body of this person. Thus, one can admit and understand the idea that the soul that survived the separation brought about by death will then be given a matter to inform, from which it will make the same body of this person, the body with which it lived, merited, and sinned. Likewise, we said that we must safeguard the fact that it is "an eschatological reality." Therefore, it is not a question of rendering to the body the life that it previously had (and in this sense, it is true to say that the resurrection is not the reanimation of a corpse). It is a completely new life, one that is different from earthly life, unimaginable, unable to be represented, though nonetheless a true life, for were this not the case, it would not be a true resurrection. On this point, Jesus's response to the Sadducees is unambiguous: "For in the resurrection they neither marry nor are given in marriage, but are like angels in heaven."[48]

Note, however, that this way of interpreting the resurrection of the body at the end of time cannot hold for Christ's resurrection. His body did not experience decomposition. It was this buried, dead body that came forth living from the tomb: "He is not here."[49] Moreover,

---

47. See §566 below.
48. Mt 22:30 (RSV).
49. Mt 28:6. See Mk 16:6 and Lk 24:6. On this topic, see M.-J. Nicolas, *Théologie de la résurrection*, 143–50.

there is the Hypostatic Union, which makes Jesus's body and soul to be the body and soul of the Word. On the cross, Christ's soul was separated from His body, and this was a true death. However, Jesus's inanimate corpse was still the body of the Word. For this reason, it could not have been abandoned to decomposition. For this to be so, it was necessary that it be united anew, in its individuality, to the soul. On the other hand, it is true to say that the life that the resurrected Christ received at the resurrection is a new life and that He was the first to enter into another existence, eschatological existence, into which those who believe in Him must enter, following Him and with Him.

Concerning this "eschatological" existence, we have the mysterious words of St. Paul: "What is sown is perishable, what is raised is imperishable ... It is sown a physical body, it is raised a spiritual body ... The first man was from the earth, a man of dust; the second man is from heaven. As was the man of dust, so are those who are of the dust; and as is the man of heaven, so are those who are of heaven."[50] These are difficult texts.[51] To claim that St. Paul holds that the resurrected body is a "pure spirit" would be to completely misunderstand the place that he accords to the body as something that is constitutive of the person. This would likewise involve a complete misunderstanding of the novelty of the resurrection in relation to the state that the person is placed into by death. We can say that it is not a "biological body" just as we said that it is not a question of re-iterating earthly life. "Spiritual body," or "heavenly body," or again a "glorious body"[52] all mean: the body, wholly transparent to the spirit and to the glory that fills the life of the just. It is a "spiritualized" body, a pure manifestation and ontological support for the soul, not weighing it down, no longer enclosing it within its opacity, as it did during earthly life. It is a body entirely submitted to the spirit. However, little more can be said concerning it.

---

50. 1 Cor 15:42–48 (RSV).

51. See Maurice Carrez, "L'herméneutique paulinienne de la résurrection," in *La résurrection du Christ et l'exégèse moderne, Lectio divina* 50 (Paris: Cerf, 1969), 55–73.

52. Phil 3:21 (RSV).

3. The judgment

{548} "He ascended to heaven, whence He will come to judge the living and the dead."[53] The judgment of the world by God is also an essential datum of biblical eschatology. What characterizes New Testament eschatology is that this power and task of judging "has been given to the Son by the Father."[54] "[God] has fixed a day on which He will judge the world in righteousness by a man whom He has appointed, and of this He has given assurance to all men by raising Him from the dead."[55] The judgment is intimately connected to the resurrection.[56] From the perspective of the community (i.e., the general judgment), it is presented as a kind of sorting. Thus, we have the parable of the wheat and weeds[57] and the parable of the fish and the fishnet.[58]

However, this judgment is often presented not as a future event, but rather as one that is contemporary, as one being exercised in the world: "For judgment I came into this world, that those who do not see may see, and that those who see may become blind."[59] "And this is the judgment, that the light has come into the world, and men loved darkness rather than light."[60] It seems to be a completely interior judgment. This conception is more particularly Johannine, which led Loisy to say that the fourth Gospel substitutes mysticism for eschatology. Nonetheless, we can find characteristic elements of traditional eschatology in St. John: the tribulation heralding the messianic times, the last day, and the coming of Jesus.[61] For him, the judgment is not something that is only immanent but is also an external event: "Now is the judgment of this world, now shall the ruler of this world be cast out"[62]; "that we may have confidence for the

---

53. See Donatien Mollat, "Jugement," in *Dictionnaire de la Bible*, 4:1321–94.
54. Jn 5:22.
55. Acts 17:31 (RSV).
56. See Jn 5:27–29.
57. See Mt 13:24–30, 36–43.
58. See Mt 13:47–50.
59. Jn 9:39 (RSV).
60. Jn 3:19 (RSV).
61. See Jn 6:39, 40, 44, 54; 11:24; 16:21–22.
62. Jn 12:31 (RSV).

day of judgment."[63] On the other hand, this conception of an immanent judgment is also found, though in a less marked fashion, in St. Paul: "For anyone who eats and drinks without discerning the body eats and drinks judgment upon himself. That is why many of you are weak and ill, and some have died";[64] "knowing that such a person is perverted and sinful; he is self-condemned";[65] "Therefore God sends upon them a strong delusion, to make them believe what is false, so that all may be condemned who did not believe the truth but had pleasure in unrighteousness";[66] likewise, in the Letter to the Hebrews: "For the word of God is living and active … discerning the thoughts and intentions of the heart."[67]

Therefore, there is a kind of antinomy. On the one hand, the judgment is presented as a future event connected to the Parousia of the Lord. On the other hand, it is presented as a present and interior reality (even if it is translated by external punishments) connected only to the presence of the Lord in the world from the time of the Incarnation. The synthesis of these two perspectives is easily found in the continuity that we have noted between the two comings of the Lord. The Parousia will be the dazzling manifestation of everything that the Lord did through His (hidden) presence alone and through His redemptive work. Although Scripture often presents the universal judgment in the form of an immense gathering at Christ's tribunal, with a majestic judicial apparatus and a public sentence, in accord with the well-known literary genre of apocalypses, it will also be interior to man. The mere presence of the glorious Christ in the midst of resurrected humanity will bring about the division between the elect and the reprobate, through the manifested evidence of the righteousness of the former and the unworthiness of the latter.[68]

---

63. 1 Jn 4:17 (RSV).
64. 1 Cor 11:29–30 (RSV).
65. Ti 3:11 (RSV).
66. 2 Thes 2:11–12 (RSV).
67. Heb 4:12 (RSV).
68. See the collected volume, "Nous sommes jugés maintenant," *Vie Spirituelle* 108, no. 494 (1963).

4. The "redemption of the universe"

{549} St. Paul speaks in gripping terms about the universe's expectation: "For the creation waits with eager longing for the revealing of the sons of God."[69] How should we conceive of this transformation of the world at the end of time, "the new heavens and the new earth"? According to St. Paul, it is essentially a liberation: "for the creation was subjected to futility, not of its own will but by the will of him who subjected it in hope; because the creation itself will be set free from its bondage to decay and obtain the glorious liberty of the children of God."[70]

In short, we can say the following. This "futility" is not the fragile condition of the material creature which is corruptible by its very nature—that is, called to disappear—but, instead, is the disorder introduced into it by man's contaminated freedom, which turns it away from its ordinary finality by making it serve his sin. This also corrupts creation by not respecting its internal order, rhythm, etc. Here, one can think of contemporary problems pertaining to ecology. By making man's subjection to material creation cease, the "freedom of the sons of God" paradoxically assures the liberation of material creation, which by its nature is submitted to man, though to man who is rectified and who uses it according to its proper finalities. This calls to mind St. Francis of Assisi's "Canticle of the Sun" or St. John of the Cross's prayer: "Mine are the heavens and mine is the earth. Mine are the nations ... all things are mine; and God Himself is mine and for me, because Christ is mine and all for me."[71]

At the end of time, this corruptible world will have come to an end. One cannot represent the new heavens and new earth as a mere renewal of this world, merely freed from its horrors. In fact, we can-

---

69. Rom 8:19. See Lyonnet, *Les étapes de l'histoire*, ch. 8; *Lumen Gentium*, no. 9; *Gaudium et Spes*, no. 2.

70. Rom 8:20–21 (RSV).

71. See John of the Cross, *Oeuvres complètes*, 1305. [Tr. note: Translation taken from St. John of the Cross, "The Sayings of Light and Love," no. 27, in *The Collected Works of Saint John of the Cross*, rev. ed., trans. Kieran Kavanaugh and Otilio Rodriguez (Washington, DC: ICS Publications, 1991), 87–88.]

not represent it to ourselves. If it is certain that man's bodily life will be exempt from corruption, and therefore from the conditions that it knows here below (i.e., nourishing itself, sleeping, reproducing itself, etc.), the material world which will be its framework will not be made of corruptible realities. What more can one say?

5. *The end of the world*

{550} In conformity with the apocalyptic literary genre, all the depictions of the Parousia are pictorial images using the wholly material imagery that had by then become classic (cosmic unrest, trumpets, the valley of Jehoshaphat, and so forth). It is clear (and admitted by all) that these images do not intend to be (and are not) a description of what will really take place, but function only as an evocation.

Nonetheless, one point stands out from all these texts, and it is a point that indeed seems to be constitutive of the *eschata*: the "end of the world" will not be the terminus of a natural development, like the ultimate fructification of the universe having arrived at its fulfillment through its internal and natural progression. Instead, it will represent the interruption of such an evolution, which of itself is indefinite. Here, at the "end of the world," God will sovereignly intervene, through an intervention that is as sovereign as was the creative act. "The heavens will be rolled up like a scroll."[72] But, more clearly: "For as the lightning flashes and lights up the sky from one side to the other, so will the Son of man be in his day."[73]

6. *Salvation in history*

{551} To say that salvation is in history is to say that man's salvation is in the midst of being accomplished and that it is accomplished in accord with a historical process. This process, begun at creation itself, includes four phases: *the phase prior to sin; the preparatory phase*, which has the distant annunciation of salvation (in

---

72. Rv 6:14. [Tr. note: Fr. Nicolas incorrectly cites 7:14.]
73. Lk 17:24 (RSV).

the proto-evangelium immediately following the Fall) and then the promise of Christ (to Israel); *the decisive phase* which spans the time from Jesus's Incarnation to His resurrection, during which the redemption of the world was brought about; and finally, *the phase of progressive realization*, that is, the phase of man's free participation in the salvation brought about by Christ, a participation that will occur in history, so that it may emerge, outside of history, in the eternity of God, where the resurrected Christ is already established.

This "salvation history" is completely penetrated by eschatology. It is a history which is guided along and goes forward toward a terminus. This terminus is Christ's return, with the ultimate effect of the redemption: the resurrection of the dead and the eschatological kingdom. This kingdom is not of this world. The millenarist illusion (founded on a false interpretation of Rv 20:1–5) consists in imagining that history would find its fulfillment *in history itself*.[74] This is in the background of the naïve infatuation for (true or false) visions and apparitions that announce in general—or at least are interpreted as announcing—a definitive victory of the "good" over the wicked in this world.[75] In reality, the only future that Scripture announces and promises, beyond faith and the cross, is the return of Christ which will bring history to its end. Nothing presented here below to us by the Christian faith is a self-sufficient end; it is wholly stretching toward the future, wholly a promise: "In this hope we were saved."[76]

III. ESCHATOLOGY AND WORLD HISTORY

{552} There is another problem to be answered, one that is grave in itself and that has a burning relevance. In short, what is the relationship between this "salvation history" and "world history" in its onward march? Has the latter become negligible, a residue, meaning

---

74. See Rv 20:2. Also, note j in *Traduction Oecuménique de la Bible* on this passage.
75. J.-H. Nicolas, "Hospitalité eucharistique et oecuménisme," *Nova et Vetera* 50 (1975): 152–58 and 168–87.
76. See Rom 8:24 (RSV).

that the events that are produced in the world would be meaningful only inasmuch as they are engaged in salvation history? Is it identical with salvation history, meaning that the events that comprise world history would be in themselves charged with a saving meaning and orientation? Or, rather, are we faced here with two histories that do not overlap, each having its own meaning and orientation, meaning that the events which make up the warp and woof of men's earthly lives would be indifferent to salvation?[77]

A. WORLD HISTORY IS NOT IDENTICAL WITH SALVATION HISTORY

{553} In various forms, an entire theological current today tends to make the movement of history toward man's progress coincide with the eschatological movement of salvation history, thus making the dynamism of the world's development coincide with the Christian hope founded on the promise of Christ's return. A typical formulation of this highly influential conception can be found in what is called the "utopian Marxism" of Ernst Bloch.[78] In this line, we likewise can find Jürgen Moltmann[79] and what is called "political theology,"[80] as well as liberation theology (or liberation theologies).[81]

From the perspective of eschatological theology, this conception is characterized by the claim that eschatological expectation finds its necessary mediation in the earthly transformations that man is called to bring about. Christian hope must be concretized in earthly

---

77. See J.-H. Nicolas, "Le Christ centre et fin de l'histoire," *Revue thomiste* 81 (1981): 357–80.

78. See Ernst Bloch, *Le Principe Espérance*, vols. 1–2 (Paris: Gallimard, 1976 / 1982).

79. See Moltmann, *Théologie de l'espérance* and *Le Dieu crucifié. La croix du Christ, fondement et critique de la théologie chrétienne* (Paris: Cerf, 1974).

80. Principally the work of Johann-Baptist Metz, "Les rapports entre l'Eglise et le monde à la lumière d'une théologie politique," in *Théologie du Renouveau, I–II* (Paris: Cerf, 1968), 33–47.

81. See Juan Gutiérrez González, *Teología de la Liberación. Evaporación de la Teología (La obra de Gustavo Gutiérrez vista desde ella misma)* (Mexico City: Jus, 1975); Georges Cottier, "Difficultés d'une théologie de la libération," *Les Quatre Fleuves* 2 (1974): 64–81.

hopes. The Christian dynamism of man's salvation takes its form in willing and undertaking the action that saves man from his earthly servitudes. This is expressed in an arresting manner by Ernst Bloch when he designates this earthly object of hope by means of the expression "penultimate events." An expression of this outlook can be found, though in a quite different but nonetheless convergent form, in the conceptions expressed by Teilhard de Chardin concerning "Christogenesis."[82]

Such conceptions presuppose a postulate, at once arbitrary in itself and in contradiction to Christian eschatology, in short: by its internal movement, world history would tend toward the goal of salvation history, toward Christ's definitive victory, the achievement of the Redemption. To make world history coincide with salvation history runs two grave risks.

On the one hand, it risks sacralizing the temporal and political orders by turning them away from their own finality in order to make them serve religious ends, not without running the risk of contaminating these religious ends themselves. Moreover, all those who would not adhere to the Christian faith and would refuse to adhere to it would fall outside of such a sacralization. Indeed, one can accept a political end and be completely engaged in it while rejecting the Christian faith in the service of which one would claim to put it.

On the other hand, there is the risk of desacralizing the faith, something that is a more present danger. Such a desacralization would represent the dissolution of Christianity, which is essentially founded on faith in Jesus Christ, the Son of God, the Savior. Indeed, it is clear that effort expended in transforming the world can be accomplished just as well by those who refuse to recognize Christ as being the terminus and mover of such efforts, even to the point of refusing to maintain that this effort would indeed have a finality. Moreover, the revolutionary effort to which liberation theology in-

---

82. See de Chardin, *Oeuvres*, 9:81ff. and 209ff.; Claude Cuénot, *Pierre Teilhard de Chardin. Les grandes étapes de son évolution* (Paris: Plon, 1958), fifth part; and Henri de Lubac, *La pensée religieuse de P. Teilhard de Chardin* (Paris: Aubier, 1962), ch. 18.

vites us does not of itself call for any reference to the Gospel, even if Christians participate in such an effort under the inspiration of their faith in the Gospel. Will it be said that such efforts are evangelical of themselves? A positive answer would ultimately be opposed to the apostolic preaching, meaning that one would come to receive the Gospel without having faith in Jesus Christ, the Son of the God who saves.

Certainly, it is not completely false to say that the movement of world history plays a kind of mediating role in relation to the movement of salvation history when the former is correctly oriented by men's freedom, for when it is correctly oriented in this way, it tends toward earthly freedom and the dignity of the human person respected in political society, and there can be no doubt that the freedom of the children of God of itself has, as a presupposition, freedom in the world shared among men. Indeed, it is a presupposition and also a demand. However, one must add that the converse is not true. Earthly freedom does not by itself bring the freedom of the children of God, which is a gift of grace, requiring the acceptance of grace by human freedom, faith. Thus, if human effort toward man's liberation is not ordered to the freedom of the children of God by itself but, rather, by the will of the believer who participates in this effort and who faithfully pursues the end toward which it tends (thus being able to fully collaborate with non-believers without experiencing any hesitations),[83] it cannot coincide with the movement of salvation history which itself tends by its own internal orientation toward the realization of the freedom of the children of God. And earthly freedom is not the required passage toward this freedom of the children of God because its absolute model, Jesus Christ, suffered the deprivation of every earthly freedom: the cross.

---

83. See Jacques Maritain, "Discours pour l'ouverture de l'Assemblée de l'Unesco à Mexico," *Nova et Vetera* (1948): 1–14.

B. WORLD HISTORY TENDS, OF ITSELF, TO AN IMMANENT AND UNDETERMINED END

{554} The "natural end of the world" is the end toward which the world tends by its own movement, the end toward which it is intrinsically ordered by the orientation of the forces that compose it. We must first note that this end can only be a horizon and not a definite terminus after which there could no longer be history. It is essential to human history that it be moving, meaning that a contradiction is involved in the claim that it would ultimately lead to a terminus that would at once be its ultimate outcome and fulfillment.[84]

Eschatology is what posits a terminus for history. Salvation history will cease as a form of history but will do so because salvation will have been accomplished. The "already" that it bears in itself will have totally consumed the "not yet." At the same time, the history of the world will have been brought to a halt—not by a fulfillment but, instead, by an interruption, as (for the individual) death interrupts life, preventing it from pursuing its course which of itself is indefinite. Thus, world history does not have "last events" (just as, properly speaking, there were not "first events," for creation is not an "event"). Therefore, there likewise are not "penultimate events." The various objectives that one can give oneself over to (e.g., revolution, the establishment of a just order, the equitable redistribution of the riches of the world, etc.) can be envisioned only as being the point of departure for new developments in human history, not as its end.

---

84. This point seems to contradict what was said earlier, namely that history necessarily includes the idea of a terminus in which history must be brought to completion. A first response is that the reality of historicity is sufficiently assured by being able to conceive and represent the terminus toward which history tends as being something real, even if it recedes to the degree that it is approached. This would thus be the idea of a utopia ("a non-place, a place that exists nowhere"), introduced by Ernst Bloch and which has become a key notion of the theology of hope and liberation theology. A more profound response would be, perhaps, that the very notion of history necessarily implies that man, who is the subject of history, has an supra-historical destiny. On such a conception, history would not exist if man did not have in himself something that survives the end of history and the end of the world.

In sum, the end of world history is the realization of the *temporal man*, his personal, social, and political development on earth. The end of salvation history is the definitive entrance of *man, the child of God*, into communion with the Divine Persons in Christ. These two ends are not reducible to one another. The former is immanent to history and not determinate. It is a horizon. The latter is transcendent, determinate, and promised before coming to its realization, though as something situated beyond this material universe and beyond history. The former prepares for the latter only indirectly; the latter neither completes nor fulfills the former, for it interrupts history.

C. World History Is Often in Conflict with Salvation History

1. *The opposition of world history to salvation history*

{555} World history does not homogeneously develop along an ascending line, unswervingly progressing toward the good. The idea of continuous progress is a myth. World history also develops according to a descending line toward evil (e.g., the recrudescence of torture in the modern world, the spreading of the scourge of drugs, increasing permissiveness of laws in the domain of abortion, soon of euthanasia, and so forth). These two lines are interwoven, and it is difficult to say whether a given moment of history is a summit or a valley (in fact, it can be a summit in some aspects and a valley in others that are no less important).[85] To the degree that the movement of history tends toward evil, it is opposed to the building up of the city of God.[86] However, something more profound is involved here. Even when world history ascends upward, it often happens to enter into conflict with salvation history, for the most authentic human values, such as freedom, science, and art, may indeed be consciously pursued as absolutes, seeking to abolish God and exalt man's pride, as well as his desire to be independent from God.

---

85. See Jacques Maritain, *Pour une philosophie de l'histoire* (Paris: Seuil, 1957), 23–24 and 57–65.

86. See Henri-Irénée Marrou, *Théologie de l'histoire* (Paris: Seuil, 1968), 53–59.

In our personal lives, *self-love* is good and necessary, provided that it passes over into love of God above all, including ourselves (so that such love may indeed reappear there, now rectified and purified). Without this, man encloses himself in self-love, and the loftier the achievements to which this *amor sui* pushes him, to that degree does he, in his prideful dissimilitude, assert himself against God.[87] If this disordered *amor sui* is the mover of what is realized in world history, these deeds are done in opposition to the coming of the kingdom of God, not in harmony with it.

However, this point must be nuanced, for "self-love" and "love of God" are directly concerned with persons—that is, with their intention and the way that they pursue and use what is realized in history. The latter can be good in themselves, and in that case, they can be used by this or that person in view of the kingdom of God. Nonetheless, they have a collective character, and the intention which has, in fact, driven one to promote them is weighed down with a burden that is opposed to the eschatological kingdom. This is striking in modern culture, both in freedom conceived as radical independence from every rule other than the requirements of life in society (e.g., complete moral freedom) and in a social and political structure in which [economic] exchanges between men would be ameliorated, though to the detriment of every spiritual dimension [of the human person].

This opposition between world history and salvation history has the consequence that it sometimes can happen that salvation history's finality will require a given believer to turn away from a historical objective that is good and intrinsically desirable because, in this given case, this objective cannot be obtained guiltlessly or because it presents a concrete obstacle to the kingdom of God. Conscientious objection is born from this sort of conflict. The Christian is preserved from a fallacious optimism regarding the world by being aware of the opposition often asserted against salvation history by

---

87. See J.-H. Nicolas, "Amour de soi, amour de Dieu, amour des autres."

world history as the latter follows the line of its own, proper development. This is true even when this "optimism" is formed out of a "surmounted pessimism," for although pessimism is bad, its antidote is hope, not optimism.

2. *The opposition of salvation history to world history*

{556} However rightly oriented world history may be, the essential character of one's activity when participating in it is a concern with effectiveness and success. Intention without success has no value. (Here, consider the not-wholly-unjustified criticisms made by Alaine Peyrefitte against the primacy of intention over results that was part of the "French evil.")[88] Is this the case for salvation history? Similarly, Teilhard de Chardin critiqued a "morality of intention" conceived as being indifferent to results,[89] and not without some justification. St. Thomas distinguishes two acts that are related to the end: *velle*, which is a simple resting in the end considered as being worthy of being pursued; *intendere*, namely, an act of will aiming to obtain this end, placing into action the appropriate means for obtaining this end.[90] Only the latter act is capable of setting one off into action. If the end is good and if I should pursue it (e.g., a missionary should pursue the end of evangelizing a region to which he has been sent, founding or strengthening the Church in this region, bringing about the authentic conversion of a people to Christ and the Church), it is clear that I cannot be content with *velle* and must go all the way to *intendere*, which implies that I would thus will that this deed be realized.

Failure renders such a willing vain, and if the intention was indeed real, such failure cannot help but be something painful. I cannot *resign myself to it*, even if I must abandon it in a state of defeat. Being defeated involves being reached in one's own willing—that is, in one's very person. If, at this moment, I say, "Intention alone

---

88. Alain Peyrefitte, *Le mal français* (Paris: Plon, 1976), ch. 42.
89. De Chardin, *Oeuvres*, vol. 4 (*Le milieu divin*).
90. *ST* I-II, q. 12, a. 1, ad 4.

counts," this can only be understood from the perspective of my own personal destiny. God sees the depths of hearts and wills. He will repay one's intention of serving Him and one's neighbor, even if this intention was not able to reach a successful fruition on account of insurmountable obstacles. However, this requires that we are here concerned with a true "intention," truly "willing to succeed." Such an act of will necessarily includes the hope of success, determination to succeed, and determination to overcome obstacles as well as to pursue the effort at hand. An act of will that would begin with a kind of detachment from success would, in fact, not be an authentic intention.

Nonetheless, it remains the case that failure, which in world history contradicts one's action and renders it vain, paradoxically (and mysteriously) in salvation history is a means for success itself—if not the means for the success of this particular action, at least the means for the general success of salvation history. The cross of Christ is placed at the center of salvation history as, at once, the failure of His mission and the means of its success. And in what followed [afterward in the Church], there was the great, paradoxical issue concerning the desire for martyrdom. Martyrdom, which is a failure of the [Christian's] mission, is also the means for its success: the Church is founded on the martyrdom of the apostles. Whence, we have the paradoxical adage: *sanguis martyrum semen christianorum* [the blood of the martyrs is the seed of Christians].

The opposition between salvation history and world history finds its arresting manifestation in the cross.[91] The cross forbids us from thinking that these two histories have a self-evident, mutual agreement. In particular, it forbids us from condemning the Church, as so often happens, on account of her "inefficacy," on account of the—all-too-contestable, alas—fact that she no longer has (or does not have) any influence upon the common conscience of men and society. Many Christians and many priests are upset by this lack of

---

91. See J.-H. Nicolas, *Contemplation et vie contemplative*, ch. 4.

an audience for the Gospel message, and they accuse the Church of having forgotten this audience. It is certain that an ever-renewed effort must be undertaken in order to enable all to hear this message. However, we contradict the cross of Jesus Christ by claiming that the truth and necessity of the message must be judged on the basis of the results of our efforts. Jesus died abandoned by all, outside the gates of the city. How many inhabitants of Corinth, Ephesus, and Rome heard and received the word of Paul? How many even knew who Paul was?

D. The Interconnection between World History and Salvation History

{557} This opposition is not the last word. We will not say, with Barth, that the Word of God definitively judges and condemns history, for it is a fact that salvation history is accomplished on earth and through the very events of world history. Each person is called to live, through a single, unified life, this twofold orientation found together in the very events of history.

1. The subordination of the end of world history to the end of salvation history

{558} God is the Creator of the world and the Lord of history. He sovereignly leads it to the definitive end that is the consummation of salvation history. Man serves one and the same God when he expressly pursues the ends of salvation history and when he participates in world history with all his heart, all his soul, and all his strength. The deviations of world history in relation to salvation do not denounce history as being something evil in itself, nor the world as something [utterly] condemned. Historical objectives have been assigned to man by God Himself (when He enjoined him to "till the garden and keep it").[92] Therefore, they can be pursued with righteousness. Indeed, righteousness very often even requires one

---

92. Gn 2:15.

to pursue them, although this righteousness can require one to renounce them in a given circumstance.

In man's life, his activity in the service of the temporal objectives of human history must be subordinated to his activity oriented toward the ultra-historical end of salvation history, for it is his final end. However, this subordination in no way abolishes the value of the temporal end, for man is a temporal being who marches toward eternity by temporal steps. He has a twofold vocation, and both vocations come from God: the vocation to be a child of God and the vocation to be a child of the earth. Therefore, his life will not be bifurcated if he actively subordinates his temporal vocation to his eternal vocation.

2. What this subordination consists in

{559} Earthly objectives are not the necessary and sufficient mediating activities for eschatological ends, as earthly objectives can be pursued without one being occupied with eschatological ends, by rejecting the latter and setting oneself in opposition to them. However, they are a possible (and in some sense required) mediation for them. For example, charity should indeed be mediated by an efficacious attempt to establish justice on earth, at least in the sense that the person who would be disinterested in injustice could not, without self-deception, claim that he pursues charity. Similarly, the freedom of the children of God is naturally mediated by freedom on earth, and it would be false (and, perhaps odious) to announce the freedom of the children of God while overlooking the oppressed conditions of those to whom it is announced, etc. The Christian can unify his two vocations by pursuing earthly objectives as mediating activities in relation to eschatological values—and also as refracting them on the level of history. What we must say, however, is that they remain distinct, and this explains how certain people can be called to dedicate themselves to eschatological values without the mediation of earthly values.

3. *The Christian and history*

{560} Man is at once the one who makes history and the one who is made in history. However, man himself can be envisioned from two perspectives: according to his temporal destiny (or, vocation) or according to his supra-temporal destiny (or, vocation).

Envisioning man according to his temporal destiny. Here, we must recognize that man is mortal, that all his realizations are like the passing leaves on a tree, and that history will entirely fall into nonbeing: "We other civilizations now know that we are mortal."[93] Can we speak of a judgment by God over history? Only men can be judged (for they alone are free and therefore responsible), and they are the object only of the eschatological judgment. Does it make sense to form an idea of "temporal punishments" which would strike the nations and groups in history? Certainly, God is the one who guides history along its paths, and everything that happens falls under His Providence. Nonetheless, we must distinguish general Providence from personal Providence. By the former, God rules the world by means of natural or free second causes whose unfolding activity He (ordinarily) respects, even permitting sins—that is, not preventing them and ordering their consequences to the good. By the latter, He makes everything that happens serve the final good of the elect.[94] Thus, a nation is not conquered, crushed, or split apart because its leaders or people have been particularly sinful. (Most often, its conquerors equally deserve great or greater chastisements.) Rather, it is conquered because it showed itself to be less strong, on account of causes that fall simply to the various factors on which the events depend. (However, one cannot draw an example for this from Israel's history, for its history is recounted to us in the Bible exclusively from the perspective of salvation history.)

Envisioning man according to his supra-temporal destiny. From this perspective, world history is the factual support of salvation history.

---

93. Paul Valéry, *Oeuvres* (Paris: La Pléiade, 1957), 1:988.
94. See Rom 8:28.

God's design consists in saving man through ways He has prepared from all eternity, ways by which God makes history move along, thus leading it to its own proper ends without disregarding human freedom and the spontaneity of other second causes. Man will be judged on his free cooperation in salvation history. To say that he will be "judged based on love"[95] is to say that he is engaged either for or against God in each of his free acts. However, this does not prevent him from having a temporal object to be realized as the immediate object of this free act. Indeed, love itself is what pushes one toward this realization, unless, in a given case, this is a form of counter-love.

IV. ESCHATOLOGY AND CHRISTIAN EXISTENCE

A. The Eschatological Dimension of Christian Existence

{561} While historical objectives are set before man like an indefinite horizon, the individual who pursues them must one day abandon the pursuit of them. Death will place an end to his quest and will make him pass out of history—and he is aware of this fact. However, he also has a very profound and existential feeling concerning his survival, a feeling that is profoundly wounded both by the death of others and by the certitude that he too will die. The individual's only definitive future is found in eschatological ends, a future in which he will exist without end. However, this presupposes that he really tends toward this future, and that he not look upon it as though it were solely a solution to his present situation, a replacement coming to him externally, something which thus would not be an end truly pursued by him.

This places the person on earth in a very difficult interior state of tension. He must live in time for temporal objectives and, simultaneously, in hope of a future situated outside and beyond time. This tension represents the eschatological dimension of Christian exis-

---

95. "A la tarde de la vida te examinarán en el amor": Juan de la Cruz, *Avisos*, 59.

tence. Hence, eschatology is no longer a mere "physics of the last things" [*fins dernières*], a more or less imaginative description of the *letzte Dinge* ["last things"]. Rather, it consists in extracting and placing in light the ultimate finality of existence and that of man's action on earth. Now the "end" (in the sense of, "the goal") is the very principle of action from its beginning. It is in relation to the end that one validly judges what the agent ought to be, as he ought to act.

More surely than in the final treatises of the *Summa theologiae* (which were added to it under the title of "Supplement," even though, as is well known, they were drawn from the commentary on the *Sentences*), St. Thomas's eschatology is found as the point of departure and beginning of the *Secunda pars*, which is dedicated to man's return to God, to what I here call "Christian existence." Likewise, it is found [near] the beginning of the *Tertia pars* as a topic that brings out the meaning of the Christian sacraments, which are signs of the future, signs of Christ's return, efficacious symbols of "the already and the not yet," something especially true for the Eucharist.

These insights are prolonged by the notion of the Church as a sacrament, an idea that is modern in its elaboration,[96] enabling us to better place the eschatological dimension of the Church herself in relief: the Church is a society (in this world and therefore in relation to other institutions of this world), but she is an eschatological society. That is, the End that gives the Church her specification, being, and unity is the eschatological end situated beyond time, not a historical end situated in time.

Pure horizontalism in one's conception of the Church (and, consequently, in one's conception of the Christian life) is radically absurd. There is absolutely no historical and temporal end—and consequently no behavior referred to such an end—that would or could belong to man's historical finalities, setting aside consideration about his membership in the Church of Christ. And, consequently, there is no historical and temporal end which could give the Church her

---

96. See sect. 1, ch. 1 of the next volume.

own consistency, by means of which she would differ from every other human institution. For example, the Church can and must take a position and act, even in a very concrete manner, in favor of peace, of social justice, against torture, etc. She can and must do this as soon as *she exists as a specific society*, irreducible to every other, that is, as soon as she exists as the Church. However, this would not suffice for making her exist as such [i.e., according to her inner nature precisely *as the Church*], for a human society can also (and must) do all of these sorts of things.

The Christian is not a "being made for death." He is a being [made] for eternal life. Nonetheless, temporal death is the necessary condition for his passage to eternal life. For this reason, as a Christian, he is occupied with the thought of death and familiar with it, not being able to think about the eschatological end without thinking about it.

B. The Temporal Dimension of Christian Existence

{562} This eschatological dimension would be false and distorted if it were not balanced by another dimension, the temporal dimension of Christian existence. (Examples of such possible distortion: "to live as if one must die on this same day"; "at the moment of making a decision ask what, at the point of death, you would wish to have decided at this moment"; "I will continue to play ball."[97]) Above, we noted Teilhard de Chardin's critique concerning the primacy given to intention over action. He formulates this conception as saying, "While earthly objectives have no value in themselves, you can love them for the occasion that they offer you for proving your fidelity to the Lord."[98] He critiques this position (one that, in fact, can be critiqued), though he does so in a way that is quite contestable in itself. According to him, in order to dedicate ourselves to earthly

---

97. [Tr. note: The final expression is attributed to St. Aloysius Gonzaga in response to an inquiry asking him what he would do if he knew his death was imminent, knowing this to be his calling at this moment.]

98. De Chardin, *Oeuvres*, vol. 4 (*Le milieu divin*), 36–38.

undertakings, we absolutely need to think that the result of our actions will not be lost and that the work of our hands will be eternalized and saved. Man cannot put himself to work and persevere in it if he does not have the conviction that the work of his hands (and of his spirit as well) will be eternalized and saved. Thus, his solution is to say that every [human] effort cooperates in bringing the world to completion *in Christo Jesu*.

His solution is the same as the one we already criticized for identifying the movement of history toward earthly objectives with the proper movement of salvation history. We can also note that it is more imaginary than real. Not only is the earthly city which man builds by his efforts passing, but also, in his very process of building, many objectives pursued with passion and at least partially realized fall into the abyss of time. How do things stand with regard to the great civilizations of past days? What about the cathedrals that have been swallowed up by the passing of time?

It is certainly false to say that human work's only value consists in the conformity of man to God's will when he performs such deeds. First of all, there are great human works (e.g., technical, scientific, artistic, civilizational works, and so forth) which may or may not have been done in the spirit of such conformity, though having a value in themselves, independent of such conformity. Secondly, and more profoundly, God who is as wise as He is powerful would not wish that man be delivered to the pursuit of these objectives if they were not good in themselves and worthy of being willed and pursued.

The true solution is different. Two things can be said about these objectives. On the one hand, they have a proper value for man, meaning that by themselves they deserve to be pursued, as much by Christians as by non-Christians. (For this reason, if the Christian's intention is right, he thus conforms himself to God's will in his own pursuit of such objectives.) On the other hand, they can be present to Christian awareness as the mediation (a non-necessary but legitimate one) for eschatological objectives. However, their fleeting nature should be squarely acknowledged, and man can and must pursue them while knowing quite well that they will one day pass away (as he knows that he himself, who is passionate in pursuing them, will be carried off by death). Man, who is a temporal being through his earthly dimension can and must act for temporal objectives—that is, for objectives that are doomed to destruction. The symphonies of Beethoven will no longer exist when there are no men living on earth to perform and enjoy them.

Thus, although the Christian can dedicate himself with all his strength, and above all with all his spirit, to the building up of a temporal work, he nonetheless retains in his depths—in the awareness that he has of his participation, through the loftiest part of his spirit and through grace, in God's transcendence over time—a kind of distance in relation to the end pursued and of the action for attaining it. He has the feeling that he is not entirely engaged in this activity—not that he is voluntarily reserved but, rather, because he is aware that something in him does not allow itself to be engaged. This is what is sometimes called our "eschatological reserve."

A concrete consequence follows from this. For a Christian, to the degree that he acts in accord with his faith, earthly failure does not swallow him up entirely, however complete such failure may be. When he has lost everything on earth, hope is still possible for him. This point can also be found in Teilhard de Chardin.[99] However, it is poorly integrated into the whole of his thought because it is not sufficiently distinguished into its two (temporal and eschatological) dimensions, and he is unable to resolve the problem presented by the complete extinction of the temporal dimension of our activity.

C. Eschatological Hope and Earthly Hopes

{563} Hope is the necessary subjective condition for every enterprise. One cannot be engaged without willing (*intendere*) the goal and, as one wills it, without holding that it is possible. Therefore, in order to be real, the Christian's temporal engagement must include

---

99. See ibid., 99.

participation in men's hopes, in their troubles, in their fears, in their angers, in their joys, and so forth. All this is part of the temporal dimension [of man's existence]. As a theological virtue, hope has the eschatological end as its object. It is a distinct object, but it is not separated off, meaning that it can be mediated by temporal objectives.

Hope rests on the divine promise. First of all and directly, the divine promise is focused on eschatological goods: on eternal life with God, not on earthly happiness; on the resurrection, not on preservation from death. Therefore, theological hope can survive the loss of every earthly hope (as in the person condemned to death after a thwarted revolt).

However, to the degree that eschatological goods are mediated by earthly goods, the divine promise conditionally extends to them (conditioned by the dispositions of general Providence), and earthly hopes can be animated by theological hope. In this sense, we can admit that the promises of eschatology make room for earthly hopes. This does not mean that success would be promised. Rather, as Jean-Gabriel Ranquet[100] notes, it means that "there is a difference of nature, not of structure" between the two of them. On the one hand, earthly hope can subjectively prepare for theological hope (though it can also turn one away from it). On the other hand, theological hope can animate earthly hope.

D. The Eschatological Witness of Religious Life

{564} What[101] justifies religious life—and, generally speaking, the choice of the evangelical counsels—in relation to humanity's earthly tasks is precisely the fact that temporal ends are not the necessary means for arriving at eschatological goods. The latter can be willed immediately. "Immediately": this is only fully valid for the "contemplative life," which includes the renunciation of every earthly objective. However, this is worthwhile only if the theological objective, the ardent search for God, is really substituted for such earthly

---

100. Jean-Gabriel Ranquet, *J'espère en Jésus-Christ* (Paris: Desclée de Brouwer, 1964), 25.
101. See *Lumen Gentium*, no. 43.

objectives. The former absolutely sets the pursuit of every earthly objective in a subordinate position, which implies the renunciation of everything that the theological objective does not command. When such a renunciation is made, earthly objectives are no longer pursued according to their own, proper value, independent in itself from the ordination to the theological order.[102]

The case is slightly different for the active life, where earthly objectives are also pursued for themselves (e.g., education). However, they are of interest to the person who has "renounced the world" only as mediating eschatological goods. The missionary has not left his family, friends, and country in order to contribute to a work of civilization—much less to a work of colonization. Instead, he has left them in order to announce the Gospel, and all of his activity, even that which is civilizing, is attracted by this predominant goal as to its pole.

Such a renunciation testifies to the superiority of eschatological goods over temporal goods. It is certain that, although earthly goods can mediate the seeking of eschatological goods, they are also, at least for sinful man, opaque. They mask eschatological goods as much as they lead to them. The end of the act of renunciation (if it is "true") and of the whole life that it inaugurates (if it is "authentic") is not to throw discredit on earthly values. Rather, their end is to proclaim the relativity of such values and the fact that they necessarily fade away before eschatological values.

---

102. See J.-H. Nicolas, *Contemplation et vie contemplative*, ch. 6.

12

From Final Eschatology to Intermediary Eschatology

{565} The traditional conception of an intermediate state between earthly death and the final resurrection, during which the soul separated from the body continues to live—either in eternal happiness with God, in a state of definitive rejection by God, or in a sorrowful, purifying expectation up to the moment when it is judged worthy of entering, in its own turn, into glory and happiness—raises problems and doubts in theology. The root of such difficulties is found in a reluctance to admit the possibility that the soul would exist in separation from the body.

To many, this seems to be a thesis that is characteristic of a dualistic Greek anthropology, which would be incompatible with Semitic anthropology, which is resolutely unitary and provides the foundation for the biblical doctrine of salvation. Such a dualist anthropology would involve a theologically unacceptable misunderstanding both of the body as an essential constitutive element of man and of death as the real destruction of his being. Moreover, it raises metaphysical problems that seem insoluble according to some. Such an existence, which must be a human one (because it is a question of a human soul and of the human person) would be inhuman or, rather, a-human because it is cut off from every possible relation with the world of men. How are we to conceive of this span of duration in which man's existence would be extended, hypothetically situated outside of space and time?

Thus, it is proposed that this intermediate state should be gathered up into an instant, into which individual eschatology would be concentrated in its totality, an instant that would include, at the moment of death, the realization of each person's eschatology, including the resurrection and, possibly, the purifications of purgatory. What theological position should we have concerning these difficulties and this proposed solution?

I. THE RESURRECTION IMPLIES THE SURVIVAL OF THE SOUL

{566} Death is an ascertainable fact. It certainly includes the irreversible phenomenon of the complete cessation of an individual's vital functioning, followed ineluctably by the dissolution of his body, which is equally ascertainable. If this bodily life is the whole of the person's life, we must say that at this moment the person has purely and simply ceased to exist, has died, as is the case for other animals.

However, we believe in the resurrection. How could we conceptualize the resurrection of a being that has totally ceased to exist, which no longer exists? To what life could he be *restored* if he from whom it was first taken has fallen into pure nonbeing precisely through this loss? In response, it is said that the resurrection is an act of God's omnipotence. Doubtlessly, this is true, but again, in order for there to be a resurrection, one would need to be able to designate a subject that, under the divine action, passes from death to life. There is not a passage from nonbeing to being, and if the Divine Omnipotence purely and simply brings into existence that which previously in no manner had existence, this is not a resurrection but, instead, an act of creation. Indeed, some do speak about the resurrection as being an act of creation.[1]

---

1. See Oscar Cullmann, *Immortalité de l'âme ou résurrection des corps?* (Neuchâtel:

However, this is an utter abuse of language, concealing a contradiction. For a created being, creation is an absolute beginning. The so-called resurrected person, which in reality would be [re-]created, would be an absolutely new being, and not the former being that, on this hypothesis, would have totally and definitively sunk into nonbeing. It is inconceivable and absurd that this being would need to correspond to the actions of the preceding person to whom it is only fictively connected by a constructed relation, not even by reason but by the imagination. It is inconceivable to say that it would depend in some way either on the benefits which God bestowed upon the first [instance of this person] (i.e., the vocation, redemption, the communication of redemption by the sacraments, in a word redemptive and ecclesial grace) or on the acts of freedom that did (or did not) correspond to these benefits. If this new person is "saved," it is not by Christ, for Christ was given to the world, and this [newly created] person never existed in the world. He never was part of it. If such is the case for all the saved, we can say that Christ died in vain.

Paradoxically, in order to receive a new life, the person who suffered death would need to still have a kind of existence and therefore a kind of life. Here, there is an intuition that one finds, so it seems, at the most remote stages of reflection on death. The "descent into Sheol" affirmed by ancient Israel, the descent into hell among the Greeks, the active presence (whether beneficial or dangerous) of ancestors in animism, the transmigration of souls in doctrines of metempsychosis—all this is concerned with one and the same person who lived in the midst of men, who died, and who continues to live by an indistinct, latent, often pitiable existence, but one that is not pure nonbeing. At this stage of thought, one finds no philosophical elaboration and no religious explanation of this state. Rather, as it were, here in its pure form, we find only the muffled feeling that death does not bring everything to an end for the human being. In Israel, the idea of resurrection was formed on the basis of this sen-

---

Delachaux et Nieslé, 1959), 48–51: an idea taken up by many authors, whether Protestant or Catholic.

From Final Eschatology to Intermediary Eschatology

timent (and, quite obviously, under the progressive action of revelation).

For the theologian, the survival of the soul seems to be the only explanation capable of rendering intelligible this survival of the person beyond his own death without which faith in the resurrection itself would be emptied of all content, a purely verbal affirmation without any purchase on reality. Indeed, the person can continue to exist and live after death only if part of him survives. This part is certainly not bodily because, obviously, through death everything that is bodily in the person ceases to live a human life (and any life whatsoever), to exist as a human body, as the body of this person, of any person. Thus, the part that survives can be only incorporeal, invisible, non-extended, and spiritual. In a word, it is what one calls the "soul." It is what continues to exist, stripped of all bodiliness by bodily death. It is what one calls the "separated soul."

Some people oppose against this the hypothesis of an instantaneous resurrection, which would mean that the soul would never exist without a body. We must first observe that this hypothesis is intelligible only within a rigorously hylomorphic anthropology. Indeed, according to such an anthropology, it is perfectly conceivable that the soul, separated from the body that it animates, could immediately be the form of another body, under the resurrecting action of God, made out of a matter to which this action would unite it. This new body would be fully its own. It would be the same body with which and by which it lived on earth, acting and suffering, meriting and sinning, for this former body would be the source of the new body's individuality, which it lost when it became disconnected from it. Therefore, it is not impossible that it would transfer it onto another matter in order to make the same body out of it. Many theologians today, faithful to the tradition of high scholasticism, conceive of the resurrection along such lines (at whatever moment it may be brought about). Their explanation seems not only acceptable but, indeed, the only one capable of rendering an account of the mystery of the resurrection, with an exception being made for Christ's resurrection.[2] However, it is not clear how a great number of contemporary theologians explain this immediate resurrection while simultaneously repudiating such hylomorphism as belonging to outdated philosophical explanations.

In any case, far from suppressing the survival of the separated soul, this hypothesis postulates it. Indeed, one must admit that the soul is capable of an existence that is independent from the body that it animates, so that it might be able to reconstruct this body, in some way, from new matter. If the soul were to pass away with the body, immediate resurrection is as inconceivable as a resurrection postponed to a later moment of duration. And if the soul does not pass away with the body, but instead continues to exist when the body passes away, this is because it can live without the body. In short, faith in the resurrection implies the survival of the person after his earthly death, a survival that can be conceived only if the person, who once existed bodily-spiritually now exists solely as spiritual, reduced to the soul alone.

II. NEW TESTAMENT ESCHATOLOGY, AS BOTH GLOBAL AND SIMULTANEOUS, ASSUMES AN ENDURING INTERMEDIARY STATE

{567} The central event of New Testament eschatology is the Parousia, the return of Christ. All the eschatological events are connected to this event, not only chronologically, but above all by a connection of dependence: the end of the world, the resurrection of the dead, the general judgment, the definitive and public verdicts of mercy and of condemnation. Obviously, Christ's return is situated at the end of human history. Therefore, we must situate all the eschatological events at the end of human history.

To take the general resurrection announced by Scripture and break it up into an indefinite, consecutive series of individual resur-

---

2. See §547 above.

rections would involve (whether or not one wishes) the substitution of a multitude of individual eschatologies in place of a collective eschatology. The immediate subject of the latter is mankind taken together, as well as each person inasmuch as he or she belongs to the human community. By contrast, the former multitude of individual eschatologies would only be connected by Christ's promise made to each person (though a promise that is one and the same for all). What would the Parousia then mean? It would mean that each person encounters Christ at his death. This is not the New Testament's eschatology, precisely the one to which theology today returns with such insistence. From this perspective, the hypothesis of an immediate resurrection can considered to be anachronistic.

However, salvation cannot really concern the whole of humanity if it does not at the same time concern each person who makes up that whole ensemble. Only persons can be "saved," by the salvation accomplished by Christ, which consists in entrance into the communion of the Divine Persons, realized by a love—the Father's love and Christ's redemptive love—offered to each person, a love that each person can freely accept or refuse. Now, the time of salvation for a person is enclosed within strict historical limits, within the salvation history that concerns the whole of humanity. This gives birth to the problem of the intermediary state: namely, the situation of persons, reduced to their soul alone, who must await the fulfillment of salvation history in order that the eschatological events may come about as the necessary fulfillment of God's Salvific Action and of Christ's redemptive action for all and for each person.

After hesitations that lasted centuries, the Church's Magisterium definitively determined that, from the time of their death, these persons are judged by God for the way they lived, and that, in accord with this judgment, they receive either eternal life in light in glory with the Trinity—possibly preceded by a period of painful purification—or the "second death," damnation.[3] This does not repre-

---

3. See Benedict XI, Constitution *Benedictus deus* (D.-*Sch.* nos. 1000–1002).

sent a surreptitious return to an individual eschatology but, rather, is a question of an anticipated participation in general eschatology. It could be compared, *mutatis mutandis*, to the grace one receives in advance *in voto sacramenti*. (Hesitations concerning such an eschatology have been justly raised by utterly conscientious theologians, who did not wish for there to be such an eschatology, one so different from what Scripture announces, yet who did not see how to avoid it other than by pushing the realization of individual salvation to the end of time—something which also stands in contrast to other teachings of the same Scripture.) One can pursue the aforementioned comparison and say that, just as *in voto sacramenti* one cannot receive the *res et sacramentum* that is the directly ecclesial (and therefore communal) effect of the sacrament,[4] so too when the person individually arrives at the end of the journey of salvation, he does not receive by anticipation the resurrection, which is a directly collective, ecclesial effect (because the Church is the community of salvation).

However, against this idea of a duration in the hereafter, some theologians recall that time concerns only temporal beings. One would thus like to reduce the intermediary state to an instant. In this instant, above the time from which the person is thus freed, he would rejoin the last events. If need be, he would traverse the trial of purification in this unique instant prior to his entrance into glory. However, this involves a rather truncated philosophy of time and duration. In truth, those who speak along these lines not seem to conceive that there would be any middle between time (i.e., our time), which obviously only pertains to bodily beings, and eternity, which pertains only to God. To be "freed" from earthly time is not to be free of every kind of time. It is not to become like God, perfectly and totally present to oneself, without the least succession and without the least change. This would exclude not only every succession in a duration to come but also every succession in a past dura-

---

4. See §761 in the next volume.

From Final Eschatology to Intermediary Eschatology

tion. It would eliminate the successive being, which would thus "become"—a claim that is contradictory—a perfectly immobile being, without a past as without a future. In the pure spirit that is the separated soul, there necessarily is succession, even if it is a discontinuous succession of acts, each of which is instantaneous. A measure exists for this discontinuous succession, which we can indeed call a "time" because we have no other word, though it is not earthly time. However, no more is it eternity.

He who would think that a unique instant of this discontinuous time would coexist with the whole of our time (at least the whole of the time that would elapse between the moment of death for the person who enters into this new time and the final events) would certainly thereby express a poor metaphysics, not perceiving the inseparable connection between existence and duration, attributing an infinite duration to a finite existence. In any case, as regards our purposes here, this hypothesis faces a more immediately theological objection: the eschatological future is made up of events whose characteristic is that they depend immediately and exclusively on God's will. It is inconceivable that, solely by its ontological structure and its existence, a created being would have a grip over these events and would make them arrive for itself. The intermediary state can be theologically conceived only as a situation of pure expectation in relation to the *eschata*, about which the Lord himself proclaimed: "But of that day or that hour no one knows ... but only the Father."[5]

Need we add that the New Testament gives valuable indications concerning this gap between the fulfillment of one's personal destiny and the eschatological fulfillment? In the Gospel of Luke, there is the parable of the rich man of Lazarus[6] and the reflections that follow the parable of the clever steward,[7] as well as Jesus's words on the cross to the good thief, "Today, you will be with me in paradise," which stands in striking contrast with the prayer to which

---

5. Mk 13:32 (RSV).
6. See Lk 16:19–31.
7. See Lk 16:9–12.

he responds: "Jesus, remember me when you come into your kingdom."[8] There is also Jesus's response to the Sadducees, which the three Synoptic Gospels relate: "He is not God of the dead, but of the living,"[9] whereas His interlocutors spoke of the future resurrection. There is also Paul who, in 2 Corinthians, begins to envision an encounter with Christ after death, though before the Parousia and the resurrection: "we would rather be away from the body and at home with the Lord."[10]

III. THE IMMORTALITY OF THE SOUL CAN BE UNDERSTOOD IN A MANNER PERFECTLY CONSISTENT WITH BIBLICAL ANTHROPOLOGY

{568} To oppose the affirmation of the immortality of the soul to that of the resurrection as though they fell under two irreconcilable anthropologies, one Greek and the other biblical, is forced and artificial. Indeed, biblical anthropology welcomed the doctrine of the immortality of the soul without in the least renouncing that of the resurrection. This is because the immortality of the soul in no way implies a dualistic anthropology. Moreover, Greek anthropology is not itself necessarily dualistic. Whatever may be the case concerning the Stagirite's authentic theory concerning the separated intellect, someone like Thomas Aquinas knew how to draw a resolutely unitary anthropology from Aristotle, an anthropology enabling us to fully grant bodiliness its role as a constitutive element of the human person and likewise enabling us to acknowledge that death is an evil whose subject is the human person.

According to such an anthropology, the human soul is not, properly speaking, united to the body—as is most often said—but rather to the matter, totally undetermined in itself, which it informs and forms and constructs from within, from which it makes a human

---

8. Lk 23:42–43 (RSV).
9. Mt 22:32 (RSV). See Mk 12:27 and Lk 20:38.
10. 2 Cor 5:8 (RSV). See Phil 1:20–24. [Tr. note: Fr. Nicolas incorrectly cites 1 Cor 5:8.]

body, this individual human body. So considering things, we can and must say that the human person *is* his body, thus connecting back to what is essential in the biblical conception. He is his body because the human body does not exist without the soul. It includes the soul as its principle of existence and, therefore, of life and movement. And the soul itself exists for the body, from the time of its creation, in order to make it exist, so that the soul is implied in its existence, life, and action.

Nonetheless, the soul is not totally submerged in matter, and this is indicated by the fact that the human person performs activities that are immaterial (i.e., thought, love, freedom). Nonetheless, although it is immaterial, this activity is not independent of the body, for this activity is intrinsically conditioned by a bodily activity—perception, imagination, and the passions. The soul's transcendence must not be represented as the elevation of one part of itself over the matter that it informs. The soul is not a kind of quantified reality. It is wholly in each part of the body. Rather, this transcendence must be understood as being a form of interiority, deep within which the soul retains its independence from matter, for it is the source of an activity in which matter does not participate, an operative independence which indicates an ontological independence. And still, it is a virtual ontological independence because, in its native condition, the soul exists only as united to this matter. Its existence is that of the person, and the matter exists with it through this same existence, of which it is the source and principle, though not the distinct possessor.

It is at the moment of death that this virtual independence becomes actual. Death affects the body, given that it is the cessation of bodily life. It destroys the body inasmuch as it is a human body. Because the soul is indestructible on account of its spirituality, it is not itself destroyed by this death. Thus, it becomes the sole holder of the existence which, initially and up to his moment, was common to it and the body. However, the body no longer exists. [As was observed by Étienne Gilson:]

When the body dies, this means that the soul ceases to make it exist. Why would the latter, by this fact, cease to exist? Its body is not what gives it being. The soul is what gives existence to the body. The soul receives its own existence only from God. However, if it preserves its existence, it thus could not lose its individuation: "What makes a given thing to have existence makes it be individuated." Therefore, just as the soul owes its existence in its body to the divine power [*efficace*] and not to the body, so too it owes its existence without its body to this same power... The immortality of the soul is that of its "esse." The survival of its "esse" therefore entails that of its individuation.[11]

If the person is defined as a "being," a subject of existence endowed (at least at his root) with consciousness, love, and freedom, we must say that the soul that thus exists separated is a person, the same person who hitherto was this body animated by this soul. Therefore, at the moment of death, the personality of the composite takes refuge in the soul alone, which subsists indestructibly. Therefore, the person was not destroyed by death, but nonetheless it lost a constitutive part. He is an ontologically truncated person—and this is doubtlessly the reason why St. Thomas thought that he should say that the separated soul is not a person,[12] even though, in fact, the way that he conceives of the life of the saints in the hereafter can belong only to persons, to the same persons as they were here below. However, this shows the very exacting sense that he had for the unity of the human being in his complexity.

IV. THE IMMORTALITY OF THE SOUL

A. The Reality of Earthly Death and the Immortality of Soul

{569} Given that the soul is immortal, it does not die. However, the person does. Such is the paradox involved in death. For all that, the person does not entirely cease to exist and therefore does not entire-

---

11. Étienne Gilson, *Le thomisme, introduction à la philosophie de Saint Thomas d'Aquin*, 5th ed. (Paris: Vrin, 1945), 273–74.

12. See *ST* I, q. 29, a. 1, ad 5.

ly cease to live. We must recognize that this existence is a philosophical enigma, and one is tempted by the agnosticism of someone like Cajetan, who doubted that one could philosophically establish the soul's immortality, given this enigma, which according to him, appeared to be unresolvable for the person who only had the light of reason for trying to disentangle it.[13] As a matter of fact, it can be established with certitude. However, for someone who does not know that the Divine Life can be granted to him, the life of this truncated person, reduced to his soul alone, seems like a kind of non-life, for the spiritual activity of a human person is conditioned by his bodiliness, and the efforts that St. Thomas deploys in showing how God could compensate for it are far from convincing in nature.[14] Interestingly, one could connect this life with that of the dead in Sheol.

The Church's belief that the souls of the just are admitted to the Beatific Vision before the resurrection suppresses the enigma and substitutes a mystery for it. Indeed, the Beatific Vision (along with the beatific love which is an integral part of it) is a mystery. We need not insist on this point here. It removes the enigma because once the mystery is accepted by faith, we can then understand how the soul would have a pure, intense, and utterly fulfilling spiritual activity, the Trinity itself, in its luminous and transparent essence—it is osbcure only for the intellect that attains it only by faith, in the night, so long as it is not yet elevated to the level of its utterly pure and transcendent light—substituting itself for every concept elaborated by the created mind, thus rendering every bodily conditioning impossible and useless both for knowledge and for love.

However, what about the souls who are not admitted immediately to the Beatific Vision? What about those who are rejected? It seems that the mystery of the Beatific Vision can illuminate the enigma for their cases as well. For it makes clear the depths which exist

---

13. See Thomas de Vio Cajetan, *Scripta philosophica. Commentaria in De Anima Aristotelis*, ed. H. Laurent (Rome, 1938), introduction, xxxiv–xxxv. Étienne Gilson, "Cajetan et l'humanisme théologique," *Archives d'histoire doctrinale et littéraire du Moyen Age* 22 (1955): 114–15.

14. See *ST* I, q. 89, a. 1.

in the created spirit, depths that, in fact, are a complete aspiration toward God prior to every particular act of willing, an aspiration which is realized in the Beatific Vision and which renders the Vision possible. (And while this indeed holds for the blessed themselves, who are satisfied, it is equally true for every man's spirit, for the blessed soul itself is able to be filled in this way precisely inasmuch as it is a human spirit.) Therefore, one can indeed suspect that an intense spiritual activity exists in the separated soul who does not see God, one comprised of knowledge of one's self as wholly tending toward God, as well as a knowledge of God, itself also independent of every bodily conditioning, reaching its deepest point through the desire that it arouses, a desire that is experienced in all of its purity precisely because of the abolition of all bodiliness. For the "souls in Purgatory," this knowledge and desire are super-elevated and unified by the theological virtues. For the souls of the damned, such knowledge and desire are painfully wrenching, given that the spirit is thus intimately divided by the obstinate rejection of this God, even though he knows and feels the fact that he was made for Him.

B. The Immortality of the Soul and Meaning of the Resurrection

{570} However, if the soul is filled by the Beatific Vision, what meaning does the resurrection still have? What can the soul expect from it? We must simply respond that grace, even at the summit and fullness that it attains in the Beatific Vision, does not suppress nature and does not substitute for it. The person is truncated in his being by bodily death—which was not only the death of the body, but also his death inasmuch as he is bodily—and this wound exists in it ontologically, even if it is not psychologically felt as something painful, given the complete fruition experienced in the Vision which makes him blessed. It is known by him as being a deficiency (though one that is only provisional). Without a doubt, it is also known by him as an anomaly, and he knows with certitude that it will be suppressed. The certitude of this reintegration is part of his actual beatitude.

From Final Eschatology to Intermediary Eschatology 479

On a plane that is more existential and closer to our experience, one can say that for the Christian who will die, Christian faith responds to our horror at the thought of death by proclaiming this certitude of the resurrection, not belief in the immortality of the soul, which in the doctrine of salvation is only the condition for the possibility of the resurrection. This is why we would fashion quite a bad theology were we to replace the resurrection of the dead in the "Credo" with the immortality of the soul, as Karl Rahner wryly suggested to "classical" theologians.[15]

V. THE DURATION OF THE INTERMEDIARY STATE AND EARTHLY TIME

{571} We can think of duration only in temporal terms, according to our earthly time. However, the intermediary state is not measurable by this time. It is measurable by a discontinuous time, and we have no [direct] means of representing such a time to ourselves. Discontinuous time is made up of instants; the eschatological events, whether they be anticipated for the individual person ([i.e.], the judgment, potential purgation and its stages, the entrance into the Beatific Vision or damnation [*rejet*]) or whether they arrive for all simultaneously ([i.e.,] the Parousia, resurrection, and general judgment) take place in instants of this discontinuous time. A moment (perhaps a continuous line, according to a hypothesis proposed by Jacques Maritain)[16] of earthly time corresponds to each of these [discontinuous] moments.

However, there is no common measure between the distance separating two of these discontinuous instants and the time that joins together two corresponding earthly instants. That is, our temporal language loses all meaning if one applies it to the duration of

---

15. See Karl Rahner, "La résurrection de la chair," in *Ecrits théologiques* (Paris: Desclée de Brouwer, 1966), 4:77.
16. See Jacques Maritain, *La philosophie bergsonienne* (Paris: Téqui, 1948), lvii–lviii.

the intermediary state. This is above all the case if this temporal language, as always happens, is freighted with psychological connotations related to time such as it is lived through and experienced by us. It is a perfectly futile enterprise for one to count the durations of eschatological anticipation in the intermediary state (in particular, the duration of the purgative trials in the hereafter) by using days, years, and centuries. It is likewise perfectly futile for one to imagine, according to one's own experience of time, the feeling experienced on account of this duration's slow, onward flow.

CONCLUSION

{572} The survival of the person reduced to his soul after bodily death poses difficult problems, as much on the level of philosophy as on that of theology. They are not insoluble, although the resolution of such problems will always remain "irritating" for our mind, given its inability to represent to itself this life outside of time and space as well as its inability to conceive of it, for all our thought is conditioned by time and space. Above all it is incapable of conceiving that the person who lives in this way, stripped of bodiliness, is the same person who lived on earth in a bodily manner. Nonetheless, it must affirm this for the grave and imperious reasons that we recalled above.

Even if the affirmation of the immortality of the soul remains problematic for the theologian on the level of philosophy, he is bound to hold it as something true and indubitable, something necessarily implied in faith's affirmations concerning eschatology, for the resurrection becomes unintelligible if the human person is totally destroyed and abolished by bodily death. However, given that the body obviously is utterly destroyed by death, the person can survive only in a non-bodily manner. He must also admit that the state of the person thus reduced to the soul by itself will persist up to the Parousia, for it is only when Christ returns that all men together will be resurrected. Granted, the problems raised by this are difficulties, grave ones; however, they are in no way impossibilities. While contemporary theology has indeed rediscovered the importance of faith's affirmations concerning the comprehensive, collective character of eschatology, we must say that any denial of the intermediary state seems to be incompatible with these very affirmations.

13

The Last Things, Considered from the Perspective of One's Individual Destiny

{573} Eschatology first of all concerns the Church, the community of believers that extends, virtually, to all men because all are called to be incorporated into Christ. However, in the Church, eschatology is concerned with each person, for each person is called to participate in the eschatological goods. This means that there is room for a personal eschatology within a communal (or, ecclesial) eschatology. Such a personal eschatology is what classical theology called "the last things." The rediscovery (or, at least, the reclaiming) of the ecclesial dimension of eschatology in no way justifies the claim that the study of the last things would be vain and pointless, for eschatology itself is what would become vain and pointless if it did not involve the destiny proper to the persons who compose the Church.

Therefore, we can and must (albeit briefly) study the last things, not as an addition to eschatology, but as something existentially included in it. Classically, the last things were distinguished in a fourfold way: death, particular judgment, eternal life (in certain cases with its preamble, purgatory), and in the case of the personal and obstinate refusal of salvation, the definitive failure that is damnation, the second death.

I. DEATH CONSIDERED IN RELATION TO THE REALIZATION OF THE CHRISTIAN VOCATION

A. The Christian Meaning of Death

We[1] will not here discuss death from a medical perspective, nor ethically (e.g., problems of euthanasia, abortion, and so forth), nor pastorally ([i.e.,] preparation for death).

1. Death is the destruction of the human person

{574} From the philosophical perspective, if one admits that the principle of human life, the soul (above all its spirituality), is indestructible, death will be defined as being the dissolution of the human composite, the spiritual part alone remaining after the cessation of bodily life (and therefore the abolition of the body inasmuch as it is a part of the human composite). If this indestructibility is not admitted, death is the pure and simple abolition of the human being (i.e., of the human person). We have seen that this cannot be reconciled with faith in eschatology.

However, the human person cannot be conceived of as a spiritual being enclosed within a bodily sheath. He is a spiritual-bodily being. The body is part of the human person. Thus, death, which is the

---

1. For this whole section, a bibliographical indication: Jacques Choron, *La mort et la pensée occidentale* (Paris: Payot, 1969); André Feuillet, "Mort du Christ et mort du chrétien d'après les épîtres pauliniennes," *Revue biblique* (1959): 481–513; *Le Christ Sagesse de Dieu* (Paris: Gabalda, 1966); *Le prologue du IVe évangile* (Paris: Desclée de Brouwer, 1968); André Godin, "La mort a-t-elle changé?" *Lumen Vitae* 26 (1971): 295–318; Grelot, "La théologie de la mort dans l'Écriture Sainte; Vladimir Jankélévitch, *La mort* (Paris: Flammarion, 1966); Elisbeth Kübler-Ross, *Les dernier instants de la vie* (Genève: Labor et Fides, 1975); Chrysostome Larcher, *Études sur le livre de la Sagesse* (Paris: Gabalda, 1968), ch. 4; Gustave Martelet, *L'au-delà retrouvé. Christologie des fins dernières* (Paris: Desclée de Brouwer, 1974); Jean-Hervé Nicolas, "Compte rendu du livre de Martelet, L'au-delà retrouvé," *Vie Spirituelle* (1976): 284–88; Georges Nossent, "Mort, immortalité, résurrection," *Nouvelle revue théologique* 91 (1969): 614–30; Karl Rahner, "Pour une théologie de la mort," *Ecrits théologiques*, vol. 3 (Paris: Desclée de Brouwer, 1963); Aimé Solignac, "Immortalité," in *Dictionnaire de spiritualité ascétique et mystique*, 7:1601–4. Also, see the anthologized texts: *Le sens chrétien de la mort, Vie Spirituelle* 108, no. 492 (1963); *Nous sommes jugés maintenant. Vie Spirituelle* 108, no. 494 (1963); *Immortalité* (Neuchâtel: Delachaux et Niestlé, 1958).

dissolution of the human composite, is, by that very fact, a dissolution of the person, its destruction. It is a destruction whose cause is obviously primarily external. Death comes to interrupt the person's process of development, which of itself does not have a terminus (as we saw in the case of the end of the world in general). However, in contrast to the end of the world, the object of this "aggression" is a conscious and free person, one who is able to "take up" his death and make it his own through a free act, the act of dying. (For an analysis of the "act of dying" as a supreme act of freedom, see the profound considerations offered by Karl Rahner and the excellent exposition of these insights by Geffré.)[2]

Through this act of freedom, death takes place within the person's destiny. However, this is intelligible only in faith and in hope, because for the person who can consider death only as being the pure and simple terminus of his personal destiny (naturally, this would prevent it from being, properly speaking, a personal destiny) such an act of freedom can be conceived only as being a fatalistic resignation or Stoic stiffening before hostile forces, the person refusing to allow himself to be pierced to his depths and in his consciousness by these forces at the very moment when they prevail over him.

For him who has faith and who hopes in Christ's promises, this act of freedom will not only be the acceptance of death through submission to God's will. It will first of all be the act by which, taking up all of his existence and renouncing all of opposed free acts, he chooses Christ and His kingdom, accepting and ratifying his belonging to Christ—unless, conversely, his act would be the rejection of Christ and the refusal to believe. Thus, it will be the act by which the human person, who must make himself through his freedom, completes himself and gives himself his definitive form.

Of course, such freedom does not exist without grace's involvement. On the one hand, death (conceived of as being the interrup-

---

2. See Karl Rahner, "Pour une théologie de la mort," in *Ecrits théologiques*, vol. 3 (Paris: Desclée de Brouwer, 1963); Claude Geffré, "La mort comme nécessité et comme liberté," *Vie Spirituelle* 492 (1963): 271.

tion and destruction of human life) simultaneously falls under general Providence (i.e., the ensemble of second causes and of God as the First Cause making them act, each according to its nature and existential situation) and under personal Providence, making all these causes' effects enter into the destiny of this person, loved for himself, led by the ways of general Providence to the fulfillment of his own personal vocation, though also being able to fail in this fulfillment through his own freely willed refusal.[3] On the other hand, God's grace is not lacking for man to be able to consummate, or take up anew, the ultimate choice of belonging to Christ. However, by his freedom, man can also choose to evade this grace.

2. *Death as an effect of sin*

{575} In Scripture and tradition, in the ordinary and extraordinary teaching of the Church, death is presented as being an effect of sin—an effect of original sin, not of the personal sins of the person who dies. Man was created immortal, and death has come through the fault of one man: "Therefore as sin came into the world through one man and death through sin, and so death spread to all men because (or, the condition being fulfilled that)[4] all men sinned."[5] The death in question here is the "death of the ungodly"—that is, the death of the soul (i.e., the second death), though also bodily death as its figure and shadow. We can say that it is bodily death inasmuch as total separation from God, who is life, is symbolized and realized by it.

For everyone obviously admits that, in the first intention [of creation and the grace given to Adam, along with its preternatural effects], man was not made to live indefinitely on earth, in an earthly life. Thus, in any event, man's earthly life would have ceased, even if it would have happened without a true death, through a realization

---

3. On the distinction between general Providence and personal Providence, see J.-H. Nicolas, *L'amour de Dieu et la peine des hommes*, ch. 9. Also, §560 above.
4. See Lyonnet, *Les étapes de l'histoire*, 94–99.
5. Rom 5:12 (RSV).

of the mysterious "transformation" spoken of by St. Paul[6] regarding those who will be startled to life by the trumpet announcing the end of the world. If this would have been a death, it would not have been the death of the ungodly but, instead, the death of the just, which we find the Bible evoking in relation to the death of the patriarchs.[7] Would it have been, perhaps, a death followed by an immediate resurrection?

Therefore, death is the effect of sin as a metaphysical catastrophe, not as a biological event. Death, as such, is concretely realized for man in his current condition. Thus, death is, at once, *contrary to nature* (and it is experienced as such) and *in accord with nature*. It is contrary to nature if we consider the aspiration to live forever, as well as man's feeling that he is made to live forever, along with the feeling of transcendence over material nature experienced by the human person precisely as such. However, death is also *in accord with nature*, if we consider the fact that, through his material component, the same person bears within himself a principle of corruptibility that is part of this physical nature submitted to change and to corruption. Finally, it is *supernatural* if we consider the person as being made in the image of God, natively preserved from death (with the nuances noted above) and submitted to death as a consequence of the rupture in man's relationship with God brought about through sin.

3. *Death as the means of redemption*

{576} We have seen how and why Christ redeemed us through His sacrificial death.[8] The Incarnate Word freely assumed this death, as the destruction painfully suffered by living beings, when He assumed human nature in the existential situation in which human nature was placed by Adam's sin (i.e., in its sinful condition) and also when He was delivered to death for our salvation. It is by voluntarily participating in His death that the Christian fully partici-

---

6. See 1 Cor 5:4 and 15:51.
7. See Nicolas, *L'amour de Dieu et la peine des hommes*, 43–44.
8. See §§492ff. above.

pates in the redemption that Christ brought about by dying and being resurrected.[9] Thus, for the Christian following in Christ's footsteps, death becomes the means for Redemption.

As Christ's own death culminated in the resurrection, which manifested its meaning, so too the Christian's death must culminate in the resurrection, which will be the ultimate fulfillment of the redemption: "The last enemy to be destroyed is death."[10] Thus, the marvelous "ingenuity" of God's love made death, which was simultaneously the effect and sign of the true death (i.e., the definitive rupture with God, the absolute failure of the human destiny), into the very means by which man was snatched from sin, reestablished in his dignity and grandeur as a child of God, and finally, the means by which immortality will be returned to him at the resurrection.

4. The Christian's death as the ultimate conformation to Christ in his earthly life

{577} Thus, by assuming our death and making it into the means of our redemption, Christ transformed it and gave it a positive value, whereas by itself it was purely negative. In his earthly life, the believer gradually comes to participate in Christ's death, allowing himself to be configured to Him in three stages: internally by faith; externally though symbolically through baptism and the other sacraments; and, on the basis of that, through all the existential sufferings and pains accepted in union with His cross up to death, which is the ultimate earthly conformation to Christ the redeemer.[11] Obviously, this is not an automatic process. Just as one must believe freely, and just as baptism must be free, so too the death that conforms man to Christ in His death must be a "free" death. Here again we find ourselves faced with the idea of the "act of dying."

9. See §494.
10. 1 Cor 15:26 (RSV).
11. See *ST* III, q. 66, a. 12.

B. The "Act of Dying" in the Warp and Woof of the Acts That Constitute Earthly Life

{578} The "act of dying" cannot be considered as a species of action differing from other actions. What characterizes it is the fact that it is the last act of freedom. Like every act of freedom, it is conditioned, on the one hand by all the limitations of human freedom, on the other by one's prior acts of freedom. It is not a "pure act of freedom." However, because it is the last act of earthly life and therefore immediately precedes man's passage to life beyond earth, it is situated "at the juncture of time and eternity."[12]

1. The continuity of supra-terrestrial life in relation to earthly life

{579} Certainly, according to Scripture, life in the hereafter is prepared for by the life led by man on earth, by the use that he there makes of his freedom. Therefore, there is continuity between the two, even if there must also be a rupture and a disjunction. This continuity is assured by three principles: the permanence of the person, the eschatological meaning of the sacraments, and the fact that charity never disappears.

a) The permanence of the human person

We have seen that despite the person's dissolution through death, he is the one who survives through his spiritual component, the soul. The same person who lived on the earth now lives—in conditions that cannot be imagined—beyond earth and history. This person is the one who will be resurrected when his body is returned to him (i.e., when the composite is revived). This is the only way that we can intelligibly express the meaning of this fundamental scriptural theme, doing so in a way that is befitting in relation to God's justice. St. Paul expresses this theme in the following way (though it is found expressed in a hundred different manners in the New Testa-

---

12. See Jean-Hervé Nicolas in the anthology volume "Le sens chrétien de la mort," *Vie Spirituelle* 108, no. 492 (1963).

ment): "For we must all appear before the judgment seat of Christ, so that each one may receive good or evil, according to what he has done in the body."[13]

b) The eschatological meaning of the sacraments

The sacraments make the Christian participate in the complete mystery of Christ, who embraces all time and who, Himself, is beyond time and eschatological. To be baptized in Christ is to exist in the dead and resurrected Christ. The resurrected Lord is the one who vivifies us through the Eucharist and whose coming will be announced by the community "until He comes [in glory]." If the person who receives the sacraments must entirely disappear, meaning that an entirely new person must "be with Christ," the sacraments would be pointless. Admittedly, they themselves belong to the earthly phase of the Christian life. However, they come to their culmination in the meeting with Him whom they signify and render present so that the Christian might be united to Him during his earthly life. They come to their culmination in the hereafter.[14]

c) Charity never dies

Again, this is a fundamental theme [of our faith]: the charity with which one loves God on earth is the same charity as that with which the person who perseveres to the end eternally loves Him. Similarly, this same point involves us in the subject of how eternal life already begins in charity and the life of grace.

2. *The final choice*

{580} During his earthly life, man can always modify his freedom's orientation. Up to the last moment, he can either turn toward the "living and true God" or, on the contrary, can turn away from Him.[15] Afterward, his free choice is fixed in the last choice of his

---

13. 2 Cor 5:10 (RSV). [Tr. note: Fr. Nicolas incorrectly cites 2 Cor 5:12.]
14. See sect. 1, ch. 4 of the third part of this text.
15. See Ezek 18.

earthly life—not by an arbitrary decision of God, but because his person, reduced to its spiritual component, is totally and irreversibly engaged in the orientation that he freely gave himself. This orientation remains free, but freedom does not consist in the ability to change. On the contrary, the ability to change arises from the particular limitations and conditions that free will takes on in the bodily conditions of its exercise on earth. Thus, the person's destiny—that is, eschatological salvation or loss—definitively depends on this last choice.

a) Questions

Generally speaking, man's exercise of free will is encumbered with a thousand servitudes. Indeed, this seems to be especially true at the moment of death. Therefore, it is difficult to admit the idea that the eternal fate of the person who made it could depend on a choice that in reality has so little freedom. Thus, theologians have taken great pains in order to exempt this choice from all the conditions that would diminish its freedom.

b) Unverifiable and contestable solutions

{581} Some have imagined that this final choice would take place in an incorporeal manner at the first moment of the life hereafter, not at the last moment of earthly life. Therefore, it would be made in full light and in full freedom, disengaged from all the obstacles coming from forms of ignorance, prejudices, bad habits, and external pressures. Such a solution is unacceptable both philosophically and theologically.

Philosophically, it presupposes the tremendous claim that the human person would fully be himself only when he ceases to be fully human! Thus, it presupposes that human freedom (which, moreover, is so strenuously proclaimed) begins to be seriously exercised only when free will finally (!) finds itself extracted from its human conditions of existence and exercise. *Theologically*, it ends up emptying all the content out of the great biblical theme that man must be judged by the way that he uses his free will on earth. On such a hypothesis, the whole of earthly life (and therefore, the whole of human history) is reduced to insignificance. The person's destiny would begin only at the moment when man is situated outside the world and outside of history. Thus, what would history be if not a vain and cruel theater, leaving the pursuit of serious matters to the domain laying beyond history? If it is said that this choice depends on prior choices, this fundamental error is hardly corrected, for that choice either strictly depends on them (and, thus, the hypothesis becomes useless) or the person can renounce them (and, in this case, the dependence in question is purely verbal).

Others (Boros, Glorieux, Geffré), all the while recognizing that the final choice is accomplished at the last moment of earthly life, have proposed the hypothesis that the person would enjoy a wholly new, unconditioned freedom to choose for or against God at this last moment:

> Death would coincide with man's first fully personal act. Thus, it would be the privileged place of self-awareness, freedom, the encounter with God, and his decision in relation to his eternal destiny. Death would thus realize the fulfillment of our human dynamism and would exhaust all of our possibilities of choice. This final act is not situated before or after death. It coincides with the very moment of death.[16]

First of all, we must note that this is a pure, absolutely unverifiable hypothesis which significantly goes against what can be verified concerning the state of the person at the moment of death. Moreover, it has a disadvantage which is similar (though in an attenuated form) to what we noted from the philosophical perspective for the preceding: it is quite strange to hear it said that "man's first truly personal act" would occur at the moment of death! This disastrously devalues human life (and, therefore, history). Likewise, from the theological perspective, this excessively relativizes the importance of our earthly choices in relation to our supra-terrestrial destiny and

---

16. Geffré, "La mort comme nécessité et comme liberté," 273.

how those choices are involved in our relationship with God. In all of this, what would become of the important insights we explained above concerning the fact that eschatology has already begun?

Certainly, God can illuminate whomever He wishes and however He wishes at the moment of death. This falls to the unpredictability of grace. However, grace ordinarily does not contradict nature. It is probable that such graces occur, though at a time when the person is existentially capable of a human act. And, psychologically, it can only be a question of a human act that is like other human acts, one submitted to other servitudes and that is also aided (and doubtlessly more efficaciously) by the same aids [as other acts]: a weakening of the attraction of earthly goods, an attenuation (sometimes a suppression) of human influences that are opposed to the movement of grace, and an intervention of other influences that go in the direction of grace (a priest, family, and so forth). One can always hope that someone may be converted "between the bridge and the river," and even between immersion and asphyxiation!

What does not seem to be acceptable in this hypothesis is the affirmation that the last moment of the person's development on earth would naturally be a summit of personal life and of freedom, while supernaturally being a summit of the intensity of grace. The last moment is such only because nothing else follows it. It is not qualitatively different from the preceding moments. Ordinarily, during these last moments of his earthly life, the person is extremely diminished in his capacities for acting and making decisions. It is wholly arbitrary to affirm that he is more capable at this moment than at a previous one to freely come to a decision in relation to God and to Christ.

c) A response to the question posed

{582} One's last human act neither necessarily nor always (nor, doubtlessly, ordinarily) coincides with the last moment of earthly life. On the other hand, there is no reason to think that the last human act is superior to others from the perspective of the exercise of freedom, knowledge, and determination. (Indeed, there are many reasons to think that the contrary is the case.)

The question is posed falsely when one asks how the person's supra-terrestrial destiny could depend on an act that is as hardly-free and as weak as the last human act ordinarily is. A human act depends on those that preceded it. What is decisive is the willing of the ultimate end implied in the final choice. Most often, the actual choice, even a very weak and very conditioned one, occurs in accord with the willing of the end, which was able to be elicited much earlier and in full freedom—and which was reinforced in the choices that followed it.

If this willing is good, if the person is voluntarily oriented toward Christ, this is what endures in the last choice by the grace of God. If it is evil, the same grace of God can act on the will so that he may revoke this evil willing at the moment of death. For this to be the case, this last act does not need to have a superior personal quality. Indeed, it is true that the deep and often-unperceived—though, nonetheless, spiritually dominating—principle in all of our choices is our decision in relation to Christ. Precisely because of the weakness in which the person finds himself at the end of life, the pressure exercised by the same object of choice upon his will (most often by the intermediary of the sensibility) is attenuated, perhaps to the point of being extinguished. This attenuation doubtlessly favors bringing this fundamental decision into the foreground.

Nonetheless, we must not minimize the redoubtable power of saying "no" that is connected to the exercise of freedom. All the prior choices made through the course of one's existence had the effect of strengthening and rooting this fundamental decision into the will itself so that, at this moment when it appears in greatest relief to consciousness, what predominates (at least psychologically) is the pressure of the priorly taken and unrevoked decision. If it is a decision against Christ, a rejection, it can only be revoked by a true conversion. Such a conversion is possible both from the perspective of grace, obviously, and psychologically, for it takes place in the spiritual depths of the person and does not require a complicated process of deliberation. However, it is a conversion that can be refused. If it is a decision for Christ, there are few reasons one can think of for revoking it at this moment when it is easier for the person who made such a decision, especially quite some time ago, to maintain it rather than revoke it. In this, we can see the classical solution's superiority over the ones mentioned above, holding that one's prior life would have so little weight in assuring the rectitude of one's last choice.

II. THE PARTICULAR JUDGMENT

{583} Earlier, we spoke about the eschatological judgment.[17] There is no doubt that Scripture most often and most extensively speaks to us about God's judgment in the form of a general judgment at the end of time. Nonetheless, there is also the judgment that has been exercised from the time of the first coming of the Word, solely by Jesus's presence in the midst of men and, above all, by His cross and resurrection. Beyond this, is there a particular judgment that would be part of the intermediary eschatology, one that would await each person immediately after his death?

Mollat shows that there are indications for this in the Gospels (e.g., the parable of the poor man Lazarus and the wicked rich man; the words of Jesus to the penitent thief) and in St. Paul.[18] In the Church's tradition, one must take note of prayer for the dead and the cult of the martyrs which both existed from the first centuries onward. However, only in the fourteenth century (in 1336) was it defined by Pope Benedict XII that the souls who have left this world receive their retribution without delay—that is, the Beatific Vision (sometimes preceded by the purifications of purgatory) or damnation—without prejudice to the general judgment on the day when all men will appear with their bodies before the tribunal of Christ

---

17. See §548 above.
18. 2 Cor 5:8; Phil 1:23.

so that they may render account of what they did, for good or evil, during their bodily life.[19]

This does not mean that the idea of a "particular judgment" was new for the Church. It is a truth that gradually emerged, so that it may reach this moment of its maturation. It emerged within the complex of the revelation of general eschatology, as was more generally the case for the idea of an intermediary eschatology. What was said concerning the judgment in general holds for the particular judgment as well. It is a question of a completely interior judgment, in which our consciousness [*conscience*], freed from forms of ignorance and its own dissimulations, will be a pure echo of God's judgment. However, two questions can be posed.

A. The Judgment of Works Performed on Earth

{584} Will God's judgment be concerned with all that was said or done? It is necessary to illuminate such affirmations by Ezekiel 18 and 33:11–16, as well as the numerous affirmations of the New (and the Old) Testament which hold that "God forgets sins." In reality, it is always the person who is judged, for he is the one who engages himself in relation to God through his free acts (in the obedience of love or in the disobedience of counter-love). However, precisely speaking, he engages himself through his acts—primarily through his internal acts, though also through his external acts and their effects (i.e., through his works), for the internal act is expressed and realized in the external act.

Unlike the human judge, who reaches the person only through his acts, passing from works to external acts, from there to interior acts, and from there to the very person who acts, God first reaches the "heart," that is, the intimate depths of the person, and, from there, reaches his acts and his works. Through conversion, the sinner separates himself from his past acts and works. They are no longer

---

19. See note 3 above. [Tr. note: Fr. Nicolas cites "111," perhaps referring to note 3 above, where he cites a text by him concerning the distinction between general Providence and personal Providence.]

his own. His present self repudiates them. They fall into the abyss of mercy and are lost. They are no longer judged. Conversely, if he turns away from God, his good works are what are separated from him and are no longer his own.

Taking these "conversions" (to good or evil) into account, the person makes himself through his free acts. God judges him at the moment when he leaves this life, such as he has made himself, such as he is, henceforth forever fixed in his essential choice, either adhering to Christ or rejecting Him. So too, he will be aware of having become what he is and of having become so freely. He will be aware of having made himself be what he is. That is why this judgment will in no way be contested by anyone. God will be proclaimed just by all, both by those who are found to be just (by grace) and by those who are condemned on account of their sin.

B. The Relation of the "Particular Judgment" to the "General Judgment"

{585} Here again, as in the whole of this question concerning eschatology, we must guard against every form of anthropomorphism. Succession does not exist in God. God judges man through a single judgment. It reaches men as a whole (general judgment) and each man personally (particular judgment). From the perspective of the created person, the sequence of the two judgments will be that of the judgment itself followed by its public manifestation. The former is internal and personal, being produced immediately after death, and it will reappear as being included in the latter in the general judgment. Properly speaking, this will not be a new judgment. As was said for intermediary eschatology in general,[20] it is an anticipation of the final judgment, in a way that is somewhat analogous to how the grace of justification granted to a "righteous person outside [the Church]" is an anticipation of baptismal justification.

---

20. See §567 above.

III. THE DEFINITIVE ENTRY INTO THE KINGDOM

{586} Jesus came to announce the kingdom of God, a kingdom immediately realized in His person though one that will appear in glory on His "day." All those who have believed in Him and have confessed and followed Him must enter into this kingdom. This is the object of Christian hope. In Scripture, the joy promised to believers is described by a host of images, some mythical (e.g., heaven and the liturgy that takes place in it)[21] and others figurative (a new Jerusalem, a new people, a new holy earth, and so forth). All of this calls to mind a radical metamorphosis of human life, though presented as being the transfiguration and definitive realization of the concrete experience first granted to the people of Israel, then, above all, to the Church sacramentally. The theologian must seek to understand what this transfiguration will consist in, a transfiguration which will simultaneously be a form of continuity and form of rupture.

A. Life with Christ Beyond Death

{587} In the fourth Gospel, life with Christ beyond death is the ultimate promise of Jesus: "that where I am you may be also."[22] Likewise, in the Book of Revelation, the elect are with the Lamb and follow Him wherever He goes.[23] In Paul, the continuity between life here below with Christ and life with Christ again in the hereafter is expressed in a gripping manner.[24] However, he notes that the Holy Spirit, thanks to whom all this is given, constitutes the first fruits of our inheritance,[25] the beginning of eternal life.[26] Thus, the ultimate object of hope[27] is nothing other than life with Christ be-

---

21. See Rv 4:5 and 7:9–11.
22. Jn 14:3 (RSV).
23. See Rv 14:4.
24. See Rom 6; Col 2:12–13; Eph 2:5–6; Gal 2:19–20.
25. See 2 Cor 1:22 and Eph 1:13–14.
26. See Rom 8:23.
27. See Rom 8:24–25.

yond death: nothing, even death itself, could separate us from the love of God that is in Christ Jesus.[28] Thus, "God will bring with him those who have fallen asleep."[29] We will be with Him forever. Christ died for us so that, "Whether we wake or sleep we might live with Him."[30]

This plural ("we") emphasizes the communitarian aspect of this life with Christ, though Paul is not unaware of its personal aspect: "My desire is to depart and be with Christ, for that is far better. But to remain in the flesh is more necessary on your account."[31] And: "So we are always of good courage; we know that while we are at home in the body we are away from the Lord, for we walk by faith, not by sight. We are of good courage, and we would rather be away from the body and at home with the Lord."[32] Similarly, Jesus's promise to the good thief: "Today you will be with me in Paradise."[33] Thus, the life of the Christian on earth is already a life with and in Christ in faith, and this life will blossom forth into "sight" and "glory" in the next world.

B. Participation in the Condition of the Resurrected Christ

{588} What is promised to "those who die in the Lord"[34] is participation in the condition of the resurrected Christ: "For if we have been united with Him in a death like his, we shall certainly be united with Him in a resurrection like His."[35] For them, as for Christ, ultimate salvation will consist in victory over the last enemy, death, so that death may be swallowed up in the victory. We have already spoken about the eschatological existence to which the resurrection gives us access.[36] All that we can say is that, as in the case of Christ,

---

28. See Rom 8:35–39.
29. 1 Thes 4:14 (RSV); see 4:14–17.
30. 1 Thes 5:10 (RSV).
31. Phil 1:23–24 (RSV); see 1:20–24.
32. 2 Cor 5:6–8 (RSV).
33. Lk 23:43 (RSV).
34. Rv 14:13.
35. Rom 6:5 (RSV).
36. See §547 above.

our entire being will partake in eternal life with God. The concept of life is certainly not foreign to our experience. However, the concept of a life integrally divinized by the Holy Spirit's action, and for this reason participating in the "glory of God," is situated outside our experience. "Life with God" will include the "redemption of our bodies."[37] What we await and what all creation awaits with us is "the revealing of the sons of God" in "glorious liberty."[38]

The object of our hope is not that our spiritual and immortal soul will escape the material world wherein the body would imprison it. On the contrary, our hope is that, passing through death as through a trial, our entire being—integrally body and soul and (mysteriously) assimilated to that of the resurrected Christ—will participate in the divine glory in a universe that has been transformed, not annihilated.

C. The Beatific Vision

{589} As regards intermediary eschatology, we have seen that even though the ordinary eschatological outlook expressed in Scripture is communitarian and ecclesial in nature, there is room not only for each person's participation in eschatological goods but, also, for an anticipatory participation in these goods by the person who dies in the course of salvation history. This anticipated participation does not include bodily resurrection, which is awaited. What does it consist in? It consists in the Beatific Vision in which the primary object of Christian hope, the promise of participation in the Divine Life, is realized in its essence. In the first part of this text, we examined the problems raised by the Beatific Vision in relation to our knowledge of God through grace as well as in relation to the full fructification of the human person.[39]

What we must note here is that, however important the role of the (spiritualized) bodily order may be in eschatological goods, the Beatific Vision (with the love that is inseparable from it) is the cen-

---

37. See Rom 8:23 (RSV).
38. Rom 8:19–21 (RSV).
39. See §§170–76 in the previous volume.

ter and focus of the eschatological fullness and joy. This love and vision together are the created person's participation in the Trinitarian life. "Being with Christ" consists in entering into a full and living communion with Him in that which makes up His life (what already made up His life here below, even if it was in some way hidden by flesh), namely His life with the Father, the knowledge and love of the Father. He returned to the Father, and through the Beatific Vision and love, the faithful rejoin Him in the Father. The mysterious "spiritualization" of the resurrected body spoken of by St. Paul will irradiate from this wholly spiritual center, this *apex animae* or this "depth" in which the person will be united to the Trinity.

Jesus's words, "All the rest will be given to you in addition," here find their ultimate and loftiest application. "Heaven" includes all the goods that can fill the person who has arrived at the eschatological terminus. However, they flow from the essential good that is personal life with the Divine Persons and are given to him by way of addition.

D. The Beatific Vision and the Bodily Resurrection

{590} It was an error to conclude from this, as was the tendency of a number of scholastic theologians, that the resurrection of the body and of all the goods that it would bring would have no importance in reality. All of this was called "accidental beatitude," and "accidental" was understood basically as meaning "superfluous." In general, this is an abuse of the primacy rightly accorded (but which must be wisely so accorded) to the essence in the constitution of a reality. There are "accidental perfections" that come from outside and remain superficial. However, there are also accidental perfections that have their root in the essence. They can be hidden, either provisionally (because the conditions for their emergence are not yet realized) or definitively (because external obstacles prevent this emergence). In this case, the realities in question already virtually exist (e.g., a human person whose intellectual and moral faculties are not yet developed) or already exist but are hindered (e.g., a human person whose mental faculties are arrested in their development, as in those who have profound intellectual disabilities). However, what is lacking for this person, all the while being "accidental" in the philosophical sense, concurs to his integrity, meaning that he is diminished without it. This is lacking for him.

The situation of the blessed prior to the resurrection could be compared to the child who provisionally lacks the full exercise of his physical and intellectual means. This is a limping analogy, given that, in contrast, the blessed person is utterly filled in his spiritual faculties. The analogy bears upon this point: bodily glorification is an integral part of the human person's beatitude, and it flows from the spiritual glory that he receives through the Beatific Vision and love. Nonetheless, it is not produced immediately, for it postulates an act of God, which is part of Providence and will take place only at the moment fixed by the Father, on the day of the Lord.

Does this introduce a shadow, namely, suffering, into beatitude? In the Book of Revelation, we see the mysterious impatience of the martyrs in heaven, calling out for vengeance on the inhabitants of the earth.[40] However, this text is not concerned with the issue of the resurrection. We are prevented on two heads from thinking of such a form of impatience that would translate into a kind of suffering. On the one hand, all eschatological goods are included in the glory of the vision as in their source and principle, so that, when the bodily goods are granted, they will not be added but, instead, will only extend the joy that is already there, bringing it to its full fructification. On the other hand, all such eschatological goods are experienced as being certain and, in some way, as already present for the soul that is indissolubly united to God, who can communicate them at a moment to come and indeed intends to do so. They will not be superfluous. They are as certain as though they were already there. More than the certitude of faith (which includes the fear of separating oneself from the source of the good), this certitude is a presently lived certitude in

---

40. See Rv 6:9–11.

a maturation that can be prevented by nothing, for it depends exclusively on the all-powerful and all-loving will of God, whose promise is certain.

IV. BETWEEN THE DEATH OF THE RIGHTEOUS AND THEIR ENTRANCE INTO THE KINGDOM: PURGATORY

{591} After having taught for many centuries that a purifying trial exists beyond death, destined for those who, having died in charity, still must expiate for the sins committed during their earthly lives, the Church solemnly defined this doctrine at the Council of Trent, against the denials expressed by the Reformers—first, in the decree on justification[41] and then in the course of the twenty-fifth session.[42] This affirmation of faith meets with two kinds of difficulties. On the one hand, it seems foreign to Scripture and poorly founded on ancient tradition. Moreover, it poses problems for theological reasoning.[43]

A. The Scriptural and Traditional Foundations of the Doctrine of Purgatory

{592} The idea of a purifying fire, on the one hand, and that of a category of the dead, on the other, intermediaries between the perfectly good and the totally wicked, who are in need of expiation, come from Judaism and influenced the [early] Christians ... It is of little importance that, following the rabbis in conceiving of purgatory as being a compartment of Gehenna, Christians represented it as a place of torture differing from Hell only by its duration ... All Christians believed in the divine holiness, that "nothing impure will enter into the Heavenly Jerusalem,"[44] and that, with-

---

41. Session 6, can. 30.
42. See *Decretum de Purgatorio*, December 3, 1563: D.-Sch., no. 1820.
43. See Yves-Marie Congar, "Le Purgatoire," in *Le mystère de la mort et de sa célébration*, ed. A. M. Rouget (Paris: Cerf, 1951), 279–336; Albert Michel, "Purgatoire," in *Dictionnaire de théologie catholique*, 13:1163–1326; Ceslas Spicq, "Purgatoire," in *Dictionnaire de la Bible*, 9:555–56; "Fegefeuer," *Lexikon für Theologie und Kirche*, 2nd edition, ed. J. Höfer und K. Rahner (Freiburg i.B., 1957ff.), 4:49–55; and the anthology text *Se purifier pour voir Dieu*. *Vie Spirituelle* 108, no. 491 (1963).
44. Rv 21:27.

out sanctification, nobody will see God.[45] They equally thought that no just person was totally free from sin. Therefore, since Christ had opened heaven and promised the vision of God to sinners pardoned by virtue of His blood … it was self-evident that they were thinking of a complete purification prior to this vision. And since Scripture teaches that the living can efficaciously intercede for the dead, they used the term "purgatory" for the situation of expectation wherein these latter—so to speak, always on the way [toward heavenly bliss]—still have the possibility of "making satisfaction" to the divine justice. It is at least the case that the process of purification and sanctification essential to salvation is prolonged and brought to its end in the intermediary state. One cannot speak of an innovation in faith; rather, this represents a progressive growth in awareness concerning the data of Revelation.[46]

From the perspective of tradition, what is the most anciently attested (already in Tertullian) is prayer for the dead, especially the offering of the Eucharist for them. Here, the affirmation of purgatory is not found in a dogmatic form but, instead, as a practice of prayer implying such an affirmation. *Lex orandi, lex credendi.*

B. THEOLOGICAL REFLECTION ON THE DOCTRINE OF PURGATORY

1. The theological aporias that the doctrine of purgatory resolves (in faith)

{593} It is not a question of demonstrating the doctrine of purgatory *a priori*. What was said above appeals to the "sense of faith" such as it developed in the Church, even if reasons that were more or less theological in nature played a role in this development. However, we do not believe in purgatory because of these theological reasons; we believe in it because it is the faith of the Church. However, this doctrine responds to difficulties that "the entrance into the kingdom" raises for believing reason. By means of such a response, it can be more easily assimilated by this reason.

---

45. See Heb 12:14.
46. Spicq, "Purgatoire," 555.

a) The continuity of the human person's destiny and the spiritual unpreparedness of the soul for death

{594} We have seen that a fundamental theme of biblical eschatology is that human destiny, begun by vocation and consummated in glorification, is accomplished through the "steps" of earthly life. The grace of the children of God is the seed of glory. By developing this seed in faith and by living in accord with the requirements of divinization, man is prepared on earth to inherit the kingdom with Christ.

However, it is a fact that few Christians live fully in accord with their grace of divinization. Few are really "occupied" with God, with living with the Divine Persons. Many, doubtlessly, come back to God at the last moment without anything in their preceding life having prepared them for living with God for all eternity. How could we conceive of such an immediate passage to the fully divinized life as anything other than a complete rupture with what they were and with what they willed during their earthly life?

Certainly, just as one cannot exclude the possibility of conversion at the moment of death, one cannot exclude an instantaneous preparation for grace. What one can say is, first of all, that most of the time there is no indication of such a spiritual transformation. Moreover, what can be verified concerning the normal course of events in the dying generally does not favor this hypothesis in any way. It would be of the order of the miraculous, and there is no promise in this direction.

The theologian's mind can find satisfaction in the idea that spiritual preparation is pursued after death in the form of a purification (which, as we have seen, itself poses many problems) from everything that at the moment of death inhibited the development of the spiritual seed of grace.

b) The continuity of the human person's destiny and the soul's moral unpreparedness for death

{595} There is more still to be said, and here we face a more delicate matter. Eschatology is wholly dominated by confidence in God's justice. Can we admit that someone who multiplied his sins during his life would be immediately admitted into the kingdom after death without doing penance? What would become of our responsibility before God in the use of our freedom?

The problem is much more urgent and can take on a harrowing form when it is a question of grave and multiple transgressions and injustices committed against men. The desire for justice, in the form of an intervention by "the sovereign" and especially by God, who loves and who can do all things, is an uncontrollable aspiration in the hearts of the poor and the oppressed. The indifference of the divine judge in relation to offenses suffered by His "litigants" can be experienced only as being an injustice and a lack of love—an indifference in relation to the oppressed, on the pretext of showing mercy toward the oppressor.

This sentiment is something completely different than vengeance (although the spirit of vengeance can often be mingled with it). For poor people who are despised, socially persecuted, and physically annihilated by injustice, it is a question of being "recognized" by Him who is the universal judge. How could He be so other than through manifestations of His severity toward the oppressor? This is the sense in which the mysterious text of Revelation 6:9–11, cited earlier, must be understood. Above all, we must call to mind the scriptural passages expressing Yahweh's indignation against oppressors, expressions that were taken up by Christ in the Gospels with the promise of divine vengeance.

Certainly, this irrepressible aspiration to justice (for one's self and for others) seems to be contradicted and, as it were, paralyzed by charity, which wills the good of all, including that of the oppressor. The response, given first by Christ's example and that of the saints, is that we are to call for the sinner's conversion, which also requires the oppressor acknowledge his wrongdoing, repent, and thereby restore the oppressed person's dignity. However, we have seen that conversion also includes satisfaction. How is one to think that there will not be, here below or hereafter, a satisfaction imposed upon injustice (and not only on injustice toward one's brothers but on sinners in general)? In this, the theologian is faced with the aporia that faith in purgatory resolves.

2. *The problems of post-mortem reparation of already-pardoned sins*

{596} Although the doctrine of purgatory resolves certain theological aporias, it also raises a number of problems. How is one to conceive that sins that have already been pardoned (for, he who has charity has the Holy Spirit, who always brings the remission of sins) would still need to be "expiated"? Is not the idea of a conditional pardon contradicted by the revelation of God's mercy? On the other hand, how is one to conceive of an "expiation" in the next life? This cannot be a kind of "satisfaction," for satisfaction is part of the state of way (*status viae*). It is a course of action by which one returns to God. He who dies in charity is united to God definitively, and his free will is irreversibly engaged in love (and, therefore, in union).

a) Sufficient and imperfect conversion

We have seen that satisfaction (or, acts of penitence) proceed from interior penitence, from "penitent love." It is by them that the expiation of sins occurs. The intensity, quantity, and duration of expiation is more so inversely proportional to the intensity of the penitent love than directly proportional to the greatness of the offenses. Paradoxically, however, penitent love takes the place of satisfaction, in the sense that satisfaction draws from it all of its value before God so that satisfaction adds nothing to it, except the fact that it expresses and concretizes it on account of man's spiritual-bodily nature.

In short, the saint does not make satisfaction in order to obtain the pardon of his sins but, rather, does so because he has obtained the pardon of them. Indeed, this is so even if he did not have to obtain this pardon for himself, or when he makes satisfaction for the sins of another. (The latter is clear with regard to the wholly unique case of Christ.)[47] Consequently, at death, when man's bodily dimen-

---

47. See §493 above.

sion is (provisionally) abolished, with love alone remaining, neither needing nor having the possibility for expression, it immediately produces its fruit: union with God, which God alone can bring about (the gift of the "light of glory" which alone capacitates him for the Beatific Vision), although the created spirit is immediately ready for it *if he totally loves.*

Unless he lacks something as regards love itself. This is the quite-frequent case of a charity that is authentic but mingled with an insufficiently subordinated and integrated self-love. (We cannot here develop this theme, which is of great importance in the moral and spiritual life.)[48] "One does not love you, Lord, when one loves something (or someone) outside of you without loving it for You":[49] given the complexity of the human person, his difficulty, his quasi-impossibility of being totally engaged in his love, even the principal love which dominates (i.e., the love of the Last End), it regularly happens that charity is thus mixed and imperfect. Therefore, through such charity, the person does totally not give himself to God in such love, without that charity losing its authenticity. It is with such a mixed charity that the just person commits venial sins.

What is the role of past sins in this imperfection? We have seen that inasmuch as sin is past it is totally pardoned: God no longer recalls it. However, we have also seen that past sin would remain in the form of the persistent attachment to the "deceptive good" for the sake of which one sinned. Conversion includes the rejection of this attachment and the preference of the divine good to created goods. However, insofar as the love of God (in which conversion essentially consists) can be imperfect and mixed with attachment to the creature which, without prevailing, remains there as it were in a silent fashion, this rejection is imperfect by this very fact. To the degree that one's attachment to the "deceptive good" (i.e., to oneself) persists, the past sin still remains in the will, in the spiritual being of the person. It is not God who measures His pardon. It is the creature

---

48. See J.-H. Nicolas, *Contemplation et vie contemplative*, ch. 3.
49. St. Augustine, *Les Confessions, Oeuvres de St. Augustine* 14 (Paris: Desclée de Brouwer, 1949ff.), bk. 10, ch. 29. See *ST* II-II, q. 186, a. 3.

who opposes a semi-obstacle to the divine pardon. The creature is incompletely pardoned because he remained incompletely pardonable, in his very conversion. By the same fact, the creature is not disposed to receive the gift of glory and to "enter into the kingdom." It is necessary that he be purified.

b) The impossibility of making satisfaction beyond death

{597} Satisfaction, properly speaking, belongs to the state of way. It is the process of returning to God undertaken by the person who sinned and has received pardon for his sins. By this undertaking, charity is amplified and intensified by being expressed and taking shape in acts of penitence. At the same time, he is purified, for inasmuch as these actions are inspired by charity, they detach him from the apparent good.

At death, the state of way ceases. Totally and definitively engaged in relation to the chosen ultimate Last End, the person is united to Him and "holds" Him inasmuch as it is possible for him. He can neither be detached from Him, nor approach more closely to Him. Effective union can occur only by a gift from God (the "light of glory"), but the soul no longer can do anything more in order to merit this gift or in order to prepare himself for it. The impurity of his charity, which we discussed above, is a lack of preparation, a counter-disposition to this gift. However, he can no longer do anything in order to prepare himself for it. The past weighs upon him, upon his present, but this present is definitive (there no longer is a future), and he can himself do nothing in order to modify it.

Therefore, he cannot "make satisfaction." God alone can act on him in order that he be purified, and thus made ready to enter into the kingdom.

Doubtlessly, this purifying action could be a simple pardon (as we have seen for the pardoning of man in general).[50] In this case, by His grace, God would bring about the conversion of the will, de-

---

50. See §482 above.

taching it in a single stroke from its attachments to that which is not God. Charity itself, stirred up by grace, would purify the will of its impurities by its blazing heat. Therefore, we cannot speak of purgatory being necessary, involving a necessity that would be imposed on God Himself. Therefore, one just as much cannot speak of a predetermined quantity of punishment. In purgatory's liberation, what is primordial is God's free will, and it is here that the Church's "suffrages" intervene, especially the offering of the Eucharistic sacrifice, for it is always on account of the satisfaction offered by Christ on the cross that sins are remitted.

The reasons that we proposed earlier can serve to explain *a posteriori* why God imposes an expiation—the very fact of this expiation being an object of faith. This expiation, which is not a "satisfaction," is a penalty, a punishment. However, it only imperfectly realizes the notion of punishment, for the latter includes the idea that the inflicted suffering is contrary to the sinner's will. The will of the person who died in charity is perfectly conformed to God's will. It does not "suffer" the punishment. It accepts it, for what it "suffers," on the contrary, is the weight of its past. Mere punishment is not an "expiation," for it leaves the person who undergoes it at an interior (voluntary) distance from God. We could call the punishment suffered in purgatory an "expiatory punishment."

c) The punishments of purgatory

{598} The current representation of the punishments of purgatory as a kind of "temporary hell" with torments ([e.g.,] fire) has no foundation, either in revelation or in theological reflection. It is certain that the souls of purgatory are definitively united to God by charity, in faith, which radically differentiates them from the situation of the damned and from the latter's experience. It is also certain that after death the human person is reduced to his spiritual component, which completely excludes all suffering other than spiritual suffering.

We can think that this suffering consists precisely in the delay of the Vision. Mystics on earth are witnesses to such a torment. They are, however, very imperfect witnesses, for whatever may be their detachment from the things of the earth, their aspiration to live can rest somewhat upon the goods of the earth in which they participate. The soul in purgatory exists in a situation in which all the goods of the earth, all created goods, are taken from him, in a situation in which God is his only good, and if the soul is not deprived of Him, it is at least distant from Him. We must doubtlessly add to this torment the pain which is inherent to penitence, which we spoke about above: the acute pain at having offended God.

As regards the "duration" of this torment, we can in no way measure it because we do not know its measure, which is the "discontinuous time" that measures the spiritual creature. We must only maintain that this non-representable, inconceivable "duration" materially depends on the power of the attachments to the creature with which the will was burdened at the moment of death so that, whatever may be the gravity of the faults committed, he who dies in a complete act of charity, thus breaking free of all the kinds of his attachments, has nothing for which to expiate. Moreover, it formally depends on the divine act of pardoning, which falls under God's unconditioned freedom, which is also motivated by the Church's "suffrages."

Note, however, that there are two meanings of "perfect contrition." It is said that the sinner who, at the moment of death, makes an act of "perfect contrition," receives pardon for his sins and salvation. Does this mean that he avoids purgatory? In well-articulated theology, "perfect contrition" is the equivalent of "contrition," that is, repentance for sins inspired by charity.[51] What was said earlier about "imperfect (though authentic) contrition" obviously holds for conversion at the moment of death, whether it is brought about by means of the sacrament of penance or without it. What renders purgatory purposeless is perfect charity, that is, the charity that, by its intensity and its completeness excludes and destroys all attachments

---

51. See sect. 4, ch. 2 of the next volume.

to sin. If, at the moment of death the sinner—the greatest sinner—is converted in this way by "perfect contrition," meaning "inspired by perfect charity," there is nothing remaining for which he must make expiation.[52]

V. EXCLUSION FROM THE KINGDOM, THE "SECOND DEATH"

{599} Jesus came into the world in order to free man from his sins and to lead him to eternal life. Eternal life, communion in glory with the Divine Persons, is the kingdom of God to which all are called, for Christ died for all men. However, we have seen that man must freely accept salvation, for the kingdom of God is the kingdom of love, and one can love only freely. Love can be rejected. The power to say "Yes" includes the power to say "No." Man has in his freedom the redoubtable power of rejecting salvation, which is brought about by the conjunction of God's grace and his freedom.

The opposite of salvation is "perdition." To reject salvation is to be lost. To reject it definitively is perdition from man's perspective. From God's perspective, it is exclusion from the kingdom when His grace has been decidedly rejected. This is the second death spoken of in the Book of Revelation.[53] The term "damnation" can express these two perspectives. In the active sense of the term, damnation is one's exclusion by God. In the passive sense of it, it is the situation of the person who is lost.[54]

---

52. See Thérèse of the Infant Child Jesus, *Manuscrits autobiographiques* (Lisieux: Carmel de Lisieux, 1957), 313n1 and 321–22.
53. See Rv 20:6 and 20.
54. See J.-H. Nicolas, "La seconde mort du pécheur et la fidélité de Dieu," *Revue thomiste* 79 (1979): 25–49; "Enfer," in *Dictionnaire de spiritualité ascétique et mystique*, 4:729–45; "Crainte et tremblement," *Vie Spirituelle* 99 (1958): 227–54; *L'amour de Dieu et la peine des hommes*, 107–18; also see the texts gathered in *L'enfer, éternelle absence*, Vie Spirituelle 108, no. 490 (1963); and *L'Enfer* (Paris: Cerf, 1949).

A. What Is Revealed about Hell

1. First of all, hell is exclusion from the kingdom of Christ

{600} Christ announced the kingdom of God. Salvation consists in the definitive entrance into this kingdom wherein eternal life perpetually springs forth. However, He posits conditions for entering it, conditions taken up by the apostles: first and primarily faith (as the engagement of the whole person) and also the "wedding garment," a symbol of charity.

In speaking of the last judgment,[55] Christ tells of how those who are "blessed of my Father," who receive a share in the kingdom that was "prepared for you from the foundation of the world," are separated from the "cursed" who are sent "into the eternal fire prepared for the devil and his angels." This image of a sorting returns many times in the parables of the kingdom, as does the idea of exclusion (e.g., the parable of the virgins, of the servant who abuses the power that he received, and so forth). The idea of exclusion is taken up by Paul[56] and by the Book of Revelation.[57]

2. The punishments of hell

{601} In the New Testament, the punishments of hell are described to us in the classic language of apocalyptic writings. We are presented with violent images, which are dominated by that of fire, though also darkness, boiling tar, and so forth. We must look upon these as mere images, and there is no need to privilege the image of fire among the various ones that are presented to us. Moreover, despite the efforts expended by theologians of the Middle Ages in their explanations of this matter, the idea that fire could afflict spiritual beings like the angels and separated souls is inconceivable. For the case of men after the resurrection, it seems that incorruptibility would be the general condition of all bodily beings in "eschatological time," and

---

55. See Mt 25:31–46 (RSV).
56. See 1 Cor 6:9–10 and Gal 5:19–21.
57. See Rv 22:14–15.

therefore it seems that there is no longer place for a bodily suffering except if it is a question of the reverberation of spiritual suffering upon the sensibility. On the other hand, the classical representations of hell give God the role of being the tormenter, which is religiously unacceptable, even if one were to say that He exercised it through interposed persons. (In Dante's *Inferno*, the devils are the ones who are the torturers. However, God indeed is the one who hands the damned over to them to be tortured in accord with their crimes.)

The punishments of hell, such as it can be known from Scripture (when one has submitted the apocalyptic "representations" to a serious hermeneutic), can be understood only in function of the goodness and fullness that exists in the kingdom, from which the damned are excluded. It is the privation of "eternal life," the "second death." Apocalyptic images of hell strive only to translate, in the form of violent metaphors, the severity of this pain, one that is wholly spiritual. (Doubtlessly, after the resurrection, it is also sensible, but this comes about by the reverberation of the spiritual upon the sensible.)

3. *The definitive character of damnation*

{602} It does not seem possible to understand Scripture's numerous affirmations of the definitive character of exclusion from the kingdom in anything but a proper sense. They are "corrected" or "mitigated" by no text. From Origen to our own days,[58] theologians have attempted to provide a foundation for the idea that damnation would be brought to a halt through mercy's intervention. Such an idea rests on theological hypotheses that are not only unverifiable (that is, no assertion of Scripture supports them, even by way of allusion) but, more importantly, are contrived, for Scripture makes no place for a "conversion" that would occur during eschatological duration. The Church has always taught that damnation is perpetual.

---

58. See Maurice Nédoncelle, "Démythisation et conception eschatologique du mal," in *Le mythe de la peine* (*Colloque Castelli*) (Paris: Aubier, 1961), 195–222; Gaston Fessard, "Enfer éternel ou salut universel," in *Le mythe de la peine* (*Colloque Castelli*) (Paris: Aubier, 1961), 223–55.

B. Theological Reflection on the Dogma of Damnation

1. *The concrete possibility of damnation*

{603} The central difficulty aroused in the believer's mind by the idea of damnation is that it seems opposed to God's love and mercy. First of all, we must recognize that we are faced here with a mystery. The same revelation that reveals to us God's overflowing love, His intention to save all men, as well as His omnipotence and the perfect efficacy of the redemption brought about by Christ, also speaks to us about His wrath against the sinner and reveals Him to us as being ruthless in punishment (at least in appearance).

The only theological key for attempting to approach this mystery is that which was provided at the beginning: the love of God is offered to man's freedom; salvation is not made up of things; it is a Someone, the Trinity offering a share in His life. It is only through love that one shares in someone's life, above all the life of three Divine Persons, who are pure subjects, pure Persons, who give only themselves and, in being given, give the whole of themselves. He who refuses to love rejects God, His communion, His salvation. The act of rejection from the kingdom by God follows upon the rejection of the kingdom by the creature.

However, can God not, through His all-powerful grace, change the creature's will and make it freely say yes? In the case of man during this life, where his will remains, to the end, capable of returning, we must simply say that he is pursued by grace up to his last moment. However, he likewise can refuse grace up to this last moment. (It is impossible for us here to dwell at greater length on the mystery of the relations existing between grace and freedom.) If it is a question of the creature (freely) fixed in his rejection (i.e., the angel from the time of his first rejection and man from the moment when death fixes his freedom in its ultimate commitment),[59] such a divine

---

59. See *ST* I, q. 64, a. 1.

intervention (one that is certainly possible from the perspective of God's omnipotence) seems impossible from the perspective of His wisdom and—paradoxically—from that of the divine goodness, for this would be to act against the creature's freedom and to break him (even if God, who created freedom, is powerful enough to reestablish the creature in the good after having broken it in its false and evil commitment).

As long as man lives, there remains a part of his voluntary being (i.e., of his will) by which he is not committed: this fundamental ordination to God, which is never realized adequately in a choice, even that of the ultimate end, even when performed in the most deliberate manner. This will forever retains a point of contact whereby it remains at grace's disposal. Grace can act upon this point of contact in order to modify the evil choice from within and to make it *turn back from this choice through conversion*. This is no longer the case after death. Then, without any reservation, the soul completely wills what it has chosen. In the case of an evil choice, it unreservedly wills its own self, separated from God, and this choice is the unqualified rejection of God. On account of the unqualified nature of this choice, it is definitive, without any possible return. Were God to act on this will in order to return it to Him, such an action would not go in the direction of its freedom but against it.

When we think of the terrible stakes at play, we will have a tendency to think that God's love could indeed here allow itself to be less scrupulous in respecting freedom. It is here above all that our sense of mystery and of the divine transcendence must intervene. The "respect" that God has for His creature is one aspect of the very love that drove Him to create, out of a love which has creation as its effect and expression. It is a respect that envelops each being in what is proper to it, though which fully merits being called "respect" only when it is addressed to a personal and free creature. Here, we have the mysterious and transcendent paradigm of this respect for the person's dignity, which is today perceived more than ever as being the first principle that must rule the relations between persons.

By refusing to impose an unwanted salvation upon His free and personal creatures, God treats them like persons.

2. The reason for the perpetuity of damnation

{604} A number of theologians (for example Scotus) have held that the perpetuity of damnation is the result of a divine decision, a punishment which God decided would be perpetual. Such a conception ends up rendering the question of the relationship between damnation and mercy absolutely unresolvable. At bottom, the great number of theologians who are tempted to think that God places a terminus to damnation reason, more or less consciously, as though God's will were what makes the punishment be perpetual. This gives rise to the hypothesis that the divine severity can last only for a time. If one judges, with St. Thomas, that the reason for the perpetuity of damnation is not first of all in God but, instead, in the damned person, this aporia can be overcome. God perpetually rejects the damned person because the latter refuses His love.

However, if the damned person does not want the kingdom, how are we to understand the idea that exclusion from it would be so painful for him? First, we must say that this kingdom that he refuses is the only place where he can be happy. There is no other beatitude for him than that which flows from communion with the Divine Persons. By refusing this communion, he is deprived of this beatitude and finds nothing in its place. Damnation represents a complete failure, for all the goods that he willed on earth as substitutes for the divine good that was offered to him no longer exist for him in the next life. However, more profoundly still, he misses this communion with the Divine Persons at the very moment that he rejects it, for he remains "made for God," called to this communion, completely retaining a tendency toward it. By the rejection in which he persists, he is interiorly torn from that which he holds onto above all else. In other words, he is torn apart by this self-attachment which in fact leads him to reject his only true fulfillment.

Thus, one cannot fail to ask, "Under the pressure of this experience, why would he not repudiate this disastrous choice?" Here we encounter a mystery, not the mystery of God, but that of freedom: the irreversibility of a choice made once and for all. The damned person remains attached, by the whole of his will, to this "self" who does not cease to deceive him. The experience of this deception does not suffice to make him reconsider his refusal to love. Moreover, would someone really come to love God were he to return to Him only because he has not found self-love to provide the fullness that he sought therein?

3. *Can one hope that none will be damned?*

{605} Some would wish that this were so (e.g., von Balthasar and Martelet). It is certainly true that every speculation on the number of the damned is vain. Instinctively, one leans toward the hypothesis that they are not many. However, from the perspective of the divine mercy and of our pity, a single one would already be one too many. We can hope for the salvation of another person[60]—a hope that is certain from the perspective of the divine goodness on which it rests and is uncertain from the perspective of the other person's freedom, over which we have no sway. Therefore, we can hope for the salvation of each man. Is it not possible that this could be hope in the effective salvation of all men? This latter assertion involves a sophism. The proposition, "All men will be saved," is not an object of hope. It is either true or false, and the intellect has no means of being certain that it is true.

Can one equally say, "There is no certitude that it would be false?" Perhaps, although Scripture speaks much of damnation as an eventuality realized for certain people. However, such an argument cannot be considered absolutely probative, for as we have seen, it is clear that revelation does not furnish us with a description of the future, a "futurology," but rather, with knowledge of the future inasmuch as it can illuminate our present. The only knowledge of dam-

---

60. See *ST* II-II, q. 17, a. 3.

nation which man presently stands in need of is knowledge of its concrete possibility. St. Thomas makes a kind of static argument that some must be damned: "In a multitude of beings capable of failing, it is necessary that some fail."[61] This cannot be retained, for the love of God is not obviously bound by a necessity of this kind.[62]

Even less can one retain the theological argument that God would draw glory from the damned, as manifesting His justice and His severity, even though such an argument could lay claim to certain texts of Scripture. However, it is one thing to say that God can draw said good from the damnation of some and another thing to say that damnation is in some manner necessary for God's glory. On the other hand, one could say that a single damned person is a failure for mercy and that God's love cannot suffer failure. In response, we must say that the damned places himself outside of mercy, and once again, mercy consists in offering man a salvation that calls for his consent. To force this consent would also represent a failure on the part of mercy.

Conclusion

{606} The Church is wholly eschatological. That is, she is conceived only in function of the kingdom of God. She stretches out toward that kingdom, and her mission is to lead men to it. Indeed, she is already this kingdom, "pilgrim and crucified." Already, she is resurrected with Christ, all the while partaking in His cross and death.

The meaning of the Church's eschatological dimension prevents one from understanding her as a worldly reality and from judging her in function of this world's scale of values. And nonetheless, she exists in the world. It is on the world that she acts, and it is before it that she renders testimony to the values and realities of another world, the eschatological world. This is so because the meaning of her eschatological dimension must not encourage her to be lazy. Eschatology is not a refuge but, instead, a stimulant for acting in the present in accordance with the Christian future which is the return of Christ.

---

61. *ST* I, q. 48, a. 2, ad 3. See *SCG*, bk. 3, ch. 71 and 94; *De ver.*, q. 5, a. 4, ad 4.

62. Thus, I cannot maintain my own prior use of this argument by St. Thomas.

This is just as true for how the "last things" must be viewed in relation to each person's life. They are not an alibi allowing one to neglect temporal ends. If these latter are obviously relativized by the pursuit, in faith, of eschatological ends, they are not, for all that, abolished or annihilated. They are present to the Christian's awareness as true ends, capable of mobilizing his hopes and energies. Obviously, exclusion from the kingdom is not itself an end but, rather, failure in the pursuit of the end. If its concrete possibility has been revealed, this is more so meant to be a warning than a threat. The ultimate end of the Christian life is the entrance into the kingdom to which all men are called by Christ, toward which the Christian must consciously stretch forth through his acts and through hope during his earthly life.

Conclusion to the Second Part

We have considered Christology as being a prolongation of the study of the Trinitarian mystery because it can be understood only in light of the mission of the Son who is sent by the Father. Moreover, in studying Christ and His redemptive work, we were also led to the second moment in the dogmatic synthesis that we are attempting to present: the return to the Trinity by man created in the image of the Trinity and for the Trinity. Indeed, through the redemptive Incarnation, the image of the Trinity has been restored in man. This image was damaged by sin, but under the action of grace which conforms him ever more completely to Jesus Christ, man gradually arrives at perfect conformity and likeness to the Trinity in eternal life.

Grace: we still must ask ourselves how it is given to us. Grace is the Holy Spirit acting in the believer, first in order to make him a believer and, then, in order to purify him by the remission of sins and to divinize him, leading him to complete divinization. Now, the Holy Spirit has been given to the Church. He brought her to birth from Christ's open side, just as He had overshadowed the conception of the Incarnate Word, and He leads her through history up to the Parousia. By and in the Church, He is given to each of the Church's members—first, to make each person (in an ever-increasing manner) a member of the Church and, then, in order to lead all of them together into the fullness of Christ. It is Christ who communicates Him—Christ in whose soul He remains in His fullness and from whom He derives all the others. The sacraments are the means for this derivation: above all the primordial sacrament that is the Church and, then, the seven sacraments by which the Church visibly continues in the world Christ's redemptive action, having itself become invisible but never ceasing to be exercised in order that it may save men under the sacramental signs.

Thus, the Holy Spirit, the vital and unifying principle of the Church, brings *the dispersed children of God* back to the Trinity by virtue of Christ's blood and of His redemptive love. As we saw at the end of the first volume of this work, the mission of the Holy Spirit is connected with the mission of the Son, not so that the Spirit's mission may be substituted for Christ's but, rather, so that throughout the time that separates Christ's two comings—the time of the Church—He may make Christ's mission successfully reach its own ultimate end. This prolongation of the Son's mission by the mission of the Holy Spirit is what we must study now in a third and final[1] part: THE CHURCH AND THE SACRAMENTS.

---

1. [Tr. note: "Final" from the perspective of the first three volumes, which make up one set, although this translation series includes a fourth volume including the supplementary volume that Fr. Nicolas wrote after completing this course's publication.]

Works Cited

Adnès, Pierre. "Mariage spirituel." In *Dictionnaire de spiritualité ascétique et mystique, doctrine et histoire*, vol. 10, edited by Marcel Viller, Ferdinand Cavalerra, et al., 388–408. [Paris: Beauchesne, 1977.]
Alberigo, Giuseppe. *Conciliorum oecumenicorum decreta*. Fribourg: Herder, 1962.
Albert the Great. *Opera Omnia*. Edited by Emil Borgnet. Paris: Vives, 1890–99.
Aldama, José Antonio de. "La maternité virginale de Notre-Dame." In *Maria*, 7:119–52. Paris: Beauchesne, 1964.
Alfaro, Juan. "La formula definitoria de la inmaculada concepción." in *Virgo Immaculata*, vol. 2, 201–75. Rome: Pontificia Academia Mariana Internationalis, 1956.
Anselm of Canterbury. *Pourquoi Dieu s'est fait homme*. Edited and translated by René Roques. SC 91. Paris: Cerf, 1963.
Audet, Thomas-André. "Approches historiques de la Somme théologique." *Etudes d'histoire littéraires et doctrines* 17 (1962): 7–32.
Augustine of Hippo. *La Cité de Dieu*. *Oeuvres de St. Augustine* 33–37. Paris: Desclée de Brouwer, 1959–60.
———. *Les Confessions*. *Oeuvres de St. Augustine* 14. Paris: Desclée de Brouwer, 1949ff.
———. *De diversis quaestionibus LXXXIII liber unus*. *Oeuvres de St. Augustine* 10. Paris: Desclée de Brouwer, 1949ff.
———. *De genesi ad litteram*. *Oeuvres de St. Augustine* 48–49. Paris: Desclée de Brouwer, 1949ff.
———. *De Natura et Gratia*. *Oeuvres de St. Augustine* 21:222–412. Paris: Desclée de Brouwer, 1966.
———. *Opus imperfectum contra Julianum*. PL 45:1049–1608.
———. *De peccatorum meritis et remissione*. PL 44:109–200.
Balić, Carolus. *Joannes Duns Scotus Doctor immaculatae conceptionis*. Rome: Academia Mariana Internationalis, 1954.
———. *La pensée de Scot sur l'Immaculée Conception*. Rome: Academia Mariana Internationalis, 1954.

Works Cited

Balthasar, Hans Urs von. *Liturgie cosmique. Maxime le Confesseur*. Paris: Aubier, 1957.

———. "Eschatologie." In *Questions théologiques aujourd'hui*, vol. 2, 269–97. Paris: Desclée de Brouwer, 1963.

———. *La foi du Christ*. Paris: Cerf, 1968.

———. *Le mystère pascal*. In *Mysterium Salutis: Dogmatique de l'histroire du salut*, 12:13–275. Paris: Cerf, 1972.

Basly, Déodat de. *Scotus-Docens, ou Duns Scot enseignant la philosophie, la théologie, la mystique, Supplément de La France franciscaine*. Paris: La France Franciscaine, 1934.

———. *Inopérantes offensives contre l'Assumptus Homo, Supplément à La France franciscaine*. Paris: La France Franciscaine, 1935.

Bavel, Tarcisius van. *Recherches sur la christologie de Saint Augustin: l'humain et le divin dans le Christ d'après Saint Augustin*. Fribourg: Éditions universitaires, 1954.

Benoît, Pierre. *Passion et resurrection du Seigneur*. Paris: Cerf, 1966.

———. "Préexistence et incarnation." *Revue biblique* (Paris) 77 (1970): 5–29.

Berten, I[gnace]. "Bulletin de Christologie protestante." *Revue des sciences philosophiques et théologiques* 54 (1970): 128–65.

Billot, Louis. *De Ecclesiae Sacramentis: Commentarius in tertiam partem S. Thomae*. Rome: Apud aedes Universitatis gregorianae, 1924.

Bloch, Ernst. *Le Principe Espérance*. Vols. 1–2. Paris: Gallimard, 1976 / 1982.

Blondel, Maurice. *La pensée*. Vols. 1–2. Paris: Aubier, 1934.

Blondel, Maurice, and Pierre Teilhard de Chardin. *Correspondance*. Edited by Henri de Lubac. Paris: Beauchesne, 1965.

Boff, Leonardo. *Jésus-Christ libérateur*. Paris: Cerf, 1974.

Bonnefoy, Jean-François. "La question hypothétique, 'Utrum si Adam non pecasset' au XIIIe siècle." *Revista Española de Teologia* 14 (1954): 327–68.

———. *La primauté du Christ selon l'Ecriture et la Tradition*. Rome: Herder, 1959.

Bossuet, Jacques-Bégnigne. *Oeuvres oratoires de Bossuet*. Edited by J. Lebarq. Paris: Desclée, 1914–26.

Bouyer, Louis. *Le trône de la sagesse*. Paris: Cerf, 1957.

———. *Le Fils éternel*. Paris: Cerf, 1974.

Brandon, S., ed. *Saviour God: Companion Studies in Concept of Salvation Presented to E. O. James*. Manchester: Manchester University Press, 1963.

Braun, François-Marie. *La Mère des fidèles*. Paris / Tournai: Casterman, 1954.

———. *Jean le théologien*. Paris: Gabalda, 1959–72.

Bur, Jacques. *Médiation mariale*. Paris: Desclée de Brouwer, 1955.

Calvin, Jean. *Institution chrétienne*. Genève: Labor et Fideles, 1967.

Caggiano, E. M. "De mente Joannis Duns Scoti circa rationem Incarnationis." *Antonianum* 32 (1957): 311–34.

Cajetan, Tommaso de Vio. *De immaculata conceptione Beatae Mariae Virginis, Opuscula Omnia*. Vol. 2. Venice, 1594.

Works Cited

———. *Scripta philosophica. Commentaria in De Anima Aristotelis.* Edited by Hyacinthus Laurent. Rome: Angelicum, 1938.
Cambe, Michel. "La 'charis' chez S. Luc." *Revue biblique* 70 (1963): 193–207.
Camelot, Pierre-Thomas. *Ephèse et Chalcédoine.* Histoire des Conciles Oecuméniques 2. Edited by G. Dumeige. Paris: Orante, 1962.
Cantalamessa, Raniero. *La Cristologia di Tertulliano.* Fribourg: Éditions Universitaires, 1962.
Cantone, Carlo. "Dio in divenire, una nuova gnosi." *Salesianum* 37 (1975): 69–91.
Capreolus, Johannes. *Defensiones Theologiae Divi Thomae Aquinatis.* Edited by Thomas Pegues and Ceslaus Paban. Vol. 6. Turonibus: Sumptibus Alfred Cattier, 1906.
Carrez, Maurice. "L'herméneutique paulinienne de la resurrection." In *La resurrection du Christ et l'exégèse moderne,* Lectio divina 50, 55–73. Paris: Cerf, 1969.
Catão, Bernard. *Salut et Rédemption chez S. Thomas d'Aquin.* Paris: Aubier, 1955.
Cerfaux, Lucien. *Le Christ dans la théologie de saint Paul.* Paris: Cerf, 1954.
Chardin, Pierre Teilhard de. *Oeuvres.* 13 vols. Paris: Seuil, 1955–76.
Chenu, Marie-Dominique. *Introduction à l'étude de Saint Thomas d'Aquin.* Paris: Vrin, 1954.
Choron, Jacques. *La mort et la pensée occidentale.* Paris: Payot, 1969.
Congar, Yves-Marie. "Le Purgatoire." In *Le mystère de la mort et de sa célébration,* edited by Aimon-Marie Rouget, 279–336. Paris: Cerf, 1951.
———. *Sainte Eglise.* Unam Sanctam 41. Paris: Cerf, 1963.
———. "La Personne-Eglise." *Revue thomiste* 71 (1971): 613–64.
Corvez, Maurice. "Le problème de dieu." *Revue Thomiste* 67 (1967): 65–104.
Cottier, Georges. "Difficultés d'une théologie de la libération." *Les Quatre Fleuves* 2 (1974): 64–81.
Cousins, Evert H. "La temporalité de Dieu dans la théologie du devenir." In *Temporalité et Aliénation,* 139–59. Paris: Aubier Montagne, 1975.
Cuénot, Claude. *Pierre Teilhard de Chardin. Les grandes étapes de son evolution.* Paris: Plon, 1958.
Cullmann, Oscar. *Immortalité de l'âme ou résurrection des corps?* Neuchâtel: Delachaux et Nieslé, 1959.
———. *La foi et le culte de l'Église primitive.* Neuchâtel: Delachaux et Niestlé, 1963.
———. *Christ et le temps.* Neuchâtel: Delachaux et Niestlé, 1966.
———. *Christologie du Nouveau Testament.* Neuchâtel: Delachaux et Niestlé, 1966.
Cyril of Alexandria. *Saint Cyrille d'Alexandrie. Deux dialogues christologiques.* SC 97. Edited by Georges-Matthieu de Durand. Paris: Cerf, 1964.
Daniélou, Jean. *Théologie du Judéo-christianisme.* Paris: Desclée, 1958.
———. *Les évangiles de l'enfance.* Paris: Seuil, 1967.
Dante. *La Monarchie.* In *Oeuvres complètes.* Bibliothèque de la Pléiade. Paris: Gallimard, 1965.
Diepen, Herman. "La critique du baslisme selon Saint Thomas." *Revue thomiste* 50 (1950): 82–118, 290–329.

———. *Théologie de l'Émmanuel*. Paris: Desclée de Brouwer, 1960.

———. "L'assumptus homo patristique." *Revue thomiste* 63 (1963): 225–45, 363–88; 64 (1964): 32–52, 364–86.

Dillenschneider, Clément. *Marie au service de notre rédemption*. Haguenau: Maison Saint-Gérard, 1947.

Dockx, Stanislas. *Fils de Dieu par grâce*. Paris: Desclée de Brouwer, 1948.

Dodd, Charles Harold. *Conformément aux Écritures*. Translated by R. Guého and J. Trublet. Paris: Seuil, 1968.

———. *Le fondateur du christianisme*. Translated by Paul-André Lesort. Paris: Seuil, 1972.

Dondaine, Hyacinthe-François. "Notes doctrinales thomistes." In *Saint Thomas d'Aquin. Somme théologique, La Trinité*, 1:214–58, 2:383–453. Paris: Cerf, [1946].

———. "Bulletin de théologie dogmatique." *Revue des sciences philosophiques et théologiques* 35 (1951): 609–13.

Dumeige, Gervais. *Textes Doctrinaux du Magistere de L'Eglise sur La Foi Catholique*. [Paris: Édition de l'Orante, 1969.]

Dupuy, Michel. *Bérulle et le sacerdoce*. Paris: Lethielleux, 1969.

Duquoc, Christian. *Christologie II: le Messie*. Paris: Cerf, 1972.

Durrwell, François-Xavier. *L'Eucharistie, présence du Christ*. Second edition. Paris: Éditions Ouvrières, [1971].

L'Enfer. Paris: Cerf, 1949.

L'enfer, éternelle absence. Vie Spirituelle 108, no. 490 (1963).

Fabro, Cornelio. *Participation et causalité selon Saint Thomas d'Aquin*. Paris: Vrin, 1961.

Febrer, Mateo. *El concepto de persona y la unión hipostática. Revisión tomista del problema*. Valencia: Editorial F.E.D.A, 1951.

Feiner, Johannes, and Magnus Löhrer, eds. *Mysterium Salutis: Dogmatique de l'histoire du salut*. Vol. 1. Paris: Cerf, 1969.

Fessard, Gaston. "Enfer éternel ou salut universel." In *Le mythe de la peine (Colloque Castelli)*, 223–55. Paris: Aubier, 1961.

Feuillet, André. "Mort du Christ et mort du chrétien d'après les épîtres pauliniennes." *Revue biblique* 66 (1959): 481–513.

———. "Le temps de l'Église d'après le IVe Evangile et l'Apocalypse." *Maison-Dieu* 65 (1961): 60–79.

———. "L'hymne christologique de l'épître aux Éphésiens." *Revue biblique* 72 (1965): 481–506.

———. *Le Christ Sagesse de Dieu*. Paris: Gabalda, 1966.

———. "Les 'Ego eimi' du IVe évangile." *Revue des Sciences Religieuses* 54 (1966): 5–22, 213–40.

———. "Le logion sur la rançon." *Revue des sciences philosophiques et théologiques* 51 (1967): 365–402.

———. "Les trois grandes prophéties de la Passion et de la Résurrection." *Revue thomiste* 67 (1967): 533–60; 68 (1968): 41–75.

———. *Le prologue du IVe évangile.* Paris: Desclée de Brouwer, 1968.
———. *Le sacerdoce du Christ et de ses ministres.* Paris: Editions de Paris, 1972.
———. *Christologie paulinienne et tradition biblique.* Paris: Desclée de Brouwer, 1973.
———. *Jésus et sa Mère d'après les récits lucaniens et d'après S. Jean.* Paris: Gabalda, 1974.
———. "La découverte du tombeau vide en Jn 20, 3–10 et la foi au Christ ressuscité." *Esprit et Vie* 19 (1977): 257–84.
Foi et Salut selon S. Paul. Analecta biblica 42. Rome: Institut Biblique Pontifical, 1970.
Füglister, Notker. "Les bases vétérotestamentaires de la christologie du Nouveau Testament." In *Les préparations de l'événement Jésus-Christ,* 161–325. Paris: Cerf, 1973.
Galot, Jean. "Eschatologie." In *Dictionnaire de spiritualité ascétique et mystique, doctrine et histoire,* vol. 4, edited by Marcel Viller, Ferdinand Cavalerra, et al., 1020–59. Paris: Beauchesne, [1960].
———. "L'immaculée conception de Notre-Dame." In *Maria,* 7:10–116. Paris: Beauchesne, 1964.
———. "Le mystère de l'assomption." In *Maria,* 7:155–237. Paris: Beauchesne, 1964.
———. *La conscience de Jésus.* Paris: Lethielleux, 1971.
———. *Vers une nouvelle christologie.* Gembloux: Duculot, 1971.
———. *Il mistero della sofferenza di Dio.* Assisi: Cittadella Editrice, 1975.
———. *Dieu, souffre-t-il?* Paris: Lethielleux, 1976.
Galtier, Paul. "L'enseignement des Pères sur la vision béatifique dans le Christ." *Recherches des sciences religieuses* 15 (1925): 54–68.
———. "Satisfaction." In *Dictionnaire de théologie catholique,* vol. 14, edited by Alfred Vacant, Eugène Mangenot, Emile Amann, 1129–1210. Paris: Letouzey et Ané, 1939.
———. *L'unité du Christ. Être. Personne. Conscience.* Paris: Beauchesne, 1939.
———. "La conscience humaine du Christ. A propos de quelques publications récentes." *Gregorianum* 32 (1951): 525–68.
———. "S. Cyrille d'Alexandrie et S. Léon le Grand à Chalcédoine." In *Das Konzil von Chalkedon,* vol. 1, edited by Alois Grillmeier and Heinrich Bacht, 345–87. Würzburg: Echter-Verlag, 1951.
Garrigues, Juan-Miguel. "La personne composée du Christ d'après S. Maxime le Confesseur." *Revue Thomiste* 74 (1974): 181–204.
Garrigou-Lagrange, Reginald. *Le sens commun.* Fourth edition. Paris: Desclée de Brouwer, 1936.
———. *Christ: The Savior.* Translated by Bede Rose. St. Louis: Herder, 1950.
———. *De beatitudine.* Turin: R. Berruti, 1951.
———. *The Trinity and God the Creator.* Translated by Frederic C. Eckhoff. St. Louis: Herder, 1952.
———. "The Subordination of the State to the Perfection of the Human Person

According to St. Thomas.» In *Philosophizing in Faith: Essays on the Beginning and End of Wisdom*, translated by Matthew K. Minerd, 183–204. Providence, RI: Cluny, 2019.

Geffré, Claude. "La mort comme nécessité et comme liberté." *Vie Spirituelle* 492 (1963): 264–80.

Gélin, Albert. "Le sacerdoce du Christ d'après l'épître aux Hébreux." In *Études sur le sacrement de l'ordre*, 43–76. Paris: Cerf, 1957.

———. "Le sacerdoce de l'ancienne alliance." In *La Tradition sacerdotale*, 27–60. Paris: Mappus, 1959.

Gervais, Michel. "Incarnation et immutabilité divine." *Revue des Sciences Religieuses* 50, no. 3 (1976): 215–43.

Gilson, Étienne. *Le thomisme, introduction à la philosophie de Saint Thomas d'Aquin*. Fifth edition. Paris: Vrin, 1945.

———. "Cajetan et l'humanisme théologique." *Archives d'histoire doctrinale et littéraire du Moyen Age* 22 (1955): 11–136.

Gironés, Gonzalo. *La humanidad salvada y salvadora*. Valencia: Anales del Seminario de Valencia, 1969.

Glorieux, Palémon. "Le mérite du Christ selon Saint Thomas." *Revue des Sciences Religieuses* 20 (1930): 622–49.

Gnilka, Joachim. "Rédemption." In *Encyclopédie de la Foi*, 4:11–13. Paris: Cerf, 1967.

Godin, André. "La mort a-t-elle changé?" *Lumen Vitae* 26 (1971): 295–318.

Goedt, Michel de. "Bases bibliques de la maternité spirituelle." In *Etudes Mariales*, 3–53. Paris: Lethielleux, 1959.

Gregory of Nazianzen. *Orationes*. PG 35–36.

Grelot, Pierre. "La théologie de la mort dans l'Écriture Sainte." *Vie Spirituelle Supplément* 77 (May 1966): 143–93.

Grillmeier, Alois. "L'image du Christ dans la théologie d'aujourd'hui." In *Questions théologiques aujourd'hui*, 2:91–136. Paris: Desclée de Brouwer, 1963.

———. *La Christ dans la tradition chrétienne. De l'âge apostolique à Chalcédoine (451)*. Paris: Cerf, 1973.

Gross, Jules. *La divinisation du chrétien d'après les Pères grecs, contribution historique à la doctrine de la grâce*. Paris: Gabalda, 1938.

Guéroult, Martial. *Malebrance, II–II: Le cinq abîmes de la providence*. Paris: Aubier, 1959.

Guillet, Jacques. "Le titre biblique de Dieu vivant." In *L'homme devant Dieu, Mélanges offerts au P. H. de Lubac*, 1:11–23. Paris: Aubier, 1963.

———. "Les récits évangéliques de la résurrection." *Les Quatre Fleuves* 15–16 (1982): 7–21.

Gutiérrez-González, Juan. *Teología de la Liberación. Evaporación de la Teología (La obra de Gustavo Gutiérrez vista desde ella misma)*. Mexico City: Jus, 1975.

Henry, Paul. "Kénose." In *Dictionnaire de la Bible*, vol. 5, edited by Louis Pirot and Robert André, 7–161. Paris: Letouzey et Ané, 1950.

Héris, Charles-Vincent. *Le mystère du Christ*. Paris: Revue des jeunes, 1928.

———. "Le Verbe incarné." In *Saint Thomas d'Aquin. Somme théologique*. Paris: Cerf, n.d.

Hocedez, Edgar. *Quaestio de unico esse in Christo a doctoribus saeculi XIII disputata, Textus et documenta, Series theologica* 14. Rome: Pontificia Universitas Gregoriana, 1933.

Iammarone, Luigi. "Il 'divenire di Dio' et Giovanni Duns Scoto." *Miscellanea Francescana* 77 (1977): 45–94.

Ignatius of Antioch. *Letter to the Smyrnaeans*. In St. Ignatius of Antioch and St. Polycarp of Smyrna, *Lettres*, edited by Pierre-Thomas Camelot, OP. SC 10bis. Paris: Cerf, 1958.

Immortalité. Neuchâtel: Delachaux et Niestlé, 1958.

Irenaeus of Lyon. *Adversus Haereses, libri quinquie, Libri I–II*. In *Bibliotheca sanctorum Patrum et scriptorium ecclesiasticorum*, edited by Ubaldo Mannucci. Rome: [Ex Officina Typographica Forzani et Socii, 1907].

Jankélévitch, Vladimir. *La mort*. Paris: Flammarion, 1966.

Jeremias, Joachim. *Théologie du Nouveau Testament*. Vol. 1. Translated by Josse Alzin and Arthur Liefooghe. Paris: Cerf, 1973.

Jésus le Sauveur. Lumière et Vie 15 (1954).

John of the Cross. *Oeuvres complètes*. Translated by Spanish by P. Cyprien de la Nativité de la Vierge, OCD. Edited by P. Lucien-Marie de Saint-Joseph, OCD. Paris: Desclée de Brouwer, 1959.

John Damascene. *De fide orthodoxa*. PG 94, 784–1228.

Jossua, Jean-Pierre. *Le salut. Incarnation ou mystère pascal chez les Pères de l'Eglise, de Saint Irénée à Saint Léon le Grand*. Paris: Cerf, 1968.

Jouassard, Georges. "Marie à travers la patristique: Maternité divine, virginité, sainteté." In *Maria*, 1:69–158. Paris: Beauchesne, 1949.

Journet, Charles. *L'Église du Verbe incarné*. Vols. 1–3. Paris: Desclée de Brouwer, 1951–69.

———. *Esquisse du développement du dogme marial*. Paris: Alsatia, 1954.

Kasper, Walter. *Jésus le Christ*. Paris: Cerf, 1976.

Kelly, John Norman Davidson. *Initiation à la doctrine des Pères de l'Église*. Translated by Celsas Tumner. Paris: Cerf, 1968.

Kirchmeyer, Jean. "Grecque (Église)." In *Dictionnaire de spiritualité ascétique et mystique, doctrine et histoire*, vol. 6, edited by Marcel Viller, Ferdinand Cavalerra, et al., 808–72. Paris: Beauchesne, 1967.

Koehler, Theodore. "Les principales interpretations traditionnelles de Jn 19, 25–27." In *Etudes Mariales*, 119–55. Paris: Lethielleux, 1959.

Krempel, Anton. *La doctrine de la relation chez Saint Thomas, exposé historique et systématique*. Paris: Vrin, 1952.

Kübler-Ross, Elisabeth. *Les dernier instants de la vie*. Genève: Labor et Fides, 1975.

Küng, Hans. *Incarnation de Dieu. Introduction à la pensée théologique de Hegel comme prolégomènes à une christologie future*. Translated by E. Galichet and C. Haas-Smets. Paris: Desclée de Brouwer, 1973.

Lafont, Ghislain. *Structures et méthode dans la Somme théologique de Saint Thomas d'Aquin*. Paris: Desclée de Brouwer, 1961.
Lagrange, Marie-Joseph. *Le messianisme chez les Juifs*. Paris: Gabalda, 1909.
Lamarche, Paul. "L'hymne de l'épître aux Éphésiens et la kénose du Christ." In *L'homme devant Dieu, Mélanges offerts au P. H. de Lubac*, 147–58. Paris: Aubier, 1963.
———. "Le prologue de S. Jean." *Recherches des sciences religieuses* 52 (1964): 497–537.
De la Taille, Maurice. *Mysterium fidei. De augustissimo Corporis et Sanguinis Christi sacrificio atque sacramento*. Paris: Beauchesne, 1921.
———. "Actuation créée par l'Act incréé." *Recherches des sciences religieuses* 18 (1928): 253–68.
Lalande, André. *Vocabulaire technique et critique de la philosophie*. 7th ed. Paris: P.U.F., 1956.
Larcher, Chrysostome. *Études sur le livre de la Sagesse*. Paris: Gabalda, 1968.
Lubac, Henri de. *La pensée religieuse de P. Teilhard de Chardin*. Paris: Aubier, 1962.
Laurentin, René. *Le titre de co-rédemptrice*. Paris: Lethielleux, 1951.
———. *Marie, L'Église et le sacerdoce*. Vols. 1–2. Paris: Lethielleux, 1952–53.
———. *Structure et théologie de Luc I–II*. Paris: Gabalda, 1959.
———. *Court traité sur la Vierge Marie*. Paris: Lethielleux, 1967.
———. "Bulletin sur la Vierge Marie." *Revue des sciences philosophiques et théologiques* 55 (1970): 269–328.
———. *Les évangiles de l'enfance du Christ. Vérité de Noël au-delà des mythes*. Paris: Desclée de Brouwer, 1982.
Lebreton, Jules. *Les origines du dogme de la Trinité*. Vols. 1–2. Paris: Beauchesne, 1919.
Legrand, Lucien. *La virginité dans la Bible*. Paris: Cerf, 1964.
Léon-Dufour, Xavier. *Les évangiles et l'histoire de Jésus*. Paris: Seuil, 1963.
Leroy, Vincent. "Bulletins." *Revue thomiste* 73 (1973): 486–98.
———. "L'union selon l'hypostase d'après Saint Thomas d'Aquin." *Revue thomiste* 74 (1974): 205–43.
———. "Bulletin de patristique." *Revue thomiste* (1979): 627–54.
———. "Leonardo Boff, Jésus-Christ libérateur." *Revue thomiste* 79 (1979): 500–503.
Leuba, Jean-Louis. "Temps et Trinité. Esquisse d'herméneutique doctrinale." In *Temporalité et Aliénation. Actes du Colloque organisé par le Centre international d'Etudes humanists et par l'institute d'Etudes philosophiques de Rome (Rome, 3–8 jan. 1975)*, 365–75. Paris: Aubier Montaigne, 1975.
Liébaert, Jacques. *L'incarnation*, vol. 1: *Des origines à Chalcédoine*. Paris: Cerf, 1968.
Lossky, Vladimir. *Théologie mystique de l'Église d'Orient*. Paris: Aubier, 1944.
Lot-Borodine, Myrrha. *La déification de l'homme*. Paris: Cerf, 1970.
Luneau, Auguste. *L'histoire du salut chez les Pères de l'Eglise*. Paris: Beauchesne, 1964.
Luther, Martin. *Commentary on Galatians. Martin Luthers Werke*. Vol. 40. Weimar, 1883ff.

Lyonnet, Stanislas. *Le récit de l'Annonciation et la maternité divine.* Rome: Institute Biblique Pontifical, 1956.

———. *De peccato et redemptione*, vol. 1: *De notione peccati.* Rome: Pontificio Instituto Biblico, 1957.

———. *De peccato et redemptione*, vol. 2: *De vocabulario redemptionis.* Rome: Pontificio Instituto Biblico, 1960.

———. *Les étapes de l'histoire du salut selon l'épître aux Romains.* Paris: Cerf, 1969.

———. "Péché." In *Vocabulaire de théologie biblique*, edited by Xavier Léon-Dufour, 936–46. Paris: Cerf, 1970.

Malevez, Léopold. "L'Église dans le Christ. Étude de théologie historique et théologique." *Revue des Sciences Religieuses* 25 (1935): 257–91 and 418–40.

———. "La gratuité du surnaturel." *Nouvelle revue théologique* 15 (1953): 561–86 and 673–68.

———. "Le Christ et la foi." *Nouvelle revue théologique* 88 (1966): 1009–43.

Malmberg, Felix. *Über den Gottmenschen.* Freiburg: Herder, 1960.

Mansi, Johannes Dominicus. *Sacrorum Conciliorum nova et amplissima Collectio.* Florence, 1758ff.; Venice, 1799ff.; Paris / Arnhem / Leipzig, 1901–27.

Maria in Sacra Scriptura: Acta congressus mariologici in Republica Dominicana anno 1965 celebrati. Rome: Pontificia Academia Mariana Internationalis, 1965.

Maritain, Jacques. *Du régime temporal et de la liberté.* Paris: Desclée de Brouwer, 1933.

———. "La dialectique immanent du premier acte de liberté." In *Raison et raisons*, 131–65. Fribourg: Egloff, 1947.

———. "Discours pour l'ouverture de l'Assemblée de l'Unesco à Mexico." *Nova et Vetera* (1948): 1–14.

———. *La philosophie bergsonienne.* Paris: Téqui, 1948.

———. "Sur la notion de subsistence." *Revue thomiste* 54 (1954): 242–56.

———. *Pour une philosophie de l'histoire.* Paris: Seuil, 1957.

———. *Carnet de notes.* Paris: Desclée de Brouwer, 1965.

———. *De la grâce et de l'humanité de Jésus.* Paris: Desclée de Brouwer, 1967.

———. "A propos de l'École Française." *Revue thomiste* 71 (1971): 463–79.

Marrou, Henri-Irénée. *Théologie de l'histoire.* Paris: Seuil, 1968.

Martelet, Gustave. *L'au-delà retrouvé. Christologie des fins dernières.* Paris: Desclée de Brouwer, 1974.

La maternité spirituelle de Marie, Actes du VIIIe congrès marial national, Lisieux 5–9 July 1961. Paris: Lethielleux, 1962.

Maximus the Confessor. *Questions to Thallassius.* PG 90.

Mersch, Emil. *Le corps mystique du Christ. Études de théologie historique.* Vols. 1–2. Paris: Desclée de Brouwer, 1951.

Metz, Johann-Baptist. "Les rapports entre l'Eglise et le monde à la lumière d'une théologie politique." In *Théologie du Renouveau, I–II*, 33–47. Paris: Cerf, 1968.

Michel, A[lbert]. "Hypostatique (Union)." In *Dictionnaire de théologie catholique*, vol. 7, edited by Alfred Vacant, 437–78 and 485–86. Paris: Letouzey et Ané, 1922.

———. "La messe chez les théologiens postérieurs au concile de Trente. Essence et efficacité." In *Dictionnaire de théologie catholique*, vol. 10, edited by Alfred Vacant et al. Paris: Letouzey et Ané, 1928.

———. "Purgatoire." In *Dictionnaire de théologie catholique*, vol. 13, edited by Alfred Vacant et al., 1163–1326. Paris: Letouzey et Ané, 1936.

Milano, Andrea. "Il 'divinire di Dio' in Hegel, Kierkegaard e san Tommaso d'Aquino." *Studi Tomistici* 3:284–94. Rome: Città Nuova Editrice, 1974.

Mitterer, Albert. *Dogma und Biologie der heiligen Familie nach dem Weltbild des Hl. Thomas von Aquin und dem der Gegenwart.* Vienna: Herder, 1952.

Molari, C[arlo]. "Aspetti metafisici et funzionali della conscienza umana di Cristo." *Divinitas* 4 (1960): 261–88.

Molinari, Paolo. "Caractère eschatologique de l'Église pérégrinante et ses rapports avec l'Église céleste." In *Augustinus Magister, Congrès international augustinien, Paris, 21–24 September 1954, Communications. Études augustiniennes*, 3:1193–1208. Paris: Études Augustiniennes, 1954.

Mollat, Donatien. "Jugement." In *Dictionnaire de la Bible*, edited by Louis Pirot and Robert André, 4:1321–94. Paris: Letouzey et Ané, 1950.

Moltmann, Jürgen. *Théologie de l'espérance*. Paris: Cerf, 1970.

———. *Théologie de l'espérance, II. Débats*. Paris: Cerf, 1973.

———. *Le Dieu crucifié. La croix du Christ, fondement et critique de la théologie chrétienne*. Translated by Bernard Fraigneau-Julien. Paris: Cerf, 1974.

Mouroux, Jean. *Le mystère du temps*. Paris: Aubier, 1962.

Muhlen, Heribert. *Die Veränderlichkeit Gottes al Horizont einer zukünftigen Christologie. Auf dem Wege zu einer Kreuzestheologie in Auseinandersetzung mit der altkirchlichen Theologie*. Münster, 1969.

———. *La mutabilità di Dio come orizzonte di una cristologiafutura. Verso una teologia delle croce in discussion con la cristologia delle Chiesa antica*. Translated by Rosino Gibellini. Brescia: Queriniana, 1974.

Nédoncelle, Maurice. "Démythisation et conception eschatologique du mal." In *Le mythe de la peine. Colloque Castelli*, 195–222. Paris: Aubier, 1961.

Nicolas, Jean-Hervé. "Essence et substance." *Revue thomiste* 47 (1947): 517–23.

———. "Chronique de théologie dogmatique." *Revue thomiste* 53 (1953): 415–31.

———. "Compte-rendu du livre de Febrer M., El concepto de persona y la union hipostatica." *Revue thomiste* 55 (1955): 186–88.

———. "Amour de soi, amour de Dieu, amour des autres." *Revue thomiste* 56 (1956): 5–42.

———. "Crainte et tremblement." *Vie Spirituelle* 99 (1958): 227–54.

———. "L'innocence originelle de la Nouvelle Eve." In *Etudes Mariales*, 15–35. Paris: Lethielleux, 1958.

———. "Réactualisation des mystères rédempteurs dans et par les sacrements." *Revue thomiste* 58 (1958): 20–54.

———. "Enfer." In *Dictionnaire de spiritualité ascétique et mystique, doctrine et histoire*, vol. 4, edited by Marcel Viller, Ferdinand Cavalerra, et al., 729–45. Paris: Beauchesne, [1960].

———. *La virginité de Marie. Étude théologique*. Fribourg: Éditions universitaires, 1962.

———. "L'unité d'être dans le Christ selon S. Thomas d'Aquin." *Revue thomiste* 65 (1965): 229–60.

———. *Dieu connu comme inconnu*. Paris: Desclée de Brouwer, 1966.

———. *L'amour de Dieu et la peine des hommes*. Paris: Beauchesne, 1969.

———. *Les profondeurs de la grâce*. Paris: Beauchesne, 1969.

———. "Vierge jusque dans l'enfantement." *Ephemerides Mariologicae* 21 (1971): 377–82.

———. "L'Act pure de saint Thomas et le Dieu vivant de l'Evangile." *Angelicum* 51 (1974): 511–32.

———. "Universalité de la médiation du Christ et salut de ceux qui ne connaissent pas le Christ." In *Acta del Congressso internazionale Tommaso d'Aquino nel suo settimo centenario*, 4:261–73. Naples, 1976.

———. "Aimante et bienheureusement Trinité" in *Révue thomiste* 78 (1978): 271–91.

———. "La seconde mort du pécheur et la fidélité de Dieu." *Revue thomiste* 79 (1979): 25–49.

———. *Contemplation et vie contemplative en christianisme*. Fribourg / Paris: Éditions Universitaires / Beachesne, 1980.

———. "Le Christ centre et fin de l'histoire." *Revue thomiste* 81 (1981): 357–80.

Nicolas, Marie-Joseph. *Theotokos, le mystère de Marie*. Paris: Desclée de Brouwer, 1965.

———. *Théologie de la résurrection*. Paris: Desclée, 1982.

Nossent, Georges. "Mort, immortalité, résurrection." *Nouvelle revue théologique* 91 (1969): 614–30.

Nous sommes jugés maintenant. Vie Spirituelle 108, no. 494 (1963).

Pannenberg, Wolfhart. *Esquisse d'une christologie*. Translated by Arthur Liefooghe. Paris: Cerf, 1971.

Parente, Pietro. "Unità ontological e psicologica de l'Uomo-Dio." *Euntes docete* 5 (1952): 337–401.

———. *L'Io di Cristo*. Brescia: Morcelliana, 1955.

Patfoort, Albert. *L'unité d'être dans le Christ d'après Saint Thomas. A la croisée de l'ontologie et de la christologie*. Paris: Desclée de Brouwer, 1964.

———. "Bulletin de théologie dogmatique. Christologie." *Revue des sciences philosophiques et théologiques* 51 (1967): 312–17.

———. "Compte-rendu du livre de Pannenberg W., Autour d'une problématique théologique." *Angelicum* 51 (1974): 128–38.

Peyrefitte, Alain. *Le mal français*. Paris: Plon, 1976.

Pius XI, Pope. *Miserentissimus redemptor*. Encyclical Letter. May 8, 1928. Available at www.vatican.va.

Potterie, Ignace de la. *La vérité dans Saint Jean*. Vols. 1–2. Rome: Biblical Institute Press, 1977.

Potvin, Thomas R. *The Theology of the Primacy of Christ Acording to St. Thomas and Its Scriptural Foundations*. Fribourg: Éditions Saint Paul, 1973.

Pozo, Cándido. *Teología del más allá*. Madrid: Biblioteca de Autores Cristianos, 1968.

Rahner, Karl. "Eschatologie." In *Lexikon für Theologie und Kirche*, vol. 3, edited by Josef Höfer and Karl Rahner, 1094–96. Second edition. Freiburg im Breisgau: Herder, 1957ff.

———. "Dieu dans le Nouveau Testament." In *Ecrits théologiques*, 1:13–111. Paris: Desclée de Brouwer, 1959.

———. "Problèmes actuels de christologie." In *Ecrits théologiques*, 1:115–81. Paris: Desclée de Brouwer, 1959.

———. "Essai d'une esquisse de Dogmatique." In *Ecrits théologiques*, 4:9–50. Paris: Desclée de Brouwer, 1963.

———. "Pour une théologie de la mort." In *Ecrits théologiques*, vol. 3. Paris: Desclée de Brouwer, 1963.

———. "Réflexions théologiques sur l'Incarnation." In *Ecrits théologiques*, 3:81–101. Paris: Desclée de Brouwer, 1963.

———. "L'immaculée conception." In *Ecrits théologiques*, 4:145–59. Paris: Desclée de Brouwer, 1966.

———. "La résurrection de la chair." In *Ecrits théologiques*, 4:71–88. Paris: Desclée de Brouwer, 1966.

———. "Le concept du mystère dans la théologie catholique." In *Ecrits théologiques*, 8:51–103. Paris: Desclée de Brouwer, 1967.

———. "Considérations dogmatiques sur la psychologie du Christ." In *Exégèse et dogmatique*, 187–210. Paris: Desclée de Brouwer, 1967.

———. "Dieu Trinité fondement transcendant de l'histoire du salut." In *Mysterium Salutis: Dogmatique de l'histoire du salut*, 6:13–135. Paris: Cerf, 1971.

Ranquet, Jean-Gabriel. *J'espère en Jésus-Christ*. Paris: Desclée de Brouwer, 1964.

Rey, Bernard. "Théologie trinitaire et révélation biblique." *Revue des sciences philosophiques et théologiques* 54 (1970): 636–53.

———. *Le cheminement des premières communautés chrétiennes à la découverte de Dieu*. Paris: Cerf, 1972.

Riedmatten, Henri de. *Les actes du procès de Paul de Samosate, Étude sur la christologie des IIIe and IVe siècles*. Fribourg: Éditions Saint Paul, 1952.

Rigaux, Béda. *Dieu l'a ressuscité*. Gembloux: Duculot, 1973.

Rivière, Jean. *Le dogme de la rédemption. Étude historique*. Paris: Lecoffre, 1905.

———. "Sur les premières applications du terme 'satisfactio.'" *Bulletin de littérature ecclésiastique* 25 (1924): 285–97 and 353–69.

———. *Le dogme de la Rédemption. Étude historique*. Louvain: Bureaux de la Revue, 1931.

———. "Rédemption." In *Dictionnaire de théologie catholique*, vol. 13, edited by Alfred Vacant et al., 1912–2004. Paris: Letouzey et Ané, 1936.

Robert, André, and André Feuillet. *Introduction à la Bible*. Paris: Desclée de Brouwer, 1959.

Rohof, Jan. *La sainteté substantielle du Christ dans la théologie scolastique*. Fribourg: Éditions Saint Paul, 1952.

Works Cited   535

Rondet, Henri. *Gratia Christi*. Paris: Beauchesne, 1948.
———. *Essai sur la théologie de la grâce*. Paris: Beauchesne, 1964.
Rousseau, Olivier. "Autour de l'idée de la royauté du Christ." *Concilium* 11 (1966): 115–26.
Sabourin, Léopold. *Rédemption sacrificielle. Une enquête exégétique*. Paris: Desclée de Brouwer, 1961.
Salmanticenses. *Collegii Salmanticensis cursus theologicus*. Vols. 1–20. Paris: Palmé, 1897.
Scheeben, Matthias-Joseph. *Les mystères du christianisme*. Paris: Desclée de Brouwer, 1947.
Scheffczyk, Leo. "Die heilsökonomische Trinitätslehre des Rupert von Deutz und ihre dogmatische Bedeutung." In *Kirche und Überlieferung. Festschrift für J. R. Geiselmann*, 90–118. Freiburg: Herder, 1960.
Schmaus, Michael. "Sendung." In *Lexikon für Theologie und Kirche*, vol. 9, edited by Josef Höfer and Karl Rahner. Second edition. Freiburg im Breisgau: Herder, 1957ff.
Schmitt, Joseph. *Jésus ressuscité dans la prédication apostolique, étude de théologie biblique*. Paris: Gabalda, 1949.
———. "Le Christ Jésus dans la foi et la vie de la naissante Église." *Lumière et Vie* 15 (1954): 23–42.
———. *Sophrone de Jérusalem*. Paris: Beauchesne, 1972.
Schnackenburg, Rudolf. "La christologie du Nouveau Testament." In *Mysterium Salutis: Dogmatique de l'histoire du salut*, 10:13–236. Paris: Cerf, 1974.
Schönborn, Christoph. *L'icône du Christ, Fondements théologiques*. Paradosis XXIV. Fribourg: Éditions Universitaires, 1976.
Schoonenberg, Piet. *L'homme et le péché*. Translated by Michel Martron. Tours: Mame, 1967.
———. *Il est le Dieu des hommes*. Translated by M. Claes. Paris: Cerf, 1973.
Schwalm, Marie-Benoît. "Individualisme et solitarité." *Revue Thomiste* 6 (1898): 66–99.
———. *Leçons de philosophie sociale*. Vol. 2. Paris: Bloud & Cie, 1911.
Scipioni, Luigi. *Ricerche sulla cristologia del "Libro di Eraclide" di Nestorio. La formulazione teologica e il suo contest filosofico*. Fribourg: Éditions Universitaires, 1956.
Se purifier pour voir Dieu. *Vie Spirituelle* 108, no. 491 (1963).
Seckler, Max. *Le salut et l'histoire*. Paris: Cerf, 1967.
Seiller, Léon. "La psychologie humaine du Christ et l'unicité de personne." *Franziskanische Studien* 31 (1949): 40–76 and 246–74.
Le sens chrétien de la mort. *Vie Spirituelle* 108, no. 492 (1963).
Solignac, Aimé. "Immortalité." In *Dictionnaire de spiritualité ascétique et mystique, doctrine et histoire*, vol. 7, edited by Marcel Viller, Ferdinand Cavalerra, et al., 1601–14. Paris: Beauchesne, [1971].
Spicq, Ceslas. *L'épître aux Hébreux*. Vols. 1–2. Paris: Gabalda, 1952.

———. "Purgatoire." In *Dictionnaire de la Bible*, vol. 9, edited by Henri Cazelles, André Feuillet, et al., 555–65. Paris: Letouzey et Ané, [1979].
Synave, Paul. "La passion du Christ et les droits du démon." In *Saint Thomas d'Aquin. Somme théologique, La Vie de Jésus*, 3:270–78. Paris: Cerf, n.d.
Ternus, Joseph. "Das Seelen-und Bewußtseinsleben Jesu." In *Das Konzil von Chalkedon*, vol. 3, edited by Alois Grillmeier and Heinrich Bacht, 81–237. Würzburg: Echter-Verlag, 1962.
Tertullian. *Adversus Praxean*. Corpus Christianorum Series Latina 2.
Theodore of Mopsuestia. *Homélies catéchétiques*. Edited by Raymond Tonneau and Robert Devresse. *Studi e Testi* 145. Vatican City: Biblioteca Apostolica Vaticana, 1949.
Thérèse of the Infant Child Jesus. *Manuscrits autobiographiques*. Lisieux: Carmel de Lisieux, 1957.
Thomas Aquinas. *In duodecim libros Metaphysicorum Aristotelis expositio*. Edited by M.-R. Cathala and R. M. Spiazzi. Rome, 1950.
———. *Quaestio disputata De unione verbi incarnati*. Edited by W. Senner, B. Bartocci, and K. Obenauer. Stuttgart: Frommann-Holzboog, 2011.
———. *Scriptum super libros sententiarum magistri Petri Lombardi episcopi Parisiensis*. Vols. 1–3. Edited by Pierre Mandonnet. Paris: Lethielleux, 1929–33.
———. *Sancti Thomae de Aquino opera omnia*. Leonine edition. Rome, 1882–. Vols. 4–12, *Summa Theologiae*. Vols. 13–15, *Summa Contra Gentiles*. Vol. 22.2/1, *Quaestiones disputatae de veritate*.
Tixeront, Joseph. *Histoire des dogmes*. 3 vols. Paris: Gabalda, 1905–11.
Tor, B. Nicolau. "El primado absolute de Cristo en el pensamiento Luliano." *Estúdios Lulianos* 2 (1958): 297–313.
Trembelas, Pangiotis N. *Dogmatique de l'Église orthodoxe catholique*. Vols. 1–3. Paris: Desclée de Brouwer, 1957.
Turner, Henry Ernest William. *The Patristic Doctrine of Redemption*. London: [Mowbray, 1952].
Valéry, Paul. *Oeuvres*. Vols. 1–2. Paris: La Pléiade, 1957–60.
Vanhoye, Albert. "Le Christ grand-prêtre selon He 2, 17–18." *Nouvelle revue théologique* 91 (1969): 449–74.
Vatican Council II. *Lumen Gentium*. November 21, 1964. Available at www.vatican.va.
———. *Gaudium et Spes*. December 7, 1965. Available at www.vatican.va.
La Vierge Marie dans la Constitution sur l'Église, Etudes Mariales. Paris: Lethielleux, 1965.
Welte, Bernhard. "Homousios hemin. Gedanken zum Verständnis und zur theologischen Problematik der Kategorien von Calkedon." In *Das Konzil von Chalkedon*, vol. 3, edited by Alois Grillmeier and Heinrich Bacht, 51–80. Würzburg: Echter-Verlag, 1962.
Wessels, Cletus. *The Mother of God. Her Physical Maternity: Reappraisal*. River Forest, Ill., 1964.

Index

Adnès, Pierre, 323
Alberigo, Giuseppe, 42
St. Albert the Great, 280
Aldama, José Antonio, 311
Alexander of Hales, 280
Alfaro, Juan, 336
St. Anselm of Canterbury, 342, 343, 344, 345, 346, 350, 351, 360, 365, 372
Apollinarism, 24, 26, 27, 28, 29, 33, 38, 42, 43, 82, 171, 217
Apollinarius, 24, 26, 27, 42, 43
Arianism, 26, 27, 28, 29, 42, 171, 382
Aristotle, 474
Arius, 26, 27, 42, 171
Assumptus-homo theory of Hypostatic Union, 40, 80–86
Athanasius of Alexandria, 25, 26, 27, 31, 32, 43, 51, 171, 243
Audet, Thomas-André, 280
St. Augustine of Hippo, 23, 40, 51, 169, 170, 172, 174, 177, 305, 312, 318, 324, 325, 326, 345, 356, 408, 507

Balić, Carolus 328, 329
Von Balthasar, Hans Urs, 111, 148, 203, 277, 278, 425, 426, 517
Basly, Déodat de, 80, 82
Van Bavel, Tarcisius, 40
Beatific Vision: in hereafter among the redeemed, 499–502; limitations of beatific character of Christ's Vision *in via*, 252; relationship with resurrected body, 500–502; see "Christ's knowledge *in via*"
Benedict XII (Pope), 494
Benoît, Pierre, 125, 127, 368, 378
Berten, Ignace 130
Billot, Louis, 60, 66, 116
Blondel, Maurice, 265, 273, 284
Bodily glorification, 151, 255, 256, 257, 501
Boff, Leonardo, 41
Bonnefoy, Jean-François, 280, 333
Book of Heraclides, 31
Bossuet, Jacques-Bégnigne, 348
Bouyer, Louis, 10, 13, 15, 17, 18, 19, 20, 171, 172, 268, 295, 403, 406
Braun, François-Marie, 15, 202, 340, 380, 399, 400, 403
Bultmann, Rudolff, 22
Bur, Jacques, 403, 406

Caggiano, E. M., 280
Cajetan, Thomaso de Vio, 51, 63, 64, 66, 106, 116, 254, 264, 265, 281, 301, 332, 333, 477
Calvin, John, 347
Cambe, Michel, 295
Camelot, Pierre-Thomas, 4, 31, 32, 33, 34, 35, 54
Cantalamessa, Raniero, 23
Cantone, Carlo, 111
Capreolus, John, 60
Carrez, Maurice, 442
Catão, Bernard, 261, 351, 359, 371, 372

Celsus, 22
Cerfaux, Lucien, 340, 378, 379
Chalcedon (Council), 3, 4, 12, 22, 24, 31, 33, 34, 35, 36, 37, 38, 39, 43, 44, 87, 104
Christ's holiness: capital grace, 159–60, 286, 362, 366; fullness of grace, 145–59; hypostatic union and grace, 139–45; involved having neither faith nor hope, 147–52
Christ's knowledge in via: Christ's self-consciousness, 192–204; natural knowledge, 162–75; question concerning infused knowledge had in via, 182, 183, 188, 189 synergy of Christ's vision of the Divine Essence and naturally acquired knowledge, 186–92; vision of the Divine Essence, 175–92
Christ's twofold activity: autonomy of Christ's will, 225–27; basic data of faith, 217–18; Christ's prayer to the Father, 385; instrumental causality and subordinate activities of Christ, 244–49; relationship between person, nature, and activity, 218–23; theandric activity (as proposed in ancient Church), 223–25; submission of Christ to the Father, 381–92 Thomas's solution regarding the complete subordination of Christ's human will to Divine Will, 227–43
De Chardin, Pierre Teilhard 265, 284, 449, 454, 461, 463
Chenu, Marie-Dominique, 103
Choron, Jacques 483
Communication of Idioms, 130–33
Congar, Yves-Marie, 106, 287, 396, 425, 502
Constantinople I (Council), 42
Constantinople II (Council), 104, 218, 311
Constantinople III (Council), 43, 218
Comprehensor, 155, 180, 181, 186, 211, 250, 253
Corvez, Maurice, 68, 117
Cottier, Georges, 448
Cousins, Evert H., 111
Cullmann, Oscar, 11, 13, 15, 16, 17, 293, 340, 427, 428, 467

Cyril of Alexandria, 31–36, 43, 49, 54, 145, 171, 287

St. Damasus I (Pope), 28, 29, 40, 42
Daniélou, Jean, 293, 295
Dante, 346, 347, 513
Death: Christian conception, 483–87; act of dying and ultimate state of soul after death, 488–94
Diepen, Herman, 40, 54, 59, 80, 85, 116, 193, 194, 224, 225, 226
Dillenschneider, Clément, 403
Dioscorus, 43
Docetism, 42, 126, 157
Dockx, Stanislas, 394
Dodd, Charles Herald, 4, 18
Dondaine, Hyacinthe-François, 80, 235
Dumeige, Gervais, 4, 31, 35, 51
Dualistic Christological errors summarized, 43–44
Dupuy, Michel, 426
Duquoc, Christian, 351
De Durand, Georges-Matthieu, 319

Ephesus (Council), 31, 33, 296, 311, 456
Ephesus ("Robber Council"), 34
Eschatology: eschatological dimension of Christian existence, 459–61; general remarks, 425–26; New Testament eschatology, 427–30; relationship to salvation history, 431–38; relationship to world history, 447–59, 463–64; religious life as eschatological witness, 464–65; see Final Judgment, Intermediary state, Parousia, "Recapitulation of all things in Christ: redemption of the universe," Resurrection
Eustathius of Antioch, 28
Eutyches, 34, 43

Fabro, Cornelio, 69
Febrer, Mateo, 59, 60, 422
Feiner, Johannes, 261
Lessard, Gaston 513
Feuillet, André, 11, 18, 109, 122, 145, 176, 177, 202, 262, 295, 308, 314, 341, 378, 380, 399, 403, 427, 483

Fittingness of the Incarnation of the Word, 102–3
Flavian of Constantinople, 23, 34
Füglister, Notker, 4, 7

Galot, Jean, 111, 112, 156, 178, 179, 193, 194, 195, 196, 197, 199, 200, 201, 224, 231, 295, 324, 339, 426
Galtier, Paul, 36, 80, 86, 107, 108, 113, 170, 193, 194, 199, 224, 225, 227, 239, 351
Garrigou-Lagrange, Réginald 88, 368
Garrigues, Juan-Miguel, 105
Geffré, Claude, 373, 484, 491
Gélin, Albert 380
Gervais, Michel 4, 31, 111
Gilson, Étienne 475, 476, 477
Gironés, Gonzalo, 403
Glorieux, Palémon, 288, 491
Gnilka, Joachim, 341
Gnosticism, 135
Godin, André, 483
De Goedt, Michel 403
Gregory Nazianzus, 277
Gregory of Nysa, 145, 278, 322, 342
Grillmeier, Alois, 10, 11, 12, 22, 25, 26, 27, 28, 29, 30, 32, 34, 35, 36, 47, 51, 70, 71, 74, 80, 86, 92, 144
Gross, Jules 145
Guéroult, Martial, 265
Guillet, Jacques, 341, 378
Günther, Anton, 72

Hell and damnation, 511–18
Henry, Paul, 109
Héris, Charles-Vincent, 396
Hocedez, Edgar, 119
Hypostatic Union: assumptive action of Trinity upon the humanity of Jesus, 114–15; criticism of various theories of appropriation of human nature to the Word (actuation by uncreated act, actuation by subsistence, appropriation by consciousness-union, *assumptus-homo* theory), 66–86; "composite person," 47, 104–5, 239, 383, 384, 413; depersonalization of Christ's human nature, 66–67; "human personality" of Christ, 105–10, 128, 133, 231, 307, 383, 384, 413; immutability of the Word in the Incarnation, 110–14; "in persona" not "in natura", 50–56; kenosis of Word, 109–14; Patristic use of soul–body unity as model, 51–52; pre-existence of Christ, 122–30; Rahner on "united unity" and "united unity," 99–102; subsistence and Jesus's humanity, 57–66; Thomistic explanation of union as a real relation 86–98; unity of *esse*, 115–22

Iammarone, Luigi, 111
Ignatius of Antioch, 21, 26, 28, 42, 146
Immortality of the Soul, 474–79
Intermediary state: duration in relation to time, 479–80; scriptural foundations, 470–74; see Immortality of the Soul; see Purgatory
Instrumental Causality, 244–46; Christ's humanity is an instrument of His divinity, 243–49
St. Irenaeus of Lyons, xiii, 21, 106, 171, 275, 342, 400

Jankélévitch, Vladimir, 483
Jeremias, Joachim, 17, 19
Jesus's own self-testimony: awareness of the being son of God, 19–20; "Son of Man" and Suffering Servant, 17–19
St. John Damascene, 54, 243
John of Antioch, 31
St. John Chrysostom 39, 145
St. John of the Cross, 240, 445
Johannine Christology: communication of divine filiation to those who believe, 15; preexistence of logos, 14; Christ presented as eternal Word acting in the world, 14–15
Jossua, Jean-Pierre, 261, 277, 287, 375
Jouassard, Georges, 311, 324, 334
Journet, Charles 286, 295, 394, 397, 398, 403, 423, 426, 430, 440
Judgment: general judgment, 496–97; particular judgment, 494–96; scriptural data, 443–45
St. Justin Martyr, 21

Kasper, Walter, 36
Kelly, John Norman Davidson, 39, 44, 135
Kirchmeyer, Jean, 277
Koehler, Theodore, 403
Krempel, Anton, 88
Kübler-Ross, Elisabeth, 483
Küng, Hans, 111

Lafont, Ghislain, 103, 290, 394
Lagrange, Marie-Joseph, 9, 176
Lalande, Marie-Joseph, 193
Lamarche, Paul, 109
De La Taille, Maurice 66, 67, 68, 69, 70, 72, 399
Larcher, Chrysostome, 483
Laurentin, René, 295, 296, 308, 311, 318, 319, 325, 338, 339, 400, 403, 404
Lebreton, Jules 169
Legrand, Lucien, 322
Leontius of Byzantium, 171
St. Leo I (Pope), 22, 23, 34, 224, 225
Léon-Dufour, Xavier, 295
Leroy, Vincent, 41, 99, 117, 128, 277
Leuba, Jean-Louis, 111
Liébaert, Jacques, 23, 51
Logos-Anthropos Christology, 24, 27–32, 39
Logos-Sarx Christology, 24–27, 32, 33, 39
Löhrer, Magnus, 261
Lossky, Vladimir, 78
Lot-Borodine, Pyrrha, 277
De Lubac, Henri, 109, 265, 449
Luneau, Auguste, 293
Luther, Martin, 347
Lyonnet, Stanislas, 261, 295, 325, 341, 351, 445, 485

Malchion of Antioch, 24
Malevez, Léopold, 72, 75, 76, 77, 148, 287, 290, 291, 292
Malmberg, Felix, 144
Mansi, Johannes Dominicus 223
Maritain, Jacques, 117, 155, 156, 159, 182, 185, 189, 190, 194, 195, 201, 202, 323, 354, 368, 398, 450, 452, 479
Marrou, Henri-Irénée, 452
Martelet, Gustave, 483, 517

Mary, mother of God: divine maternity, 296–302; grace as Mother of God, 303–10; growth in grace, 339 Immaculate Conception, 325–34; perpetual virginity, 311–24; preservation from all sin, 334–38; role in association with Christ's sacrifice, 400–407
St. Maximus the Confessor, 105, 170, 277, 278
Mediation by Christ: mediation in Christ Himself and in His action, 411–14; roles attributed in the Savior in the Old Testament, 5–10; roles as Reconciler, Revealer, and Priest, 415–17; subordinate mediation in the mystical body of Christ, 418–24
Melanchthon, Philip, 347
Meritorious nature of Christ's human acts: general considerations, 249–55; meriting of bodily glorification and salvation of all mankind, 255–59
Mersch, Emil, 286, 287
Milano, Andrea 111
Mitterer, Albert, 322
Molari, Carlo, 193
Molinari, Paolo, 426
Mollat, Donatien, 426, 427, 443, 494
Moltmann, Jürgen, 111, 374, 432, 433, 435, 436, 438, 439, 448
Monist Christological errors summarized, 41–43
Monoergism, 217
Monophysitism, 22, 34, 43, 51, 54 104, 196, 217, 223
Monothelitism, 43, 217, 225
Motive and End of Incarnation, 263–85
Mouroux, Jean, 176, 178, 191, 194, 195, 276
Muhlen, Heribart, 111
Mystical body of Christ, 258, 367, 406, 420

Nédoncelle, Maurice, 203, 513
Nestorianism, 31–36, 44, 49, 82, 110,
Nestorius, 29, 31, 32, 33, 39, 44, 49, 110
Nicene Creed, 51, 262
Nicaea II (Council), 37
Nicolas, Jean-Hervé, 58, 71, 98, 111, 117,

193, 199, 311, 325, 370, 379, 386, 422, 432, 483, 488
Nicolas, Marie-Joseph, 295, 363, 372, 375
Nossent, Georges, 483

Odo Rigaldus, 280
Origen, 24, 25, 172, 277, 342, 513

Pannenberg, Wolfhart, 129, 130
Passion of Christ: see Salvation
Passions in Christ, 208, 209, 218–22
Parente, Pietro, 224
Parousia, 427, 431, 438, 439, 444, 446, 470, 471, 474, 479
Patfoort, Albert, 117, 130
Paul of Samosata, 24, 44
Pauline Christology: divine filiation, 10–11; lordship of Christ, 13; preexistence, 11–13
Peter the Lombard, 80, 105, 106, 389
Peyrefitte, Alain, 454
Bl. Pius XI (Pope), 173
Pius XII (Pope), 173
De la Potterie, Ignace 416
Potvin, Thomas, 275
Pozo, Cándido, 426
Priesthood of Christ, 380–81, 395–400, 407–10
Primacy of Christ, 275–76, 282–85, 290–94
Proclus of Constantinople, 34
Pseudo-Dionysius, 118, 223
Purgatory, 502–11

Quicumque (Athanasian) Creed, 51

Rahner, Karl, 47, 71, 72, 73, 74, 75, 76, 78, 79, 89, 91, 92, 99, 102, 112, 113, 173, 182, 189, 190, 194, 195, 211, 272, 292, 333, 373, 394, 425, 426, 479, 483, 484, 502
Ranquet, Jean-Gabriel, 464
Recapitulation of all things in Christ: critique of notion of Cosmic Christ, 284; critique of theories of ontological inclusion, 286–88; dynamic inclusion, 289; filiation in Christ, 392–94; inclusion in Christ's grace, 290–94, 366–70; redemption of the universe, 445–46

Relation, important role played in theology, 93–94
Resurrection: implies immortality of the soul, 467–70; of Christ 14, 16, 44, 150, 151,152, 155 174, 175, 180, 249, 327, 338, 255, 293, 429, 433, 441, 447; of those who are damned, 512, 513; of those saved in Christ, 440–42, 443, 497–99; see "Salvation: soteriological value of Christ's resurrection"
Rey, Bernard, 126, 128
De Riedmatten, Henri 28, 44
Rigaux, Béda, 378
Rivière, Jean, 341, 343, 346, 347, 348, 349, 350, 351
Robert, André, 202
Robert Grosseteste, 281
Rohof, Jan, 153
Rondet, Henri, 286, 394
Rousseau, Olivier, 397
Rupert of Deutz, 279

Sabourin, Léopold, 341, 363, 399
Salmanticenses, 281
Salvation: Christ's freedom in the passion, 373–75; critical examination of St. Anselm's theory, 342–46; critique of explanation by appeal to "rights of the devil," 341–43; critique of minimizing explanations (Abelard, Socinus, Schoonenberg), 348–50; critique of penal substitutionary theories, 346–48; explanation by vicarious satisfaction, 350–73; general observations, 261–62, 340–41; soteriological value of Christ's resurrection, 152, 375–79, 435, 440, 447, 498, 499
Scheeben, Mattias, 394, 402
Scheffczyk, Leo, 279
Schmaus, Michael, 72, 74, 75, 78, 102, 103
Schmitt, Joseph, 17, 377, 378
Schnackenburg, Rudolf, 377
Schönborn, Christoph, 217
Schoonenberg, Piet, 111, 128, 349
Schwalm, Marie-Benoît, 368
Scipioni, Luigi, 31

Bl. Scotus, John Duns, 59, 80, 118, 119, 120, 279, 280, 281, 328, 329, 332, 334, 360, 516
Seckler, Max, 103, 425
Seiller, Léon, 80, 83, 86
Solignac, Aimé, 483
Spicq, Teslas, 380, 396, 397, 502, 503
Suárez, Francisco, 69, 70
Synave, Paul, 341

Ternus, Joseph, 70
Tertullian, 21, 22, 23, 311, 351, 503
St. Thérèse of Lisieux, 551
Theodore of Mopsuestia, 29, 30, 39, 51
Theodotus of Byzantium, 44
St. Thomas Aquinas, passim.
Thurian, Max, 296, 315, 325, 331, 333
Tixeront, Joseph, 225
Tor, B. Nicolau, 265

Trent (Council), 334, 341, 502, 326
Trembelas, Pangiotis N., 177
Turner, Henry Ernest William, 341

Valéry, Paul, 458
Vanhoye, 380
Vatican II (Council), vii, 98, 286, 296, 425, 426
Viator, 155, 178, 180, 181, 186, 211, 212, 250, 253, 254, 336, 388, 407, 409
St. Victor I (Pope)

Welte, Bernard, 74, 272
Wessels, Cletus, 320
World history, and temporal dimension of Christian existence, 461–63; see "Eschatology: relationship to world history," "Eschatology: eschatological dimension of Christian existence"

ALSO IN THE
THOMISTIC RESSOURCEMENT SERIES

Series Editors: Matthew Levering
Thomas Joseph White, OP

Liturgical Theology in Thomas Aquinas
Sacrifice and Salvation History
Franck Quoëx

Principles of Catholic Theology
Book One: On the Nature of Theology
Thomas Joseph White, OP

Reading the Song of Songs with St. Thomas Aquinas
Serge-Thomas Bonino, OP
Translated by Andrew Levering with Matthew Levering

Divine Speech in Human Words
Thomistic Engagements with Scripture
Emmanuel Durand
Edited by Matthew K. Minerd

Revelations of Humanity
Anthropological Dimensions of Theological Controversies
Richard Schenk

The Trinity
On the Nature and Mystery of the One God
Thomas Joseph White, OP

www.ingramcontent.com/pod-product-compliance
Lightning Source LLC
Chambersburg PA
CBHW070713020526
44107CB00078B/2358